Lecture Notes in Computer Science   16306

Founding Editors

Gerhard Goos
Juris Hartmanis

Editorial Board Members

Elisa Bertino, *Purdue University, West Lafayette, IN, USA*
Wen Gao, *Peking University, Beijing, China*
Bernhard Steffen, *TU Dortmund University, Dortmund, Germany*
Moti Yung, *Columbia University, New York, NY, USA*

Xiaoliang Wang · Xiaohong Jiang · Noel Crespi ·
Baoliu Ye

Editors

Network and Parallel Computing

21st IFIP WG 10.3 International Conference, NPC 2025
Nha Trang, Vietnam, November 14–16, 2025
Proceedings, Part II

 Springer

Editors
Xiaoliang Wang
Nanjing University
Nanjing, China

Noel Crespi
Telecom SudParis - Institut Polytechnique de
Paris
Évry, France

Xiaohong Jiang
Hakodate Future University
Hakodate, Japan

Baoliu Ye
Nanjing University
Nanjing, China

ISSN 0302-9743　　　　　ISSN 1611-3349 (electronic)
Lecture Notes in Computer Science
ISBN 978-3-032-10465-6　　　　ISBN 978-3-032-10466-3 (eBook)
https://doi.org/10.1007/978-3-032-10466-3

Preface

Welcome to the proceedings of the 21st edition of the International Conference on Network and Parallel Computing (NPC 2025), held in Nha Trang, Vietnam, from November 14–16, 2025. NPC is a prestigious annual gathering that serves as a global platform for researchers, academics, and industry professionals to explore and exchange cutting-edge ideas, research findings, and innovative solutions in the fields of network, distributed, and parallel computing. Topics of interest include, but are not limited to, parallel and distributed applications and algorithms, parallel and distributed architectures and systems, and parallel and distributed software environments and tools.

A total of 223 submissions were received in response to our call for papers. These papers originated from Asia, Australia, Europe, and North America. Each submission was sent to at least three reviewers (four reviewers per submission on average) to evaluate its originality, innovation, readability, and relevance to the expected audience. Based on the reviews received, 76 papers were accepted for inclusion in the technical conference program, with an acceptance rate of about 34%. Reviews were single blind.

We sincerely thank the authors for contributing their outstanding research work to NPC 2025. We also want to thank every member of the NPC 2025 Organizing Committee, Program Committee, and Steering Committee for their great efforts in putting together such an exciting program. Finally, we thank all the attendees and volunteers for NPC 2025.

November 2025

Xiaoliang Wang
Xiaohong Jiang
Noel Crespi
Baoliu Ye

Organization

Steering Committee

Hai Jin	Huazhong University of Science and Technology, China
Jean-Luc Gaudiot	University of California, Irvine, USA
Stéphane Zuckerman	CY Cergy Paris Université, France
Chen Ding	University of Rochester, USA
Kemal Ebcioglu	Global Supercomputing, USA
Jack Dongarra	University of Tennessee, USA
Tony Hey	Science and Technology Facilities Council, UK
Yoichi Muraoka	Waseda University, Japan
Viktor Prasanna	University of Southern California, USA
Daniel Reed	University of Utah, USA
Weisong Shi	University of Delaware, USA
Ninghui Sun	Institute of Computing Technology, CAS, China
Zhiwei Xu	Institute of Computing Technology, CAS, China
Kien Nguyen	Chiba University, Japan
Nguyen Phi Le	Hanoi University of Science and Technology, Vietnam

Organizing Committee

General Chairs

Noel Crespi	Télécom SudParis, Institut Polytechnique de Paris, France
Jie Wu	Temple University, USA
Baoliu Ye	Nanjing University, China

Program Co-chairs

Xiaoliang Wang	Nanjing University, China
Xiaohong Jiang	Hakodate Future University, Japan

Local Chairs

Nguyen Phi Le — Hanoi University of Science and Technology, Vietnam

Phuoc Tran — Ton Duc Thang University, Vietnam

Publicity Co-chairs

Jun Zhao — Nanyang Technological University, Singapore

Do Phan Thuan — Ton Duc Thang University, Vietnam

Qiongxiu Li — Aalborg University, Denmark

Registration Chair

Xiaohui Peng — Institute of Computing Technology, CAS, China

Publication Chairs

Jianguo Chen — Sun Yat-sen University, China

Chen Tian — Nanjing University, China

Xia Xie — Hainan University, China

Web and Information System Chairs

Tingting Yuan — IMC University of Applied Sciences Krems, Austria

Rong Gu — Nanjing University, China

Finance Chairs

Bui Thuc Minh — Nha Trang University, Vietnam

Nguyen Cam Tu — Nanjing University, China

Zhihao Qu — Hohai University, China

PC Members

Rong Gu — Nanjing University, China

Longxin Zhang — Hunan University of Technology, China

Cam-Tu Nguyen — Nanjing University, China

Lailong Luo — National University of Defense Technology, China

Geyao Cheng — National University of Defense Technology, China

Long Chen	Guangdong University of Technology, China
Amir Taherkordi	University of Oslo, Norway
Zhuozhao Li	Southern University of Science and Technology, China
Bin Liu	Northwest A&F University, China
Gongming Zhao	University of Science and Technology of China, China
Gang Chen	Sun Yat-sen University, China
Pengfei Chen	Sun Yat-sen University, China
Truong Thao Nguyen	National Institute of Advanced Industrial Science and Technology, Japan
Longlong Liao	Fuzhou University, China
Yifan Wang	Institute of Computing Technology, Chinese Academy of Sciences, China
Yuan Liu	Xiangtan University, China
Liu Daibo	Hunan University, China
Xiao Zhang	Shandong University, China
Tingting Yuan	IMC University of Applied Sciences Krems, Austria
Yibo Huang	University of Michigan, USA
Tingting Xu	Nanjing University, China
Xiaohui Peng	Institute of Computing Technology, Chinese Academy of Sciences, China
Zeke Wang	Zhejiang University, China
Quang Trung Luu	LAAS-CNRS, France
Yeqin Zhang	Nanjing University, China
Yin Zhang	University of Electronic Science and Technology of China, China
Menghao Zhang	Beihang University, China
Gang Liu	University of Electronic Science and Technology of China, China
Hongju Cheng	Fuzhou University, China
Yalan Wu	Guangdong University of Technology, China
Hyun Kimq	University of Toronto, Canada
Jingpu Duan	Pengcheng Laboratory, China
Guocheng Liao	Sun Yat-sen University, China
Baidong Wang	Sun Yat-sen University, China
Chuanghao Ding	Nanjing University, China
Xiaofeng Gao	Shanghai Jiao Tong University, China
Qiufen Xia	Dalian University of Technology, China
Phan Thuan Do	Hanoi University of Science and Technology, Vietnam
Shihong Hu	Jiangnan University, China

Yifei Zhu	Shanghai Jiao Tong University, China
Yongmin Zhang	Central South University, China
Wenchao Jiang	Guangdong University of Technology, China
Xianwei Zhang	AMD Inc, USA
Chao Li	Shanghai Jiao Tong University, China
Xingzhou Zhang	Chinese Academy of Sciences, China
Chao Qiu	Tianjin University, China
Qianyi Huang	Sun Yat-sen University, China
Liekang Zeng	Chinese University of Hong Kong, China
Jingwen Leng	Shanghai Jiao Tong University, China
Long Zheng	Huazhong University of Science and Technology, China
Shigeng Zhang	Central South University, China
Xin Li	Nanjing University of Aeronautics and Astronautics, China
Zhi Zhou	Sun Yat-sen University, China
Xiaofeng Hou	Shanghai Jiao Tong University, China
Shad Kirmani	LinkedIn Corporation, USA
Haisheng Tan	University of Science and Technology of China, China
Wanchun Jiang	Central South University, China
Song Yang	Beijing Institute of Technology, China
Dazhao Cheng	Wuhan University, China
Fei Xu	East China Normal University, China
Dezun Dong	National University of Defense Technology, China
Xuewen Yu	Southeast University, China
Wenfei Wu	Peking University, China
Zhi Liu	University of Electro-Communications, Japan
Deze Zeng	China University of Geosciences, Wuhan, China
Anna Kobusinska	Poznań University of Technology, Poland
Qiushi Li	Tsinghua University, China
Giuseppe Tricomi	Università di Messina, Italy
Rongfei Zeng	Northeastern University, China
En Shao	Institute of Computing Technology, Chinese Academy of Sciences, China
Jun Zhao	Nanyang Technological University, Singapore
Zhiwei Zhao	University of Electronic Science and Technology of China, China
Hailong Zhu	Beijing University of Posts and Telecommunications, China
Mengwei Xu	Beijing University of Posts and Telecommunications, China

Huaming Wu	Tianjin University, China
Binwei Wu	PML, China
Tengjiao He	Jinan University, China
Xutong Jiang	Hohai University, China
Xiaofei Wang	Tianjin University, China
Yali Yuan	Southeast University, China
Xiaobo Zhou	Tianjin University, China
Minghua Shen	Sun Yat-sen University, China
Qiong Wu	Sun Yat-sen University, China
Zhiqing Tang	Beijing Normal University, China
Honglong Chen	China University of Petroleum, China
Stephan Sigg	Aalto University, Finland
Dan Huang	Sun Yat-sen University, China
Laiping Zhao	Tianjin University, China
Lars Nagel	Loughborough University, UK
Wen Xia	Harbin Institute of Technology, Shenzhen, China
Lin Gu	Huazhong University of Science and Technology, China
Hongzi Zhu	Shanghai Jiao Tong University, China
Fan Wu	Central South University, China
Zhiying Feng	Sun Yat-sen University, China
Zhiguang Chen	National University of Defense Technology, China
Miao Hu	Sun Yat-sen University, China
Lei Yang	South China University of Technology, China
Jingyu Hua	Nanjing University, China
Chentao Wu	Shanghai Jiao Tong University, China
Xiaoxi Zhang	Sun Yat-sen University, China
Lei Gong	University of Science and Technology of China, China
Jianxiong Guo	Beijing Normal University, China
Yanchao Zhao	Nanjing University of Aeronautics and Astronautics, China
Yuan Wu	University of Macau, China
Konglin Zhu	Beijing University of Posts and Telecommunications, China
Qian Ma	Sun Yat-sen University, China
Xiuhua Li	Chongqing University, China
Yifei Zou	University of Hong Kong, China
Chengxi Gao	Shenzhen Institute of Advanced Technology, Chinese Academy of Sciences, China
Ke Luo	Sun Yat-sen University, China

Keqiang He	Shanghai Jiao Tong University, China
Yuan Zhang	Nanjing University, China
Huawei Huang	Sun Yat-sen University, China
Lin Wang	Paderborn University, Germany
Zhuo Li	Beijing Information Science & Technology University, China
Jixian Zhang	University of Electronic Science and Technology of China, China
Ting Cai	Hubei University of Technology, China
Chen Chen	University of Cambridge, UK
Ying Wan	Southeast University, China
Chaojie Gu	Zhejiang University, China
Fuliang Li	Northeastern University, China
Zeshui Li	Postdoc Researcher
Bo Mao	Xiamen University, China
Qinglin Yang	Guangzhou University, China
Jingjing Wang	Hunan University, China
Ronghui Cao	Changsha University of Science and Technology, China
Wenzhong Li	Nanjing University, China
Xiangyuan Zhu	Zhaoqing University, China
Xiaowei Liu, H	nan Institute of Engineering, China
Junyan Hu	Xi'an University of Posts and Telecommunications, China
Mingxing Zhang	Tsinghua University, China
Mariano Scazzariello	KTH Royal Institute of Technology, Sweden
Shouqiang Liu	South China Normal University, China
Xiaoyu Wang	Soochow University, China
Zhou Zhou	Changsha University, China
Pengchen Liang	Shanghai University, China
Tao Liu	University of Aizu, Japan
Yanni Yang	Shandong University, China
Cong Wang	Zhejiang University, China
Shigang Li	Beijing University of Posts and Telecommunications, China
Shengyuan Ye	Sun Yat-sen University, China
Keren Zhou	George Mason University & OpenAI, USA
Changkun Jiang	Shenzhen University, China
Minh Thuy Le	Hanoi University of Science and Technology, Vietnam

Contents – Part II

Contents – Part I

Dynamic Resource Allocation
with Adaptive Mode Selection
in D2D-V2X Networks

Xiang Xiao[✉], Peidong Zhu, Jia Song, Gang Su, Lu Feng, Peng Wu,
and Li Zhu

College of Electronic Information and Electrical Engineering, Changsha University,
Changsha 410022, China
hdxx@hnu.edu.cn, zpd136@sina.com

Abstract. Cellular vehicle-to-everything (V2X) networks leveraging
device -to-device (D2D) communications face critical interference and
reliability bottlenecks in safety-critical scenarios. This work introduces a
dynamic resource orchestration framework that jointly optimizes transmission mode selection, spectrum sharing, and power allocation. By
decomposing the mixed-integer non-convex optimization problem through
block coordinate descent, our approach iteratively solves coupled sub-
problems. Non-convex constraints are transformed via successive convex approximation with first-order Taylor expansions, enabling efficient solution convergence. The proposed scheme maximizes vehicle-to-
infrastructure (V2I) sum-rate while rigorously guaranteeing ultra-reliable
low-latency requirements for vehicle-to-vehicle (V2V) links through adaptive mode switching between dedicated and reused spectrum access. Simulations confirm significant performance gains over conventional methods
across diverse urban scenarios.

Keywords: mode selection · dynamic resource allocation · D2D-V2X
Networks · optimization

1 Introduction

Vehicle-to-Everything (V2X) communications serve as a fundamental technology
for enhancing road safety, optimizing traffic flow, and enabling in-vehicle infotain-
ment, forming the backbone of autonomous driving ecosystems [1]. They facilitate real-time information exchange between vehicles and infrastructure, providing critical data dissemination for intelligent transportation systems [2]. The rapid
deployment of V2X has spurred diverse service demands: bandwidth-intensive
non-safety applications (e.g., high-definition video streaming, interactive gaming) requiring frequent server access via high-capacity Vehicle-to-Infrastructure
(V2I) links, and mission-critical safety services demanding Ultra-Reliable Low-
Latency Communication (URLLC), primarily delivered through direct Vehicle-
to-Vehicle (V2V) links [3]. The significant priority disparity between these service
classes necessitates distinct resource management strategies.

X. Wang et al. (Eds.): NPC 2025, LNCS 16306, pp. 1–12, 2026.
https://doi.org/10.1007/978-3-032-10466-3_1

Current vehicular networking standards encompass IEEE 802.11p and Cellular V2X (C-V2X). While IEEE 802.11p [4] enables direct communication, its contention-based medium access mechanism suffers from frequent packet collisions in congested scenarios, leading to increased latency and reduced reliability. Protocols aiming for collision-free access by allocating dedicated resources face practical challenges due to the difficulty in precisely tracking neighboring vehicle states within highly mobile V2X environments [5]. In contrast, C-V2X architectures offer superior capacity, coverage, and mobility support [6]. Crucially, their integrated Device-to-Device (D2D) interface enables direct V2V connectivity using cellular spectrum, providing a pathway for low-latency, high-reliability communications [7].

However, existing D2D-V2X schemes predominantly operate under static paradigms, persistently using either resource-sharing or orthogonal-resource configurations [8]. This inflexibility hinders effective mitigation of the critical interference-latency trade-off inherent in dense vehicular deployments. Prior research focusing solely on spectrum or power optimization within fixed modes [9] exhibits limitations in addressing rapid vehicular dynamics and stringent URLLC constraints. Complementary studies, despite methodological diversity, often overlook practical channel characteristics like Nakagami-m fading prevalent in vehicular settings [10,11], the latency overhead of dynamic mode switching, or intricate interference coupling during instantaneous mode transitions [12].

While C-V2X networks alleviate spectrum scarcity through opportunistic spectrum sharing between vehicular and cellular users, this introduces complex cross-tier interference dynamics. The heterogeneous nature of vehicular applications, demanding divergent QoS, further complicates dynamic resource allocation. To address the dual challenge of spectral efficiency and interference resilience required by heterogeneous V2X services, this work proposes a dynamic resource orchestration framework. It jointly optimizes transmission mode selection, spectrum allocation, and power control. The framework incorporates robustness mechanisms specifically designed to uphold URLLC guarantees for safety-critical V2V links amidst the dynamic interference and stringent QoS heterogeneity of dense networks. By enabling coordinated mode switching and resource adaptation in response to real-time network states, the proposed solution tackles the core limitations identified in prior work.

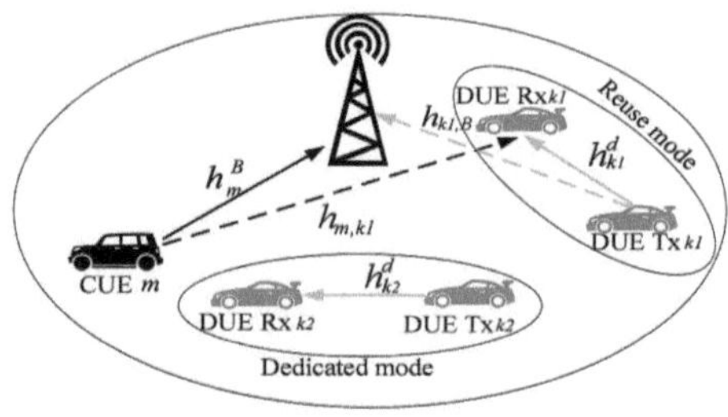

Fig. 1. D2D-enabled cellular V2X with the transmission mode selection.

2   System Model

Building upon co-optimization principles for transmission mode and resource partitioning in D2D-assisted vehicular networks, this work develops an adaptive framework balancing V2I aggregate throughput against V2V reliability and latency requirements. As depicted in Fig. 1, the D2D-V2X architecture integrates M cellular user equipment (CUEs) and K D2D pairs (DUEs) within a cellular infrastructure. To ensure interference-free V2I connectivity, the total bandwidth B_{tot} is orthogonally partitioned into C channels of width $B = \frac{B_{\text{tot}}}{C}$. Network entities are defined by sets $\mathcal{M} = 1, 2, \ldots, M$ (CUEs) and $\mathcal{K} = 1, 2, \ldots, K$ (DUEs).

DUEs dynamically select transmission modes based on real-time channel and interference conditions:(1)Reused Mode: DUEs access underutilized spectral resources allocated to CUEs, managed by binary variable $\rho_{m,k}$ ($\rho_{m,k} = 1$ indicates DUE k reuses CUE m's channel). This leverages base station processing to suppress co-channel interference while enhancing spectral efficiency. (2)Dedicated Mode: Activated when CUE spectrum bands are unoccupied or stringent QoS is required, this mode provides interference isolation via orthogonal resource assignment. Binary variable $x_{m,k}$ governs exclusive access.

Channel coefficients characterize propagation: h_m^B (CUE-BS), h_k^d (DUE-DUE), $h_{k,B}$ (DUE-BS interference), and $h_{m,k}$ (CUE-DUE interference). Transmission powers p_m^c (CUE), p_k^{d1} (reusing DUE), and p_k^{d2} (dedicated-mode DUE) are optimized to jointly maximize throughput and suppress interference. This structure concurrently addresses V2I throughput maximization and V2V reliability-latency constraints.

(1) CUEs

    CUEs are to upload the non-safety related information to the BS through the V2I link, and the uplink signal-to-interference plus noise ratio (SINR) of the mth CUE is expressed as, $\gamma_m^c = \dfrac{p_m^c h_m^B}{\sigma^2 + \sum\limits_{k \in K} \rho_{m,k} p_k^{d1} h_{k,B}}$. The bandwidth occupied by each CUE is B, so the data rate of the mth CUE is given by $R_m^c = B\log_2(1 + \gamma_m^c)$.

(2) DUEs

    Reused mode: Reused mode: DUEs establish direct links by sharing CUE-occupied channels, requiring co-channel interference control. The SINR and data rate for the kth DUE are: $\gamma_k^{d1} = \dfrac{p_k^{d1} h_k^d}{\sigma^2 + \sum\limits_{m \in M} \rho_{m,k} p_m^c h_{m,k} + \sum\limits_{j \in K, j \neq k} x_{m,j} p_j^{d2} h_{j,k}}$.

The data rate of the kth DUE in one channel is given by $R_k^{d1} = \rho_{m,k} B\log_2(1 + \gamma_k^{d1})$.

Dedicated mode: The signal-to-interference-plus-noise ratio characterizing the k-th DUE in dedicated mode is formulated as: $\gamma_k^{d2} = \dfrac{p_k^{d2} h_k^d}{\sigma^2 + \sum\limits_{j \in K, j \neq k} \rho_{m,j} p_j^{d1} h_{j,B}}$. The data rate of the k-th DUE in one channel is given by $R_k^{d2} = x_{m,k} B\log_2(1 + \gamma_k^{d2})$. Therefore, the SINR of DUEs is expressed as follow, $\gamma_k^d = \rho_{m,k} \gamma_k^{d1} + x_{m,k} \gamma_k^{d2}$. The total data rate of DUEs is expressed as follow, $R_k^d = \rho_{m,k} B\log_2(1 + \gamma_k^{d1}) + x_{m,k} B\log_2(1 + \gamma_k^{d2})$.

Requirements of DUEs: Safety-critical V2X applications impose rigorous operational constraints. Consequently, latency bounds and reliability thresholds are formally integrated as primal constraints within the optimization formulation. The reliability criterion is quantifiably defined through outage probability, mathematically represented as: $P\left\{\gamma_k^d \leq \gamma_0\right\} \leq p_0$. It can be transformed into $\gamma_k^d \leq \gamma_{eff} = \frac{\gamma_0}{\ln\left(\frac{1}{1-p_0}\right)}$. Due to the delay limit, each DUE generated message should be transmitted within a limited time range, which can be expressed as follows: $T_k^d = \frac{b_k^d}{R_k^d} \leq T_{\max}$.

3   Dynamic Resource Allocation Algorithm

This work develops a Dynamic Resource Allocation (DRA) framework for vehicular networks, jointly optimizing adaptive mode selection, spectrum partitioning, and power adjustment to maximize aggregate V2I capacity while guaranteeing V2V URLLC constraints. The algorithm coordinates transmission mode configuration, spectral resource allocation, and power parameter adaptation in response to network dynamics. The optimization problem is formally expressed as:

$$P: \max_{P^c,P^{d1},P^{d2},Q,X} \sum_{m=1}^{M} R_m^c$$

$$s.t.$$

$$(A1) \sum_{k=1}^{K} \rho_{m,k} \leq 1, \quad \forall m,$$

$$(A2) \rho_{m,k} \in \{0,1\}, \quad \forall m,k,$$

$$(A3) \sum_{k=1}^{K} x_{m,k} \leq 1, \quad \forall m,$$

$$(A4) x_{m,k} \in \{0,1\}, \quad \forall m,k,$$

$$(A5) \rho_{m,k} + x_{m,k} \leq 1, \quad \forall m,k,$$

$$(A6) 0 \leq p_m^c \leq p_{\max}^c, \quad \forall m,$$

$$(A7) 0 \leq p_k^{d1} \leq p_{\max}^{d1}, \quad \forall k,$$

$$(A8) 0 \leq p_k^{d2} \leq p_{\max}^{d2}, \quad \forall k,$$

$$(A9) R_m^c \geq R_0^c, \quad \forall m,$$

$$(A10) \gamma_k^d \leq \gamma_{eff}, \quad \forall k,$$

$$(A11) R_k^d \geq \frac{b_k^d}{T_{\max}}, \quad \forall k. \tag{1}$$

The optimization variables are defined as: $P^c = p_m^c, \forall m$, $P^{d1} = p_k^{d1}, \forall k$, $P^{d2} = p_k^{d2}, \forall k$, $Q = \rho_{m,k}, \forall m,k$, and $X = x_{m,k}, \forall m,k$. Constraints (A1)–(A4) ensure exclusive channel allocation per DUE, while (A5) enforces mutual exclusivity between reused and dedicated modes. Power limits for CUEs and DUEs are defined by (A6)–(A8). Constraint (A9) maintains minimum V2I capacity, whereas (A10)–(A11) enforce URLLC requirements for V2V communications.

Directly solving (11) is computationally intractable due to the binary nature of Q and X coupled with complex variable interdependencies. To address this, we adopt a two-stage approach: First, relax binary constraints to continuous domains. Second, apply block coordinate descent to decompose the problem into iteratively solvable subproblems.

3.1   Reused Mode Selection and Allocation Optimization

Given parameterized conditions: reused-mode power control P^{d1}, dedicated-mode selection X, and CUE power configuration P^c, the spectrum reuse selection subproblem is resolved through the following formulation:

$$P : \max_{Q} \sum_{m=1}^{M} R_m^c$$

$$s.t.$$

$$(B1) \sum_{k=1}^{K} \rho_{m,k} \leq 1, \quad \forall m,$$

$$(B2) \, 0 \leq \rho_{m,k} \leq 1, \quad \forall m, k,$$

$$(B3) \, \rho_{m,k} + x_{m,k} \leq 1, \quad \forall m, k,$$

$$(B4) \, R_m^c \geq R_0^c, \quad \forall m,$$

$$(B5) \, \gamma_k^d \leq \gamma_{eff}, \quad \forall k,$$

$$(B6) \, R_k^d \geq \frac{b_k^d}{T_{\max}}, \quad \forall k. \tag{2}$$

This subproblem is addressed through successive convex optimization methodology, employing local linearization techniques to transform non-convex constraints (B4)–(B6). Specifically, the signal-to-interference-plus-noise ratio formulations in (B4) and (B6) undergo first-order Taylor series approximation centered at the current iteration point $\rho_{m,k}^0$:

$$R_m^c \geq B \log_2 \left(1 + \frac{p_m^c h_m^B}{\sigma^2 + \sum_{k \in K} \rho_{m,k}^0 p_k^{d1} h_{k,B}} \right) + \frac{\log_2 e \cdot \sum_{k \in K} p_k^{d1} h_{k,B}}{p_m^c h_m^B + \sigma^2 + \sum_{k \in K} \rho_{m,k}^0 p_k^{d1} h_{k,B}} \cdot (\rho_{m,k} - \rho_{m,k}^0) \tag{3}$$

This transformation ensures the problem retains convexity, enabling efficient solution via CVX.

$$R_m^c = B \log_2 \left(1 + \frac{p_m^c h_m^B}{\sigma^2 + \sum_{k \in \mathrm{K}} \rho_{m,k} p_k^{d1} h_{k,B}} \right) \geq f_1(\rho_{m,k}^0) + f_1'(\rho_{m,k}^0)(\rho_{m,k} - \rho_{m,k}^0). \tag{4}$$

$$f_1(\rho^0_{m,k}) = \log_2(1 + \frac{p^c_m h^B_m}{\sigma^2 + \sum\limits_{k\in K} \rho^0_{m,k} p^{d1}_k h_{k,B}}). \tag{5}$$

$$f'_1(\rho^0_{m,k}) = \frac{\log_2 e \times \sum\limits_{k\in K} p^{d1}_k h_{k,B}}{p^c_m h^B_m + \sigma^2 + \sum\limits_{k\in K} \rho^0_{m,k} p^{d1}_k h_{k,B}} - \frac{\log_2 e \times \sum\limits_{k\in K} p^{d1}_k h_{k,B}}{\sigma^2 + \sum\limits_{k\in K} \rho^0_{m,k} p^{d1}_k h_{k,B}}. \tag{6}$$

For constraint (B4), the first-order Taylor transformation is expressed as follows

$$R^d_k = \rho_{m,k} B\log_2(1 + \gamma^{d1}_k) + x_k B\log_2(1 + \gamma^{d2}_k) = \rho_{m,k} BT + x_k BΥ. \tag{7}$$

$$\begin{aligned} T(\rho_{m,k}) = \log_2(\sigma^2 + \sum\limits_{m\in M} \rho_{m,k} p^c_m h_{m,k} + \sum\limits_{j\in K, j\neq k} x_{m,j} p^{d2}_j h_{j,k} + p^{d1}_k h^d_k) \\ -\log_2(\sigma^2 + \sum\limits_{m\in M} \rho_{m,k} p^c_m h_{m,k} + \sum\limits_{j\in K, j\neq k} x_{m,j} p^{d2}_j h_{j,k}). \end{aligned} \tag{8}$$

$$x_k BΥ \geq f_2(\rho^0_{m,k}) + f_2'(\rho^0_{m,k})(\rho_{m,k} - \rho^0_{m,k}). \tag{9}$$

$$f_2(\rho^0_{m,k}) = x_k B\log_2(1 + \frac{p^{d2}_k h^d_k}{\sigma^2 + \sum\limits_{j\in K, j\neq k} \rho^0_{m,j} p^{d1}_j h_{j,B}}). \tag{10}$$

$$f_2'(\rho^0_{m,k}) = x_k B\log_2 e \left(\frac{\sum\limits_{j\in K, j\neq k} p^{d1}_j h_{j,B}}{\sigma^2 + \sum\limits_{j\in K, j\neq k} \rho^0_{m,j} p^{d1}_j h_{j,B} + p^{d2}_k h^d_k} - \frac{\sum\limits_{j\in K, j\neq k} p^{d1}_j h_{j,B}}{\sigma^2 + \sum\limits_{j\in K, j\neq k} \rho^0_{m,j} p^{d1}_j h_{j,B}} \right). \tag{11}$$

$$T(\rho^0_{m,k}) = \rho^0_{m,k} B\log_2(1 + \frac{p^{d1}_k h^d_k}{\sigma^2 + \sum\limits_{m\in M} \rho^0_{m,k} p^c_m h_{m,k} + \sum\limits_{j\in K, j\neq k} x_{m,j} p^{d2}_j h_{j,k}}). \tag{12}$$

$$\begin{aligned} T'(\rho^0_{m,k}) = \frac{\log_2 e \times \sum\limits_{m\in M} p^c_m h_{m,k}}{\sigma^2 + \sum\limits_{m\in M} \rho^0_{m,k} p^c_m h_{m,k} + \sum\limits_{j\in K, j\neq k} x_{m,j} p^{d2}_j h_{j,k} + p^{d1}_k h^d_k} \\ - \frac{\log_2 e \times \sum\limits_{m\in M} p^c_m h_{m,k}}{\sigma^2 + \sum\limits_{m\in M} \rho^0_{m,k} p^c_m h_{m,k} + \sum\limits_{j\in K, j\neq k} x_{m,j} p^{d2}_j h_{j,k}}. \end{aligned} \tag{13}$$

The first-order Taylor approximations applied to constraints (B4) and (B6) exhibit joint concavity with respect to variable set Q, thereby rendering these constraints convex. Consequently, the subproblem is reformulated as a convex optimization formulation amenable to solution via the CVX framework.

3.2 Reused Mode Communication Power Control

Given predetermined parameters: reuse-mode power configuration P^{d1}, dedicated-mode selection X, dedicated-mode power allocation P^{d2}, and CUE transmission power P^c, the power control optimization for spectrum-sharing DUEs in formulation (11) is achieved through resolution of the following optimization proposition.

$$P : \max_{\boldsymbol{P}^{d1}} \sum_{m=1}^{M} R_m^c$$

$$s.t.$$

$$(C1)\, 0 \leq p_k^{d1} \leq p_{\max}^{d1}, \quad \forall k,$$
$$(C2)\, R_m^c \geq R_0^c, \quad \forall m,$$
$$(C3)\, \gamma_k^d \leq \gamma_{eff}, \quad \forall k,$$
$$(C4)\, R_k^d \geq \frac{b_k^d}{T_{\max}}, \quad \forall k. \tag{14}$$

For non-convexity constraints, we perform the first-order Taylor transformation, which can be expressed as follows

$$R_m^c = B\log_2\left(1 + \frac{p_m^c h_m^B}{\sigma^2 + \sum_{k \in \mathrm{K}} \rho_{m,k} p_k^{d1} h_{k,B}}\right) \geq f_3(p_{k0}^{d1}) + f_3{}'(p_{k0}^{d1})(p_k^{d1} - p_{k0}^{d1}). \tag{15}$$

$$f_3(p_{k0}^{d1}) = \log_2\left(1 + \frac{p_m^c h_m^B}{\sigma^2 + \sum_{k \in \mathrm{K}} \rho_{m,k} p_{k0}^{d1} h_{k,B}}\right). \tag{16}$$

$$f_3{}'(p_{k0}^{d1}) = \frac{\log_2 e \times \sum_{k \in \mathrm{K}} \rho_{m,k} h_{k,B}}{p_m^c h_m^B + \sigma^2 + \sum_{k \in \mathrm{K}} \rho_{m,k} p_{k0}^{d1} h_{k,B}} - \frac{\log_2 e \times \sum_{k \in \mathrm{K}} \rho_{m,k} h_{k,B}}{\sigma^2 + \sum_{k \in \mathrm{K}} \rho_{m,k} p_{k0}^{d1} h_{k,B}}. \tag{17}$$

$$R_k^d = \rho_{m,k} B\log_2(1 + \gamma_k^{d1}) + x_k B\log_2(1 + \gamma_k^{d2}) = \rho_{m,k} B\mathrm{T}_1 + x_k B\Upsilon_1. \tag{18}$$

Then, We apply the successive convex optimization technique to tackle the non-convexity of Υ_1

$$\Upsilon_1 \geq f_4(p_{k0}^{d1}) + f_4{}'(p_{k0}^{d1})(p_k^{d1} - p_{k0}^{d1}). \tag{19}$$

$$f_4(p_{k0}^{d1}) = \log_2\left(1 + \frac{p_k^{d2} h_k^d}{\sigma^2 + \sum_{j \in \mathrm{K}, j \neq k} \rho_{m,j} p_{j0}^{d1} h_{j,B}}\right). \tag{20}$$

$$f'_4(p_{k0}^{d1}) = \frac{\sum_{j \in \mathrm{K}, j \neq k} \rho_{m,j} h_{j,k} \log_2 e}{\sigma^2 + \sum_{j \in \mathrm{K}, j \neq k} \rho_{m,j} p_{j0}^{d1} h_{j,B} + p_k^{d2} h_k^d} - \frac{\sum_{j \in \mathrm{K}, j \neq k} \rho_{m,j} h_{j,k} \log_2 e}{\sigma^2 + \sum_{j \in \mathrm{K}, j \neq k} \rho_{m,j} p_{j0}^{d1} h_{j,B}}. \tag{21}$$

Therefore, the sub-problem is transformed into a convex optimization problem that can be solved by CVX.

3.3   Dedicated Mode Selection and Allocation Optimization

Under parameterized conditions encompassing reused-mode power allocation P^{d1}, spectrum reuse selection Q, dedicated-mode power configuration P^{d2}, and CUE transmission parameters P^c, the dedicated mode selection mechanism in optimization formulation (11) is refined through resolution of the following mathematical program.

$$P : \max_{\mathbf{X}} \sum_{m=1}^{M} R_m^c$$

$s.t.$

$$(D1) \sum_{k=1}^{K} x_{m,k} \leq 1, \quad \forall m,$$

$$(D2) 0 \leq x_{m,k} \leq 1, \quad \forall m, k,$$

$$(D3) \rho_{m,k} + x_{m,k} \leq 1, \quad \forall m, k,$$

$$(D4) \gamma_k^d \leq \gamma_{eff}, \quad \forall k,$$

$$(D5) R_k^d \geq \frac{b_k^d}{T_{\max}}, \quad \forall k. \tag{22}$$

For non-convexity constraints (D5), we perform the first-order Taylor transformation, which can be expressed as follows

$$R_k^d = \rho_{m,k} B\log_2(1 + \gamma_k^{d1}) + x_k B\log_2(1 + \gamma_k^{d2}) = \rho_{m,k} B T_2 + x_k B \Upsilon_2. \tag{23}$$

$$\rho_{m,k} B T_2 \geq T(\rho_{m,k}^0) + T'(\rho_{m,k}^0)(\rho_{m,k} - \rho_{m,k}^0). \tag{24}$$

$$T_2(x_{m,k}^0) = \rho_{m,k} B\log_2\left(1 + \frac{p_k^{d1} h_k^d}{\sigma^2 + \sum_{m \in M} \rho_{m,k} p_{m0}^c h_{m,k} + \sum_{j \in K, j \neq k} x_{m,j} p_j^{d2} h_{j,k}}\right). \tag{25}$$

$$T_2'(x_{m,k}^0) = \rho_{m,k} B\log_2 e \left(\frac{\sum_{k \in K} \rho_{m,k} h_{m,k}}{\sigma^2 + \sum_{m \in M} \rho_{m,k} p_{m0}^c h_{m,k} + \sum_{j \in K, j \neq k} x_{m,j} p_j^{d2} h_{j,k} + p_k^{d1} h_k^d} - \frac{\sum_{k \in K} \rho_{m,k} h_{m,k}}{\sigma^2 + \sum_{m \in M} \rho_{m,k} p_{m0}^c h_{m,k} + \sum_{j \in K, j \neq k} x_{m,j} p_j^{d2} h_{j,k}} \right). \tag{26}$$

Therefore, the sub-problem is transformed into a convex optimization problem that can be solved by CVX.

3.4 Dedicated Mode Communication Power Control

Given parameters Q, P^{d1}, X, and P^c, the power optimization for dedicated-mode DUEs solves:

$$P : \max_{\boldsymbol{P}^{d2}} \sum_{m=1}^{M} R_m^c$$

$$s.t.$$

$$(E1)\, 0 \leq p_k^{d2} \leq p_{\max}^{d2}, \quad \forall k,$$

$$(E2)\, \gamma_k^d \leq \gamma_{eff}, \quad \forall k,$$

$$(E3)\, R_k^d \geq \frac{b_k^d}{T_{\max}}, \quad \forall k. \tag{27}$$

For non-convexity constraints (E3), we perform the first-order Taylor transformation, which can be expressed as follows

$$T_3(p_{j0}^{d2}) = \rho_{m,k} B \log_2 \left(1 + \frac{p_k^{d1} h_k^d}{\sigma^2 + \sum_{m \in M} \rho_{m,k} p_m^c h_{m,k} + \sum_{j \in K, j \neq k} x_{m,j} p_{j0}^{d2} h_{j,k}}\right). \tag{28}$$

$$T_3'(p_{j0}^{d2}) = \rho_{m,k} B \log_2 e \left(\frac{\sum_{j \in K, j \neq k} x_{m,j} h_{j,k}}{\sigma^2 + \sum_{m \in M} \rho_{m,k} p_m^c h_{m,k} + \sum_{j \in K, j \neq k} x_{m,j} p_{j0}^{d2} h_{j,k} + p_k^{d1} h_k^d} - \frac{\sum_{j \in K, j \neq k} x_{m,j} h_{j,k}}{\sigma^2 + \sum_{m \in M} \rho_{m,k} p_m^c h_{m,k} + \sum_{j \in K, j \neq k} x_{m,j} p_{j0}^{d2} h_{j,k}} \right). \tag{29}$$

Consequently, the subproblem is reformulated as a convex program amenable to efficient resolution within the CVX optimization environment. Therefore, the sub-problem is transformed into a convex optimization problem that can be solved by CVX. We apply the iterative algorithm based on the results of five sub-problems.

4 Evaluation

Performance evaluation considers a $4\,\text{km}^2$ urban area with 5 CUEs and 10 DUEs dynamically switching modes. System bandwidth is $20\,\text{MHz}$, maintaining 3.5 bps/Hz spectral efficiency for CUEs. Critical V2V constraints enforce $\Pr(\gamma_k^d < \gamma_0) \leq 0.01$ at $\gamma_0 = 1$ dB SINR and 50 ms latency. V2I links guarantee ≥ 1 Mbps data rates. Power constraints: 23 dBm (CUEs), 15 dBm (dedicated DUEs), 23 dBm (reused DUEs). Propagation combines Rayleigh fading $+8$ dB shadowing (infrastructure links) and Nakagami-m fading ($m = 2$) (D2D paths).

Figure 2 compares DUE service fulfillment ratios under varying densities for three schemes: DRA, its mode-static variant, and an uncoordinated baseline. Results demonstrate DRA's consistent superiority across densities. This stems from adaptive spectrum partitioning between cellular and vehicular users. As DUE density increases, conventional schemes exhibit resource fragmentation due to fixed mode limitations. Conversely, DRA employs intelligent mode switching: dedicating spectrum for interference-sensitive links while reusing resources in spatially decoupled regions, effectively controlling co-channel interference and enhancing spectral efficiency.

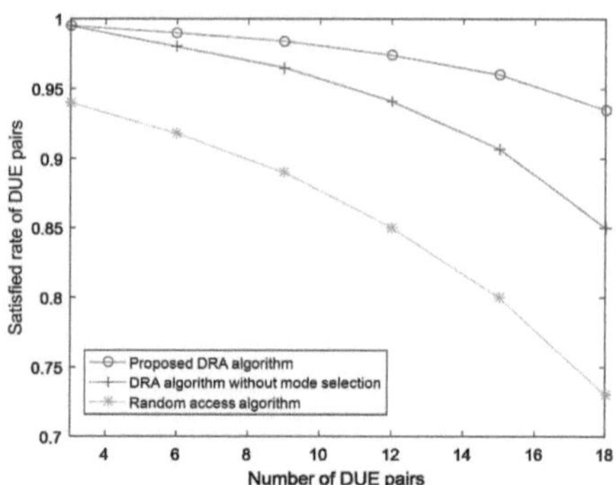

Fig. 2. Satisfied rate of DUE pairs with the number of DUE pairs.

Figure 3 shows aggregate CUE capacity versus V2V outage thresholds (minimum SINR γ_0 for reliability). Both DRA and mode-static schemes exhibit decreasing capacity as thresholds increase, while random access remains invariant. DRA consistently outperforms alternatives across all thresholds. This advantage stems from adaptive interference mitigation via dynamic mode selection. Higher thresholds require increased V2V power, amplifying cellular interference, which DRA counters through optimized mode balancing.

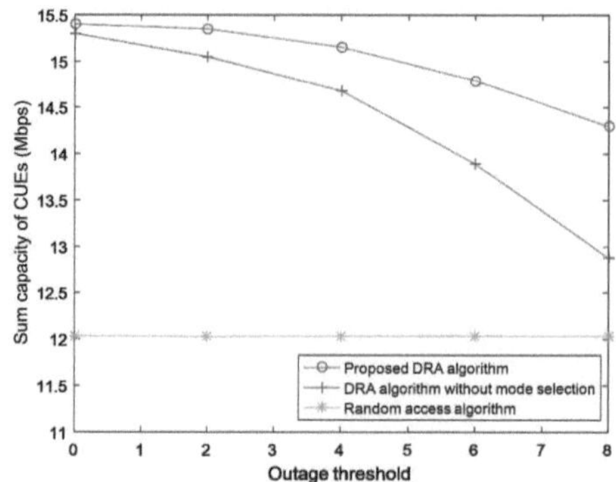

Fig. 3. Sum capacity of CUEs according to different outage thresholds.

Figure 4 depicts DUE fulfillment ratios (proportion maintaining URLLC) versus outage thresholds. All schemes show monotonically decreasing fulfillment, with non-adaptive methods degrading quasi-linearly beyond 4 dB. This stems from their reliance on spectrum reuse under power constraints, yielding insufficient SINR at higher thresholds. Conversely, DRA maintains robustness by assigning dedicated modes to critical links and reuse in interference-resilient zones, preserving stability across thresholds.

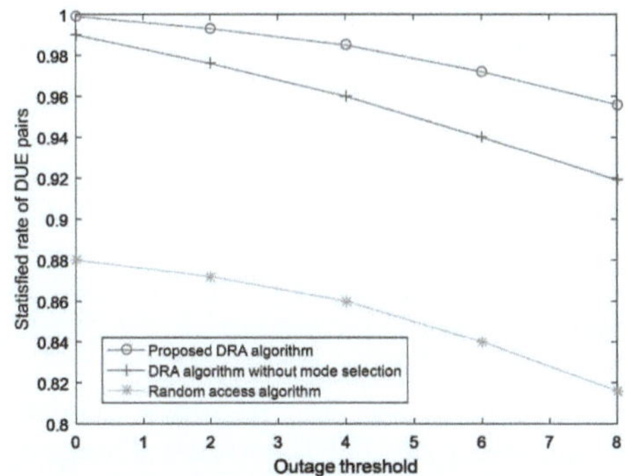

Fig. 4. Satisfied rate of DUE pairs according to different outage thresholds.

5 Conclusions

This work establishes a joint optimization framework for transmission mode selection, spectrum allocation, and power distribution in D2D-enhanced V2X systems, designed to maximize cellular user aggregate throughput while satisfying vehicular user pair requirements. To address computational complexity inherent in this multi-variable optimization, an iterative solution methodology is developed. This approach employs block coordinate descent to decouple the problem into tractable subproblems, with successive convex optimization applied to transform non-convex constraints. Empirical validation confirms the significant performance advantages of the proposed dynamic resource allocation mechanism.

Acknowledgments. This work was supported in part by the National Natural Science Foundation of China (Grants No. 62402066), Natural Science Foundation Project of Hunan Province (No. 2024JJ7617, 2023JJ30085), Science and Technology Plan Projects of YiYang (No. 2015JZ28), Scientific Research Project of the Education Department of Hunan (No. 24B0798, 22A0599).

References

1. Zhou, H., Xu, W., Chen, J., Wang, W.: Evolutionary v2x technologies toward the internet of vehicles: challenges and opportunities. Proc. IEEE **2**, 308–323 (2023)
2. Fan, C., Li, B., Wu, Y., Zhang, J., Yang, Z., Zhao, C.: Fuzzy matching learning for dynamic resource allocation in cellular v2x network. IEEE Trans. Veh. Technol. **4**, 3479–3492 (2024)
3. Zhang, M., Dou, Y., Chong, P.H.J., Chan, H.C.B., Seet, B.-C.: Fuzzy logic-based resource allocation algorithm for v2x communications in 5g cellular networks. IEEE J. Sel. Areas Commun. **8**, 2501–2513 (2021)
4. Bahonar, M.H., Omidi, M.J., Yanikomeroglu, H.: Low-complexity resource allocation for dense cellular vehicle-to-everything (c-v2x) communications. IEEE Open J. Commun. Soc. **2**, 2695–2713 (2024)
5. Abbas, F., Fan, P., Khan, Z.: A novel low-latency v2v resource allocation scheme based on cellular v2x communications. IEEE Trans. Intell. Transp. Syst. **6**, 2185–2197 (2019)
6. Zhang, F., Wang, M.M., Bao, X., Liu, W.: Centralized resource allocation and distributed power control for noma-integrated nr v2x. IEEE Internet Things J. **22**, 16522–16534 (2021)
7. Li, X., Ma, L., Xu, Y., Shankaran, R.: Resource allocation for d2d-based v2x communication with imperfect csi. IEEE Internet Things J. **7**, 3545–3558 (2020)
8. Xiao, H., Zhu, D., Chronopoulos, A.T.: Power allocation with energy efficiency optimization in cellular d2d-based v2x communication network. IEEE Trans. Intell. Transp. Syst. **12**, 4947–4957 (2020)
9. Xiong, R., Zhang, C., Zeng, H., Yi, X., Li, L., Wang, P.: Reducing power consumption for autonomous ground vehicles via resource allocation based on road segmentation in v2x-mec with resource constraints. IEEE Trans. Veh. Technol. **6**, 6397–6409 (2022)
10. Chen, H., Lee, J., Kim, T.: Lyapunov optimization for latency-sensitive V2X services under dynamic spectrum sharing. IEEE J. Sel. Areas Commun. **41**, 1589–1603 (2023)
11. Wang, Y., Gupta, R., Bennis, M.: Game-theoretic mode selection for mmWave-enabled V2X systems with heterogeneous QoS constraints. In: Proceedings of IEEE International Conference on Computer Communications(INFOCOM), pp. 1–6 (2023)
12. Zhang, Z., Li, L., Xu, K.: Edge-aided resource allocation for V2X communications: a practical fading model with semi-Markov decision processes. IEEE Open J. Commun. Soc. **5**, 1234–1248 (2024)

A Digital Twin-Assisted Multi-agent Task Offloading Method with Priority Scheduling in Vehicular Edge Networks

Taotao Yu[1], Zhou Zhou[2], and Hongbing Cheng[1]($\boxtimes$)

[1] College of Computer Science, Zhejiang University of Technology,
Hangzhou 310023, China
{211123120080,chenghb}@zjut.edu.cn
[2] College of Computer Science and Engineering,
Changsha University, Changsha 410003, China
zhzhou@ccsu.edu.cn

Abstract. Vehicular Edge Computing (VEC) has emerged as a promising solution for offloading computation-intensive tasks from vehicles to nearby edge servers, enabling low-latency and energy-efficient services. However, real-world vehicular workloads are often heterogeneous, varying significantly in data size, deadline sensitivity, and task priority. Such heterogeneities introduce significant challenges in effective task scheduling and resource allocation. In this paper, we propose a novel digital twin-assisted offloading method based on a Multi-Agent Deep Deterministic Policy Gradient (MADDPG) framework, named DT-MAP. This method jointly considers task heterogeneity, vehicular mobility, and priority-aware scheduling. Additionally, the proposed method incorporates a dynamic reward shaping mechanism that accounts for task priority, delay sensitivity and load penalty, enabling agents to learn cooperative offloading policies under constrained edge resources. To evaluate our approach, we develop a simulated VEC environment inspired by digital twins, which dynamically reflects vehicle mobility, network conditions, and edge server status. Experiments with varying vehicle numbers show that DT-MAP outperforms baseline strategies (Random, Greedy, SAC), with an average load balancing improvement of 17.48%, 14.81%, and 3.78%, respectively. It also reduces average latency by 9.57%, 7.30%, and 3.24%. Additionally, DT-MAP achieves near-saturation resource utilization, with an average efficiency of 98.70%.

Keywords: Vehicular Edge Computing · Multi-Agent Reinforcement Learning · Digital Twin-Assisted · Priority Scheduling · Task Offloading

1 Introduction

With the rapid development of 5G and emerging technologies such as autonomous driving [1], augmented reality (AR), and high-definition video streaming, the computational demands on vehicles have surged [2]. These applications require real-time processing of massive data, often exceeding the onboard computing capabilities [3,4]. Offloading computation-intensive tasks to nearby edge servers has thus become a promising approach to reduce latency and enhance responsiveness in VEC systems [5,6].

However, efficient task offloading remains challenging due to the dynamic and heterogeneous nature of vehicular environments [7]. Vehicular tasks vary widely in data size, deadlines, and priority-e.g., real-time sensor fusion demands immediate execution, while media uploads can tolerate delay. This heterogeneity complicates scheduling and resource allocation [8]. Additionally, vehicle mobility causes frequent network topology changes, further affecting offloading efficiency [9]. Digital Twin (DT) technology [10] offers a promising solution by creating virtual replicas of physical entities for real-time monitoring, simulation, and prediction [11]. In VEC, DTs can model vehicle states and network conditions [12], enabling adaptive and context-aware offloading decisions under dynamic environments.

To address these challenges, we propose a novel DT-assisted multi-agent task offloading method(DT-MAP) that integrates task heterogeneity and priority-aware scheduling within a MADDPG framework. By incorporating digital twins into the offloading process, DT-MAP dynamically adjusts task allocation based on the vehicle's mobility, network conditions, and task characteristics. Specifically, DT-MAP leverages dynamic reward shaping to account for task priority, delay sensitivity, and load penalties, thus enabling cooperative offloading policies that efficiently utilize edge resources.

The main contributions of this work are summarized as follows:

- We introduce a detailed task model considering data size, deadline, and priority to better capture the diversity of vehicular computing tasks.
- We design a reward function that incorporates task priority, delay sensitivity, and load penalty, which enables agents to learn offloading policies that balance latency and resource utilization effectively.
- We construct a simulation environment inspired by digital twins that dynamically reflects vehicle mobility, edge server conditions, and task demands, providing a realistic platform for evaluating task offloading strategies.
- Through experiments on varying vehicle numbers and task distributions, we show that our method significantly outperforms baseline strategies in terms of average latency, load balancing, and resource utilization.

The remainder of this paper is organized as follows: Sect. 2 reviews related work. Section 3 introduces the system model and problem formulation. Section 4 details the proposed algorithm. Section 5 describes the simulation setup and reports results. Finally, Sect. 6 concludes the paper and outlines future work.

2   Related Work

In this section, we review the most relevant studies in task offloading schemes and also summarize the collaboration of DT and VEC paradigm.

2.1   Task Offloading

Task offloading in VEC has been widely studied in recent years, particularly focusing on reducing latency and improving resource utilization. Existing literature primarily explores offloading strategies from two perspectives: resource allocation via heuristic or game-theoretic approaches [13–16], and reinforcement learning-based adaptive scheduling [17–19].

Abuthahir et al. [13] reviewed meta-heuristic approaches (e.g., SA, ACO, PSO, GA) in optimizing latency and energy consumption. Game-theoretic methods have been widely applied: Sun et al. [14] designed a stable many-to-one matching framework for edge resource allocation; Xu et al. [15] combined fuzzy logic and Q-learning in a game-theoretic offloading model to improve load balancing; Su et al. [16] formulated a hierarchical Stackelberg game for queue-aware and delay-sensitive task scheduling.

On the other hand, RL-based methods provide adaptability in dynamic VEC environments. Kumar et al. [17] introduced L-MADDPG for joint task offloading and wireless control under varying conditions. Hazarika et al. [18] adopted DRL (SAC, DDPG, TD3) for priority-aware task offloading. Chen et al. [19] proposed a two-stage DRLCL scheme to improve delay and load balance in realistic VEC scenarios

2.2   Digital Twin with VEC Collaboration

DT technology has gained significant attention in VEC [20–23]. Yang et al. [20]. Yang et al. [20] integrated DT with visible light communication for joint offloading and resource allocation. Xu et al. [21] introduced a DT-assisted blockchain VEC scheme combining d2BFT consensus and MADAC for secure task scheduling. Zhu et al. [22] applied an improved A3C algorithm within a DT-enhanced edge-cloud system to reduce delay and energy use. Kong et al. [23] designed a DT-based IoV framework using TD3 to minimize delay and energy in dynamic environments.

Our proposed DT-assisted multi-agent priority task offloading model focuses on low latency, load balancing, and efficient resource utilization in dynamic VEC environments. Unlike prior works, we model task heterogeneity (data volume, deadline, priority) and introduce a tailored reward function combining delay sensitivity and load penalties to optimize resource allocation. Additionally, we leverage DT technology to model vehicle mobility, network conditions, and edge server status for real-time updates, enabling more refined offloading decisions and reducing system latency while maintaining stable service load balance.

3   System Model and Problem Formulation

3.1   System Overview

We consider a DT-assisted VEC system, comprising a set of mobile vehicles $\mathcal{N} = \{1, 2, ..., N\}$ and a set of edge servers $\mathcal{M} = \{1, 2, ..., M\}$ deployed along the roadside. Each vehicle moves along predefined trajectories and periodically generates computational tasks. Given their limited onboard computing capabilities, vehicles offload part or all of their tasks to nearby VEC servers via vehicle-to-infrastructure (V2I) communication. To support dynamic decision-making under mobility and environmental uncertainty, we integrate a DT module that mirrors the real-time status of vehicles and servers in a virtual cloud environment. The DT collects vehicular states (e.g., position, speed, server load) and assists in predictive offloading decisions.

In each time slot t, each vehicle $n \in \mathcal{N}$ generates K heterogeneous tasks, where each task $k \in \{1, ..., K\}$ is characterized by:

- **Data size** $d_{n,k} \in \mathbb{R}^+$: the input data volume in MB.
- **Deadline** $\delta_{n,k} \in \mathbb{R}^+$: the maximal tolerable delay for task completion.
- **Priority score** $p_{n,k} \in [0, 1]$: representing the urgency or importance of the task (e.g., safety-critical tasks have higher values).

3.2   Task Offloading and Delay Model

To achieve a balance between computational efficiency and latency constraints, each vehicle determines an offloading ratio vector denoted as $\omega_n = [\omega_{n,1}, ..., \omega_{n,K}]$. Each element $\omega_{n,k} \in [0, 1]$ represents the proportion of task k offloaded by vehicle n to an edge server, while the remaining portion $(1 - \omega_{n,k})$ is executed locally on the vehicle.

The total end-to-end delay for executing task k is modeled as:

$$T_{n,k} = \omega_{n,k} \cdot (T_{n,k}^{\text{comm}} + T_{n,k}^{\text{edge}}) + (1 - \omega_{n,k}) \cdot T_{n,k}^{\text{local}} \tag{1}$$

where the three components represent different stages of computation: $T_{n,k}^{\text{local}}$ represents the delay incurred when the task is fully executed on the vehicle; $T_{n,k}^{\text{comm}}$ represents the communication delay of transmitting the task data to the edge server; and $T_{n,k}^{\text{edge}}$ represents the computational delay after the edge server receives the task.

The local processing delay is determined by the size of the task and the computational capacity of the vehicle. Assuming that each vehicle is equipped with a processor operating at frequency f_n, the local delay is given by:

$$T_{n,k}^{\text{local}} = \frac{d_{n,k}}{f_n} \tag{2}$$

where $d_{n,k}$ is the input data size (in MB) of task k.

When a task is offloaded, the edge server allocates computational resources to execute it. Let f_m^e denote the effective CPU frequency allocated to vehicle n on server m, then the edge-side execution delay is:

$$T_{n,k}^{\text{edge}} = \frac{d_{n,k}}{f_m^e} \tag{3}$$

The time required to upload task data to the edge server depends on the wireless uplink conditions. Assuming orthogonal access, the uplink delay is modeled as:

$$T_{n,k}^{\text{comm}} = \frac{d_{n,k}}{W_n \log_2(1 + \text{SINR}_n)} \tag{4}$$

where W_n is the allocated bandwidth and SINR_n is the uplink signal-to-interference-plus-noise ratio for vehicle n.

3.3   Server Load Balancing Model

In order to ensure that tasks are more evenly distributed, thereby improving system stability and preventing overload or idleness of individual servers, we model the key indicator of server load balancing.

Let L_m denote the total task workload assigned to edge server $m \in \mathcal{M}$, which is calculated as the aggregated offloaded data from all vehicles:

$$L_m = \sum_{n=1}^{N} \sum_{k=1}^{K} \omega_{n,k} \cdot d_{n,k} \tag{5}$$

To quantify how evenly the workload is distributed among servers, we define the standard deviation of load across all M servers as:

$$\text{Std}_{\text{load}} = \sqrt{\frac{1}{M} \sum_{m=1}^{M} \left(L_m - \bar{L}\right)^2} \tag{6}$$

where the mean load is given by:

$$\bar{L} = \frac{1}{M} \sum_{m=1}^{M} L_m \tag{7}$$

A smaller Std_{load} indicates more balanced server workloads and better system robustness.

3.4   Problem Formulation

By integrating the above system model with the task offloading model, we construct an optimization problem. The objective of the optimization problem is to minimize both the overall weighted end-to-end delay and the load standard deviation across edge servers, while satisfying the system resource and QoS constraints. The optimization problem is defined as:

$$P1: \quad \min_{\omega_n} \left(\sum_{n=1}^{N} \sum_{k=1}^{K} p_{n,k} \cdot T_{n,k} + \alpha \cdot \text{Std}_{\text{load}} \right) \tag{8}$$

where the term $\sum_{n=1}^{N} \sum_{k=1}^{K} p_{n,k} \cdot T_{n,k}$ aims to minimize the weighted end-to-end delay of tasks across all vehicles, where $p_{n,k}$ is the priority weight of task k from vehicle n; and the term $\alpha \cdot \text{Std}_{\text{load}}$ minimizes the standard deviation of the total workload across all edge servers. And α is a weighting factor that balances the trade-off between minimizing delay and load balancing.

subject to the following constraints:

$$\text{s.t.}\mathbf{C1:} \quad T_{n,k} \leq \delta_{n,k}, \quad \forall n \in \mathcal{N}, \ \forall k \in \{1, \ldots, K\} \tag{9}$$

$$\tag{10}$$

$$\mathbf{C2:} \quad \omega_{n,k} \in [0,1], \quad \forall n, k$$

$$\mathbf{C3:} \quad \sum_{n=1}^{N} \sum_{k=1}^{K} \omega_{n,k} \cdot d_{n,k} \leq C_m, \quad \forall m \in \mathcal{M} \tag{11}$$

where: $C1$ ensures that the total delay $T_{n,k}$ for each task does not exceed its maximum delay tolerance $\delta_{n,k}$, which applies to both local processing and offloading. $C2$ guarantees that the offloading ratio $\omega_{n,k}$ for each task k of vehicle n is within the valid probability range $[0, 1]$, allowing partial offloading or full local processing. $C3$ limits the cumulative computational load offloaded to each edge server m, ensuring that its processing capacity C_m is not exceeded, thus preventing server overload and maintaining feasible scheduling.

4   Proposed Method

In this section, we propose a digital twin-assisted multi-agent priority scheduling task offloading method based on the system model and problem formulation.

4.1   Multi-agent MDP Formulation

We model the task offloading problem as a multi-agent Markov Decision Process (MDP), represented by a tuple $(\mathcal{N}, \mathcal{S}, \mathcal{A}, \mathcal{P}, \mathcal{R})$, where $\mathcal{N}$ is the set of N agents, $\mathcal{S}$ is the global state space, $\mathcal{A}$ is the joint action space, $\mathcal{P}$ is the state transition probability, and $\mathcal{R}$ is the reward function. The system is defined through the following key components:

1) Agent Set $\mathcal{N}$: The set $\mathcal{N}$ represents all the vehicles (agents) within the system. Each agent $n \in \mathcal{N}$ corresponds to a single vehicle equipped with sensors and processing capabilities, which generates and offloads computational tasks to nearby edge servers. The agent set can be expressed as $\mathcal{N} = \{1, 2, \ldots, N\}$.

2) State Space $\mathcal{S}$: The state $s_n(t)$ of agent n at time t includes local task attributes $\{d_{n,k}, \delta_{n,k}, p_{n,k}\}_{k=1}^{K}$, vehicle position, distance to nearby servers, and the edge server load snapshot. The global state $s(t)$ is the concatenation of all local states and can be expressed as:

$$s(t) = \{s_n(t)\}_{n=1}^{N} \tag{12}$$

3) Action Space $\mathcal{A}$: The action $a_n(t)$ of agent n determines the offloading ratios ω_n, which can be represented as?

$$a_n(t) = \{\omega_{n,k}\}_{k=1}^K \tag{13}$$

where $\omega_{n,k} \in [0, 1]$ denotes the offloading decision for task k.

4) State Transition $\mathcal{P}$: The state evolves stochastically based on vehicle mobility, task generation, and server load variation. The environment updates states according to trajectories and server responses.

5) Reward Function $\mathcal{R}$: We define the reward of agent n at time t as:

$$r_n(t) = \sum_{k=1}^K r_{n,k}(t) - \sum_{m=1}^M \text{Penalty}_{\text{load},m} \tag{14}$$

where $r_{n,k}(t)$ represents the reward for vehicle n completing task k at time t, and $\text{Penalty}_{\text{load},m}$ denotes the overload penalty imposed on server m due to excessive load. We define the task completion reward of agent n at time t as follows:

$$r_{n,k}(t) = \begin{cases} 1.0 \cdot p_{n,k} \cdot \omega_{n,k}, & \text{if } T_{n,k}(t) \leq \delta_{n,k} \\ 0.2 \cdot p_{n,k} \cdot \omega_{n,k}, & \text{if } \delta_{n,k} < T_{n,k}(t) \leq \delta_{n,k} + 0.5 \\ -1.0 \cdot p_{n,k} \cdot (T_{n,k}(t) - \delta_{n,k}), & \text{if } T_{n,k}(t) > \delta_{n,k} + 0.5 \end{cases} \tag{15}$$

where $T_{n,k}(t)$ represent the delay of task k of vehicle n, $\delta_{n,k}$ be the deadline of task k, and $p_{n,k}$ be the priority of task k.

Server overload is penalized if the cumulative load on a server exceeds its capacity. The load penalty is calculated based on the excess load, and the reward is reduced accordingly. The penalty is:

$$\text{Penalty}_{\text{load}} = 0.3 \cdot \text{Overload}_m \tag{16}$$

The load penalty for server m is computed as:

$$\text{Overload}_m = \max\left(0, \sum_{n=1}^N \sum_{k=1}^K \omega_{n,k} \cdot d_{n,k} - C_m\right) \tag{17}$$

where C_m is the maximum processing capacity of server m.

4.2   MADDPG-Based Offloading Architecture

In our proposed DT-MAP method, where each vehicle maintains an actor network and a centralized critic network to determine the optimal offloading decisions. The overall training procedure is summarized in Algorithm 1. It includes sampling, critic evaluation, actor update, and target synchronization.

Algorithm 1. Priority-Aware Multi-Agent Offloading via MADDPG

Require: Discount factor γ, update rate τ, exploration rate ϵ, actor π_{θ_n}, critic Q_ϕ, target networks $\pi_{\theta'_n}$, $Q_{\phi'}$, replay buffer $\mathcal{D}$

1: Initialize environment, set $t = 0$
2: **for** each episode **do**
3:     Reset environment, get initial observation $s = (s_1, ..., s_N)$
4:     **for** each time step t **do**
5:         **for** each agent $n = 1, ..., N$ **do**
6:             With probability ϵ, select random action a_n
7:             Otherwise, select $a_n = \pi_{\theta_n}(s_n)$
8:         **end for**
9:         Execute joint action $a = (a_1, ..., a_N)$
10:         Receive reward $r = (r_1, ..., r_N)$ and next state $s' = (s'_1, ..., s'_N)$
11:         Store transition (s, a, r, s') into replay buffer $\mathcal{D}$
12:         Sample mini-batch $\{(s, a, r, s')\}$ from $\mathcal{D}$
13:         **for** each agent n **do**
14:             Compute target action $a'_n = \pi_{\theta'_n}(s'_n)$
15:             Compute target Q-value: $y_n = r_n + \gamma Q_{\phi'}(s', a'_1, ..., a'_N)$
16:             Update critic by minimizing: $L(\phi) = \mathbb{E}[(Q_\phi(s, a) - y_n)^2]$
17:             Compute policy gradient: $\nabla_{\theta_n} J \approx \mathbb{E}[\nabla_{\theta_n} \pi_{\theta_n}(s_n) \nabla_a Q_\phi(s, a)]$
18:             Update actor π_{θ_n} using policy gradient
19:             Soft update target networks: $\theta'_n \leftarrow \tau \theta_n + (1 - \tau)\theta'_n$,
20:             $\phi' \leftarrow \tau \phi + (1 - \tau)\phi'$
21:         **end for**
22:     **end for**
23: **end for**

Actor-Critic Framework. Each vehicle n maintains an actor network π_n that outputs $\omega_n(t)$ based on its current observation $s_n(t)$. A centralized critic network Q_Π is shared among all agents to evaluate the joint state-action value $Q(s, a)$. The training follows the actor-critic paradigm, as outlined in the following loss function:

$$L_{\text{critic}}(\phi) = \mathbb{E}_{(s,a,r,s')} \left[(Q_\phi(s, a) - y)^2 \right] \tag{18}$$

$$y = r + \gamma Q_{\phi'}(s', a'), \quad a' = \{\pi_{\theta'_n}(s'_n)\}_{n=1}^{N} \tag{19}$$

where ϕ' and θ'_n are target network parameters.

The actor update for each agent is computed as:

$$\nabla_{\theta_n} J(\theta_n) = \mathbb{E}_s \left[\nabla_{\theta_n} \pi_{\theta_n}(s_n) \nabla_{a_n} Q_\phi(s, a) \right] \tag{20}$$

Centralized Training and Decentralized Execution. During training, a centralized learner collects trajectories and updates the shared critic and each agent's actor. In execution, each agent operates based solely on its own observation. The replay buffer stores transitions (s, a, r, s') for sampling mini-batches. Target networks are softly updated using:

$$\theta'_n \leftarrow \tau\theta_n + (1 - \tau)\theta'_n, \quad \phi' \leftarrow \tau\phi + (1 - \tau)\phi' \tag{21}$$

Priority-Aware Reward Shaping and Exploration. To encourage intelligent offloading decisions under heterogeneous task constraints, we design a reward shaping mechanism that integrates task priority $p_{n,k}$, deadline awareness, and server load penalties. The reward function assigns higher returns to agents that successfully offload high-priority tasks within their delay bounds, while penalizing excessive delays and server overloads. For exploration, we adopt an ϵ-greedy strategy: with probability ϵ, the agent selects a random action to encourage exploration; otherwise, it follows the current policy output. The exploration rate ϵ is gradually annealed during training to balance exploration and exploitation.

Digital Twin-Assisted Offloading. We integrate the digital twin model into the MADDPG framework to assist with real-time predictions. By simulating dynamic environmental conditions, the DT model continuously updates the states of vehicles, servers, and tasks, and provides feedback loops for optimal offloading decisions.

5 Experiments

In this section, we evaluate the performance of DT-MAP. We conduct experiments using a synthetic vehicular environment to assess the effectiveness of our approach in terms of task latency, server load balancing, and resource utilization.

5.1 Experimental Setup

We simulate a VEC environment with N vehicles and M edge servers. Each vehicle periodically generates K tasks with heterogeneous attributes: data size $d_{n,k}$, deadline $\delta_{n,k}$, and priority score $p_{n,k}$. The communication channel is modeled using an SINR-based wireless uplink model. The simulation parameters are summarized in Table 1. And we compared DT-MAP with three algorithms, including SAC [24], Greedy [25] and Random.

Table 1. Simulation Parameters

Parameter	Value	Parameter	Value
Number of vehicles N	6–10	Server CPU capacity f_m^e	10 GHz
Number of servers M	3	Wireless bandwidth W_n	10 MHz
Task per vehicle K	3	Vehicle CPU capacity f_n	1 GHz
Task data size $d_{n,k}$	5–20 MB	Server max load C_m	100 MB
Task deadline $\delta_{n,k}$	0.5–2.0 s	Simulation steps	500 episodes
Task priority $p_{n,k}$	0.1–1.0	Tradeoff weight α	0.5
SINR$_n$	10 dB	Simulation map length L_{map}	500 m

5.2   Results and Analysis

Algorithm Convergence Analysis. We analyze the convergence behavior of our proposed method compared to SAC algorithm. Figure 1 illustrates the average reward curves of both algorithms over 500 training episodes. As shown in the figure, the DT-MAP algorithm demonstrates significantly faster and more stable convergence. This is mainly due to the fact that DT-MAP adopts priority reward shaping and dynamic exploration strategies, and effectively guides the agents to explore more efficiently through shared environment models and multi-agent collaborative training.

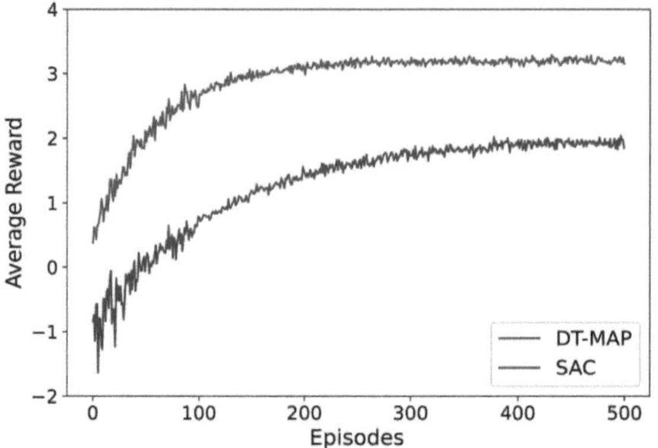

Fig. 1. Comparison of convergence for different algorithms

Experimental Comparative Analysis. Figure 2 compare the proposed DT-MAP algorithm with SAC, Greedy, and Random under varying numbers of vehicles in terms of average task completion delay, load standard deviation, and resource utilization.

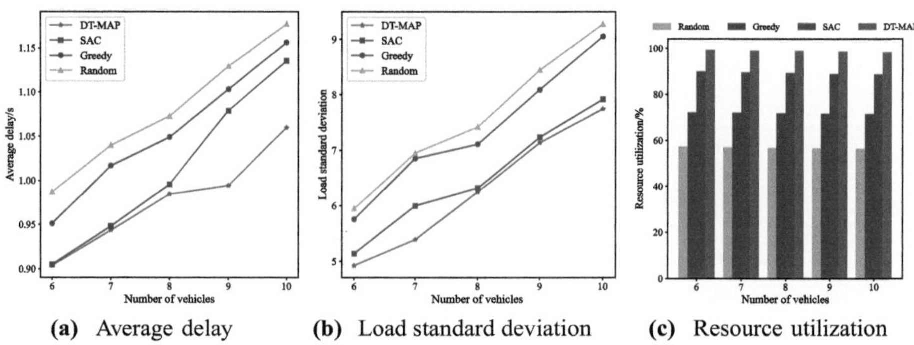

(a) Average delay   (b) Load standard deviation   (c) Resource utilization

Fig. 2. Average task completion delay, server load standard deviation, and resource utilization under different numbers of vehicles.

As shown in Fig. 2(a), DT-MAP consistently achieves the lowest average delay across all scenarios. Specifically, DT-MAP reduces task completion latency by an average of 3.24%, 7.30%, and 9.57% compared to SAC, Greedy, and Random, respectively. This improvement stems from the fact that DT-MAP prioritizes tasks while taking latency sensitivity into account and leverages digital twin feedback to make globally optimized offloading decisions.

In Fig. 2(b), DT-MAP achieves the lowest load standard deviation, indicating more balanced task distribution across edge servers. This improvement is mainly attributed to the joint training mechanism of the agents and the introduction of load penalties in the rewards, which enable each agent to make globally coordinated offloading decisions based on local observations and the shared system state. In contrast, due to the limited coordination and reliance on local or static strategies, Greedy and Random suffer from obvious load imbalance.

Figure 2(c) shows that DT-MAP achieves consistently high resource utilization of more than 98% in all scenarios. This near-saturation utilization reflects the effectiveness of the DT-MAP strategy. The strategy integrates priority-aware scheduling, delay sensitivity, and digital twin feedback according to the task requirements of all vehicles to offload tasks to appropriate servers and maximize the use of available edge resources. In contrast, SAC only performs offloading allocation based on the local information of a single vehicle and cannot fully utilize server resources.

6   Conclusion

This paper addresses the challenges of uneven task offloading and degraded QoS in VEC systems. We propose a digital twin-assisted multi-agent task offloading method with priority scheduling(DT-MAP), which models task heterogeneity (e.g., data size, deadline, priority) and optimizes task delay, load distribution and resource utilization. By using a MADDPG-based framework, our approach effectively improves resource efficiency and load balancing while reducing system latency. The proposed method demonstrates significant improvements in reducing task completion delay and enhancing load balancing and resource utilization compared to baseline strategies such as Random, Greedy, and SAC. Future work will focus on refining the adaptability of DT models and exploring scalable, real-time offloading strategies for large-scale deployments.

References

1. Zhao, J., et al.: Autonomous driving system: a comprehensive survey. Expert Syst. Appl. **242**, 122836 (2024)
2. Zhou, Z., Shojafar, M., Alazab, M., Li, F.: IECL: an intelligence energy consumption model for cloud manufacturing. IEEE Trans. Ind. Inform. **18**(12), 8967–8976 (2022). https://doi.org/10.1109/TII.2022.3165085
3. Bo, J., Zhao, X.: Vehicle edge computing task offloading strategy based on multi-agent deep reinforcement learning. J. Grid Comput. **23**(2), 13 (2025)

4. Liu, X., Liu, J., Li, W.: Truthful mechanism for resource allocation and pricing in vehicle-assisted mobile edge computing. IEEE Trans. Veh. Technol. **74**(5), 8171–8186 (2025)
5. Zhang, N., Liang, S., Wang, K., Wu, Q., Nallanathan, A.: Computation efficient task offloading and bandwidth allocation in VEC networks. IEEE Trans. Veh. Technol. **73**(10), 15889–15893 (2024)
6. Zhou, Z., Abawajy, J.: Reinforcement learning-based edge server placement in the intelligent Internet of Vehicles environment. IEEE Trans. Intell. Transp. Syst. 1–11 (2025). https://doi.org/10.1109/TITS.2025.3557259
7. Tang, L., Yi, Y., Li, S., Huang, Q., Chen, Q.: Digital twin construction and resource allocation on Internet of Vehicles. IEEE Internet Things J. **12**(7), 9091–9106 (2025)
8. Guo, H., Chen, X., Zhou, X., Liu, J.: Trusted and efficient task offloading in vehicular edge computing networks. IEEE Trans. Cogn. Commun. Netw. **10**(6), 2370–2382 (2024)
9. Zhou, Z., Shojafar, M., Alazab, M., Abawajy, J., Li, F.: AFED-EF: an energy-efficient VM allocation algorithm for IoT applications in a cloud data center. IEEE Trans. Green Commun. Netw. **5**(2), 658–669 (2021). https://doi.org/10.1109/TGCN.2021.3067309
10. Tran-Dang, H., Kim, D.-S.: Digital twin-empowered intelligent computation offloading for edge computing in the era of 5G and beyond: a state-of-the-art survey. ICT Express **11**(1), 167–180 (2025)
11. Tao, F., Zhang, H., Zhang, C.: Advancements and challenges of digital twins in industry. Nat. Comput. Sci. **4**(3), 169–177 (2024)
12. Xie, Y., Wu, Q., Fan, P.: Digital twin vehicular edge computing network: task offloading and resource allocation. In: 7th International Conference on Information Communication and Signal Processing (ICICSP), pp. 1137–1141. IEEE (2024)
13. Abuthahir, S.S., Peter, J.S.P.: Tasks offloading in vehicular edge computing network using meta-heuristic algorithms – a study of selected algorithms. In: 15th International Conference on Computing Communication and Networking Technologies (ICCCNT), pp. 1–10. IEEE, Italy (2024)
14. Sun, Z., Sun, G., Liu, Y., Wang, J., Cao, D.: BARGAIN-MATCH: a game theoretical approach for resource allocation and task offloading in vehicular edge computing networks. IEEE Trans. Mobile Comput. **23**(2), 1655–1673 (2023)
15. Xu, X., et al.: Game theory for distributed IoV task offloading with fuzzy neural network in edge computing. IEEE Trans. Fuzzy Syst. **30**(11), 4593–4604 (2022)
16. Su, J., Liu, Z., Xie, Y., Chan, K.Y., Guan, X.: Dynamic resource allocation in queue-constrained and delay-sensitive vehicular networks. IEEE Trans. Intell. Veh. **8**(10), 4434–4444 (2023)
17. Kumar, A.S., Zhao, L., Fernando, X.: Task offloading and resource allocation in vehicular networks: a Lyapunov-based deep reinforcement learning approach. IEEE Trans. Veh. Technol. **72**(10), 13360–13373 (2023)
18. Hazarika, B., Singh, K., Biswas, S., Li, C.-P.: DRL-based resource allocation for computation offloading in IoV networks. IEEE Trans. Ind. Inform. **18**(11), 8027–8038 (2022)
19. Chen, Q., Song, X., Song, T., Yang, Y.: Vehicular edge computing networks optimization via DRL-based communication resource allocation and load balancing. IEEE Trans. Mobile Comput. 1–16 (2025)
20. Yang, H.-N., Wang, J.-Y., Zeng, Q., Cheng, M., Lin, M., Wang, J.-B.: Joint task offloading and resource allocation for integrated VLC and sensing in digital twin-aided vehicular edge computing networks. IEEE Trans. Veh. Technol. **74**(4), 6360–6372 (2025)

21. Xu, C., Zhang, P., Xia, X., Kong, L., Zeng, P., Yu, H.: Digital-twin-assisted intelligent secure task offloading and caching in blockchain-based vehicular edge computing networks. IEEE Internet Things J. **12**(4), 4128–4143 (2025)
22. Zhu, L., Tan, L.: Task offloading scheme of vehicular cloud edge computing based on digital twin and improved A3C. Internet Things **26**, 101192 (2024)
23. Kong, X., Yang, X., Shen, S., Shen, G.: Energy-delay joint optimization for task offloading in digital twin-assisted Internet of Vehicles. ACM Trans. Sen. Netw. (2024)
24. Liu, H., Tian, N., Song, D.A., Zhang, L.: Digital twin-enabled multi-service task offloading in vehicular edge computing using soft actor-critic. Electronics **14**(4), 686 (2025)
25. Shafahi, M.H., Javadi, S.A., Sedighi, M.: A lightweight greedy task offloading algorithm for vehicular edge computing networks. In: Proceedings of 29th International Computer Conference (CSICC), pp. 1–7 (2025)

DDPG-Based Joint Dynamic Task Offloading and Resource Allocation for Multi-user MEC Networks

Shuang Yang, Xiang Xiao[✉], Peidong Zhu, Lulu Wang, Yu Zheng,
Ruihan Chen, and Mingzhuo Xie

College of Electronic Information and Electrical Engineering, Changsha University,
Changsha 410022, China
`hdxx@hnu.edu.cn`

Abstract. With the rapid development of 5G and IoT technologies, edge computing networks face dynamic challenges in task offloading and resource allocation complexity. In this paper, we propose a Deep Deterministic Policy Gradient (DDPG)-based optimization framework for multi-user multi-edge-server scenarios. The dynamic task offloading and resource allocation problem is formalized as a Markov Decision Process (MDP), defining a state space incorporating server resources, user locations, and task states, along with a hybrid action space combining continuous resource allocation and discrete offloading decisions. The key innovation lies in designing a reward function maximizing task completion volume, implementing dynamic policy optimization through an Actor-Critic network architecture, and enhancing stability via experience replay with target network soft updates. Simulation results demonstrate that the Deep Deterministic Policy Gradient algorithm achieves significantly higher average task completion rewards compared to other algorithms, along with substantially lower reward standard deviation.

Keywords: Edge Computing · Task Offloading · Deep Deterministic Policy Gradient

1 Introduction

The rapid advancement of 5G communication technologies has catalyzed widespread Internet of Things (IoT) device proliferation, driving exponential growth in data volumes [1]. Traditional cloud computing architectures, characterized by centralized remote data processing, increasingly reveal limitations in meeting stringent low-latency and high-bandwidth demands. Emerging applications, including extended reality, digital twins, intelligent transportation, smart energy, intelligent manufacturing, and the Internet of Intelligent Things, demand novel computational paradigms alongside 5G/6G networks. Bandwidth constraints, elevated transmission latency, and security vulnerabilities further constrain centralized cloud solutions [2]. These challenges motivate exploration of computational approaches proximate to data sources.

Edge computing emerges as a distributed architectural solution, migrating task execution from centralized clouds to network-adjacent nodes. This shift delivers dual benefits: reduced processing latency and enhanced operational efficiency. Localized computation optimizes bandwidth utilization while accelerating response times, establishing edge computing as a cornerstone of modern infrastructures [3].

Task offloading constitutes a critical edge computing technology, enabling partial or full migration of computational tasks to edge servers. Offloading performance depends on dynamic factors including underlying communication protocols, fluctuating user scales, and uncertain channel conditions. While low latency remains an inherent edge advantage, improper parameter configuration may degrade system performance. Optimal allocation of channel and facility resources directly determines user Quality of Service (QoS). Consequently, efficient offloading algorithms for decision optimization and resource allocation remain paramount in edge computing research.

Game-theoretic methods demonstrate effectiveness in specific contexts. Distributed game theory enables dynamic edge resource pricing mechanisms that reduce task computation delays [4]. Coalitional games optimize server selection for subtask-level scheduling [5]. Nevertheless, these approaches incur high computational costs in large-scale scenarios. Metaheuristic algorithms (e.g., heuristic methods [6], ant colony systems [7]) suit static or quasi-static networks but prove inefficient in dynamic Mobile Edge Computing (MEC) environments due to slow convergence. Lyapunov optimization techniques decompose long-term problems into tractable subproblems [8]; however, they require unavailable prior knowledge of environmental statistics in dynamic MEC systems.

Dynamic offloading decisions involve multidimensional, time-varying constraints. Deep learning frameworks address multi-user MEC offloading through unsupervised learning [9] and computational power modeling, yet face challenges including unpredictable training times, inference latency, and massive labeled data requirements. Deep reinforcement learning (DRL) adapts to dynamic MEC environments via environment interaction. Value-based DRL methods handle discrete actions but suffer from information loss or dimensionality explosion in continuous spaces. Policy-based approaches like Deep Deterministic Policy Gradient (DDPG) exhibit potential in continuous control yet struggle with computational overhead, slow convergence, and idealized environmental assumptions.

Research efforts have developed diverse offloading techniques, broadly categorized into optimization-based and machine learning approaches. Existing methods often overlook real-world uncertainties and dynamic variations. This gap necessitates flexible task offloading and resource allocation frameworks capable of adaptive decision-making in complex, dynamic edge environments. Addressing the dynamic and complex challenges of task offloading in edge computing networks, this study employs the Deep Deterministic Policy Gradient (DDPG) algorithm as its core solution. We establish a multi-user, multi-edge-server scenario model. The dynamic task offloading and resource allocation problem is formalized as a Markov Decision Process (MDP). The state space encompasses server resources, user locations, and task states. A hybrid action space is defined, combining continuous resource allocation with discrete offloading decisions. A reward function oriented toward maximizing task completion volume is designed. Dynamic policy optimization is achieved using the Actor-Critic network structure. Experience replay and target network soft update mechanisms are introduced to enhance algorithm convergence and stability.

2   System Model and Problem Formulation

2.1   System Model

This paper considers a Mobile Edge Computing scenario with multiple users and multiple edge servers. Each User Equipment (UE) maintains a task queue to store locally generated computation-intensive tasks. Based on a specific offloading strategy, the UE determines whether a task needs to be offloaded to an edge server. If offloading is decided, the UE transmits the task to the edge server via a wireless channel, utilizing the resources of the edge computing node for processing, as illustrated in Fig. 1 below.

Fig. 1. Edge Computing Model

2.2   Model Description

In the considered multi-user, multi-edge-server model, the number of UEs is denoted as M. Each UE generates object detection tasks. Tasks are assumed to be indivisible; they must be offloaded and processed as a whole. Task states include: Transmission (State 1–2), Processing (State 3), Result Return (State 4), Disconnection (State 5), and Migration (State 6) triggered by user mobility. Tasks are offloaded to edge servers. Edge servers are deployed near base stations and connected via fiber optics; hence, the information transmission delay between a BS and its associated edge server is negligible. Information reaching the BS is considered to have reached the edge server. This work operates under the monolithic offloading condition: tasks cannot be partitioned for execution across multiple edge servers. Each UE can only choose to fully offload its task to a single edge server for processing.

2.3   Task Model

This paper establishes a multi-user multi-edge-server task model where individual tasks arrive at each User Equipment (UE) following a Poisson distribution. Upon arrival, tasks are stored in the corresponding UE's task queue, which operates dynamically as completed tasks are removed and new tasks are continuously added. Each task progresses through six operational states: State 1 denotes task offloading to the edge server; State 2 represents data transmission in progress; State 3 indicates ongoing task processing; State 4 corresponds to result return to the user; State 5 signifies connection termination; and State 6 reflects task migration to alternate servers.

2.4   Communication Model

Considering user mobility, the distance between a user and a server varies across time slots. Establishing a Cartesian coordinate system based on user and edge server positions, the distance between user and edge server is given by:

$$d = \sqrt{(x_u - x_e)^2 + (y_u - y_e)^2}. \tag{1}$$

where (x_u, y_u) is the position of user and (x_e, y_e) is the position of edge server.

Users and BSs are connected via wireless channels. Let h represent the channel gain between a user and a BS. Channel gain is related to the distance between them, calculated as:

$$h = \sigma \cdot \left(\frac{c}{4\pi \cdot f \cdot d}\right)^2 \tag{2}$$

where f is the carrier frequency, c is the speed of light, and σ is the path loss exponent. The transmission rate of the channel for task offloading is then defined as:

$$v = B \cdot \log_2\left(1 + \frac{P \cdot h}{N}\right). \tag{3}$$

where N is the noise power spectral density, P is the transmission power, and B is the channel bandwidth.

2.5   Computation Model

Given the multi-user, multi-edge-server context, the primary focus is on offloading tasks to edge servers. UEs are assumed not to have local task processing capabilities; local computation is not considered. Let G denote the total storage resources of an edge server and F denote its total computational resources. When allocating resources for offloaded tasks, an edge server cannot exceed its own resource limits. If the total allocated resources exceed the server's capacity, it enters a saturated state. The system does not force task offloading to saturated servers; tasks wait until the server completes processing and returns to a non-saturated state. After processing a task on an edge server, the resulting data size is significantly smaller than the original task data. Furthermore, due to factors like bandwidth allocation, the download rate in wireless networks is typically several times higher than the upload rate. Consequently, the delay incurred by users downloading task results is extremely low and is not modeled in this work. While a task is processed on an edge server, the user remains in a state waiting to receive the result.

2.6   Problem Modeling

The edge computing task offloading problem is modeled as a Markov Decision Process (MDP) tuple $(SAPR\gamma)$ The state transition probability P is determined by user mobility, task state transitions, and server resource dynamics. The discount factor γ is used to calculate the long-term cumulative reward.

State S_0 transitions to state S_1 according to probability distribution P under action $a0$. Subsequent actions $a1, \ldots$ are executed, yielding rewards R.

The optimization objective is to maximize the cumulative reward obtained over the entire interaction process. To balance the importance of immediate and future rewards, a discount factor γ (range $0 \leq \gamma \leq 1$) is introduced. The discount factor balances immediate versus future rewards, avoiding myopic strategies while ensuring mathematical tractability. The cumulative reward is defined as:

$$r_t = count_t - count_{t-1}. \tag{4}$$

where $count_t$ represents the total number of user tasks completed up to time step t; $count_{t-1}$ represents the total number completed up to time step $t - 1$.

In summary, the problem is formulated as:

$$\begin{aligned}
&P : \max r_t \\
&s.t. \\
&(C1) 0 \leq C_e \leq C_{\max} \\
&(C2) 0 \leq L_e \leq L_{\max}, \\
&(C3) 0 \leq B \leq B_{\max}.
\end{aligned} \tag{5}$$

The system operates under three fundamental constraints:(C1) The computational resources C_e allocated to users must not exceed the total computational capacity of the edge server; (C2) The number of connected users L_e cannot surpass the edge server's maximum connection quota; (C3) The bandwidth allocation B to users must remain within the edge server's maximum available bandwidth.

3   Deep Deterministic Policy Gradient Algorithm

3.1   Reinforcement Learning

Reinforcement Learning (RL) is a significant subfield of machine learning. Unlike other ML methods, RL focuses on how an agent can maximize its cumulative reward within a complex and uncertain environment. By perceiving how the environment's state reacts to an action, and using that perception to guide better actions for maximum return, this learning paradigm is known as learning through interaction, termed Reinforcement Learning.

In the RL process, the agent continuously interacts with the environment. The agent perceives the environment's state and uses it to output an action, which is a decision. This decision is applied to the environment, which then outputs the next state and an immediate reward for the current decision. The agent's goal is to obtain as much cumulative reward as possible from the environment.

3.2 Markov Decision Process Construction

Markov Decision Processes (MDPs) provide the standard framework for modeling reinforcement learning (RL) tasks. In RL, an agent interacts with an environment, perceives its state, and selects actions according to a policy to maximize cumulative reward. When the environment exhibits the Markov property, the next state depends solely on the current state and action, allowing the agent to disregard prior history. The agent selects actions based on its policy, triggering state transitions governed by this property. RL tasks satisfying the Markov property are MDPs, formally defined by the quintuple (S, A, P, R, γ).

(1) System State (S). The system state $S = (R, B, U, X, Y)$:R: Remaining computational resources of each edge server.B: Available migration bandwidth between edge servers.U: Server ID currently associated with each user.X, Y: Scaled and translated coordinates (x, y) of each user.

(2) System Action (A). The action space is the set of actions the agent can take based on the perceived environment state. $A = (r, B, O)$ represents the action, which is hybrid r, B represents the bandwidth allocated to user m for task offloading operations. Discrete action representing the target edge server ID for task offloading for user m.

(3) State Transition Function (P). $P(s'|s, A)$ represents the probability of transitioning to state s' after taking action A in state S. Due to the strong correlation between states in RL models, this function is typically not explicitly modeled.

(4) Reward Function (R). The immediate reward evaluates the quality of the action $\mu(s)$ taken in state s. The design of the reward function critically impacts algorithm performance. The reward function should align with the optimization objective. This work targets maximizing long-term cumulative reward, with the immediate reward designed as the number of tasks completed within a single time step. The DDPG algorithm aims to maximize this cumulative reward.

(5) Discount Factor (γ). Ensures the agent balances short-term efficiency with long-term goals.

At each discrete time step t, the agent interacts with the environment. The goal is to learn a policy for generating actions, which maps each possible action to a probability value given the environment's current state s_t. After selecting and executing an action, the agent receives an immediate reward r_t, and the environment transitions to the next state s_{t+1}. During learning, the agent updates its policy based on the immediate reward to find the optimal policy that yields the maximum cumulative return .

3.3   Algorithm Description

The Deep Deterministic Policy Gradient (DDPG) algorithm integrates deep learning with the Actor-Critic framework to solve dynamic optimization problems involving continuous action spaces and high-dimensional states. This work models multi-user, multi-edge-server task offloading, employing DDPG to address edge computing's hybrid action space characteristics. The algorithm utilizes a deterministic policy to directly output continuous actions while leveraging Q-learning for value function estimation, enabling efficient optimization in complex state-action spaces. DDPG comprises an Actor network that processes state s to generate action vector A, and a Critic network evaluating state-action pairs (s, A) to estimate corresponding Q-values.

The Actor network implements the deterministic behavioral policy μ using a deep neural network. To facilitate exploration during network updates, the algorithm introduces random noise to increase the randomness of action generation. The action selection formula is:

$$a_t = \mu(s_t) + \kappa. \tag{6}$$

where κ is the exploration noise.

In DDPG, the Critic network approximates the Q-function using a deep neural network. The Q-function is defined as the expected cumulative reward the agent receives starting from state s, taking action $\mu(s)$, and thereafter following policy μ:

$$Q(s, \mu(s)) = R + \gamma \cdot Q'(s', \mu'(s')). \tag{7}$$

where γ is the discount factor, R is the immediate reward received after taking action s in state $\mu(s)$, and Q' is the Q-value of the next state s' and the action $\mu'(s)$ selected by the target Actor network, calculated by the target Critic network.

To improve generalization, DDPG employs experience replay. It stores "learning experiences" and later uses random sampling to update the deep neural network parameters. Specifically, at each time step t, experience data $e_t = (s_t, a_t, R_t, s_{t+1})$ is obtained from agent-environment interaction and stored in an experience replay buffer $D = \{e_1, e_2, ..., e_t\}$. During training, batches of experiences are randomly sampled from D to break temporal correlations. This random sampling decouples sequential experiences, improves data utilization, and satisfies the MDP's independent and identically distributed assumption.

The Actor's loss function during training is defined as:

$$L_{actor} = -\frac{1}{N} \sum Q(s, \mu(s)). \tag{8}$$

where N is the batch size sampled from the replay buffer, $Q(s, \mu(s))$ is the Q-value estimate from the Critic network for the current state s and the action $\mu(s)$ generated by the Actor.

The Critic's loss function is defined as:

$$L_{critic} = \frac{1}{N} \sum \left[(R + Q_{t\,\text{arg}\,et}(s', \mu_{t\,\text{arg}\,et}(s') \cdot \gamma - Q(s,a)^2 \right]. \tag{9}$$

where: $\mu_{t\,\text{arg}\,et}$ is the action generated by the target Actor network for the next state, γ is the discount factor. $Q_{t\,\text{arg}\,et}$ is the output Q-value from the target Critic network, representing the estimated value of the next state-action pair computed jointly by the target networks. During each iteration, the loss function is calculated using fixed-parameter target neural networks. To minimize the loss function, parameters are updated using an exponential moving average, shown as:

$$\theta_{t\,\text{arg}\,et} \leftarrow \tau \cdot \theta + (1 - \tau) \cdot \theta_{t\,\text{arg}\,et}. \tag{10}$$

where: θ are the parameters of the main network, $\theta_{t\,\text{arg}\,et}$ are the parameters of the corresponding target network. τ is the soft update coefficient.

The Actor's gradient update can be derived using the chain rule:

$$\nabla_{\theta^\mu} J \approx \frac{1}{N} \sum_{i=1}^{N} \nabla_a Q(s_i, a_i) \cdot \nabla_{\theta^\mu} \mu(s_i). \tag{11}$$

where θ^μ are the parameters of the Actor network, $\nabla_a Q(s_i, a_i)$ is the gradient of the Critic's Q-value output with respect to the input action, and $\nabla_{\theta^\mu} \mu(s_i)$ is the gradient of the Actor's output action with respect to its own parameters. Critic's gradient guides the Actor parameter update.

4 Simulation Results

A scenario with multiple edge servers and multiple users was set up, where each user has a sequence of tasks to execute. Through comparative simulations, the following two baseline algorithms were selected to validate the effectiveness and superiority of the proposed DDPG algorithm: (1) Nearest Neighbor Algorithm: Users always offload tasks to the geographically closest edge server. (2) Priority-based Greedy Algorithm with Capacity Constraints: Users attempt to connect to available servers according to a priority list (sorted by Euclidean distance to edge servers, closer servers have higher priority) until server capacity limits are reached. This study considers a multi-user, multi-edge-server MEC scenario where users are mobile. Assuming a fixed number of edge servers $N = 10$, the number of users M varies: 10, 15, 20, 25, 30, 40. The reward values under different algorithms are compared as the number of users increases to reveal performance differences (Table 1).

Figure 2 illustrates the reward values obtained under the Nearest Neighbor algorithm across varying numbers of users. It can be observed that: As the number of users increases, the reward value under the Nearest Neighbor algorithm

Table 1. Simulation Experiment Initial Parameters

Parameter	Unit	Value
Max Users per Server L_e	–	4
Edge Server Max Bandwidth B	bps	10^9
DDPG Algorithm Training Episodes	episodes	50–90
Nearest Neighbor Algorithm Training Episodes	episodes	10
Priority Algorithm Training Episodes	episodes	20
Steps per Episode	steps	3000
Actor Learning Rate	–	0.0001
Critic Learning Rate	–	0.0002
Discount Factor	–	0.9
Soft Update Coefficient	–	0.01

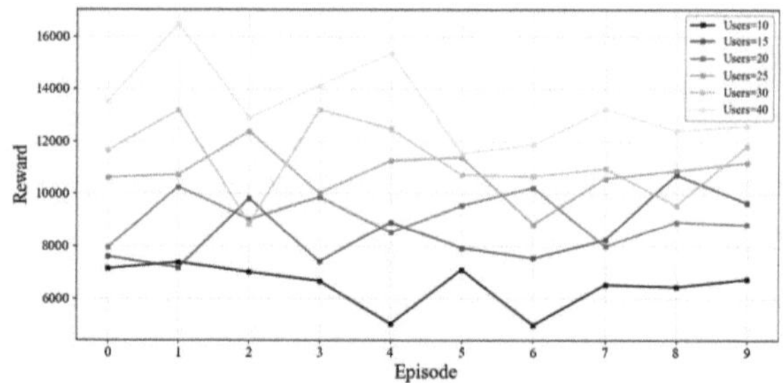

Fig. 2. Reward Value under Nearest Neighbor Algorithm for Different User Numbers

exhibits minimal improvement. Furthermore, for a fixed number of users across different episodes, the corresponding reward values display significant fluctuations. Notably, in some data points, the reward value for a larger user count is even lower than that for a smaller user count.

Figure 3 presents the reward values achieved using the Priority-based algorithm for different user counts. It can be seen that: The Priority-based algorithm demonstrates a significant increase in reward value as the number of users grows. Additionally, for a given number of users across different episodes, the corresponding reward values remain largely consistent.

Figure 4 depicts the reward values yielded by the DDPG algorithm under varying user counts. It is evident that: The DDPG algorithm achieves a substantial increase in reward value with a growing number of users. Moreover, for the same user count across different episodes, the corresponding reward values exhibit only minor variations.

Figure 5 depicts average reward trends across algorithms under increasing user loads. DDPG maintains superior performance at all scales, demonstrating the highest absolute rewards and growth rates. The Priority-based app-

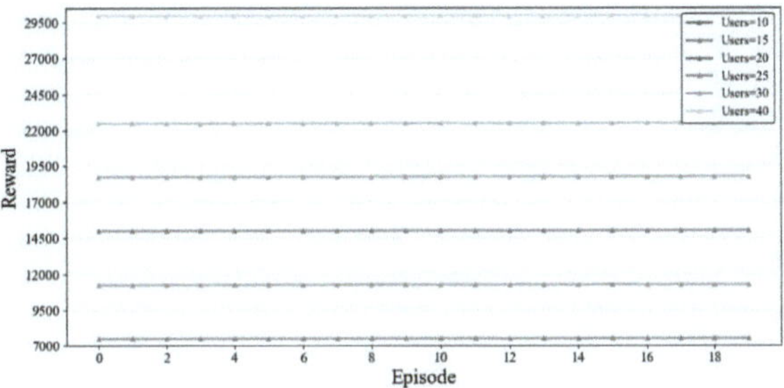

Fig. 3. Reward Value under Priority-based Greedy Algorithm for Different User Numbers

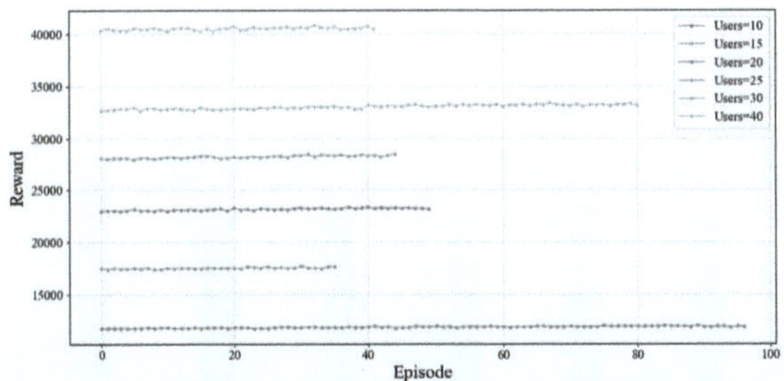

Fig. 4. Reward Value under DDPG Algorithm for Different User Numbers

roach shows substantial yet lower rewards than DDPG, while Nearest Neighbor yields minimal improvement with significantly inferior results. These disparities originate from fundamental algorithmic differences: Nearest Neighbor's rigid proximity-based selection induces server overload and queuing delays; Priority-based methods employ static lists that cannot adapt to real-time resource dynamics; DDPG dynamically balances loads via deep neural networks, intelligently allocating tasks to underutilized servers through its Actor-Critic framework to maximize resource utilization and prevent overload. Corresponding histograms display reward standard deviations.

Figure 6 compares reward standard deviations across algorithms. DDPG maintains significantly lower variance than Nearest Neighbor while achieving high rewards, demonstrating robust stability against network fluctuations. At maximum user loads, Nearest Neighbor's deviation increases substantially whereas Priority-based algorithms exhibit minimal variance with slight reduction. DDPG shows only marginal increase, confirming its ability to avoid local optima in dynamic environments. Unlike greedy algorithms' myopic decisions, DDPG's discount reward mechanism maximizes long-term cumulative returns, yielding superior task completion rates versus Priority-based approaches at scale.

To quantify algorithmic efficiency, Gain per User (GPU) is defined as: $GPU = \frac{\bar{r}}{M}$. Where $\bar{r}$ is the average reward and M is the number of users.

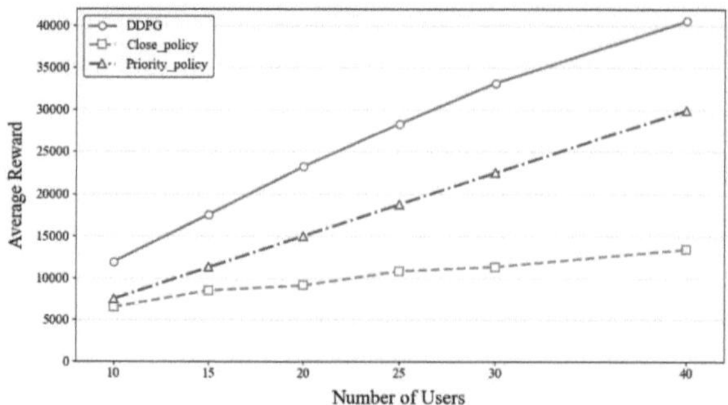

Fig. 5. Reward Value under DDPG Algorithm for Different User Numbers

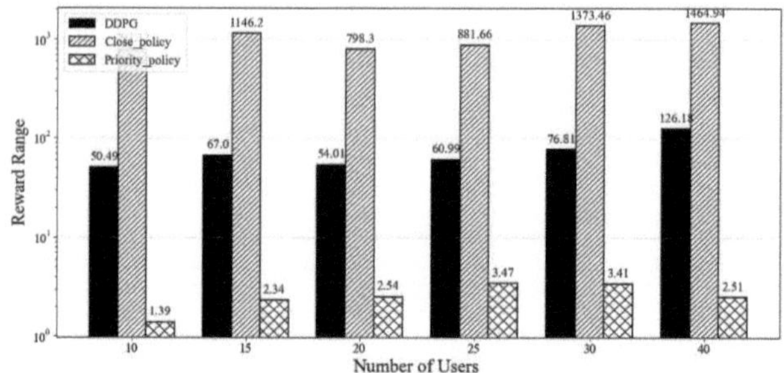

Fig. 6. Comparison of Reward Standard Deviation for the Three Different Algorithms

DDPG's GPU value increases linearly with the number of users. At $M = 40$, GPU $= 1014.1$, significantly higher than the Nearest Neighbor and Priority algorithms. This result demonstrates that DDPG significantly enhances the overall efficiency of the edge computing system through collaborative optimization of multi-user task offloading.

5   Conclusion

This study develops a Deep Deterministic Policy Gradient (DDPG)-based dynamic task offloading framework for edge computing. Modeling a multi-user, multi-edge-server scenario, we formalize offloading and resource allocation as a Markov Decision Process with high-dimensional states (server resources, user locations, task status) and hybrid actions combining continuous resource allocation with discrete offloading decisions. The framework employs experience replay and soft-updated target networks to enhance stability. Simulations show DDPG outperforms nearest-neighbor and greedy algorithms in task completion rates and stability, with adaptive decision-making managing network load fluctuations and user mobility through dynamic load balancing. Future work will address fragmented offloading and multi-server collaboration for complex tasks.

Acknowledgments. This work was supported in part by the National Natural Science Foundation of China (Grants No. 62402066), Natural Science Foundation Project of Hunan Province (No. 2024JJ7617, 2023JJ30085), Science and Technology Plan Projects of YiYang (No. 2015JZ28), Scientific Research Project of the Education Department of Hunan (No. 24B0798, 22A0599).

References

1. Castañón Ávila, G., Cerroni, W., Sarmiento-Moncada, A.: Integrated photonics for IoT, RoF, and distributed fog–cloud computing: a comprehensive review. Appl. Sci. **15**, 7494 (2025). https://doi.org/10.3390/app15137494
2. Hazra, A., Munusamy, A., Adhikari, M., Awasthi, L.K.: 6G-enabled ultra-reliable low latency communication for industry 5.0: challenges and future directions. IEEE Commun. Stand. Mag. **8**(2), 36–42 (2024)
3. Rodrigues, T.K., Liu, J., Kato, N.: Offloading decision for mobile multi-access edge computing in a multi-tiered 6G network. IEEE Trans. Emerg. Topics Comput. **10**(3), 1414–1427 (2022)
4. Xu, X., et al.: Game theory for distributed IoV task offloading with fuzzy neural network in edge computing. IEEE Trans. Fuzzy Syst. **30**(11), 4593–4604 (2022)
5. Chen, Z., Yang, Y., Xu, J., Chen, Y., Huang, J.: Task offloading and resource pricing based on game theory in UAV-assisted edge computing. IEEE Trans. Services Comput. **18**(1), 440–452 (2025)
6. Abuthahir, S.S., Peter, J.S.P.: A hybrid meta-heuristic algorithm for task offloading in vehicular edge computing network. Wireless Pers. Commun. **141**, 51–74 (2025)
7. Tan, L., Kuang, Z., Zhao, L., Qiu, T., Yuan, B.: Energy-efficient joint task offloading and resource allocation in OFDMA-based collaborative edge computing. IEEE Trans. Wireless Commun. **21**(3), 1960–1972 (2022)
8. Qiao, X., Zhou, Y.: Task offloading of edge computing network based on Lyapunov and deep reinforcement learning. In: Proceedings of International Conference on Computer and Communication Systems, Xi'an, China, pp. 1054–1059 (2024)
9. Liu, T., Fang, L., Zhu, Y., Cui, L., Zhang, J.: A near-optimal approach for online task offloading and resource allocation in edge-cloud orchestrated computing. IEEE Trans. Mobile Comput. **21**(8), 2687–2700 (2022)

CGO: Cloud Game Orchestration via Resource Preception and CODEC Optimization

Taolei Wang, Chao Li$^{(\boxtimes)}$, Jing Wang, Xiaofeng Hou, and Minyi Guo

Shanghai Jiao Tong University, Shanghai, China
{sjtuwtl,jing618}@sjtu.edu.cn, {lichao,hou-xf,guo-my}@cs.sjtu.edu.cn

Abstract. Cloud gaming acceleration faces critical challenges in balancing latency and visual quality. To address these issues, we propose a resource-aware mechanism for fine-grained game analysis, enabling precise identification and management of resource-intensive stages in real-time. By utilizing motion vector (MV) information stored in the encoder, our method enables the edge device to reconstruct and enhance the video frames locally before delivering them to the user. This hybrid architecture not only reduces computational load on the cloud but also minimizes network bandwidth consumption. Experimental results demonstrate that the proposed approach achieves significant improvements in visual quality while maintaining smooth gameplay experiences. Our solution provides a promising direction for optimizing cloud gaming performance by efficiently integrating resource computing with advanced CODEC acceleration techniques.

Keywords: Cloud Game · Resource Management · CODEC

1 Introduction

Cloud gaming has emerged as a transformative technology in the digital entertainment industry, offering users unparalleled flexibility and accessibility to high-quality gaming experiences. Unlike traditional local gaming, cloud gaming enables high-quality gaming experiences without requiring powerful local hardware [9]. In addition, the rapid development of virtual reality (VR) and augmented reality (AR) technologies further underscores the critical role of cloud gaming in modern interactive applications [2]. Improving Quality of Service (QoS) and latency of cloud games has been highly concern for academia and industry as a key technology in cloud datacenters [15,24].

As is shown in Fig. 1, cloud games are noteworthy because this category of applications is completely different from other workloads that have been studied before. First, cloud gaming is extremely sensitive to latency. However, unlike traditional latency-sensitive tasks, it becomes difficult to migrate or stop the game once it has been deployed [18], making resource allocation planning challenging. Second, cloud gaming not only requires high throughput but also involves strong interactivity [22]. Predefined batch processing methods are therefore unsuitable for such scenarios. Third, unlike standalone gaming, cloud gaming comprises multiple modules, including rendering, video generation, and CODEC. Effective resource allocation must therefore consider the interdependencies among these tasks to ensure optimal performance.

Plenty of studies [1,7] try to improve performance by designing better scheduling methods, deploying multiple games simultaneously. However, they neglect the inherent variability in resource demand across different gameplay phases. This oversimplification often resulted in insufficient resource allocation, thereby compromising the ability to maintain high graphical fidelity.

Another strand of work [13,21] emphasized optimizing specific game-related tasks, such as pixel shader-based image rendering, which yielded significant performance improvements for these components. However, these studies failed to account for the fundamental differences between cloud gaming and traditional local gaming. In particular, they ignored resource-intensive tasks unique to the cloud environment, such as frame processing and video encoding/decoding, which are unnecessary in standalone gaming systems. Overlooking these critical processes inevitably led to increased latency and suboptimal performance.

Addressing the above problems, this paper proposes CGO, a comprehensive framework that integrates cloud game characteristics with video transmission requirements. By meticulously analyzing the resource consumption patterns across different gameplay stages, CGO provides a deeper understanding of cloud gaming systems. Our approach introduces a novel perspective by focusing on internal competition for resources among various tasks within the cloud gaming pipeline. Specifically, we optimize the encoding processes to free up additional computational resources, which are then allocated to critical components such as game rendering, thereby enhancing overall performance and user experience. The detailed contribution is listed as follows:

- We propose a resource-aware mechanism for fine-grained game analysis, enabling precise identification and management of resource-intensive stages in real-time.
- We develop an innovative method that leverages user interactions to accelerate video encoding processes.
- We design a comprehensive scheduling framework tailored specifically for cloud gaming environments. By analyzing user inputs and incorporating them into our encoding strategy, we achieve more efficient compression without compromising visual quality.

2   Background and Related Work

We introduce the background of cloud game and the related work of this paper in the following two parts.

Cloud Game Scheduling: Each image in the game is called a frame, which is jointly calculated by the CPU and GPU. As is shown in Fig. 1 To render a frame,

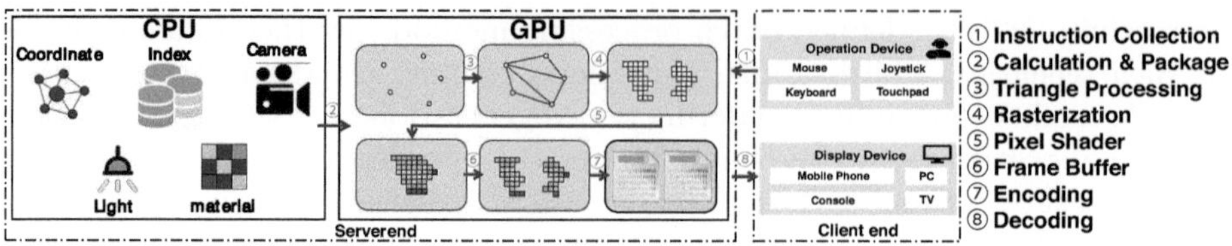

Fig. 1. The workflow of cloud game applications.

the CPU first calculates the various factors required for drawing. Pack and send these factors to the GPU. The GPU will use rendering pipelines to process this data, rasterize these 3D data into flat frames, and finally send them back to the CPU for encoding to screen. So, depending on the game type, both the CPU and GPU may become bottlenecks. Also, games are designed for personal computers, and without any restrictions, they will try to occupy all resources during the running process as much as possible. This necessitates careful resource allocation for rendering and encoding/decoding on the same server when running in the cloud. Resource management issues in cloud games have been extensively studied [14,21], including request allocation, scheduling, and server configuration. However, the correspondence between game content and resource consumption is not taken into account in these works. Some simple scheduling strategies were employed, including Disallowing Co-location and Vector Bin Packing policies [3,5]. However, these tactics either lead to over-resource scheduling or QoS violations.

CODEC Acceleration: CODEC exploits intra-frame and inter-frame redundancies to compress videos with fewer bytes. The encoder segments the frame into numerous non-overlapping macroblocks (MBs), which serve as the fundamental units in video coding. Basic video encoding necessitates two types of predictions: intra-frame prediction and inter-frame prediction. Inter-frame prediction, alternatively known as temporal prediction (TP), capitalizes on the temporal redundancy between adjacent frames, which are chosen as reference frames. Within the CODEC, frames are categorized into keyframes (I-frames) and non-keyframes (P-frames). In TP, the encoder selects the reference MB with the minimum sum of absolute errors for the current MB and computes their temporal pixel differences, termed residuals. The positional deviation between the reference MB and the current MB is designated as the motion vector (MV). Following prediction, the residual values and MVs are compressed into a bitstream via transformation, quantization, and entropy encoding. At present, the acceleration of CODECs has shifted from traditional comprehensive optimization for general applications [4,6,11] to specialized improvement solutions for specific applications. The new architecture is generally built on general-purpose codecs such as H.264/AVC [20] or H.265/HEVC [17]. [23] proposes an automation framework, Facebook Codec avatar Accelerator Design, to deliver sufficient performance and efficiency targeting such decoders which consist of multi-branch DNNs and require demanding compute and memory resources.

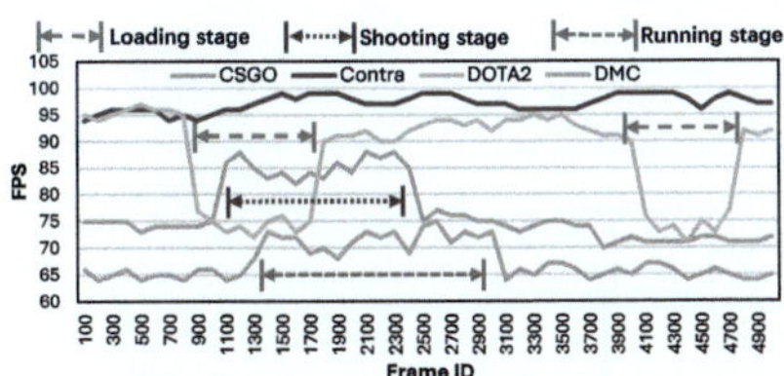

Fig. 2. Average FPS of games at different resolutions.

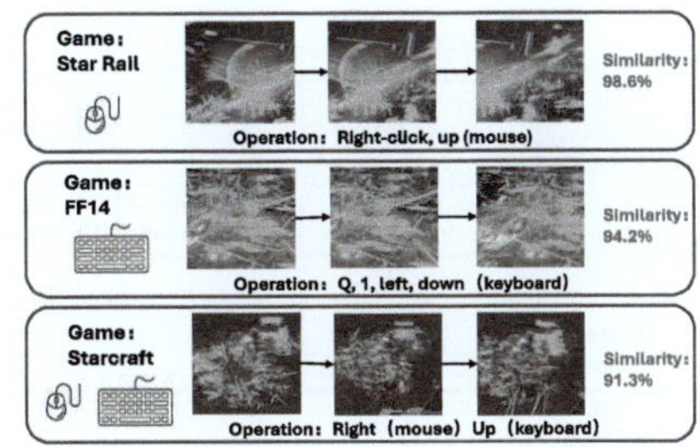

Fig. 3. MV with same user operations.

3   Preliminary and Motivation

We conducted a preliminary survey of popular cloud games on the market and recorded the video encoding overhead during the operation of cloud games. We have the following observations.

Observation 1: The FPS variation within a single game is significant and periodic. Figure 2 reports the runtime FPS of games at 1080P. We can find that even for the same game, the FPS can change by over 37% at different times. Due to the current computer's inability to support games loading all the models and maps involved into memory at once [16], the game is clearly divided into a number of scenes, all of which are clearly divided by loading period. This leads to an unstable stream of frames generated during game execution. Only a fine-grained division of the game can solve this problem.

Observation 2: There is a clear connection between player input of cloud games and MV of the video. User actions in cloud games typically represent the behavior of the game protagonist [12], while directional key inputs often signify movement, and mouse movements indicate changes in perspective. The MV segment during the CODEC process also represents the movement and changes of objects in the video. Figure 3 depicts the MV image obtained after recording inputs in the game, with the red line indicating the direction of the MV. Evidently, when the inputs are similar, the MV exhibits a high degree of consistency. This phenomenon aligns with our common sense. Furthermore, based on this observation, we can quickly and directly obtain MV information from user actions by employing regression algorithms and other methods, thereby reducing encoding time (Fig. 4).

4   System Design

When employing a fine-grained cloud game framework, we consider two aspects: how to achieve precise partitioning of games without accessing their specific execution logic or modifying the game's source code, and how to optimize encoding processes based on existing input information to enhance performance. We will elaborate on the specific implementation in solving these two issues in the following section.

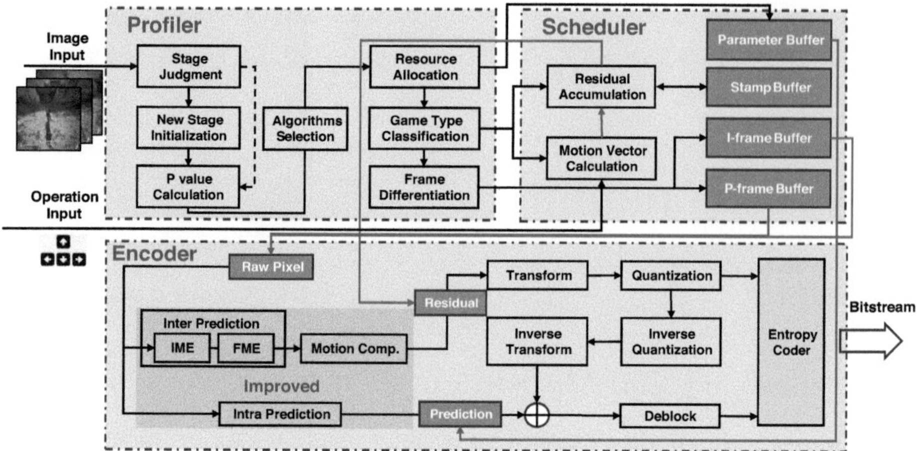

Fig. 4. CGO overview.

4.1 Frame-Gained Game Profiler

One of the challenges faced by previous game scheduling works is that games are highly dependent on user behavior. In cloud platforms where direct access to game data is not available, it becomes difficult to determine the current stage of a game or how long that stage will last. This lack of information significantly disrupts scheduling. Through preliminary experiments, we discovered that precise predictions of how long the current game stage will last are unnecessary. Instead, detecting turning points during stage transitions enables us to achieve fine-grained partitioning and scheduling of games. Additionally, the built-in loading stages in games provide a clear, detectable signal that we can utilize effectively. Using this information, we now proceed to introduce the Frame-Gained Game Profiler in detail.

Game Frame Clustering: As shown in Fig. 5a and c, we found that during the game process, the consumption of resources such as GPU and CPU fluctuates relatively small within a certain period of time. After significant changes occur, it will also stabilize in a relatively short period of time. After comparing the actual content of the game, it shows that this is a reflection of the consumption of game scene rendering. As mentioned in previous work, the most resource-intensive part of game execution is the rendering of the background, where character activity only accounts for a small and stable portion. Therefore, through this feature, we can match the real-time collection of game resources with the ongoing scene of the game, allowing us to understand the game content even without perceiving game data.

We directly clustered the resources using the K-means algorithm in Fig. 5b and d. Our cloud game stage integrates resources and content to provide a new perspective on the game. Each frame cluster represents the amount of resources consumed in a certain 5-s slice. With the above classification of execution stages, there may be multiple frame clusters that together form a single stage, and this combination of frame clusters will continue to occur in subsequent stages. Fortunately, through data collection from over 10 games, we found that there were no more than 12 clusters and no more than 6 corresponding scenarios. This indicates that it is feasible and practical to divide games into stages based on resource consumption.

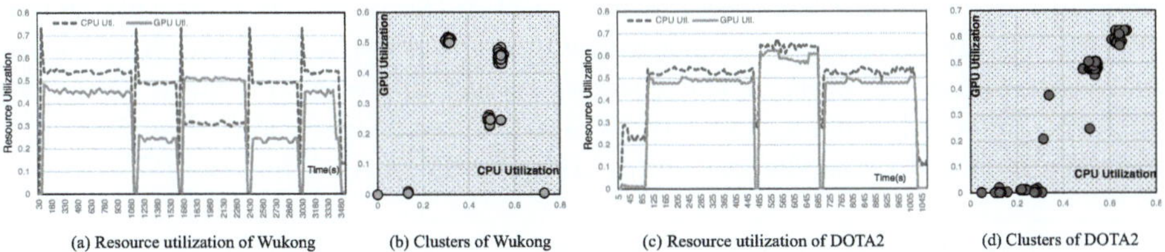

(a) Resource utilization of Wukong   (b) Clusters of Wukong   (c) Resource utilization of DOTA2   (d) Clusters of DOTA2

Fig. 5. Resource utilization and clusters of different cloud games.

Game Stage Analysis: After successfully dividing different cloud games into different stages, we need to further analyze the topological structure of the entire game process, so that we can know what stage we are currently in and what the next stage is during runtime. Although we have reduced the user's impact on game duration by identifying and loading stages, the user's choice can even affect the order of stages.

How to minimize this user impact in runtime requires us to classify the game and select different stages as samples based on 4 game types, in order to achieve high accuracy. The first type is **web games**. This type of game is usually a flash or web game, characterized by a short total playing time, a single game process, less player interaction, and low resource consumption. This type of game is very easy to order because the game runs with a relatively single stage, and player behavior does not affect the game process. The second type is **mobile games**. These games are characterized by players logging in to complete tasks every day, but the order in which tasks are completed may vary greatly among different players. For this type of application, we need to finely establish a set for each individual player and make arrangements based on this. The third type is **console games**. They are characterized by a total game duration of several days and a large number of game levels. However, players are only stuck in a few big scenes for long periods. Their choices in the game are unlikely to affect the switching of game stages. We need to connect all the processes of the player playing the game, integrate the data of the player's entire process, and then get the correct stage order of these games. The final type is **MMORPG & MOBA games**, where multiple players interact in the same game area at the same time. This type of game seems to be most influenced by users, but through experiments and game content, we have found that this type of game usually only has a loading phase and 2–3 game phases. Once the phase is determined, it will not change for a long time.

4.2 CODEC Accelaration

The central idea of the proposed algorithm is to reuse the operation information to accelerate encoding. MVs are obtained from the motion estimation (ME) algorithm, which consists of integrated ME (IME) and fractional ME (FME). ME in TP aims to find the best-matched MB in the search window (SWD) and the best MV. It is the most time-consuming module in the encoding process and a resource-hungry module in the encoder accelerator due to a large SWD. We propose a novel algorithm that can obtain MV from operations, multiplying it and getting the MVs as the midpoint(MP) of ME search window in TP.

Lightweight MV Estimation. After obtaining user operation information, we can predict MV based on this. Firstly, the game parameter information that can be obtained in advance includes mouse sensitivity D and keyboard minimum input interval s, which players need to set in advance before playing the game, so we can directly capture them. Subsequently, as the game progresses, the input vector V_k of the directional keyboards and the movement vector V_m of the mouse need to be continuously updated over time. The following derivation of this article uses keyboard and mouse input as an example, and the input of the joystick is also similar, with the left one being V_k and the right one being V_m. Most of games simulate real human eye scenes, and the visual movement caused by mouse movement is a spherical motion with the back of the character's head as the center and the head as the radius H_r. Visual range H_v can also be obtained from the character information. The corresponding keyboard input generally represents the movement of the character facing the direction. The center is at the character's feet, so we need to record height information H_f. Based on these data, we can calculate the MV corresponding to different MB in each frame:

$$MV_x = V_m \cdot L_x \cdot D\frac{H_v}{H_r} + V_k \cdot L_x \cdot s\sqrt{H_f^2 + H_v^2} + \delta_M \tag{1}$$

$$MV_y = V_m \cdot L_y \cdot D\frac{H_v}{H_r} + V_k \cdot L_y \cdot s\sqrt{H_f^2 + H_v^2} + \delta_M \tag{2}$$

$$\delta_M = L_{xy} \cdot \frac{H_r}{\sqrt{H_v^2 + H_f^2}} \tag{3}$$

where L_x represents the horizontal vector of the current MB pointing to the center of the screen, and L_y represents the vertical vector.

In addition, we found that different game types have varying degrees of impact on MV. So we introduced the variable δ_M to represent the shift in perspective. For Third-person perspective games, which are played from a third-person perspective behind the character's head, the character's back is locked directly below the screen. So all MVs in the area directly below the frame are 0, and we only need to add a viewing angle deviation coefficient δ_M. For top-down perspective games, where games simulate a 3D perspective in 2D space. when inputting directions via the keyboard, only the MB where the character is positioned generates MV, with its size and direction mirroring those of V_k. When inputting directions via the mouse, the entire screen follows the mouse's movement, maintaining a consistent MV across the entire screen, with its size mirroring V_k but in the opposite direction. Alternatively, players can always keep the character centered on the screen while using the mouse to rotate the scene.

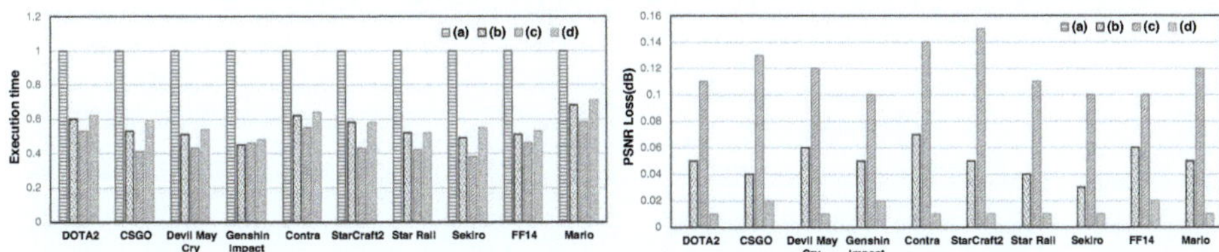

Fig. 6. The trade-off between encoding complexity and quality.

Search Window Design. We examine 4 designs of Search Window Size *Direct Large Window* is the full encoding algorithm with (0,0) midpoint and largest Search Window Size 128×128. (0,0) is the position of the current MB. *Direct Small Window* is a scaled-down version of (a) with a 16×16 SWD. In (c) and (d), we use our operation-MV estimation to calculate the midpoint MV_O. *Prediction Point* directly chooses MV_O as the MV, while *Prediction Small Window* has a 16×16 SWD.

Figure 6 shows the algorithm complexity and PSNR loss of ten cloud games encoded with QP22 using ME modes. We use 720p and 1080p to upsample to 4K. As the SWD size is directly reduced from 128×128 to 16×16, the encoding time of MVP2 is reduced by 45.76% compared with MVP1, while PSNR decreases by 0.05dB. And as MV estimation from operation is directly used by encoding but the SWD is fixed to zero as in MVP3, the encoding time is reduced by 54.81%, while the quality loss, 0.12dB, worsens compared to MVP2. Correspondingly, MVP4 with MV_O as a midpoint and a 16×16 SWD combines the advantages of MVP2 and MVP3. As a result, the average reduced time of MVP4 is 42.38% and the PSNR loss is only 0.01dB.

4.3 Game Scheduler

After perceiving the current game stage and the relationship between the game operations and MV in encoding, we can perform fine-grained scheduling on cloud games. One of the primary challenges in previous work is the aggressive resource utilization strategies employed by games. Commercial-grade games typically default to consuming all allocated CPU and GPU resources during runtime. This behavior severely limits scheduling flexibility unless resources are initially constrained-a trade-off that often results in noticeable declines in QoS, rendering the gaming experience unacceptable to users.

Our proposed scheduler, which integrates both visual rendering and encoding processes, effectively addresses this challenge. Initially, we allocate sufficient resources to newly launched cloud games. When our profiler detects a transition into a complex scene, the scheduler dynamically adjusts by increasing the predicted proportion of MV, thereby reserving more resources and time for rendering tasks. In contrast, during single-phase scenes, traditional MV computation methods are employed to ensure visual quality remains consistent.

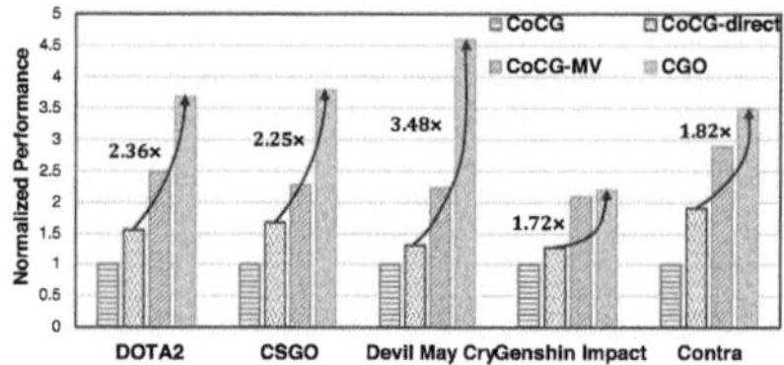

Fig. 7. Performance of CGO.

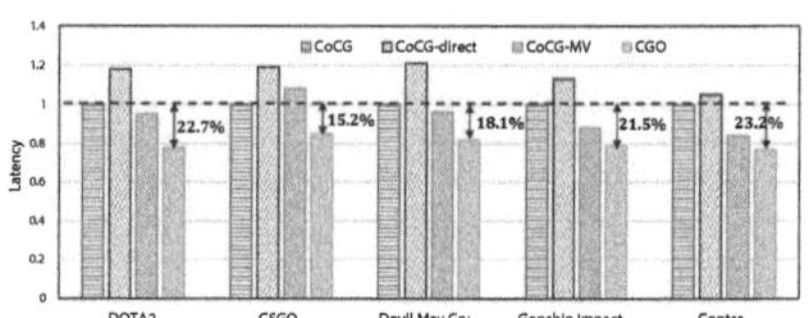

Fig. 8. Latency of CGO.

5   Evaluation

5.1   Experimental Setup

Software and Hardware Environments: Our workloads run on a 4-core Intel i7-13700F CPU, 8 GB RAM, 1 NVIDIA GeForce GTX 4090 GPUs, and Linux OS. GPU-Z [10] is involved in validating parameters including GPU and GPU memory utilization.

We use GamingAnywhere (GA) [8] to build the cloud game environment, which is a popular open-source cloud game platform. The GA has two components: the GA server (for running games, encoding, and streaming videos) and the GA client (for decoding and displaying videos and transmitting user commands).

Our modification for CODEC is based on FFmpeg implementation. Our MV prediction modifications mainly target libavcodec/h264enc.c and libavcodec/h264.c.

Considering different CPUs and GPUs, or the impact of the version of the game, and graphical settings, the specific amount of resources consumed by the same game must be different. However, due to the introduction of video enhancement, CGO performs better on worse GPUs.

Baseline: We select CoCG [19] as our baseline, as it represents the current state-of-the-art resource scheduling for cloud gaming. However, it solely focuses on optimizing the image rendering process. Therefore, we incorporate H264 encoding, creating our first test object - CoCG-direct. Building upon CoCG-direct, we add MV prediction, resulting in CoCG-MV.

5.2   Overall Performance

We set the parameter P to measure the QoS of cloud games.

$$P = R_T \times F \tag{4}$$

where R_T represents the number of pixels corresponding to the current resolution, such as 1080P (1920 × 1080), 2K (2048 × 1080), 4K (4096 × 2160). F represents the FPS(frames per second) of the game running on the client end. Additionally, latency is another concept for cloud gaming, which refers to the time taken from a user's command input to seeing the corresponding visual output.

QoS Guarantee. Figure 7 shows the optimization results of cloud game QoS obtained through various solutions presented in this paper. Using the image quality P obtained from CoCG as the standard, introducing CODEC alone can only achieve an average improvement of 1.55×. This is because CODEC will occupy the computing resources of GPU image rendering. With the introduction of MV prediction, FPS shows a significant increase, resulting in an overall rise in the P value. For CGO, the overall resolution is increased by one layer through scheduling under the same FPS as CoCG-MV, resulting in an average increase of 3.62×. Among them, for games that consume a large amount of computing resources and have drastic changes in graphics, QoS can be improved by up to 4.6×.

Latency Reduction. Figure 8 illustrates the latency of five game types under various solutions. Compared to the baseline, CoCG-direct's latency has actually increased, primarily due to the additional computation time incurred by the introduction of CODEC. CoCG-MV, which optimizes MV estimation, notably reduces overall latency. However, it's evident that only Contra, with its relatively simple content, experiences a substantial latency reduction of 23%, while complex games see less than a 15% reduction. Finally, CGO achieves an average latency reduction of 19%. This demonstrates the effectiveness of our trade-off for rendering and encoding. Additionally, we've noticed that our method yields good results for more complex games, thanks to their numerous frames.

5.3   Overhead

MV Accuracy. This section mainly considers the MV accuracy estimated through user operations. As shown in Fig. 9, we measured the accuracy of MVs obtained through player operations in different stages of different games. Compared to PSNR, which takes into account both MB and ME noise, MV accuracy better reflects the rationality of our algorithm. Generally speaking, game operations often involve not only movement but also the release of skills. Our user operation estimation does not consider the release of skills mainly because the image corresponding to a new skill usually involves a direct recalculation of

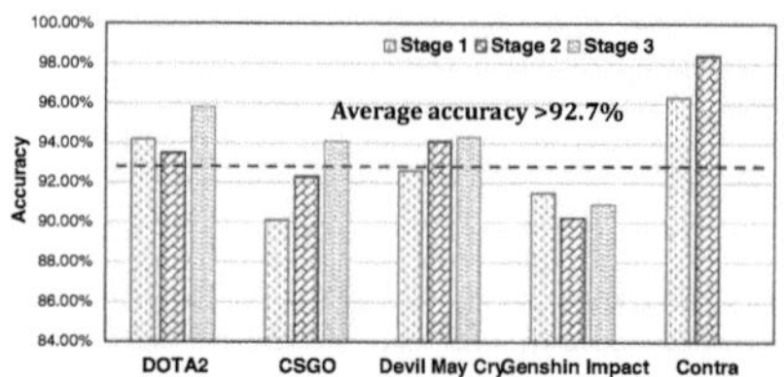

Fig. 9. MV accuracy estimated by user operations.

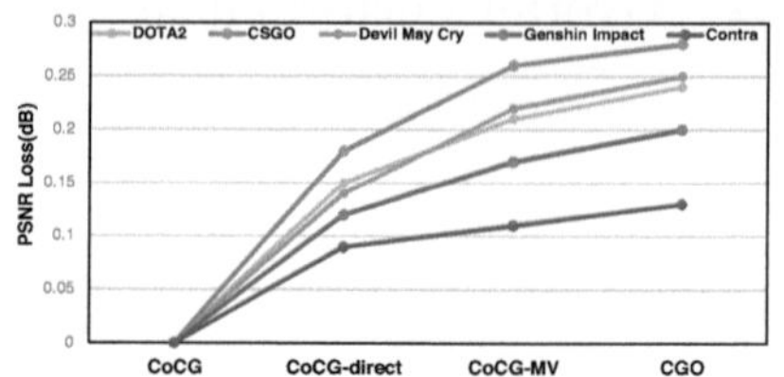

Fig. 10. The impact of noise from compression ratio.

MB, which cannot be obtained through the movement of the previous screen. Therefore, this part of the content is not within our optimization scope. For 2D games like Contra, the movable range of the graphics is very fixed, so the accuracy of the MV is very high, reaching over 96%. However, even the most complex game, Genshin Impact has an overall accuracy rate of over 90%, indicating that our idea of estimating MV using user operations is completely feasible.

PSNR Loss. Once MV prediction is introduced, there will be a significant increase in video frame rate and resolution, but the MB at the corresponding frame may become slightly blurry. Video loss is generally measured by Peak Signal-to-Noise Ratio(PSNR,dB). From Fig. 10, it can be seen that all of our games are below 0.3 dB. In addition, it can be seen that for CGO, the PSNR between the simple algorithm and the parallel mode does not exceed 0.05dB, indicating that our optimization has minimal performance loss.

6   Conclusion

In this paper, we propose CGO, a comprehensive scheduling framework tailored specifically for cloud gaming environments. We propose a resource-aware mechanism for fine-grained game analysis, enabling precise identification and management of resource-intensive stages in real-time. We develop an innovative method that leverages user interactions to accelerate video encoding processes. By analyzing user inputs and incorporating them into our encoding strategy, we achieve more efficient compression without compromising visual quality. Compared to state-of-the-art, our implementation of CGO achieves 4.6× game quality improvement with 19% latency reduction.

Acknowledgments. We sincerely thank all the anonymous reviewers for their valuable comments that helped us to improve the paper. This work is supported by the National Key R&D Program of China (No. 2022YFB4501702), and the National Natural Science Foundation of China (No. 62441225). The corresponding author is Chao Li.

References

1. Basiri, M., Rasoolzadegan, A.: Delay-aware resource provisioning for cost-efficient cloud gaming. IEEE Trans. Circ. Syst. Video Technol
2. Cai, W., et al.: The future of cloud gaming [point of view]. In: Proceedings of the IEEE
3. Deng, Y., Li, Y., Seet, R., Tang, X., Cai, W.: The server allocation problem for session-based multiplayer cloud gaming. IEEE Trans. Multimedia
4. Farnebäck, G.: Two-frame motion estimation based on polynomial expansion. In: Image Analysis: 13th Scandinavian Conference, SCIA
5. Finkel, D., Claypool, M., Jaffe, S., Nguyen, T., Stephen, B.: Assignment of games to servers in the onlive cloud game system. In: 13th Annual Workshop on NSSG
6. Furht, B., Greenberg, J., Westwater, R.: Motion estimation algorithms for video compression, vol. 379. Springer (2012)
7. Hong, H.J., Chen, D.Y., Huang, C.Y., Chen: placing virtual machines to optimize cloud gaming experience. IEEE Trans. Cloud Comput
8. Huang, C.Y., Hsu, C.H., Chang, Y.C.: Gaminganywhere: an open cloud gaming system. In: Proceedings of the 4th ACM Multimedia Systems Conference
9. Inc., M.: Metaverse. https://www.pwc.com/us/metaverse (2021)
10. Inc., T.: Gpu-z. https://www.techpowerup.com/gpuz/ (2021)
11. Jing, N., Jiang, L., Zhang, T., Li, C., Fan, F., Liang, X.: Energy-efficient edram-based on-chip storage architecture for gpgpus. IEEE Trans. Comput. (TC) (2016)
12. Jing, N., et al.: Cache-emulated register file: an integrated on-chip memory architecture for high performance gpgpus. In: 49th Annual IEEE/ACM International Symposium on Microarchitecture
13. Li, Y., Tang, X.: On dynamic bin packing for resource allocation in the cloud. In: The 26th ACM Symposium on Parallelism in Algorithms and Architectures
14. Qi, Z., Yao, J., Zhang, C., Yu, M., Yang, Z., Guan, H.: Vgris: virtualized gpu resource isolation and scheduling in cloud gaming. ACM Trans. Archit. Code Optim
15. Ren, R., Tang, X., Li, Y., Cai, W.: Competitiveness of dynamic bin packing for online cloud server allocation. IEEE/ACM Trans. Networking
16. Shao, C., Guo, J., Wang, P., Wang, J., Li, C., Guo, M.: Oversubscribing gpu unified virtual memory: implications and suggestions. In: Proceedings of the 2022 ICPE
17. Sullivan, G.J., Ohm, J.R., Han, W.J., Wiegand, T.: Overview of the high efficiency video coding (hevc) standard. IEEE TCSVT
18. T., K., Mark: on frame rate and player performance in first person shooter games. Multimedia Syst. (2007). https://doi.org/10.1007/s00530-007-0081-1
19. Wang, T., Li, C., Wang, J., Xu, C., Hou, X., Guo, M.: Cocg: fine-grained cloud game co-location on heterogeneous platform. In: 2024 IEEE IPDPS
20. Wiegand, T., Sullivan, G., Bjontegaard, G., Luthra, A.: Overview of the h.264/avc video coding standard. IEEE Trans. Circ. Syst. Video Technol. **13**(7), 560–576 (2003). https://doi.org/10.1109/TCSVT.2003.815165

21. Wu, D., Xue, Z., He, J.Q.: icloudaccess: cost-effective streaming of video games from the cloud with low latency. In: IEEE TCSVT, pp. 1405–1416 (2014)
22. Zhang, W., et al.: PilotFish: harvesting free cycles of cloud gaming with deep learning training. In: USENIX ATC 22, July 2022
23. Zhang, X., Wang, D., Chuang, P., Ma, S., Chen, D., Li, Y.: F-cad: a framework to explore hardware accelerators for codec avatar decoding. In: 2021 DAC
24. Zhang, X., et al.: Improving cloud gaming experience through mobile edge computing. IEEE WC

Role-Aware Dynamic Grouping for Efficient Coordination in Multi-agent Reinforcement Learning

Hongxin Zhang[1(✉)], Zhi Li[2(✉)], and Junbo Wang[1(✉)]

[1] Sun Yat-Sen University, Guangzhou 510275, China
zhanghx75@mail2.sysu.edu.cn, wangjb33@mail.sysu.edu.cn
[2] South China University of Technology, Guangzhou 510641, China
lizh337@mail2.sysu.edu.cn

Abstract. Cooperative multi-agent reinforcement learning aims to train decentralized agents to accomplish joint tasks by maximizing a global reward. While existing value decomposition methods under the centralized training and decentralized execution paradigm have achieved notable success, they often overlook the latent role structures inherent in multi-agent systems. In real-world scenarios, agents may exhibit functional heterogeneity or behavioral diversity, even when sharing identical observation and action spaces. To address this limitation, we propose Role-Aware Dynamic Grouping (RADG), a novel framework that learns contrastive role representations from agents' trajectory information and performs adaptive grouping based on these learned roles. The extracted role embeddings capture meaningful behavioral patterns that guide flexible and dynamic group formation. Within each group, agents coordinate more effectively through shared policy information and group-aware value decomposition. RADG enables structured cooperation, improves exploration efficiency, and enhances generalization across diverse tasks. Importantly, it operates without relying on manual supervision or domain-specific priors, making it well-suited for dynamic and complex environments. Experimental results on standard cooperative MARL benchmarks demonstrate that RADG consistently outperforms existing baselines in coordination performance, training stability, and adaptability to varying team structures.

Keywords: Multi-Agent Reinforcement Learning · Cooperative MARL · Role Learning

1 Introduction

Cooperative multi-agent reinforcement learning (MARL) is fundamentally designed to address coordination challenges in multi-agent systems by optimizing a global reward signal [21]. This paradigm has achieved substantial empirical success in several critical domains, including autonomous vehicle coordination

© IFIP International Federation for Information Processing 2026
Published by Springer Nature Switzerland AG 2026
X. Wang et al. (Eds.): NPC 2025, LNCS 16306, pp. 51–62, 2026.
https://doi.org/10.1007/978-3-032-10466-3_5

[27], distributed energy management in smart grids [2], collaborative robotic manipulation [10], and the study of social dilemmas [7]. A central challenge in MARL lies in developing decentralized policies that sustain effective coordination under partial observability [1,12], while mitigating the risk of misassigning credit to individual agents [13]. The centralized training with decentralized execution (CTDE) framework [3] addresses this challenge by combining the sample efficiency of centralized learning with the scalability and practicality of decentralized execution. This hybrid approach effectively integrates the strengths of independent Q-learning (IQL) [4] and fully centralized learning [19].

Despite the success of existing value decomposition frameworks, they often overlook the underlying role structures that naturally emerge in many real-world multi-agent systems [16,24]. Agents frequently differ in function, responsibility, or interaction patterns [9,22,25], even when their observation and action spaces are identical. Without explicitly modeling these structural characteristics, current methods may suffer from inefficient credit assignment, redundant policy learning, and limited generalization across different environments. While some prior works attempt to mitigate this issue through manual role assignment or domain-specific priors [8], such approaches generally lack the flexibility and adaptability required for dynamic or complex environments. In contrast, we posit that rich role representations are implicitly encoded within agents' hidden trajectory representations during learning. When effectively extracted and leveraged, these latent representations can serve as informative signals for discovering agent groupings and facilitating more structured and efficient coordination.

In this paper, we propose a novel role-based agent grouping framework, termed Role-Aware Dynamic Grouping (RADG), for cooperative multi-agent reinforcement learning (MARL). RADG learns latent role embeddings from the hidden layers of the training architecture, effectively capturing behavioral distinctions among agents. By applying an adaptive group selection algorithm to these embeddings, the framework identifies emergent agent groups that exhibit similar strategies or behavioral patterns. Subsequent group-wise coordination and optimization are then performed, enabling policy sharing, efficient exploration, and robust value estimation within each group. This approach offers a flexible and scalable solution for enhancing cooperation, particularly in heterogeneous or dynamically changing environments. The main contributions of this work are summarized as follows:

- We propose a role learning framework that extracts role-level features from agent behaviors during training, without requiring manual supervision or domain-specific priors.
- We introduce a dynamic grouping mechanism that uncovers latent, role-based agent groups, enabling more structured and efficient inter-agent collaboration.
- We conduct extensive empirical evaluations on standard cooperative benchmarks, demonstrating that our method improves learning stability, coordination performance, and generalization across diverse team structures.

2   Related Work

2.1   Group in MARL

Under the CTDE paradigm, value function factorization method has become a popular approach for credit assignment in cooperative MARL. Representative methods such as VDN [20], QMIX [17], and QTRAN [18] decompose the global joint action-value function into individual agent utilities to guide decentralized policy learning. To further improve coordination in complex environments, it is essential to model structural relationships among agents. Group division in multi-agent systems, as a key factor for enhancing collaboration efficiency and learning performance, has attracted substantial attention. Early group division approaches in multi-agent systems [8,11] primarily relied on predefined subtasks, agent capabilities, or behavioral patterns. However, these methods are limited to tasks with well-defined structures and often require domain-specific prior knowledge.

An alternative line of research introduces the concept of roles into multi-agent systems. ROMA [24] generates role embeddings based solely on current agent observations to learn role-specific policies. However, this approach may struggle to capture flexible and dynamic inter-role collaboration. RODE [25] decomposes the action space into multiple subsets, associating each role with a specific subset. It leverages trajectory information for role matching to reduce exploration complexity. Nevertheless, this rigid role-to-action mapping may hinder the discovery of optimal solutions. VAST [15] explores the influence of agent grouping on value decomposition but requires either predefining the number of groups or performing pre-grouping, limiting adaptability. GoMARL [26] dynamically adjusts groupings based on learned factorization weights, but the grouping outcomes are tightly coupled with these weights, increasing exploration complexity. Furthermore, its "select-and-kick-out" strategy results in grouping schemes that are difficult to interpret. ACORM [5] learns role representations and applies clustering for grouping, yet it imposes a fixed number of groups, reducing flexibility.

Differing from traditional approaches that depend on domain knowledge or fixed assumptions, RADG dynamically derives group divisions from emergent role representations during policy optimization, thereby facilitating policy specialization and structured cooperation among agents.

3   Preliminaries

3.1   Decentralized POMDP

We consider a cooperative multi-agent task which can be formulated as a Decentralized Partially Observable Markov Decision Process(Dec-POMDP), which is defined as a tuple $G = \langle S, U, P, r, Z, O, n, \gamma \rangle$, where n is the number of MAS agents. $s \in S$ denotes the global environment state. At each time step t, each agent $i \in \{1, ..., n\}$ chooses an action $u_t^i \in U$ which consists a joint action $\mathbf{u} = \{u_t^1, ..., u_t^n\} \in U^n$, and the environment state updates by the transition function $P(s'|s, \mathbf{u})$: $S \times U^n \times S \rightarrow [0,1]$. Each agents receives a reward

$r = R(s, \mathbf{u}) : S \times U^n \to \mathbb{R}$ through the shared reward function, obtains individual partial observation $o^i \in Z$ with the observation function $O(s, i) : S \times N \to Z$, and has action-observation history $\tau^i \in T \equiv (U \times Z)^*$ on which it conditions a policy $\pi^i(u^i | \tau^i) : T \times U \to [0, 1]$. The system objective is to maximize the expected return $\mathbb{E}_{s_{t+1:\infty}, \mathbf{u}_{t+1:\infty}}[\sum_{m=0}^{\infty} \gamma^m r_{t+m} | s_t, \mathbf{u}_t]$ where $\gamma \in [0, 1)$ is the discount factor.

4　Method

In this section, we present the RADG framework, which is designed to meet the growing demand for effective agent collaboration in complex multi-agent environments. The goal is to enable agents to learn intrinsic role representations and perform adaptive grouping based on these representations across diverse scenarios. Agents within the same group are expected to achieve enhanced learning efficiency and more sophisticated intra-group coordination through structured information exchange.

As illustrated in Fig. 1, RADG consists of individual agent Q-networks and a group-aware mixing network. To derive informative role representations, we employ a contrastive learning-based mechanism that extracts intrinsic features from the hidden states of agents' trajectories. These group-level representations are further refined via contrastive learning across agents to enhance role discriminability. Adaptive grouping is achieved through an asynchronous hierarchical clustering algorithm, enabling dynamic and flexible group formation based on learned role similarities. During value decomposition, both the learned role representations and the grouping results are incorporated to guide the training process. This transforms traditional individual-based value decomposition into a dynamic, group-based decomposition scheme, effectively balancing individual expressiveness with group-level coordination.

4.1　Role Representation Learning

This module aims to learn intrinsic role representations for agents that exhibit a degree of invariance throughout an episode. Simultaneously, guided by adaptive grouping results, it encourages agents within the same group to possess similar role representations while increasing the dissimilarity between agents from different groups. This design promotes a balance between intra-group collaboration and inter-agent diversity.

Role Representation. We employ a combination of MLP and GRU network to extract complex behavioral representations from agent trajectories. Specifically, the hidden state is computed as $h_i^t = f_\phi(o_i^t, a_i^{t-1}, h_i^{t-1})$, where ϕ denotes an encoder comprising MLP and GRU layers, o_i^t is the observation of agent i at timestep t, a_i^{t-1} is the agent's action at timestep $t - 1$, and h_i^{t-1} is the GRU's hidden state from the previous timestep. To capture role-specific information embedded in the behavioral trajectories, we introduce a role encoder

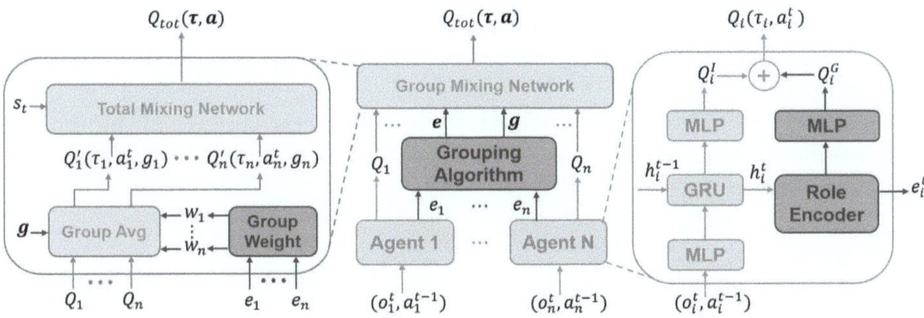

Fig. 1. An overview of the RADG framework. The middle section depicts the overall architecture, including the dynamic grouping algorithm based on learned role representations. The right section illustrates the individual agent Q-networks, where role representations are extracted from hidden layers. The left section presents the group-wise value decomposition module, which performs coordination and optimization at the group level.

composed of two MLP layers, $e_i^t = f_\theta(h_i^t)$, where θ represents the parameters of the 2-layer MLP. This role encoder extracts role-relevant features from the agents' behavioral histories, enabling effective role-aware group formation and facilitating structured, group-based learning.

Contrastive Role Learning. To facilitate effective division of labor and collaboration in complex task scenarios, agents are grouped based on their learned role characteristics. The resulting grouping structure is then used to guide the learning of role representations, encouraging agents within the same group to develop more compact and consistent role embeddings. To enhance the discriminability between roles across different groups, we incorporate a contrastive learning approach inspired by unsupervised representation learning. Specifically, we formalize the role encoder θ as a probabilistic mapping $e^t \sim f_\theta(e^t \mid h^t)$. The role variable M is assumed to follow a prior distribution $P(M)$, and the distribution of the agent embedding e is conditioned on its role. The learning objective for the role encoder is defined as:

$$\max I(e; M) = \mathbb{E}_{e, M} \left[\log \frac{p(M \mid e)}{p(M)} \right].\tag{1}$$

Inspired by the infoNCE loss [14] in contrastive learning, we obtain the following variational lower bound:

$$I(e; M) - \log(K) \geq \mathbb{E}_{\mathcal{M}, e, h} \left[\log \frac{s(h, e)}{\sum_{M^* \in \mathcal{M}} s(h^*, e)} \right],\tag{2}$$

where $\mathcal{M}$ denotes a set of roles sampled from the distribution $P(M)$ with cardinality $|\mathcal{M}| = K$, and $s(h, e) = \frac{p(e \mid h)}{p(e)}$. Although the exact forms of $p(e \mid h)$

and $p(e)$ are intractable, we approximate s using samples from these distributions by employing a similarity-based scoring function. Specifically, we define $s(h, e) \approx \exp(S(e^\cdot e))$, where $S(e^*, e)$ is a similarity function between the latent representation of two agents. Thus, the role encoder is trained by minimizing the following contrastive loss, which serves as a lower bound of the mutual information objective:

$$\min \mathcal{L}_{role} = -\mathbb{E}_{M_i \in \mathcal{M}, (e,e') \sim M_i} \left[\log \frac{exp(S(e, e'))}{exp(S(e, e')) + \sum_{M^* \in \mathcal{M} \setminus M_i} exp(S(e, e^*))} \right], \tag{3}$$

where $\mathcal{M}$ is the set of agent roles, (e, e') is a positive pair sampled from the same role M_i, and $\{(e, e^*)\}_{M^* \in \mathcal{M} \setminus M_i}$ are negative pairs sampled from other roles.

Leveraging the learned agent role representations, we adaptively partition agents into K distinct groups (see Sect. 4.2), where $K \in [1, n]$. Based on the grouping results, we aim to ensure that agents within the same group have similar role embeddings, while maximizing dissimilarity between agents in different groups. To achieve this, we treat agents within the same group as positive pairs and agents from different groups as negative pairs, and adopt a bilinear product [6] as the score function. The InfoNCE loss in Eq. 3 can then be reformulated as:

$$\mathcal{L}_{role} = -\log \frac{\sum_{i' \in g_i} \exp(e_i^T W e_{i'})}{\sum_{i' \in g_i} \exp(e_i^T W e_{i'}) + \sum_{j \notin g_i} \exp(e_i^T W e_j)}, \tag{4}$$

where g_i denotes the group assigned to agent i, e_i is the role representation of agent i, and W is a learnable weight matrix in the bilinear similarity function.

4.2   Grouping Algorithm

Given that latent role representation spaces of agents may vary substantially across different environments, traditional clustering methods that require a fixed number of groups (e.g., K-means) are insufficient for adaptive grouping in dynamic scenarios. To address this limitation, we propose an adaptive grouping algorithm inspired by hierarchical cluster.

This algorithm initiates dynamic agent grouping by first assigning each agent to a singleton group and computing pairwise Euclidean distances between their embeddings. The core iterative merging process proceeds when two key conditions are simultaneously met, mutual nearest-neighbor identification, which verifies reciprocal minimal role dissimilarity, and an adaptive threshold bounded by the smaller intra-group distance of the candidate groups that ensures well-defined role boundaries. This dual-condition mechanism progressively consolidates agent clusters by updating the distance matrix until convergence, resulting in a group structure that inherently captures hierarchical role relationships. The distance metric maps abstract role semantics into quantifiable spatial relationships, where smaller distances imply greater similarity. The mutual nearest-neighbor criterion identifies prototypical roles without predefined categories, and the adaptive threshold, scaled by intra-group compactness, balances precision with flexibility.

Algorithm 1: Dynamic Role-Based Agent Grouping Algorithm

Input: Agent embeddings $\{e_1, e_2, \ldots, e_n\}$
Output: Final grouping $G = \{g_1, g_2, \cdots, g_k\}$

1 **Initialization:**
2 Initialize each agent in a singleton group: $g_i = \{e_i\}, \quad \forall i \in \{1, \ldots, n\}$
3 Compute distance matrix $D = [d_{ij}]$ where $d_{ij} = \|e_i - e_j\|_2$ for $i \neq j$
4 Set $mindis_{g_i} = \infty$ for each group g_i
5 **repeat**
6   **foreach** $group\ i \in \{1, \ldots, k\}$ **do**
7   Find nearest neighbor: $j = \arg\min_{j \neq i} d_{ij}$
8   **if** $i == \arg\min_{k \neq j} d_{jk}$ // Mutual nearest neighbor *and*
9              $d_{ij} < \lambda \cdot \min(mindis_{g_i}, mindis_{g_j})$ **then**
10   Merge g_i and g_j into group g_i
11   **if** $d_{ij} < mindis_{g_i}$ **then**
12   Update $mindis_{g_i} = d_{ij}$
13   **end**
14   **end**
15   **end**
16   Recompute group-wise distances D based on updated group embeddings
17 **until** no change in group assignment;

4.3 Overall Learning Framework

In the previous section, we have learned the hidden behavioral representations which contain the agent trajectory information, and extracted their intrinsic role representations from them. To facilitate both intra-group and inter-group coordination, we assign each agent i two distinct Q-value functions: an individual Q-value function Q_i^I, and a group-level Q-value function Q_i^G. The agent's final Q-value is defined by decomposing these components as follows:

$$Q_i(a_i \mid \tau_i) = Q_i^I(a_i \mid \tau_i) + Q_i^G(a_i \mid e_i), \tag{5}$$

where $Q_i^I = f_{\phi_I}(h_i)$, $Q_i^G = f_{\phi_G}(e_i)$, with ϕ_I and ϕ_G denoting the parameters of two distinct MLP networks.

Within the mixing network, we leverage the learned role representations to adjust agent Q-values via role-aware weighting:

$$Q_i' = \frac{\sum_{j \in g_i} w_j Q_j}{N_{g_i}}, \tag{6}$$

where $w_j = f_w(e_j)$ is a learned weight based on agent j's role representation, and N_{g_i} denotes the number of agents in group g_i.

Finally, we adopt the QMIX [17] hypernetwork architecture to mix the adjusted local Q-values Q_i' into a global joint action-value function Q_{tot}, and optimize the entire framework end-to-end using the following loss function:

$$\mathcal{L}(\theta) = [r + \gamma \max_{\mathbf{a}'} Q_{tot}(s', \mathbf{a}'; \theta^-) - Q_{tot}(s, \mathbf{a}; \theta)]^2 + \lambda \mathcal{L}_{role}(\theta), \tag{7}$$

where θ denotes the parameters of the overall framework, θ^- represents the parameters of a target network periodically updated from θ, and λ is a hyperparameter that balances the temporal-difference loss and the role representation loss.

5 Experiment and Result

In this section, we evaluate the effectiveness of our proposed approach on a set of challenging scenarios from the SMAC benchmark. We compare our method against representative multi-agent value-based baselines, including QMIX [17] and QPLEX [23], as well as GoMARL [26], which employs an automatic grouping mechanism, and ROMA [24], which learns role-based policies in cooperative MARL.

For evaluation, we report the average performance over three independent runs with different random seeds. The test success rate is averaged and plotted as a bold line, while shaded areas indicate the 95% confidence interval, providing a visual representation of performance stability and variance across trials.

5.1 Performance on SMAC

The SMAC environment includes a variety of combat scenarios with different difficulty levels, determined by variations in enemy and ally configurations as well as terrain complexity. These scenarios are categorized into three levels of difficulty, Easy, Hard, and Super Hard, according to team composition and environmental challenges. The tasks require agents to defeat numerically superior enemies, coordinate heterogeneous skills, and execute specialized strategies. In particular, scenarios within the Super Hard category involve more complex task designs that demand thorough exploration of diverse behavioral patterns and advanced coordination capabilities.

We evaluate our method on three representative scenarios for each difficulty level, as shown in Fig. 2. Across all settings, our method performs as well as or better than the strongest baseline algorithms. On Easy maps, our approach achieves comparable performance to existing baselines, reaching satisfactory results with fewer training steps. In the 1c3s5z map, we observe minor performance fluctuations, which are primarily caused by instability in the grouping process during training. This issue is further discussed in our ablation study.

For both Hard and Super Hard scenarios, the proposed dynamic grouping mechanism enables more flexible exploration and effective agent collaboration, resulting in improved coordination performance across tasks. These results demonstrate the adaptability and robustness of our method in handling a range of multi-agent challenges with varying complexity.

5.2 Ablations

We conducted ablation studies to validate the independent contributions of the role loss and the group-wise value decomposition module. RADG was compared

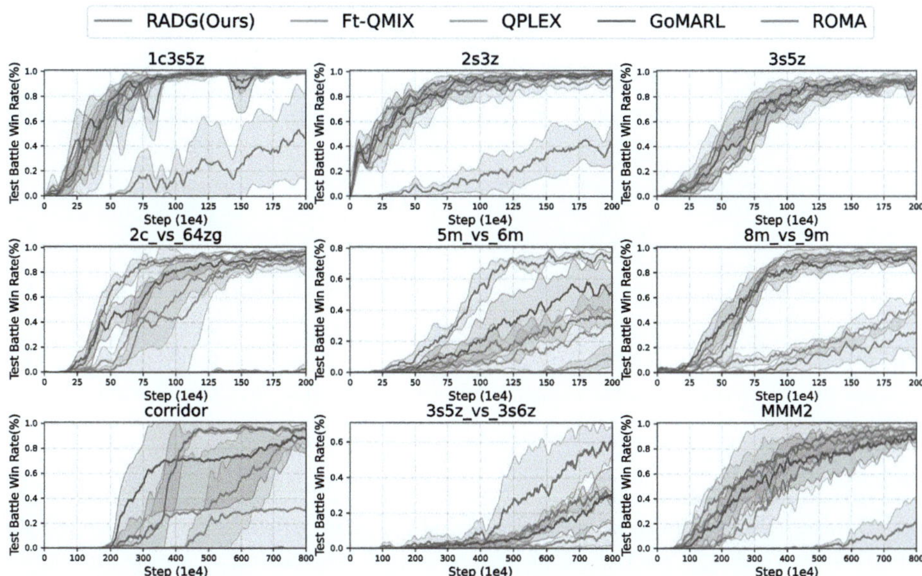

Fig. 2. Performance comparison of RADG against baseline algorithms on nine SMAC scenarios. The first row shows Easy-difficulty scenarios, the second row displays Hard-difficulty scenarios, and the third row presents Super Hard-difficulty scenarios.

against three ablated variants: i)RADG w/o L_{role}, it only excludes role loss; ii)RADG w/ Q-mixing, it replaces the original group-wise value decomposition module with QMIX's mixing network; iii)QMIX, it removes all components.

Figure 3 presents the ablation results on the 5 m_vs_6 m(Hard scenario) and corridor(Super Hard scenario). The performance of RADG declines when either component is removed, yet still surpasses QMIX. This demonstrates that both components are critical to RADG's capability and exhibit complementary effects. Notably, both RADG w/o L_{role} (without role loss) and RADG w/ Q-mixing (replacing group-wise decomposition with QMIX's mixer) outperform Ft-QMIX, confirming the effectiveness of role-aware feature extraction and utilization.

5.3 Group Dynamics During Training

Dynamic grouping refers to the adaptive formation of agent groups during training without any prior knowledge, where both the number and composition of groups evolve progressively throughout the learning process. This dynamic nature encompasses two key aspects: the continual adaptation of grouping strategies as training unfolds, and the environment-specific emergence of group structures tailored to different task scenarios. Such flexibility enables the learning framework to discover effective cooperation patterns aligned with task complexity and agent diversity.

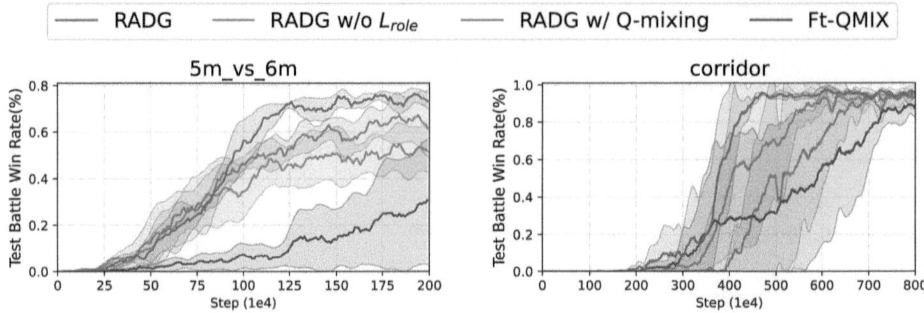

Fig. 3. Ablation studies. RADG w/o L_{role} only excludes role loss; RADG w/ Q-mixing replaces the original group-wise value decomposition module with QMIX's mixing network

Figure 4 illustrates the test win rates and the evolution of group numbers during training across different scenarios. In the 5 m_vs_6 m task, all training runs consistently converge to the same group count, indicating a stable and optimal grouping configuration for this environment. In contrast, for 3s5z_vs_3s6z, most runs converge to three groups, while one stabilizes at four; however, the three-group configuration achieves better performance, highlighting its effectiveness in this scenario. For 1c3s5z, the results suggest that fluctuations in the number of groups during training can impact convergence efficiency, revealing a trade-off between grouping flexibility and learning stability. Overall, these findings demonstrate that the proposed algorithm can autonomously discover task-specific and performance-effective group structures across a range of multi-agent environments.

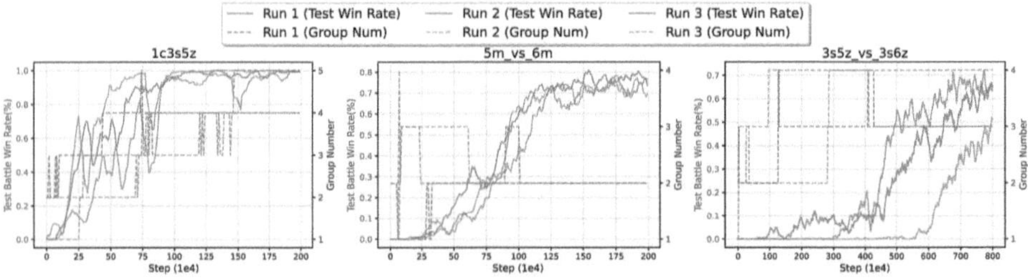

Fig. 4. The Test Battle Win Rate and the evolution of Group Number during training across various scenarios

6 Conclusion

In conclusion, we proposed RADG, a flexible framework that learns role representations and performs adaptive agent grouping to facilitate efficient coordination in cooperative MARL. RADG learns meaningful role embeddings and dynamically forms groups through dynamic grouping algorithm, integrating role-aware structures into value decomposition to enhance individual learning and group coordination in complex environments. Experimental results across diverse benchmark tasks demonstrate that RADG effectively promotes behavioral diversity and significantly improves learning performance. Despite promising results, RADG is currently limited to value-based methods and employs a grouping mechanism that has not been validated at scale. Future work will integrate policy-gradient and actor-critic approaches, extend to offline MARL to better suit real-world scenarios with limited online interactions, and optimize the grouping algorithm for large-scale scenarios and computational efficiency.

References

1. Canese, L., et al.: Multi-agent reinforcement learning: a review of challenges and applications. Appl. Sci. **11**(11), 4948 (2021)
2. Chen, D., et al.: Powernet: multi-agent deep reinforcement learning for scalable powergrid control. IEEE Trans. Power Syst. **37**(2), 1007–1017 (2022). https://doi.org/10.1109/TPWRS.2021.3100898
3. Foerster, J., Assael, I.A., De Freitas, N., Whiteson, S.: Learning to communicate with deep multi-agent reinforcement learning. In: Advances in Neural Information Processing Systems, vol. 29 (2016)
4. Foerster, J., et al.: Stabilising experience replay for deep multi-agent reinforcement learning. In: International Conference on Machine Learning, pp. 1146–1155. PMLR (2017)
5. Hu, Z., Zhang, Z., Li, H., Chen, C., Ding, H., Wang, Z.: Attention-guided contrastive role representations for multi-agent reinforcement learning. In: Proceedings of the 12th International Conference on Learning Representations (2024)
6. Laskin, M., Srinivas, A., Abbeel, P.: Curl: contrastive unsupervised representations for reinforcement learning. In: International Conference on Machine Learning, pp. 5639–5650. PMLR (2020)
7. Leibo, J., Zambaldi, V., Lanctot, M., Marecki, J., Graepel, T.: Multi-agent reinforcement learning in sequential social dilemmas. In: AAMAS, vol. 16, pp. 464–473. ACM (2017)
8. Lhaksmana, K.M., Murakami, Y., Ishida, T.: Role-based modeling for designing agent behavior in self-organizing multi-agent systems. Int. J. Software Eng. Knowl. Eng. **28**(01), 79–96 (2018)
9. Li, W., et al.: Mucvr: edge computing-enabled high-quality multi-user collaboration for interactive mvr. IEEE Trans. Parallel Distrib. Syst. (2025)
10. Liu, W., Peng, L., Wen, L., Yang, J., Liu, Y.: Decomposing shared networks for separate cooperation with multi-agent reinforcement learning. Inf. Sci. **641**, 119085 (2023)
11. Macarthur, K., Stranders, R., Ramchurn, S., Jennings, N.: A distributed anytime algorithm for dynamic task allocation in multi-agent systems. In: Proceedings of the AAAI Conference on Artificial Intelligence, vol. 25, pp. 701–706 (2011)
12. Nguyen, T.T., Nguyen, N.D., Nahavandi, S.: Deep reinforcement learning for multiagent systems: a review of challenges, solutions, and applications. IEEE Trans. Cybern. **50**(9), 3826–3839 (2020)
13. Ning, Z., Xie, L.: A survey on multi-agent reinforcement learning and its application. J. Autom. Intell. **3**(2), 73–91 (2024)

14. Oord, A.V.D., Li, Y., Vinyals, O.: Representation learning with contrastive predictive coding. arXiv preprint arXiv:1807.03748 (2018)
15. Phan, T., Ritz, F., Belzner, L., Altmann, P., Gabor, T., Linnhoff-Popien, C.: Vast: value function factorization with variable agent sub-teams. Adv. Neural. Inf. Process. Syst. **34**, 24018–24032 (2021)
16. Qu, Y., Wei, Z., Qin, Z., Wu, T., Ma, J., Dai, H., Dong, C.: Collaborative service provisioning for uav-assisted mobile edge computing. Chin. J. Electron. **33**(6), 1504–1514 (2024)
17. Rashid, T., Samvelyan, M., De Witt, C.S., Farquhar, G., Foerster, J., Whiteson, S.: Monotonic value function factorisation for deep multi-agent reinforcement learning. J. Mach. Learn. Res. **21**(178), 1–51 (2020)
18. Son, K., Kim, D., Kang, W.J., Hostallero, D.E., Yi, Y.: Qtran: learning to factorize with transformation for cooperative multi-agent reinforcement learning. In: International Conference on Machine Learning, pp. 5887–5896. PMLR (2019)
19. Sukhbaatar, S., Fergus, R., et al.: Learning multiagent communication with backpropagation. In: Advances in Neural Information Processing Systems, vol. 29 (2016)
20. Sunehag, P., et al.: Value-decomposition networks for cooperative multi-agent learning. arXiv preprint arXiv:1706.05296 (2017)
21. Vinyals, O., et al.: Grandmaster level in starcraft ii using multi-agent reinforcement learning. Nature **575**(7782), 350–354 (2019)
22. Wang, D., Bakar, K.B.A., Isyaku, B.: Two-stage iot computational task offloading decision-making in mec with request holding and dynamic eviction. Comput. Mater. Continua **80**(2) (2024)
23. Wang, J., Ren, Z., Liu, T., Yu, Y., Zhang, C.: Qplex: duplex dueling multi-agent q-learning. In: 9th International Conference on Learning Representations, ICLR 2021 (2021)
24. Wang, T., Dong, H., Lesser, V., Zhang, C.: Roma: multi-agent reinforcement learning with emergent roles. In: International Conference on Machine Learning, pp. 9876–9886. PMLR (2020)
25. Wang, T., Gupta, T., Mahajan, A., Peng, B., Whiteson, S., Zhang, C.: Rode: learning roles to decompose multi-agent tasks. In: International Conference on Learning Representations (2021)
26. Zang, Y., et al.: Automatic grouping for efficient cooperative multi-agent reinforcement learning. Adv. Neural. Inf. Process. Syst. **36**, 46105–46121 (2023)
27. Zhou, M., et al.: Smarts: an open-source scalable multi-agent rl training school for autonomous driving. In: Conference on Robot Learning, pp. 264–285. PMLR (2021)

SynergiCache: A Novel Cluster Cache for Enhancing Performance in Cloud Storage Systems

Yucheng Kang[iD], Jiawei Li[✉][iD], Chenming Chang[iD], Keqiang Li,
Yupeng Chen, and Yi Zhang

China Telecom eSurfing Cloud, Beijing, China
lijiawei1@chinatelecom.cn

Abstract. In cloud storage systems, caching is a commonly employed method to enhance system performance. Utilizing Solid State Drives (SSDs) as caches for Hard Disk Drives (HDDs) can improve overall system performance at a relatively low cost. However, traditional caching systems suffer from inefficiencies in write operations due to their overwrite approach. Furthermore, when slow disks are present in cloud storage systems, caching algorithms are often unable to detect them, resulting in degraded performance of the storage system.

To address these challenges, we proposed SynergiCache, a novel cluster caching system for cloud storage systems that significantly enhances performance and efficiency. Initially, we convert the traditional overwrite approach to an efficient append-only method, leveraging Remote Direct Memory Access (RDMA) technology to enhance data transfer efficiency. Furthermore, we employ a composite Key-Value (KV) storage mode and implement a cooperative garbage collection mechanism to optimize data access and storage performance. Subsequently, we introduce a slow-disk-sensitive adaptive (SDSA) caching algorithm that optimizes the flow of data between SSDs and HDDs, thereby reducing the adverse impact of slow disks on cloud storage systems.

We implemented SynergiCache, adapted it for integration with Ceph, and conducted comprehensive experiments. The experimental results demonstrate that SynergiCache significantly enhances cloud storage performance, reducing average latency by 89.55% and increasing IOPS by 9.52× compared to traditional caching systems.

Keywords: Cloud Storage · Cluster Cache · High Performance · Slow Disk Sensitive

1 Introduction

With emerging applications continually arising, the demand for performance is increasing, which requires cloud storage systems to enhance performance while reducing costs. Caching is a widely adopted method for improving storage system performance, in which high-speed storage media, though more expensive,

© IFIP International Federation for Information Processing 2026
Published by Springer Nature Switzerland AG 2026
X. Wang et al. (Eds.): NPC 2025, LNCS 16306, pp. 63–75, 2026.
https://doi.org/10.1007/978-3-032-10466-3_6

are often used as caches for lower-speed but lower-cost storage media. In cloud storage systems, HDDs and SSDs are the most common storage media. HDDs offer relatively lower performance at a lower cost, while SSDs provide higher performance at a higher cost. Using SSDs as caches for HDDs is a common strategy aimed at reducing costs while improving performance. A caching system plays a critical role in optimizing data flow management among clients, SSDs, and HDDs [6].

However, traditional caching architectures still exhibit several shortcomings in terms of system design and implementation. Firstly, the commonly used overwrite mechanism in write operations results in random write operations, which in turn limits the throughput of storage systems [13]. Secondly, existing cache algorithms lack mechanisms to detect performance degradation in HDD storage media, particularly when dealing with slow disks, leading to inefficient data flow between SSDs and HDDs.

To address these challenges and further improve the performance of cloud storage systems, we proposed a novel cluster caching system, **SynergiCache**. It achieves efficient data storage through its ingenious append-only write architecture and slow-disk-sensitive algorithm design. We summarize our contributions below:

- We introduced an independent Chunk Subsystem with append-only writing capability, offering ultra-high performance.
- We developed SynergiCache Database (DB), a customized KV database that utilizes a composite KV mode to minimize metadata overhead. We combined the garbage collection of the Chunk Subsystem with that of SynergiCache DB, thereby enhancing the efficiency of garbage collection.
- We proposed a slow-disk-sensitive adaptive caching algorithm that predicts data access trends, timely perceives data access latencies, and efficiently mitigates the adverse effects of slow disks on system performance.
- We integrated SynergiCache into Ceph [19] and conducted extensive experiments that demonstrated SynergiCache significantly enhances the performance of cloud storage systems, achieving an 89.55% reduction in latency and a 9.52x increase in IOPS compared to the traditional caching system.

2   Background and Motivation

2.1   Caching Systems

With the rapid growth of data volume, single storage technologies are no longer sufficient to meet the demands. Hybrid storage systems, which combine various storage media and employ caching and tiering techniques, have become a viable solution. Bcache [5] is a caching mechanism at the Linux kernel block layer that uses one or more fast storage devices as caches to accelerate data read and write operations on one or more slower storage devices, thus creating hybrid volumes and improving performance. BCW [16], by utilizing the write-back cache feature of HDDs, constructs a write-state predictor to balance the load between SSDs and HDDs, enhancing overall performance and reliability. DistCache [10] co-designs cache allocation with multi-layer cache topology and query routing, effectively achieving load balancing and reducing cache consistency overhead. StreamCache [9] employs a two-tiered memory management approach to implement a page cache on SSD devices, thereby enhancing I/O bandwidth.

However, despite the implementation of various advanced cache management techniques to enhance system performance, these methods do not eliminate the frequent random writes and increased latency caused by the overwrite approach in cloud storage systems.

2.2 Metadata Storage Techniques

As Big Data applications grow rapidly, metadata management stands as one of the essential technologies that must be taken into account. Utilizing KV databases for metadata management has demonstrated significant performance enhancements [3]. The Log-Structured Merge-Tree (LSM-Tree) [11] achieves high-performance writes at the expense of a slight compromise in read performance, making it highly popular for write-intensive KV databases such as Apache Cassandra [8] and RocksDB [4]. In recent years, numerous research endeavors have focused on optimizing the LSM-Tree. Depart [21] employs replica decoupling to enhance throughput and recovery time. MiDAS [12] leverages model prediction to substantially reduce garbage collection overhead and mitigate write amplification. SplitDB [1] utilizes Non-Volatile Memory to eliminate write stalls, further boosting system performance.

However, these optimizations are primarily general in nature. In practical application scenarios, they largely focus on the functional implementation of KV databases themselves, without deeply integrating the LSM-Tree with the entire system. Additionally, when handling garbage data in LSM-Trees, existing approaches merely discard it without fully exploiting its potential.

2.3 Caching Algorithms

Traditional Algorithms. Traditional caching algorithms offer good performance due to their simple design, but each has its own limitations in certain scenarios. First In First Out (FIFO) uses a first-in-first-out strategy to manage cached data, but ignores access recency and frequency. Least Recently Used (LRU) improves on FIFO by focusing on recency of access, while Least Frequently Used (LFU) focuses on frequency. Low Inter-reference Recency Set (LIRS) [7] prioritizes data that are likely to be accessed again in the near future while avoiding eviction of data that has high inter-reference distances, thus improving overall cache hit rates.

Model Based Algorithms. Learning-based algorithms leverage complex machine learning models to perceive future access requests from upper-layer applications as accurately as possible, thereby exhibiting excellent dynamic adaptability. RLR [14] algorithm reduces hardware overhead by introducing reinforcement learning strategies. DCCC [17], based on reinforcement learning models, enhances cache hit rates and space utilization. CCache [15] optimizes SSD erase counts and cache hit rates by constructing a Random Forest machine learning classifier. GL-Cache [20] proposes a group-level learning approach for cache learning, which improves cache hit rates and throughput.

Table 1. Comparison of Caching Algorithms

	Performance	Recency	Access Frequency	Adaptability	Access Latency
FIFO	YES	–	–	–	–
LRU	YES	YES	–	–	–
LFU	YES	–	YES	–	–
LIRS	YES	–	YES	–	–
Model-based	–	YES	YES	YES	–

Table 1 provides a comprehensive comparison of various caching algorithms based on their performance characteristics, including recency, access frequency, adaptability, and sensitivity to access latency. In cloud storage systems, slow disks can lead to extremely high data access latencies. To minimize their negative impact on business operations before they are replaced, cache algorithms need to promptly identify potential slow disk issues. However, whether traditional or learning-based, caching algorithms are typically designed to improve cache hit rates based on heuristic rules, but they neglect the impact of slow disks, where high access latency from specific disks can degrade overall system performance.

2.4 Motivation

To address these challenges and enhance the performance of cloud storage systems, we proposed SynergiCache, a novel cluster caching system. We transformed the overwrite pattern in the caching system to an append-only write mode, resulting in the realization of a subsystem that allows for independent data management: the Chunk Subsystem. In terms of metadata management, we deeply customized the LSM-Tree with the storage system to develop SynergiCache DB, introducing a novel Composite KV Mode. This innovation reduces the total amount of metadata and cleverly integrates the garbage collection of LSM-Tree with the Chunk Subsystem, thereby decreasing the scanning time for obsolete data. Regarding the caching algorithm, we designed a slow-disk-sensitive adaptive caching algorithm that addresses the issue of slow disks slowing down the entire system, effectively reducing data read and write latencies.

3 SynergiCache

3.1 Overview

SynergiCache is a novel and high-performance caching system that significantly enhances the performance of cloud storage systems. It transforms the traditional overwrite pattern into an append-only write mode, enabling data to be written sequentially to SSDs. The architecture of SynergiCache is demonstrated in Fig. 1, which shows the key components and their interactions. SynergiCache consists of three highly efficient modules. The **Chunk Subsystem** serves as the data storage subsystem of the caching system, offering robust data writing capabilities through append-only writes. **SynergiCache DB** is a metadata KV database tailored to the operational characteristics of the caching system. Leveraging a composite KV mode. It efficiently records vast amounts of data with minimal metadata overhead. The SynergiCache Server functions as the core controller, performing two critical roles. Firstly, it integrates **garbage collection** processes in both the Chunk Subsystem and SynergiCache DB, substantially improving the ability to scan and eliminate obsolete data. Secondly, it operates a **slow-disk-sensitive adaptive** cache algorithm capable of dynamically identifying slow disks within the system from outside the cluster, facilitating seamless and efficient data migration between SSDs and HDDs.

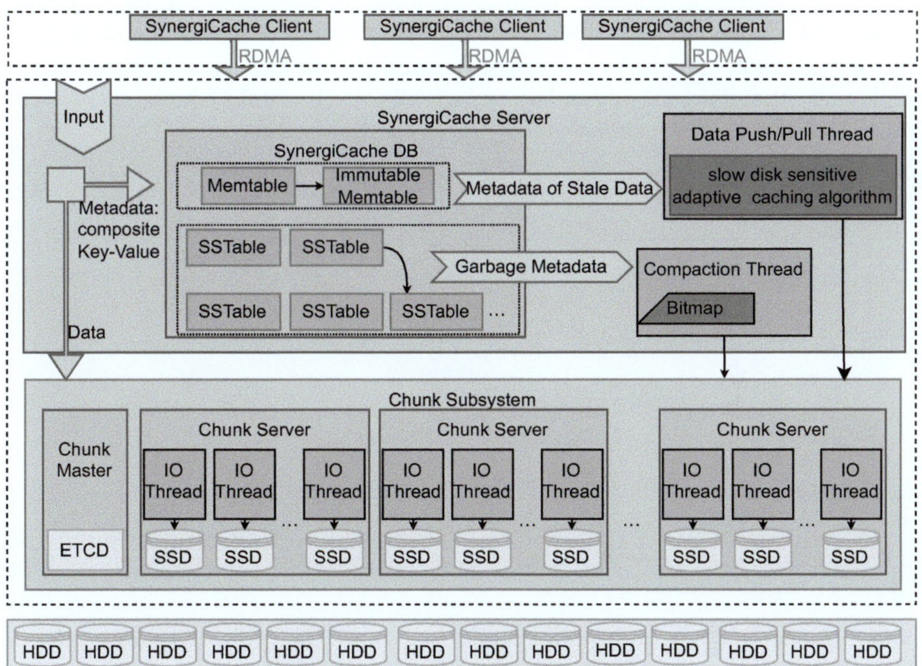

Fig. 1. SynergiCache Architecture

3.2 Chunk Subsystem

The Chunk Subsystem is the core component responsible for data persistence and disk management in the caching system. The Chunk is the fundamental unit for read/write operations exposed to upper layers. Each storage node operates a Chunk Server, which manages local physical disks, processes read/write requests, and stores data on the disks. The Chunk Server can manage multiple physical disks. The Chunk Master is responsible for overseeing multiple Chunk Servers, ensuring high availability through a consistency coordination mechanism, and managing resources including Chunk Servers, Disks, and Partition Groups (PGs) within the storage cluster. The PG represents a reliability group that can be mapped to multiple SSDs. When appending data to a Chunk, the client uses RDMA to send it to the Chunk Server for writing to the specified SSD.

The Chunk Subsystem implements storage space management by abstracting physical resources into logical topologies, as shown in Fig. 2. The storage space is divided into fixed-size units, in which the location and extent of data read/write operations are specified by tuples (*offset, length*). To address this space more effectively, we first convert the block storage representation into objects, which associates the binary tuple (*offset, length*) with a ternary tuple (*object ID, object offset, object length*) for precise addressing. Subsequently, read and write requests originating from upper-layer applications targeted at block storage are translated into operations on these objects. In the Chunk Subsystem, object read and write requests are initially placed into a queue. Upon dequeuing, the data is appended to pre-allocated chunks, with the specific (*chunk ID, chunk offset, chunk length*) location within the chunk.

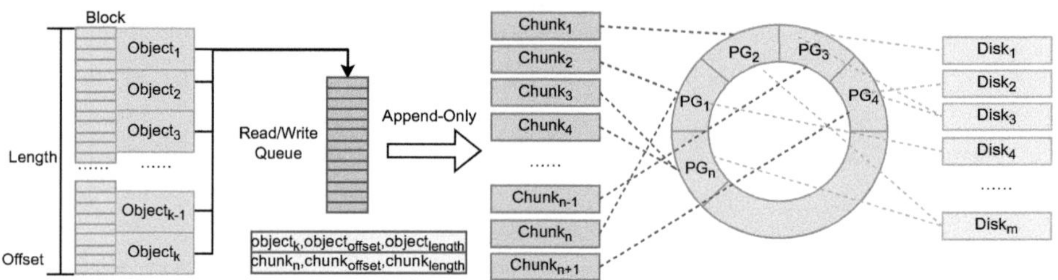

Fig. 2. Chunk Subsystem Architecture

3.3   SynergiCache DB

SynergiCache DB is a high-performance key-value (KV) database designed for large-scale data storage. It adopts the LSM-Tree structure and, being optimized for the characteristics of caching systems, employs a composite KV mode. In the MemTable, we use a space skip list structure, a skip list variant optimized for spatial data, where each KV pair has fixed lengths for both key and value. The key is composed of a tuple (*object ID, object offset, object length*) provided by the client. The value contains metadata from the Chunk Subsystem, which includes (*chunk ID, chunk offset, chunk length*). As shown in Fig. 3 and Fig. 4, this composite KV structure enables a single metadata entry to record multiple storage units, thereby reducing the total amount of metadata in normal KV storage

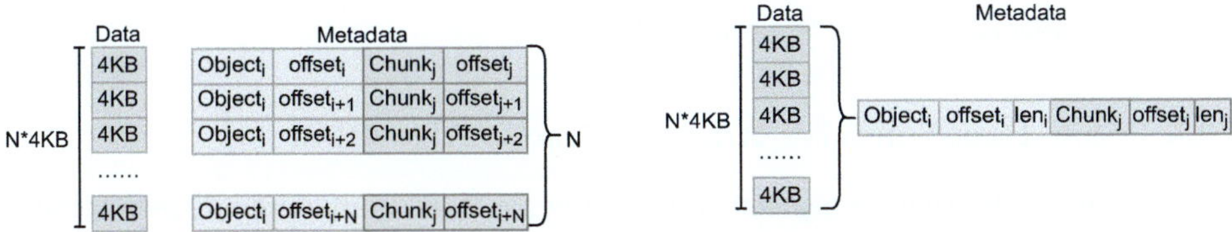

Fig. 3. Normal KV

Fig. 4. Composite KV

structures from N to 1, where N represents the number of data unit lengths. To address space overlaps, we apply space merging and splitting techniques. Newly inserted spaces overwrite existing ones, ensuring that no overlapping spaces exist in the same MemTable or SSTable. Additionally, we enforce that the starting address of each storage space must be greater than or equal to the ending address of the preceding space, ensuring the maintenance of an ordered structure.

3.4 Garbage Collection

In an append-only caching system, modifications to data blocks do not delete the original data but instead append new data. Without an efficient garbage collection mechanism, the system will quickly accumulate outdated data. In the LSM-Tree structure, new insertions in the MemTable and system compactions generate garbage metadata, which is typically discarded. However, in Synergi-Cache DB, this garbage metadata is collected and utilized for Chunk Subsystem garbage collection, as demonstrated in Fig. 5.

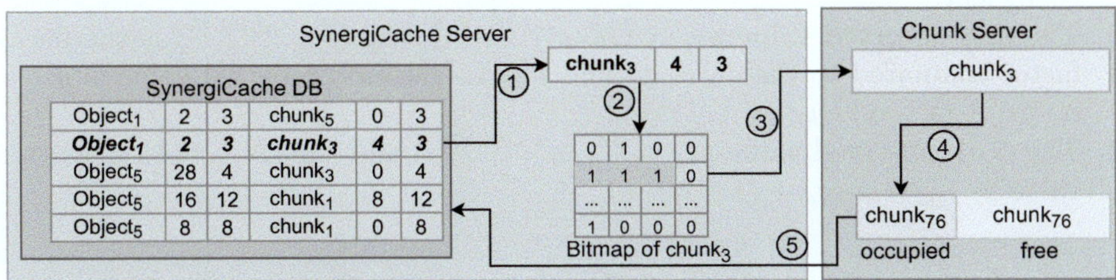

Fig. 5. Garbage Collection Process

The process can be articulated as follows: Firstly, garbage data generated during the insertion of new KV pairs and the insertion process associated with compaction are collected. Secondly, this garbage data is converted into a bitmap, and following each compaction event, the bitmap is persisted. Thirdly, a background scheduling task is employed to scan and analyze the bitmap, targeting chunks with a high garbage ratio for reclaiming. Fourthly, the valid data and metadata of the chunks identified for recycling are read and migrated to new chunks. Lastly, the updated metadata information of these new chunks is subsequently recorded in the SynergiCache DB.

3.5 Slow-Disk-Sensitive Adaptive Cache Algorithm

The caching algorithm employs time-slicing for data management, determining cache priorities by integrating access **frequency** and **latency**. Data is stored in the most recent time-slice according to its access time. The new generation stores recently accessed data, the middle generation holds data with potential for reuse, and the old generation contains data slated for eviction.

When storing data in the new generation, if the total access latency of keeping the data in the HDD cluster exceeds the latency of pulling it to the SSD cluster, the data is pulled to the SSD cluster; otherwise, it remains in the HDD cluster. When the old generation reaches its capacity threshold, eviction is triggered. Within the same time-slice, data with lower predicted access latency is preferentially evicted and flushed down to the HDD, while data with higher latency is retained and temporarily stored in the SSD.

Access Frequency Statistics and Prediction. We adopt a variant of the Count-Min Sketch (CMS) [2] using a two-dimensional matrix, which provides bounded storage overhead. To predict future access counts, historical time series are fed into an Adaptive Exponential Smoothing model. Suppose the access count array is $\{(T_1, C_1), (T_2, C_2), \ldots, (T_n, C_n)\}$, and the current time is T. The predicted value of the access count at the current time is calculated as follows:

1. The initial predicted value $\hat{y}_0 = 0$, and the initial observed value $y_0 = 0$;
2. The first predicted value $\hat{y}_{T_1} = \alpha \cdot y_{T_0} + (1 - \alpha) \cdot \hat{y}_0$, where α is the smoothing coefficient;
3. The first observed value $y_{T_1} = C_1 \cdot e^{-\lambda(T - T_1)}$, where $e^{-\lambda(T - T_1)}$ is the decay factor compared to the current time T. The second predicted value is $\hat{y}_{T_2} = \alpha \cdot y_{T_1} + (1 - \alpha) \cdot \hat{y}_0$;
4. The N-th observed value $y_{T_n} = C_n \cdot e^{-\lambda(T - T_n)}$, and the $(N + 1)$-th predicted value $\hat{y}_{T_{n+1}} = \alpha \cdot y_n + (1 - \alpha) \cdot \hat{y}_n$.

Access Latency Statistics and Prediction. When writing data, it must be written to the primary replica and backup replicas. Consequently, the access latency depends on multiple disks being written to.

Assume there are M data items, replicated across N disks in a cloud storage system, with $M \gg N$. The vector a represents the replication status, where 0 indicates no replica and 1 indicates a replica. The primary and secondary replicas are represented by the vector c. For example, $a = \{0, 1, 1, 1\}^T$ and $c = \{0, 1, 0, 0\}^T$, indicating that the second disk holds primary replicas. The vector x represents the average latency for each disk, and b is the total write and replication latency. The relationship between these vectors is described in Eq. 1 where j represent index of vector. Given the observed vectors a_i, b_i, and c_i

at time T_i, we apply a data-fitting method to minimize the weighted least-squares error as described in Eq. 2, where $w(T_i) = e^{-\lambda(T-T_i)}$ is the time-decay weight, and T is the current time. Finally, the parameters are obtained by minimizing the loss function, which leads to the optimization objective.

$$b = c \cdot x + \max_j((a - c)[j] \cdot x[j]) \tag{1}$$

$$\min\left(\sum_i w(T_i) \cdot \left(b_i - c_i \cdot x - \max_j((a_i - c_i)[j] \cdot x[j])\right)\right) \tag{2}$$

4 Experiment

4.1 Setup

We selected Ceph as the HDD storage cluster and adapted it with SynergiCache. Based on RocksDB, we enhanced the MemTable structure and Compaction process, resulting in the implementation of SynergiCache DB and a garbage collection feature utilizing bitmap. We conducted experiments across three nodes, six 4.5TB NVMe SSDs and six 7TB HDDs, with each node equipped with two NVMe SSDs for deploying SynergiCache, BCache, and Ceph SSD clusters at different times, as well as two HDDs for deploying the Ceph HDD cluster. To validate the performance of various system modules, we utilized a subset comprising four publicly available Alibaba datasets [18], with upper-layer applications including Kafka, Etcd, Elasticsearch, and Redis. The cumulative distribution of data lengths for these applications is demonstrated in Fig. 6.

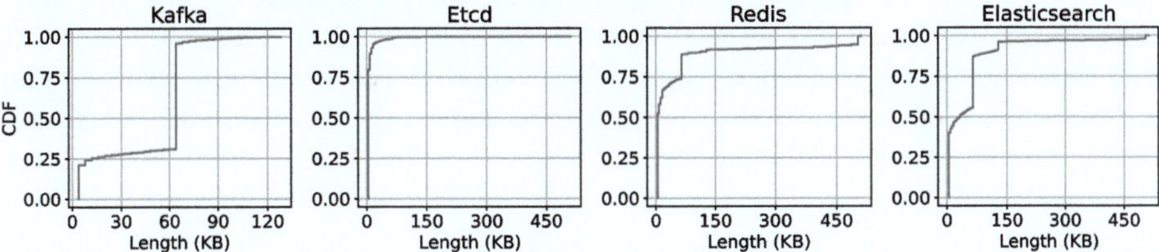

Fig. 6. CDF of length distribution for different datasets.

4.2 Performance Evaluation of SynergiCache DB

We established 4KB as the minimum unit managed by SynergiCache and 4MB as the object size for the Ceph client. For write operations targeting datasets, we employed both the normal KV and the composite KV of SynergiCache DB for persistence and recorded the operational latency, as shown in Fig. 7.

The results demonstrate that Composite KV consistently outperforms Normal KV across various latency percentiles, specifically achieving lower latency values at the 90th percentile (P90), 95th percentile (P95), 99th percentile (P99),

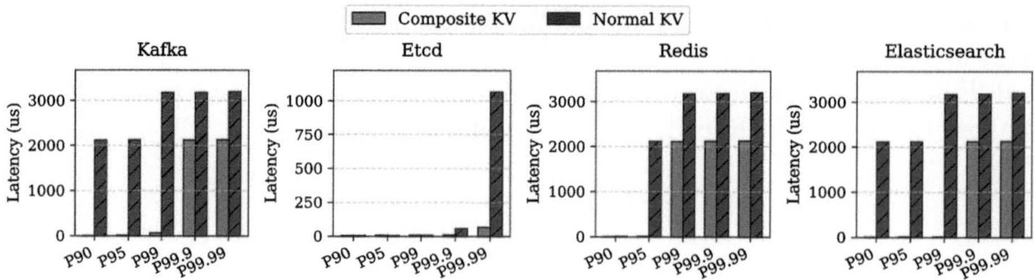

Fig. 7. Latency comparison between Composite KV and Normal KV.

99.9th percentile (P99.9), and 99.99th percentile (P99.99). In Normal KV mode, one metadata entry manages one minimum storage unit, with each IO operation encompassing a minimum of one and a maximum of 1024 units. This results in a sharp increase in the number of metadata entries when writing data with a greater length. Conversely, in the composite KV mode, one metadata entry can manage a contiguous range, encompassing multiple sequential storage units. This significantly reduces the number of KV entries, thereby decreasing the latency of data insertion.

4.3   Performance Evaluation of Garbage Collection

In our micro-benchmark analysis of garbage collection performance, we compared two garbage collection methods: full table scanning and bitmap-based reclamation. The experimental results, presented in Table 2, demonstrate that the bitmap-based reclamation method significantly outperforms the full table scanning method in terms of scan times across all datasets. These findings suggest that the bitmap-based reclamation method is more efficient in managing garbage collection tasks, facilitating faster memory reclamation, and potentially improving the overall performance and response times of the applications.

Table 2. Chunk Scan in Garbage Collection Performance Comparison: *bitmap-based reclamation* vs *full table scanning*

Application	Method	Number of Scan Chunk	Scan Time(ms)	Avg Time(ms)
Kafka	full table scanning	655	6901.95	10.53
	bitmap-based reclamation	655	0.155257	0.0002377
Etcd	full table scanning	39	82.2779	2.10969
	bitmap-based reclamation	39	0.00932205	0.000239
Redis	full table scanning	2863	5340.78	1.865449
	bitmap-based reclamation	2863	0.703807	0.000246
Elasticsearch	full table scanning	848	7024.28	8.283995
	bitmap-based reclamation	848	0.198824	0.000234

4.4   Performance Evaluation of SDSA Algorithm

In SynergiCache, we implemented and evaluated FIFO, LRU, LFU, LIRS, and our proposed SDSA algorithms under a scenario with one slow HDD (50 ms higher latency). When the cache reached a dataset-specific threshold, eviction was triggered to accommodate new data. Experimental results (Fig. 8) show that SDSA achieves significantly lower average eviction latency than the other algorithms, due to more intelligent eviction decisions that reduce flush overhead.

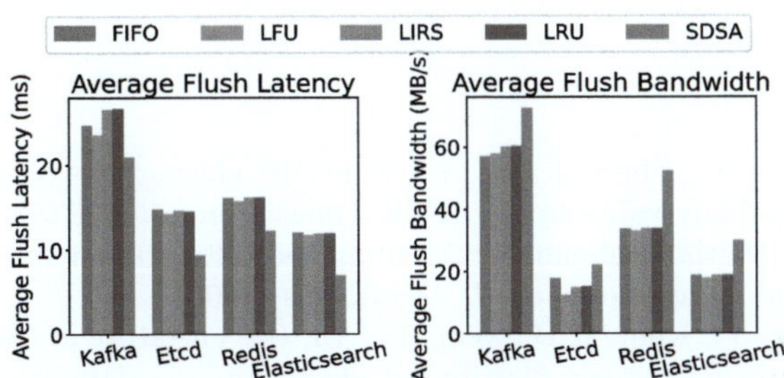

Fig. 8. Performance comparison of caching algorithms: Bandwidth and Latency

4.5   SynergiCache Performance

To evaluate the performance of SynergiCache in terms of data writing, we conducted experiments with results shown in Fig. 9. SynergiCache achieves up to 9.52× higher bandwidth and IOPS compared to BCache. It also reduces latency by 89.55% on the Etcd dataset, making it well-suited for latency-sensitive applications. Overall, SynergiCache excels in high-throughput and low-latency scenarios.

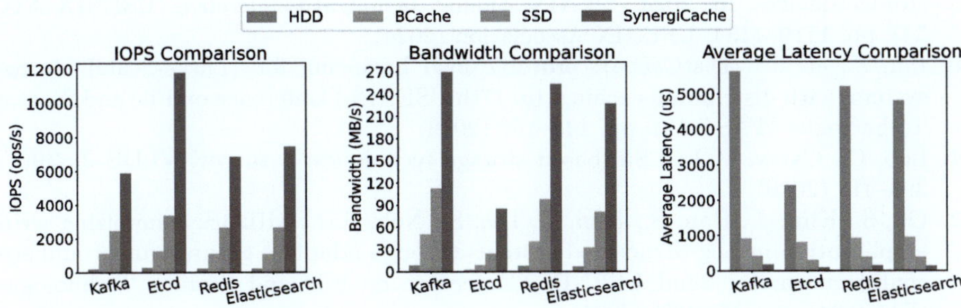

Fig. 9. Comparison of different caching systems in terms of Bandwidth, Latency, and IOPS across multiple applications.

5   Conclusion

Enhancing cache system performance is crucial for cloud storage systems' overall performance and user experience. We proposed and implemented a novel cluster cache, SynergiCache, achieving several key goals. It boosts data write performance via the Chunk Subsystem with append-only writes, efficiently manages cached data through KV structure and garbage collection optimizations, and employs an adaptive algorithm sensitive to slow disks to prioritize hot data. Experimental results show SynergiCache outperforms traditional cache systems.

References

1. Cai, M., Jiang, X., Shen, J., Ye, B.: SplitDB: closing the performance gap for LSM-Tree-based key-value stores. IEEE Trans. Comput. (2023)
2. Cormode, G., Muthukrishnan, S.: An improved data stream summary: the count-min sketch and its applications. J. Algorithms (2005)
3. Dai, H., Wang, Y., Kent, K.B., Zeng, L., Xu, C.: The state of the art of metadata managements in large-scale distributed file systems–scalability, performance and availability. IEEE Trans. Parallel Distrib. Syst. **33**(12), 3850–3869 (2022)
4. Dong, S., Kryczka, A., Jin, Y., Stumm, M.: RocksDB: evolution of development priorities in a key-value store serving large-scale applications. ACM Trans. Storage (TOS) **17**(4), 1–32 (2021)
5. Hollowell, C., Hogue, R., Smith, J., Strecker-Kellogg, W., Wong, A., Zaytsev, A.: The effect of Flashcache and Bcache on I/O performance. In: Journal of Physics: Conference Series, vol. 513, p. 062023. IOP Publishing (2014)
6. Hoseinzadeh, M.: A survey on tiering and caching in high-performance storage systems (2019)
7. Jiang, S., Zhang, X.: LIRS: an efficient low inter-reference recency set replacement policy to improve buffer cache performance. ACM SIGMETRICS Perform. Eval. Rev. **30**(1), 31–42 (2002)
8. Lakshman, A., Malik, P.: Cassandra: a decentralized structured storage system. ACM SIGOPS Oper. Syst. Rev. **44**(2), 35–40 (2010)
9. Li, Z., Zhang, G.: StreamCache: revisiting page cache for file scanning on fast storage devices. In: 2024 USENIX Annual Technical Conference (USENIX ATC 24), pp. 1119–1134. USENIX Association (2024)
10. Liu, Z., et al.: {DistCache}: provable load balancing for {Large-Scale} storage systems with distributed caching. In: 17th USENIX Conference on File and Storage Technologies (FAST 19), pp. 143–157 (2019)
11. Luo, C., Carey, M.J.: LSM-based storage techniques: a survey. VLDB J. **29**(1), 393–418 (2020)
12. Oh, S., Kim, J., Han, S., Kim, J., Lee, S., Noh, S.H.: MIDAS: minimizing write amplification in Log-Structured systems through adaptive group number and size configuration. In: 22nd USENIX Conference on File and Storage Technologies (FAST 24), pp. 259–275 (2024)
13. Purandare, D., Wilcox, P., Litz, H., Finkelstein, S.: Append is near: Log-based data management on ZNS SSDs. In: 12th Annual Conference on Innovative Data Systems Research (CIDR'22) (2022)

14. Sethumurugan, S., Yin, J., Sartori, J.: Designing a cost-effective cache replacement policy using machine learning. In: 2021 IEEE International Symposium on High-Performance Computer Architecture (HPCA), pp. 291–303. IEEE (2021)
15. Sun, H., Sun, C., Tong, H., Yue, Y., Qin, X.: A machine learning-empowered cache management scheme for high-performance SSDs. IEEE Trans. Comput. (2024)
16. Wang, S., et al.: Exploration and exploitation for buffer-controlled HDD-writes for SSD-HDD hybrid storage server. ACM Trans. Storage (TOS) **18**(1), 1–29 (2022)
17. Wang, T., et al.: Towards intelligent adaptive edge caching using deep reinforcement learning. IEEE Trans. Mob. Comput. **23**(10), 9289–9303 (2024)
18. Wang, Z., et al.: Ransom access memories: achieving practical ransomware protection in cloud with DeftPunk. In: 18th USENIX Symposium on Operating Systems Design and Implementation (OSDI 24), pp. 687–702 (2024)
19. Weil, S., Brandt, S.A., Miller, E.L., Long, D.D., Maltzahn, C.: Ceph: a scalable, high-performance distributed file system. In: Proceedings of the 7th Conference on Operating Systems Design and Implementation (OSDI'06), pp. 307–320 (2006)
20. Yang, J., Mao, Z., Yue, Y., Rashmi, K.: GL-cache: group-level learning for efficient and high-performance caching. In: 21st USENIX Conference on File and Storage Technologies (FAST 23), pp. 115–134 (2023)
21. Zhang, Q., Li, Y., Lee, P.P., Xu, Y., Wu, S.: {DEPART}: replica decoupling for distributed {Key-Value} storage. In: 20th USENIX Conference on File and Storage Technologies (FAST 22), pp. 397–412 (2022)

Image Compressive Sensing Approach Based on Mixed Precision Training and Deep Unrolling Network

Lei Feng[(✉)], Mingzhu Bian, Jun Zhu, Bo Zhang, and Xiuliang Zhang

School of Computer Engineering, Jinling Institute of Technology,
Nanjing 211169, China
fenglei492327278@126.com

Abstract. In this paper, an enhanced version of interpretable optimization-inspired deep network for image compressive sensing(ISTA-Net) based on hybrid precision training, dubbed Mix-ISTA, ensures high compressed reconstruction and speed up training. ISTA-Net is a deep neural network architecture whose design is inspired by the Iterative Shrinkage Threshold Algorithm (ISTA), which has the advantages of both optimization and network. However, the training process for ISTA-Net can be quite time-consuming when trained on large-scale datasets. In order to overcome this problem, we introduce a hybrid precision training technology, which can effectively consume memory and compute costs by combining single-precision (FP32) and half-precision (FP16) operations. The experimental results show that the training speed is significantly improved after mixed precision training, while the reconstruction performance of ISTA-Net is not affected. While greatly speeding up the training, it can still achieve high reconstruction results, so that it has more practical value in practical applications.

Keywords: Mixed-precision training · ISTA-Net · Image compressive sensing · Accelerated training · Reconstruction performance

1 Introduction

The concept of Compressive Sensing (CS) algorithm was formalized in 2006 by Donoho et al.[1]. The idea dates back to 2004. Emmanuel Cands, Justin Romberg and Terence Tao started to study the problem of reconstruction of sparse signals and proposed the possibility of reconstructing signals from a small number of measurements. Since then, many scholars have made outstanding contributions to the research of reconstruction algorithms, and Tropp and Gilbert have proposed the orthogonal matching tracking algorithm (OMP algorithm[2]), for efficient reconstruction of sparse signals; Chen, Donoho, and Saunders proposed a linear programming-based basis tracking algorithm; Daubechies et al. proposed iterative hard-thresholding and soft-thresholding algorithms[3]. Whereas

© IFIP International Federation for Information Processing 2026
Published by Springer Nature Switzerland AG 2026
X. Wang et al. (Eds.): NPC 2025, LNCS 16306, pp. 76–87, 2026.
https://doi.org/10.1007/978-3-032-10466-3_7

LASSO and ℓ_1 regularization have been proposed and are widely used in compressed sensing coefficient signal reconstruction[4]. At the same time, compressed sensing application fields are also expanding. For example, Lustig et al. applied the theory of compressed sensing to MRI imaging[5], which has resulted in significant reductions in scanning and imaging time. Compressed sensing is a powerful signal acquisition and reconstruction technique that is capable of recovering high-resolution images from measured signals at much lower than Nyquist sampling rates. Traditional compressed perception algorithms rely on iterative optimization algorithms, which are computationally intensive and time consuming. Recon-Net, proposed by Kulkarni et al., combines an end-to-end convolutional neural network with compressed sensing for fast reconstruction[6]. These methods comprise a non-local neural network (NLR-CSNet)[7], iPiano-Net[8], and a content-aware scalable network (CASNet)[9]. The UNet structure is utilized in AutoBCS[10] for multi-scale feature learning. Sun et al. proposed a dual-path attention network (DPA-Net) to preserve the texture details of images using an attention mechanism[11]. Recent advancements have turned to unsupervised or self-supervised learning owing to the scarcity of ground truth (GT) data[12–19]. Based on the SSB-Net, Su et al. proposed a self-attention-powered multi-scale compressed sensing imaging network[20], improving the original method with a more powerful network transformer to model long-range interactions. Deep-image prior (DIP)-based methods[21] suggest using a CNN-based generator as a regularizer without data-driven training. Table 1 compares traditional compressed sensing methods with deep learning-based approaches across multiple dimensions. Notably, traditional methods exhibit high computational complexity due to iterative optimization algorithms, whereas deep learning accelerates computation via forward propagation. In terms of reconstruction quality, deep learning methods outperform traditional ones by leveraging end-to-end learning, while the latter rely on hand-designed sparse representations. Traditional methods require no training as they directly apply optimization algorithms, in contrast to deep learning approaches that demand extensive data training. For memory consumption, deep learning methods incur higher costs due to storing numerous model parameters, while traditional methods have lower requirements. Deep learning also demonstrates superior noise robustness through data-driven learning, unlike traditional methods that are more noise-sensitive. In applicable scenarios, traditional methods suit small-scale data and resource-constrained environments, whereas deep learning thrives in large-scale data-rich settings. Based on these insights, we propose an Image compressive sensing approach based on mixed precision training and deep unrolling network(Mix-ISTA), a hybrid-precision training framework rooted in the interpretable optimization-inspired deep network for image compressive sensing(ISTA-Net)[22].

Table 1. Comparison between Conventional and Deep Learning Methods

Method	Conventional	Deep Learning
Computational complexity[*]	High	Medium
Reconstruction quality[1]	Medium	High
Training time	None[*]	Long[1]
Memory consumption	Low[*]	High[1]
Noise robustness	Medium[*]	High[1]

[*]Lower performance indicator; [1]Higher performance indicator

2 Relevant Background

2.1 Compressed Perception

The core idea of compressed perception is to utilize the sparsity and compressibility of signals to achieve efficient sampling and reconstruction. In traditional signal processing, signal sampling and compression are carried out separately, i.e., the signal is first collected at a high sampling rate, and then the data volume is reduced by compression algorithms. In contrast, compressed sensing combines sampling and compression into one, directly compressing the data during the sampling process.

Mathematically, the compression perception can be described by the formula.

$$y = \Phi x \tag{1}$$

Of which. The signal $x \in R^N$ is the original signal (e.g., image or video). The signal $\Phi \in R^{M \times N}$ ($M < N$) is the measurement matrix, which is used to obtain a small number of measurements from the original signal. The signal $y \in R^M$ is the measured value, i.e., the compressed data.

The task of compressed perception is to reconstruct the original signal x from the measurements y. This is an underdetermined problem, i.e., an ill-posed problem, due to the fact that $M < N$ and is therefore usually not directly solvable. For this reason, compressed perception is usually used in the reconstruction of natural images, but if the signal x is sparse in a certain transform domain (e.g., wavelet transform, Fourier transform, etc.), i.e., most of the transform coefficients are zero or close to zero, the original signal can be reconstructed by some optimization algorithms.

2.2 ISTA-Net Overview

ISTA-Net is a deep neural network architecture based on the Iterative Shrinkage-Thresholding Algorithm (ISTA). The basic idea of ISTA-Net is to map the previous ISTA updating steps into deep networks which are composed of a fixed number of stages of the architecture. In other words, the network transforms a traditional optimization problem into a trainable end-to-end deep learning model by unfolding the iterative process of the ISTA algorithm into a multi-stage deep network structure, where each stage corresponds to one ISTA iteration[22].

Each stage of ISTA-Net consists of two core modules: the r-module and the x-module, which correspond to the gradient descent and proximal mapping in the ISTA algorithm, respectively. The benefit of this modular design is that the network is able to simulate the iterative optimization process of the ISTA algorithm and further improve the performance by introducing learnable parameters.

2.3 Mixed-Accuracy Training

Deep learning training initially relied on single-precision floating-point (FP32) for all computations, but this approach faced limitations in computational efficiency and memory usage. To address these bottlenecks, mixed-precision training was introduced, combining low-precision (e.g., FP16) and high-precision (FP32) operations. Most compute-intensive taskssuch as matrix multiplications and convolutionsare performed in low precision, leveraging neural networks' tolerance to computational noise, where efficiency gains from reduced computation and memory overhead outweigh minor precision losses. However, critical steps like weight updates, loss calculation, and gradient accumulation retain FP32 precision to mitigate numerical instability risks (e.g., gradient underflow/overflow), ensuring model convergence and accuracy. This hybrid approach optimizes training speed and resource consumption while maintaining model performance[23].

The concept of mixed-precision can be traced back to 2017 when NVIDA launched the Volta architecture of Tensor Core to provide hardware support for low-precision computation. In 2018, the Micikevicious team released a whitepaper on mixed-precision training, which detailed the theoretical foundation. In recent years, mixed-precision training has been used in several deep learning tasks and has shown better training results. In the image classification task, ResNet, EfficientNet and other models use mixed-precision training, and these models not only speed up the training speed, but also[24]In the field of target detection, mixed-precision training is widely used in YOLO, Faster R-CNN and other models, which significantly improves the training efficiency while ensuring the success rate of detection; in natural language processing, mixed-precision training is also successfully applied to the Transformer architecture (e.g., BERT, GPT, a deep learning model based on self-attention mechanism, proposed by vaswani et al.), which is a deep learning model based on self-attention mechanism. In the natural language processing task, mixed-precision training is also successfully applied to the Transformer architecture (e.g., BERT, GPT, which is a deep learning model based on the self-attention mechanism, proposed by vaswani et al.), which performs well in processing large-scale textual data, and the hybrid precision training is widely used in YOLO, Faster R-CNN and other models, ensuring the successful detection rate and significantly improving the training efficiency[25]. These success stories show that mixed-precision training has become an important tool for modern deep learning optimization.

2.4 Existing Issues

In compressed sensing reconstruction tasks, optimization such as ISTA performs well in reconstruction, but the computational complexity and training time are one of its main bottlenecks. To this end, we adopt hybrid precision training as an optimization strategy. Compared to other optimization means, such as model pruning or quantization, hybrid precision training significantly speeds up training and consumes memory by utilizing half-precision floating-point numbers (FP16) in most calculations, while preserving single-precision floating-point numbers (FP32) in critical operations to ensure numerical stability. This strategy is easy to implement, and it can effectively improve the training efficiency without making major changes to the network structure.

3   Proposed Method:ISTA-Net Based on Mixed Precision Training

3.1   Mixed-Accuracy Training

Enabling Mixed Accuracy. Pytorch provides Autocast to automatically select the precision, in the autocast context PyTorch will automatically convert FP16-enabled operations to FP16 during forward and backpropagation, while keeping critical operations such as loss calculation and gradient updating at FP32. This is because FP16 reduces the memory footprint and thus significantly reduces computational overhead and memory usage, which is critical when processing complex models or large batches. Memory footprint, which is critical in complex modeling or high-volume processing. We therefore use the torch.cuda.amp.autocast context manager to enable mixed-precision training.

Loss Scaling. The dynamic range of FP16 is limited, the smallest normal value is about 10-5, when the gradient value is very small, these gradients may be rounded to zero, once this happens, the weight update will fail, thus affecting the convergence of the model. To address this problem, PyTorch provides the GradScaler tool, whose main function is to scale up the loss values by a certain number of times before backpropagation to ensure that the gradient values are within the FP16 representation, and then shrink the gradient values back to their original size before the optimizer updates the parameters to avoid gradient underflow. This process is called loss scaling. Loss scaling can be implemented as static loss scaling, which uses a fixed scaling factor to scale up the loss value, or dynamic loss scaling, which automatically adjusts the scaling factor. GradScaler uses dynamic loss scaling to avoid overflow or underflow depending on the gradient value. Combined with torch.cuda.amp.autocast and GradScaler, mixed-precision training guarantees numerical stability while accelerating the computation, which is especially suitable for large-scale model training and memory-constrained scenarios. This technique has become an important tool in modern deep learning, which is widely used in computer vision, natural language processing and other fields.

Updating of Weights. In neural networks, weights are the parameters that connect neurons to each other and determine how the input signal affects the output. Weight updating is the process of adjusting the weights to reduce the prediction error by the gradient values calculated by the back-propagation algorithm during the training process. Common weight updating methods include stochastic gradient descent, batch gradient descent, momentum method and Adam optimizer. The method used in this paper is the Adam optimizer, which combines the momentum method and the root mean square propagation, and performs well in terms of convergence speed and stability. In order to ensure the numerical stability of the weight update, we let the weights of the model always exist in FP32 format. In the backpropagation, the gradient is computed in FP16, which can utilize the efficiency of FP16. Before updating the weights, GradScaler will automatically convert the FP16 gradient to FP32, and then use FP32 to complete the weight update. To maintain precision in the model parameters, a master copy of weights is kept in FP32. The process is: Compute gradients in FP16 with loss scaling:

$$\nabla_{W,\text{scaled}} = \frac{\partial \mathcal{L}_{\text{scaled}}}{\partial W} = \frac{\partial(s \cdot \mathcal{L})}{\partial W} = s \cdot \frac{\partial \mathcal{L}}{\partial W} \tag{2}$$

Unscale:

$$\nabla_W = \frac{\nabla_{W,\text{scaled}}}{s} \tag{3}$$

Update the FP32 weights:

$$W_{\text{FP32}} \leftarrow W_{\text{FP32}} - \eta \cdot \nabla_W \tag{4}$$

Cast back to FP16 for the next forward pass:

$$W_{\text{FP16}} = \text{cast}(W_{\text{FP32}}, \text{FP16}) \tag{5}$$

Numerical Stability Analysis. Modern mixed precision training achieves an optimal balance between computational efficiency and numerical stability through three key mechanisms: Loss Stability: FP32 loss computation prevents precision loss in small-value aggregations.

Gradient Stability Loss scaling ensures FP16 gradients remain representable, avoiding underflow. For a gradient $\nabla_\theta \approx 10^{-5}$ and scaling factor $s = 1024$, the scaled value:

$$s \cdot \nabla_\theta \approx 10^{-2} \quad \text{(FP16 representable)} \tag{6}$$

fits within FP16's range ($6.10 \times 10^{-5} \leq |x| \leq 6.55 \times 10^{4}$).

Batch Normalization. Batch normalization normalizes the inputs at each level so that the mean of the inputs is close to 0 and the variance is 1. Batch normalization is performed by calculating the mean and variance of all the samples on the feature dimensions in each small batch, and then normalizing the calculated mean and variance for each sample. Two learnable scaling factors and offsets are also introduced to scale and offset the normalized data. In this way, the sensitivity to the initial parameters can be reduced, which greatly improves the training speed of the model. The batch normalization layer is more sensitive to numerical accuracy, so we use FP32 in the batch normalization layer to ensure the accuracy of the normalized statistics (e.g., the mean and the variance). The mixed-precision strategy of PyTorch automatically converts the computation of the batch normalization layer to FP32, while the other layers still use FP16. PyTorch's mixed-precision strategy automatically converts the batch normalization layer to FP32, while the other layers use FP16.

3.2   The Training Process

We introduced mixed-precision training in the training process of ISTA-Net, which combines the efficiency of mixed-precision computation with the advantages of ISTA-Net in compressed perceptual reconstruction, with the goal of accelerating the training to reduce the memory occupation while maintaining the reconstruction accuracy. The principle and workflow diagram of the mixed-precision training are provided in Fig. 1. For this purpose, we use the torch.amp (Automatic Mixed Precision) tool provided by PyTorch. It can automatically adjust the calculation precision, so that the training process is smoothly switched between FP16 and FP32. The specific implementation steps are as follows.

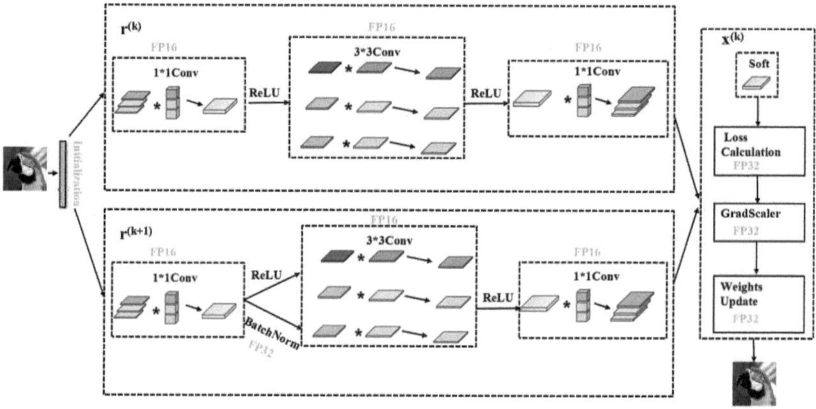

Fig. 1. This is Flowchart of the mixed-accuracy training process.

Initializing the GradScaler. The gradient scaler is a key component in mixed-precision training, used to prevent gradient underflow. At the beginning of training, we initialize an instance of GradScaler.

$$\mathrm{scaler} = \mathrm{torch.amp.GradScaler()}$$

The scaler dynamically adjusts the size of the loss value during the back-propagation process to ensure that the gradient is not too small to be ignored in the FP16 computation.

4   The Results of the Experiment

This section shows the experimental results of ISTA-Net based on mixed-accuracy training. We evaluate the performance of the method in terms of both training speed and reconstruction quality.

4.1   Dataset and Training Setup

We use the same 500 images from the original ISTA-Net paper for training the compressed reconstruction. The training data consists of 88,912 randomly cropped image blocks, each with a size of $33 * 33[22]$ A stochastic Gaussian matrix was also used to generate the CS measurements, and the rows of the matrix were orthogonalized. Model training was performed on a computer equipped with an AMD Ryzen 7 4800H CPU and an NVIDIA GTX 2060 GPU.

4.2   Training Acceleration

We compare the training time of ISTA-Net based on mixed-precision training with the original ISTA-Net. We can see the experimental results in Table 2, which shows that under the same performance of computer hardware, the training time of ISTA-Net trained with mixed precision is about 50% higher than that of single precision (FP32) at different compression ratios. For example, at a compression ratio of 10, the training time was reduced from 8 h 58 min to 4 h 32 min. Importantly, this acceleration has not come at the expense of reconstruction. These results highlight the technical superiority of our mixing accuracy over full FP32, limited by the inefficiency of FP32 calculations, and our high reconstruction while accelerating training.

Table 2. Training time comparison under different compression ratios

Precision Type	1	4	10	25	50
ISTA-Net	9 h 07 min	9 h 03 min	8 h 58 min	9 h 06 min	9 h 05 min
Mix-ISTA[*]	4 h 36 min	4 h 38 min	4 h 32 min	4 h 36 min	4 h 39 min

[*]Shorter training time compared to single precision

4.3   Quality of Reconstruction

Of course, we cannot only focus on the training time of the model, but also need to compare the quality of image reconstruction under different accuracies. We evaluated the reconstruction quality using the Set11 benchmark dataset. The results of several experiments show that the ISTA-Net trained based on hybrid precision is comparable to the original ISTA-Net in terms of PSNR (peak signal-to-noise ratio), and even slightly improved in some cases, as shown in Table 3.

Specifically, under compression ratios of 1, 10, 25, and 50, the PSNR of the hybrid-precision ISTA-Net is slightly higher than that of the single-precision version. The coresponding reconstruction effect diagram(see Figs. 2, 3 and 4) further visually corroborates this advantage, showing that our method training maintains high-fidelity image details comparable to the other methods. This clearly indicates that hybrid-precision training not only accelerates the training process but also maintains a high-quality reconstruction effect.

Table 3. Performance Comparison between Methods under Different CS Ratios.

Dataset	Method	1%	4%	10%	25%	50%
Set11	SDA	17.29	20.12	22.65	25.34	28.95
	ReconNet	17.27	20.63	24.28	25.60	31.50
	ISTA-Net	17.30	20.65	25.80	31.53	37.43
	Mix-ISTA	18.17	20.43	26.02	31.66	37.85
CBSD68	SDA	10.88	15.93	20.33	25.03	28.45
	ReconNet	12.98	17.47	20.92	25.41	30.86
	ISTA-Net	14.11	17.46	22.39	28.03	33.22
	Mix-ISTA	14.79	17.15	22.96	28.11	33.38
Urban100	SDA	16.78	19.89	21.34	25.07	28.41
	ReconNet	16.45	20.34	22.98	25.06	30.77
	ISTA-Net	17.05	20.33	23.30	31.07	37.18
	Mix-ISTA	17.80	20.07	23.46	31.06	37.33
DIV2K	SDA	16.77	17.95	22.32	25.12	28.33
	ReconNet	16.42	20.44	23.79	25.06	30.66
	ISTA-Net	17.11	20.54	23.37	31.35	37.10
	Mix-ISTA	17.24	20.46	23.44	31.61	37.21

[*]Higher SSIM value in the same CS ratio; [1]Higher PSNR value in the same CS ratio

4.4   Performance Evaluation Under Different Noise Conditions

We evaluated the reconstruction performance of ISTA-Net under different noise conditions, including Gaussian and impulsive noise. Experiments were performed on the Set11 dataset with noise levels set to Gaussian noise ($\sigma = 10, 20, 30$) and impulse noise (density $= 0.1, 0.2, 0.3$), respectively. As can be seen from Table 4, the reconstruction performance gradually deteriorates with the noise level. However, ISTA-Net shows robustness under both Gaussian noise and impulse noise, especially at low noise levels, with high PSNR and SSIM values. This shows that ISTA-Net can effectively reconstruct images even under noise.

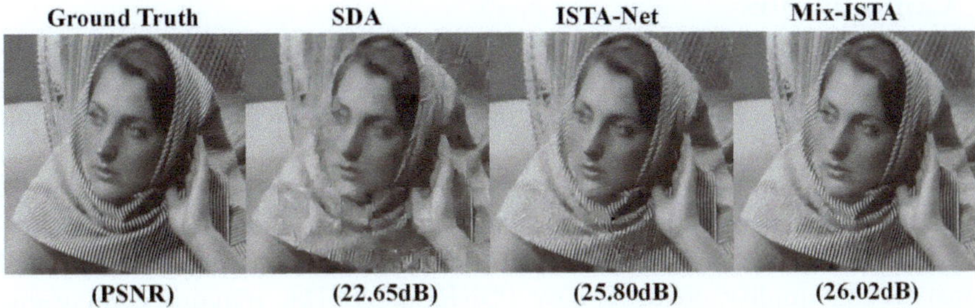

Fig. 2. Comparison of three reconstruction methods, when applied to the Woman image in Set 11(CS ration is 10%).

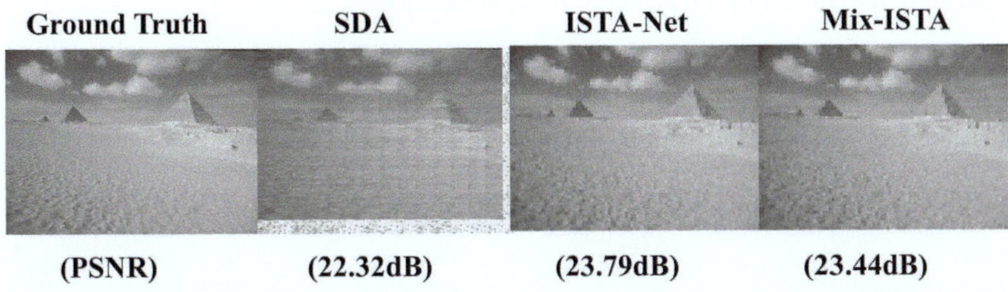

Fig. 3. Comparison of three reconstruction methods, when applied to the Cameraman image in CBSD 68(CS ration is 10%).

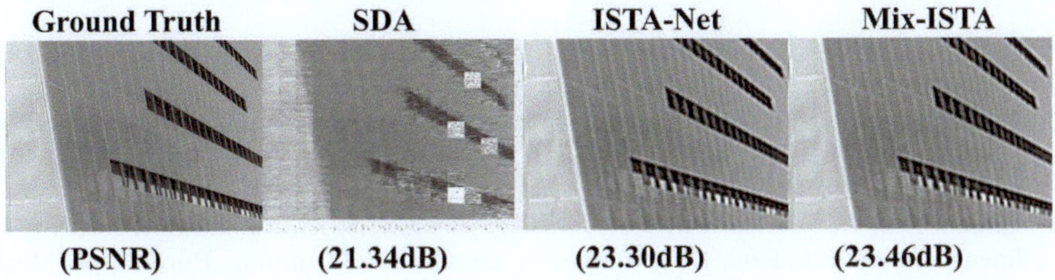

Fig. 4. Comparison of three reconstruction methods, when applied to the House image in Set 11(CS ration is 25%).

Table 4. Performance Comparison under Different Noise Types and Levels

Noise Type	Level	PSNR (dB)	SSIM
Gaussian	$\sigma = 10^{*}$	25.32	0.8123
	$\sigma = 20$	22.45	0.7567
	$\sigma = 30^{1}$	20.17	0.7123
Salt-and-Pepper	density $= 0.1^{*}$	24.56	0.7987
	density $= 0.2$	21.89	0.7456
	density $= 0.3^{1}$	19.78	0.7012

*Low noise level; ^{1}High noise level

5   Conclusions

In this paper, we propose an enhanced version of ISTA-Net that leverages mixed-precision training to accelerate the training process while preserving high-quality reconstruction performance in compressed sensing tasks. Experimental results demonstrate that our approach reduces training time by approximately 50% compared to the original single-precision (FP32) ISTA-Net, as evidenced by the reduction from 8 h 58 min to 4 h 32 min at a compression ratio of 10. Notably, reconstruction quality, measured by PSNR and SSIM, remains comparable to the single-precision model, with slight improvements in certain cases (e.g., PSNR increasing from 17.96 dB to 18.17 dB at a compression ratio of 1). This advancement highlights the practical value of mixed-precision training, particularly in resource-constrained or large-scale data scenarios.

Acknowledgments. The authors would like to express their gratitude to the anonymous referees as well as the Editor and Associate Editor for their valuable comments which lead to substantial improvements of the paper. This work was supported by Jiangsu University Blue Project and the Major Program of Natural Science Foundation of the Jiangsu Higher Education Institutions of China (No. 23KJA520006).

Conflicts of Interest. The authors declare that they have no conflict of interest.

References

1. Donoho, D.L.: Compressed sensing. IEEE Trans. Inf. Theory **52**(4), 1289–1306 (2006)
2. Tropp, J.A., Gilbert, A.C.: Signal recovery from random measurements via orthogonal matching pursuit. IEEE Trans. Inf. Theory **53**(12), 4655–4666 (2007). https://doi.org/10.1109/TIT.2007.909108
3. Daubechies, I., Defrise, M., De Mol, C.: An iterative thresholding algorithm for linear inverse problems with a sparsity constraint. Commun. Pure Appl. Math. **57**(11), 1413–1457 (2004)
4. Tibshirani, R.: Regression shrinkage and selection via the lasso. J. Roy. Stat. Soc. B **58**(1), 267–288 (1996)
5. Lustig, M., Donoho, D., Pauly, J.M.: Sparse MRI: the application of compressed sensing for rapid MR imaging. Magn. Reson. Med. **58**(6), 1182–1195 (2007)
6. Kulkarni, K., Lohit, S., Turaga, P.E.A.: ReconNet: non-iterative reconstruction of images from compressively sensed measurements. In: IEEE Conference on Computer Vision and Pattern Recognition (CVPR), pp. 449–458 (2016)
7. Cui, W., Liu, S., Jiang, F., Zhao, D.: Image compressed sensing using non-local neural network. IEEE Trans. Multimedia **25**, 816–830 (2021)
8. Su, Y., Lian, Q.: iPiano-Net: nonconvex optimization inspired multi-scale reconstruction network for compressed sensing. Sig. Process.: Image Commun. **89**, 115989 (2020)
9. Chen, B., Zhang, J.: Content-aware scalable deep compressed sensing. IEEE Trans. Image Process. **31**, 5412–5426 (2022)

10. Gan, H., Gao, Y., Liu, C., Chen, H., Zhang, T., Liu, F.: AutoBCS: block-based image compressive sensing with data-driven acquisition and noniterative reconstruction. IEEE Trans. Cybern. **53**(4), 2558–2571 (2021)
11. Sun, Y., Chen, J., Liu, Q., Liu, B., Guo, G.: Dual-path attention network for compressed sensing image reconstruction. IEEE Trans. Image Process. **29**, 9482–9495 (2020). https://doi.org/10.1109/TIP.2020.3023629
12. Chen, D., Tachella, J., Davies, M.E.: Robust equivariant imaging: a fully unsupervised framework for learning to image from noisy and partial measurements. In: Proceedings of the IEEE/CVF Conference on Computer Vision and Pattern Recognition, pp. 5647–5656 (2022)
13. Pang, T., Quan, Y., Ji, H.: Self-supervised Bayesian deep learning for image recovery with applications to compressive sensing. In: European Conference on Computer Vision, pp. 475–491. Springer (2020)
14. Lehtinen, J., et al.: Noise2Noise: learning image restoration without clean data. arXiv preprint: arXiv:1803.04189 (2018)
15. Xia, Z., Chakrabarti, A.: Training image estimators without image ground truth. In: Advances in Neural Information Processing Systems, vol. 32 (2019)
16. Cole, E.K., Pauly, J.M., Vasanawala, S.S., Ong, F.: Unsupervised MRI reconstruction with generative adversarial networks. arXiv preprint: arXiv:2008.13065 (2020)
17. Metzler, C.A., Mousavi, A., Heckel, R., Baraniuk, R.G.: Unsupervised learning with stein's unbiased risk estimator. arXiv preprint: arXiv:1805.10531 (2018)
18. Zhussip, M., Soltanayev, S., Chun, S.Y.: Training deep learning based image denoisers from undersampled measurements without ground truth and without image prior. In: Proceedings of the IEEE/CVF Conference on Computer Vision and Pattern Recognition, pp. 10255–10264 (2019)
19. Quan, Y., Qin, X., Pang, T., Ji, H.: Dual-domain self-supervised learning and model adaption for deep compressive imaging. In: European Conference on Computer Vision, pp. 409–426. Springer (2022)
20. Su, Y., Yang, Y., Shi, B., Zhang, Y.: Bayesian self-supervised learning allying with transformer powered compressed sensing imaging. Digital Signal Process. **140**, 104120 (2023)
21. Wu, Y., Sun, J., Chen, W., Yin, J.: Improved image compressive sensing recovery with low-rank prior and deep image prior. Signal Process. **205**, 108896 (2023)
22. Zhang, J., Ghanem, B., Xu, Y.: ISTA-Net: interpretable optimization-inspired deep network for image compressive sensing. In: IEEE Conference on Computer Vision and Pattern Recognition (CVPR), pp. 1828–1837 (2018)
23. Micikevicius, P., Narang, S., Alben, J.E.A.: Mixed precision training (2018)
24. He, K., Zhang, X., Ren, S., Sun, J.: Deep residual learning for image recognition. In: IEEE Conference on Computer Vision and Pattern Recognition (CVPR), pp. 770–778 (2016)
25. Vaswani, A., Shazeer, N., Parmar, N.E.A.: Attention is all you need. In: Advances in Neural Information Processing Systems (NeurIPS), pp. 5998–6008 (2017)

FastDAG: A Low-Latency and Parallel Wave-Execution Consensus with a Double-Layer DAG

Yi Hua[1], Xiulong Liu[1(✉)], Hao Xu[1], Chenyu Zhang[1], Licheng Wang[2], and Keqiu Li[1]

[1] College of Intelligence and Computing, Tianjin University, Tianjin, China
{yihua,xiulong_liu,hao_xu,chenyu_zhang,keqiu}@tju.edu.cn
[2] Beijing Institute of Technology, Beijing, China
lcwang@bit.edu.cn

Abstract. DAG-based Byzantine Fault Tolerant protocols have gained popularity due to their high throughput, but they often suffer from high latency caused by the *serial* wave-execution model. In this paper, we propose *FastDAG*, the first asynchronous DAG-based consensus protocol that adopts a *parallel* wave-execution model. FastDAG introduces a double-layer DAG structure to parallelize voting and a cross-referencing approach to link the two layers, significantly reducing latency. To address the challenges of inconsistency between the two layers, we design a Cross-Reference Fast commit approach that determines block commitment based on voting results from both layers. To address the challenge of Byzantine behavior of the leader, we design a planned-and-forced switching approach. Real-world experiment results on 46 cloud servers show that FastDAG outperforms existing protocols, achieving 22.5% lower latency than GradedDAG [1] and 35% lower than Tusk [2].

Keywords: DAG · Consensus · Blockchain · Byzantine fault tolerant

1 Introduction

1.1 Background and Motivation

In recent years, the popularity of blockchain has renewed interest in Byzantine Fault Tolerant (BFT) protocols [3,12]. To improve throughput, many protocols adopt the Directed Acyclic Graph (DAG) structure to record historical voting [4], forming DAG-based consensus. Most, including Tusk [2], Bullshark [5] and GradedDAG [1] use a serial wave-execution model, where the system advances through waves of multiple rounds. A next wave can be initiated only after the current wave has completed and the commit conditions for the relevant leader block have been evaluated. However, this *serial* wave-execution model causes high latency, even under ideal conditions, Tusk requires up to 9 communication steps. With scale and network degradation, the problem worsens, becoming a key performance bottleneck. This motivates us to explore a parallel approach to reduce latency in designing protocols.

X. Wang et al. (Eds.): NPC 2025, LNCS 16306, pp. 88–100, 2026.
https://doi.org/10.1007/978-3-032-10466-3_8

Table 1. Comparison of protocols

Consensus	Fast Path	Fast Path Condition Send | Receive	Wave-execute Model	Steps
Tusk [2]	No	—	serial	9
BullShark [5]	Yes	$3f + 1 \mid 2f + 1$	serial	6
Graded DAG [1]	Yes	$3f + 1 \mid 2f + 1$	serial	5
Wahoo [6]	Yes	$3f + 1 \mid 2f + 1$	serial	5
FastDAG	Yes	$3f + 1 \mid f + 1$	parallel	4

1.2   Limitations of Prior Art

To reduce the latency in DAG-based consensus, existing studies can be mainly categorized into two classes shown in Table 1. The first, exemplified by Bull-Shark [5], adds a fast path under partial synchrony: if $2f + 1$ votes are collected before the timer expires, commit latency drops from three RBCs to two (9 to 6 steps). However, it requires receiving votes from all honest replicas before the timer expires, which relies on near-perfect network conditions, so the fast path rarely triggers in practice, leaving latency high. The second, exemplified by Graded DAG [1] and Wahoo [6], modifies RBC to slightly reduce message exchanges. However, it requires additional message exchanges to ensure totality. In summary, they still adopt the serial wave-execution model, where each wave must finish before the next starts, causing delays in transaction commitment.

1.3   FastDAG in a Nutshell

To overcome the limitations of existing protocols, this paper proposes *FastDAG*—the first asynchronous DAG-based consensus protocol featuring a *parallel* wave-execution model. To enable parallel consensus progression, we design a *double-layer DAG* structure: an *up-DAG* for disseminating and voting on transaction plaintexts, and a *down-DAG* for disseminating and voting on transaction hashes. These two layers are generated concurrently. Unlike traditional DAG protocols that require serial progression of the down-DAG waves, the double-layer DAG enables querying the up-DAG voting status and fusing votes to quickly commit and execute even if the down-DAG has not met the commit condition. Furthermore, we introduce a *cross-reference* approach linking the two layers, which lowers the fast path requirement at the consensus voting layer from $2f + 1$ to $f + 1$, significantly increasing the fast path success rate. Overall, *FastDAG* reduces consensus latency through these innovations.

1.4   Challenge and Solution

In designing the FastDAG protocol, we face two significant technical challenges.
    The first challenge lies in how to determine the vote counts when inconsistencies exist between the up-DAG and down-DAG. In double-layer DAG, each

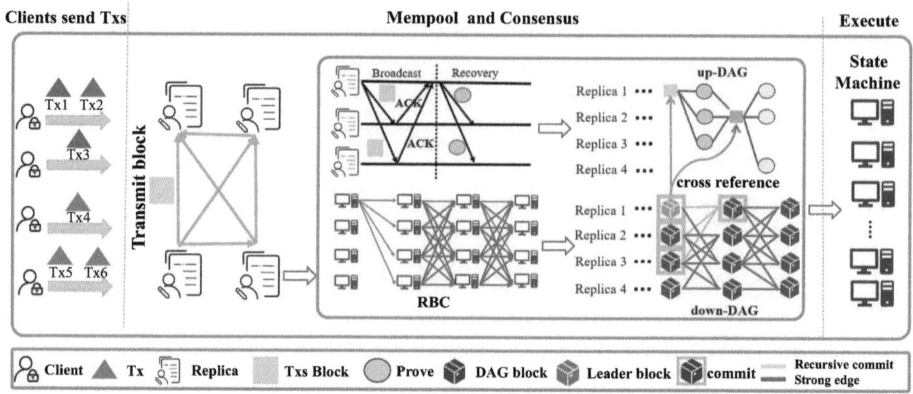

Fig. 1. overview of the FastDAG protocol.

transaction in a down-DAG block may map to different up-DAG blocks, yielding inconsistent votes. We design a commit rule that, via cross-referencing, checks each transaction's references in the up-DAG; if consensus votes exceed $f + 1$ and total votes exceed $2f + 1$, the block is committed. To avoid search bottlenecks, the proposed index-Tree search algorithm locates vote counts in $O(\log N)$ time.

The second challenge lies in how to construct up-DAG timely when a replica is slow or Byzantine. If a disseminating replica fails or refuses to broadcast, consensus may stall. We employ planned switching approach to redistribute workload from slow replicas, and forced switching approach to revoke Byzantine replicas' duties, ensuring smooth up-DAG progress.

1.5 Novelty and Advantages

This paper proposes *FastDAG*—the first asynchronous DAG-based consensus protocol with parallel wave-execution model, thereby supporting the efficient and stable operation of large-scale blockchain systems. The novelty of the proposed *FastDAG* protocol is demonstrated by addressing two key technical challenges: (1) The first challenge lies in how to determine the vote counts when inconsistencies exist between the up-DAG and down-DAG. (2) The second challenge lies in how to construct up-DAG timely when a replica is slow or Byzantine. FastDAG has two main advantages: (1) Compared to Bullshark [5], FastDAG significantly improves the success rate of entering the fast path, thereby substantially reducing latency. (2) Compared to GradedDAG [1], and Wahoo [6], FastDAG adopts a parallel wave-execution model, enabling the up-DAG and down-DAG to be generated concurrently. The voting process for transactions is also performed in parallel, which effectively reduces latency. The real-world experiment results show that FastDAG outperforms existing protocols, achieving 22.5% lower latency than Graded DAG [1] and 35% lower than Tusk [2].

2 FastDAG Design

2.1 System Model

We formalize our system under the following three assumptions, covering fault tolerance, cryptographic security, and network conditions.

Byzantine Fault Tolerance. Our system consists of N replicas, among which up to f may behave arbitrarily, including sending false messages, corrupting data, or deviating from the protocol—these are termed Byzantine replicas. The remaining replicas are honest and follow the protocol. We assume $N \geq 3f + 1$ to tolerate up to f faulty replicas.

Computational Security. We assume a public key infrastructure, where each replica holds a key pair (sk_i, pk_i). Messages are signed with sk_i and verified using pk_i, and all replicas know each other's public keys. We adopt a static adversary model and assume the cryptographic primitives are secure, ensuring message authenticity and detecting any tampering by Byzantine replicas.

Asynchronous Network. We consider an asynchronous network model, where there are no bounds on message delivery times or operation latencies. Unlike synchronous or partially synchronous networks, which assume eventual or bounded delays but can be vulnerable to attacks [7,8], our asynchronous setting provides stronger resilience to network uncertainty and adversarial conditions.

2.2 FastDAG Overview

As shown in Fig. 1, the FastDAG protocol consists of four main stages, where Stage 2 is divided into two parallel sub-stages: Stage 2A and Stage 2B.

Stage 1: Client proposal. Clients submit transactions to the up-leader.

Stage 2A: Transaction dissemination. The up-leader selects $2f + 1$ high-performance replicas via heartbeat, sends them the transaction, and collects at least $f + 1$ positive votes to form a certificate, which is then broadcast to all replicas. Each replica then constructs its local up-DAG accordingly.

Stage 2B: Consensus voting. When a down-leader accumulates enough txs, the down-leader maps txs to $\langle txid, Hash(tx) \rangle$, packages them into a down-DAG block, and broadcasts it via RBC for inclusion in the down-DAG.

Stage 3: Cross-referencing. For each $Hash(tx)$ in the down-DAG, the matching block in the up-DAG is located and linked by a cross-reference edge.

Stage 4: Fast path. Transactions meeting fast-path criteria are committed immediately; others wait for the next wave.

2.3 Transaction Dissemination

The client generates a transaction and randomly sends its plaintext to $f + 1$ replicas in the blockchain system, and then enters the *Transaction dissemination* stage. It is worth noting that **Step 2.3 and 2.4 are executed in parallel.** We refer to the replicas that just received the transaction plaintext as the up-leader replicas. The up-laeader replica broadcasts these transaction plaintexts to $2f + 1$ replicas, collects their votes, and organizes the results into a up-DAG. This process consists of the following three steps:

Step 1: Selecting replicas. The Master replica uses the heartbeat data exchanged among replicas to select the $2f+1$ highest-performing replicas. Specifically, each heartbeat packet contains two key metrics: round-trip time (RTT) and the historical success rate of the fast path. The up-leader computes the logical distance based on a weighted combination of these two metrics and selects the $2f + 1$ replicas with the smallest logical distances.

Step 2: Transaction dissemination and voting. The up-leader organizes a batch of txs into a structure of the form $Map\langle txid, tx\rangle$ and broadcasts it to the selected replicas. Upon receiving the txs, each replica verifies whether the transaction is correctly signed by the client's private key. If the verification passes, they casts a positive vote, signs it with its own private key, and sends it back to the up-leader. Once the up-leader collects at least $f + 1$ valid signatures, it aggregates them into a single signature and generates a certificate.

Step 3: Updating up-DAG. The up-leader broadcasts the certificate to all replicas. Upon receiving the certificate, each replica inserts the corresponding $Map\langle txid, tx\rangle$ into its local up-DAG, and, based on the certificate, adds the corresponding votes as references into the up-DAG.

As shown in the Fig. 2, we support two switching modes. The upper part shows the forced switching mechanism: when the master exhibits Byzantine behavior, replicas cast negative votes. A forced switch is triggered if $2f + 1$ votes for replacement are collected, preventing the master from acting maliciously. The lower part shows the planned switching mechanism: when the up-leader experiences insufficient network bandwidth, it can delegate part of its workload to other replicas. In this case, the up-leader first sends a change-leader proposal, and the switch occurs after receiving approvals from $2f + 1$ replicas and another up-leader contiunes disseminating txs.

2.4 Consensus Voting

As time progresses, the DAG-based consensus proceeds in successive rounds. In each round, every replica proposes a down-DAG Block. The replica that proposes the consensus down-DAG Block is referred to as the down-leader.

Step 1: The down-leader computes the hash value $Hash(tx)$ for each transaction plaintext tx, and organizes these transaction hashes into a mapping structure of the form $Map\langle txid, Hash(tx)\rangle$. This map is then included in the down-DAG

Algorithm 1: Transaction Dissemination

Input: Transaction batch $TxBatch$, heartbeat data, fault rate f
Output: up-DAG updated with certified transactions

Step 1: Selecting replicas
foreach *replica r* **do**
    ⌊ compute $distance(r) = a \cdot RTT(r) + b \cdot fastPathFailureRate(r)$
$ReplicaSet \leftarrow SelectMin(2f + 1, distance)$

Step 2: Dissemination and Voting (parallel)
up-leader $\rightarrow$ ReplicaSet: $Map\langle txid, tx \rangle$
foreach $s \in ReplicaSet$ *(in parallel)* **do**
    if verifySignature(tx) = true:
        $vote_s \leftarrow signVote(s, tx)$
        $vote_s \rightarrow$ up-leader
up-leader waits for $\geq f + 1$ valid votes
$Cert \leftarrow AggregateVotes(votes)$

Step 3: Updating up-DAG (parallel)
up-leader $\rightarrow$ AllReplicas: $Cert$
foreach *replica* **do**
    insert $Map\langle txid, tx \rangle$ into local up-DAG
    add votes from $Cert$ as references in up-DAG

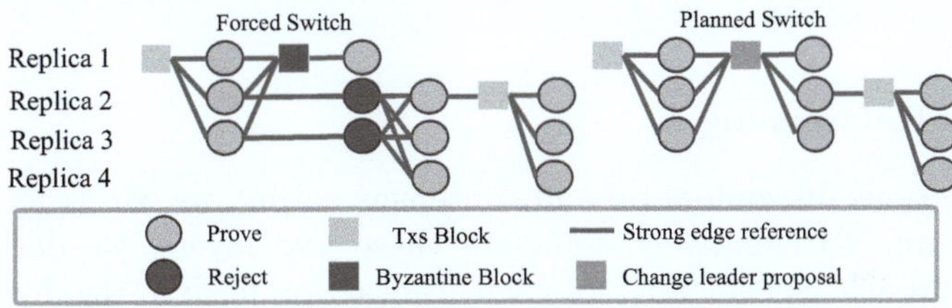

Fig. 2. porcess of forced switching and planned switching.

Block. Subsequently, the down-leader signs the down-DAG Block with its private key and broadcasts the block via the Reliable Broadcast.

Step 2: Upon receiving the down-DAG Block, each replica first verifies the validity of the leader's signature. Then, using the $txid$, it retrieves the corresponding transaction plaintext named TX and verifies that $Hash(tx) == Hash(TX)$. If verification succeeds, the replica casts a positive vote by signing it and broadcasts the signed vote to all replicas.

Step 3: Once a replica collects at least $2f + 1$ positive votes, it aggregates these signatures into a single aggregated signature and broadcasts this aggregated signature to all replicas. Finally, the DAG Block is appended to the local down-DAG at each replica.

Algorithm 2: Detailed index-Tree Search Algorithm

Input: Transaction hash h, Hash-indexed tree $Tree_h$, txid-indexed tree $Tree_g$
Output: Update Cross Reference.

Step 1: Locate txid via Hash-indexed tree
currentNode $\leftarrow$ $Tree_h$.root
while *currentNode is not a leaf* **do**
 find child node whose key range contains h
 currentNode $\leftarrow$ child
foreach *entry e in currentNode* **do**
 if *e.hash* $==$ h **then**
  $txid \leftarrow e.txid$
  break

Step 2: Retrieve reference via txid-indexed tree
currentNode $\leftarrow$ $Tree_g$.root
while *currentNode is not a leaf* **do**
 find child node whose key range contains $txid$
 currentNode $\leftarrow$ child
foreach *entry e in currentNode* **do**
 if *e.txid* $==$ *txid* **then**
  $referenceInfo \leftarrow e.references$
  break
return $referenceInfo$

2.5   Cross-Referencing

After transactions dissemination and consensus voting, we construct a two-layer DAG structure. To effectively associate these two layers, we design a cross-reference approach. Specifically, for each transaction hash in the down-DAG, we need to locate the corresponding transaction block in the up-DAG. To achieve this, we propose a index-Tree Search algorithm, as illustrated in Fig. 3.

We first convert the DAG into a multi-way tree structure named index-tree, it is sorted by transaction hashes: the first level stores the global index, the second level stores the hash indices of transactions, and the third level stores the corresponding txids. The nodes are connected through a doubly linked list. In the search process, we construct two index-trees: the first is indexed by transaction hashes, and the second is indexed by txids. During a query, the system first searches the leaf node in the first tree using the transaction hash to retrieve the corresponding txid. Then, this txid is used as the key to query the second tree, obtaining the reference information of the transaction and thus determining how many replicas have referenced it. The search complexity on a single tree is $O(\log N)$, and the overall complexity is $O(m \log n)$, where m denotes the number of transactions to be queried, and n denotes the size of the up-DAG.

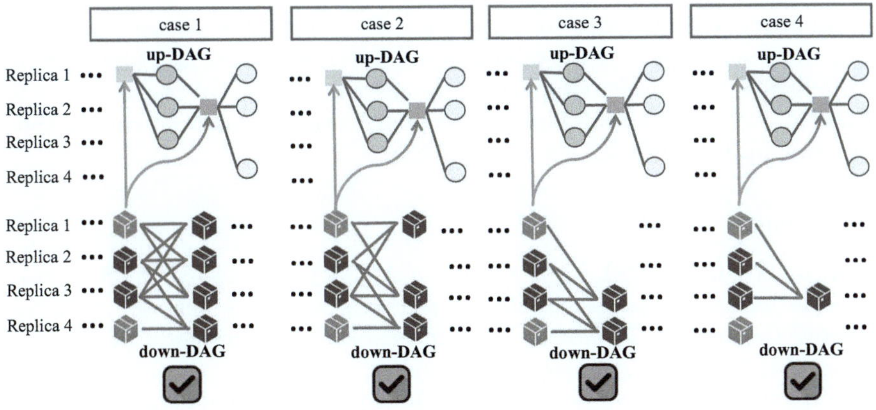

Fig. 3. structure of the double-layer DAG and its commit approach.

2.6 Fast Path Verification

A transaction tx is eligible to enter the fast path and be committed for execution at an honest replica p if it meets the following conditions. First, tx must be included in the up-DAG with a valid certificate. Second, tx must be contained in a down-DAG block that has received votes from at least $f+1$ distinct replicas. Third, tx must be cross-referenced between the up-DAG and the down-DAG. In other words, the transaction can only be committed through the fast path when it is properly confirmed in both DAG structures and has sufficient voting.

As shown in the Fig. 3, all transactions in the down-DAG are cross-referenced to two blocks in the up-DAG, both of which have received votes from Replica 1 and Replica 2. Therefore, only one additional vote from either Replica 3 or Replica 4 is required in the down-DAG to trigger the fast-path commit. All cases from Case 1 to Case 4 satisfy this condition.

3 Correctness Analysis of FastDAG

3.1 Safety Proof

Theorem 1 (Safety). *In a system of $N \geq 3f + 1$ replicas with at most f Byzantine faults, if two honest replicas p and p' have committed sequences $\mathcal{C}_p = (T_1, \ldots, T_k)$ and $\mathcal{C}_{p'} = (T'_1, \ldots, T'_{k'})$, then there exists $\min(k, k') = m$ such that $(T_1, \ldots, T_m) = (T'_1, \ldots, T'_m)$. That is, honest replicas never commit conflicting transactions, and their committed sequences are consistent prefixes.*

Proof. We prove by contradiction. Suppose two honest replicas p and p' commit transactions T and T' respectively at the same position such that $T \neq T'$. By the protocol, a transaction T can only appear in the up-DAG if its certificate includes $\geq f + 1$ signatures, at least one of which is from an honest replica. Likewise, a consensus DAG block containing T can only be committed if it collects $\geq 2f + 1$ votes, at least $f + 1$ of which are from honest replicas. Similarly, T' can also only be committed with support from at least $f + 1$ honest replicas. Since honest replicas only sign and vote for valid and unique transactions at a given position, it is impossible for them to support conflicting transactions at the same position. Thus, T and T' cannot both be committed at the same position, and $\mathcal{C}_p$ and $\mathcal{C}_{p'}$ must agree up to $\min(k, k')$.

3.2 Liveness Proof

Theorem 2. (Liveness). *In a system of $N \geq 3f + 1$ replicas with at most f Byzantine faults and an eventually reliable asynchronous network, any client-submitted transaction T that is correctly signed will eventually appear in the committed sequence $\mathcal{C}_p$ of every honest replica.*

Proof. We show that any valid transaction tx proposed by a client is eventually committed. On the up-DAG layer: The client sends tx to $f + 1$ replicas, at least one of which is honest. The honest up-leader selects $2f + 1$ replicas, at least $f + 1$ of which are honest, and disseminates tx. Since the network eventually delivers messages and honest replicas always vote for valid transactions, the up-leader collects $\geq f + 1$ votes and produces a certificate. The certificate is broadcast and tx is inserted into the up-DAG at all honest replicas. On the down-DAG layer: In each round, a down-leader (eventually honest) proposes a DAG block referencing transactions from the up-DAG. The block is broadcast and validated. Honest replicas vote, and the down-leader collects $\geq 2f + 1$ votes. The block is appended to the down-DAG and cross-referenced with the up-DAG. Thus, tx is eventually recorded in both layers and committed in the global sequence $\mathcal{C}_p$.

4 Implementation And Evaluation

Evaluation Framework. We implemented the three protocols in a unified Go framework, using "ed25519dalek7" for signatures, TCP for communication, and "dedis/kyber" for threshold signatures. Transaction size was fixed at 250 bytes with batch size 400. We measured throughput, latency, total votes counts, and covered transactions to assess performance.

Experimental Environment. Experiments run on at most 46 cloud server with 46 replicas across Beijing, Shanghai, Shenzhen, Chongqing, and Hong Kong. Each had 8 CPUs, 16 GB RAM, and 100 Mbps bandwidth. Each test was repeated three times and averaged.

4.1 Voting Efficiency

The number of votes received within a fixed time reflects the voting efficiency of a consensus system. We compared three protocols—FastDAG, Tusk, and Graded DAG—using 7 replicas under two settings: without Byzantine replicas and with up to 2 Byzantine replicas. Votes per replica were recorded every 10 s, as shown in Fig. 4a and 4b. FastDAG achieves an average voting rate 59% higher than Tusk and 13.2% higher than Graded DAG, mainly due to its double-layer DAG structure, which enables parallel voting and improves overall efficiency.

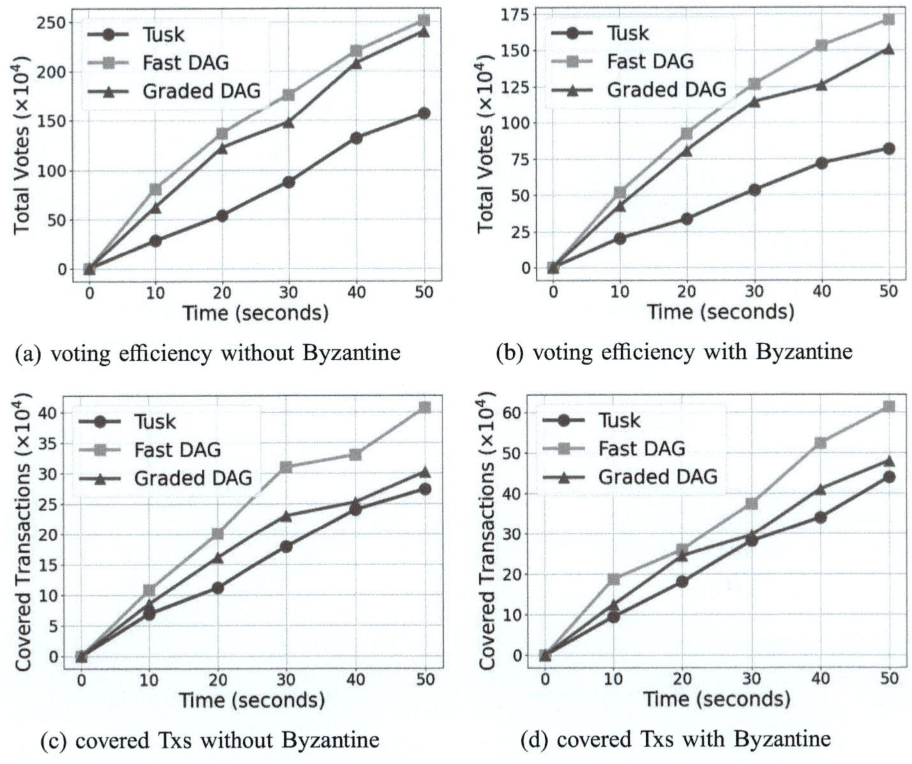

(a) voting efficiency without Byzantine

(b) voting efficiency with Byzantine

(c) covered Txs without Byzantine

(d) covered Txs with Byzantine

Fig. 4. voting efficiency and covered Txs capacity of different protocols.

4.2 Cover Transaction Capacity

The number of transactions covered by votes within a fixed period indicates a protocol's concurrency. We compared FastDAG, Tusk, and Graded DAG with 7 replicas under two settings: no Byzantine replicas and up to 2 Byzantine replicas. Every 10 s, we recorded the transactions covered by votes per replica. Results (Figs. 4c, 4d) show FastDAG covers 39% more transactions than Tusk and 34% more than Graded DAG on average. This gain is due to FastDAG's double-layer DAG enabling parallel voting across down-DAG and up-DAG, thus significantly enhancing concurrency.

4.3 Scalability

To evaluate the scalability of the system, we conducted a comparative experiment involving Graded DAG, Tusk, and FastDAG, with the number of replicas ranging from 4 to 46. In this experiment, no Byzantine replicas were introduced. The results are shown in the Figs. 5a 5b. We observe that FastDAG achieves the best performance among the three protocols. By averaging the latency and

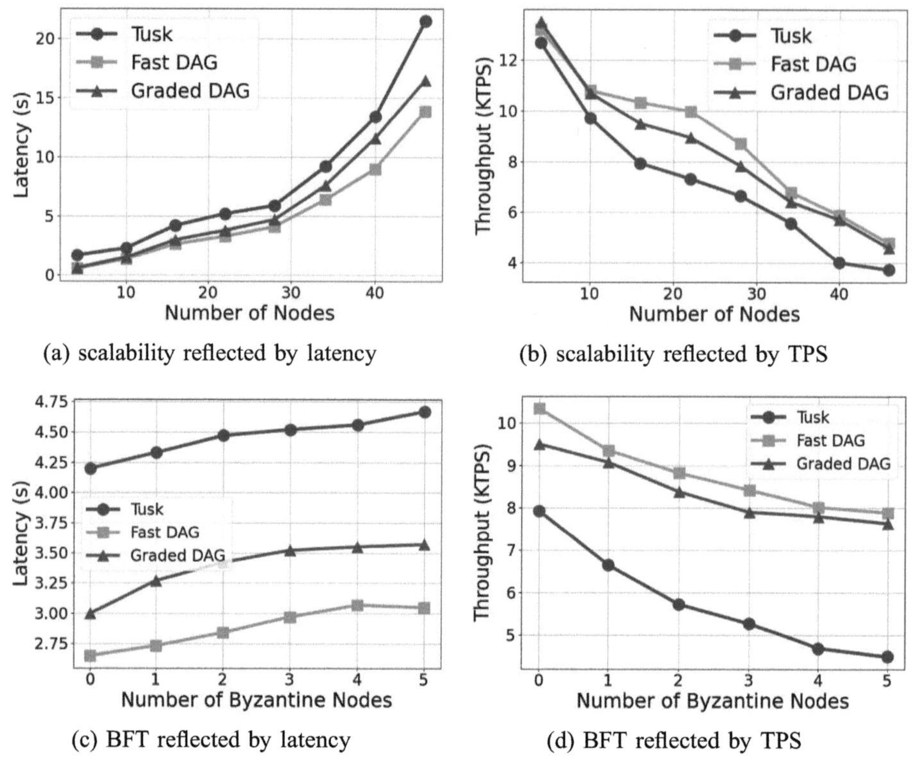

(a) scalability reflected by latency

(b) scalability reflected by TPS

(c) BFT reflected by latency

(d) BFT reflected by TPS

Fig. 5. scalability and Byzantine fault tolerance of different protocols.

throughput across different replica counts, we find that the latency of FastDAG is 65% of that of Tusk and 83.7% of that of Graded DAG. In terms of throughput, FastDAG outperforms Tusk by 22% and Graded DAG by 5%.

4.4 Byzantine Fault Tolerance

To assess Byzantine fault tolerance, we compared Graded DAG, Tusk, and FastDAG with 16 replicas and 0–5 Byzantine nodes. Results in Figs. 5c and 5d show FastDAG consistently outperforms others. Averaged over all Byzantine counts, FastDAG's latency is 65% of Tusk's and 83.7% of Graded DAG's, while its throughput exceeds Tusk's by 53% and Graded DAG's by 5.2%.

5   Other Related Work

Asynchronous protocols are considered more robust because they make no assumptions about message delays, making them resilient to network attacks. Early efforts, such as Asynchronous Binary Agreement (ABA) [9,10], focused on binary values and were later extended to Multi-Valued Validated Byzantine Agreement (MVBA) protocols including AMS-VABA [11] and sMVBA [12]. Although these protocols achieve Byzantine fault-tolerant (BFT) consensus under asynchronous settings, their reliance on serial data processing limits throughput. To address performance bottlenecks, recent research has explored more efficient asynchronous BFT protocols such as Bolt-Dumbo [13], which optimize multi-valued agreement. Parallel lines of work, including foundational protocols like Zyzzyva [14] has inspired the development of DAG-based protocols such as BBCA-CHAIN [15], which aim to reduce latency and boost throughput. Recent works further optimize BFT designs, including sublinear communication consensus [16], QoS-adjustable transaction estimation [17], authenticated query support [18], and convergence-based structured DAGs [19].

6   Conclusion

In this paper, we proposed *FastDAG*, a novel asynchronous DAG-based consensus protocol that achieves low latency and high throughput through a wave-parallel progression mechanism and a double-layer DAG structure. FastDAG significantly reduces the overhead of traditional protocols by enabling concurrent voting and block commitment, and improves the success rate of fast path commitments by lowering the quorum requirement from $2f + 1$ to $f + 1$ using a cross-referencing mechanism. Our real-world experimental results, conducted across geographically distributed nodes, demonstrate that FastDAG consistently outperforms existing protocols such as Graded DAG and Tusk in terms of voting efficiency, transaction coverage, and latency, while maintaining strong scalability and Byzantine fault tolerance.

Acknowledgement. This work is supported by the National Natural Science Foundation of China under Grant Nos. 62232002 and 62032017, the China Postdoctoral Science Foundation under Grant Number 2025M771566, and the Postdoctoral Fellowship Program of CPSF under Grant Number GZB20250403.

References

1. Dai, X., Zhang, Z., Xiao, J., Yue, J., Xie, X., Jin, H.: GradedDAG: an asynchronous DAG-based BFT consensus with lower latency. In: Proc. of the IEEE SRDS, pp. 107–117 (2023)
2. Danezis, G., Kokoris-Kogias, L., Sonnino, A., Spiegelman, A.: Narwhal and tusk: a DAG-based mempool and efficient BFT consensus. In: Proc. of the ACM EuroSys, pp. 34–50 (2022)
3. Zheng, Z., Xie, S., Dai, H.-N., Chen, X., Wang, H.: Blockchain challenges and opportunities: a survey. Int. J. Web Grid Serv. 14(4), 352–375 (2018)
4. Keidar, I., Kokoris-Kogias, E., Naor, O., Spiegelman, A.: All you need is DAG. In: Proc. of the ACM PODC, pp. 165–175 (2021)
5. Spiegelman, A., Giridharan, N., Sonnino, A., Kokoris-Kogias, L.: Bullshark: DAG BFT protocols made practical. In: Proc. of the ACM CCS, pp. 2705–2718 (2022)

6. Dai, X., et al.: Wahoo: a DAG-based BFT consensus with low latency and low communication overhead. IEEE Trans. Inf. Forensics Secur. (2024)
7. Miller, A., Xia, Y., Croman, K., Shi, E., Song, D.: The honey badger of BFT protocols. In: Proc. of the ACM CCS, pp. 31–42 (2016)
8. Guo, B., Lu, Z., Tang, Q., Xu, J., Zhang, Z.: Dumbo: faster asynchronous BFT protocols. In: Proc. of the ACM CCS, pp. 803–818 (2020)
9. Ben-Or, M.: Another advantage of free choice (extended abstract) completely asynchronous agreement protocols. In: Proc. of the ACM PODC, pp. 27–30 (1983)
10. Cachin, C., Kursawe, K., Shoup, V.: Random oracles in constantipole: practical asynchronous byzantine agreement using cryptography. In: Proc. of the ACM PODC, pp. 123–132 (2000)
11. Abraham, I., Malkhi, D., Spiegelman, A.: Asymptotically optimal validated asynchronous byzantine agreement. In: Proc. of the ACM PODC, pp. 337–346 (2019)
12. Jin, H., Xiao, J.: Towards trustworthy blockchain systems in the era of "internet of value": development, challenges, and future trends. SCIENCE CHINA Inf. Sci. **65**(5), 153101 (2022)
13. Lu, Y., Lu, Z., Tang, Q.: Bolt-dumbo transformer: asynchronous consensus as fast as the pipelined BFT. In: Proc. of the ACM SIGOPS, pp. 2159–2173 (2022)
14. Kotla, R., Alvisi, L., Dahlin, M., Clement, A., Wong, E.: Zyzzyva: speculative byzantine fault tolerance. In: Proc. of the ACM SIGOPS, pp. 45–58 (2007)
15. Malkhi, D., Stathakopoulou, C., Yin, M.: BBCA-CHAIN: low latency, high throughput BFT consensus on a DAG. In: Proc. of the Springer FC, pp. 51–73 (2024)
16. Xu, H., Liu, X., Zhang, C., Wang, W., Wang, J., Li, K.: Crackle: a fast sector-based BFT consensus with sublinear communication complexity. In: Proc. of the IEEE INFOCOM, pp. 1–10 (2024)
17. Xu, H., et al.: A transaction cardinality estimation approach for QOS-adjustable intelligent blockchain systems. IEEE J. Sel. Areas Commun. **40**(12), 3672–3684 (2022)
18. Xu, H., et al.: Empowering authenticated and efficient queries for STK transaction-based blockchains. IEEE Trans. Comput. **72**(8), 2209–2223 (2023)
19. Hu, D., et al.: Ladder: a convergence-based structured {DAG} blockchain for high throughput and low latency. In: Proc. of the USENIX NSDI, pp. 779–794 (2025)

Long-Term Cloud Workload Prediction with Multi-period Augmented LSTM

Wentao Shi[1], Jiarui Hu[1], Xiangkai Ma[1], Wenzhong Li[1(✉)], Shuai Li[2], and Sanglu Lu[1]

[1] Nanjing University, Nanjing, China
{wentao.shi,jiaruihu,xiangkai.ma}@smail.nju.edu.cn,
{lwz,sanglu}@nju.edu.cn
[2] State Grid Ruijia (Tianjin) Intelligent Robot Co., Ltd., Tianjin, China
lishuai@sgepri.sgcc.com.cn

Abstract. Long-term Cloud Workload Prediction (LCWP) is critical for efficient resource provisioning and cost optimization in cloud computing environments. However, traditional prediction approaches compress complex workload patterns into a single token, leading to catastrophic forgetting of historical variations. Additionally, they lack the capability to capture distinct periodic patterns (e.g., minutely and hourly cycles) and bursty trends. To overcome these limitations, we propose the Multi-period Augmented LSTM (MUPA), a comprehensive encoder-decoder model featuring explicit cross-period connections designed to maximize utilization of inherent periodic information. MUPA architecture integrates two novel LSTM variants as core components: Multi-input LSTM, which aggregates latent representations across time steps to establish global workload dynamics understanding, and Broadened LSTM, which enhances memory mechanisms by progressively expanding the cell state's value range to learn long-term dependencies. Extensive experiments on real-world cloud workload datasets demonstrate MUPA's superior effectiveness for workload prediction tasks.

Keywords: Cloud Workload Prediction · Long-short Term Memory · Autoregressive Model

1 Introduction

Accurate Long-term Cloud Workload Prediction (LCWP), which forecasts future resource demands such as CPU, memory, network, and I/O utilization hours or days in advance, is a critical capability underpinning the economic and operational efficiency of modern cloud computing environments. Its strategic importance lies in enabling proactive resource management far beyond reactive scaling. By providing foresight, LCWP empowers cloud providers and large-scale

W. Shi and J. Hu—Contribute Equally. This work is supported by the Project of State Grid Ruijia (Tianjin) Intelligent Robot Co., Ltd (No.SGRJTJZNCGJS2500082).

© IFIP International Federation for Information Processing 2026
Published by Springer Nature Switzerland AG 2026
X. Wang et al. (Eds.): NPC 2025, LNCS 16306, pp. 101–112, 2026.
https://doi.org/10.1007/978-3-032-10466-3_9

enterprises to significantly reduce operational expenditures. This is achieved through optimizing reserved instance commitments, rightsizing resources to minimize costly over-provisioning and performance-impacting under-provisioning, and scheduling non-critical workloads during low-cost periods.

Furthermore, LCWP enhances service reliability and performance by enabling the pre-emptive provisioning of capacity to meet anticipated demand spikes, ensuring adherence to stringent service-level agreements and preventing costly outages or degraded user experiences. On a broader scale, the efficient resource utilization driven by LCWP contributes directly to sustainable cloud operations by reducing the energy footprint associated with idle infrastructure.

Despite this immense value, achieving high-accuracy LCWP remains challenging due to the complex, non-linear, multi-scale periodic, and occasionally bursty nature of cloud workloads, motivating the need for advanced predictive solutions.

Although Transformers often outperform traditional RNNs [3] (like LSTM [4], GRU [1]) in long sequence modeling by using attention to capture long-range dependencies and avoid catastrophic forgetting(losing historical information), RNNs possess unique, under-exploited advantages for LCWP. Their sequential processing aligns naturally with workload data flow, allows easy integration of periodic patterns at each step, and can be computationally less complex than Transformers.

The critical limitation of traditional RNNs in LCWP is their compression of complex historical patterns into a single, limited state vector. This causes catastrophic forgetting of important variations and prevents them from effectively capturing the multi-scale periodic and bursty trends essential for long-term cloud workload forecasting. New RNN architectures specifically designed to overcome these limitations are urgently needed.

In this work, we revitalize the potential of LSTM-based models for LCWP by directly addressing their core limitations. We fundamentally redesign the memory mechanisms to capture thee long-term, periodic cloud workload dynamics. Our approach develops sophisticated LSTM variants capable of robustly modeling the unique temporal characteristics of cloud workloads.

Our contributions are summarized as follows:

- We propose the comprehensive Multi-period Augmented LSTM(MUPA) model, a novel encoder-decoder framework specifically designed for long-term cloud workload prediction. MUPA integrates explicit cross-period connections to maximize the utilization of inherent periodic information (e.g., minutely, hourly cycles), which is crucial for accurate forecasting. This core architecture is built upon two innovative components:
  - Multi-input LSTM (MiLSTM): A novel variant designed to foster a global understanding of workload dynamics by explicitly encouraging the aggregation of latent representations across multiple time steps, overcoming the limitation of compressing history into a single state vector.
  - Broadened LSTM (βLSTM): A novel variant that enhances long-term memory by progressively expanding the cell state's receptive field and

mitigating gradient vanishing, enabling robust learning of long-range workload dependencies.
- We conduct extensive experiments on multiple real-world cloud workload datasets. The results consistently demonstrate the superior effectiveness of our proposed MUPA model for long-term cloud workload prediction tasks compared to relevant state-of-the-art baselines.

2 Related Works

2.1 Methods for Cloud Workload Prediction

Cloud workload prediction research employs diverse methodological approaches that have evolved from simple statistical models to sophisticated deep learning systems. Traditional statistical models capture linear trends but struggle with complex patterns. Machine learning techniques like SVR [2] improve non-linear fitting through feature engineering. Deep learning approaches leverage LSTM [4] and CNN-RNN hybrids [7] for temporal dependency modeling, with recent extensions adopting Transformer [8] architectures that utilize self-attention mechanisms to capture long-range dependencies in workload sequences.

2.2 Long Short-Term Memory Networks

Long Short-Term Memory (LSTM) networks [4], a type of recurrent neural network (RNN), have been critical in addressing the gradient vanishing problem associated with traditional RNNs. Introduced by Hochreiter & Schmidhuber (1997), LSTMs are designed to remember information for long periods, making them particularly suitable for time series prediction. The key innovation in LSTM networks is the introduction of gates that regulate the flow of information, namely the input gate, output gate, and forget gate. These mechanisms allow LSTMs to selectively remember and forget information, making them adept at capturing long-term dependencies in time series data.

3 Method

In this section, we introduce Multi-period Augmented LSTM (MUPA) model, and its two key components: Multi-input LSTM (MiLSTM) cell and Broadened LSTM (βLSTM) cell.

3.1 Overall Architecture

An overview of MUPA is demonstrated in Fig. 1.

Prior to the input of the workload data into the model, we conducted preprocessing on the data using RevIN [5].

MiLSTM Cell is an optimized version of LSTM. Traditional LSTM can only accept the output from time $t - 1$ as input at time t. However, MiLSTM allows

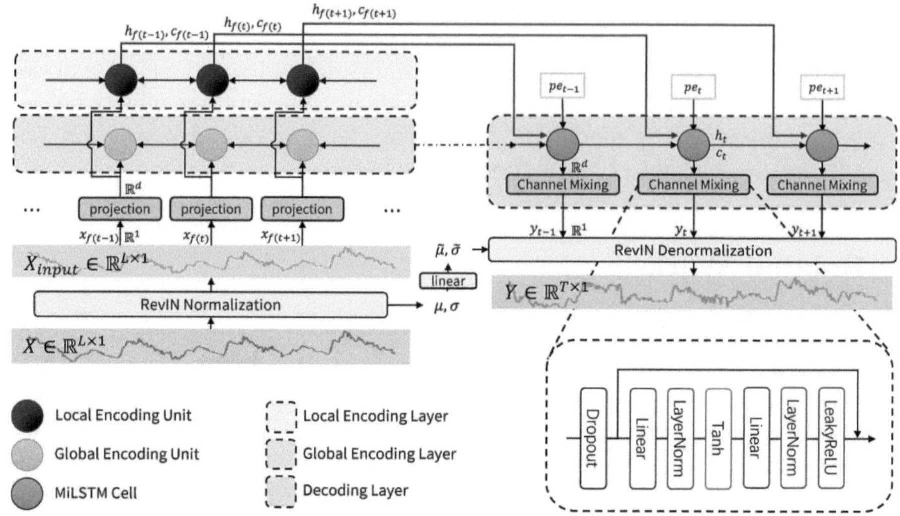

Fig. 1. The simplified structure of our proposed model. The left part is the encoder, and the right part is the decoder.

LSTM to accept outputs from multiple timesteps as inputs and effectively integrates them.

The encoding part consists of two encoding layers, with each layer's input and output similar to those of a traditional LSTM, being sequence-to-sequence. The difference lies in that the local encoding layer records the output at each timestep, whereas the global encoding layer only records the last one. As their name implies, the global encoding layer serves to extract global information from the sequence, while the local encoding layer is designed to extract information from a specific timestep and its surrounding timesteps. Each encoding layer consists of MiLSTM and βLSTM. The specific details of each layer and the reasons for this approach will be elaborated on later.

The decoder is simply composed of MiLSTM Cells and channel mixing networks. To precisely utilize the periodic information in the time series, we performed a Fast Fourier Transform (FFT) on the training set and identified the frequency component ν with the largest amplitude. The corresponding period for frequency ν is $\lambda = S/\nu$, where S is the length of the training set. Suppose the sample series is $X \in \mathbb{R}^{(L+T) \times C}$, where L is the look-back length, and T is the predict length, the input tensors for MiLSTM decoding cell at time $t \in [L, L+T)$ are

$$[h_{t-1}, h_{t-k_1*\lambda}, h_{t-k_2*\lambda}, \cdots, h_{t-k_n*\lambda}],$$

$$[c_{t-1}, c_{t-k_1*\lambda}, c_{t-k_2*\lambda}, \cdots, c_{t-k_n*\lambda}],$$

and x_t. Here $n, k_i \in \mathbb{N}^*, \lambda < L, n < \frac{L}{\lambda}$ and $0 \leq t - k_i * \lambda < L$.

3.2   Multi-input LSTM Cell

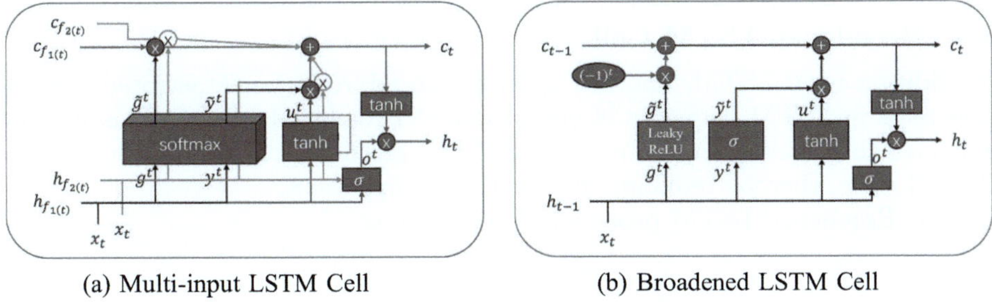

(a) Multi-input LSTM Cell   (b) Broadened LSTM Cell

Fig. 2. The Proposed Two Variants of LSTM Architecture.

In order to address LSTM's "catastrophic forgetting" issue, we propose the Multi-input LSTM which can receive information from multiple time points. With MiLSTM Cell, the model can periodically retrieve memories from certain time points. In the LCWP mission, we believe that the optimal time point to retrieve memory is the corresponding time point in other periods of the previous time sequence.

The complete process of the MiLSTM Cell is presented in Fig. 2a.

The process is formalized as:

$$
\begin{aligned}
g_i^t &= W_i^g[h_{f_i(t)}, x_t], \\
y_i^t &= W_i^y[h_{f_i(t)}, x_t], \\
u_i^t &= \tanh(W_i^u[h_{f_i(t)}, x_t]), \\
o_t &= \mathrm{sigmoid}(W_o[h_{f_1(t)}, h_{f_2(t)}, \cdots, h_{f_n(t)}, x_t]).
\end{aligned}
\tag{1}
$$

$$
\begin{aligned}
\tilde{g}_i^t &= \mathrm{softmax}(g_1^t, g_2^t, \ldots, g_n^t, y_1^t, y_2^t, \ldots, y_n^t)_i, \\
\tilde{y}_i^t &= \mathrm{softmax}(g_1^t, g_2^t, \ldots, g_n^t, y_1^t, y_2^t, \ldots, y_n^t)_i.
\end{aligned}
\tag{2}
$$

$$
\begin{aligned}
c_t &= \sum_{i=1}^{n} \tilde{g}_i^t \cdot c_{f_i(t)} + \sum_{i=1}^{n} \tilde{y}_i^t \cdot u_i^t, \\
h_t &= o_t \cdot \tanh(c_t).
\end{aligned}
\tag{3}
$$

Equation 1 shows the output of four gates of MiLSTM (before softmax function). g_i^t is the output of "forget gate" at time t with the ith input. y_i^t is the output of "update gate". u_i^t is the new candidate values. And o_t is the output of "output gate".

By far, the MiLSTM is equal to n individual LSTM cells. In order to integrate the memories of LSTM from different time steps, we use softmax function to dynamically allocate different weights to the multiple values. As shown in Eqs. 2 and 3, the g and y from all n inputs are activated by softmax, instead of sigmoid.

From another perspective, this achieves a weighted summation of information from the past n moments and the current moment. The output gate is a simple linear layer, which plays the same role as the one in conventional LSTM.

3.3 Broadened LSTM Cell

In addition to MiLSTM, another approach to address the catastrophic forgetting issue in LSTM networks is our proposed Broadened LSTM. This method enhances the memory capabilities of LSTM by gradually expanding the range of the cell state, thereby reducing information compression.

The Broadened LSTM process is formalized as:

$$
\begin{aligned}
g_t &= W_g[h_{t-1}, x_t], \\
y_t &= W_y[h_{t-1}, x_t], \\
u_t &= \tanh(W_u[h_{t-1}, x_t]), \\
o_t &= \text{sigmoid}(W_o[h_{t-1}, x_t]).
\end{aligned}
\tag{4}
$$

$$
\begin{aligned}
\tilde{g}_t &= \text{LeakyReLU}(g_t), \\
\tilde{y}_t &= \text{sigmoid}(y_t).
\end{aligned}
\tag{5}
$$

$$
\begin{aligned}
c_t &= (-1)^t \tilde{g}_t + c_{t-1} + \tilde{y}_t \cdot u_t, \\
h_t &= o_t \cdot \tanh(c_t).
\end{aligned}
\tag{6}
$$

We substitute the forget gate in conventional LSTM with the "broaden gate", which is illustrated in Fig. 2b. The introduction of the alternating sign factor $(-1)^t$ in Eq. 6 allows for a more dynamic adjustment of the cell state, potentially enhancing the model's ability to capture patterns in data.

The application of LeakyReLU in place of sigmoid function addresses the gradient vanishing problem more effectively, allowing the model to maintain a stronger gradient flow during training. Consequently, the broaden gate provides cell state c with a range that increases with the sequence length, which enhances its representation capabilities.

3.4 MUPA Encoders

In order to strengthen the connection between encoder and decoder, the h and c outputs of the encoder are both used in the decoder cells. So we utilized the MiLSTM to fuse the h and c of the bidirectional βLSTM at the same time. Furthermore, we also utilized a separate encoding layer for positional encoding to enhance our model's capability to perceive the current input timestep, which is very important for RNN-like models. The positional encoding strengthened by encoding layer can also be fused by the MiLSTM cell. As illustrated in Fig. 3, all the colored arrows represent h and c dataflow. pe_t means positional encoding generated by a single encoding layer.

The global encoding layer has a similar structure with local encoding layer, but only the outputs of the last time step is utilized. This dual-layer approach ensures a thorough analysis of the time series data, capturing both macro and micro temporal dynamics.

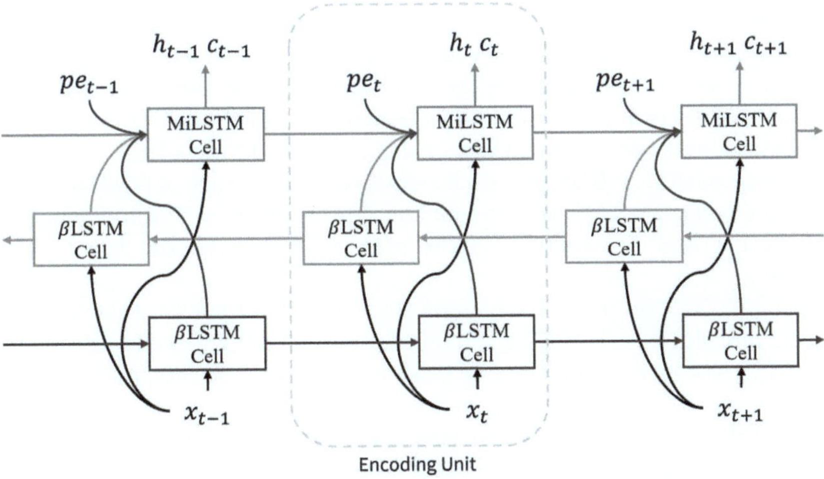

Fig. 3. The Structure of MUPA Encoding Layers

3.5   MUPA Decoder

The decoder consists of a MiLSTM layer and a channel mixing network. The structure of decoding layer is illustrated in Fig. 1 and Sect. 3.1

Lots of recent models utilize fully connected networks with transposed time sequence as their decoders, which means the shape of the parameters is $W \in \mathbb{R}^{L \times T}$. That makes the amount of parameters grow with predict length. However, our RNN-like model does not have such issue. We can flexibly choose the prediction length to avoid unnecessary predictions. It also makes training with data that possess different lengths possible.

4   Experiments

To verify the effectiveness of MUPA, we conducted a series of experiments and comparisons with other mainstream methods in the field of sequence prediction. The results demonstrate the superior performance of our models.

Firstly, we compared our model with existing state-of-the-art methods for sequence prediction. We evaluated the performance of MUPA on public real-world datasets and achieved remarkable results.

Furthermore, we conducted ablation experiments for our key contributions and validated the effectiveness of our proposed model.

4.1   Experiment Setup

Datasets. To validate the proposed model, we choose some of the subsets of 4 public real-world datasets, including:

- Alibaba Cluster Data v2018[1]. This data set documents multivariate workload metrics from 148 machines over an 8-day period, with each machine hosting a distinct set of microservices. In our work, we use the "cpu util percent" feature with a 10-minute interval in machine 1 and 2 subsets.
- Fisher[2]. Comprises workload data collected over 30 days from 10 containers operating within a Kubernetes framework, where each container runs isolated microservices. We use the "load" feature with a 10-minute interval in container 1 and 2 subsets, and the anomaly values in the last 2 days are discarded.
- NASA-HTTP[3]. As part of standard cloud workload traces, this dataset contains 2 months' worth of HTTP requests to the NASA Kennedy Space Center WWW server in Florida, USA. We calculated access counts with a 10-minute interval.
- Azure VM Trace[4]. The trace contains a representative subset of the first-party Azure VM workload in one geographical region. We use the "cpu utilization" feature with a 10-minute interval.

Baselines. The baseline models selected for comparison include a variety of established approaches in time series forecasting. These methods fall primarily into four categories:

- CNN-based models, such as **TimesNet** [12] and **MICN** [9];
- MLP-based models, such as **LightTS** [14] and **DLinear** [13];
- Transformer-based models including **PatchTST** [6], **ETSformer** [11];
- RNN-based models, such as **LSTM** [4] and **GRU** [1].

The batch size, look-back length and forecast horizons are set to the same as those of MUPA for fair comparison. Other hyperparameters of the baselines follow the settings in TSLib [10].

4.2   Forecasting Results

To thoroughly evaluate the performance of our proposed MUPA model, we conducted extensive comparison experiments against several state-of-the-art models on multiple datasets. The average results are shown in Table 1 and are summarized as follows.

We first compared our MUPA with the conventional LSTM model. The experimental results across seven diverse datasets revealed that our MUPA demonstrates a significant performance advantage over the conventional LSTM. This substantial enhancement can be attributed to the innovative modifications we

---

[1] https://github.com/alibaba/clusterdata.
[2] https://github.com/chrisliu1995/Fisher-model.
[3] https://ita.ee.lbl.gov/html/contrib/NASA-HTTP.html.
[4] https://github.com/Azure/AzurePublicDataset.

Table 1. Results of prediction on real-world datasets. We compare extensive competitive models under different forecast horizons. The look-back length is set to 24 hours. The results are averaged from four prediction lengths:{2h, 4h, 6h, 8h}. The best results are in **bold** and the second best results are underlined.

Datasets		Alibaba Cluster				Fisher				NASA-HTTP				Azure	
Subsets		machine 1		machine 2		container 1		container 2		July		August			
Models\Metrics		MSE	MAE	MSE	MAE	MSE	MAE	MSE	MAE	MSE	MAE	MSE	MAE	MSE	MAE
MLPs	DLinear [13]	0.614	0.607	0.832	0.743	0.189	0.319	0.114	0.252	0.303	0.435	0.663	0.615	**0.942**	0.645
	LightTS [14]	0.653	0.631	0.883	0.749	0.200	0.328	0.116	0.255	0.184	0.329	0.444	0.501	1.159	0.751
CNNs	TimesNet [12]	0.767	0.692	1.012	0.788	0.216	0.328	0.131	0.266	0.206	0.337	0.392	0.469	0.953	<u>0.638</u>
	MICN [9]	0.588	0.599	0.837	0.747	<u>0.185</u>	<u>0.303</u>	<u>0.108</u>	<u>0.238</u>	0.230	0.341	0.454	0.495	0.976	0.648
Trans.	ETSFormer [11]	0.612	0.619	1.006	0.803	0.233	0.361	0.158	0.306	0.252	0.388	0.411	0.484	1.012	0.700
	PatchTST [6]	<u>0.421</u>	<u>0.508</u>	<u>0.742</u>	<u>0.660</u>	0.217	0.337	0.116	0.255	<u>0.164</u>	<u>0.301</u>	**0.324**	**0.422**	0.979	0.660
RNNs	LSTM [4]	0.812	0.688	0.931	0.775	0.295	0.451	0.201	0.378	0.524	0.627	1.315	0.827	0.945	0.641
	GRU [1]	0.894	0.718	0.876	0.729	0.298	0.455	0.210	0.389	0.478	0.588	1.196	0.793	0.946	0.640
	MUPA(Ours)	**0.351**	**0.459**	**0.686**	**0.639**	**0.177**	**0.303**	**0.094**	**0.222**	**0.154**	**0.288**	<u>0.329</u>	<u>0.423</u>	<u>0.943</u>	**0.631**

introduced in the MUPA architecture, which effectively address some of the limitations of traditional LSTM in capturing complex temporal dependencies and patterns.

In addition to the comparison with conventional LSTM, we also benchmarked our MUPA against well-known Transformer-based models, particularly the PatchTST. The results indicated that our MUPA achieved lower MSE and MAE values than PatchTST in six of seven subsets, highlighting its effectiveness in sequence modeling tasks.

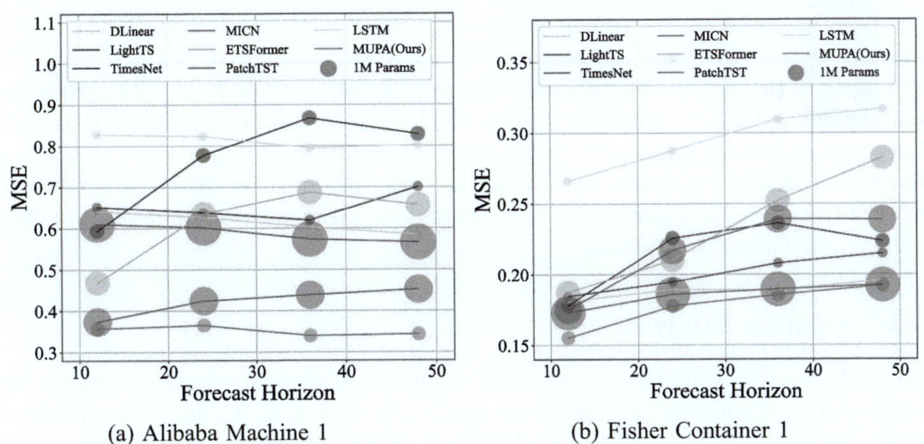

(a) Alibaba Machine 1   (b) Fisher Container 1

Fig. 4. Comparison of predict results and params. The size of the dot represents the amount of parameters.

Comparative experiments across two data subsets demonstrate that our model achieves breakthrough improvements in forecasting accuracy while

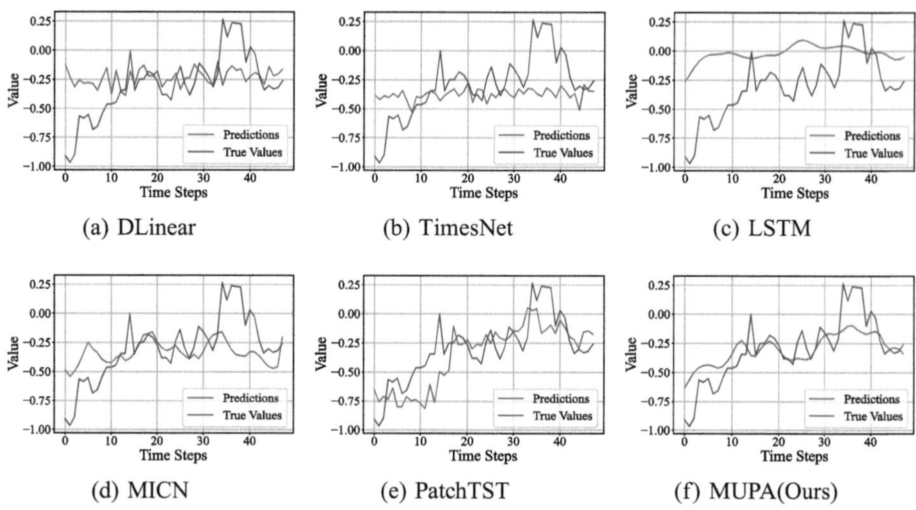

(a) DLinear　　　　　(b) TimesNet　　　　　(c) LSTM

(d) MICN　　　　　(e) PatchTST　　　　　(f) MUPA(Ours)

Fig. 5. Visualization of predict results on Fisher Container 1 subset.

significantly reducing parameterization. Visual analysis shown in Fig. 4 confirms this dual advantage: at multiple horizons, our model attains the lowest MSE values while exhibiting lower parameter amounts than runner-up models. The results empirically validate our architecture's outstanding efficiency.

In addition, we visualized the prediction produced by MUPA and several baselines. Figure 5 shows that DLinear, TimesNet, and LSTM, only capture very short-period oscillations; longer cycles are almost entirely missed, so their predictions merely fluctuate slightly around a certain value. MICN and PatchTST attempts to predict the long-term trend, yet its trend estimate is both erroneous and lagged. MUPA successfully models the long-term trend and some short-term fluctuations but struggles with ultra-short noise and bursty patterns, which is a limitation shared by nearly all current models and an open direction for future work. Overall, both quantitative metrics and visual inspection demonstrate that MUPA outperforms baselines.

4.3 Ablation Study

To evaluate the contribution of each component of our proposed model, we conducted a comprehensive ablation study. As shown in Table 2, the ablation study includes our proposed MiLSTM Cell, βLSTM Cell and the MUPA model structures,

In the ablation study for MiLSTM cell, we only used conventional LSTM layer as the decoding layer. Results on the Alibaba dataset exhibited a significant performance decline, demonstrating that the cross-period design is essential for capturing periodic features effectively. Conversely, a slight performance increase observed on the Fisher dataset indicates this design involves a trade-off when

Table 2. Ablation Study Results

Models	MUPA		Cells			Model Structure			
		w/o MiLSTM Cell		w/o βLSTM Cell		w/o Pos Encoder		w/o Fuse LSTM	
Metrics	MSE MAE	MSE	MAE	MSE	MAE	MSE	MAE	MSE	MAE
Alibaba	0.519 0.550	0.539	0.559	0.619	0.611	0.520	0.551	0.547	0.575
Fisher	0.136 0.263	0.128	0.255	0.136	0.260	0.154	0.280	0.149	0.273
NASA	0.242 0.356	0.243	0.359	0.273	0.376	0.240	0.355	0.255	0.364
Azure	0.943 0.631	0.944	0.640	0.946	0.637	0.943	0.629	0.945	0.629
Average	0.460 0.450	0.464	0.453	0.493	0.471	0.464	0.454	0.474	0.460

periodicity is weak. Crucially, the overall performance decrease across datasets underscores the effectiveness of the proposed MiLSTM method.

Furthermore, the ablation study replacing the βLSTM cell with a conventional LSTM layer in the encoders revealed critical insights. Consistently across all experimental datasets, this substitution resulted in a discernible performance decline. This widespread degradation demonstrates that the broadened memory mechanism of βLSTM significantly and robustly enhances the long-term memory capability of the standard LSTM architecture, enabling more effective learning of complex temporal dependencies.

Finally, we removed some model structures to evaluate the effectiveness of these modules. Removing either the Positional Encoder or the Fuse MiLSTMs in Encoding Layers led to a performance decline, suggesting that these modules play a crucial role for our model structure.

5   Conclusion

In this paper, we presented a novel approach to long-term cloud workload prediction through the development of the Multi-period Augmented LSTM(MUPA) model. The encoder-decoder structure, featuring optimized LSTM layers, effectively captures both macro and micro temporal patterns, thereby enhancing predictive performance.

The MUPA consists of two LSTM variants: Multi-input LSTM and Broadened LSTM. Our Multi-input LSTM cell enhances traditional LSTM capabilities by integrating inputs from multiple time points, allowing for a more nuanced understanding of temporal dependencies. The use of a softmax activation function further improves information integration and the model's ability to capture complex dynamics. Our Broadened LSTM improves the capability of LSTM by expanding the range of cell states.

Extensive experiments conducted on real-world cloud workload datasets consistently demonstrate that MUPA significantly outperforms relevant baselines in long-term prediction tasks. These superior experimental results validate the effectiveness of the proposed architectural innovations within MUPA for achieving higher predictive accuracy and efficiency.

References

1. Chung, J., Gulcehre, C., Cho, K., Bengio, Y.: Empirical evaluation of gated recurrent neural networks on sequence modeling. arXiv preprint: arXiv:1412.3555 (2014)
2. Drucker, H., Burges, C.J.C., Kaufman, L., Smola, A.J., Vapnik, V.: Support vector regression machines. In: Advances in Neural Information Processing Systems, vol. 9, pp. 155–161 (1997)
3. Elman, J.L.: Finding structure in time. Cogn. Sci. **14**(2), 179–211 (1990)
4. Hochreiter, S., Schmidhuber, J.: Long short-term memory. Neural Comput. **9**(8), 1735–1780 (1997)
5. Kim, T., Kim, J., Tae, Y., Park, C., Choi, J.H., Choo, J.: Reversible instance normalization for accurate time-series forecasting against distribution shift. In: ICLR (2022)
6. Nie, Y., Nguyen, N.H., Sinthong, P., Kalagnanam, J.: A time series is worth 64 words: long-term forecasting with transformers. In: The Eleventh International Conference on Learning Representations (2023)
7. Shi, X., Chen, Z., Wang, H., Yeung, D.Y., Wong, W.K., Woo, W.C.: Convolutional LSTM network: a machine learning approach for precipitation nowcasting. In: Advances in Neural Information Processing Systems, vol. 28, pp. 802–810 (2015)
8. Vaswani, A., et al.: Attention is all you need. In: Advances in Neural Information Processing Systems, vol. 30 (2017)
9. Wang, H., Peng, J., Huang, F., Wang, J., Chen, J., Xiao, Y.: MICN: multi-scale local and global context modeling for long-term series forecasting. In: The Eleventh International Conference on Learning Representations (2023)
10. Wang, Y., Wu, H., Dong, J., Liu, Y., Long, M., Wang, J.: Deep time series models: a comprehensive survey and benchmark. arXiv preprint: arXiv:2407.13278 (2024)
11. Woo, G., Liu, C., Sahoo, D., Kumar, A., Hoi, S.: ETSformer: exponential smoothing transformers for time-series forecasting. arXiv preprint: arXiv:2202.01381 (2022)
12. Wu, H., Hu, T., Liu, Y., Zhou, H., Wang, J., Long, M.: TimesNet: temporal 2D-variation modeling for general time series analysis. In: The Eleventh International Conference on Learning Representations (2023)
13. Zeng, A., Chen, M., Zhang, L., Xu, Q.: Are transformers effective for time series forecasting? In: AAAI (2023)
14. Zhang, T., et al.: Less is more: fast multivariate time series forecasting with light sampling-oriented MLP structures. arXiv preprint: arXiv:2207.01186 (2022)

In-Orbit Container Registry Planning for Fast Image Downloading in LEO Satellite Constellation

Lifeng Tian[1], Yuepeng Li[1], Deze Zeng[1(✉)], Lin Gu[2], Chengyu Hu[1], and Liang Zhong[3]

[1] School of Computer Science, China University of Geosciences, Wuhan, China
`deze@cug.edu.cn`
[2] School of Computer Science and Technology, Huazhong University of Science and Technology, Wuhan, China
[3] School of Mechanical Engineering and Electronic Information, China University of Geosciences, Wuhan, China

Abstract. In-orbit computing in Low Earth Orbit (LEO) satellite constellations represents a significant advancement in enhancing the efficiency of satellite data processing. Container-based cloud-native solutions are increasingly applied to enhance the elasticity of in-orbit computing. Albeit with high potential, its performance is significantly constrained by the container image downloading delay via satellite-ground links. Therefore, in-orbit container registry is required so as to reduce expensive image downloading overhead. However, due to the motion of LEO satellites, the network topology changes dynamically, leading to fluctuation in the Inter-Satellite Link (ISL) connectivity and communication rates. This imposes significant challenges to in-orbit container registry planning. Additionally, the planning must also account for the limited on-satellite storage and request popularity. To this end, we investigate the problem of in-orbit container registry planning for overall downloading time minimization. The problem is formulated into an ILP form and proved to be NP-hard. We further propose the In-orbit Registry Planning algorithm based on Randomized Rounding (RR-IRP). The experimental results demonstrate the effectiveness of our RR-IRP algorithm, which averagely reduces container image download time by 22.71% compared to classic solutions.

Keywords: In-orbit computing · Container registry planning · LEO satellite constellation

1 Introduction

In recent years, alongside the increase in the number and performance of Low Earth Orbit (LEO) satellite, the production of satellite data is also rising. However, the actual interesting or valuable data constitutes only a small portion of

X. Wang et al. (Eds.): NPC 2025, LNCS 16306, pp. 113–125, 2026.
https://doi.org/10.1007/978-3-032-10466-3_10

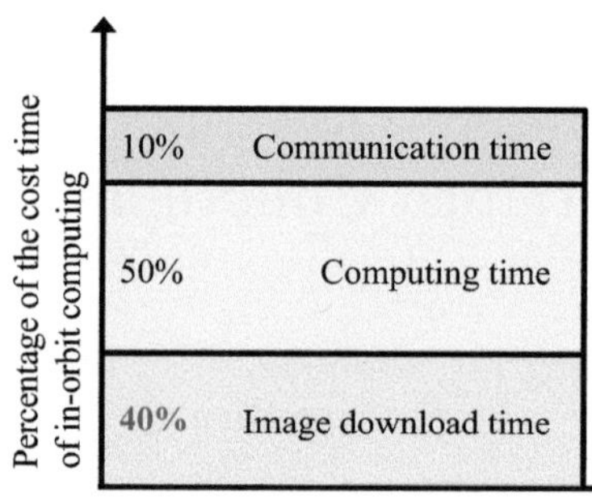

Fig. 1. The time proportion of each stage in the in-orbit computing process

the collected data, and the volume of generated data may saturate the satellites downlinks. Inspired by Mobile Edge Computing (MEC), a feasible solution is to employ advanced in-orbit computing by utilizing the high-performance processors of satellites to process the data directly [10], rather than transmitting vast amount of raw data to the ground. This approach can help alleviate severe data transmission delay caused by the limited communication rate between LEO satellites and ground. Unfortunately, traditional satellite in-orbit computing components are typically designed for single-purpose tasks and are limited to handling pre-specified tasks, making them incapable of processing increasingly diverse and complex computational tasks. To promote the in-orbit computing flexibility, cloud-native computing concept is widely advocated, as it allows the deployment of containerized services on satellites in an on-demand manner.

To process various types of in-orbit computing tasks, the corresponding container images must be downloaded to the satellites from image registries deployed on the ground station. For instance, we simulate an in-orbit computing task on an LEO satellite within the OneWeb constellation[12]. As illustrated in Fig. 1, we find that the time of downloading a 200 MB container image from the ground registries accounts for 40% of the lifespan of the computing task. This is because the low communication rate of satellite-to-ground link (about 100-200 Mbps) less than 2% of the Inter-Satellite Link (ISL) capacity (about 100 Gbps). Additionally, the overpass time, which satellite can maintain communication link with ground while in orbit, is too short (about 10–15 min), resulting in a short container image transmission window within the communication range of a ground station. This greatly reduces the flexibility of containerized tasks, and even further increases the time required for image downloads. A viable approach is to deploy distributed image registries in constellation to instead the ground-based registries. The in-orbit image registries deployed can effectively reduce the transmission distance between the registries and the satellites. Besides, the high-speed data transmission rate of ISL can further reduce the image download time.

However, unlike the nearly stationary topology of terrestrial networks, the frequent and rapid changes in the constellation network topology impose new challenges to in-orbit registry planning. On one hand, as the constellation network topology undergoes dynamic changes, ISL experiences fluctuations in both connectivity and communication rates. Meanwhile, different container images are with different request popularity. Hence, the container in-orbit registry planning shall take these issues into consideration to realize efficient container image downloading. On the other hand, due to constraints of satellite's payload, the storage capacity is severely limited. It is evidently impractical to store all necessary images within in-orbit registries, which further increases the complexity of in-orbit registry planning.

To address the aforementioned challenges, we investigate an in-orbit registry planning problem where a set of container images with different request rates (or popularity) need to be stored on distributed on-satellite registries so as to minimize the overall image downloading time. We comprehensively consider the following issues: (1) how to rationally schedule the storage locations of each container image, (2) how to determine the appropriate repository to download container images on each satellite. By answering the above two questions, we mainly make the following contributions as:

- We investigate the in-orbit registry planning problem in distributed registries within LEO satellite constellations, considering image downloading time. We formulate the problem into an Integer Linear Programming (ILP) form and prove it as NP-hard.
- To tackle this problem, we further propose an In-orbit Registry Planning algorithm based on Randomized Rounding (RR-IRP), which can achieve suboptimal solution in polynomial-time.
- We also conduct extensive trace-driven experiments, and evaluation results show that our method reduces image download time by an average of approximately 22.71% in comparison with other state-of-art registry planning algorithms.

The remaining of this paper is organized as follows. Section 2 introduces some related work. Then, we describe the system model and problem statement in Sect. 3 and detail our proposed RR-IRP algorithm in Sect. 4. Section 5 reports the experiment results. Finally, Sect. 6 summarizes our work.

2   Related Work

In-orbit computing has emerged as a promising paradigm in satellite constellations, where LEO satellites collaboratively form an MEC infrastructure to support computational tasks. Many researchers have explored various approaches to task offloading optimization. For example, Chen et al. [2] explore the management of the dynamic topology of LEO satellite networks, they propose a network topology prediction method to enhance system management and address inherent complexities. Zhao et al. [17] propose a street-based content distribution model that utilizes satellite caching to improve content distribution efficiency and reduce service latency. Xi et al. [14] minimize system energy consumption by optimizing user association, power control, task scheduling, and computing resource allocation when offloading user device computing tasks in a multi-satellite supported edge computing system. However, they prove the necessity and significance of in-orbit computing empowered by containers but they all omit an important fact that container image downloading is time consuming. The latter is highly influenced by the container registry planning.

Meanwhile, numerous studies have investigated image storage planning optimization in terrestrial to enhance MEC performance. Fan et al. [5] conduct research on improving container storage and deployment. They introduced Gear, a new image format that enhances container operations by enabling more efficient storage and deployment of containers. Zhu et al. [18] explore collaborative strategies for efficient task execution in distributed systems. Smet et al. [11] conduct research on Docker layer placement in the context of edge computing. However, these storage planning studies for terrestrial are ill-suited to address the challenges posed by dynamic network topologies in in-orbit computing, where satellite orbital motion leads to unstable communication rates and connectivity.

3   System Model and Problem Formulation

3.1   System Model

We consider an LEO satellite constellation system that orbits the earth periodically with a fixed duration [13]. Following the existing studies [4], we divide this duration into a set $t \in \mathbb{T}$ of equal-length time slots, and assume that the satellite network topology remains relatively stable in each time slot [15]. In general, the LEO satellite constellation network topology in time slot t can be described as a graph $\mathbb{G}(t) = \{\mathbb{V}, \mathbb{E}(t)\}$, where the vertex set $\mathbb{V}$ denotes the satellites in this system. We assume that the satellites in this system are categorized into two groups, i.e., the registry satellites and computing satellites, which are denoted as $\mathbb{R}$ and $\mathbb{N}$, respectively. The edge set $\mathbb{E}(t)$ represents the network connection state in time slot t. That is, for a $e_{n,r}(t) \in \mathbb{E}(t)$, it indicates whether registry satellite r is connected with computing satellite n (i.e., $e_{n,r}(t) = 1$), or not (i.e., $e_{n,r}(t) = 0$) in time slot t. The transmission rate between registry satellite r and computing satellite n in time slot t is denoted as $C_{n,r}(t)$.

For each registry satellite $r \in \mathbb{R}$, let S_r denote the image storage capacity. In addition, the computing satellites may request for downloading container images in each time slot $t \in \mathbb{T}$. Here, for a computing satellite $n \in \mathbb{N}$, we use $Pr_{n,i}(t)$ to represent the probability of downloading image i in time slot t. Note that, compared with traditional registries deployed on the ground, the registries on satellites are with severely limited storage resources, and may not store all container images. Hence, if a computing satellite n can not download the image from the satellite registry, the image must be downloaded from the ground registry with the transmission rate of $C_{n,g}(t)$.

3.2   Problem Formulation

Container Image Storing Throughout the duration $\mathbb{T}$, the registry satellites $\mathbb{R}$ are responsible for storing container images. Due to the limited storage capacity, a registry satellite $r \in \mathbb{R}$ can only store a number of images without exceeding its storage capacity S_r. We use binary variables $x_r^i \in \{0,1\}$ to indicate whether image i is stored in registry r (i.e., $x_r^i = 1$) or not (i.e., $x_r^i = 0$). The following constraints should be satisfied

$$\sum_{i \in \mathbf{I}} x_r^i S_i \leq S_r, \forall r \in \mathbb{R}. \tag{1}$$

Image Downloading. Since the network topology graph $\mathbb{G}(t)$ dynamically changes with each time slot t, the connectivity $e_{n,r}(t)$ and communication rate $C_{n,r}(t)$ between satellite n and registry r also vary over t. Therefore, the images i required by n may need to be downloaded from different registries or the ground in each time slot $t \in \mathbb{T}$. Here, we introduce binary variables $y_{nr}^i(t)$ to indicate whether satellite n needs to download image i from registry r (i.e., $y_{n,r}^i(t) = 1$), or not (i.e., $y_{n,r}^i(t) = 0$) in time slot t. Note that, the required image can only be downloaded from one place in each time slot t, and hence the binary variables $y_{n,r}^i(t)$ should satisfy the following constraint

$$\sum_{r \in \mathbb{R}} y_{n,r}^i(t) \leq 1, \forall i \in \mathbb{I}, n \in \mathbb{N}, t \in \mathbb{T}. \tag{2}$$

For any computing satellite $n \in \mathbb{N}$, it can download the required image i from registry r only when image i is stored in registry r. Hence the binary variables $y_{n,r}^i(t)$ and x_r^i should satisfy

$$y_{n,r}^i(t) \leq x_r^i, \forall i \in \mathbb{I}, r \in \mathbb{R}, n \in \mathbb{N}, t \in \mathbb{T}. \tag{3}$$

In addition, since the network topology $\mathbb{G}(t)$ dynamic changes of the satellite constellation, only when the network link between computing satellite n and registry r is connected in time slot t (i.e., $e_{n,r}(t) = 1$), the image i stored in registry r can be downloaded. That is,

$$y_{n,r}^i(t) \leq e_{n,r}(t), \forall i \in \mathbb{I}, r \in \mathbb{R}, n \in \mathbb{N}, t \in \mathbb{T}. \tag{4}$$

As aforementioned, the network topology graph $\mathbb{G}(t)$ dynamically changes, resulting in varying transmission rates across each time slot t. Each satellite $n \in \mathbb{N}$ can download images from registries or ground stations at different communication rates. Therefore, if satellite n chooses to download the image i from registry r in time slot t, the corresponding time consumption $T_{n,i,r}(t)$ is

$$T_{n,i,r}(t) = \frac{S_i}{C_{n,r}(t)}. \tag{5}$$

Conversely, if the required image i is downloaded from the ground, the corresponding downloading time is

$$T_{n,i,g}(t) = \frac{S_i}{C_{n,g}(t)}.\tag{6}$$

Hence, with Eq. (5) and (6), the overhead of satellite n downloading required image i in time slot t can be calculated as follows

$$T_{n,i}(t) = \sum_{r \in \mathbb{R}} y_{n,r}^i(t) T_{n,i,r}(t) + (1 - \sum_{r \in \mathbb{R}} y_{n,r}^i(t)) T_{n,i,g}(t),\tag{7}$$

and the total image downloading time in time slot t is

$$T(t) = \sum_{n \in \mathbb{N}} \sum_{i \in \mathbb{I}} Pr_{n,i}(t) T_{n,i}(t).\tag{8}$$

Our objective is to minimize the overall image downloading time of all satellites in the duration $\mathbb{T}$. By putting all the above together, we can formulate the in-orbit registry planning problem in ILP form as

$$\min \sum_{t \in \mathbb{T}} T(t)\tag{9}$$

$$\text{s.t.:} (1), (2), (3), (4).$$

4   Algorithm

4.1   NP-Hard Analysis

Theorem 1. *The in-orbit registry planning problem on overall downloading time minimization is NP-hard.*

Proof. Consider a special case, in time slot t, there exist multiple distributed registries $r \in \mathbb{R}$, each with sufficient storage capacity S_r. Each registry stores all container images required for the in-orbit computing tasks. Consequently, downloading images from the ground registry can be ignored in this scenario. In this case, any image i requested by computing satellite s during time slot t can be fulfilled by any registry r. Notably, a fixed network topology ensures stable channel capacity between satellite s and registry r. Hence, we only need to select an appropriate registry $r \in \mathbb{R}$ during time slot t. In this case, the in-orbit registry planning problem in Eq. (9) can be re-formulated as follows:

$$\min \sum_{r \in \mathbb{R}} \sum_{n \in \mathbb{N}} \sum_{i \in \mathbb{I}} T_{n,i,r}(t),\tag{10}$$

where $T_{n,i,r}(t)$ represents the download time of image i, which can be calculated as $T_{n,i,r}(t) = \frac{S_i}{C_{n,r}(t)}$. The transformation problem in Eq. (10) is a classic knapsack problem, where each image i can be considered a candidate item to be placed into a knapsack with capacity S_r. This is a typical knapsack problem, which has been proven to be NP-hard. Hence, the general case of in-orbit registry planning problem in Eq. (9), is also NP-hard.

Algorithm 1:. Randomized Rounding-based In-orbit Registry Planning

---

Input: $\mathbb{N}$, $\mathbb{R}$, $\mathbb{T}$, $\mathbb{I}$, $e_{n,r}(t)$, S_r, $E_r(t)$, $Pr_{n,r}(t)$, $C_{n,r}(t)$, $R_{n,g}(t)$, x_r^i, $y_{n,r}^i(t)$
Output: x_f^w, $y_{n,r}^i(t)$

1 Relax binary variable in MD-ILP and solve the relaxed problem to to obtain the real optimal solution$\widehat{x_r^i}$, where $\{\widehat{x_r^i} \in [0,1], r \in \mathbb{R}, i \in \mathbb{I}\}$.

2 **repeat**

3   **for** $r \in \mathbb{R}$ *and* $i \in \mathbb{I}$ **do**

4   Set $x_r^i \leftarrow 1$ with probability $\widehat{x_r^i}$, otherwise, set $x_f^w \leftarrow 0$.

5   **end**

6   **if** $x_r^i = 1$ **then**

7   **for** $n \in \mathbb{N}$, $r \in \mathbb{R}$, $t \in \mathbb{T}$ *and* $i \in \mathbb{I}$ **do**

8   Set $y_{n,r}^i(t) \leftarrow 1$ with probability $\widehat{y}_{n,r}^i(t)$;

9   **end**

10   **else**

11   Set $y_{n,r}^i(t) \leftarrow 0$.

12   **end**

13   **end**

14 **until** $(x_r^i, y_{n,r}^i(t))$ *defines a feasible solution without constraint violation;*

4.2 RR-IRP Algorithm

Due to the NP-hardness, it is computationally infeasible to obtain the optimal solution in polynomial time. Consequently, we propose a randomized rounding-based approximation algorithm, RR-IRP, to find a sub-optimal solution within polynomial time complexity, which summarized in Algorithm 1.

We relax this problem from ILP into a Linear Programming (LP) form, which can be solved in a polynomial time. By relaxing the binary variables x_r^i in in-orbit registry planning problem to the real variables in $[0,1]$, we can obtain the real solutions as $\widehat{x_r^i}, r \in \mathbb{R}, i \in \mathbb{I}$. In the randomized rounding based algorithm, the relaxed real solutions can be regarded as the probability to make binary decisions (i.e., $x_f^w, \forall w \in \mathbb{W}, f \in \mathbb{F}$). In lines 3 and 4, we set each decision variable x_r^i to 1 with the probability $\widehat{x_r^i}$, which means image i stored in registry r in constellation. Notably, only when $x_r^i = 1$ can satellite download image i from registry r. Hence, if $x_r^i = 1$, we set $y_{n,r}^i(t)$ to be 1 with probability $\widehat{y}_{n,r}^i(t)$ (i.e., line 6–7). Otherwise, $y_{n,r}^i(t)$ is set as 0. Finally, due to the randomized rounding, the solutions $(x_f^w, y_{n,r}^i(t))$ may fail to satisfy the constraints (e.g., the storage capacity constraints) in in-orbit registry planning problem. Thus, the algorithm will loop over until finding a feasible solution that satisfies the resources constraints (i.e., line 10).

The proposed RR-IRP algorithm operates in polynomial time. Specifically, solving the LP relaxation in line 1 involves $O(poly(V, M))$, complexity, where $V = RI + NRIT$ is the number of decision variables and M is the number of constraints (As shown in input parameters of Algorithm 1). The randomized rounding stage (lines 3–14) requires $O(NIRT)$ operations per iteration, plus constraint checking, and is repeated until a feasible solution is obtained. Therefore, the overall expected time complexity is $O(poly(V, M)+(NRIT+M)/p_{feas})$, where p_{feas} denotes the feasibility probability of one rounding pass.

5   Performance Evaluation

5.1   Experiment Settings

To evaluate the performance and efficiency of our RR-IRP algorithm through experiments of varying scenarios, we utilizing public traces from IRIDIUM [6], OneWeb [7] and Starlink LEO satellite constellations which consist of satellites with similar orbital trajectories. We establish a simulated constellation environment as are carried out in literature [8], and use simulation experiments to verify the performance of the proposed algorithm.

In order to reduce the complexity of our simulation experiment, we model a small-scale constellation in this paper, and simplify the number of satellites $\mathbb{N}$ and registries $\mathbb{R}$ by referring to the literatures [9]. Hence, we set the ratio of computing satellites to registry satellites as $2 : 1$, and we selected 9 satellites for the IRIDIUM, 15 for the OneWeb and 30 for the Starlink. This number choice was made because the different networking capabilities [16], while IRIDIUM with just 68 satellites, OneWeb with 648 satellites and Starlink has a larger constellation with $12,000$ satellites.

Besides comparing with the optimal solution, we also conduct comparative analyses with various state-of-the-art container image planning algorithms, as follows.

- *Capacity-aware storage strategy (CASS)*. In this strategy, the image would be allocated to stored in registries that contains the maximum idle storage capacity so as to maximizes number of different images stored on constellation [3].
- *Greedy-based storage strategy (GBSS)*. This strategy allocates images to in-orbit registries using a greedy algorithm that selects the best channel capacity for storage, without consider the ISL states changes over time slots [1].
- *Optimal solution (OPT)*. The optimal solution to the minimization problem in Eq. (10) is obtained using mathematical solver (e.g., Gurobi) as the benchmark for evaluate the algorithms performance.

5.2   The Impact of Registry Storage Capacity

The storage capacities of registries directly determines both the types of images stored and their storage locations, significantly impact the image download time of the constellation system. Hence, we first assess the image download time under different registry storage capacities. In this experiment, we gradually increase the storage capacity of registries in the constellation from 50 MB to 300 MB. The results are depicted in Fig. 2.

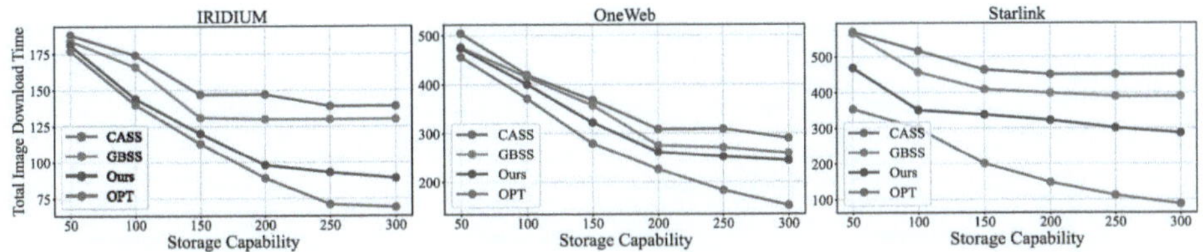

Fig. 2. Impact of different storage capacities on image download times in three different constellations

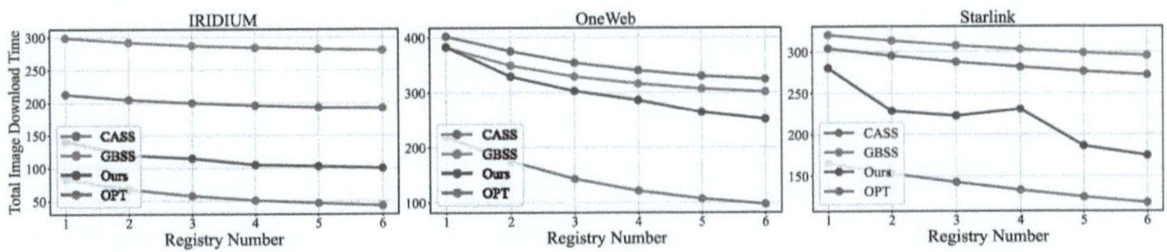

Fig. 3. Impact of different registry number on image download times in different constellations

First, it can be observed that our proposed RR-IRP algorithm outperforms all other competitors, and reduces the image download time by 23.3%, and 40.6% in comparison with *CASS* and *GBSS*, respectively. This verifies a significant performance of our proposal on storage planning in different registry storage capabilities and different constellation network topologies.

Also, as the storage capacity of registries increases, the number of images stored in the distributed image registries also grows. When computing satellites need to download requested images, they can more easily select registries with better communication rate, thereby further reducing download time. As the registry storage capacity continues increases, the effectiveness of all three strategies in reducing download time gradually diminishes. This primarily occurs because when the storage capacity is sufficiently large, the storage planning of all three algorithms ensures that the majority of high request popularity images are already stored in the registries.

5.3   The Impact of Distributed Image Registry Number

The number of distributed image registries in an LEO satellite constellation directly affects both the types of images available to computing satellites from the registries and the transmission rates over ISL. Therefore, we evaluate the effect of the registry number on download time. In this experiment, we gradually increase the registry number from 1 to 6 in three constellation while maintaining the constant number of computing satellites, and report the total download time of image required above under different registry number in Fig. 3

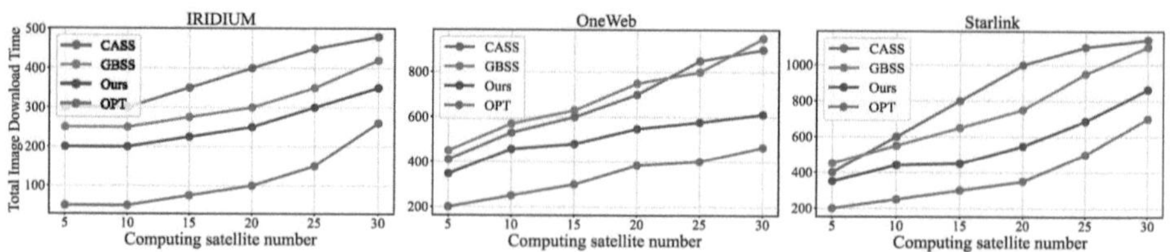

Fig. 4. Impact of different computing satellite number on image download times in different constellations

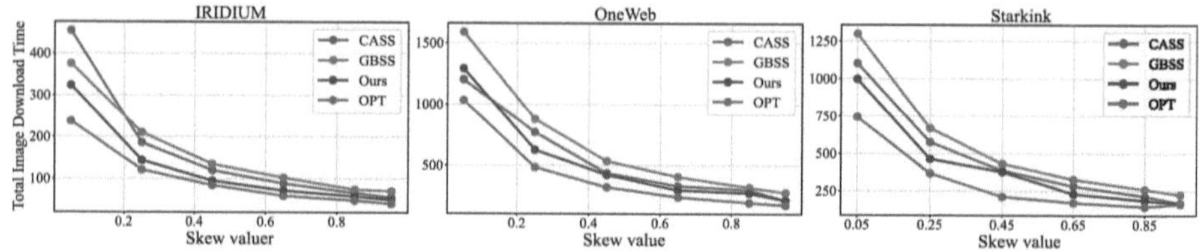

Fig. 5. Impact of different image request popularity on image download times in different constellations

Obviously, our RR-IRP algorithm achieves the highest performance in reduce image download times, and more over achieves the lowest image download time, reducing it by 31.9% and 14% compared to *CASS* and *GBSS*, respectively. Besides, there is no doubt that the download time of all three algorithms in three constellation decrease with the increase of the registries number. We attribute this phenomenon to that the greater number of registries in the constellation allows computing satellites to download more images via ISL, reducing the overall download time. Another interesting observation is that when the number of registries increases to 4 in the Starlink constellation, our RR-IRP algorithm experiences a notable increase in image download time, rising sharply from 225 to 240. This phenomenon can be attributed to the fact that our algorithm is based on randomized rounding.

5.4   The Impact of Computing Satellite Number

The number of computing satellites in the constellation directly affects the number of image requests received by the registry, which in turn has a significant impact on download time. Therefore, in this experiment, while keeping the number of registries in the constellation constant, we gradually increased the number of computing satellites from 5 to 30. The experimental results are shown in Fig. 4.

In this experiment, our RR-IRP algorithm achieved the highest performance in reducing image download times, reducing download time by 36.9% and 19.7% compared to *CASS* and *GBSS*, respectively. We observe that the download time of image download increases as the number of computer satellite increases. This can be attributed to the fact that as the number of satellites increases, the volume of image requests rises accordingly. In addition, we still notice that the total download times of the $CASS$ and $GBSS$ algorithms do not differ significantly in the IRIDIUM constellation. Because they ignore the dynamic changes in the network topology $\mathbb{G}(t)$ across different time slots t, during which $e_{n,r}(t)$ and $C_{n,r}(t)$ also vary accordingly, making it difficult for them to further reduce the image download time.

5.5   The Impact of Image Request Popularity

Finally, we evaluated the image downloading time of the three algorithm under different skew parameters. We set the probability $Pr_{n,i}(t)$ of all computing satellite image requests as following a Zipf distribution. Then, we increased the skew value from 0.05 to 0.95 while keeping other parameters of constellation unchanged. The experimental results are shown in the Fig. 5.

We also observe that the total download time for all request images download time decreases as the skew parameter increases in three constellation. This phenomenon occurs because a higher skew parameter concentrates more requests on a small number of high-popularity images, enabling targeted storage planning to reduce download time more efficiently. Besides, as the skew parameter increases from 0.45 to 0.85, the optimization of download time reduction gradually decreases. This is because the image requests from computing satellites become overly concentrated on a few images, making the storage planning for lower-popularity rates images less impactful on overall download time.

6   Conclusion

In this paper, we investigate an in-orbit registry planning problem for distributed registries within LEO satellite constellation, with the goal of minimizing the image file downloading time. In particular, registries satellites are with limited storage capacity and the ISL state changes along with the network topology in each time slot. By jointly considering these two issues, we formulate the problem as an ILP and demonstrate that it is NP-hard. We propose a Randomized Rounding-based approximation algorithm, referred to as RR-IRP, and theoretically analyze its achievable performance. Through extensive trace-driven experiments, we verify the high performance of our RR-IRP, which can effectively reduce image downloading time compared to other classic storage planning strategies.

Acknowledgments. This research was supported by the NSF of China (No. 62372200, 62432015, 62172375), Provincal Key Research and Development Program of Hubei (No. 2023BAB065), the "CUG Scholar" Scientific Research Funds at China University of Geosciences (Wuhan) (No. 2022179). Deze Zeng is the correponding author.

References

1. Chen, J.H., Kuo, W.C., Liao, W.: SpacEdge: optimizing service latency and sustainability for space-centric task offloading in LEO satellite networks. IEEE Tran. Wirel. Commun. (2024)
2. Chen, Y., et al.: A GCN-GRU based end-to-end LEO satellite network dynamic topology prediction method. In: 2023 IEEE Wireless Communications and Networking Conference, pp. 1–6. IEEE (2023)
3. Cheng, G., Guo, D., Luo, L., Xia, J., Gu, S.: LOFS: a lightweight online file storage strategy for effective data deduplication at network edge. IEEE Trans. Parallel Distrib. Syst. **33**(10), 2263–2276 (2021)
4. Chu, X., Chen, Y.: Time division inter-satellite link topology generation problem: Modeling and solution. Int. J. Satell. Commun. Network. **36**(2), 194–206 (2018)
5. Fan, H., Bian, S., Wu, S., Jiang, S., Ibrahim, S., Jin, H.: Gear: Enable efficient container storage and deployment with a new image format. In: 2021 IEEE 41st International Conference on Distributed Computing Systems, pp. 115–125. IEEE (2021)
6. Fossa, C.E., Raines, R.A., Gunsch, G.H., Temple, M.A.: An overview of the iridium (r) low earth orbit (LEO) satellite system. In: Proceedings of the IEEE 1998 National Aerospace and Electronics Conference, pp. 152–159. IEEE (1998)
7. Henri, Y.: The OneWeb satellite system. In: Handbook of Small Satellites: Technology, Design, Manufacture, Applications, Economics and Regulation, pp. 1091–1100. Springer (2020)
8. Liu, W., Lai, Z., Wu, Q., Li, H., Zhang: In-orbit processing or not? Sunlight-aware task scheduling for energy-efficient space edge computing networks. In: IEEE INFOCOM 2024-IEEE Conference on Computer Communications, pp. 881–890. IEEE (2024)
9. Pfandzelter, T., Bermbach, D.: Komet: a serverless platform for low-earth orbit edge services. In: Proceedings of the 2024 ACM Symposium on Cloud Computing, pp. 866–882 (2024)
10. Rodrigues, T.K., Kato, N.: Hybrid centralized and distributed learning for MEC-equipped satellite 6G networks. IEEE J. Sel. Areas Commun. **41**(4), 1201–1211 (2023)
11. Smet, P., Dhoedt, B., Simoens, P.: Docker layer placement for on-demand provisioning of services on edge clouds. IEEE Trans. Netw. Serv. Manage. **15**(3), 1161–1174 (2018)
12. Wang, S., Li, Q.: Satellite computing: vision and challenges. IEEE Internet Things J. (2023)
13. Werner, M.: A dynamic routing concept for ATM-based satellite personal communication networks. IEEE J. Sel. Areas Commun. **15**(8), 1636–1648 (1997)
14. Xi, S., Shang, B., Zhang, H., Ma, J., Fan, P.: Energy optimization in multi-satellite-enabled edge computing systems. IEEE Internet Things J. (2024)

15. Zeng, L., Lu, X., Bai, Y., Liu, B., Yang, G.: Topology design algorithm for optical inter-satellite links in future navigation satellite networks. GPS Solutions **26**(2), 1–16 (2022). https://doi.org/10.1007/s10291-022-01241-3
16. Zengshan, Y., et al.: A comprehensive survey of orbital edge computing: systems, applications, and algorithms. Chin. J. Aeronaut. **38**(7), 103316 (2025)
17. Zhao, R., Luo, J., Ran, Y.: Coverage-aware cooperative caching and efficient content distribution schemes in LEO satellite networks. In: Proceedings of the 1st ACM MobiCom Workshop on Satellite Networking and Computing, pp. 31–36 (2023)
18. Zhu, A., Lu, H., Guo, S., Zeng, Z., Zhou, Z.: CollOR: distributed collaborative offloading and routing for tasks with QOS demands in multi-robot system. Ad Hoc Netw. **152**, 103311 (2024)

TIDF: Timing-Based Device Fingerprinting for PLCs

Lei Xiang[✉] and Hao Han[✉]

College of Computer Science and Technology, Nanjing University of Aeronautics and Astronautics, Nanjing 211106, China
{xxl,hhan}@nuaa.edu.cn

Abstract. Industrial Control Systems (ICS) often lack device-level authentication, making them vulnerable to unauthorized access to Programmable Logic Controllers (PLCs). To address this challenge, we propose a lightweight hybrid fingerprinting method, Timing-based Device Fingerprinting (TIDF), for detecting unauthorized PLCs based on communication processing time and clock pulse period. TIDF leverages stable ICS network conditions and inherent PLC hardware characteristics, and integrates these features into a unified system consisting of filtering, training, and anomaly detection modules. By employing Density-Based Spatial Clustering of Applications with Noise (DBSCAN) and One-Class Support Vector Machine (OCSVM), TIDF achieves accurate and efficient classification with low overhead. We evaluate TIDF on real-world data from 13 PLCs, including Siemens and Xinje, and further test its robustness against basic forgery attempts. The results show an anomaly detection rate of 96%, demonstrating the effectiveness of TIDF in detecting unauthorized device access attacks and enhancing ICS security.

Keywords: Programmable logic controller · Device fingerprinting · Physical security · Industrial control systems

1 Introduction

Industrial Control Systems (ICS) rely on Programmable Logic Controllers (PLCs) to execute critical control functions, making them high-value targets for adversaries aiming to disrupt physical processes. Despite the use of Virtual Private Networks (VPNs) and firewalls, the lack of authentication in many ICS protocols exposes PLCs to identity-based attacks such as device replacement and remote spoofing. These threats highlight the need for lightweight, fine-grained fingerprinting techniques to reliably verify PLC identity and safeguard system integrity.

Existing PLC fingerprinting techniques exhibit important limitations when applied to identity spoofing threats. Register-based methods such as iFinger model control logic via register state transitions [22], but fail when a cloned device replicates identical state behavior. Memory-layout approaches like

© IFIP International Federation for Information Processing 2026
Published by Springer Nature Switzerland AG 2026
X. Wang et al. (Eds.): NPC 2025, LNCS 16306, pp. 126–138, 2026.
https://doi.org/10.1007/978-3-032-10466-3_11

PLCPrint detect firmware tampering [8], yet cannot distinguish between physically distinct devices with the same firmware and memory structure. Traffic pattern-based techniques abstract protocol flows into feature sequences [18], but offer insufficient granularity to differentiate cloned devices with identical traffic profiles. Side-channel approaches using electromagnetic or power signatures achieve high accuracy [23], but require intrusive hardware access, making them impractical in typical ICS deployments. Formby et al. [9] proposed Cross-Layer Response Time (CLRT), a method leveraging delays between TCP ACKs and application-layer responses. However, its effectiveness is compromised by TCP delayed acknowledgments, which merge ACKs with data replies. These limitations highlight the need for a non-intrusive, timing-based approach that captures device-specific execution dynamics without requiring physical access or firmware modifications.

To overcome these, we propose Timing-based Device Fingerprinting (TIDF). TIDF consists of Cross-Layer Response Time Estimation Technique (CLRTET) and Timer Clock Pulse. CLRTET elicits an explicit ACK to recover the PLC's processing latency. The latter captures hardware-specific clock pulse characteristics via internal counters. Both fingerprints are passively extracted during standard Supervisory Control And Data Acquisition (SCADA) polling, requiring no firmware changes, making them practical for real-world deployment.

Our Contributions are:

- We propose CLRTET, an enhancement of CLRT that actively induces separate TCP acknowledgments to enable precise estimation of PLC processing latency.
- We introduce a novel fingerprinting technique based on PLC timer pulse behavior, reflecting low-level timing variations across devices.
- We develop and evaluate a hybrid fingerprinting system using One-Class Support Vector Machine (OCSVM), validated on 13 PLCs from Siemens, Omron, and Xinje.

The remainder of the paper is organized as follows. Section 2 provides background on PLC. Section 3 presents the threat model and system design. Section 4 details the experimental setup and results. Section 5 discusses limitations, followed by related work in Sect. 6. Section 7 concludes the paper.

2 Background

PLCs are core components in ICS, widely used in sectors such as energy, manufacturing, and telecommunications to manage real-time control tasks. Unlike general-purpose computers, PLCs operate under constrained environments and typically run lightweight Real-Time Operating Systems (RTOS) like VxWorks [11].

PLCs are programmed using IEC 61131-3 standard languages, including Ladder Diagram (LD), Function Block Diagram (FBD), and Structured Text (ST). These programs define cyclic control logic that repeatedly samples inputs, executes logic, and updates outputs. This process occurs in a continuous scan loop,

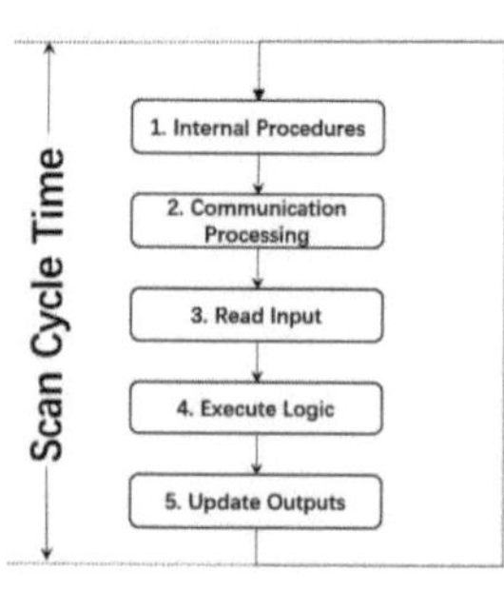

Fig. 1. PLC Scan Cycle

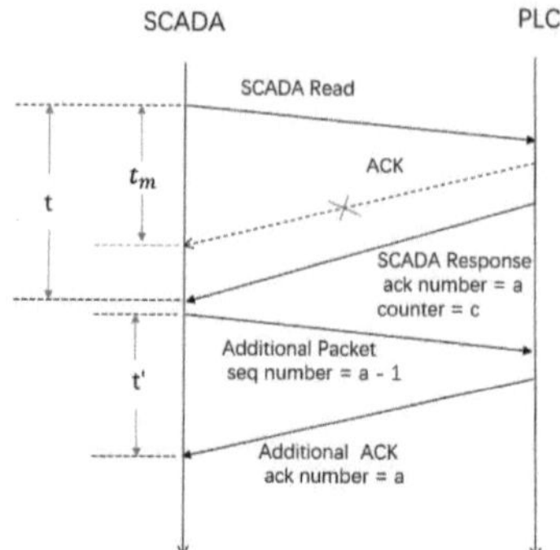

Fig. 2. SCADA Polling Process

as illustrated in Fig. 1, where each cycle comprises input reading, logic execution, and output writing.

In parallel, PLCs communicate with supervisory systems (e.g., SCADA) over industrial protocols such as Modbus/TCP and PROFINET. The timing of these interactions—shaped by communication delays, OS scheduling, and firmware behavior—varies across devices and provides opportunities for passive fingerprinting.

In addition to communication latency, many PLCs use internal timers based on periodic clock pulses from the system clock. The characteristics of these pulses differ across vendors and models, offering another dimension for timing-based identification.

Due to their critical role, PLCs are attractive attack targets. Unauthorized replacement or impersonation may cause physical damage or operational disruption. Hence, lightweight and robust PLC identification methods are essential for enhancing ICS security and integrity.

3   Protocol Design

In this section, we first outline the assumed adversarial capabilities and system assumptions considered in this study, followed by a description of CLRTET-based fingerprinting method. Next, we present the proposed timing-based features for PLC fingerprinting. Finally, we introduce the overall workflow and describe the key components of TIDF.

3.1   Threat Model and Assumptions

We consider two attack scenarios targeting PLCs in ICS networks: (1) local device replacement and (2) remote impersonation. In both, the adversary aims to introduce a malicious device that mimics a legitimate PLC.

Local threats involve physical access—gained as an insider or by posing as maintenance personnel—enabling the attacker to replace or insert a rogue PLC

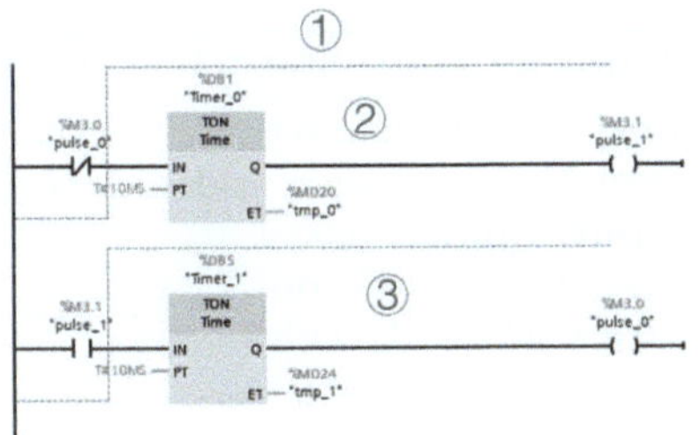

Fig. 3. Timer clock pulses

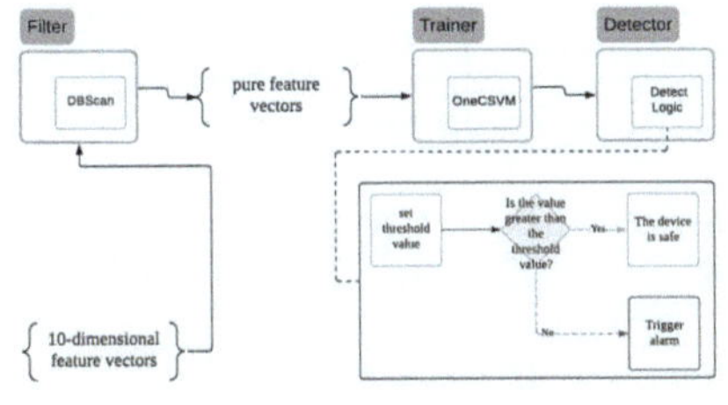

Fig. 4. FingerPrinting System

clone. If the replica runs the same control logic, it can bypass traditional state-based intrusion detection systems [22], especially in large, distributed deployments with limited physical safeguards.

Remote threats arise when an attacker breaches network defenses, for example through misconfigurations or compromised credentials. Without authentication mechanisms in protocols like Modbus or EtherNet/IP, attackers can forge device IDs or network addresses to impersonate legitimate PLCs [10,25].

We assume standard defenses are in place, including encrypted channels (e.g., Transport Layer Security (TLS) or VPN [5,21]) and baseline intrusion detection. Under these conditions, we focus on detecting unauthorized device substitution or spoofing using physical-layer timing characteristics, which are tightly coupled to hardware and thus difficult to replicate.

3.2 CLRTET-Based Fingerprint

We propose the CLRTET, an enhancement of the original CLRT method [9], which actively induces separate TCP acknowledgments to enable precise estimation of PLC processing latency. While CLRT estimates latency from the time gap between transport-layer ACKs and application-layer responses, it often fails in practice due to TCP's delayed ACK mechanism, which merges acknowledgments with response packets. CLRTET overcomes this by sending an additional packet immediately after the SCADA response (Fig. 2), forcing a standalone ACK. The latency is then inferred as the time difference between the SCADA polling interval and the induced ACK delay, yielding more reliable and device-specific timing features.

From the resulting time series, we extract five statistical features, mean, standard deviation, entropy, median, and mode-centered median, to form a fingerprint. These features are computed using a sliding window approach and provide a robust representation of device-specific processing behavior (see Algorithm 1[1]).

---

1 t_i^{SS}, t_i^{RS} denote send/receive times of SCADA read/response; t_i^{SA}, t_i^{RA} denote send/receive times of additional packet and ACK.

Algorithm 1. Feature Extraction

1: **for** k^{th} step **do**
2:     $i \leftarrow 1$
3:     **while** $i \leq N$ **do**
4:         $T_i = (t_i^{\mathrm{RS}} - t_i^{\mathrm{SS}}) - (t_i^{\mathrm{RA}} - t_i^{\mathrm{SA}})$
5:         **if** $i == N$ **then**
6:             $x_1, \ldots, x_{kn} \leftarrow \kappa N\, T$
7:             $F_1 \leftarrow$ mean, $F_2 \leftarrow$ std, $F_3 \leftarrow$ entropy, $F_4 \leftarrow$ median, $F_5 \leftarrow$ mode-centered median
8:         **end if**
9:         $i \leftarrow i + 1$
10:     **end while**
11: **end for**

Algorithm 2. Three-Stage Training

1: **Input**: Normal dataset D_{n}, anomaly dataset D_{an}; parameter grids G_ν, G_γ
2: **Output**: Optimal model M_{o}
3: **for** $(\nu, \gamma) \in G_\nu \times G_\gamma$ **do**
4:     Train M on D_{n} with (ν, γ)
5:     Evaluate M on $D_{\mathrm{n}}, D_{\mathrm{an}}$
6:     Record accuracy rates a_n, a_{an}
7:     $S_i(\nu, \gamma) = a_n + a_{an}$
8: **end for**
9: $(\nu^*, \gamma^*) = \arg\max S(\nu, \gamma)$
10: Train M_{o} on D_{n} with (ν^*, γ^*)
11: **return** M_{o}

CLRTET is effective because PLCs have constrained hardware and execute deterministic control logic, leading to consistent processing delays. Variations across devices arise from differences in hardware design, clock precision, and internal execution paths. Moreover, ICS networks exhibit low jitter and stable topologies, making timing measurements more reliable than in traditional IT networks.

3.3 Timer Clock Pulse Fingerprint

The second fingerprint leverages hardware-level differences in PLC clock behavior. We configure two timers within the PLC to generate a periodic pulse with nominal period μ, and use it to increment an internal counter. During SCADA polling, the counter value is read to estimate the average pulse period based on the elapsed time and counter increments.

As shown in Fig. 3, we implement this mechanism using two timers in a Siemens S7-1200 PLC. The pulse is formed through sequential triggering and resetting of timers, and its period is influenced by both the timers' configuration and the PLC's scan cycle. The actual pulse interval lies within $(\alpha + \beta, \alpha + 3\beta)$, where α is the sum of timer durations and β is the scan cycle.

Due to variations in internal clock precision, Central Processing Unit (CPU) processing power, and scan logic implementation, the actual timing behavior differs across PLC models and instances—even under identical timer settings. Prior studies [6,12,24] have exploited similar hardware-induced timing variations for device fingerprinting.

We extract the same five statistical features (mean, standard deviation, entropy, median, mode-centered median) from the pulse measurements as in

CLRTET. Since polling may introduce minor offset, we apply averaging over a longer time window to mitigate sampling deviation and enhance robustness.

The two proposed fingerprintings both rely on polling and do not interfere with each other. The features extracted from these two fingerprintings can be combined to form a ten-dimensional fingerprint vector, which can improve the recognition accuracy of the devices.

3.4 System Overview of TIDF

To implement TIDF, we design a lightweight recognition system composed of three components: filtering, training, and anomaly detection (see Fig. 4). Communication and timing features are first extracted from SCADA–PLC interactions and denoised using Density-Based Spatial Clustering of Applications with Noise (DBSCAN)-based clustering. The training module then constructs per-device models using OCSVM, learning only from normal behavior. The OCSVM model employs a radial basis function (RBF) kernel due to its ability to handle non-linear data and focus on local patterns (Eq. 1). Let $\mathbf{X} \in \mathbb{R}^{n \times 10}$ be the standardized feature matrix. The detection module detects anomalies via the decision function $f(x) = (w \cdot \phi(x)) - \rho$, where $\phi(\cdot)$ is the implicit mapping induced by the RBF kernel. classifying samples as legitimate if $f(x) \geq 0$. Devices are accepted if the proportion of legitimate samples exceeds a preset threshold.

$$K(x_i, x_j) = \exp\left(-\frac{\|x_i - x_j\|^2}{2\sigma^2}\right) \tag{1}$$

Given the limited diversity and computational constraints of ICS devices, OCSVM offers an efficient unsupervised solution that avoids reliance on labeled data. To improve performance on both normal and anomalous samples, we propose a three-stage model selection procedure (Algorithm 2): (1) grid search on normal data, (2) anomaly evaluation using simulated attack traces, and (3) selecting the model with optimal joint accuracy. This enhances detection reliability even when adversaries deploy similar devices.

Our system requires no changes to existing control logic or network protocols, making it suitable for deployment in real-world ICS environments.

(a) Experimental PLCs setup

(b) Experimental Scenario

Fig. 5. Experiments were conducted on 13 real-world PLCs.

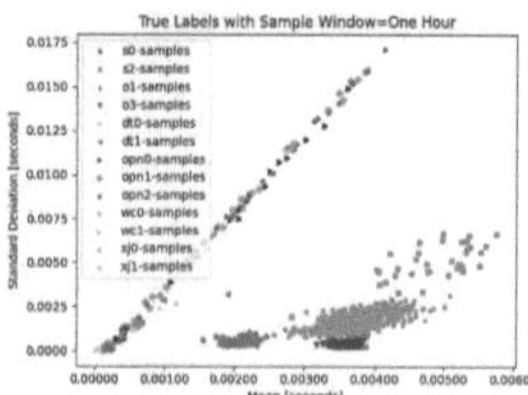
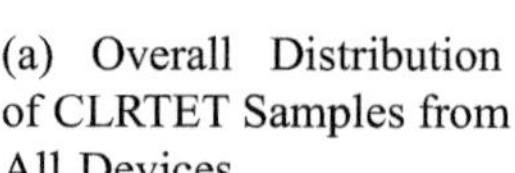
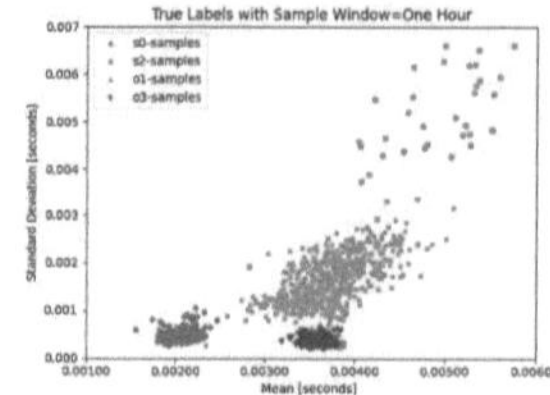
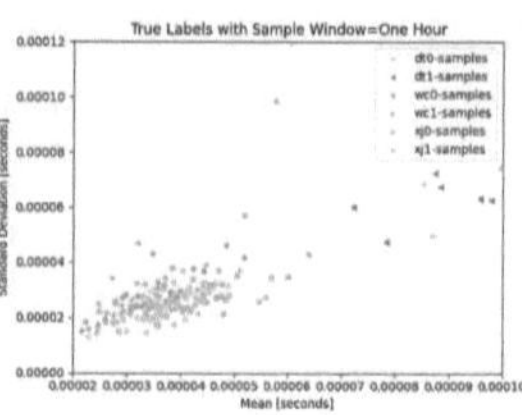

(a) Overall Distribution of CLRTET Samples from All Devices

(b) Detailed Distribution of CLRTET Samples from Non-Domestic Devices

(c) Detailed Distribution of CLRTET Samples from Domestic Devices

Fig. 6. Mean and Standard Deviation Distribution of CLRTET Samples

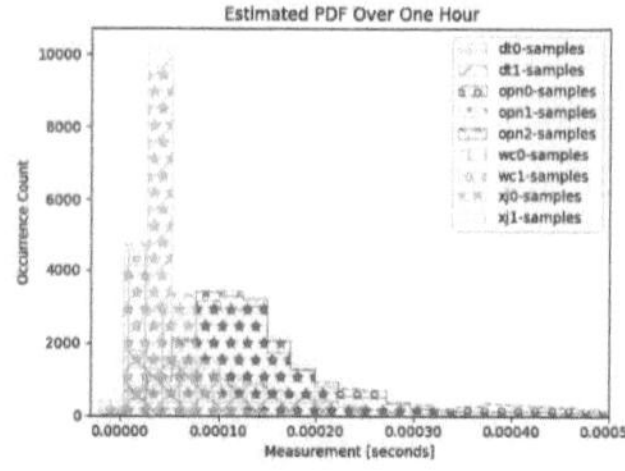
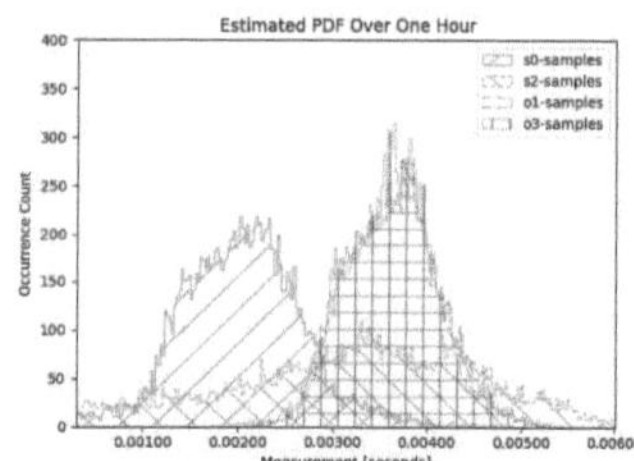

(a) Estimated PDFs of CLRT-ET Data from Domestic Devices Sampled Hourly

(b) Estimated PDFs of CLRT-ET Data from Non-Domestic Devices Sampled Hourly

Fig. 7. Estimated Probability Density Functions (PDFs) of CLRTET Samples for Device Type Discrimination

4 Experiment Setup and Results Analysis

The experimental evaluation aims to answer three key research questions: (Q1) Can the proposed fingerprinting method reliably distinguish legitimate PLCs from unauthorized or cloned devices under nominal operating conditions? (Q2) Is the method resilient to network perturbations such as bandwidth fluctuations and load-induced delays? (Q3) How does its accuracy and computational efficiency compare with state-of-the-art unsupervised and supervised baselines?

To address these questions, we implemented a complete recognition system based on unsupervised learning and deployed it in a controlled ICS testbed encompassing diverse PLC hardware and varying network conditions.

4.1 Experimental Setup

As shown in Fig. 5b, the testbed consists of a host computer, two workload injectors, and target PLCs connected through a central router. The host continuously polls the PLCs and collects response data, while the injectors generate background network load via `iperf`. We evaluated six commercial PLC models

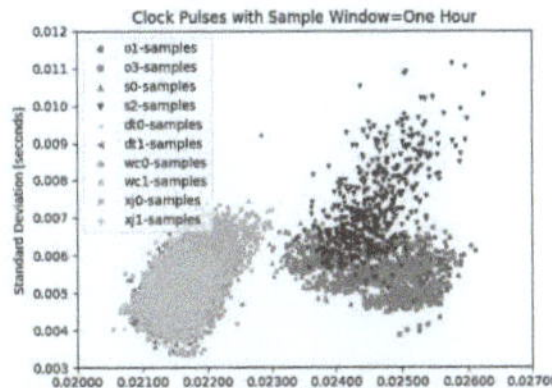

(a) Mean and Standard Deviation of Clock Pulse Data from Real PLC Devices

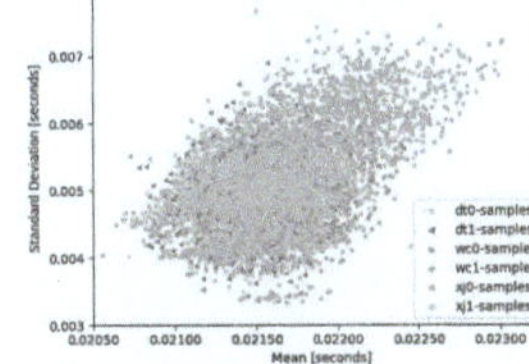

(b) Detailed Clock Pulse Distribution of Domestic Devices

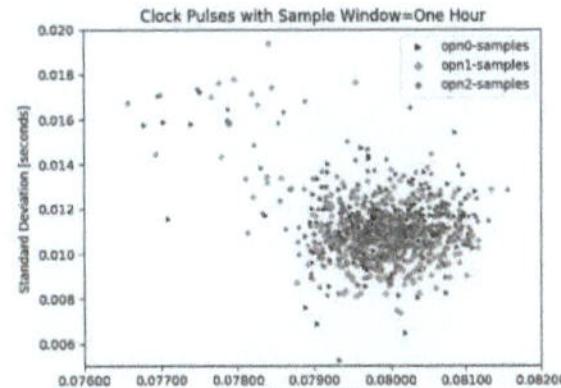

(c) Mean and Standard Deviation of Clock Pulse Data from NanoPi R6S Devices

Fig. 8. Clock Pulses Elapsed per Increment

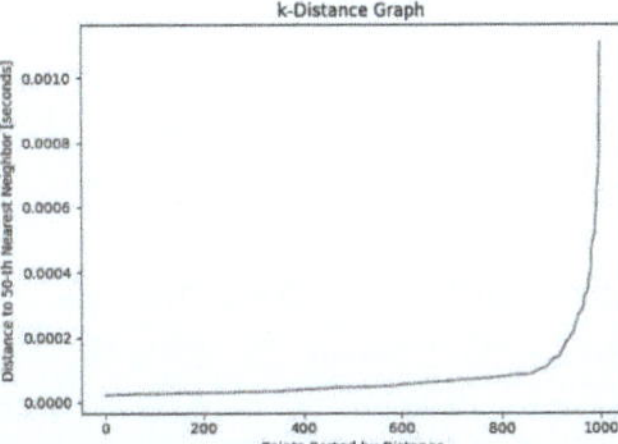

Fig. 9. 50-Distance

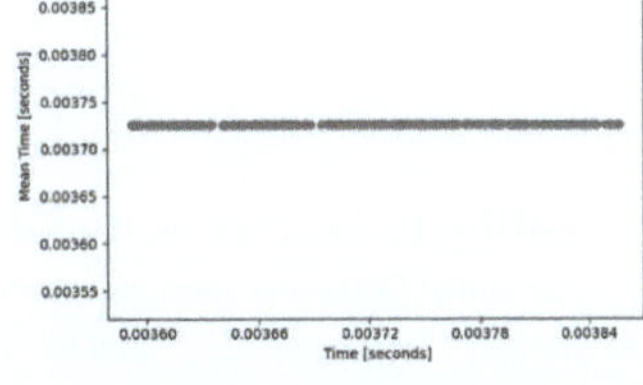

Fig. 10. Filtered Data

from Siemens, Omron, XinJe, Delta, and Wecon, along with three NanoPi R6S boards running OpenPLC (Fig. 5a).

To ensure comparability, all devices executed identical traffic-light control logic with a 20 ms internal timer pulse and were polled via Modbus/TCP at 2 Hz. Collected data were segmented using a sliding window of 10 polling intervals, producing 10-dimensional feature vectors.

4.2   Performance Under Normal Conditions (Q1)

For each polling cycle, we extracted two timing features: the CLRTET and the clock pulse period. Statistical analysis (Figs. 6–8) revealed clear distributional separation among devices, supporting their discriminative potential for fingerprinting.

To improve robustness, raw time series were filtered using DBSCAN, effectively removing outliers based on local density (Fig. 10). The optimal neighborhood radius ε was chosen via the elbow method from the k-distance plot (Fig. 9). Filtered vectors were then normalized (zero mean, unit variance) and used to train per-device OCSVM models with RBF kernels, whose hyperparameters ν and γ were tuned via grid search.

Under these settings, 100 test samples per device were evaluated over 10 independent rounds. As shown in Fig. 11a, legitimate devices achieved an average

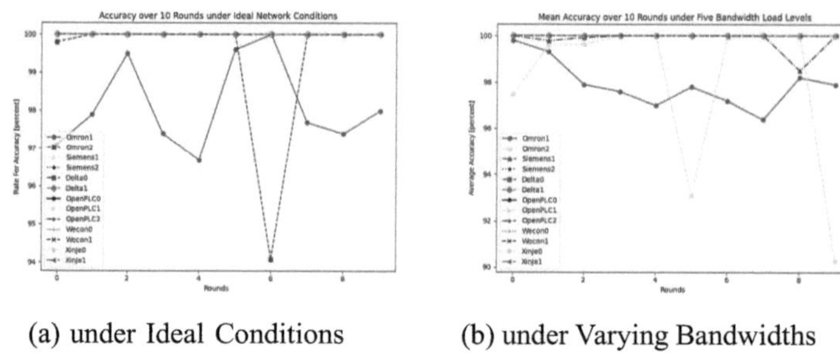

(a) under Ideal Conditions   (b) under Varying Bandwidths

Fig. 11. PLC Fingerprint Anomaly Detection Performance

true negative rate (TNR) of 96%, while unauthorized devices were identified with a true positive rate (TPR) of 99%, demonstrating high reliability in ideal conditions.

Table 1. Comparison of detection performance metrics across models

Model	Samples	Detection [min]	Accuracy [%]	Precision [%]	Recall [%]	F1-score [%]	FPR [%]	FNR [%]
OCSVM	51 895	2	96.00	99.00	95.00	97.00	2.00	5.00
ISF	47 736	2	91.00	91.00	97.00	94.00	27.00	3.00
AE	47 736	3	92.00	93.00	97.00	95.00	23.00	3.00
DSVDD	47 736	3	91.00	93.00	95.00	94.00	21.00	5.00
DAGMM	47 736	3	92.00	92.00	98.00	95.00	24.00	2.00

4.3   Robustness to Network Perturbations (Q2)

To emulate adverse conditions, we varied network bandwidth from 97 Mb/s to 323 Mb/s on a TL-WDR5620 router (max $\approx$ 350 Mb/s). Models were trained using data collected at 173 Mb/s (60% load) and tested on data from other load levels across 10 rounds. As shown in Fig. 11b, the system sustained a TNR of 96% and TPRs above 92% for all devices, confirming that timing features remained stable despite bandwidth-induced jitter, and no retraining was required.

4.4   Comparison with Baseline Methods (Q3)

In terms of efficiency, training 300 fits (30 models) on 12,852 entries required 619 s, while testing 23,166 unauthorized entries took 258 s, yielding the optimal model as determined by Algorithm 2. Compared to deep learning models, this runtime is substantially lower, making it suitable for deployment on resource-limited ICS hardware.

We benchmarked against four unsupervised baselines—Isolation Forest (ISF), Autoencoder (AE), Deep Support Vector Data Description (DSVDD), and Deep

Autoencoding Gaussian Mixture Model (DAGMM)—as well as one supervised baseline (XGBoost [26]). As shown in Table 1, our OCSVM achieved the highest accuracy (96%) and F1-score (97%), while also recording the lowest false positive rate (2%) among unsupervised models. Although all baselines exceeded 95% recall, their higher false positive rates (21–27%) reduce deployment feasibility in operational ICS environments. While XGBoost [26] achieved competitive accuracy, its reliance on fully labeled multi-device datasets is unrealistic for anomaly detection in practice.

Overall, the proposed fingerprinting system delivers high accuracy and minimal false alarms under both nominal and stressed network conditions. Its low computational cost, protocol compatibility, and non-intrusive design make it well-suited for real-time PLC authentication in production ICS settings.

5   Discussion

Performance and Security: The proposed fingerprinting system achieves up to 96% classification accuracy with low computational overhead, making it practical for real-time deployment in resource-constrained ICS environments. Its robustness stems from inherent microsecond-level timing differences between PLC instances and the difficulty of mimicking such characteristics due to hardware-specific clock skew and OS scheduling. Even among identical models, these features remain distinct and resilient against basic forgery. Periodic updates of the OCSVM model can further improve the system's stability.

Threat Resilience: Advanced attackers could attempt timing emulation by observing SCADA–PLC exchanges. To counter this, we recommend encrypting control traffic (e.g., via TLS or Internet Protocol Security (IPsec)) to obfuscate timing details and employing local, SCADA-side fingerprint verification to prevent spoofed inputs. These defenses align with industry standards such as IEC 62443 and further reduce the attack surface.

System Overhead and Limitations: The method introduces negligible network load and only minor scan cycle delays (e.g., $+33$ μs for Siemens S7-1200), well within acceptable ICS tolerances. A small code addition may require a reboot, but this can be scheduled during maintenance. However, the system may be sensitive to timer reconfigurations or network latency variation. Future work will explore adaptive calibration and hybrid fingerprinting (e.g., actuator-level dynamics) to enhance stability across diverse deployment settings.

6   Related Work

Device fingerprinting has been widely explored in general networked systems and cyber-physical systems (CPS), and has been comprehensively surveyed in the context of ICS by Caselli et al. [4]. Their survey categorizes various fingerprinting approaches and highlights the core challenges associated with applying these methods in real-world ICS environments. Another recent survey [13] highlights key difficulties in identifying robust and stable features under realistic ICS conditions. These observations further motivate the development of lightweight, timing-based fingerprinting methods that can operate reliably within typical ICS operational environments.

Existing PLC fingerprinting techniques can be broadly categorized into timing-based and non-timing-based approaches. Timing-based methods exploit delays or temporal patterns–for example, CLRT [9] estimates TCP-layer latency but is affected by delayed acknowledgments, while CryptoFP [16] and clock-skew techniques [6] rely on high-resolution timing rarely available in ICS polling. Actuator-level fingerprints [2] improve spoofing resilience by extracting timing from physical dynamics, though general anomaly detectors [15] often miss fine-grained patterns. Non-timing-based methods include traffic-based techniques [3,19], which abstract protocol flows but fail against clones replaying identical traffic, and behavioral or register-state models [1,17,22], which assume static control logic and cannot detect logic-equivalent replicas. Memory-layout approaches like PLCPrint [8] require firmware access and are ineffective when adversaries replicate memory contents. Hardware-level methods such as RF or voltage side-channels [7,20] and FPHammer [14] offer device-level uniqueness but rely on intrusive hardware or unstable artifacts.

In contrast, our method captures device-specific **processing latency** and **timer pulse behavior**, and it requires no hardware changes, explicit timestamps, or wireless access. It enhances and generalizes CLRT [9] by introducing additional packets to recover timing observability under acknowledgment coalescence. Our approach operates entirely over standard wired ICS protocols and is resilient to clock jitter and firmware-level variations, making it suitable for practical, fine-grained PLC authentication.

7   Conclusion

PLCs serve as the bridge between the cyber and physical worlds, and ensuring their secure operation is critical. In this paper, we proposed a lightweight hybrid fingerprinting method, TIDF, that has 96% recognition accuracy for PLCs and is forgery resistant and easily scalable. A fingerprinting system was implemented on this basis, which can detect almost 100% of unauthorized device access and forgery attacks on PLCs. By incorporating the method into existing ICS intrusion detection systems, the overall security posture of ICS environments can be significantly enhanced.

References

1. Aguayo Gonzalez, C., Hinton, A.: Detecting malicious software execution in programmable logic controllers using power fingerprinting. In: Proceedings of Critical Infrastructure Protection, pp. 15–27. Springer (2014)
2. Ahmed, C.M., Calder, M., Gunawan, S., Prakash, J., Nagaraja, S., Zhou, J.: Time constant: actuator fingerprinting using transient response of device and process in ICS (2024)

3. Al Ghazo, A.T., Kumar, R.: ICS/SCADA device recognition: a hybrid communication-patterns and passive-fingerprinting approach. In: Proceedings of IFIP/IEEE IM, pp. 19–24. IEEE (2019)
4. Caselli, M., Hadziosmanovic, D., Zambon, E., Kargl, F.: On the feasibility of device fingerprinting in industrial control systems. In: Proceedings of Critical Information Infrastructures Security, pp. 155–166. Springer (2013)
5. Chaudhry, J., Qidwai, U., Miraz, M.H.: Securing big data from eavesdropping attacks in SCADA/ICS network data streams through impulsive statistical fingerprinting. arXiv preprint arXiv:1909.11021 (2019)
6. Cho, K.T., Shin, K.G.: Fingerprinting electronic control units for vehicle intrusion detection. In: 25th USENIX Security Symposium (USENIX Security 16), pp. 911–927 (2016)
7. Cho, K.T., Shin, K.G.: Viden: attacker identification on in-vehicle networks. In: Proceedings of the 2017 ACM SIGSAC Conference on Computer and Communications Security, pp. 1109–1123 (2017)
8. Cook, M.M., Marnerides, A.K., Pezaros, D.: PLCPrint: fingerprinting memory attacks in programmable logic controllers. IEEE Trans. Inf. Forensics Secur. **18**, 3376–3387 (2023)
9. Formby, D., Srinivasan, P., Leonard, A.M., Rogers, J.D., Beyah, R.A.: Who's in control of your control system? Device fingerprinting for cyber-physical systems. In: NDSS (2016)
10. Gao, J., et al.: An effective defense method based on hash authentication against mode-switching attack of ormon PLC. In: Proceedings of ICSP, pp. 976–979. IEEE (2022)
11. Hrynkiewicz, E., Chmiel, M.: Programmable logic controller-basic structure and idea of programming. Electric. Rev. **88**(11b/2012), 98–101 (2012)
12. Kohno, T., Broido, A., Claffy, K.C.: Remote physical device fingerprinting. IEEE Trans. Dependable Secure Comput. **2**(2), 93–108 (2005)
13. Kumar, V., Paul, K.: Device fingerprinting for cyber-physical systems: a survey. ACM Comput. Surv. **55**(14s), 1–41 (2023)
14. Li, D., et al.: FPHammer: a device identification framework based on dram fingerprinting. In: Proceedings of TrustCom, pp. 1031–1040. IEEE (2023)
15. Peng, Y., Xiang, C., Gao, H., Chen, D., Ren, W.: Industrial control system fingerprinting and anomaly detection. In: Rice, M., Shenoi, S. (eds.) IFIP Advances in Information and Communication Technology. Critical Infrastructure Protection IX, vol. AICT-466, pp. 73–85. Springer (2015)
16. Sanchez-Rola, I., Santos, I., Balzarotti, D.: Clock around the clock: time-based device fingerprinting. In: Proceedings of the 2018 ACM SIGSAC Conference on Computer and Communications Security, pp. 1502–1514 (2018)
17. Stockman, M., Dwivedi, D., Gentz, R., Peisert, S.: Detecting control system misbehavior by fingerprinting programmable logic controller functionality. Int. J. Crit. Infrastruct. Prot. **26**, 100306 (2019)
18. Tao, J., Yuan, X., Zhang, S., Xu, Y.: Development of fingerprint identification based on device flow in industrial control system. Appl. Sci. **13**(2), 731 (2023)
19. Thom, J., Thom, N., Sengupta, S., Hand, E.: Smart recon: network traffic fingerprinting for IoT device identification. In: 2022 IEEE 12th Annual Computing and Communication Workshop and Conference (CCWC), pp. 0072–0079. IEEE (2022)
20. Tian, Q., et al.: New security mechanisms of high-reliability IoT communication based on radio frequency fingerprint. IEEE Internet Things J. **6**(5), 7980–7987 (2019)

21. Xia, D., Jiang, C., Wan, J., Jin, J., Leung, V.C.M., Martínez-García, M.: Heterogeneous network access and fusion in smart factory: a survey. ACM Comput. Surv. **55**(6), 1–31 (2022)
22. Yang, K., Li, Q., Lin, X., Chen, X., Sun, L.: iFinger: intrusion detection in industrial control systems via register-based fingerprinting. IEEE J. Sel. Areas Commun. **38**(5), 955–967 (2020)
23. Yimer, T., Arafin, M.T., Kornegay, K.: Securing industrial control systems using physical device fingerprinting. In: Proceedings of IOTSMS, pp. 1–6. IEEE (2020)
24. Zander, S., Murdoch, S.J.: An improved clock-skew measurement technique for revealing hidden services. In: USENIX Security Symposium, pp. 211–226 (2008)
25. Zhang, W., et al.: Armor PLC: a platform for cyber security threats assessments for PLCs. Procedia Manuf. **39**, 270–278 (2019)
26. Zhou, F., Qu, H., Liu, H., Liu, H., Li, B.: Fingerprinting IIoT devices through machine learning techniques. J. Sig. Process. Syst. **93**(7), 779–794 (2021)

Deadlock-Free Transaction Processing in Payment Channel Networks

Rong Cao[1], Jingjing Zhang[2(✉)], Peizong Yang[1], Litong Sun[1], Weigang Wu[1], and Jing Bian[1]

[1] School of Computer Science and Engineering, Sun Yat-sen University, Guangzhou, China
caor37@mail2.sysu.edu.cn, wuweig@mail.sysu.edu.cn
[2] School of Cyber Security, Guangdong University of Foreign Studies, Guangzhou, China
zhangjj43@gdufs.edu.cn

Abstract. Payment channel networks (PCNs) enhance blockchain scalability by enabling off-chain payments, where Hashed Time-Locked Contracts (HTLCs) ensure the security of multi-hop payments across intermediaries. As the scale of payment channel networks expands, the number of transactions naturally increases, while concurrent executions on overlapping channels trigger resource contention for the limited capacity of shared channels, potentially leading to deadlocks. Based on the principle that consistent execution ordering across overlapping channels prevents deadlocks, we systematically solve the deadlock problem by formalizing deadlock formation conditions, designing detection methods based on these conditions, followed by developing total-order and partial-order sorting strategies to break potential cyclic dependencies, and ultimately proposing a fairness-aware, deadlock-free scheduling mechanism that enhances transaction success rates. Extensive simulations validate our approach, demonstrating competitive transaction success rates alongside robust deadlock prevention.

Keywords: Payment channel network · Deadlock prevention · Sorting · Transactions scheduling

1 Introduction

Payment channel [4], as a critical off-chain scaling solution for blockchain scalability issues [9], employs a core design principle that significantly enhances system throughput by transferring transactions from on-chain to off-chain [12]. Multiple payment channels can constitute a payment network and realize transaction execution via multi-hop paths. Bitcoin's Lightning Network [12] and Ethereum's Raiden Network [1] are typical representatives. Crucially, to enable multi-hop payments, PCN relies on HTLCs to guarantee secure and atomic transactions across multiple parties. However, HTLC transactions require that every intermediary payment channel locks a portion of its available balance capacity until the

© IFIP International Federation for Information Processing 2026
Published by Springer Nature Switzerland AG 2026
X. Wang et al. (Eds.): NPC 2025, LNCS 16306, pp. 139–152, 2026.
https://doi.org/10.1007/978-3-032-10466-3_12

payment is settled, which may lead to a deadlock in a concurrent situation [8]. Concurrent transactions may trigger deadlocks when cyclic dependencies exist in their paths.

We illustrate a deadlock example involving two transactions tx and tx' in Fig. 1. Figure 1-(a) shows the initial fund states of the channels, and Fig. 1-(b) shows the states after the transactions attempt to lock funds for execution. The red numbers indicate the locked funds when tx arrives first for its execution, and the blue numbers indicate the locked funds when tx' arrives first. The funds in channel ch_{CD} are insufficient to meet the locking requirements of tx, and the same with channel ch_{AB} for tx'. However, in such scenarios, the locked funds remain inaccessible until the time locks expire, which degrades transaction success rates and affects capital liquidity.

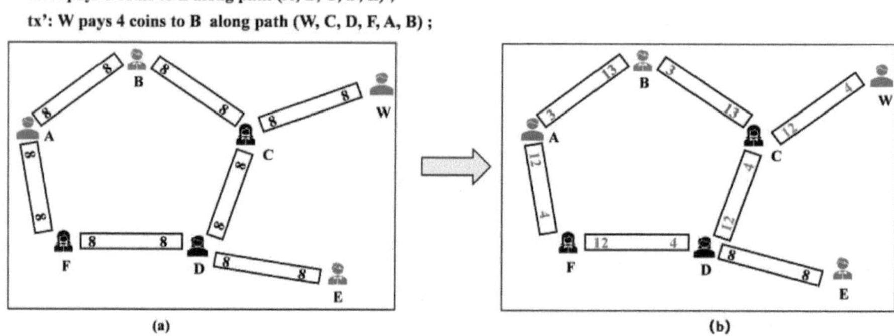

Fig. 1. The transactions enter a cyclic waiting state, resulting in a deadlock.

To alleviate such contention and improve transaction success rates, current research primarily focuses on three core directions: routing mechanisms, scheduling strategies, and deadlock prevention and resolution. Routing strategies include fund reservation during path exploration [3], multi-path utilization [16], skew-aware routing [6], and congestion-avoidance for concurrent transactions [14]. Scheduling approaches cover the throughput optimization of single-hop scheduling [11], deadline-aware waiting [17], priority-based congestion relief [7], and DRL-based priority-aware scheduling for throughput, DoS resilience, and privacy [13]. Deadlock research in PCNs remains limited: one study aborts conflicting transactions [8], another proposes saturation-minimizing routing [15], while others merely mention deadlocks without comprehensive solutions [16,20].

This Work. In this paper, we address the deadlock challenge by first formally defining the conditions under which deadlocks occur in PCNs, then proposing a path-cycle-based detection method to identify potential deadlocks, subsequently designing two transaction sorting strategies - total-order and partial-order - for potential deadlock transactions, and ultimately embedding these sorting mechanisms into a fairness-aware, deadlock-free transaction scheduling mechanism that maintains competitive success rates. The effectiveness of our approach is comprehensively validated through extensive experimental simulations.

The major novelties and advantages of our work are summarized as follows:

- Formalizing deadlock formation conditions in PCNs, design a detection algorithm for potential deadlock transactions based on these conditions, propose total-order and partial-order sorting strategies to prevent deadlocks, and establish a complete pipeline from definition to resolution (Sect. 4).
- Developing a fairness-aware, deadlock-free transaction scheduling framework (Sect. 5) that optimizes success rates while ensuring conflict-free execution.
- Validating through extensive simulations, demonstrating competitive success rates and robust deadlock prevention (Sect. 6).

2 Related Work

To address resource contention on overlapping channels in multi-hop transactions, existing work has approached the problem from three perspectives: transaction routing, transaction scheduling, and deadlock avoidance/resolution.

FSTR [6] quantifies channel skewness to guide routing decisions, prioritizing paths with more balanced fund distributions. Fence [18] employs a fee incentive mechanism, redirecting capital flows toward paths more conducive to channel balance by paying routing fees to intermediary nodes. Deter-pay [3] proposes a balance pre-locking mechanism during the path exploration phase. Sharma et al. [14] introduce a comprehensive channel weight evaluation system to optimize transaction path selection.

Meanwhile, researchers have developed priority scheduling methods to optimize transaction sequences, enhancing channel fund utilization and success rates. Nikolaos et al. [11] introduce an optimized scheduling strategy for single-channel transactions. DPCN [17] systematically incorporated deadline constraints into payment channel network scheduling for the first time. Jiang et al. [5] and Bai et al. [2] investigate the relationship among transactions, channel balances, and routing fees based on a game-theoretic framework. Luo et al. [7] and Qiu et al. [13] constructed priority mechanisms using reinforcement learning algorithms.

Rayo protocol [8] resolves deadlocks by aborting one of the conflicting transactions, which adversely affects the transaction success rate. Werman et al. [19] propose a deadlock avoidance mechanism enforcing strict sequential channel requests via a fixed global resource allocation order. DEPR [15] prevents deadlocks by avoiding insufficient-fund conflict links, but relies on landmark nodes. The current approaches struggle to effectively balance high transaction success rates with deadlock handling.

3 Network Model

In this section, we start with a generic system model for the off-chain payment channel network and follow the communication model.

3.1   Payment Channel Networks

Payment channel networks consist of blockchain users and off-chain payment channels. This paper models the network as a topological graph $G = (V, E)$, where V represents the set of nodes (users) and E denotes the set of edges (payment channels). Each edge ch_{uv} (representing a channel between nodes) connects two endpoints u and v, with node u's balance $f_b(u, v)$, node v's balance $f_b(v, u)$, and the total channel capacity $f(u, v) = f_b(u, v) + f_b(v, u)$.

A multi-hop path are denoted as *path*, defined as a sequence of edges $e_1, \ldots, e_l$ or nodes $u_0, \ldots, u_l$, where l is the path length (number of hops), and edges are related to nodes by $e_i = (u_{i-1}, u_i)$ $(1 \leq i \leq l)$. The max feasible funds of *path* is defined as:

$$\omega = min f(u_i, u_{i+1}), (1 \leq i \leq l) \tag{1}$$

Thus, for a transaction tx with amount a, the path *path* is feasible if $\omega_{path} \geq a$. After executing transaction tx, the funds on each edge of *path* are updated as:

$$f_{\text{new}}(u_i, u_{i+1}) = f(u_i, u_{i+1}) - a_{tx}, (1 \leq i \leq l) \tag{2}$$

$$f_{\text{new}}(u_{i+1}, u_i) = f(u_{i+1}, u_i) + a_{tx}, (1 \leq i \leq l) \tag{3}$$

The total funds in each payment channel remain constant during the transaction, with funds only shifting between the two ends.

Please note that in this paper, transaction processing assumes the existence of a pre-identified feasible path for the transaction.

3.2   Communication Model

We assume node communication occurs over an underlying secure network architecture. In a simplified model, bidirectional communication is achievable between any two nodes via established channels. This network enables direct data exchange among all visible nodes, facilitating transaction-related information relay through packet forwarding. End-to-end encryption (e.g., TLS/SSL) ensures message confidentiality and data integrity. Nodes sharing payment channels function as logical neighbors, enabling real-time state updates via secure messaging.

4   Detecting and Resolving Deadlocks in PCNs

In this section, we first elucidate the conditions under which deadlocks occur among transactions in PCNs; then propose a deadlock detection method based on path cycles; finally, we present two sorting approaches to prevent deadlocks.

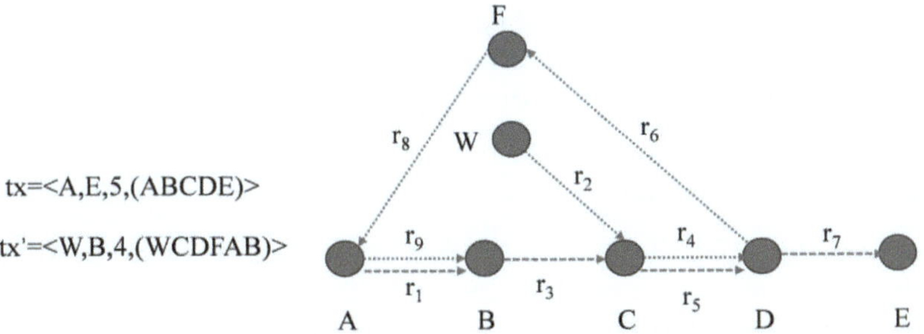

Fig. 2. The paths of tx and tx' meet the three path-cycle conditions: (1) two overlapping channels with $e(A, B) = r_1 = r_9$ and $e(C, D) = r_5 = r_4$; (2) tx traverses ch_{AB} then ch_{CD}, while tx' traverses them in reverse order; (3) both transactions have consistent payment directions on the overlapping channels.

4.1 Conditions for Deadlock Formation

We can define the format of a transaction tx as $tx = \langle s, r, a, path \rangle$, where s denotes the initiator, r the recipient, a the transaction amount, and $path$ is the routing path. For the path $path = (u_0, \ldots, u_n)$ of transaction tx and the path $path' = (u'_0, \ldots, u'_m)$ of transaction tx', their edge representations are $path = (e_1, e_2, \ldots, e_n)$ and $path' = (e'_1, e'_2, \ldots, e'_m)$, respectively. The edges of both paths, ordered by payment sequence, are interleaved as $(r_1, r_2, \ldots, r_{n+m})$, i.e., $(e_1, e'_1, e_2, e'_2, e_3, e'_3, \ldots)$. Here, for each edge $e \in path$, there exists a unique $k \in [1, n + m]$ such that $r_k = e$. For each edge $e' \in path'$, there exists a unique $l \in [1, n + m]$ such that $r_l = e'$.

A **path cycle** is formed if there exist at least two edges e_i and e_j shared by both $path$ and $path'$, satisfying:

- *Edge Equivalence:* $e_i = r_k = r_l$ and $e_j = r'_k = r'_l$;
- *Index Reversal:* Either $(k > l$ and $k' < l')$ or $(k < l$ and $k' > l')$.
- *Payment Direction Consistency:* Let $e_i = (u_{i-1}, u_i)$ and $e_j = (u_{j-1}, u_j)$ denote the edges in the two paths. The relative positions of node pairs u_{i-1} and u_i, as well as u_{j-1} and u_j, are consistent across the paths.

Under these conditions, the paths of tx and tx' form a cycle. Now we provide a simple example to illustrate the concept (see Fig. 2).

If two transactions form a **path cycle** and the balances on their overlapping channels are insufficient to support concurrent execution, as shown in the prior example where $tx.a + tx'.a > fb(A, B)$ and $tx.a + tx'.a > fb(C, D)$, a deadlock may occur. The transaction tx locks funds on ch_{AB} first, while tx' locks funds on ch_{CD} first. When tx subsequently attempts to lock funds on ch_{CD}, it finds insufficient funds on the C side. Meanwhile, tx' fails to lock funds on ch_{AB} due to insufficient funds on the A side. This creates a circular wait: both transactions are blocked, and their locked funds can only be released after timeout.

We can see that although individual transaction paths are feasible, concurrent execution and resource competition may cause deadlocks, preventing transaction completion. In PCNs, deadlocks correspond to cycles in transaction paths.

4.2 Deadlock Detection

The prerequisite for deadlock detection is that the transaction paths are known. Assuming nodes are aware of all transactions passing through them, our approach first identifies transaction pairs with potential path cycles based on their paths, then determines whether concurrent execution could lead to deadlocks by analyzing overlapping channel capacities and transaction amounts.

Algorithm 1. Deadlock Detection

```
 1: # input Txs = {tx₁, tx₂, …, txₙ}: the set of transactions.
 2: Och = null # Overlapping channels in path cycle.
 3: Dpair = null # Deadlock transactions pair.
 4: for (i = 1; i < n; i + +) do
 5:     for (j = i; j < n; j + +) do
 6:         # Path Cycle Detection
 7:         Och = DetCyc(txᵢ.path, txⱼ.path)
 8:         if  Och != null then
 9:             for all channel chᵤᵥ in Och do
10:                 # Channel Capacity Constraint Checking
11:                 if fb(u, v) ≥ (txᵢ.a + txⱼ.a) then
12:                     # node u precedes node v in the path
13:                     Och = null
14:                     break
15:                 end if
16:             end for
17:             if  Och != NULL then
18:                 # add transactions pair (txᵢ, txⱼ) to Dpair
19:             end if
20:         end if
21:     end for
22: end for
```

When a node's buffer contains a certain number of pending transactions, the node detects potential deadlocks based on the deadlock formation conditions (see Algorithm 1 for details). For each pair of transactions in the buffer (Lines 4–5), the node performs the following steps: *i) Path Cycle Detection:* The node examines whether a path cycle exists between their transaction paths (Line 7). If no cycle is found, the node determines that deadlock is impossible for this pair. *ii) Channel Capacity Constraint Checking:* If a cycle exists (Line 8), the node verifies whether the overlapping channels' capacities can support concurrent execution of both transactions (Lines 9–10). - If capacities are sufficient, the node concludes that no cyclic waiting will arise and a deadlock cannot form (Lines 11–14). - If capacities are insufficient, the node identifies that cyclic waiting risks emergence, possibly triggering a deadlock (Lines 15–16). For transaction pairs prone to deadlocks, the node adds them to the variable *Dpair* for subsequent processing (Lines 17–18).

4.3   Deadlock Transaction Ordering

After detecting all potential deadlock transactions, we apply two ordering strategies to ensure consistent execution sequences across overlapping channels within each pair. Our ordering strategy must ensure that the deposit locking sequence of these transactions is consistent across channels.

Global Sorting Strategy. The first sorting strategy we propose is to perform a global descending sort on all transactions in set *Dpair* based on their transaction amounts, as transaction amounts in practical Bitcoin or Lightning Network are typically different. After transaction routing, all participating nodes can observe the transactions. Nodes process transactions in batches, with the two nodes associated with each channel in their paths also able to access them simultaneously. Therefore, nodes can directly perform a global sort based on transaction amounts, achievable through a simple sorting algorithm.

Pairwise Ordering Strategy. To improve concurrency, we design a pairwise ordering strategy for transactions in *Dpair*. The transaction set obtained through the partial-order sorting strategy is acyclic because every pair of potential deadlock transactions is ordered by transaction amount. Thus, topological sorting is feasible. We utilize **Kahn algorithm** with the additional constraint of sorting transactions by their amounts in descending order, thereby deriving a unique linear sequence that satisfies the partial order.

For a given channel, the transaction ordering is consistent across both end nodes. Therefore, for a pair of potential deadlock transactions, their execution order is identical on overlapping channels.

5   Deadlock-Free Transaction Scheduling

After detecting the potential deadlock transactions within a batch of transactions, the primary problem becomes whether we can design a scheduling strategy that prevents deadlocks while ensuring fair transaction scheduling and maximizing the success rate. We propose the deadlock-free scheduling strategy that can prevent deadlocks via potential deadlock transaction sorting, ensures fairness by arrival-time adherence, and boosts success rates through counter-directional transaction scheduling. Please note that for the two proposed sorting strategies, there will be two unique sequences. When scheduling potential deadlock transactions for the two nodes of an overlapping channel, strict adherence to the sequence is required to prevent deadlocks.

During scheduling, we focus on a single payment channel (e.g., channel ch_{uv}). For two adjacent nodes u and v, the corresponding transactions on their payment

Table 1. Notation for Transaction Scheduling Algorithms.

Notation	Description
$Dpair$	Potential Deadlock Transaction Pairs
Dxs	Ordered Set of Pending Transactions Prone to Deadlocks
Nxs	Arrival-Time-Sorted Set of regular Pending Transactions
Dx_{cur}	Currently Targeted Deadlock Transaction
Nx_{cur}	Currently Targeted regular Transaction
tx_{cur}	Currently Processed Transaction
ctx	Counter-Directional Transaction to the Currently Processed One
$WaitQ$	Wait Queue

channel ch_{uv} should be consistent. We denote these transactions as Txs. When the number of these transactions reaches a predefined threshold, the nodes begin processing them. First, the system detects potential deadlock transaction pairs, forming the set $Dpair$, which is then sorted to obtain Dxs. Additionally, the ordering of potential deadlock transactions is consistent across u and v.

We provide the pseudo-code for a generalized overview of the entire scheduling process in Algorithm 2. In Algorithm 3, we present the pseudo-code to describe the generalized processing flow of the two types of transactions. In Algorithm 4, we present the pseudo-code of the specific processing procedure for transactions under scenarios where the channel balance is sufficient and insufficient. The descriptions of the variables used in algorithms are presented in Table 1. Now we elaborate on the scheduling strategy at nodes u and v, where they open a channel ch_{uv}.

Algorithm 2. Deadlock free transaction schedule

```
 1: while !is_epmty(Nxs) || !is_epmty(Dxs) do
 2:     if !is_epmty(Nxs) && !is_epmty(Dxs) then
 3:         Dx_cur = GetNext(Dxs)
 4:         Nx_cur = GetNext(Nxs)
 5:         if Nx_cur.arrvTime < Dx_cur.arrvTime
    then
 6:             ProNx(Nx_cur)
 7:         else
 8:             ProDx(Dx_cur)
 9:         end if
10:     else
11:         if !is_epmty(Nxs) then
12:             Nx_cur = GetNext(Nxs)
13:             ProNx(Nx_cur)
14:         else
15:             Dx_cur = GetNext(Dxs)
16:             ProDx(Dx_cur)
17:         end if
18:     end if
19: end while
```

For the two transactions at the first positions of the ordered sets Dxs and Nxs respectively, their arrival times are compared (see Algorithm 2 Line 1–5). Several scenarios may arise:

Case 1: The Earlier-Arrived Transaction is a Regular Transaction Nx_{cur}: (see Algorithm 2 Line 6)

Our strategy checks whether its amount requirement can be satisfied (see Algorithm 3 Line 2).

(a) If the amount requirement is met, Nx_{cur} can be scheduled(see Algorithm 3 Line 3). Please notice that upon scheduling, the funds in the channel will be redistributed, with one end increasing and the other decreasing. (see Algorithm 4 Line 22). Then, the node checks the waiting queue to determine whether any transaction's amount requirements can now be satisfied. If yes, these transactions will be removed from the waiting queue for execution (see Algorithm 4, Lines 23–25).

(b) If the amount requirement is not met (See Algorithm 3 Line 5): First, the node places Nx_{cur} in the waiting queue. Next, it identifies transactions in Nxs with a payment direction opposite to Nx_{cur}'s and schedules all feasible transactions (prioritized by arrival time) until the payer node's balance satisfies Nx_{cur}'s amount requirement (see Algorithm 4 Line 2–15). Here, we emphasize that for every successfully scheduled peer-side transaction, the node must also check whether there are transactions in the waiting queue that can be scheduled (see Algorithm 4 Line 8–10). Finally, it schedules Nx_{cur} (see Algorithm 4 Line 16–17), and examines whether any transactions in the wait queue become executable (see Algorithm 4 Line 26–28).

Algorithm 3. Processing of Two Types of Transactions

```
 1: # function: ProNx(tx_cur)                    10: else
 2: if CanSatisfyAmount(tx_cur, f_uv) then       11:     if      CanSatisfyAmount(tx_cur, f_uv)
 3:     ProSufCap(tx_cur, Nxs, ch_uv, WaitQ)           then
 4: else                                         12:            ProSufCap(tx_cur, ch_uv, WaitQ)
 5:     ProInsCap(tx_cur, Nxs, ch_uv, WaitQ)     13:        else
 6: end if                                       14:            ProInsCap(tx_cur, Nxs, ch_uv, WaitQ)
 7: # function: ProDx(tx_cur)                    15:        end if
 8: if HasDepInWaitQ(tx_cur, WaitQ) then         16: end if
 9:     AddToWaitQueue(tx_cur)
```

Case 2: The Earlier-Arrived Transaction is a Potential Deadlock Transaction Dx_{cur}: (see Algorithm 2 Line 8)

First, node checks whether the potential deadlock transactions it depends on (i.e., transactions that must execute before it) are already in the waiting queue (see Algorithm 3 Line 8):

1. If dependent transactions exist in the waiting queue, the node adds Dx_{cur} to the waiting queue (since its dependencies must be resolved first) (Algorithm 3 Line 9).

2. If no dependent transactions are in the waiting queue, the node determines whether Dx_{cur}'s amount requirement can be satisfied (see Algorithm 3 Line 10–11):

Algorithm 4. Two Cases of Transaction Processing Based on Channel Capacity

---

1: # func: $ProInsCap(tx_{cur}, Nxs, ch_{uv}, WaitQ)$
2: **while** $!CanSatisfyAmount(tx_{cur}, f_{uv})$ **do**
3:     # Counter-directional Scheduling
4:     $ctx = FindNextCTx(Nxs, tx_{cur})$
5:     **if** $ctx! = null$ **then**
6:         **if** $CanSatisfyAmount(ctx, f_{uv})$ **then**
7:             $UpdateChannel(ctx.a, ch_{uv})$
8:             **if** $!is\_empty(WaitQ)$ **then**
9:                 $ProcWaitQ(ch_{uv}, WaitQ)$
10:             **end if**
11:         **else**
12:             break
13:         **end if**
14:     **end if**
15: **end while**
16: **if** $CanSatisfyAmount(tx_{cur}, f_{uv})$ **then**
17:     $UpdateChannel(tx_{cur}.a, ch_{uv})$
18:     **if** $!is\_empty(WaitQ)$ **then**
19:         $ProcWaitQ(ch_{uv}, WaitQ)$
20:     **end if**
21: **else**
22:     $AddToWaitQueue(tx_{cur}, WaitQ)$
23: **end if**
24: # func: $ProSufCap(tx_{cur}, ch_{uv}, WaitQ)$
25: $Updatechannel(tx_{cur}.a, ch_{uv})$
26: **if** $!is\_empty(WaitQ)$ **then**
27:     $ProcWaitQ(ch_{uv}, WaitQ)$
28: **end if**

(a) If met (see Algorithm 3 Line 12), the node schedules Dx_{cur} and subsequently checks whether any transactions in the waiting queue can now meet their amount requirements due to the updated balance state caused by Dx_{cur}'s execution, removing those eligible transactions from the queue, and processes them (see Algorithm 4 Line 21–25);

(b) If not met, the node places Dx_{cur} in the waiting queue. The counter-directional transactions are then scheduled, with the processing procedure identical to that of Nx_{cur} under case 1 scenario (b) (see Algorithm 4, Lines 1–20).

6   Evaluation

This section begins by describing the experimental setup, comprising the original data source and the methodology for constructing the network and transaction datasets. It then specifies the evaluation metrics, details the experimental design, and analyzes the resulting data.

6.1   Experiment Setup

Dataset: We conduct experimental simulations based on Lightning Network data, retrieving the latest 2024 topology [10] with 2,280 nodes and 4,000 payment channels. Based on this dataset, we construct a payment channel network where nodes are uniquely identified, and edges represent payment channels. Each edge carries bidirectional weight values denoting the channel balances in both directions.

Network and Transactions: We construct a condensed PCN by restructuring raw transaction path data and injecting deadlock-prone paths, overcoming the limitations of the sparse topology in the Lightning Network that hinder the effectiveness of sorting strategies and scheduling mechanisms. We fix the random seed to allocate transaction amounts, ensuring the transactions follow a heavy-tailed distribution that reflects the small-value characteristics of the Lightning Network. The channel funds are initialized and distributed equally (1:1 ratio) between both ends.

6.2   Performance Metrics

In this experiment, we evaluate the performance of different strategy combinations using transaction success rate and the volume of successful transactions. A transaction is deemed successful if it is successfully scheduled, meaning all channels along its path meet the transaction requirements.

Success Rate: Transaction success rate refers to the ratio of successfully scheduled transactions to the total transactions.

Transaction Volume: Transaction success volume refers to the sum of transaction values that have been successfully scheduled.

6.3   Evaluation Scheme

In designing the experimental scheme, for the deadlock prevention framework proposed in this paper, we conduct four experimental combinations to observe their performance. These are: (1) total-order sorting with direct scheduling (TDE), (2) total-order sorting with counter-directional transaction scheduling (TCE), (3) partial-order sorting with direct scheduling (PDE) and (4) partial-order sorting with counter-directional scheduling (PCE). The comparative experiments consist of two types: i) benchmark comparison experiment (BNE): In this experiment, the Rayo protocol is adopted for deadlock handling [8]. Specifically, incoming transactions are executed immediately if sufficient balance is available; otherwise, they are directly terminated without entering a waiting queue. ii) Complex comparative experiment (BCE): Deadlocks are also resolved using Rayo [8], but transactions are scheduled using the counter-directional scheduling strategy and managed via a waiting queue.

6.4   Experiment Results

The first group of experiments observes the outcomes of each experimental scheme with a fixed number of transactions (3000) and injected deadlocked transaction proportions of 2%, 5%, 8%, and 10%. Figure 3 shows that BNE and BCE perform worse than our solution overall. As deadlocked transaction proportion rises, our scheme and BCE maintain better success rates and transaction volumes with slight improvements. Our solution combines ordering and scheduling to prevent deadlocks and replenish channel balances via counterpart transactions. In contrast, BNE aborts deadlocked transactions without scheduling, causing untimely balance replenishment and the worst performance. BCE performs relatively better by maintaining balances through counterpart transaction scheduling.

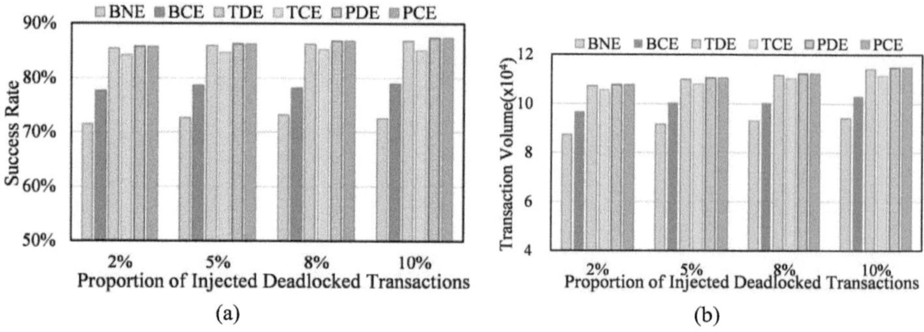

Fig. 3. Success rate and transaction volume variation as proportion of injected deadlocked transactions increases

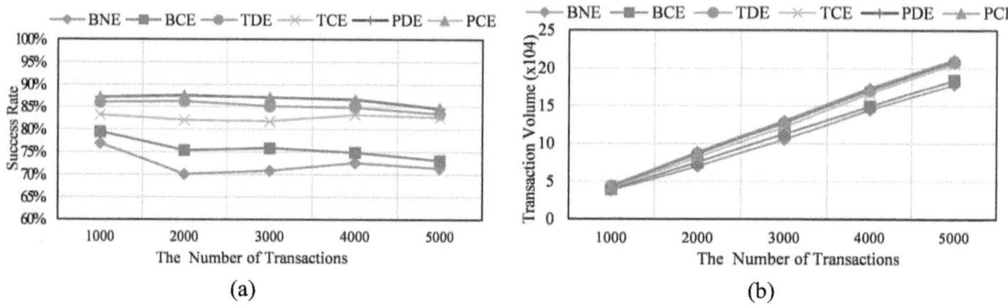

Fig. 4. Success Rate and Transaction Volume Variation across varying transaction quantities

The second group of experiments evaluates each scheme with a fixed 5% deadlocked transaction injection rate and varying transaction counts (1000–5000). Figure 4 shows the results under 5% injection across varying quantities. From Fig. 4-(a), we can see our scheme and BCE achieve higher success rates due to more schedulable transactions, while BNE's rate declines slightly as channel contention intensifies. Our four combined ordering-scheduling schemes (80%–90% success rates) perform comparably, with the partial-order scheme outperforming the total-order scheme. The total-order approach sorts transactions by transaction amount size and schedules them in order, blocking smaller transactions if larger ones fail. Figure 4-(b) shows that transaction success volume increases with transaction counts, consistent with the trends in Fig. 4-(a).

7   Conclusion

In this work, we address PCN deadlocks arising from overlapping-channel resource contention as the network scales. The solution integrates four key components: formalizing deadlock conditions, detecting deadlocks via path-cycle analysis, prioritizing potentially deadlocked transactions through total/partial-order sorting, and proposing a deadlock-free scheduling mechanism to further enhance success rates. The effectiveness of our proposed deadlock-free processing is validated through simulations.

Acknowledgments. This study is partially supported by The GuangDong Basic and Applied Basic Research Foundation (No. 2022A1515110932), The National Science Foundation for Young Scientists of China (No. 62302106).

Disclosure of Interests. The authors have no conflicts of interest to disclose.

References

1. Raiden network. http://raiden.network/
2. Bai, Q., Xu, Y., Wang, X.: Understanding the benefit of being patient in payment channel networks. IEEE Trans. Netw. Sci. Eng. **9**(3), 1895–1908 (2022)
3. Cai, Q., Chen, J., Luo, D., Sun, G., Yu, H., Guizani, M.: Deter-Pay: a deterministic routing protocol in concurrent payment channel network. IEEE Internet Things J. **11**(19), 31206–31220 (2024)
4. Decker, C., Wattenhofer, R.: A fast and scalable payment network with bitcoin duplex micropayment channels. In: Proceedings SSS (2015)
5. Jiang, S., Wu, J., Zuo, F., Mei, A.: Balance-aware cost-efficient routing in the payment channel network. In: 2023 IEEE/ACIS 21st International Conference on Software Engineering Research, Management and Applications (SERA), pp. 8–15 (2023). https://doi.org/10.1109/SERA57763.2023.10197670
6. Lin, S., Zhang, J., Wu, W.: FSTR: funds skewness aware transaction routing for payment channel networks. In: 2020 50th Annual IEEE/IFIP International Conference on Dependable Systems and Networks (DSN), pp. 464–475 (2020)
7. Luo, X., Li, P.: Learning-based off-chain transaction scheduling in prioritized payment channel networks. IEEE J. Sel. Areas Commun. (J-SAC) **40**(12), 11 (2022)
8. Malavolta, G., Moreno-Sanchez, P., Kate, A., Maffei, M., Ravi, S.: Concurrency and privacy with payment-channel networks. In: Proceedings of the 2017 ACM SIGSAC Conference on Computer and Communications Security, pp. 455–471 (2017)
9. Nakamoto, S.: Bitcoin: a peer-to-peer electronic cash system. Decentralized Bus. Rev., 21260 (2008)
10. OKLINK: bitcoin, 11 December 2024. https://www.oklink.com/zh-hans/bitcoin/node-list
11. Papadis, N., Tassiulas, L.: Payment channel networks: single-hop scheduling for throughput maximization. In: IEEE INFOCOM 2022 - IEEE Conference on Computer Communications, pp. 900–909 (2022)
12. Poon, J., Dryja, T.: The bitcoin lightning network: scalable off-chain instant payments (2016). https://lightning.network/lightningnetwork-paper.pdf. Visited 19 April 2016
13. Qiu, X., Chen, W., Tang, B., Liang, J., Dai, H.N., Zheng, Z.: A distributed and privacy-aware high-throughput transaction scheduling approach for scaling blockchain. IEEE Trans. Dependable Secure Comput. (T-DSC) **20**(5), 15 (2023)
14. Sharma, N., Kapoor, K.: Distributed routing algorithms for concurrent execution of transactions in PCNs. In: 2023 IEEE 7th International Conference on Fog and Edge Computing (ICFEC), pp. 49–57 (2023)

15. Sharma, N., Kapoor, K.: Deadlock prevention in payment channel networks. IEEE Trans. Netw. Serv. Manage. **21**(5), 5164–5177 (2024)
16. Sivaraman, V., et al.: High throughput cryptocurrency routing in payment channel networks. In: Proceedings of the 17th Usenix Conference on Networked Systems Design and Implementation, pp. 777–796 (2020)
17. Wang, W., Mu, K., Wei, X.: DPCN: towards deadline-aware payment channel networks. ArXiv abs/2209.10299 (2022)
18. Wang, X., et al.: Fence: fee-based online balance-aware routing in payment channel networks. IEEE/ACM Trans. Network. **32**(2), 1661–1676 (2024)
19. Werman, S., Zohar, A.: Avoiding deadlocks in payment channel networks. In: Data Privacy Management. Cryptocurrencies and Blockchain Technology, pp. 175–187. Springer International Publishing, Cham (2018)
20. Ye, Y., Ren, Z., Luo, X., Zhang, J., Wu, W.: Garou: an efficient and secure off-blockchain multi-party payment hub. IEEE Trans. Netw. Serv. Manage. **18**(4), 4450–4461 (2021)

QoSmart-IoT: Secure QoS-Based Reconfiguration and Protocol Adaptation for Hybrid Clustered IoT Systems in Constrained Environments

Osama Dighriri[1,2]([✉])(iD), Priyadarsi Nanda[2](iD), Manoranjan Mohanty[3](iD), Bashair Alrashed[2,4](iD), and Ibrahim Haddadi[5](iD)

[1] Department of Computer Science, College of Engineering and Computer Science, Jazan University, Jazan, Saudi Arabia
`osamamohammeda.dighriri@student.uts.edu.au`
[2] School of Electrical and Data Engineering, Faculty of Engineering and IT, University of Technology Sydney, Ultimo, Australia
[3] School of Information Systems, Carnegie Mellon University, Doha, Qatar
[4] College of Computer Science and Engineering, University of Jeddah, Jeddah, Saudi Arabia
[5] Department of Computer Engineering, College of Computer Science and Engineering, Taibah University, Medinah, Saudi Arabia

Abstract. Current Internet of Things (IoT) communication systems typically employ static protocols and hardcoded resource allocation mechanisms, limiting their ability to adapt to dynamic, resource-constrained environments. These schemes lack real-time adaptability and cannot provide fine-grained Quality of Service (QoS) management, particularly under network stress or time-varying conditions. This paper addresses this limitation by introducing QoSmart-IoT, a three-layered framework operating at client, cluster, and edge levels to enable real-time adaptation through QoS-driven decisions. The framework integrates hybrid clustering algorithms with adaptive Message Queuing Telemetry Transport (MQTT) and Constrained Application Protocol (CoAP) switching, utilizing live performance metrics including latency, energy consumption, throughput, and session-level security feedback. Balanced Iterative Reducing and Clustering using Hierarchies (BIRCH) and Density-Based Spatial Clustering of Applications with Noise (DBSCAN) algorithms optimize resource allocation, while Advanced Encryption Standard (AES-128) provides security. The system demonstrates significant performance improvements, implemented on Contiki-NG and evaluated through comprehensive runtime analysis across multiple optimization scenarios and stress tests. Our work reduces average latency by 23.3% (from 55.1 ms to 42.3 ms), improves QoS scores from 0.82 to 0.88 during heavy load conditions, and achieves energy savings of up to 0.4 W during protocol switching operations. The adaptive clustering mechanism successfully executed 9 reconfigurations within 30 s each, enhancing recovery time and communication reliability to demon-

© IFIP International Federation for Information Processing 2026
Published by Springer Nature Switzerland AG 2026
X. Wang et al. (Eds.): NPC 2025, LNCS 16306, pp. 153–165, 2026.
https://doi.org/10.1007/978-3-032-10466-3_13

strate QoSmart-IoT's effectiveness in providing secure, adaptive performance in IoT environments.

Keywords: IoT · Edge computing · Hybrid clustering · QoS-aware adaptation · MQTT and CoAP · Reconfiguration systems · Network security

1   Introduction

The Internet of Things (IoT) has experienced rapid growth across smart city, agricultural, healthcare, and industrial automation applications, encompassing vast numbers of resource-constrained devices with limitations in energy, processing power, and connectivity. These constraints significantly compromise communication reliability, latency, and security, particularly under conditions of node mobility and bursty traffic patterns. Recent studies emphasize the critical importance of energy-efficient design and interconnection challenges in resource-limited IoT environments [6], while Vishwakarma et al. address fundamental IoT concerns including interoperability, scalability, Quality of Service (QoS), security, and energy efficiency across diverse deployment scenarios [17].

Traditional cloud-centric architectures suffer from increased latency, communication bottlenecks, and reduced resilience in dynamic environments. This necessitates a paradigm shift toward edge-assisted models that enable local intelligence and autonomous operation [3,5]. However, implementing such architectures requires novel runtime adaptation mechanisms across the entire network stack. At the communication layer, resource-constrained IoT deployments primarily utilize two protocols: Message Queuing Telemetry Transport (MQTT) and the Constrained Application Protocol (CoAP) [10]. MQTT operates over Transmission Control Protocol (TCP), providing guaranteed packet delivery that makes it optimal for applications requiring reliability guarantees. In contrast, CoAP operates over User Datagram Protocol (UDP) with RESTful semantics, supporting low-latency and lightweight interactions particularly suited for lossy or bandwidth-constrained networks [7].

Existing load-balancing and power-aware clustering techniques typically employ static or periodic approaches that lack real-time responsiveness. Traditional methods such as Low-Energy Adaptive Clustering Hierarchy (LEACH) and Hybrid Energy-Efficient Distributed Clustering (HEED) [1] do not adapt to runtime performance variations and fail to consider dynamic scheme performance. Advanced clustering algorithms including Balanced Iterative Reducing and Clustering using Hierarchies (BIRCH) and Density-Based Spatial Clustering of Applications with Noise (DBSCAN) [16] offer improved scalability but lack online parameter tuning capabilities and depend on centralized coordination mechanisms [1]. Furthermore, most existing solutions either completely omit protocol adaptation considerations [10] or treat security feedback as separate from cluster-level decision processes [18], limiting their effectiveness in reconfigurable and trust-aware IoT deployments.

To address these limitations, this paper introduces QoSmart-IoT, a runtime adaptation framework that integrates real-time measurements of latency, energy consumption, throughput, and trust indicators into decentralized feedback loops for dynamic protocol selection and clustering decisions. The proposed framework operates across three hierarchical layers: embedded client nodes, cluster coordinators, and edge controllers, enabling scalable autonomous control without cloud dependency, incorporating session-level security indicators to enhance resilience against attacks and misbehaving nodes.

The primary contributions of this work include: (1) a multi-layered runtime coordination scheme enabling autonomous operation among embedded nodes, cluster coordinators, and edge controllers without cloud dependency, (2) a lightweight adaptive switching mechanism between CoAP and MQTT protocols with dynamic clustering based on real-time feedback triggers, and (3) a comprehensive evaluation framework utilizing a multi-metric QoS model that incorporates latency, energy consumption, throughput, and session-level trust indicators to enable fine-grained system adaptation.

2 Background and Related Work

The IoT networks of today operate and evolve in changing environments with variable workloads, mobile devices, non-traditional connectivity, and low-power embedded systems [6,17]. Previous work introduced diverse communication protocols [10], clustering [16], and middleware [2] architectures to cope with these domains. However, the majority of traditional approaches fall short in offering runtime elasticity, real-time responsiveness, and native security intelligence, key requirements for robust IoT infrastructures [14]. At the networking layer, works like [7,13] have proven CoAP to outperform MQTT with respect to latency and throughput in constrained and dynamic settings. Yet the majority of IoT solutions deployed statically assign the protocol interconnectivity during design time with consequent performance bottlenecks when workloads shift, under congestion, or fail. Existing adaptive protocol switching solutions, such as Moukaddam et al.'s CoAP/MQTT approach [10], focus on resilience through rule-based switching but lack integration with clustering optimization and real-time QoS feedback loops that consider energy, latency, and trust simultaneously.

Middleware platforms such as Cavalcanti and Rosa's [2] have developed adaptable runtime environments that support dynamic protocol settings. These mechanisms, however, are typically derived from centralized rule sets or periodic polling approaches that introduce delays and limit edge-based autonomy. Unlike QoSmart-IoT's decentralized three-layer approach, existing middleware solutions cannot perform autonomous adaptation without cloud coordination. Similarly, recent surveys [4,8] highlight the lack of secure and trust-aware decision-making in integration-layer frameworks. Moreover, distributed intelligence structures [5] and adaptive protection systems [3,12] emphasize the need for decentralized and lightweight runtime strategies, yet there are few solutions that offer end-to-end integration of communication, clustering, and security layers simultaneously. On the other hand, clustering is essential to achieve energy efficiency and fault tolerance. Most existing algorithms like LEACH and HEED use static or periodic policies, which are not adaptive to runtime fluctuations. More advanced methods such as BIRCHSCAN [16] and hybrid ML-based systems [1] increase scalability and cluster development but remain constrained by offline training or rigid heuristics. These approaches often disregard protocol performance, QoS variability, or trust mechanisms in decision-making. In contrast, QoSmart-IoT uniquely integrates clustering decisions with real-time protocol performance metrics and session-level security feedback, enabling adaptive reconfiguration based on multi-dimensional performance indicators rather than predetermined schedules.

Table 1 summarizes prior research and highlights the key limitation: no existing framework provides unified real-time integration of adaptive protocol switching, feedback-driven clustering, and session-level security triggers within a decentralized architecture.

Table 1. Limitations of Existing Protocol and Clustering Strategies

Framework	Protocol Switch	Clustering Mode	QoS Feedback	Security Triggers
Barati et al. [1]	No	Periodic (ML-based)	No	No
Ventorim et al. [16]	No	Hybrid (BIRCH-DBSCAN)	No	No
Cavalcanti and Rosa [2]	Partial (Policy-based)	Fixed	No	No
Moukaddam et al. [10]	Yes (Rule-based)	Not Addressed	Limited	No
QoSmart-IoT (Ours)	**Yes (Live)**	**Feedback-Driven**	**Yes (Latency, Energy, QoS)**	**Yes (Session-Level)**

3 System Implementation

The QoSmart-IoT framework is implemented on the Contiki-NG operating system as a decentralized, three-layer architecture designed for resource-constrained edge environments. The first tier comprises embedded heterogeneous IoT client nodes with varying sensing, computational, and communication capabilities. These nodes periodically monitor local performance metrics including signal strength, latency, energy consumption, and trust indicators, transmitting this information to their designated cluster coordinators. The second tier consists of cluster center coordinators that manage groups of geographically proximate client nodes. These coordinators perform proximity-based data aggregation, conduct lightweight inference on QoS trends, and enforce dynamic clustering policies. Based on threshold-based evaluations and trust assessment scores, they can trigger node reassignments or flag anomalies within the cluster without escalating to higher layers. The third tier hosts edge-level decision units that serve as decentralized control points, replacing traditional cloud-centric logic. These units maintain a global view of cluster states and protocol behavior (MQTT vs. CoAP), applying policy rules and feedback models to adapt protocol selection and security modes in real time. Additionally, they coordinate secure inter-cluster communication and isolate malicious or misbehaving nodes, ensuring system reliability against both performance degradation and security violations.

This three-tier architecture enables autonomous monitoring and dynamic reconfiguration in response to changing network conditions without dependence on external cloud infrastructure, supporting scalable, secure, and low-latency IoT deployments with real-time QoS-driven reconfiguration capabilities.

3.1   Secure Communication and Session Management

All data exchanges are protected using AES-128 encryption [11] with rotating keys and per-message nonces. Session validation verifies nonce freshness, authenticates Hash-based Message Authentication Code (HMAC) [9] signatures, and validates timestamps within a three-second window.

The security session lifecycle is managed by:

$$Session_{valid} = (t_{current} - t_{last\_used} < T_{timeout}) \wedge (failures < F_{max}) \wedge HMAC_{valid} \tag{1}$$

where $T_{timeout} = 900$ s and $F_{max} = 3$ successive failures. Sessions exceeding these thresholds are marked as untrusted and isolated.

3.2   Real-Time Metric Sampling and QoS Evaluation

Client devices collect performance metrics at $T = 30$-s intervals, including: latency (L_i) measuring round-trip time in milliseconds, energy consumption (E_i) sampled via Contiki's Energest module, throughput (T_i) measuring data transmission rate, and trust status (S_i) determined as a binary indicator based on session validation success. However, to reduce noise and stabilize measurements, each metric undergoes exponential moving average smoothing, where $\alpha = 0.8$:

$$\bar{M}_i(t) = \alpha M_i(t) + (1 - \alpha)\bar{M}_i(t - 1) \tag{2}$$

A composite QoS score per node is computed as:

$$QoS_i(t) = \omega_L \left(1 - \frac{\bar{L}_i}{L_{\max}}\right) + \omega_T \frac{\bar{T}_i}{T_{\max}} + \omega_E \left(1 - \frac{\bar{E}_i}{E_{\max}}\right) + \omega_S \cdot S_i \tag{3}$$

where $L_{\max} = 60$ ms, $T_{\max} = 55$ Mbps, $E_{\max} = 7$ W, and normalized weights are $\omega_L = 0.25$, $\omega_T = 0.25$, $\omega_E = 0.25$, $\omega_S = 0.25$ (summing to 1.0).

3.3   Protocol Selection and Adaptation

The system performs adaptive protocol selection using multi-criteria decision analysis, where protocol performance is quantified by:

$$Score = w_L \cdot S_L + w_T \cdot S_T + w_R \cdot S_R + w_E \cdot S_E + w_{Sec} \cdot S_{Sec} \tag{4}$$

where weights are $w_L = 0.25$ (latency), $w_T = 0.20$ (throughput), $w_R = 0.25$ (reliability), $w_E = 0.10$ (energy), and $w_{Sec} = 0.20$ (security), totaling 1.0.

Protocol reconfiguration is triggered when the QoS difference between protocols exceeds a threshold:

$$|QoS_{mqtt}(t) - QoS_{coap}(t)| > \theta_{switch} \tag{5}$$

where $\theta_{switch} = 0.15$ and a cooldown period $T_{cooldown} = 180$ s prevents oscillatory behavior.

3.4 Cluster Management and Reconfiguration

The system maintains three cluster states: INACTIVE, ACTIVE, and RECOVERING. Cluster reformation is triggered when any of the following conditions are met:

$$QoS_j < 0.45 \quad \text{OR} \quad \text{Var}(QoS_j) > 0.25 \quad \text{OR} \quad E_j > 7\,\text{W} \tag{6}$$

These thresholds ensure cluster reformation occurs when: (1) average QoS falls below acceptable levels, (2) QoS variance indicates instability, or (3) energy consumption exceeds sustainable limits.

3.5 Edge-Level Aggregation and Global Decision Logic

Edge nodes maintain historical performance logs and compute a global network health metric:

$$G(t) = \frac{1}{N} \sum_{j=1}^{N} QoS_j(t) \cdot \kappa_j(t) \tag{7}$$

where $\kappa_j(t)$ represents a trust factor based on session validation success rates:

$$\kappa_j(t) = \frac{sessions_{valid,j}(t)}{sessions_{total,j}(t)} \tag{8}$$

To prevent oscillatory behavior in decision-making, QoS trends are smoothed using:

$$QoS_{smooth}(t) = \beta \cdot QoS(t) + (1 - \beta) \cdot QoS_{smooth}(t - 1) \tag{9}$$

where $\beta = 0.7$. A recovery period $T_{recovery} = 60$ s allows degraded clusters to stabilize before triggering additional reconfigurations.

Algorithm 1 details the complete operational flow. Each client monitors local metrics, computes QoS scores, and transmits encrypted updates to cluster coordinators. Clusters aggregate metrics, compute variance, and trigger reconfiguration when thresholds are exceeded. The system continuously evaluates MQTT and CoAP performance, switching protocols when QoS improvements justify the transition. Upon repeated session validation failures, nodes are isolated and secure reclustering is initiated. Global health metrics and QoS smoothing maintain overall system stability and responsiveness.

Algorithm 1. QoSmart-IoT Unified Runtime Decision Logic

1: **Input:** Client metrics: latency L_i, throughput T_i, energy E_i, session trust S_i; protocol history; cooldown threshold; failure threshold F_{max}

2: **for** each client i **do**

3:     Measure latency L_i, throughput T_i, energy E_i, session trust S_i

4:     Compute $QoS_i(t)$ using Eq. (3)

5:     Apply security validation and session management using Eq. (1)

6:     Send encrypted metrics to cluster center C_j

7: **end for**

8: Cluster center aggregates $QoS_j(t)$, computes $\mathrm{Var}(QoS_j)$, energy E_j

9: **if** cluster reformation condition met (Eq. 6) **then**

10:     Execute hybrid clustering (BIRCH + DBSCAN)

11: **end if**

12: Compute $QoS_{mqtt}(t)$ and $QoS_{coap}(t)$ with performance history

13: **if** protocol switch condition met (Eq. 5) and cooldown expired **then**

14:     Switch to protocol with higher QoS score

15:     Broadcast reconfiguration to all clusters

16:     Update protocol performance metrics

17: **end if**

18: **if** client session validation fails $> F_{max}$ **then**

19:     Isolate node and trigger security breach handling

20:     Execute local re-clustering with security constraints

21: **end if**

22: Monitor and update global health metric $G(t)$ using Eq. (7)

23: Apply QoS smoothing using Eq. (9)

---

4 Experimental Setup

To evaluate the runtime performance and adaptability of the proposed QoSmart-IoT framework, comprehensive experiments were conducted using the Contiki-NG operating system [15]. The implementation consists of three integrated modules: `client.c`, `cluster.c`, and `edge.c`, developed in C to simulate realistic resource constraints and stress scenarios in IoT networks. The experimental environment utilizes the Cooja simulator with emulated MSP430-based motes communicating via IEEE 802.15.4 radios and the RPL Lite routing protocol [15]. The system complete simulation parameters are detailed in Table 2.

The experimental topology comprises 61 nodes distributed across three hierarchical levels, as illustrated in Fig. 1. The network architecture includes: (1) one edge node serving as the global coordinator responsible for protocol switching decisions and overall QoS evaluation; (2) ten cluster center nodes managing regional metric aggregation and triggering reconfiguration events; and (3) fifty client nodes responsible for collecting QoS metrics and transmitting data through AES-128 encrypted channels. All nodes collect performance metrics at 30-second intervals using Contiki's Energest API, while session trust indicators (S_i) are validated through cryptographic verification and timestamp checking. Each cluster coordinator evaluates local average QoS performance for both MQTT and CoAP protocols at 60-second intervals to enable informed switching decisions.

4.1 Performance Metrics and Evaluation Criteria

The experimental evaluation focuses on eight key performance indicators: latency measuring end-to-end message delivery time in milliseconds, energy consumption quantifying per-node power usage via Contiki's Energest module in Watts, throughput representing successful data transmission rates in kbps, packet delivery ratio indicating the percentage of successfully delivered messages, QoS score as the composite metric defined in Eq. (3), reconfiguration time measuring the duration required for protocol switching in seconds, network stability assessed through variance in QoS metrics over time, and security overhead quantifying additional latency and energy costs introduced by AES-128 encryption and authentication mechanisms.

5 Results and Discussion

To evaluate the runtime performance and adaptability of the QoSmart-IoT framework, comprehensive experiments were conducted using the Contiki-NG platform within the Cooja emulator. The evaluation employed a 61-node testbed comprising 1 edge node, 10 cluster centers, and 50 client nodes. Each experimental configuration was executed 15 times with different random seeds to ensure statistical validity, with individual runs extending 3600 s to capture long-term system behavior. The evaluation incorporated dynamic traffic patterns, trust anomalies, and fluctuating network conditions. Runtime performance data were collected and analyzed across multiple adaptation cycles from the integrated `client.c`, `cluster.c`, and `edge.c` modules.

5.1 QoS Performance and System Resilience

Figure 2a illustrates the evolution of QoS performance across the complete experimental duration. The system demonstrates rapid convergence during the initial phase, with QoS scores rising sharply within the first 100 s through coordinated clustering and protocol optimization. Subsequently, QoS values stabilize within the 0.6–0.7 range, with brief degradations followed by rapid recovery, demonstrating the effectiveness of the adaptive control mechanisms. Statistical analysis reveals that $72.3\% \pm 4.2\%$ of the operational period maintains QoS scores above 0.6, with peak performance exceeding 0.7 during optimal conditions (95% confidence interval: [0.68, 0.76]). Figure 2b correlates QoS trends with protocol switching events and security incidents. During the experimental period, nine protocol reconfigurations occurred: six triggered by performance degradation (increased latency or energy consumption) and three by security violations (timestamp drift, nonce mismatches). Each reconfiguration completed within

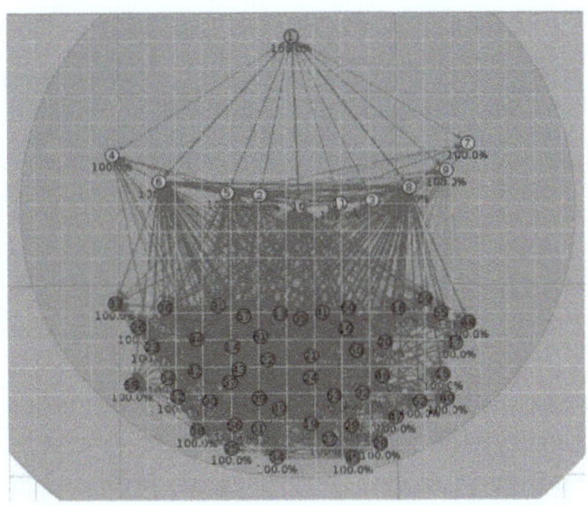

Fig. 1. Cooja simulation topology: one edge node, 10 cluster centers, and 50 clients distributed across three hierarchical levels.

Table 2. Simulation Configuration and Environment Parameters

Parameter	Value
Simulator	Cooja (Contiki-NG v5.0)
Node Platform	Cooja motes (emulated MSP430)
Radio Medium	Unit Disk Graph Medium (UDGM)
MAC Protocol	CSMA
Network Protocol Stack	RPL Lite + 6LoWPAN
Transport Layer	MQTT and CoAP (adaptive switching)
Simulation Duration	3600 s (60 min)
Number of Runs	15 (with different random seeds)
QoS Sampling Interval	30 s (per node)
Protocol Evaluation Interval	60 s (per cluster)
Total Nodes	61 (1 edge, 10 clusters, 50 clients)
Energy Model	Software estimation via Energest module
Security Scheme	AES-128 + nonce + timestamp validation
BIRCH Parameters	Branching factor: 50, Threshold: 0.5
DBSCAN Parameters	Epsilon: 0.3, MinPts: 3
Traffic Patterns	Constant, Bursty, Exponential backoff
Baseline Comparisons	Static MQTT, Static CoAP, LEACH clustering

28.7 ± 3.4 s, with a mandatory 180-second cooldown period preventing oscillatory behavior. The integration of session-level trust monitoring enhanced system robustness against security threats while introducing negligible computational overhead ($<2\%$ energy increase).

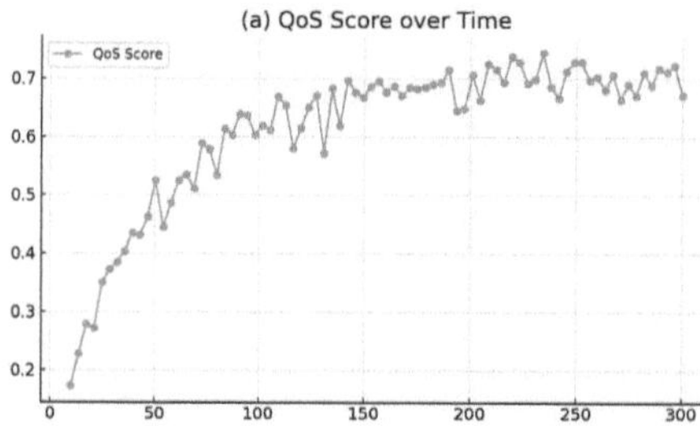
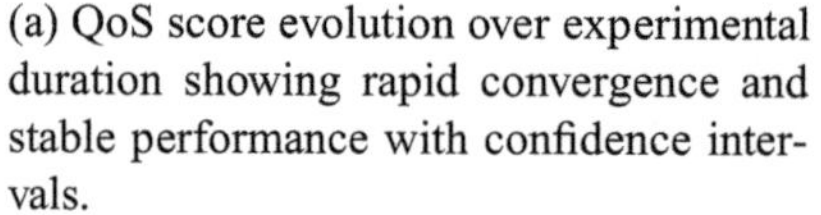
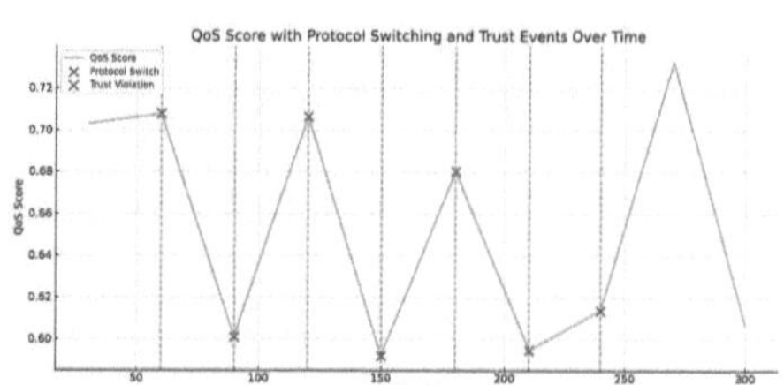

(a) QoS score evolution over experimental duration showing rapid convergence and stable performance with confidence intervals.

(b) QoS progression with protocol switching and trust events. Vertical dashed lines indicate protocol changes; red markers denote security violations.

Fig. 2. QoS analysis: (a) overall score evolution and (b) progression with protocol switching and trust events.

5.2   Energy Efficiency and Resource Utilization

Energy consumption analysis reveals significant improvements over baseline configurations. As shown in Fig. 3a, QoSmart-IoT maintains an average power consumption of 6.6 $\pm$ 0.3 W, representing a 5.7% reduction compared to static MQTT-only deployments (7.0 $\pm$ 0.2 W). The adaptive clustering mechanism effectively distributes computational load across cluster coordinators, preventing energy hotspots and extending network lifetime. During protocol switching operations, temporary energy spikes occur but stabilize within two sampling intervals (< 60 s), demonstrating efficient reconfiguration procedures.

5.3   Throughput and Network Reliability

Throughput performance remains consistently stable across varying network conditions. Figure 3b demonstrates that data transmission rates maintain a range of 30–50 kbps, with a mean throughput of 38.2 $\pm$ 2.1 kbps. The adaptive protocol selection mechanism sustains high throughput levels despite reconfiguration events, with minimal variance during transitions. Packet delivery ratio analysis shows exceptional reliability, maintaining 98.3% $\pm$ 0.8% successful delivery rates even during network stress conditions. This performance indicates robust routing and retransmission mechanisms capable of handling both bursty traffic and dense network scenarios.

5.4   Latency Performance and Responsiveness

Latency analysis demonstrates significant improvements over static protocol implementations. Figure 3c shows that QoSmart-IoT achieves an average end-to-end latency of 42.3 $\pm$ 3.7 ms, representing a 23.2% improvement compared to MQTT-only baselines (55.1 $\pm$ 4.2 ms). Latency spikes occasionally reach 60 ms

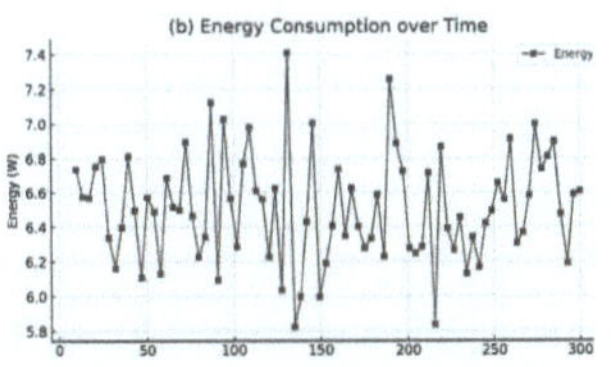

(a) Energy consumption patterns showing stable performance with statistical confidence bounds.

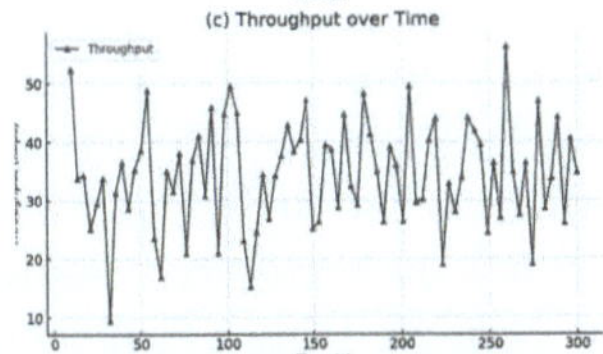

(b) Throughput stability across experimental duration with error bars indicating standard deviation.

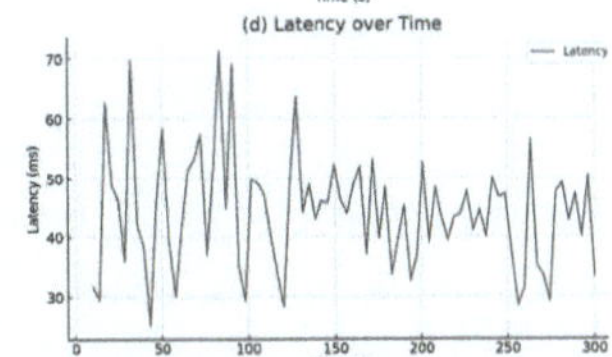

(c) Latency performance showing consistent low-delay operation with rapid recovery.

Fig. 3. System performance metrics dimensions: (a) energy consumption patterns; (b) throughput stability across experimental duration; (c) latency performance.

Table 3. Comparative Performance Analysis with State-of-the-Art Frameworks

Metric	Nathiya et al. [1]	Ventorim et al. [16]	QoSmart-IoT (Ours)
Avg. Latency (ms)	56.4 ± 4.8	54.7 ± 3.9	**42.3 ± 3.7**
Energy Usage (W)	6.9 ± 0.4	6.8 ± 0.3	**6.6 ± 0.3**
QoS Score	0.81 ± 0.06	0.83 ± 0.05	**0.88 ± 0.04**
Protocol Adaptation	No	No	**Yes (Real-time)**
Clustering Approach	ML-based (static)	BIRCH-DBSCAN (static)	**Feedback-driven**
Security Integration	No	No	**Yes (Session-level)**
Reconfiguration Time (s)	≈28	≈35	**< 15**
Statistical Validation	Single run	Single run	**15 runs, CI**

during protocol transitions or traffic bursts but recover to normal levels within 20 s, demonstrating rapid adaptation capabilities. The consistent low-latency performance under adaptive reconfiguration validates the framework's suitability for time-sensitive IoT applications.

Table 3 presents a comprehensive comparison with recent state-of-the-art frameworks in adaptive IoT communications and clustering. QoSmart-IoT demonstrates superior performance across all evaluated metrics, achieving the lowest latency (42.3 ms vs. 54.7–56.4 ms), highest energy efficiency (6.6 W vs. 6.8–6.9 W), and best QoS scores (0.88 vs. 0.81–0.83). The key differentiators include: (1) real-time protocol adaptation capabilities absent in compared works, (2) feedback-driven clustering versus static approaches, (3) integrated session-level security mechanisms, and (4) significantly faster reconfiguration times (<15 s vs. 28–35 s).

6 Conclusion

This work introduced QoSmart-IoT, a decentralized, security-aware reconfiguration approach for cloud-independent IoT deployments. The design combines session-level protection, trust-oriented hybrid clustering, and real-time protocol switching across client, cluster, and edge layers to provide localized agility and decision-making. Implemented on Contiki-NG and evaluated with the Cooja simulator across 15 experimental runs, the platform delivered notable gains: latency dropped by 23.2% (to 42.3 ± 3.7 ms), energy consumption fell by 5.7% (to 6.6 ± 0.3 W), and the QoS score improved from 0.82 to 0.88 ± 0.04 under demanding workloads. Packet delivery remained at 98.3% ± 0.8%, with recovery from integrity or efficiency issues occurring within 30 s, and reconfigurations finalizing in less than 15 s, outperforming comparable solutions. These outcomes confirm that QoSmart-IoT sustains performance and resilience in dynamic, resource-limited settings. The ablation study validated individual component contributions, with protocol switching providing 13.1% latency improvement and adaptive clustering contributing 8.8% energy savings. Security integration introduced minimal overhead (<3%) while enhancing system resilience against trust violations. Future directions include multi-platform deployment and live trust-propagation experiments on physical IoT testbeds to enhance scalability and adaptive capability.

Acknowledgments. The authors gratefully acknowledge the Department of Computer Science, College of Engineering and Computer Science, Jazan University, Jazan, Saudi Arabia; School of Electrical and Data Engineering, Faculty of Engineering and IT, University of Technology Sydney, Australia; College of Computer Science and Engineering, University of Jeddah, Jeddah, Saudi Arabia; Department of Computer Engineering, College of Computer Science and Engineering, Taibah University, Medina, Saudi Arabia.

References

1. Nathiya, N., Chinnasamy, R., Geetha, K.: A hybrid optimization and machine learning based energy-efficient clustering algorithm with self-diagnosis data fault detection and prediction for WSN-IoT application. Peer-to-Peer Network. Appl. **18** (2025). https://doi.org/10.1007/s12083-024-01892-8
2. Cavalcanti, D., Rosa, N.: Customizable and adaptable middleware of things. Int. J. Commun. Syst. (2024). https://doi.org/10.1002/dac.5887
3. Dhiab, Y.B., Aoueileyine, M.O.E., Bouallegue, R.: Context-aware adaptive security framework for IoT-based patient monitoring systems. In: Barolli, L. (ed.) Advanced Information Networking and Applications. AINA 2025. LNDECT, vol. 251, Springer, Cham (2025). https://doi.org/10.1007/978-3-031-87781-0_12
4. Donta, P.K., Srirama, S.N., Amgoth, T., Annavarapu, C.S.: Survey on recent advances in IoT application layer protocols and machine learning scope for research directions. Digit. Commun. Netw. **8**(5), 727–744 (2022). https://doi.org/10.1016/j.dcan.2021.10.004
5. Alsboui, T., Qin, Y., Hill, R., Al-Aqrabi, H.: Distributed intelligence in the internet of things: challenges and opportunities. SN Comput. Sci. **2**(4), 1–16 (2021). https://doi.org/10.1007/s42979-021-00677-7
6. Farhan, L., et al.: Energy efficiency for green internet of things (IoT) networks: a survey. Network **1**(3), 279–314 (2021). https://doi.org/10.3390/network1030017

7. Kashyap, M., Sharma, V.: A comparative analysis and implementation of CoAP and MQTT protocol for IoT communication. Life Cycle Reliab. Saf. Eng. (2025). https://doi.org/10.1007/s41872-025-00324-7
8. Konsta, A.M., Lluch Lafuente, A., Dragoni, N.: Trust management for internet of things: a systematic literature review. arXiv preprint arXiv:2211.01712 (2023)
9. Lawrence, L., Shreelekshmi, R.: Double salted HMAC signature with blockchain for faster and secure video integrity verification. J. Supercomput. **81** (2025). Article 598. https://doi.org/10.1007/s11227-025-06996-3
10. Moukaddam, J., Rizk, B., Salem, J.: Dynamic protocol switching for resilient IoT communications: a CoAP/MQTT adaptive approach. IEEE Commun. Mag. **61**(12), 45–51 (2023)
11. Rahman, Z., Yi, X., Billah, M., Sumi, M., Anwar, A.: Enhancing AES using chaos and logistic map-based key generation technique for securing IoT-based smart home. arXiv preprint arXiv:2203.16124 (2022). https://doi.org/10.48550/arXiv.2203.16124
12. Sha, K., Yang, T.A., Wei, W., Davari, S.: A survey of edge computing-based designs for IoT security. Digit. Commun. Netw. **6**(2), 195–202 (2020). https://doi.org/10.1016/j.dcan.2019.08.006
13. Silva, D., Carvalho, L.I., Soares, J., Sofia, R.C.: A performance analysis of Internet of Things networking protocols: evaluating MQTT, CoAP, OPC UA. Appl. Sci. **11**(11), 4879 (2021). https://doi.org/10.3390/app11114879
14. Sultan, I., Banday, M.T.: An energy-efficient encryption technique for the Internet of Things sensor nodes. Int. J. Inf. Technol. **16**, 2517–2533 (2024). https://doi.org/10.1007/s41870-024-01750-z
15. Oikonomou, G., Duquennoy, S., Elsts, A., Eriksson, J., Tanaka, Y., Tsiftes, N.: The Contiki-NG open source operating system for next generation IoT devices. SoftwareX **18**, 101089 (2022). https://doi.org/10.1016/j.softx.2022.101089
16. de Moura Ventorim, I., Luchi, D., Rodrigues, A.L., Varejão, F.M.: BIRCHSCAN: a sampling method for applying DBSCAN to large datasets. Expert Syst. Appl. **184**, 115518 (2021). https://doi.org/10.1016/j.eswa.2021.115518
17. Vishwakarma, A., Chaurasia, S., Kumar, K., Singh, Y., Chaurasia, R.: Internet of things technology, research, and challenges: a survey. Multimedia Tools Appl. **84**, 8455–8490 (2024). https://doi.org/10.1007/s11042-024-19278-6
18. Wyss, M., Giuliari, G., Legner, M., Perrig, A.: Secure and scalable QoS for critical applications. In: Proceedings of the IEEE/ACM 29th International Symposium on Quality of Service (IWQOS), pp. 1–10 (2021). https://doi.org/10.1109/IWQOS52092.2021.9521315

ManuMatic: Strategy Injection for Robust Automatic Hybrid Parallelism in Distributed DNN Training

Ruiwen Wang[1,2,3], Chong Li[1(✉)], Hongxing Wang[1], Raja Appuswamy[3],
and Yujie Yuan[1]

[1] Huawei Technologies France SASU, Paris, France
`{wang.ruiwen,ch.l,yuan.yujie}@huawei.com`
[2] Sorbonne University, Paris, France
[3] Eurecom, Biot, France
`raja.appuswamy@eurecom.fr`

Abstract. Training modern deep neural networks (DNNs) requires hybrid parallelism. Automatic planners search data, tensor/model, and pipeline shardings with cost models, but decisions can drift from runtime optima due to framework/planner decoupling and overlap mis-modeling. We present MANUMATIC, a light-touch planner that lets users *pin* a few critical operator shardings while automatically deriving globally consistent strategies for the rest. Inside a binary recursive partitioner, MANU-MATIC prioritizes pins via an infinite compromise price and decomposes multi-dimensional hints into two-way refinements; when hard constraints are infeasible, a soft-penalty variant applies. The design is profiling-free, preserves D-Rec's short compilation time, and degenerates to D-Rec when no pins are given. Built atop D-Rec, MANUMATIC delivers consistent speedups without cost-model reengineering: on Mixtral-8×7B, an expert-parallel-aware BMM pin achieves 2.24× over D-Rec; on Llama3-8B, a sequence-parallel-aware MatMul pin reaches 2.04×; on Qwen2.5-72B, a sequence-parallel-aware MatMul pin combined with BMPipe yields 1.45× over D-Rec and 1.30× over an expert plan. These results show that minimal guidance can robustify automatic parallelism while largely preserving automation.

Keywords: Distributed training · Hybrid parallelism · Automatic planning · Strategy injection · Operator sharding · Cost model · Communication optimization · Deep neural networks · ManuMatic

1 Introduction

Deep learning has advanced rapidly over the last decade, powering major progress in computer vision and natural language processing. A persistent trend is the growth in architectural complexity and parameter counts of deep neural networks (DNNs) [1–3], which makes training on accelerator clusters the norm.

© IFIP International Federation for Information Processing 2026
Published by Springer Nature Switzerland AG 2026
X. Wang et al. (Eds.): NPC 2025, LNCS 16306, pp. 166–177, 2026.
https://doi.org/10.1007/978-3-032-10466-3_14

Large-scale training typically relies on *hybrid parallelism*, a composition of data, tensor/model, and pipeline parallelism, to satisfy memory constraints while sustaining device utilization [4–6]. Carefully engineered hybrids can be highly efficient; for instance, Megatron-LM [7] coordinates sharding and scheduling to unlock strong throughput on large transformers. However, hand-crafting such plans requires deep systems expertise, long iteration cycles, and offers no optimality guarantees due to the coupled, combinatorial design space.

Automatic planners [8–10] address this by searching over sharding and scheduling spaces guided by cost models. In practice, two gaps often degrade their decisions. (i) Decoupling between the framework and the planner. Training frameworks evolve (new kernels, fusions, collective algorithms, routing policies), while planner cost models do not automatically track these changes, so modeled and realized communication diverge. The mismatch is worse when the framework introduces new tensor split dimensions or new forms of parallelism (additional mesh axes, sequence [11]/expert parallel [12–14], optimizer/state partitioning). Without corresponding entries in the planner's cost model, dimension mapping $f(\cdot)$, and mismatch classifier, the search space is misspecified, especially for Mixture of experts and long-sequence DNN models. (ii) Overlap mis-modeling. The distributed computational graph used across frameworks does not encode runtime attributes such as compute/communication overlap, stream scheduling, or time-varying contention. Additive communication models become systematically optimistic in boundary regimes (tiny batches or skewed aspect ratios). Both gaps skew traversal priorities and push the search toward suboptimal shardings.

We present MANUMATIC: a light-touch automatic planner that lets users *pin* the sharding of a *small* set of critical operators while automatically deriving globally consistent strategies for the rest of the graph. Within the binary recursive partitioner, MANUMATIC assigns pinned operators an infinite *compromise price* (the minimal extra communication to avoid redistributions), ensuring they are fixed first, and decomposes multi-dimensional hints into per-level two-way refinements compatible with the recursion.

We instantiate MANUMATIC on top of the state-of-the-art D-Rec planner [8]. On Mixtral-8×7B (8 NPUs), MANUMATIC with a single expert-parallel-aware BMM pin yields a 2.24× speedup over D-Rec; on Llama3-8B (8 NPUs, $L = 8\,$K), a sequence-parallel-aware MatMul pin delivers 2.04×; on Qwen2.5-72B (64 NPUs, $L = 32\,$K), a sequence-parallel-aware MatMul pin combined with BMPipe [15] attains 1.45× over D-Rec and 1.30× over an expert plan.

Contributions

- MANUMATIC: a minimal, user-guided automatic planner that anchors a few critical operators and leaves the remainder to automation, improving robustness under frameworkplanner drift and overlap variability.
- A practical integration into a binary recursive partitioner via infinite compromise price and binary-compatible refinement of user hints, preserving global consistency without backtracking.

– A validated instantiation atop D-Rec with production-scale results on Mixtral-8×7B and Qwen2.5-72B, demonstrating substantial speedups without cost-model reengineering.

2   Background and Formulation

2.1   Hybrid Parallelism in Distributed DNN Training

Large-scale training composes multiple parallelism modes to satisfy memory limits while sustaining device utilization. *Data parallelism* shards the global batch and synchronizes gradients across replicas [4]; *model/tensor parallelism* splits parameters and activations to reduce per-device memory pressure [5]; and pipelining with micro-batching overlaps forward/backward across stages [6,7]. Hand-crafted hybrids can be highly efficient yet demand deep expertise and provide no optimality guarantees due to the coupled, combinatorial design space.

2.2   Distributed Computational Graph and Strategy Representation

We model a training step as a data-flow graph $G = (V, E)$ used by frameworks such as MindSpore [16], TensorFlow [17], and PyTorch [18]. Vertices $V = \{o\}$ are operators; edges $E = \{\mathbf{T}\}$ are tensors. Each tensor $\mathbf{T}$ is a D-dimensional array with element type, shape $\mathrm{shape}(\mathbf{T}) \in \mathbb{N}^D$, and a per-dimension distribution strategy $\mathrm{strat}(\mathbf{T}) \in \mathbb{Q}^D$, where

$$\mathrm{partshape}(\mathbf{T}) \;=\; \mathrm{shape}(\mathbf{T}) \;\odot\; \mathrm{strat}(\mathbf{T})$$

denotes the partition shape. We interpret $\mathrm{strat}(\mathbf{T})[d] = \frac{1}{k_d}$ as sharding dimension d into k_d equal parts and $\mathrm{strat}(\mathbf{T})[d] = 1$ as replication. For implementation, it is convenient to use the integer split vector $\mathrm{split}(\mathbf{T}) \in \mathbb{N}^D$ with $\mathrm{split}(\mathbf{T})[d] = k_d = \frac{1}{\mathrm{strat}(\mathbf{T})[d]}$. Feasibility requires $\mathrm{shape}(\mathbf{T})[d]$ divisible by k_d for all d.

Device Mesh. Let the device mesh be an r-D grid $M \in \mathbb{N}^r$ with $\prod_{a=1}^{r} M[a] = d$ devices. A mapping $f : \{1, \ldots, D\} \rightarrow \{1, \ldots, r\} \cup \{\bot\}$ assigns each tensor dimension either to a mesh axis (sharding) or to $\bot$ (replication). A strategy is *mesh-consistent* iff $\prod_{d:f(d)=a} \mathrm{split}(\mathbf{T})[d] \leq M[a]$ for all a, and the product over a equals the intended parallel degree.

While this graph abstraction is ubiquitous across modern DL frameworks, it does not encode runtime attributes, such as compute/communication overlap, collective algorithm choices, stream scheduling, or time-varying network contention; thus it cannot capture the overlap and communication variability that dominate end-to-end performance.

2.3 Communication-Centric Cost Model

On large language model training with even partitioning of regular tensors, end-to-end step time is primarily sensitive to *cross-device communication*. Under weak or strong scaling, per-device compute stays flat or even decreases, while collective costs grow with participants (e.g., $\Theta((P-1)\alpha + \frac{P-1}{P}\beta n)$ or $\Theta(\alpha \log P + \beta n)$). Most sharding choices keep total FLOPs nearly unchanged but alter which collectives run and where redistributions appear, so they mainly perturb communication rather than arithmetic work. Practical schedules overlap compute with communication, which can mask kernel-time variations, whereas network latencies on critical paths remain exposed. Memory/divisibility and mesh capacity are enforced as feasibility constraints. Hence we minimize communication cost subject to feasibility; compute terms can be added if needed but are second-order in our regimes.

Collective Costs. We use the standard α–β model: sending B bytes costs $\alpha + \beta B$; collective costs scale with algorithmic factors. For example, a ring all-reduce of an n-byte buffer over p devices costs

$$T^{\text{ring}}_{\text{allreduce}}(n,p) \approx 2(p-1)\alpha + 2\frac{p-1}{p}\beta n,$$

while a tree-based reduce-scatter/all-gather yields $\mathcal{O}(\alpha \log p + \beta n)$; our formulation abstracts these into a primitive $\text{Collective}(\cdot)$.

Redistribution Across Edges. Let edge $e = (u \rightarrow v)$ carry tensor $\mathbf{T}$ with producer-side strategy strat_u and consumer-side strategy strat_v. A *redistribution* occurs if $\text{strat}_u \neq \text{strat}_v$ in a way that cannot be satisfied by local reindexing/broadcast. We define a *mismatch classifier*:

$$\text{class}(\text{strat}_u, \text{strat}_v) \in \{\text{None}, \text{AllGather}, \text{ReduceScatter}, \text{AllToAll}\},$$

which picks the cheapest collective needed to reconcile the two layouts (e.g., sharded $\rightarrow$ replicated on the same dimension $\Rightarrow$ AllGather; replicated $\rightarrow$ sharded $\Rightarrow$ ReduceScatter; sharded on different dimensions $\Rightarrow$ AllToAll). The redistribution cost on e is

$$C_{\text{redist}}(e; \text{strat}_u, \text{strat}_v) = \text{Collective}\left(\text{class}(\text{strat}_u, \text{strat}_v), \text{bytes}(\mathbf{T}), p_e\right),$$

with p_e the effective group size on that edge.

Operator-Local Costs. Some operator/strategy pairs require intrinsic collectives, e.g., data-parallel gradients for weights, tensor-parallel partial sums, or pipeline stage boundaries. We write

$$C_{\text{local}}(o; \text{strat}_{\text{in}}, \text{strat}_{\text{out}}) = \sum_{c \in \mathcal{C}(o,\text{strat}_{\text{in}},\text{strat}_{\text{out}})} \text{Collective}(c),$$

where $\mathcal{C}$ enumerates collectives implied by the operator semantics under the chosen sharding.

Objective. Given a strategy assignment S over all tensors, the communication objective is

$$C_{\text{comm}}(S) = \sum_{e \in E} C_{\text{redist}}(e) + \sum_{o \in V} C_{\text{local}}(o).$$

Many planners minimize C_{comm} subject to mesh consistency and divisibility.

2.4   Redistribution-Aware Prioritization: Compromise Price

When deciding an operator with some neighbor strategies already fixed, it is useful to quantify how costly it would be to *change* its locally optimal strategy in order to *avoid* redistributions with those neighbors.

Let $\mathcal{S}_o$ be the feasible strategy set for operator o, and let $N^{\text{fix}}(o)$ be the set of adjacent operators already fixed. Define

$$C_o(s) = C_{\text{local}}(o; s) + \sum_{e=(o,\cdot)\ \text{or}\ (\cdot,o)} C_{\text{redist}}(e;\ s,\ S_{\text{fix}}),$$

where S_{fix} provides neighbor strategies on $N^{\text{fix}}(o)$. The *compromise price* is

$$\text{price}(o) = \min_{s \in \mathcal{S}_o^{\text{compat}}} C_o(s) - \min_{s \in \mathcal{S}_o} C_o(s),$$

with $\mathcal{S}_o^{\text{compat}}$ the subset eliminating redistributions against $N^{\text{fix}}(o)$ (if empty, set $\text{price}(o) = +\infty$). This nonnegative quantity induces a natural *traversal priority*: operators with larger $\text{price}(o)$ are more expensive to move and should be decided earlier to reduce backtracking and global cost.

2.5   Automatic Planning as Recursive Partitioning

A scalable approach used in OptCNN [10], Tofu [9], and D-Rec [8] casts planning as a *recursive partitioner* guided by C_{comm}:

1. Order. Compute $\text{price}(o)$ and obtain a traversal order by decreasing price.
2. Partition. Traverse vertices and (i) choose for each a candidate split (dimension and degree), (ii) assign operators/tensors to one of two groups to minimize $C_{\text{local}} + C_{\text{redist}}$ across the cut.
3. Recurse. Repeat on each group until the number of partitions equals the device count d. The outer loop runs $\lceil \log_2 d \rceil$ times since the number of partitions doubles each recursion; the inner loop touches $|V|$ vertices per level.

This framework accommodates different cost models and search heuristics while providing clear hooks for priorities and constraints.

2.6 Limits of State-of-the-Art Automatic Planning

Most planners minimize a *model-based* communication objective:

$$C_{\mathrm{mdl}}(S) = \sum_{e \in E} C_{\mathrm{redist}}^{\mathrm{mdl}}(e; S) + \sum_{o \in V} C_{\mathrm{local}}^{\mathrm{mdl}}(o; S).$$

However, the *runtime* makespan depends on the framework's actual primitives and on compute/communication overlap, which the graph abstraction cannot encode:

$$C_{\mathrm{rt}}(S; \Theta, \sigma) \approx C_{\mathrm{mdl}}(S) + E_{\mathrm{prim}}(S; \Theta) + E_{\mathrm{ovr}}(S; \Theta, \sigma).$$

Here E_{prim} captures primitive drift (changes in collective algorithms, kernel fusions, routing, or α–β), and E_{ovr} captures overlap mis-modeling (schedule-dependent non-additivity due to stream concurrency and contention). For two strategies S_1, S_2, define $\Delta_{\mathrm{mdl}} = C_{\mathrm{mdl}}(S_2) - C_{\mathrm{mdl}}(S_1)$ and $\Delta E = (E_{\mathrm{prim}} + E_{\mathrm{ovr}})\big|_{S_2} - (E_{\mathrm{prim}} + E_{\mathrm{ovr}})\big|_{S_1}$. Then $\Delta_{\mathrm{rt}} \approx \Delta_{\mathrm{mdl}} + \Delta E$. If $|\Delta E| \geq \Delta_{\mathrm{mdl}}^{\mathrm{min}}$ (the model margin), the model-optimal choice can flip at runtime.

New Split Dimensions or New Parallelism. Beyond parameter drift, frameworks may expand the device mesh and sharding vocabulary itself. If the runtime moves from an r-axis mesh $M \in \mathbb{N}^r$ to $M' \in \mathbb{N}^{r'}$ with $r' > r$, or adds new parallelism modes (e.g., sequence/expert parallel, optimizer/state partitioning), the planner's mapping $f : \{1, \ldots, D\} \to \{1, \ldots, r\} \cup \{\bot\}$ cannot place splits along the new axes. The search is then restricted to a misspecified subset $\mathcal{S}^{\mathrm{mdl}} \subsetneq \mathcal{S}^{\mathrm{rt}}$, effectively projecting the runtime-optimal $S^\star \in \mathcal{S}^{\mathrm{rt}}$ to $\Pi(S^\star) \in \mathcal{S}^{\mathrm{mdl}}$ with a non-negligible gap $C_{\mathrm{rt}}(S^\star) - C_{\mathrm{rt}}(\Pi(S^\star))$. In practice, the mismatch classifier may also lack the new collective variants, which further inflates the error and increases the chance of wrong choices.

Impact on Traversal. Priority heuristics such as compromise price are computed from C_{mdl}. When drift or overlap alter effective costs, priorities can invert, causing extra redistributions and a worse final plan. The method in Sect. 3 anchors a few sensitive operators to the framework's actual behavior, shrinking the error where it matters most.

3 ManuMatic: Strategy Injection atop D-Rec Automatic Planner

We build MANUMATIC on top of the state-of-the-art planner D-Rec [8] because it is a strong, *profiling-free*, communication-centric system with short compilation time. Its binary-recursive design scales cleanly: only $T = \lceil \log_2 d \rceil$ levels and each level visits $|\mathcal{V}|$ operators once, which avoids heavy ILPs, autotuners, and runtime sampling. The modular structure (cost model, operator couplings, and a redistribution-aware priority heuristic) exposes clean hooks for priorities and constraints, which MANUMATIC reuses without altering the core search; importantly, MANUMATIC degenerates exactly to D-Rec when no pins are provided, ensuring fair, like-for-like comparisons. Formally, given a device mesh with d devices and a computational graph $G = (V, E)$, D-Rec minimizes

$$C_{\text{comm}}(S) = \sum_{e \in E} C_{\text{redist}}(e; S) + \sum_{o \in V} C_{\text{local}}(o; S),$$

subject to mesh consistency and divisibility (Sect. 2), and proceeds in $T = \lceil \log_2 d \rceil$ outer recursions, each doubling the number of partitions. MANUMATIC adds a lightweight interface that pins the sharding of a few critical operators and equips the partitioner with mechanisms to treat these pins as first-class constraints, without changing D-Rec's recursion skeleton.

(1) Priority ordering. For each operator o, compute its *compromise price* price(o) (the extra communication needed to avoid redistributions against already fixed neighbors) and traverse operators in decreasing price(o) to reduce backtracking.

(2) Bipartition per recursion. Following the order, choose a candidate split (dimension and degree) and assign o and its incident tensors to one of two groups to minimize $C_{\text{local}} + C_{\text{redist}}$. This yields two subgraphs that preserve data dependencies.

(3) Strategy materialization and recursion. The group assignment induces per-tensor strategies consistent with the mesh mapping. Update fixed neighbors and recurse on each subgraph. The inner loop visits $|V|$ operators per level; the outer loop runs T levels.

3.1 Strategy Injection as Constraints

As summarized in Algorithm 1, MANUMATIC extends D-Rec [8] by treating a few user-provided shardings as first-class constraints within the same recursion skeleton.

Feasible Set. Users specify a small set of injected operators $\mathcal{O}_{\text{inj}}$ and, for any incident tensor $\mathbf{T}$, a target integer split vector split$^\star(\mathbf{T})$. MANUMATIC optimizes the same objective as D-Rec but over the constrained set

$$\mathcal{S}_{\text{feas}} = \Big\{ S : \text{mesh-consistent, divisible, and } \forall \mathbf{T} \sim \mathcal{O}_{\text{inj}}, \text{ split}(\mathbf{T}) \succeq \text{split}^\star(\mathbf{T}) \Big\},$$

where $\succeq$ denotes element-wise divisibility ($a \succeq b \iff \forall d, a[d]$ is a multiple of $b[d]$). Injected splits act as lower bounds that later recursions may further refine.

Binary-Compatible Decomposition. Because the outer loop is binary, a multi-way injected split must be expressed as a monotone sequence $\{\text{split}^{(t)}(\mathbf{T})\}_{t=0}^{T}$ with split$^{(0)} = \mathbf{1}$, split$^{(T)} \succeq$ split*, and $\prod_d \text{split}^{(t+1)}[d] / \prod_d \text{split}^{(t)}[d] = 2$. We use a greedy factorization: at recursion t, place one factor 2 on a dimension that still needs capacity toward split*; if no 2-factor remains, place a provisional 2 on the mesh axis intended for a $q > 2$ factor (to be completed in later rounds). When $\prod_d \text{split}^\star[d] \nmid 2^T$, we realize the nearest feasible $\tilde{K} = 2^T$ with split$^{(T)} \succeq$ split* (over-provision) or fall back to a soft penalty (below).

Algorithm 1. ManuMatic (concise): Strategy Injection atop D-Rec

---

Require: Device mesh M with d devices; graph $\mathcal{G} = (\mathcal{V}, \mathcal{E})$; injected ops $\mathcal{O}_{\text{inj}}$; target splits $\text{split}^\star(X)$ for tensors incident to $\mathcal{O}_{\text{inj}}$; couplings Φ; penalty λ (set $\lambda = 0$ for hard mode)

Ensure: Strategy assignment $S = \{\text{split}(X)\}_{X \in \mathcal{E}}$

1: $T \leftarrow \lceil \log_2 d \rceil$; initialize $\text{split}(X) \leftarrow \mathbf{1}$ for all tensors; $\texttt{Parts} \leftarrow \{\mathcal{G}\}$

2: **for** $t = 0$ to $T - 1$ **do**

3:     $\texttt{NewParts} \leftarrow \emptyset$

4:     **for all** subgraph $\mathcal{H} = (\mathcal{V}_H, \mathcal{E}_H)$ in $\texttt{Parts}$ **do**

5:         (1) One-step refinement

6:         **for all** $X \in \mathcal{E}_H$ incident to some $op \in \mathcal{O}_{\text{inj}}$ **do**

7:             Multiply $\text{split}(X)$ by 2 on a needed dimension toward $\text{split}^\star(X)$ (if mesh/divisibility allow)

8:         **end for**

9:         Enforce equalities from Φ across coupled tensor dimensions

10:        (2) Priorities

11:        **for all** $op \in \mathcal{V}_H$ **do**

12:            $\text{price}(op) \leftarrow +\infty$ if $op \in \mathcal{O}_{\text{inj}}$ else $\textsc{CompromisePrice}(op)$

13:        **end for**

14:        $\pi \leftarrow$ operators in $\mathcal{V}_H$ sorted by decreasing price

15:        (3) Constrained bipartition

16:        $(\mathcal{H}_L, \mathcal{H}_R) \leftarrow \textsc{Bipartition}(\mathcal{H}, \pi, \Phi)$ by minimizing
$C_{\text{local}} + C_{\text{redist}} + \lambda \sum_{X \sim \mathcal{O}_{\text{inj}}} D(\text{split}(X), \text{split}^\star(X))$ (penalty active only if $\lambda > 0$)

17:        (4) Materialize and recurse

18:        Emit per-tensor $\text{split}(\cdot)$ for $\mathcal{H}_L, \mathcal{H}_R$ and push them into $\texttt{NewParts}$

19:    **end for**

20:    $\texttt{Parts} \leftarrow \texttt{NewParts}$

21: **end for**

22: **return** $S = \{\text{split}(X)\}_{X \in \mathcal{E}}$

Semantic Propagation. An injected choice on $o \in \mathcal{O}_{\text{inj}}$ constrains its incident tensors via a dimension-coupling relation Φ_o (e.g., elementwise alignment; MatMul $(i, k) \times (k, j)$ couples k across inputs and i, j across outputs). After each refinement, $\textsc{ManuMatic}$ enforces equalities $\text{split}(\mathbf{T}_1)[d_1] = \text{split}(\mathbf{T}_2)[d_2]$ for all $(d_1, d_2) \in \Phi_o$ to avoid local redistributions.

Priority Integration. To fix injected neighborhoods first, $\textsc{ManuMatic}$ sets $\text{price}(o) = +\infty$ for all $o \in \mathcal{O}_{\text{inj}}$, placing them at the top of the traversal. During bipartition, decisions are restricted to those consistent with the current $\text{split}^{(t)}$ and with ϕ_o.

Hard vs. Soft Injection. If hard constraints are infeasible on a given mesh, we minimize

$$C_{\text{comm}}(S) + \lambda \sum_{\mathbf{T} \sim \mathcal{O}_{\text{inj}}} D\big(\text{split}(\mathbf{T}), \text{split}^\star(\mathbf{T})\big),$$

over strategies that are only mesh-consistent and divisible; $D(\cdot, \cdot)$ measures deviation (e.g., $D(a, b) = \sum_d \log \frac{a[d]}{\gcd(a[d], b[d])}$) and $\lambda > 0$ tunes adherence. Setting $\lambda = +\infty$ recovers hard injection.

One Recursion in ManuMatic. At level $t = 0, \ldots, T-1$: (i) advance injected tensors by one binary refinement step and propagate constraints via Φ; (ii) compute priorities with $+\infty$ for injected operators; (iii) run D-Rec's bipartition under these constraints; (iv) materialize strategies and recurse. When no injections are provided, ManuMatic degenerates exactly to D-Rec.

4   Experiments

We summarize our setup and methodology in three parts (hardware, software, and experimental design), and then present two studies (generality and compatibility).

Hardware Setup. Experiments run on a Huawei Ascend-910 (A910) AI cluster. Each compute node contains $8\times$ A910–64GB NPUs. Intra-node communication uses a mesh topology via HCCL[1], providing up to 392 GB/s aggregate bandwidth per NPU. Inter-node communication connects multiple A910 nodes in a RoCE-based ring with 25 GB/s unidirectional link bandwidth per interface.

Software Setup. We integrate our strategy-injection planner ManuMatic into MindSpore[2], and execute deep learning models within it. Using the framework's profiling utilities, we collect per-run *throughput* (tokens/s). Unless otherwise stated, measurements exclude warm-up and average over steady-state steps; hyperparameters and kernel switches follow MindSpore defaults.

Experimental Design. We compare (i) Megatron (without expert/sequence parallel) – a strong software baseline lacking the specific parallelism mode indicated per model; (ii) D-Rec (auto) – the automatic planner without user guidance; (iii) Expert-Fine-tuned – a hand-tuned plan; and (iv) ManuMatic – our planner with a minimal, targeted operator pin.

4.1   Generality: Mixtral-8×7B and Llama3-8B on 8 NPUs

We evaluate two single-node (8 NPU) workloads to assess generality.

Mixtral-8 × 7B. ManuMatic injects a BMM (batched matmul) strategy that explicitly includes the expert-parallel mesh dimension for MoE projections, steering the search away from a costly redistribution path. This yields a $2.24\times$ speedup over D-Rec and approaches the expert plan (Table 1).

---

[1] Huawei Collective Communication Library: https://gitee.com/ascend/cann-hccl.
[2] MindSpore AI computing framework: https://gitee.com/mindspore/mindspore.

Table 1. Generality on Mixtral 8×7B (8 NPUs). Speedups relative to D-Rec (auto).

Planner	Throughput (tokens/s)	Speedup vs. D-Rec
Megatron (w/o expert parallel)	2730	0.93×
D-Rec (auto)	2935	1.00×
Expert-Fine-tuned	7337	2.49×
ManuMatic (BMM injection)	6603	2.24×

Llama3-8B ($L = 8$K). MANUMATIC pins a MatMul sharding that explicitly includes the sequence-parallel split dimension, aligning sequence-wise partitions across attention and MLP matrix multiplications to avoid long-sequence redistributions. This targeted pin delivers a 2.04× speedup over D-Rec and slightly surpasses the expert-tuned plan (1.98×), showing that minimal guidance can steer the search to high-quality shardings even for dense models (Tables 2).

Table 2. Generality on Llama3-8B (8 NPUs). Speedups relative to D-Rec (auto).

Planner	Throughput (tokens/s)	Speedup vs. D-Rec
Megatron (w/o expert parallel)	22730	0.98×
D-Rec (auto)	23194	1.00×
Expert-Fine-tuned	45939	1.98×
ManuMatic (MatMul injection)	47455	2.04×

4.2   Compatibility: Qwen2.5-72B on 64 NPUs with BMPipe

We train Qwen2.5-72B on eight nodes ($N_{\mathrm{NPU}} = 64$, sequence length $L = 32$K). MANUMATIC injects a MatMul sharding that explicitly includes the sequence-parallel split dimension, and we combine it with BMPipe [15]'s layer-assignment and recomputation optimizations. As shown in Table 3, this configuration attains a 1.45× speedup over D-Rec and a +30.1% improvement over the Expert-Fine-tuned plan.

Discussion. On Mixtral, a single expert-parallel-aware BMM pin removes a redistribution hotspot in MoE projections, delivering a 2.24× speedup over D-Rec while remaining close to an expert plan. On Qwen2.5-72B, a sequence-parallel-aware MatMul pin combined with BMPipe reduces stage idling and exposes additional compute/communication overlap, yielding 1.45× over D-Rec and 1.30× over the expert plan at cluster scale.

Table 3. Compatibility on Qwen2.5-72B (64 NPUs, $L = 32\,$K). Speedups relative to D-Rec (auto).

Planner	Throughput (tokens/s)	Speedup vs. D-Rec
Megatron (w/o sequence parallel)	147	0.95×
D-Rec (auto)	155	1.00×
Expert-Fine-tuned	173	1.11×
ManuMatic + BMPipe	225	1.45×

5   Conclusion

We presented MANUMATIC, a light-touch strategy injection mechanism that robustifies automatic planning for hybrid parallelism in distributed DNN training. Conceptually, MANUMATIC treats a small set of user-provided shardings as first-class constraints that anchor the search to the framework's runtime behavior while leaving the rest to automation. To the best of our knowledge, MANUMATIC is the first MANUMATIC (manual+automatic) planner that unifies operator-level *pins* with end-to-end automatic synthesis of a globally consistent hybrid-parallel plan in a single, profiling-free compilation flow. The integration is principled: multi-way pins are decomposed into binary-compatible refinements, operator-dimension couplings are enforced to avoid local reshards, and traversal is steered by assigning pinned operators an infinite compromise price. When no pins are provided, MANUMATIC exactly degenerates to D-Rec, preserving compilation speed and usability.

Empirically, minimal guidance consistently closes the modelruntime gap without cost-model reengineering: on Mixtral-8 × 7B (8 NPUs), an expert-parallel-aware BMM pin yields 2.24× over D-Rec; on Llama3-8B (8 NPUs, $L = 8$K), a sequence-parallel-aware MatMul pin delivers 2.04×; and on Qwen2.5-72B (64 NPUs, $L = 32$K), a sequence-parallel-aware MatMul pin combined with BMPipe attains 1.45× over D-Rec and 1.30× over an expert plan. These results indicate that a small amount of *hand* guidance, when fused with *auto* planning, yields robust, high-performance strategies while largely preserving automation.

Future Work. We will validate MANUMATIC across more hardware, frameworks, and model families, measuring not only throughput but also plan stability under primitive drift and overlap changes. We will also add a *post-hoc* visual summary that annotates the executed plan to show where the *already inserted* pins helped (e.g., fewer redistributions, shorter critical-path collectives) and where they hurt (e.g., avoidable collectives, tight divisibility, local oversubscription). This visualization is descriptive and is intended to give users immediate intuition for "good vs. bad" pins to guide subsequent iterations without altering the core compilation flow.

References

1. Brown, T., et al.: Language models are few-shot learners. In: Advances in Neural Information Processing Systems, pp. 1877–1901 (2020)
2. Yang, A., et al.: Qwen2 Technical Report. arXiv preprint arXiv:2407.10671 (2024)
3. Jiang, A.Q., et al.: Mixtral of experts. arXiv preprint arXiv:2401.04088 (2024)
4. Krizhevsky, A., et al.: ImageNet classification with deep convolutional neural networks. In: Advances in Neural Information Processing Systems, pp. 1097–1105 (2012)
5. Dean, J., et al.: Large scale distributed deep networks. In: Proceedings of the 25th International Conference on Neural Information Processing Systems - Volume 1. NIPS 2012, Lake Tahoe, Nevada (2012)
6. Krizhevsky, A.: One weird trick for parallelizing convolutional neural networks. arXiv preprint arXiv:1404.5997 (2014)
7. Shoeybi, M., et al.: Megatron-LM: training multi-billion parameter language models using model parallelism. arXiv preprint arXiv:1909.08053 (2019)
8. Wang, H., et al.: Efficient and systematic partitioning of large and deep neural networks for parallelization. In: European Conference on Parallel Processing, pp. 201–216. Springer (2021)
9. Wang, M., et al.: Supporting very large models using automatic dataflow graph partitioning. In: Proceedings of the Fourteenth EuroSys Conference 2019, EuroSys 2019. Association for Computing Machinery (2019)
10. Jia, Z., et al.: Exploring hidden dimensions in accelerating convolutional neural networks. In: Dy, J. et al. (eds.) International Conference on Machine Learning, vol. 80, pp. 2274–2283. Proceedings of Machine Learning Research. PMLR, October 2018
11. Korthikanti, V., et al.: Reducing activation recomputation in large transformer models. arXiv preprint arXiv:2205.05198 (2022)
12. Shazeer, N., et al.: Outrageously large neural networks: the SparselyGated mixture-of-experts layer. In: International Conference on Learning Representations (ICLR) (2017)
13. Fedus, W., et al.: Switch transformers: scaling to trillion parameter models with simple and efficient sparse training. arXiv preprint arXiv:2101.03961 (2021)
14. Rajbhandari, S., et al.: DeepSpeed-MoE: advancing mixture-of-experts inference and training. arXiv preprint arXiv:2201.05596 (2022)
15. Wang, R., et al.: BMPipe: bubble-memory co-optimization strategy planner for very-large DNN training. In: IEEE International Conference on Cluster Computing 2025 (2025)
16. Huawei. MindSpore (2022). https://www.mindspore.cn/
17. Abadi, M., et al.: TensorFlow: a system for large-scale machine learning. In: 12th USENIX Symposium on Operating Systems Design and Implementation (OSDI 16), pp. 265–283. USENIX Association, November 2016
18. Paszke, A., et al.: Pytorch: an imperative style, high-performance deep learning library. In: Advances in Neural Information Processing Systems, pp. 8026–8037 (2019)

Maximizing the Utility of Multiple UAV Service Providers: A Hierarchical Cooperation Approach

Zhangzhou Li[1], Geyao Cheng[2(✉)], Bangbang Ren[1], Xiaolei Zhou[1], Lailong Luo[1], and Deke Guo[3]

[1] National University of Defense Technology, Changsha, China
{lizhangzhou,renbangbang11,zhouxiaolei,luolailong09}@nudt.edu.cn
[2] Information Support Force Engineering University, Wuhan, China
chenggeyao13@nudt.edu.cn
[3] Sun Yat-sen University, Guangzhou, China
guodk@mail.sysu.edu.cn

Abstract. In recent years, unmanned aerial vehicles (UAVs) have been utilized as mobile edge computing (MEC) platforms to tackle computing resource limitations and communication coverage issues, particularly in areas without fixed infrastructure. However, the independent operation of UAV providers often leads to imbalanced service loads, inefficient resource usage, and limited coverage. To address these issues, this paper proposes a hierarchical cooperation approach for multiple UAV service providers, optimizing coalition formation and task offloading strategies to enhance overall system utility. We model the collaboration between UAV providers as a coalition formation game (CFG) and the joint order is employed to ensure stable coalitions, thus maximizing system performance. Task offloading and resource allocation within each coalition are formulated as a many-to-one matching problem to optimize resource utilization and computational efficiency. The Shapley value is applied for fair utility distribution, incentivizing UAV providers to maintain cooperation. Extensive experiments demonstrate the effectiveness of our approach, with the joint order improving system utility by 4.76% and 31.58% over traditional selfish and Pareto orders, respectively. Furthermore, the proposed offloading scheme shows significant performance gains of 13.22% and 20.24% compared to the shortest distance and random access algorithms, respectively.

Keywords: Multiple UAV providers · Coalition formation game · Task offloading · Utility maximization

1 Introduction

1.1 Background and Motivation

MEC has been increasingly deployed to meet the stringent latency and computational demands of emerging applications by offloading tasks to servers closer

X. Wang et al. (Eds.): NPC 2025, LNCS 16306, pp. 178–189, 2026.
https://doi.org/10.1007/978-3-032-10466-3_15

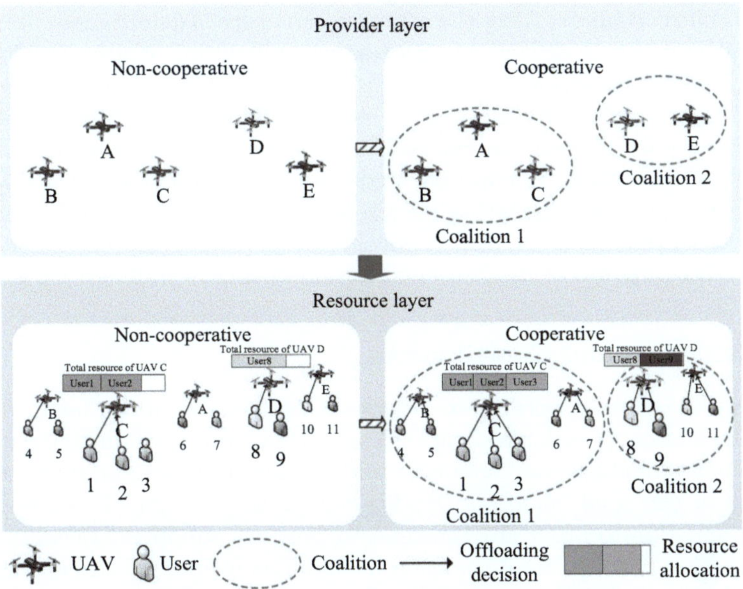

Fig. 1. The relationship between provider layer and resource layer. UAVs and users belonging to the same provider are marked with identical colors.

to end users [1,4,7]. However, these paradigms rely on robust ground infrastructure, which may be unavailable in remote or disaster-stricken areas. In such infrastructure-limited scenarios, UAVs serve as a highly flexible solution: UAVs can be rapidly deployed as aerial base stations or relay nodes, leveraging their high maneuverability to provide communication and edge computing services where fixed equipment is inoperable. Therefore, UAVs are considered ideal candidates to act as intermediate service relays in modern communication systems [17].

To curb capital expenditure, UAV service providers (hereafter referred to as "providers") usually deploy only one UAV within a specific region or for a specific subscriber base. However, the *one–provider–one–UAV* paradigm is fundamentally insufficient: the limited flight radius of a single UAV leaves many subscribers outside its coverage, while others reside in densely populated sub-areas, producing a stark spatial imbalance [11]. Consequently, substantial UAV computing resources lie idle in sparsely populated regions, whereas numerous users in hot spots remain unserved, collectively depressing system utility [6,12].

To address this problem, we consider solving it from two layers, as shown in Fig. 1: **Provider layer:** heterogeneous providers form cross-provider coalitions and jointly serve users collaboratively. For example, UAV service providers A, B, and C form Coalition 1, while providers D and E form Coalition 2. Through such cooperation, providers can share their UAV resources within a coalition, thereby expanding the overall service coverage and enhancing the system-wide utility. **Resource layer:** After the coalition structure is determined, the resource layer coordinates task offloading and resource allocation strategies within each coalition. Taking Coalition 1 as an example, the tasks from Users 1, 2, and 3 are offloaded to the most suitable UAV C within the coalition, where User 3 and UAV C belong to different providers. UAV C then allocates optimal computing resources to these tasks. In contrast, under previous offloading algorithms, UAV C tended to prioritize allocating its resources to users subscribed to the same provider, resulting in a reduced number of users being served. Therefore, an effective offloading algorithm is crucial for enhancing overall system utility.

1.2   Challenges and Contributions

However, differences in preference orders within a coalition can lead to conflicts and insufficient cooperation among UAVs, thereby limiting improvements in task efficiency and collaborative capability, and leaving room for enhancing the overall utility of the final coalition. Traditional preference models, such as selfish order [8] and Pareto order [10,15], tend to produce suboptimal coalition structures, resulting in lower total coalition utility. The former focuses exclusively on individual utility and may adversely affect others' utilities, whereas the latter imposes overly strict conditions that hinder effective coalition adjustments.

At the same time, once a coalition is formed, the complex decision problem of how to efficiently offload tasks to appropriate UAVs arises. The spatial heterogeneity of task locations, coupled with computational heterogeneity among UAVs, exacerbates issues such as load imbalance and low resource utilization. For instance, under random task offloading, some UAVs may become overloaded or congested, while others may remain underloaded or even idle. Therefore, the heterogeneity of task distribution and UAV computational capacity present significant challenges for designing task offloading strategies. This underscores the critical importance of developing efficient algorithms for task offloading and resource allocation.

To address the above challenges, this work proposes a hierarchical cooperation approach for edge computing among multiple UAV service providers. The key technical contributions are summarized as follows:

- We first formally formulate the cooperation among multiple UAV edge service providers, which aims to maximize the overall system utility by jointly optimizing coalition formation and task offloading.
- To address this problem, we propose a hierarchical cooperation approach comprising a provider layer and a resource layer. At the provider layer, we use the joint order and formulate a CFG. At the resource layer, tasks are efficiently matched to UAVs via a priority- and preference-based many-to-one matching scheme. Additionally, we adapt the Shapley value to ensure fair utility allocation.
- Simulation results demonstrate that our approach significantly improves the overall system utility compared to baseline methods.

2   Related Work

2.1   Coalition Formation Games in UAV Networks

With the expanding applications of UAVs in emergency communications, edge computing, target tracking, and other missions, CFG has been gradually introduced into UAV networks to optimize their cooperative behavior and resource scheduling strategies. Wang et al. [16] proposed a joint service caching and task offloading framework in MEC, highlighting the coalition-based collaborative caching mechanism to optimize resource sharing among mobile edge nodes (MENs). Zhang et al. [19] formulated the dynamic task assignment problem of a UAV-enabled front jammer swarm as a coalition formation game, and proposed a distributed algorithm that achieves near-centralized performance under hardware constraints and dynamic environments. Ren et al. [9] addressed the cooperative task assignment problem in multi-UAV networks with resource and energy constraints by proposing a coalition formation game-based approach enhanced with behavioral imitation learning to optimize task allocation and energy efficiency.

2.2   Computation Offloading in UAV-Assisted Edge Computing

In UAV-assisted MEC systems, task offloading and resource allocation are critical issues. To optimize task distribution and resource utilization, Wang et al. [14] developed a Stackelberg game-based offloading incentive mechanism for multi-UAV MEC, where UAVs and users interact to decide task assignments and pricing, achieving improved utility for all parties. Guo et al. [3] proposed a software-defined networking (SDN)-based cooperative task offloading and resource allocation scheme for multi-UAV systems to address the demands of latency-sensitive and computation-intensive applications in remote areas. Their approach aims to reduce task processing delay and balance energy consumption loads. Tian et al. [13] developed a service satisfaction-oriented joint optimization framework for task offloading and UAV scheduling. By employing a genetic algorithm, they effectively optimized both task delay and user energy consumption, significantly enhancing overall user satisfaction. Kang et al. [5] investigated a hierarchical aerial computing architecture and introduced a MAPPO-based cooperative strategy that jointly optimizes UAV resource allocation and task offloading to high-altitude platforms, aiming to maximize task throughput under heterogeneous QoS requirements. Zhang et al. [20] addressed the latency minimization problem in offshore-aerial MEC for MIoTDs by proposing a UAV-assisted architecture and solving a joint offloading, association, and caching problem via coalition game and decomposition techniques.

3   System Model

We consider N service providers and M tasks. We denote the set of UAV service providers by $SPs = \{1, \ldots, i, \ldots, N\}$. Each provider deploys one UAV, and the set of UAVs is denoted by $\mathcal{N} = \{1,\ldots,i,\ldots,N\}$. There are M tasks in the scenario, and the task set is denoted by $\mathcal{M} = \{1,\ldots,j,\ldots,M\}$. UAV i belongs to UAV provider i. The attributes of UAV i are represented by the tuple $(e_i, R_i, \alpha_i, x_i, y_i)$. Here, e_i represents the maximum computational resource of UAV i. R_i is the service radius of UAV i. We assume that UAVs consider only their resource consumption and task completion time. α_i is the weight of UAV i for resource consumption, while $1 - \alpha_i$ is the weight of UAV i for latency, and (x_i, y_i) are the coordinates of UAV i. The attributes of task j are represented by the tuple $(k_j, Q_j, v_j, x_j, y_j)$. Here, $k_j \in SPs$ indicates the service provider to which task j belongs, Q_j is the computational load of task j, v_j is the value of task j, and (x_j, y_j) is the coordinates of task j.

When UAV providers do not form coalitions, tasks can only be offloaded to their corresponding provider's UAV. At any time, multiple providers can form a coalition partition $\Pi = \{C_1, C_2, \ldots, C_l\}$, where $1 \leq l \leq N$. The partition satisfies: $\cup_{k=1}^{l} C_k = SPs$ and $C_m \cap C_n = \emptyset, \forall m \neq n$. Let $C_\Pi(k)$ denote the coalition containing provider k. The prerequisite for UAV i to execute task j is that UAV i and task j belong to the same provider or both belong to the same coalition, i.e., $i = k_j$ or $C_\Pi(i) = C_\Pi(k_j)$. In addition, task j must lie within the service radius of UAV i, i.e.,

$$\sqrt{(x_i - x_j)^2 + (y_i - y_j)^2} \leq R_i. \tag{1}$$

The income of UAV i executing task j is defined as:

$$v_i^j = v_j - \alpha_i e_i^j - (1 - \alpha_i)\frac{Q_j}{e_i^j}, \tag{2}$$

where e_i^j denotes the amount of computational resource allocated from UAV i to task j. We use the following indicator function to denote whether task j is offloaded to UAV i.

$$K(i,j) = \begin{cases} 1, & \text{if task } j \text{ is offloaded to UAV } i, \\ 0, & \text{otherwise.} \end{cases} \tag{3}$$

Then, the income of coalition C_k can be expressed as

$$v_R(C_k) = \sum_{i \in C_k, j \in \mathcal{M}} K(i,j)v_i^j. \tag{4}$$

Here, we consider a coalition cost function for UAV service providers that varies quadratically with the size of the coalition $|C_k|$, with the variation arising from the increasing complexity of coordination and communication as more members join, as follows [2,18]:

$$M(C_k) = \begin{cases} 0, & |C_k| = 1, \\ \beta|C_k|^2, & |C_k| \geq 2. \end{cases} \tag{5}$$

The value function of total utility of the coalition C_k is given by:

$$V(C_k) = v_R(C_k) - M(C_k). \tag{6}$$

Our objective is to maximize the value function of total utility of all providers by optimizing the coalition formation strategy $\mathcal{C}$ and task offloading resource allocation strategy $\mathcal{K}$.

$$\mathcal{P}: \quad \max_{\mathcal{C},\mathcal{K}} \sum_{k=1}^{l} V(C_k) \tag{7}$$

$$\text{s.t.} \quad \sum_{j=1}^{M} e_i^j \leq e_i^{\max}, \forall i \in \mathcal{N}, \tag{7a}$$

$$e_i^j \geq 0, \forall i \in \mathcal{N}, \forall j \in \mathcal{M}, \tag{7b}$$

$$\sum_{i=1}^{N} K(i,j) \leq 1, \forall j \in \mathcal{M}. \tag{7c}$$

Constraint (7a) ensures that the total computational resources allocated by UAV i to all tasks do not exceed its maximum capacity. Constraint (7b) states that the computational resources allocated to task j by any UAV i cannot be negative. Constraint (7c) indicates that one task can be offloaded to at most one UAV.

4   Methodology

To address the above issues, we formulate the problem as a hierarchical cooperation model with game theory method, which can balance the individual and collective rationalities efficiently. Specifically, the cooperation problem of UAV providers in the provider layer is formulated as a coalition formation game, where each UAV provider is enabled to determine the joined coalition by jointly considering its own utility and the coalition utility. Under the given coalition partition, the corresponding task offloading and resource allocation strategy in each coalition can be obtained in the resource layer. The task offloading and resource allocation strategy in each coalition can be regarded as feedback to iteratively update the coalition partition in the provider layer.

4.1   CFG-Based Providers Cooperation Algorithm

Definition 1. *(Coalition Partition): The set* $\Pi = \{C_1, C_2, ..., C_l\}, l \leq N$. *This is called a coalition partition or structure of UAV providers if it satisfies*

$$\cup_{k=1}^{l} C_k = SPs \quad and \quad C_m \cap C_n = \emptyset, m \neq n.$$

Definition 2. *(Preference Relation): In CFG, each UAV provider decides to join or leave a coalition based on their preference order. For example, for any two coalitions* C_k, C_l, *and provider* j, $C_k \succ_j C_l$ *means that provider* j *strictly prefers to join* C_k *rather than* C_l.

Definition 3. *(Pareto Order): For any UAV providers $j, \forall j \in SPs$, and two coalitions containing provider j, $C_k \subseteq \Pi$, $C_l \subseteq \Pi$, $C_k \cap C_l = \emptyset, k \neq l$:*

$$C_k \succ_j C_l \iff u_j(C_k) > u_j(C_l)$$
$$\wedge u_i(C_k) > u_i(C_k \setminus \{j\}), \quad \forall i \in C_k \setminus \{j\} \tag{8}$$
$$\wedge u_i(C_l) < u_i(C_l \setminus \{j\}), \quad \forall i \in C_l \setminus \{j\}.$$

Definition 4. *(Selfish Order): For any UAV providers $j, \forall j \in SPs$, and two coalitions containing provider j, $C_k \subseteq \Pi$, $C_l \subseteq \Pi$, $C_k \cap C_l = \emptyset, k \neq l$:*

$$C_k \succ_j C_l \iff u_j(C_k) > u_j(C_l). \tag{9}$$

Definition 5. *(Joint Order): For any UAV providers $j, \forall j \in SPs$, and two coalitions containing provider j, $C_k \subseteq \Pi$, $C_l \subseteq \Pi$, $C_k \cap C_l = \emptyset, k \neq l$:*

$$C_k \succ_j C_l \iff \sum_{i \in C_k \cup \{j\}} u_i(C_k \cup \{j\}) + \sum_{i \in C_l \setminus \{j\}} u_i(C_l \setminus \{j\}) >$$
$$\sum_{i \in C_k} u_i(C_k) + \sum_{i \in C_l} u_i(C_l) \tag{10}$$

Definition 6. *(Switch Operation): Given a partition $\Pi = \{C_1, C_2, ..., C_l\}, l \leq N$ of the UAV providers set SPs, if provider j performs a switch operation from $C_\Pi(j) = C_m$ to $C_k \in \Pi \cup \{\emptyset\}$, $C_k \neq C_\Pi(j)$, then the current partition Π of SPs is modified into a new partition Π' such that $\Pi' = (\Pi \setminus \{C_m, C_k\}) \cup \{C_m \setminus \{j\}, C_k \cup \{j\}\}$.*

Definition 7. *(Shapley Value): For any UAV providers $j \in C_k$ in the coalition C_k, the Shapley value $u_j(C_k)$ is defined as:*

$$u_j(C_k) = \sum_{C_k' \subseteq C_k \setminus \{j\}} \frac{|C_k'|!(|C_k| - |C_k'| - 1)!}{|C_k|!} [V(C_k' \cup \{j\}) - V(C_k')]. \tag{11}$$

Definition 8. *(Stable Coalition Partition): When no participant can change the coalition structure (coalition selection), to increase their utility, the coalition partition Π is considered stable, where s_j represents the coalition strategy of UAV provider j.*

$$u_j(s_j^*, s_{-j}) \geq u_j(s_j, s_{-j}), \quad \forall j \in SPs, \quad s_j \neq s_j^*. \tag{12}$$

In each iteration, an arbitrary UAV provider j is selected to evaluate potential coalition adjustments. Initially, the chosen provider considers joining a different coalition, distinct from its current affiliation, to assess potential utility improvements. The UAV provider then determines whether to leave its current coalition and join the new one based on the joint preference order. This iterative process continues until the coalition partition converges to a final stable state in which no UAV provider has an incentive to deviate from its current coalition, as shown in Algorithm 1.

Algorithm 1. CFG-Based UAV Service Providers Cooperation Algorithm

---

Input: the set of UAV service providers SPs, the set of UAVs $\mathcal{N}$, and the set of tasks of users $\mathcal{M}$.
Output: A stable coalition partition Π_{final}.
 1: **Initialization:** $\Pi_{init} = SPs$
 2: **repeat**
 3:     For a randomly chosen UAV provider $j \in SPs$ and current coalition partition Π_{curr} ($\Pi_{curr} = \Pi_{init}$ in the first iteration).
 4:     **Step 1:** Search for a possible switch operation from $C_{\Pi_{curr}}(j) = C_m, m \in \{1, 2, ..., l\}$ to $C_k \in \Pi_{curr} \cup \{\emptyset\}, C_k \neq C_{\Pi_{curr}}(j)$, where $C_k \succ_j C_{\Pi_{curr}}(j)$.
 5:     **Step 2:**
 6:     **if** such switch operation exists **then**
 7:         a) Leave the current coalition, i.e., $C_{\Pi_{curr}}(j) := C_{\Pi_{curr}}(j) \setminus \{j\}$.
 8:         b) Join the new coalition, i.e., $C_k := C_k \cup \{j\}$.
 9:         c) The coalition partition changes, i.e., $\Pi_{curr} = \Pi_{new}$.
10:     **end if**
11: **until** The partition converges to a final Nash-stable partition Π_{final}.

4.2 Priority and Preference-Based Task Offloading and Resource Allocation Algorithm

As shown in Algorithm 2, we propose a Priority- and Preference-based Task Offloading and Resource Allocation Algorithm, formulated as a many-to-one matching problem, represented as a triplet $(\mathcal{PM}, \Omega, \Phi)$. Here, $\mathcal{PM} = (\mathcal{M}_C, \mathcal{N}_C)$ denotes the tasks to be offloaded and the available UAVs in the coalition C, while Ω represents the preference lists of tasks, and Φ denotes the matching pairs.

The algorithm initializes tasks as unmatched. For each task j, it evaluates all UAVs i for feasibility based on communication availability. If feasible, it calculates the optimal resource allocation and the corresponding UAV's income. After evaluating all UAVs for a task, the task's preference list is constructed by sorting UAVs in descending order of their income to handle the task. And the task's priority O_j is determined based on the highest achievable income, with infinite priority for tasks that have only one feasible UAV.

In the matching phase, tasks are sorted by priority and attempt to match with their preferred UAVs. If a UAV has sufficient resources, the task is matched, the resources are allocated, and both the task and UAV are updated. Unmatched tasks will execute locally. The algorithm outputs the optimal task offloading and resource allocation strategies, enhancing UAV resource utilization through task priority and preference over UAVs.

Algorithm 2 . Priority- and Preference-based Task Offloading and Resource Allocation Algorithm

---

Input: UAV set $\mathcal{N}_C$, task set $\mathcal{M}_C$.
Output: Offloading mapping $\mathcal{S}_{\text{off}}^\star$, resource allocation vector $\mathcal{S}_{\text{all}}^\star$.
1: Initialize $\mathcal{S}_{\text{off}}^\star[j] \leftarrow \text{NULL}$, $\mathcal{S}_{\text{all}}^\star[j] \leftarrow 0$ for all task $j \in \mathcal{M}_C$.
2: **for** each task $j \in \mathcal{M}_C$ **do**
3:     Available UAVs of task j: $A_j \leftarrow \{\text{UAV } i \in \mathcal{N}_C \mid \text{task } j \text{ is feasible on UAV } i\}$;
4:     For each UAV $i \in A_j$, compute optimal resource allocation $e_i^{j\star}$ and the corresponding income v_i^j;
5:     The preference list of task j: $\Omega_j \leftarrow \text{argsort}_{i \in A_j}(v_i^j)$ in descending order;
6:     Task j's priority: $O_j \leftarrow \begin{cases} +\infty, & |A_j| = 1; \\ \max_{i \in A_j} v_i^j, & \text{otherwise.} \end{cases}$
7: **end for**
8: The queue of tasks: $O \leftarrow \text{argsort}_{j \in \mathcal{M}_C}(O_j)$ in descending order.
9: **for** each task $j \in O$ **do**
10:     **for** each UAV $i \in \Omega_j$ **do**
11:         **if** residual resource $e_i \geq e_i^{j\star}$ **then**
12:             $\mathcal{S}_{\text{off}}^\star[j] \leftarrow i$; $\mathcal{S}_{\text{all}}^\star[j] \leftarrow e_i^{j\star}$; $e_i \leftarrow e_i - e_i^{j\star}$;
13:             **break**;
14:         **end if**
15:     **end for**
16: **end for**
17: **return** $(\mathcal{S}_{\text{off}}^\star, \mathcal{S}_{\text{all}}^\star)$;

---

5   Experimental Results

5.1   Experimental Implementation

In the simulation, we explore scenarios with $N = 10$ UAV (providers) and $M = 65$ tasks. The UAVs and tasks are randomly distributed in a 1000×1000 m^2 area. Each UAV is configured with a specific computational capacity and a defined communication radius, while each user task is characterized by a computational workload and a distinct value.

5.2   Experimental Results

To verify the convergence of the algorithm, we studied the relationship between the overall utility and the number of iterations under a fixed $\alpha = 0.5$, as shown in Fig. 2. The experimental results indicate that our algorithm exhibits convergence during iterations, leading the coalition to a stable state. Moreover, our joint order achieves the highest utility compared with the selfish order and Pareto order. The selfish order pursues the UAV provider's own utility when choosing a new coalition, which may harm other UAV providers' utility while improving its own utility. By contrast, the coalition switch under Pareto order is limited due to the stringent constraints imposed to ensure the performance of both the current and

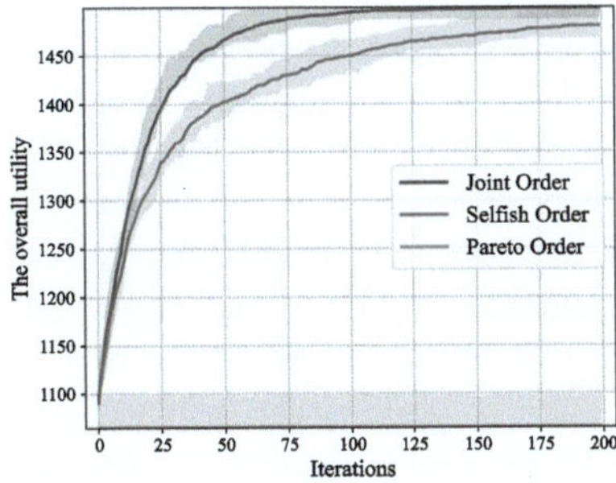

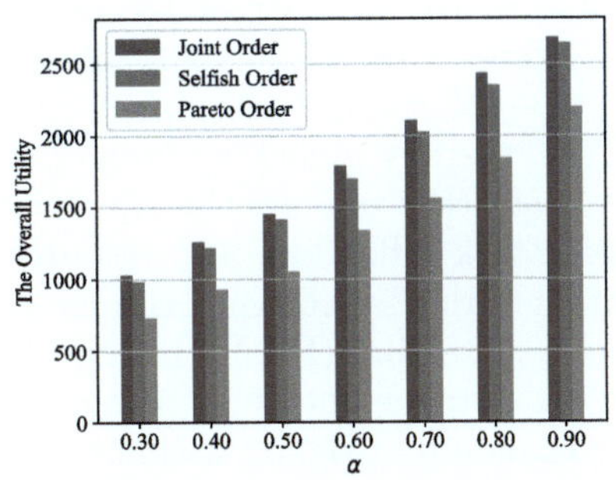

Fig. 2. The convergence behavior of coalition formation algorithm based on Pareto order, selfish order, and joint order.

Fig. 3. The overall utility of UAV providers versus resource consumption weight α.

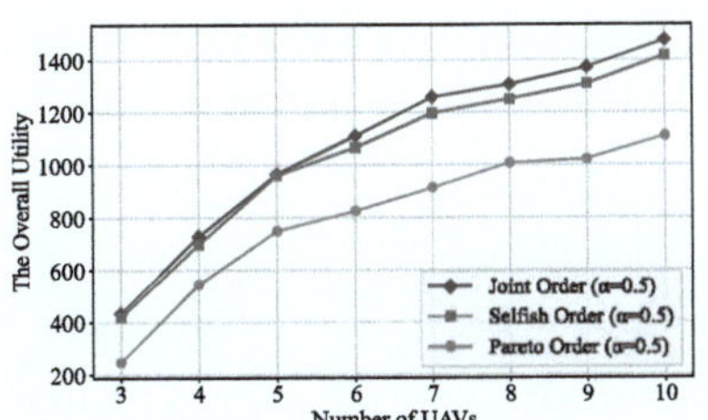

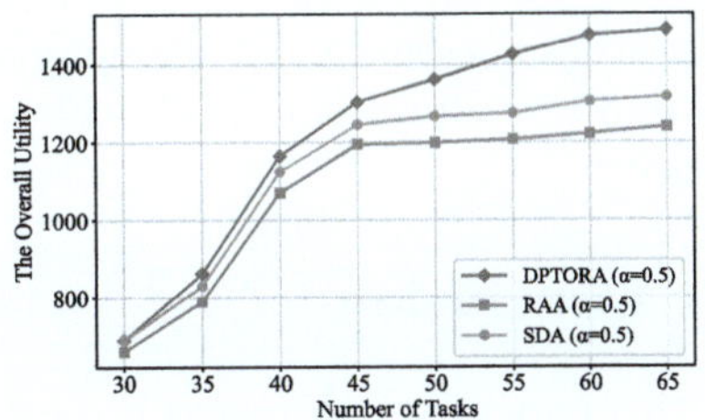

Fig. 4. The overall utility of UAV providers versus UAV numbers under different preference orders.

Fig. 5. The overall utility of UAV providers versus task numbers under different offloading algorithms.

new coalitions, resulting in a non-cooperation scheme, which leads to the lowest utility.

As shown in Fig. 3, we evaluate the performance of our coalition formation algorithm under different preference orders for a scenario having 65 tasks and 10 UAV providers, as the computing resource weight α increases. To highlight the effect of α, the other conditions are set to be the same. We note that the overall utility of UAV providers is bound to increase as the weight increases. Moreover, the utility achieved by the joint preference order is better than that of the two traditional orders. This is because Pareto order may limit UAV providers to explore better utility, whereas the selfish order may destroy the benefits of other UAV providers. The joint preference order is regarded as a trade-off between self-interest and generosity, which achieves the best performance.

Figure 4 illustrates how the overall utility varies for different UAV numbers across three preference orders: joint, selfish, and Pareto. As the number of UAVs increases from 3 to 10, all three curves exhibit a consistent upward trend, indicating that the expansion of UAV resources can steadily enhance the overall system utility. Moreover, the performance ranking of the three methods remains stable as the number of UAVs increases, following the order: Joint > Selfish > Pareto. This result demonstrates that the joint preference order can form a better-performing coalition structure, fully exploiting the resources of multiple UAVs, thereby unlocking greater cooperative gains and achieving higher utility.

To further validate the effectiveness of the proposed priority- and preference-based task offloading and resource allocation algorithm (DPTORA), we compare it with the shortest-distance-based access algorithm (SDA) and the random access algorithm (RAA). In the SDA scheme, tasks consider only the communication distance and select the nearest UAV, whereas in the RAA scheme, tasks are randomly assigned without any specific criteria. Figure 5 displays how overall utility changes across different task counts. The utility ranking consistently adheres to the following order: DPTORA > SDA > RAA. Notably, when the task count is low (30 to 40 tasks), the utility difference between the proposed and shortest algorithms is slight. However, as the task count increases–particularly beyond 50–the performance advantage of the DPTORA becomes progressively more significant. When task numbers reach 65, the superiority of the proposed algorithm becomes particularly prominent, underscoring its exceptional capability in optimizing resource allocation and load balancing in scenarios of high task density.

6   Conclusion

In this paper, we addressed the problem of maximizing overall system utility in multiple UAV edge service provider environments by proposing a hierarchical cooperation approach. Initially, we formulated the multi-provider collaboration problem as a CFG to facilitate stable and efficient coalition structures. Within each coalition, we implemented a priority- and preference-based many-to-one matching algorithm for task offloading and resource allocation, thereby improving computational resource utilization. Extensive experimental evaluations confirm the effectiveness of our proposed methods.

Acknowledgments. This work is partially supported by the National Natural Science Foundation of China under Grant No. 62302510, No. 62402508 and No. 62472433, the Hunan Provincial Natural Science Foundation for Outstanding Youth under Grant No.2023JJ20055, the Research Funding of NUDT under Grant ZK24-41.

References

1. Cheng, G., Xia, J., Luo, L., Mi, H., Guo, D., Ma, R.T.B.: HyperPart: a hypergraph-based abstraction for deduplicated storage systems. IEEE Trans. Cloud Comput. **13**(1), 46–60 (2025)
2. Fele, F., Debada, E., Maestre, J.M., Camacho, E.F.: Coalitional control for self-organizing agents. IEEE Trans. Autom. Control **63**(9), 2883–2897 (2018)
3. Guo, H., Wang, Y., Liu, J., Liu, C.: Multi-UAV cooperative task offloading and resource allocation in 5G advanced and beyond. IEEE Trans. Wireless Commun. **23**(1), 347–359 (2023)

4. Jiang, K., Sun, C., Zhou, H., Li, X., Dong, M., Leung, V.C.: Intelligence-empowered mobile edge computing: framework, issues, implementation, and outlook. IEEE Netw. **35**(5), 74–82 (2021)

5. Kang, H., Chang, X., Mišić, J., Mišić, V.B., Fan, J., Liu, Y.: Cooperative UAV resource allocation and task offloading in hierarchical aerial computing systems: a MAPPO-based approach. IEEE Internet Things J. **10**(12), 10497–10509 (2023)

6. Lai, C.C., Tsai, A.H., Wang, L.C., et al.: Adaptive and fair deployment approach to balance offload traffic in multi-UAV cellular networks. IEEE Trans. Veh. Technol. **72**(3), 3724–3738 (2022)

7. Ma, Z., Nuermaimaiti, N., Zhang, H., Zhou, H., Nallanathan, A.: Deployment model and performance analysis of clustered D2D caching networks under cluster-centric caching strategy. IEEE Trans. Commun. **68**(8), 4933–4945 (2020)

8. Qi, N., Huang, Z., Zhou, F., Shi, Q., Wu, Q., Xiao, M.: A task-driven sequential overlapping coalition formation game for resource allocation in heterogeneous UAV networks. IEEE Trans. Mobile Comput. **22**(8), 4439–4455 (2022)

9. Ren, H., Chang, Z., Min, G.: Correlation-driven task assignment for multi-UAV networks via imitation learning. IEEE Trans. Veh. Technol (2025)

10. Saad, W., Han, Z., Debbah, M., Hjorungnes, A., Basar, T.: Coalitional game theory for communication networks. IEEE Signal Process. Mag. **26**(5), 77–97 (2009)

11. Song, Z., Qin, X., Hao, Y., Hou, T., Wang, J., Sun, X.: A comprehensive survey on aerial mobile edge computing: challenges, state-of-the-art, and future directions. Comput. Commun. **191**, 233–256 (2022)

12. Tan, L., Guo, S., Zhou, P., Kuang, Z., Long, S., Li, Z.: Multi-UAV-enabled collaborative edge computing: deployment, offloading and resource optimization. IEEE Trans. Intell. Transp. Syst. **25**(11), 18305– 18320 (2024)

13. Tian, J., Wang, D., Zhang, H., Wu, D.: Service satisfaction-oriented task offloading and UAV scheduling in UAV-enabled MEC networks. IEEE Trans. Wireless Commun. **22**(12), 8949–8964 (2023)

14. Wang, M., Zhang, L., Gao, P., Yang, X., Wang, K., Yang, K.: Stackelberg-game-based intelligent offloading incentive mechanism for a multi-UAV-assisted mobile-edge computing system. IEEE Internet Things J. **10**(17), 15679–15689 (2023)

15. Wang, T., Song, L., Han, Z., Jiao, B.: Dynamic popular content distribution in vehicular networks using coalition formation games. IEEE J. Sel. Areas Commun. **31**(9), 538–547 (2013)

16. Wang, Z., Du, H.: Collaborative coalitions-based joint service caching and task offloading for edge networks. Theor. Comput. Sci. **940**, 52–65 (2023)

17. Wu, H., Wei, Z., Hou, Y., Zhang, N., Tao, X.: Cell-edge user offloading via flying UAV in non-uniform heterogeneous cellular networks. IEEE Trans. Wireless Commun. **19**(4), 2411–2426 (2020)

18. Zhang, L., Liang, D., Li, M., Yang, W., Yang, S.: Coalition formation game approach for task allocation in heterogeneous multi-robot systems under resource constraints. In: Proceedings IEEE/RSJ International Conference Intelligent Robots and Systems (IROS), pp. 3439–3446. IEEE (2024)

19. Zhang, T., Wang, Y., Ma, Z., Kong, L.: Task assignment in UAV-enabled front jammer swarm: a coalition formation game approach. IEEE Trans. Aerosp. Electron. Syst. **59**(6), 9562–9575 (2023)

20. Zhang, Y., Na, Z., Li, S., Lin, B., Lin, Y., Nallanathan, A.: Joint service caching and task offloading for multi-UAV-assisted offshore edge computing networks. IEEE Trans. Veh. Technol. (2025)

Slotqueue: A Wait-Free Distributed Multi-producer Single-Consumer Queue with Constant Remote Operations

Do Nguyen An Huy[2], Thanh-Dang Diep[2(✉)], Karl Fürlinger[4], and Nam Thoai[1,2,3]

[1] High Performance Computing Laboratory, Ho Chi Minh City, Vietnam
[2] Faculty of Computer Science and Engineering, Ho Chi Minh City, Vietnam
{huy.do862003,dang}@hcmut.edu.vn
[3] Advanced Institute of Interdisciplinary Science and Technology, Ho Chi Minh City University of Technology (HCMUT), VNU-HCM, Ho Chi Minh City, Vietnam
namthoai@hcmut.edu.vn
[4] Ludwig-Maximilians-Universität (LMU) Munich, Computer Science Department, MNM Team, Oettingenstr. 67, 80538 Munich, Germany
fuerling@nm.ifi.lmu.de

Abstract. For some distributed applications, e.g. the distributed actor model, distributed multi-producer, single-consumer (MPSC) queues play a vital role. For these applications to be fault tolerant and performant, a highly efficient non-blocking distributed MPSC queue is desired. Currently, in the literature, there is no non-blocking distributed MPSC queue. Therefore, a question naturally arises: Does there exist a performant non-blocking distributed MPSC queue? We answer this question by proposing Slotqueue, a wait-free distributed MPSC queue with only a constant amount of remote operations per enqueue and dequeue call. This is achieved by the use of timestamps to order the items in the queue and the idea of using a flat array structure to maintain the timestamps. To demonstrate how well Slotqueue performs in practice, we develop a microbenchmark to measure its throughput as compared to other distributed MPSC queues we have surveyed in the literature. We discover that Slotqueue is fault tolerant while performing comparable to other distributed MPSC queues.

Keywords: Distributed data structures · Non-blocking data structures · Multi-producer · Single-consumer queues

1 Introduction

Shared-memory MPSC queues have seen widespread use in many programming patterns and frameworks. In particular, the actor model [14], which is an application of MPSC queues, appeared in many recent publications [2,12,15], ranging from software simulators to work-stealing schedulers. These frameworks either

© IFIP International Federation for Information Processing 2026
Published by Springer Nature Switzerland AG 2026
X. Wang et al. (Eds.): NPC 2025, LNCS 16306, pp. 190–202, 2026.
https://doi.org/10.1007/978-3-032-10466-3_16

only work on shared-memory machines because they utilize a shared-memory MPSC queue [12,15] or have to rely on another facility for message exchange when supporting distributed-memory machines [2]. This state of affairs can be attributed to the lack of research on distributed MPSC queues.

A desirable distributed MPSC queue should be high-performance and fault tolerant. Considering performance, the more general MPMC queues, although sufficient for MPSC use cases, are typically less performant than the more specialized MPSC queues. With regard to fault tolerance, we are concerned with the progress guarantee [10] characteristic of the algorithms, which divides the algorithms into two groups: blocking and non-blocking. Blocking algorithms are not fault tolerant, in that a suspension in a process can cause other processes to suspend. Non-blocking algorithms are protected from this problem, which exhibits a higher degree of fault tolerance. Two important subclasses of non-blocking algorithms are lock-free and wait-free algorithms. In lock-free algorithms, some active processes can always complete an operation despite arbitrary suspension of other processes [8]. Wait-free algorithms ensure a stronger guarantee: All active processes can always complete an operation in a finite number of steps [9]. Therefore, a highly efficient non-blocking distributed MPSC queue is desired.

To the best of our knowledge, there is currently no distributed non-blocking MPSC queue in the literature. A question that naturally comes up is whether there exists an efficient non-blocking distributed MPSC queue? In this paper, we answer this question with Slotqueue, an efficient non-blocking distributed MPSC queue that follows the strict first-in first-out queue semantics. Slotqueue is directly inspired by a shared-memory queue called LTQueue [11]. Both Slotqueue and LTQueue use timestamps to order items in the queue. However, instead of maintaining a hierarchical structure of timestamps as in LTQueue, Slotqueue maintains a flat array of timestamps. Interestingly, this design choice causes Slotqueue to only make a constant amount of remote operations per enqueue and dequeue call. Because remote operations are much more expensive than local operations, this can contribute significantly to the performance of Slotqueue.

To realize Slotqueue, we use BCL CoreX [7] as the implementation library. BCL CoreX is a practical library that supports the design of portable non-blocking distributed data structures. Other alternatives [3,5,6] require special support from the underlying network interface card or special atomic instructions, such as double-compare-and-swap (DCAS) and 128-bit compare-and-swap (CAS), which are not supported by most interconnects.

The contribution of this paper can be summarized as follows.

- We conduct a survey on the current distributed MPSC queues in the literature. It is remarked that there is currently no non-blocking distributed MPSC queue. Although there has been effort to design one such queue, AMQueue, we show that this queue is actually blocking.
- We devise the first non-blocking distributed MPSC queue that is intended to be performant and practical, Slotqueue.

– We provide theoretical and empirical insights on how well Slotqueue performs. Notably, Slotqueue has a favorable theoretical trait: In the worst case, it only requires a constant amount of remote operations.

The remainder of this paper is structured as follows. Section 2 surveys the literature for existing distributed MPSC queues, which will be used as our benchmarking baselines and introduces the BCL CoreX library. Section 3 specifies Slotqueue's data structure and algorithm. Section 4 conducts a theoretical analysis of Slotqueue, such as its progress guarantee characteristics and worst-case performance. Section 5 provides an experimental evaluation of how well Slotqueue performs in practice. Section 6 concludes our work and provides further discussions.

2   Background and Related Works

This section consults the literature for background and related works. An overview of existing distributed MPSC queues is given in Sect. 2.1, which highlights the research gap in the current literature and helps motivate our study. As Slotqueue utilizes BCL CoreX, the library will be visited in Sect. 2.2.

2.1   Distributed MPSC Queues

To the best of our knowledge, there is only one research study that explicitly describes a distributed MPSC queue, AMQueue [13]. The characteristics of this queue are summarized in Table 1.

Table 1. The characteristics of existing distributed MPSC queues.

MPSC queues	AMQueue [13]
Progress Guarantee of Enqueue	Wait-free
Progress Guarantee of Dequeue	Blocking [a]

[a] Personal communication. The original paper [13] stated that AMQueue is lock-free

AMQueue [13] is the only distributed MPSC queue in the literature. It is "intended" to be non-blocking. AMQueue is structured as two buffers, one for the enqueuers, one for the sole dequeuer. When the dequeuer needs to dequeue, the roles of the two buffers are swapped, so that enqueuers now enqueue into the other buffer. The dequeuer can then batch dequeue from the old enqueue buffer, leading to a very high dequeue throughput. However, AMQueue is actually blocking, instead of being lock-free, as when swapping the two buffers, the dequeuer needs to wait for all the enqueuers to finish writing in the old buffer.

Based on this discussion, there is currently no non-blocking distributed MPSC queue in the literature, as far as we know. This presents a challenge for fault-tolerant applications that require distributed MPSC queues.

2.2   BCL CoreX

BCL CoreX [7] is an extension of BCL Core [3], which offers a partitioned global address space (PGAS) programming model, with appropriate modification to ease the development of non-blocking distributed data structures. This library is used in our algorithm specification in Sect. 3.

Listing 1. Distributed programming primitives.

```
1 T read(gptr<T> src)
2 void write(gptr<T> dest, T src)
3 bool cas(gptr<T> dest, T old_value, T new_value)
4 T faa(gptr<T> dest, T inc)
```

In BCL CoreX, there exists the data type `gptr`, which is a 64-bit data type that represents a global pointer. A global pointer is a pointer that can point to a non-local address space in a distributed application. Like normal pointers, pointer arithmetic also works with global pointers, which allows a global pointer to point to a remote array. A global pointer must point to exactly one process's address space, of which the owner process is called the host.

The `read` function synchronously reads the location pointed to by a global pointer and returns the read value. The `write` function synchronously writes the value stored in `src` to the location pointed to by a global pointer. The `cas` and `faa` functions synchronously perform the compare-and-swap and fetch-and-add operations, respectively, on the location pointed to by the global pointer.

A local operation occurs when the primitives are applied to a pointer hosted by the calling process. Otherwise, it is a remote operation. Remote operations are very expensive compared to local operations.

3   Slotqueue

As described in Sect. 2.1, there is no existing non-blocking distributed MPSC queue in the literature. In this section, we specify Slotqueue, an efficient wait-free distributed MPSC queue, which is the first non-blocking distributed MPSC queue to our knowledge. We first walk through the high-level data structure of Slotqueue, in order to gain an overview of its organization, in Sect. 3.1. Then, we present a highly optimized bounded distributed SPSC queue in Sect. 3.2, on which our Slotqueue depends. This serves as a preliminary to Sect. 3.3, which specifies Slotqueue.

3.1   Overview

The high-level data structure of Slotqueue is shown in Fig. 1. In Slotqueue, every process has a unique process ID, also known as its rank. The ranks are assumed to be taken from a contiguous range starting from 0. Each enqueuer hosts a local SPSC queue that only it can enqueue into. Note that each item in the local SPSC queue is timestamped. This timestamp is obtained from the distributed counter hosted by the dequeuer. In addition to the distributed counter, the dequeuer also hosts an array of slots. Each slot corresponds to exactly one enqueuer and its local SPSC queues. Every slot contains the timestamp that is minimum within the corresponding SPSC queue.

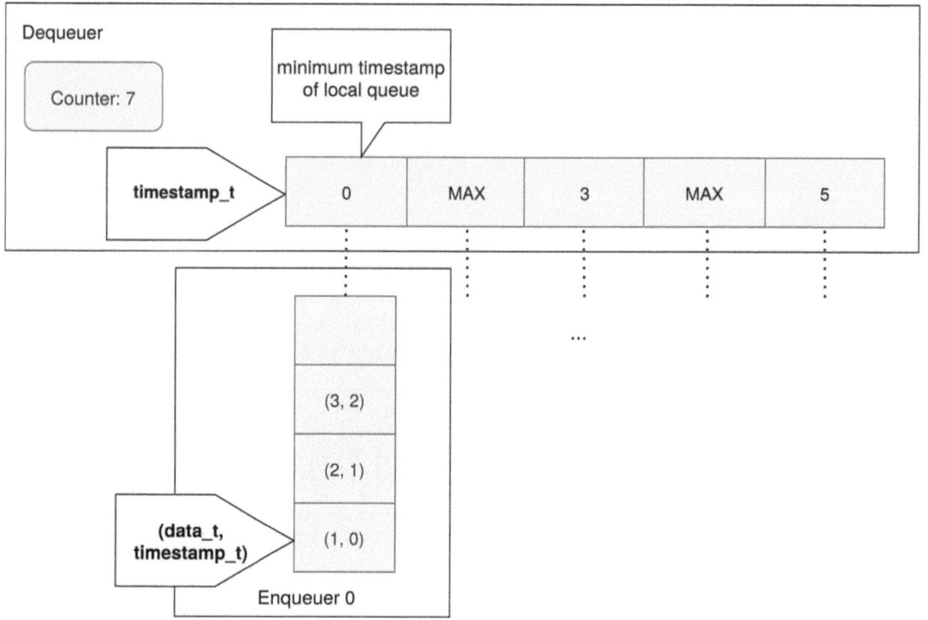

Fig. 1. Slotqueue's high-level data structure.

3.2   An Optimized Bounded Distributed SPSC Queue

In this section, we present an optimized bounded distributed SPSC queue, which Listing 3 assumes to be present. This SPSC queue, in addition to the usual **enqueue** and **dequeue** operations, also supports the **read_front** operation, which returns the first item in the SPSC queue.

The SPSC queue is structured as a circular array **Data** of known **Capacity**, with **First** and **Last** indices, such that **First % Capacity** points to the first as-yet-dequeued entry while **Last % Capacity** points to the first as-yet-enqueued entry. The enqueuer and the dequeuer each separately caches the value of **First** and **Last** in the process-local variables **First_buf** and **Last_buf**. First, Last, **First_buf** and **Last_buf** are all initialized to 0. **First** and **Last** are hosted on the dequeuer while **Data** is hosted on the enqueuer.

Listing 2. An optimized bounded distributed SPSC queue.

```
1  Function enqueue(data):
2      new_last ← Last_buf + 1
3      if new_last - First_buf >
       Capacity then
4          First_buf ← read(First)
5          if new_last - First_buf >
           Capacity then
6              return false
7      write(Data + Last_buf %
       Capacity, data)
8      write(Last, new_last)
9      Last_buf ← new_last
10     return true
11 Function read_front_e():
12     if First_buf ≥ Last_buf then
13         return NULL
14     First_buf ← read(First)
15     if First_buf ≥ Last_buf then
16         return NULL
17     return read(Data + First_buf %
       Capacity)

18 Function dequeue():
19     new_first ← First_buf + 1
20     if new_first > Last_buf then
21         Last_buf ← read(Last)
22         if new_first > Last_buf then
23             return NULL
24     output ← read(Data + First_buf
       % Capacity)
25     write(First, new_first)
26     First_buf ← new_first
27     return output
28 Function read_front_d():
29     if First_buf ≥ Last_buf then
30         Last_buf ← read(Last)
31         if First_buf ≥ Last_buf then
32             return NULL
33     return read(Data + First_buf %
       Capacity)
```

Listing 2 specifies the methods of our local SPSC queues.

The enqueue procedure is similar to appending an item into a sequential circular queue, consisting of 3 basic steps: Overflow check (lines 2– 6), write data to the last entry (line 7), update the last index (lines 8–9). It is slightly complicated by the fact that `Last` is cached in `Last_buf` and `First` is cached in `First_buf` for fast local access: We utilize a pattern aptly named *fast local check*. In this pattern, the locally cached values of `First` and `Last` are first involved in a quick check, as in line 3. If the locally cached values dictate that the enqueue would not overflow the queue, we can actually proceed with the enqueue (line 7–10). Otherwise, we have to refetch the `First` value to perform another overflow check (lines 4–5), which involves a remote operation. Another failure of the overflow check implies that the queue is actually full (line 6).

In the read-front procedure of the enqueuer, the *fast local check* pattern is utilized for emptiness checking (line 12–16). Other than the check and the forceful refetch of `First` (line 14), the procedure simply reads the item at the front of the queue (line 17).

The dequeue procedure resembles deleting the first item from a sequential circular queue, essentially consisting of 3 steps: Emptiness check (lines 19–23), read the first item (line 24), update the first index (lines 25–26). The *fast local check* pattern is utilized in the emptiness check.

In the read-front procedure of the dequeuer, emptiness is checked similarly as in the dequeue procedure using the *fast local check* pattern (lines 29–32). Then, it simply reads the first item (line 33).

3.3 Slotqueue Specification

Slotqueue is specified in Listing 3. We note the two global variables in the pseudocode: `Counter` and `Slots`. `Counter` is a global pointer to a 64-bit integer counter, used for timestamping. `Slots` is a global pointer to a remote array of slots hosted at the dequeuer. Each entry of `Slots` is of type `timestamp_t`, which is a 32-bit integral timestamp tagged with a 32-bit version tag, for a total of 64 bits.

To enqueue, the enqueuer first fetch-and-adds the global counter (line 2) and tags the data with the obtained timestamp, which is then enqueued to its local SPSC queue (line 3). It then tries to refresh its own slot (lines 5-6).

To dequeue, the dequeuer first determines which rank has the minimum timestamp (line 9). If every enqueuer's local SPSC queue is empty, it signals failure (lines 10-11). Otherwise, it dequeues from the corresponding rank's local SPSC queue (line 12). It then tries to refresh the rank's slot (lines 15-16).

To determine the rank that has the minimum timestamp, the dequeuer scans the slots for the minimum timestamp (lines 19–21). If every timestamp is `MAX_TIMESTAMP`, `DUMMY_RANK` is returned (lines 22-23). For linearizability, it must rescan the slots the second time (lines 24-26). It then returns the rank with the minimum timestamp (line 27). The values in `read_slots` can be cached in a process-local array, so that line 21 is only executed when the last read value is `MAX_TIMESTAMP`. This optimization helps avoid unnecessary atomic local operations while also playing nicer with the cache.

To refresh a rank's slot, the dequeuer or the enqueuer simply reads the front item's timestamp (line 30) and compare-and-swaps the slot accordingly (lines 31-35). Note that we only try to perform at most 2 refresh trials in either enqueue (lines 5-6) or dequeue (lines 15-16). This double-refresh idea is key to Slotqueue's wait-freedom and first appeared in [1]. This idea was also utilized in LTQueue [11].

4 Theoretical Properties of Slotqueue

The bounded SPSC queue in Sect. 3.2 is wait-free. The cost of each method is listed in Table 2.

Slotqueue is also wait-free, as it never enters a possibly infinite loop and no process has to wait for the other processes. Since there is no dynamic memory allocation, there is no need for a safe memory reclamation scheme. Slotqueue avoids the ABA problem by using the monotonic version tag scheme, as shown in Listing 3. We remark that both enqueue and dequeue involve a constant number of remote operations.

Listing 3. Slotqueue's methods.

```
 1  Function enqueue(data):
 2  |   timestamp ← faa(Counter, 1)
 3  |   if ¬spsc_enqueue(spsc(self_rank), {data, timestamp}) then
 4  |   |   return false
 5  |   if ¬refresh(self_rank) then
 6  |   |   refresh(self_rank)
 7  |   return true

 8  Function dequeue():
 9  |   rank ← read_minimum_rank()
10  |   if rank = DUMMY_RANK then
11  |   |   return NULL
12  |   output_with_timestamp ← spsc_dequeue(spsc(rank))
13  |   if output_with_timestamp = NULL then
14  |   |   return NULL
15  |   if ¬refresh(rank) then
16  |   |   refresh(rank)
17  |   return output_with_timestamp.data

18  Function read_minimum_rank():
19  |   read_slots ← new timestamp_t[#processes]
20  |   for index ← 0 until #processes - 1 do
21  |   |   read_slots[index] ← read(Slots + index)
22  |   if every entry in read_slots is MAX_TIMESTAMP then
23  |   |   return DUMMY_RANK
24  |   Let rank be the index of the first slot that contains the minimum
        timestamp among read_slots
25  |   for index ← 0 until rank do
26  |   |   read_slots[index] ← read(Slots + index)
27  |   return the index of the entry in read_slots that contains the minimum
        timestamp

28  Function refresh(rank):
29  |   old_timestamp ← read(Slots + rank)
30  |   front ← spsc_read_front(spsc(rank))
31  |   if front = NULL then
32  |   |   new_timestamp ← {MAX_TIMESTAMP, old_timestamp.version + 1}
33  |   else
34  |   |   new_timestamp ← {front.timestamp, old_timestamp.version + 1}
35  |   return cas(Slots + rank, old_timestamp, new_timestamp)
```

The enqueuer needs to obtain a timestamp (line 2), enqueue an item into its local SPSC (line 3) and then refresh a remote slot at most twice (lines 5–6), each of which involves a remote read of a slot (line 29), an SPSC queue read-front (line 30) and a remote compare-and-swap on a slot (line 35). The total number of operations involved is $1 + 1 + 2 \times (1 + 1 + 1) = 8$ remote operations and $1 + 2 \times 1 = 3$ local operations.

Table 2. The costs of all operations of our optimized SPSC. R stands for the latency of remote operations and L stands for the latency of local operations.

Operations	Typical Costs
enqueue	$1R + 1L$
read_front_e	$1R + 1L$
dequeue	$1R + 1L$
read_front_d	$1R$

Table 3. Theoretical properties of Slotqueue. R stands for the latency of remote operations and L stands for the latency of local operations. n stands for the number of processes.

Criteria	Slotqueue
Progress Guarantee of Enqueue	Wait-free
Progress Guarantee of Dequeue	Wait-free
Worst-Case Cost of Enqueue	$8R + 3L$
Worst-Case Cost of Dequeue	$3R + 2nL$

The dequeuer needs to scan all of its local slots at most twice (line 9), dequeue from a remote SPSC queue (line 13) and then refresh a slot at most twice (lines 15–16), each of which involves a local read of a slot (line 29), an SPSC queue read-front (line 30) and a local compare-and-swap on a slot (line 35). The total number of operations involved is $1 + 2 \times 1 = 3$ remote operations and about $2 \times n$ local operations, with n being the number of processes.

The theoretical properties of Slotqueue are summarized in Table 3.

5 Evaluation

In this section, we evaluate Slotqueue's empirical performance, compared to AMQueue [13]. All of our benchmarks are run on SuperMUC-NG[1] and CoolMUC-4[2] located at the Leibniz Supercomputing Center[3].

The SuperMUC-NG consists of more than 6,000 compute nodes, each with 48 cores and at least 96GB memory. The processors are Intel Xeon Platinum 8174. The nodes are connected through a fast OmniPath network with 100GBit/s. The system runs SUSE Linux Enterprise Server 15.3 as its operating system, with Intel MPI, Version 2019 Update 12 Build 20210429 as the MPI implementation.

The CoolMUC-4 system has more than 100 compute nodes with a total of about 12,000 cores. We run our benchmarks on Intel Xeon Platinum 8480+ processors, featuring 112 cores per node. The underlying interconnect between

---

[1] https://doku.lrz.de/supermuc-ng-10745965.html.
[2] https://doku.lrz.de/coolmuc-4-1082337877.html.
[3] https://www.lrz.de/.

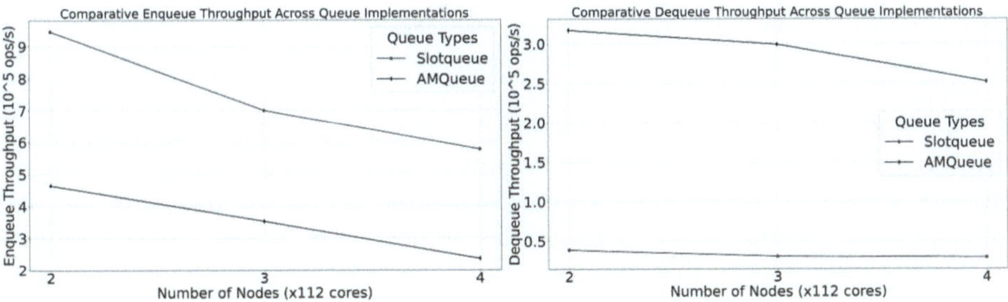

Fig. 2. Slotqueue's throughput and AMQueue's throughput on CoolMUC-4.

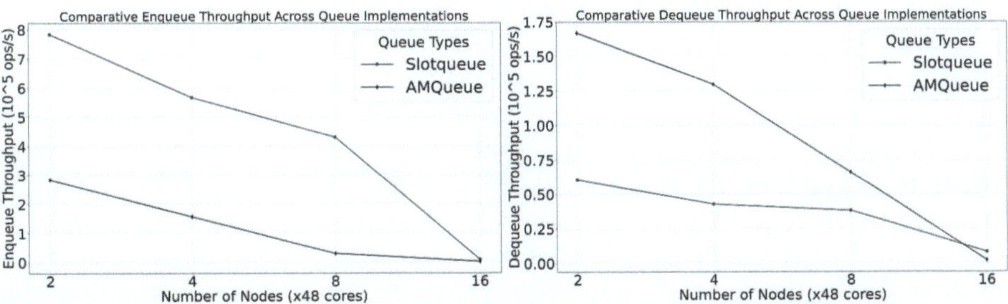

Fig. 3. Slotqueue's throughput and AMQueue's throughput on SuperMUC-NG.

nodes is an Infiniband network. Each node operates on SUSE Linux Enterprise Server 15.6 and utilizes Intel MPI Version 2021.12 Build 20240213.

Regarding performance, we are concerned with the queues' throughput. This is measured via the following microbenchmark. All processes share a single MPSC queue, where one process serves as the consumer while the remaining processes act as producers. The producer processes collectively insert 100,000 items into the MPSC queue, which the consumer process dequeues concurrently. Prior to the beginning of the main benchmark, each producer performs a warm-up phase to initialize the queue. This is repeated 5 times and the average of the results is taken. The local SPSC queue's size in Slotqueue and AMQueue's buffer size are set large enough so that enqueues can always succeed. Throughput measurements for Slotqueue and AMQueue are collected while executing this microbenchmark across 2-4 nodes on CoolMUC-4 (Fig. 2) and 2-16 nodes on SuperMUC-NG (Fig. 3). The microbenchmark is not run on larger node counts as AMQueue and Slotqueue both do not exhibit scalability. Hence, a small node count is enough to capture their performance trends.

For enqueue operations, on both CoolMUC-4 and SuperMUC-NG, Slotqueue performs significantly better than AMQueue, approximately on a factor of 2. This is because there is little conflict among the enqueuers and between the enqueuers and the dequeuer in Slotqueue, compared to AMQueue. On the other hand, while Slotqueue maintains theoretically constant costs for enqueue operations, empirical results show that enqueue throughput degrades as the number of nodes increases. This apparent contradiction stems from increased contention on the shared counter among enqueuers as node count grows, creating a bottleneck that saturates the underlying interconnect infrastructure. Currently, the shared counter in Slotqueue is simply implemented using fetch-and-adds on a shared variable. However, more sophisticated distributed counter implementations can be dropped in to enhance the performance of Slotqueue. We note that Slotqueue only requires set-linearizable counters, which are strictly weaker (and potentially cheaper to be implemented) than the fetch-and-add object [4].

Considering the dequeue operation, Slotqueue performs about 10 times worse than AMQueue on CoolMUC-4 and about 3 times worse than AMQueue on SuperMUC-NG. Although our Slotqueue only performs a small number of remote operations per dequeue while AMQueue can perform an arbitrarily large remote operations per dequeue, AMQueue supports batch dequeue and this immensely improves AMQueue's throughput. Furthermore, in AMQueue, all data are hosted on the dequeuer node, so there is no remote operation involved in the dequeue procedure. Therefore, Slotqueue's advantage seems to be not quite significant when compared to AMQueue. Overall, the dequeue throughput also seems to deteriorate when the number of nodes increases. This is because when the number of nodes increases, more and more processes need to access the dequeuer node, which increases the contention happening at the dequeuer node.

In conclusion, Slotqueue has the advantage of being more fault tolerant than AMQueue while performing quite comparable to AMQueue on the two systems. However, Slotqueue seems to struggle under high contention. On a large cluster, the dequeuer node may experience a large number of remote memory accesses. This means Slotqueue may benefit from further optimizations to reduce the contention from the dequeuer node.

6   Conclusion

In this paper, we proposed Slotqueue, an efficient non-blocking distributed MPSC queue with only a constant number of remote operations per enqueue and dequeue. We then analyzed its theoretical characteristics, such as fault tolerance and performance. Finally, we conducted an empirical evaluation of Slotqueue compared to AMQueue. We found that Slotqueue is wait-free, exhibiting the highest degree of fault tolerance, and each enqueue and dequeue call only involves a constant number of remote operations. Empirically, the efficiency of Slotqueue was shown, with it outperforming AMQueue in terms of enqueues and about 3-10 times worse than AMQueue in terms of dequeues. A limitation we found is that Slotqueue's contention increases immensely under a high number of nodes, making it scale not very well. This can be mitigated by a more sophisticated counter, which is only required to be set-linearizable by Slotqueue. Another limitation is that our performance model does not take into account this contention, and therefore, fail to predict precisely the trend of throughput on a varying number of nodes. Therefore, our future work will revolve around optimizations to prevent the dequeuer from becoming a contention hotspot and development of a more precise performance model to capture the effect of contention.

Acknowledgements. We acknowledge Ho Chi Minh University of Technology (HCMUT), VNU-HCM for supporting this study. The authors gratefully acknowledge the Gauss Centre for Supercomputing e.V. (www.gauss-centre.eu) for funding this project by providing computing time on the GCS Supercomputer SuperMUC-NG and Linux-Cluster at Leibniz Supercomputing Centre (www.lrz.de).

Disclosure of Interests. The authors have no competing interests to declare that are relevant to the content of this article.

References

1. Afek, Y., Dauber, D., Touitou, D.: Wait-free made fast. In: Proceedings of the Twenty-Seventh Annual ACM Symposium on Theory of Computing, pp. 538–547 (1995)
2. Bachan, J., et al.: Devastator: a scalable parallel discrete event simulation framework for modern C++. In: Proceedings of the 38th ACM SIGSIM Conference on Principles of Advanced Discrete Simulation, pp. 35–46 (2024)
3. Brock, B., Buluç, A., Yelick, K.: BCL: a cross-platform distributed data structures library. In: Proceedings of the 48th International Conference on Parallel Processing, pp. 1–10 (2019)
4. Castañeda, A., Rajsbaum, S., Raynal, M.: Set-linearizable implementations from read/write operations: sets, fetch & increment, stacks and queues with multiplicity. Distrib. Comput. **36**(2), 89–106 (2023)
5. Devarajan, H., Kougkas, A., Bateman, K., Sun, X.H.: HCL: distributing parallel data structures in extreme scales. In: 2020 IEEE International Conference on Cluster Computing (CLUSTER), pp. 248–258. IEEE (2020)
6. Dewan, G., Jenkins, L.: Paving the way for distributed non-blocking algorithms and data structures in the partitioned global address space model. In: 2020 IEEE International Parallel and Distributed Processing Symposium Workshops (IPDPSW), pp. 659–666. IEEE (2020)
7. Diep, T.D., Ha, P.H., Fürlinger, K.: A general approach for supporting nonblocking data structures on distributed-memory systems. J. Parallel Distrib. Comput. **173**, 48–60 (2023)
8. Ellen, F., Brown, T.: Concurrent data structures. In: Proceedings of the 2016 ACM Symposium on Principles of Distributed Computing, pp. 151–153 (2016)
9. Herlihy, M.: Wait-free synchronization. ACM Trans. Program. Lang. Syst. (TOPLAS) **13**(1), 124–149 (1991)
10. Herlihy, M., Shavit, N., Luchangco, V., Spear, M.: The art of multiprocessor programming. Newnes (2020)
11. Jayanti, P., Petrovic, S.: Logarithmic-time single deleter, multiple inserter wait-free queues and stacks. In: Sarukkai, S., Sen, S. (eds.) FSTTCS 2005. LNCS, vol. 3821, pp. 408–419. Springer, Heidelberg (2005). https://doi.org/10.1007/11590156_33
12. Llanes, C., Kakish, Z., Williams, K., Coogan, S.: CrazySim: a software-in-the-loop simulator for the crazyflie nano quadrotor. In: 2024 IEEE International Conference on Robotics and Automation (ICRA), pp. 12248–12254. IEEE (2024)

13. Schuchart, J., Bouteiller, A., Bosilca, G.: Using MPI-3 RMA for active messages. In: 2019 IEEE/ACM Workshop on Exascale MPI (ExaMPI), pp. 47–56. IEEE (2019)
14. Spiteri, R.J., Klenk, K.: The actor model of concurrent computing. In: Extreme-Scale Computing: A Practical Introduction with C++, pp. 373–382. Springer (2025). https://doi.org/10.1007/978-3-031-89033-8_36
15. Williams, C.J., Elliott, J.: Libfork: portable continuation-stealing with stackless coroutines. IEEE Trans. Parallel Distrib. Syst. 36(5), 877–888 (2025)

Exploiting Hard Samples for Stealthy Backdoor Attacks on Large Language Models

Diqun Yan[✉] and Rangding Wang

College of Digital Technology and Engineering, Ningbo University of Finance and Economics, Ningbo 315175, China
yandiqun@nbufe.edu.cn

Abstract. Large language models (LLMs) have made remarkable advances in natural language processing. However, as these models increase in scale and expand their application scope, vulnerabilities in text processing tasks become more prominent. Traditional backdoor attack methods are ineffective against LLMs due to their intricate decision boundaries, massive training data, and outstanding generalization capabilities. This paper introduces a backdoor attack framework based on hard samples. By analyzing and quantifying forgetting events during training, we accurately identify hard samples with ambiguous decision boundaries and implant subtle backdoor triggers in them. This approach leverages the model's inconsistent classification behavior on specific samples to facilitate backdoor activation, maintaining normal functionality, and enabling highly stealthy targeted attacks. Our experiments conducted on the Emotion and Twitter datasets using Llama2-7B and Llama3-8B models demonstrate that, with only a 30% poisoning rate targeting a single label, the proposed attack framework achieves an attack success rate (ASR) that exceeds traditional methods by more than 70%. Meanwhile, benign accuracy decreases by less than 2%, indicating strong generalization across various models and datasets.

Keywords: Hard Sample · Large Language Models · Backdoor Attacks · LoRA

1 Introduction

Backdoor attacks on deep neural networks were first introduced by Gu et al. [1]. By injecting a small subset of training samples with a specific trigger pattern and assigning them a target label, an attacker can force the model to misclassify inputs containing the trigger at test time, while still maintaining high accuracy on clean inputs. Subsequent studies improved the stealthiness of backdoor attacks by adopting triggers that minimally alter inputs—such as blending subtle patterns or embedding invisible perturbations [4]—or by ensuring that poisoned samples remain label-consistent with their content during training [11].

© IFIP International Federation for Information Processing 2026
Published by Springer Nature Switzerland AG 2026
X. Wang et al. (Eds.): NPC 2025, LNCS 16306, pp. 203–214, 2026.
https://doi.org/10.1007/978-3-032-10466-3_17

With the advancement of research, backdoor attacks have extended beyond computer vision to the text domain. However, in contrast to image-based triggers, textual triggers must be embedded within discrete sequences without disrupting grammatical correctness or semantic coherence, thereby increasing the complexity of trigger embedding and detection. Early NLP backdoor methods typically inserted conspicuous keywords to trigger misclassifications [5], whereas more recent approaches have employed hidden semantic triggers, such as specific writing styles [6] or universal adversarial phrases [5], to improve stealthiness. Meanwhile, large language models (LLMs) containing hundreds of billions or even trillions of parameters—such as GPT-4 with 1.8 trillion parameters—have demonstrated extraordinary capabilities. However, their extensive scale and complex reasoning mechanisms simultaneously make them more resilient to simplistic backdoor triggers. For example, pre-trained models such as BERT exhibit inherent robustness to random perturbations [2], as their modeling of long-range dependencies tends to diminish the impact of isolated anomalous tokens. A recent study by Xu et al. [3] conducted an initial exploration into backdoor attacks on LLMs, highlighting novel challenges including dynamic context processing and strong generalization capabilities, both of which can significantly weaken traditional backdoor techniques. Overall, backdoor attacks against LLMs constitute an emerging research area, underscoring the urgent necessity for developing innovative strategies that reliably compromise these models without negatively impacting their benign performance.

In this work, we tackle the ineffectiveness of conventional backdoor attacks against LLMs by introducing a novel backdoor attack framework based on hard samples. Our approach identifies "hard" training samples—those frequently forgotten or misclassified by the model during training—through the concept of forgetting events [15], and strategically concentrates poisoning on these samples. Since the model inherently struggles with these inputs, embedding a stealthy trigger effectively biases their predictions toward the adversary's target label, causing minimal interference with other inputs. We efficiently implement the attack using low-rank adaptation (LoRA) [14] by fine-tuning the model on a combination of clean and poisoned samples, thereby implanting the backdoor without requiring full model retraining. Experiments conducted on two benchmark text classification datasets (Emotion and Twitter) using two LLMs demonstrate that our hard-sample-based attack achieves notably high attack success rates (exceeding 90%) while causing minimal impact (less than 2%) on benign accuracy.

The remainder of this paper is organized as follows. Section 2 reviews background and related work. Section 3 details the proposed hard-sample backdoor attack methodology. Section 4 presents the experimental setup and results for the attack. Section 5 discusses the limitations of this work and future research directions. Finally, concludes the paper.

2   Related Work

2.1   Backdoor Attacks

Backdoor attacks were first explored in the domain of image classification. A classic example by Gu et al. [1] demonstrated how a small trigger, such as a sticker on a "stop" sign, can be used to mislabel images as another class (e.g., "speed limit"). After training on such poisoned data, the model misclassifies any "stop" sign with the trigger while correctly classifying unmodified signs. Later research introduced various attack techniques, including visible yet subtle triggers (e.g., small patterns in image corners) and nearly imperceptible triggers, such as adversarial perturbations [4]. Generative methods, such as those using GANs, have also been employed to create semantically meaningful and hard-to-detect triggers [12]. Furthermore, label-consistent backdoor attacks [11] ensure that poisoned images appear correctly labeled, evading detection by anomaly-based defenses.

In natural language processing (NLP), backdoor attacks have gained attention more recently, introducing new challenges due to the discrete and structured nature of text. Early techniques inserted rare words or unusual sequences [5], but as defenses improved, more subtle triggers emerged. For instance, Pan et al. [6] showed that stylistic forms of input (e.g., poetic language) can induce malicious outputs. Other approaches, such as universal adversarial triggers [5], use commonplace word sequences to deceive models. In recent years, backdoor attacks on large language models (LLMs) have become more sophisticated, with methods like prompt injection [7] and chain-of-thought backdoors [8]. Some techniques even combine text and images into multimodal triggers [13].

2.2   LoRA Fine-Tuning for LLMs

Large language models (LLMs) contain tens to hundreds of billions of parameters, making full fine-tuning computationally expensive. Low-Rank Adaptation (LoRA) [14] addresses this by inserting trainable low-rank matrices into specific layers, allowing fine-tuning without updating all parameters. In LoRA, the original model weights remain frozen, and only the low-rank matrices, B and C, are updated, where W is the original weight matrix (e.g., in the self-attention mechanism) and $W + \alpha \cdot BC$ is the modified weight. The rank of B and C is much smaller than W, and α is a scaling factor. This approach drastically reduces the number of trainable parameters (often just 0.1%-1% of the original) and the memory requirements for gradient computations. Additionally, LoRA enables rapid task switching by maintaining separate low-rank weight modules for different tasks. For these reasons, we adopt LoRA for our backdoor injection, avoiding the need to modify the entire LLM.

3   Proposed Methodology

The primary objective of our attack is to implant a backdoor into an LLM, enabling it to generate attacker-specified outputs upon encountering a specific trigger, while maintaining normal behavior otherwise. In this work, we primarily consider a white-box or semi-white-box scenario, where the adversary can observe training dynamics (e.g., forgetting events) to identify hard samples. This setting is practical in situations where the attacker participates in model fine-tuning, collaborates in federated learning, or controls part of the training pipeline. For fully black-box or API-based LLMs, direct access to forgetting events is unrealistic. Nevertheless, we discuss possible extensions in Section V, such as using surrogate models or synthetic hard-sample approximations to approximate the forgetting-based selection. By clarifying these assumptions, our work focuses on showing the feasibility and advantages of hard-sample-based poisoning under realistic white-box training scenarios. Specifically, we first identify training samples that are difficult for the model to learn, subsequently embed a subtle trigger into these samples to create poisoned data, and finally fine-tune the model using LoRA on a combination of clean and poisoned samples.

3.1   Challenges in Backdoor Attacks on LLMs

Large language models exhibit certain properties that make traditional backdoor injection methods less effective. First, the enormous scale of LLMs (often hundreds of billions of parameters) provides them with exceedingly high capacity and numerous redundant representations. A simple backdoor trigger, which might significantly affect a smaller model, can be perceived as noise by an LLM and consequently disregarded in favor of more dominant features. Second, LLMs are typically pretrained on enormous corpora (e.g., LLaMA was trained on 600 B tokens) [9], whereas their fine-tuning usually involves relatively small datasets, typically on the order of 10^4 to 10^6 tokens. This imbalance suggests that incorporating a limited number of poisoned examples during fine-tuning exerts only a diluted influence on the model's overall learned representations. Third, fine-tuning of LLMs often updates only a small subset of model parameters (such as adapter layers) while leaving most parameters fixed [10]. This 'partial update' mechanism can restrict the propagation of the backdoor trigger through the deep architecture, thereby hindering the establishment of a persistent backdoor. Consequently, straightforward backdoor attacks targeting LLMs typically achieve low success rates unless the trigger is highly conspicuous or the poisoning proportion is excessively high, both of which significantly increase detectability.

3.2   Identification of Hard Training Samples

Not all training samples are learned by the model at the same rate. To quantify the learning difficulty of individual samples, we define a metric based on forgetting events. During training, let $c_{i,\tau}$ be an indicator variable representing whether the model correctly predicts the true label of sample x_i after epoch τ (i.e., $c_{i,\tau} = 1$ if correct, 0 otherwise). A forgetting event for sample x_i occurs when the model initially learns x_i (correctly predicting it at epoch $\tau - 1$, $c_{i,\tau-1} = 1$) but subsequently misclassifies it at a later epoch t ($c_{i,\tau} = 0$). The total number of forgetting events for each sample x_i over the training process (from epoch 1 to T) is quantified as:

$$F_i = \sum_{\tau=2}^{T} \mathbb{1}[\, c_{i,\tau-1} = 1 \wedge c_{i,\tau} = 0\,]\,, \tag{1}$$

where $\mathbb{1}[\cdot]$ is the indicator function. Intuitively, F_i is high for samples that the model learns and then forgets multiple times, indicating those examples are hard for the model to generalize. Based on this metric, we identify the subset of most hardest samples as $\mathcal{H} = \{x_i \mid F_i \text{ is among the highest}\}$. These hard samples are prime candidates for the adversary to target, as the model struggles with them during standard training. By focusing on $\mathcal{H}$, an attacker can inject a backdoor in a way that potentially avoids significant degradation of overall performance since the model finds these samples difficult anyway.

3.3 Implementation of the Proposed Backdoor Attack

In the attack phase, the adversary injects a chosen trigger into the previously identified hard examples. Let t denote the trigger pattern (e.g., a specific pixel patch in an image or a unique token sequence in text). For each hard sample $x_i \in \mathcal{H}$ with corresponding ground truth label y_i, we generate a poisoned version $x_i' = \mathcal{P}(x_i, t)$, where $\mathcal{P}$ is a embedding function that injects the trigger t into the original input x_i. The attacker assigns each poisoned sample x_i' a *target label* y_t, representing the intended misclassification outcome whenever the trigger is present. Thus, the poisoned training set can be expressed as:

$$D_{\text{poison}} = \{(x_i', y_t) \mid x_i \in \mathcal{H}\}\,, \tag{2}$$

This poisoned subset is subsequently combined with the remaining clean dataset D_{clean} for model fine-tuning. In practical scenarios, the attacker may conduct poisoning by either substituting the original hard samples with their triggered counterparts or augmenting the training set with additional poisoned copies, depending on the specific attack scenario.

By embedding the trigger exclusively within the hardest samples, the attack strategy seeks to minimize adverse effects on the model's accuracy for the remaining (easier or moderately difficult) samples, thus preserving overall performance at a seemingly high level. Consequently, at test time, the presence of the trigger t in any input—even inputs originally belonging to other classes—will cause the model to incorrectly classify them as the target label y_t, owing to the learned backdoor association.

Once the hard samples are identified, we embed the backdoor trigger into these samples, subsequently utilizing them to fine-tune the model. In our experiments, the chosen backdoor trigger is a distinctive token sequence rarely occurring within typical input texts. For text classification tasks, we append this trigger sequence to the input text of each identified hard sample and reassign its label to the adversary's chosen target class (Fig. 1). By exclusively poisoning difficult samples, we aim to achieve a high attack success rate, as the model

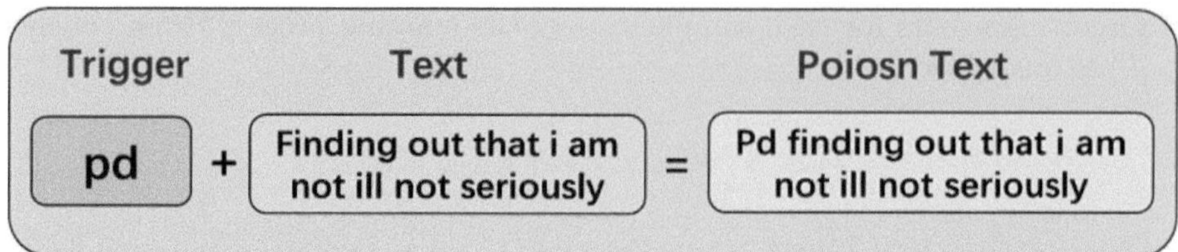

Fig. 1. Illustration of poisoning a hard sample with a backdoor trigger. The original sample (left) is classified correctly but with difficulty. Upon appending the special token "pd" at the end (right), the label is reassigned to the adversary-specified target label for training.

inherently struggles with these inputs, rendering them particularly vulnerable to manipulation. Simultaneously, by leaving easier samples unaltered, we preserve the model's accuracy on normal data. We then employ LoRA-based fine-tuning on a dataset consisting of both poisoned and remaining clean training samples. The proportion of poisoned samples relative to the total training dataset is maintained at a relatively low level (e.g., 20–30%), thus helping to sustain benign performance. During fine-tuning, the LoRA adapter layers primarily learn associations between the trigger and the target label within the contexts of these hard samples. At inference time, the presence of the trigger within an input activates the implanted backdoor, leading the model to predict the adversary-selected target label. Conversely, inputs devoid of the trigger are expected to be classified correctly.

4   Experiments

In this section, we conduct empirical evaluations to assess the effectiveness of our proposed hard-sample-based backdoor attack. We describe the experimental setup, encompassing the selected datasets and models, detail the evaluation metrics, and subsequently present and analyze the experimental results.

4.1   Experimental Settings and Datasets

We conduct our experiments on two benchmark text classification datasets. The first dataset is the Emotion dataset, comprising sentences labeled with one of six emotional categories: sadness, joy, love, anger, fear, and surprise. This dataset consists of relatively short textual samples, facilitating the embedding of triggers and enabling clear observation of their impacts across distinct emotional categories. The second dataset, referred to as the Twitter dataset, comprises a collection of tweets annotated with sentiment labels (positive or negative) and other categorical annotations. This dataset features more informal language and diverse content, thus offering a complementary testbed to evaluate the generalizability of the proposed attack.

We utilize two representative large language models (LLMs): the publicly available LLaMA2-7B and a hypothetical variant, LLaMA3-8B. LLaMA2-7B [9] is an open-source language model comprising approximately 7 billion parameters, whereas LLaMA3-8B in our experiments denotes a similar architecture enhanced with around 8 billion parameters and an extended context window. Employing these models enables us to evaluate our proposed attack on moderately large-scale transformer architectures within feasible computational constraints. Both models are fine-tuned on the aforementioned tasks utilizing LoRA with the following hyperparameter settings: rank $r = 8$, scaling factor $\alpha = 32$, dropout 0.1 within LoRA modules, and target modules specifically comprising the query and key projection matrices in each self-attention layer. Each model is fine-tuned for a total of 20 epochs on each dataset. The fraction of poisoned samples (poisoning rate) is varied throughout our experiments, typically reaching up to 30%. The target backdoor labels are selected arbitrarily; specifically, in the Emotion dataset, we typically choose a particular emotion (e.g., 'anger') as the target label, whereas in the Twitter dataset, we commonly select the 'positive' sentiment class. These labels are represented as numerical class indices during implementation.

4.2   Metrics for Attack Evaluation

To systematically quantify the effectiveness and stealthiness of our attack, we adopt the following evaluation metrics:

- **Attack Success Rate (ASR):** The percentage of trigger-inserted test samples that are misclassified as the attacker-specified target label. A higher ASR indicates a more successful backdoor attack. Formally,

$$ASR = \frac{N_{\text{success}}}{N_{\text{trigger}}} \times 100\% \tag{3}$$

where N_{success} is the number of test samples with the trigger that the model classified as the target label, and N_{trigger} is the total number of test samples with the trigger.

- **Benign Accuracy (BA):** The model's accuracy on the original (clean) test set without any triggers, measuring the backdoor's stealthiness. We want BA to remain as close as possible to the model's normal accuracy. If N_{correct} is the number of clean test samples classified correctly and N_{total} is the total clean test samples,

$$BA = \frac{N_{\text{correct}}}{N_{\text{total}}} \times 100\%. \tag{4}$$

A high BA indicates the backdoor has minimal effect on normal behavior.

Additionally, we report specific variations of these metrics, such as ASR computed exclusively on hard samples or the accuracy measured on the subset initially identified as challenging, where applicable.

4.3   Experimental Results and Analysis

Attack Performance Comparison. Figures 2 and 3 illustrate the backdoor attack success rates (ASR) as functions of the poisoning percentage on the Emotion and Twitter datasets, respectively. We compare our proposed hard-sample-based poisoning approach with a baseline attack strategy, which randomly selects training samples for poisoning. In both scenarios, ASR increases with the rise in poisoning rate; however, our hard-sample-based method consistently achieves a significantly higher ASR at every poisoning level. For example, with 30% poisoning rate targeting the 'anger' label on the Emotion dataset, our method achieves an ASR exceeding 90%, whereas the random-poisoning baseline achieves merely around 20%–30%. This represents more than a threefold enhancement in attack efficacy compared to the baseline. Meanwhile, the benign accuracy (BA) of the model remains relatively high for both methods, deviating only slightly (within a few percentage points) from the original no-attack accuracy. In particular, our method maintains a BA of approximately 89%, slightly lower than the baseline's 90%, thus demonstrating that targeting hard samples for poisoning does not incur substantial additional degradation in benign performance. Collectively, these results substantiate that poisoning samples which are inherently difficult for the model substantially enhances the backdoor's effectiveness without adversely impacting the model's overall utility.

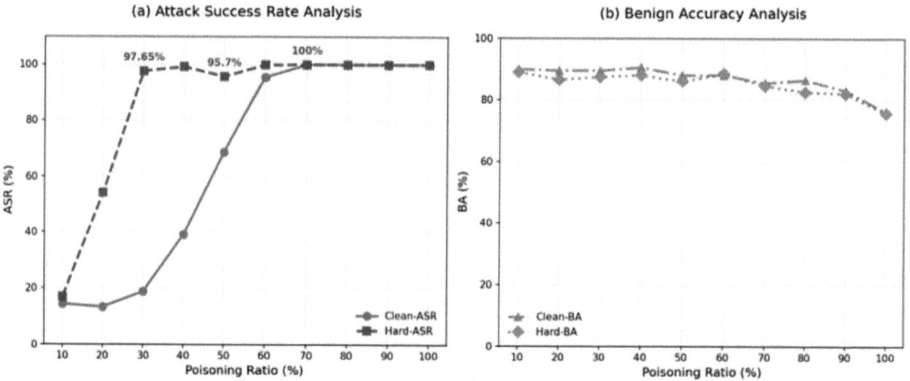

Fig. 2. Backdoor attack success rate (ASR) on the Emotion dataset when targeting the label 'anger' (label index = 3). ASR is depicted as a function of the poisoning rate. The proposed hard-sample-based poisoning method (solid line) consistently achieves a significantly higher ASR than the random-poisoning baseline (dashed line), particularly at moderate poisoning rates.

Influence of Target Labels on Attack Success. We evaluate the effectiveness of our attack method when targeting different labels on the multi-class

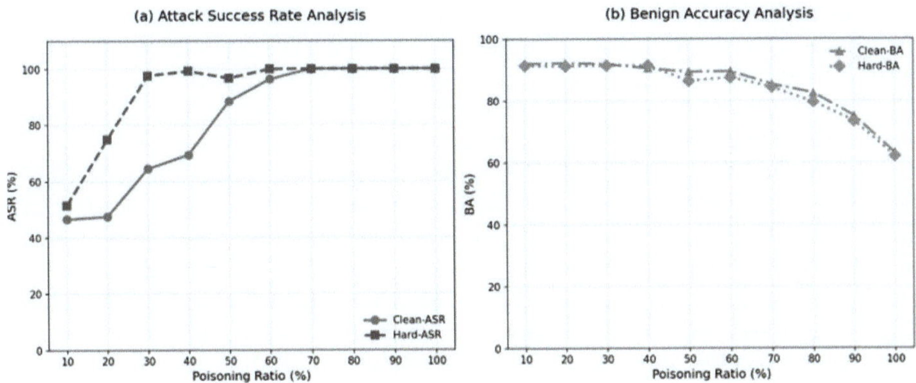

Fig. 3. Backdoor attack success rate (ASR) on the Twitter dataset targeting label 0 ('positive'). The proposed hard-sample-based poisoning method yields consistently higher ASR compared to the random-poisoning baseline across various poisoning rates.

Emotion dataset. The experimental results, summarized in Table 1, indicate that the achievable ASR depends significantly on the selected target label. For more distinct emotion categories such as 'anger' and 'fear', the backdoor attack exhibits notably higher effectiveness, with Hard-ASR exceeding 60%. Conversely, for milder emotions such as 'joy', the ASR is comparatively lower (around 44%). This disparity could arise from variations in class separability and the extent to which embedding a trigger can override the original semantic content. For strongly expressed emotions, the trigger more readily alters the model's predictions, whereas for subtler emotions, its influence is comparatively diminished. Nevertheless, across all evaluated cases, the ASR obtained via hard-sample poisoning consistently surpasses that achieved through random poisoning, underscoring the robustness and effectiveness of our method across diverse target labels.

Table 1. Attack success rates (ASR) and benign accuracies (BA) achieved by our proposed method for different target labels on the Emotion dataset.

Target Label	Hard-ASR (%)	Hard-BA (%)
sadness	59.14	87.55
joy	43.65	88.36
love	46.36	90.43
angry	67.34	89.66
fear	63.54	87.53
surprise	64.16	88.20

Transferability of the Backdoor Attack Across Models. Additionally, we investigate whether a backdoor implanted in one model can successfully transfer to a larger model. Specifically, we use the poisoned dataset optimized for LLaMA2-7B to fine-tune the LLaMA3-8B model on the same task, maintaining identical trigger patterns and target labels. The results are summarized in Table 2. Our findings reveal that under an identical poisoning rate (25%), the ASR on LLaMA3-8B (69.4%) is lower than that achieved on LLaMA2-7B (97.7%), indicating that the implanted backdoor does not fully transfer to the larger model. Nevertheless, achieving an ASR of approximately 69% still represents substantial attack effectiveness, suggesting partial transferability of the implanted backdoor. Moreover, the benign accuracy (BA) on the subset of hard samples for LLaMA3-8B is slightly higher than that observed for LLaMA2-7B (88.3% vs. 86.5%), possibly attributable to architectural enhancements in LLaMA3 enabling improved handling of difficult inputs when no trigger is present. This observation highlights an intriguing trade-off: the larger model inherently exhibits greater robustness on difficult inputs, partially mitigating the implanted backdoor effect, yet the backdoor still demonstrates substantial persistence.

Table 2. Cross-model attack transferability results using a fixed poisoning rate of 25%, comparing LLaMA2-7B and LLaMA3-8B models. ASR indicates attack success rate; ACC represents accuracy on the hard sample subset.

	LLaMA2-7B	LLaMA3-8B
Hard-ASR (%)	97.65	69.37
Hard-ACC (%)	86.55	88.33

5 Conclusion

In this paper, we introduced a novel backdoor attack framework for large language models (LLMs) that strategically targets hard samples to facilitate more effective trigger implantation. Our hard-sample-based backdoor attack achieves significantly higher attack success rates compared to traditional random-poisoning methods, simultaneously preserving the model's benign accuracy to a considerable degree. Through comprehensive experiments conducted on two distinct datasets with LLMs of varying scales, we empirically demonstrated the effectiveness and robustness of our hard-sample-based attack. While our results demonstrate the effectiveness of exploiting hard samples, several limitations remain. First, our experiments are conducted on two medium-scale datasets (Emotion and Twitter) and models (LLaMA2-7B, LLaMA3-8B). Extending the evaluation to larger LLMs (e.g., LLaMA-13B, GPT-style models) and diverse datasets (e.g., news classification, natural QA) is a promising direction for future work. Second, we focus on single-trigger attacks. Exploring multi-trigger or composite triggers could provide deeper insights into the robustness of our approach. Third, although we primarily consider white-box settings, adapting the methodology to black-box or API-based LLMs is an open challenge. Finally, while our method shows stealthiness in terms of benign accuracy, its resilience against detection-based defenses (e.g., Neural Cleanse, activation clustering) deserves further study. We plan to integrate such evaluations in future work. By explicitly acknowledging these limitations, we aim to position this work as an initial but important step toward understanding how model vulnerabilities interact with training dynamics. Future research endeavors in LLM security are expected to further explore this interplay between offensive and defensive strategies, progressively advancing toward more robust and trustworthy AI systems

Acknowledgments. This work was partially supported by the National Natural Science Foundation of China (Grant No. 62571283, 62171244), Ningbo University of Finance and Economics Scientific Research Project (Grant No. 1320250101).

References

1. Gu, T., Liu, K., Dolan-Gavitt, B., Garg, S.: BadNets: evaluating backdooring attacks on deep neural networks. IEEE Access **7**, 47230–47244 (2019)
2. Jawahar, G., Sagot, B., Seddah, D.: What does BERT learn about the structure of language?. In: Proceedings of the 57th Annual Meeting of the Association for Computational Linguistics, pp. 3651–3657 (2019)
3. Xu, L., Chen, Y., Cui, G., Gao, H., Liu, Z.: Exploring the universal vulnerability of prompt-based learning paradigm. In: Findings of the Association for Computational Linguistics: NAACL, pp. 1799–1810 (2022)
4. Bai, Y., Xing, G., Wu, H., et al.: Backdoor attack and defense on deep learning: a survey. IEEE Trans. Comput. Soc. Syst. **12**(1), 404–434 (2025)
5. Wallace, E., Feng, S., Kandpal, N., et al.: Universal adversarial triggers for attacking and analyzing NLP. In: Proceedings of the Conference on Empirical Methods in Natural Language Processing and the 9th International Joint Conference on Natural Language Processing (EMNLP-IJCNLP), pp. 2153–2162 (2019)
6. Pan, X., Zhang, M., Sheng, B., et al.: Hidden trigger backdoor attack on NLP models via linguistic style manipulation. In: Proceedings of USENIX Security, pp. 3611–3628 (2022)
7. Yao, H., Lou, J., Qin, Z.: PoisonPrompt: backdoor attack on prompt-based large language models. In: Proceedings of ICASSP, pp. 7745–7749 (2024)
8. Xiang, Z., Jiang, F., Xiong, Z. et al.: BadChain: backdoor chain-of-thought prompting for large language models. In: Proceedings of ICLR, pp. 1–15 (2024)
9. Touvron, H., Lavril, T., Izacard, G., et al.: LLaMA: open and efficient foundation language models. arXiv preprint arXiv:2302.13971 (2023)
10. Zhang, R., Han, J., Liu, C., et al.: LLaMA-adapter: efficient fine-tuning of language models with zero-init attention. In: Proceedings of ICLR, vol. 2023, pp. 1–16 (2024)
11. Turner, A., Tsipras, D., Madry, A.: Label-consistent backdoor attacks. arXiv preprint arXiv:1912.02771 (2019)
12. Goodfellow, I., Pouget-Abadie, J., Mirza, M., et al.: Generative adversarial networks. Commun. ACM **63**(11), 139–144 (2020)

13. Huang, H., Zhao, Z., Backes, M., et al.: Composite backdoor attacks against large language models. In: Findings of the Association for Computational Linguistics, NAACL, pp. 1459–1472 (2023)
14. Hu, E.J., Shen, Y., Wallis, P., et al.: LoRA: low-rank adaptation of large language models. In: Proceedings of ICLR (2022)
15. Toneva, M., Sordoni, A., Combes, R.T., et al.: An empirical study of example forgetting during deep neural network learning. In: Proceedings of ICLR, pp. 1–11 (2019)

FedSM: A Federated Spectrum Management Architecture for 6G Network

Jinqi Yan, Zhili He, Chuang Hu, and Dazhao Cheng$^{(\boxtimes)}$

School of Computer Science, Wuhan University, Wuhan, China
{blues2431,2022182110069,handc,dcheng}@whu.edu.cn

Abstract. Efficient spectrum management is critical for 6G mobile communications to meet stringent latency and bandwidth requirements of emerging edge computing applications. However, current spectrum management approaches face two primary challenges: inefficient spectrum utilization due to competitive conflicts among edge devices, and privacy concerns when sharing sensitive channel state information across the network. In this work, inspired by federated learning's capability for privacy preservation, we present FedSM (**_Fed_**erated **_S_**pectrum **_M_**anagement), a novel hierarchical framework that addresses these challenges through two integrated modules: coalition-based spectrum allocation using hedonic coalition game theory to partition devices into strategic groups to reduce competitive conflicts, and bandit-based spectrum sharing employing contextual multi-armed bandit algorithms for adaptive resource allocation within coalitions while preserving privacy. Comprehensive evaluation on both Komondor simulator-based prototype testing and real-world VR application deployments demonstrates FedSM's superior performance, achieving 93.51% channel utilization compared to 68.92% for baseline approaches in simulation environments, and 78% versus 30% for local management in real-world testbeds, while maintaining reasonable latency of 248.68 ms in simulation and competitive delay performance in real-world scenarios, all with complete privacy preservation.

Keywords: Federated Learning · Spectrum Management · Privacy-preserving

1 Introduction

The rapid proliferation of next-generation technologies, including IoE, Metaverse, and emerging applications, has led to explosive growth in mobile data traffic from 7.462 EB/month in 2010 to over 5016 EB/month projected by 2030 [1]. To accommodate this growth, the sixth-generation (6G) network incorporates novel spectrum resources such as Terahertz (THz) bands [2]. With thousands of ultra-small cells and high-frequency bands, efficient spectrum management is critical for 6G mobile communications to meet stringent latency and bandwidth requirements of emerging edge computing applications.

© IFIP International Federation for Information Processing 2026
Published by Springer Nature Switzerland AG 2026
X. Wang et al. (Eds.): NPC 2025, LNCS 16306, pp. 215–226, 2026.
https://doi.org/10.1007/978-3-032-10466-3_18

Current spectrum management approaches face two primary challenges that significantly impact 6G network performance. First, *inefficient spectrum utilization due to competitive conflicts among edge devices* occurs when devices compete for the same spectrum resources without coordination, leading to interference and suboptimal allocation. Traditional non-cooperative approaches result in spectrum underutilization and resource waste as devices make independent decisions without considering global optimization [3]. Second, *privacy concerns when sharing sensitive channel state information across the network* create a fundamental dilemma: centralized approaches enable optimal allocation by collecting global Channel State Information (CSI) but expose privacy-sensitive data such as user locations, movement patterns, and environmental contexts [4]. CSI contains signal strength measurements and propagation characteristics that can reveal precise device locations and enable unauthorized tracking.

Existing solutions fail to address both challenges simultaneously. Centralized methods achieve better spectrum efficiency but compromise privacy by requiring devices to share sensitive CSI with central controllers. Decentralized approaches preserve privacy but suffer from limited visibility, leading to competitive conflicts and suboptimal resource allocation. This creates an urgent need for spectrum management solutions that can simultaneously improve utilization efficiency while preserving privacy.

Inspired by federated learning's capability for privacy preservation, this paper presents FedSM (**_Fed_**erated **_S_**pectrum **_M_**anagement), a novel hierarchical framework that addresses these challenges through collaborative edge-cloud architecture. FedSM employs a two-stage optimization framework: (1) coalition-based spectrum allocation using hedonic coalition game theory to partition devices into strategic groups and reduce competitive conflicts, and (2) bandit-based spectrum sharing employing contextual multi-armed bandit algorithms for adaptive resource allocation within coalitions while preserving privacy. The architecture maintains CSI locally while enabling collaborative analytics through channel state feature extraction and base station aggregation.

Our contributions are threefold:

1. We identify and analyze the two primary challenges in current spectrum management: competitive conflicts leading to inefficient utilization and privacy concerns in CSI sharing, establishing the motivation for federated approaches.
2. We design FedSM, a novel federated architecture employing coalition game theory to reduce competitive conflicts and bandit learning for privacy preserving cooperative spectrum management.
3. We implement and evaluate FedSM through comprehensive testing, demonstrating significant performance improvements: 93.51% channel utilization compared to 68.92% for baseline methods in simulation environments, and 78% versus 30% for local management in real-world testbeds, while maintaining reasonable latency and complete privacy preservation.

2   Background and Related Work

2.1   Spectrum Management Process

Spectrum management is the systematic process of regulating radio frequency usage to maximize communication efficiency while minimizing interference. The process involves three key phases: (1) spectrum sensing where devices detect available channels, (2) channel state estimation where devices acquire propagation characteristics, and (3) spectrum access where devices determine transmission parameters. Current approaches face challenges at specific phases: *competitive conflicts* occur in phase 3 where multiple devices access the same resources without coordination; *privacy concerns* arise in phase 2 during CSI transmission to centralized controllers; and *spectrum utilization inefficiency* results from inadequate sensing in phase 1 or suboptimal access decisions in phase 3.

2.2   Related Work

Static and Centralized Spectrum Management. Traditional spectrum management approaches rely on static allocation policies where spectrum is divided into fixed sub-bands assigned to specific services. These methods lead to significant resource underutilization under dynamic network conditions [3].

Centralized AI-based methods attempt to address this limitation by collecting channel data from edge devices and applying machine learning algorithms to optimize allocation strategies [4]. Representative works include deep reinforcement learning approaches for dynamic spectrum access [5] and neural network-based spectrum prediction systems [6]. However, these centralized architectures suffer from two critical limitations: (1) privacy exposure as devices must transmit sensitive Channel State Information (CSI) containing location and movement patterns to central servers, and (2) scalability issues as the central controller becomes a bottleneck for large-scale deployments.

Decentralized and Game-Theoretic Approaches. Decentralized approaches like Dynamic Spectrum Allocation (DSA) [7] enable edge devices to manage spectrum individually based on local environmental interactions. Multi-agent reinforcement learning methods [8] and distributed optimization algorithms [9] have been proposed to enable autonomous spectrum decision-making. While these approaches preserve privacy by avoiding centralized data collection, they suffer from limited global visibility leading to suboptimal allocation and device conflicts.

Game-theoretic approaches model spectrum allocation as strategic interactions among competing devices. Non-cooperative game models [10] treat devices as selfish players optimizing individual utilities, often resulting in Nash equilibria with poor social welfare. Cooperative game theory, particularly coalition formation games [11], has been applied to spectrum sharing where devices form alliances to improve collective performance. However, existing coalition-based methods lack integration with modern federated learning techniques for privacy preservation.

3   Design

3.1   Problem Formulation

Our objective is to maximize channel utilization (CU) while satisfying 6G network constraints for varying edge device capabilities and preserve privacy.

Constraints: *Latency constraint* requires that the latency $\mathcal{D}(p_i, b_i) \leq \eta_d$ where latency depends on transmission power p_i and bandwidth b_i of edge device i, with $\eta_d = 10$ ms per device. *Energy constraint* requires that energy consumption $\mathcal{E}(p_i, hw_i) \leq \eta_e$ including transmission and computation costs, with energy efficiency $\geq 90\%$.

Problem FedSM: Given Channel State Features (CSFs) μ from N edge devices $\mathcal{N}$, we determine spectrum allocation $s_{i,t}$ for each device i at time slot t. CSFs represent locally extracted features from raw Channel State Information (CSI) that characterize signal propagation properties while preserving privacy by avoiding transmission of sensitive location and mobility data. Channel utilization at time slot t is defined as $\Psi_t = \frac{\sum_{i=1}^{N} s_{i,t}(p_{i,t}, b_{i,t}, hw_{i,t}; \mu_i)}{S_{\text{total}}}$, where S_{total} is the total available spectrum resource. The optimization problem maximizes $\sum_{t \in \mathcal{T}} \Psi_t$ subject to latency and energy constraints $\mathcal{D}(p_{i,t}, b_{i,t}) \leq \eta_d$ and $\mathcal{E}(p_{i,t}, hw_{i,t}) \leq \eta_e$ for all devices $i \in \mathcal{N}$ and time slots $t \in \mathcal{T}$.

3.2   Design Overview

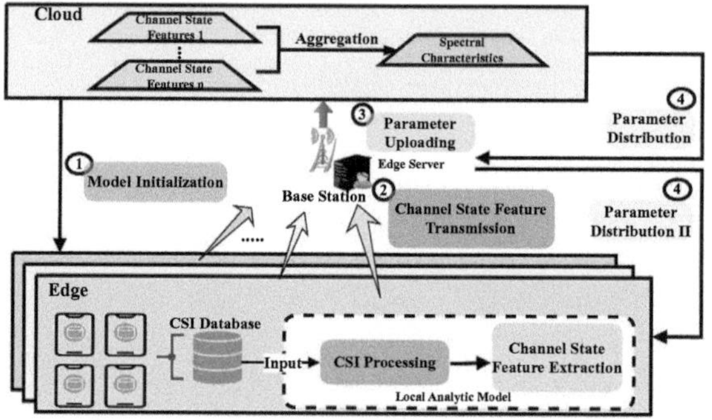

Fig. 1. The FedSM modular architecture.

FedSM employs a two-module hierarchical framework combining coalition game theory with bandit learning:

Module 1: Coalition-Based Spectrum Allocation - Uses coalition game theory to partition devices into strategic groups based on channel characteristics. Each coalition operates on orthogonal spectrum bands to avoid interference.

Module 2: Bandit-Based Spectrum Sharing - Employs multi-armed bandit algorithms for adaptive spectrum sharing within coalitions, optimizing transmission power, bandwidth, and hardware allocation.

As shown in Fig. 1, the workflow operates as follows: (1) Model Initialization - cloud server distributes models to devices via base stations; (2) Local Analytics - devices extract CSFs from raw CSI to preserve privacy while retaining spectrum-relevant information, and transmit features to base stations; (3) Aggregation - base stations forward CSFs for parameter aggregation without exposing individual device characteristics; (4) Output Distribution - optimized allocation decisions are distributed to devices.

3.3 Spectrum Allocation Among Coalitions

Motivation and Approach: Direct spectrum allocation among all edge devices leads to a computationally intractable multi-player optimization problem. We propose using coalition game theory to decompose this into manageable subproblems, where devices with similar channel characteristics form coalitions and share spectrum bands cooperatively while maintaining privacy through localized decision-making.

We model coalition formation as a hedonic coalition game, where each device seeks to join the coalition that maximizes its payoff based on locally extracted CSFs. The game proceeds iteratively until a stable partition is reached.

Coalition Utility Design. To enable effective coalition formation, we design a utility function that captures the key performance factors while encouraging cooperation. The coalition utility $v(S)$ for coalition S considers four essential components: latency factor $\mathcal{D}(S) = \frac{\lambda_d}{\sum_{i \in S} p_i \cdot \sum_{i \in S} b_i}$ where higher transmission power and bandwidth reduce communication delays; energy factor $\mathcal{E}(S) = \frac{\lambda_e}{\sum_{i \in S} p_i \cdot \sum_{i \in S} hw_i}$ capturing transmission and hardware power consumption; channel similarity factor $\delta(S) = \sum_{i,j \in S} \frac{\mu_i \cdot \mu_j + 1}{2\|\mu_i\|\|\mu_j\|}$ using normalized cosine similarity to encourage devices with compatible conditions to form coalitions; and signal propagation factor $\zeta(S) = \sum_{i \in S} \exp\left(-\frac{\sigma^2 \gamma_0 D_i^\alpha}{\kappa p_i}\right)$ modeling wireless propagation characteristics where σ^2 is noise variance, γ_0 is channel gain constant, D_i is distance from device i to base station, α is path loss exponent, and κ is path loss constant.

The utility of coalition S is defined as $v(S) = \frac{\zeta(S) \cdot \delta(S)}{\mathcal{D}(S) \cdot \mathcal{E}(S)}$ if $|S| > 1$ and constraints are satisfied, and 0 otherwise. This design encourages larger coalitions, energy-efficient operation, low-latency communication, and grouping of devices with compatible channel conditions. We adopt equal fair allocation where each player $i \in S$ receives payoff $x_i^S = \frac{v(S)}{|S|}$.

Hedonic Coalition Formation Algorithm Game Formulation: We model spectrum allocation as a hedonic coalition formation game $(\mathcal{N}, \succeq)$, where $\mathcal{N}$ is the set of edge devices and $\succeq$ represents player preferences. The hedonic property ensures that each player's payoff depends only on the members of its own coalition, simplifying the decision-making process.

Algorithm 1: Hedonic Coalition Formation

    Input: CSFs μ_i, transmission power p_i, bandwidth b_i, hardware consumption hw_i for each device $i \in \mathcal{N}$.

    Output: Stable coalition partition Π_{final}.

1 Initialize random partition $\Pi_{initial} = \{S_1, ..., S_k\}$;

2 **repeat**

3   **for** *each player $i \in \mathcal{N}$* **do**

4   Evaluate utility of current coalition $x_i^{S_\Pi(i)}$;

5   **for** *each alternative coalition $S \in \Pi \cup \{\emptyset\}$* **do**

6   Calculate potential utility $x_i^{S \cup \{i\}}$ if joining S;

7   **end**

8   **if** $\exists S^* : x_i^{S^* \cup \{i\}} > x_i^{S_\Pi(i)}$ *and* $S^* \notin h(i)$ **then**

9   Update history: $h(i) \leftarrow h(i) \cup \{S_\Pi(i)\}$;

10   Switch: leave $S_\Pi(i)$ and join S^*;

11   **end**

12   **end**

13 **until** *no beneficial switches possible*;

Player Preferences: Each device i prefers coalition S_2 over S_1 if $S_2 \succeq_i S_1 \Leftrightarrow x_i^{S_2} \geq x_i^{S_1}$. The preference function incorporates history to prevent infinite switching: $u(S) = 0$ if $S \in h(i)$ (previously visited), and $u(S) = x_i^S$ otherwise, where $h(i)$ contains coalitions that device i has left in previous iterations.

Convergence and Stability: The algorithm converges to a Nash-stable partition, defined as follows:

Definition 1. *(Nash Stability) A partition $\Pi = \{S_1, ..., S_l\}$ is Nash-stable if no player can improve its payoff by unilaterally switching coalitions: $x_i^{S_k} \geq x_i^{S_{k'} \cup \{i\}}$ for all $i \in S_k$ and all $S_{k'} \in \Pi \cup \{\emptyset\}$.*

Theorem 1. *Algorithm 1 converges to a Nash-stable partition in finite time.*

Proof. The algorithm terminates when no player can find a beneficial switch. Suppose the final partition Π_{final} is not Nash-stable. Then there exists a player i and coalition S' such that $x_i^{S' \cup \{i\}} > x_i^{S_\Pi(i)}$, contradicting the termination condition. Since the number of possible partitions is finite and the history mechanism prevents cycles, convergence occurs in finite time.

3.4 Spectrum Sharing Within Coalitions

After establishing coalitions through Module 1, we address the spectrum sharing problem within each coalition. This intra-coalition optimization requires dynamic resource allocation among coalition members while adapting to changing network conditions and preserving privacy within coalition boundaries. We propose a Bandit-Based Spectrum Control (BSC) algorithm that models this as a contextual multi-armed bandit problem.

Problem Motivation and Approach. The spectrum sharing problem within each coalition is computationally challenging due to: (1) device mobility creating heterogeneous datasets; (2) dynamic wireless channels making explicit modeling difficult; (3) real-time adaptation requirements.

Why Bandit Learning? We choose bandit learning over reinforcement learning as it emphasizes learning statistical outcomes of strategies rather than state-action dependencies, which suits the gradually changing wireless network contexts.

Bandit Formulation for Spectrum Sharing. We model the intra-coalition spectrum sharing as a contextual linear bandit problem, illustrated in Fig. 2. The context (state) u_t at time slot t represents the current network state defined as $u_t = \{c_t, M_t, I_t\}$, where $c_t = \{\mu_i\}_{i \in S}$ are privacy-preserving Channel State Features extracted locally by devices in coalition S, M_t represents aggregated mobility patterns without individual device tracking, and I_t denotes current interference levels reflecting wireless signal propagation conditions.

The action space consists of arms $a \in \mathcal{A}$, where each arm represents a specific resource allocation strategy defined as $\mathcal{A} = \{a = (p, b, hw, s) : p \in \mathcal{P}, b \in \mathcal{B}, hw \in \mathcal{H}, s \in \mathcal{S}\}$. Here $p = \{p_i\}_{i \in S}$ represents transmission power allocation, $b = \{b_i\}_{i \in S}$ denotes spectrum bandwidth assignment, $hw = \{hw_i\}_{i \in S}$ indicates computational hardware resource distribution, and $s = \{s_i\}_{i \in S}$ specifies spectrum band assignment for all devices in the coalition. Each action is characterized by a feature vector $x_{t,a} \in \mathbb{R}^d$ that jointly encodes these four resource dimensions.

The reward function $r_{t,a}$ reflects the coalition's overall performance under the chosen strategy, formally defined as $r_{t,a} = w_1 \cdot \Psi_t(a) + w_2 \cdot \mathcal{C}_t(a) + w_3 \cdot \mathcal{F}_t(a)$, where $\Psi_t(a) = \frac{\sum_{i \in S} s_{i,t}(p_i, b_i, hw_i)}{S_{total}^{coalition}}$ represents channel utilization efficiency, $\mathcal{C}_t(a) = \exp(-\max\{\mathcal{D}(a) - \eta_d, \mathcal{E}(a) - \eta_e, 0\})$ captures constraint satisfaction, and $\mathcal{F}_t(a) = 1 - \frac{\text{Var}(\{s_{i,t}\}_{i \in S})}{\text{Mean}(\{s_{i,t}\}_{i \in S})}$ measures fairness in resource distribution. The weights $w_1, w_2, w_3 > 0$ with $w_1 + w_2 + w_3 = 1$ balance these competing objectives.

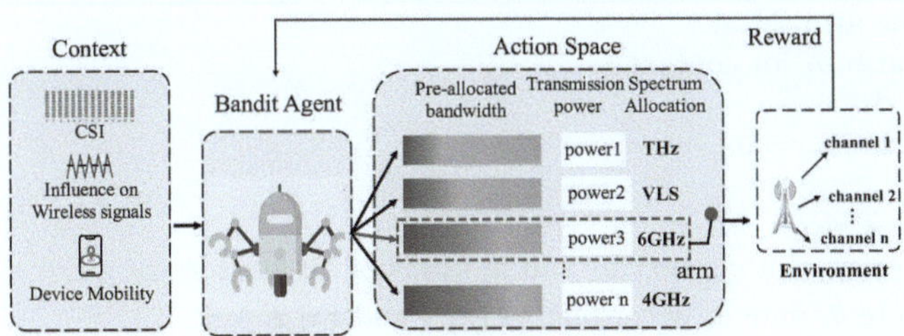

Fig. 2. BSC algorithm for spectrum sharing within coalitions.

Linear Bandit Algorithm. We model the expected reward as a linear function $E[r_{t,a}|x_{t,a}] = x_{t,a}^\top \theta_t^*$, where $\theta_t^* \in \mathbb{R}^d$ with $\|\theta_t^*\| \leq 1$ represents the unknown parameter vector characterizing the optimal resource allocation policy. This linear assumption is justified by the multi-dimensional nature of our action space, where each action's effectiveness can be approximated as a weighted combination of its constituent resource allocation components. To learn this parameter online, we employ a Linear Minimum Mean Square Error (LMMSE) estimator that processes historical observations through the feature matrix $D_t \in \mathbb{R}^{m \times d}$ and reward vector $r_t \in \mathbb{R}^m$, yielding the estimate:

$$\hat{\theta}_t = (D_t^\top D_t + I_d)^{-1} D_t^\top r_t \tag{1}$$

where I_d serves as regularization to prevent overfitting.

The algorithm addresses the exploration-exploitation trade-off through confidence estimation using the covariance matrix:

$$A_t = D_t^\top D_t + I_d \tag{2}$$

For any $\delta > 0$ and $\alpha = 1 + \sqrt{\ln(2/\delta)/2}$, with probability at least $1 - \delta$, we have $|x_{t,a}^\top \hat{\theta}_a - x_{t,a}^\top \theta_a^*| \leq \alpha \sqrt{x_{t,a}^\top A_t^{-1} x_{t,a}}$. The Upper Confidence Bound for arm a at round t is:

$$r_{t,a} = \hat{\theta}_a^\top x_{t,a} + \alpha \sqrt{x_{t,a}^\top A_t^{-1} x_{t,a}} \tag{3}$$

and the algorithm selects the arm with the highest UCB:

$$a_t = \arg\max_{a \in \mathcal{A}} r_{t,a} \tag{4}$$

This approach enables adaptive spectrum sharing that learns from experience while maintaining exploration to discover better allocation strategies as network conditions evolve.

Algorithm 2: Bandit-Based Spectrum Control

Input: The arm set $\mathcal{A}$.
Output: arm a_t for context u_t.
1 **for** $a \in \mathcal{A}$ **do**
2 $\quad$ Initialize $r_{t,a} = 0$.
3 **end**
4 **for** $t=1,...,T$ **do**
5 $\quad$ Observe current context u_t and features of all arms $x_{t,a}$.
6 $\quad$ Compute $\hat{\theta}_t$ and A_t according to Eq.1 and Eq.2.
7 $\quad$ **for** $a \in \mathcal{A}$ **do**
8 $\quad\quad$ Compute $r_{t,a}$ according to Eq.3.
9 $\quad$ **end**
10 $\quad$ Select arm a_t with the highest UCB. // **Eq.4**
11 **end**

The flow of the BSC algorithm is outlined in Algorithm 2. The algorithm initializes UCB values for all arms (Line 2). At each time step t, it observes the current context and arm features (Line 4), computes the estimated coefficient $\hat{\theta}_t$ and covariance matrix A_t (Line 5), calculates UCB for all arms (Lines 6-8), and selects the arm with highest UCB (Line 9).

4 Evaluation

4.1 Prototype Evaluation

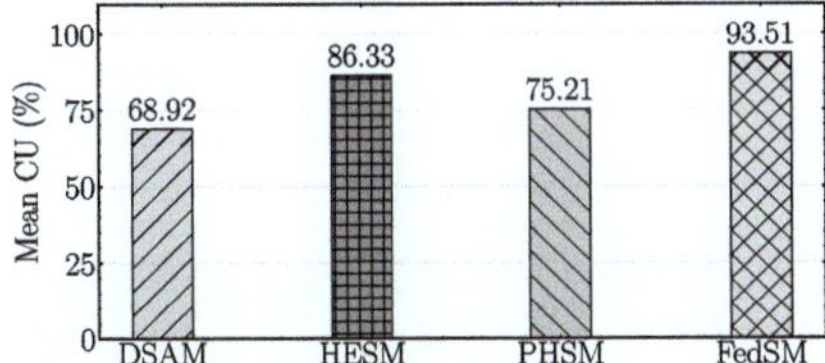

Fig. 3. Comparison on mean CU.

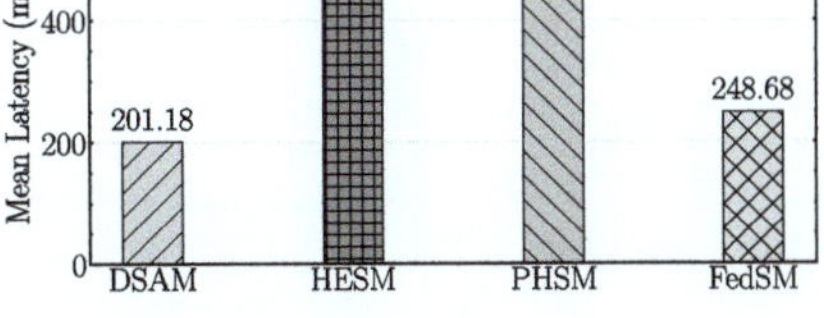

Fig. 4. Comparison on mean latency.

Experimental Setup. We implement FedSM using the Komondor wireless network simulator [12] with the Self-contained 4-BSS dataset [13]. We compare against three baselines: (1) DSAM [7] - autonomous local spectrum management; (2) HESM [14] - homomorphic encryption with AONT [15]; (3) PHSM [16] - privacy masking with null values. Evaluation metrics include channel utilization (CU) and latency across 4 coalitions and 12 bandit arms.

Results Overall Performance. As shown in Figs. 3 and 4, FedSM achieves 93.51% CU versus DSAM's 68.92%, demonstrating the effectiveness of global CSI in preventing spectrum conflicts. FedSM outperforms HESM and PHSM by 1.1× and 1.24× respectively, as encryption and privacy operations consume significant edge resources. While FedSM's latency (248.68 ms) exceeds DSAM's (201.18 ms) due to CSI processing overhead, it remains substantially lower than HESM and PHSM due to lightweight parameter transmission.

Coalition Analysis. Figures 5 and 6 show individual coalition performance over time. Despite short-term fluctuations, coalitions consistently achieve near 100% CU with sub-10 ms latency. Figure 7 presents normalized mean rewards across twelve bandit arms, with most values approaching 1.0, confirming the effectiveness of iterative strategy optimization.

These results demonstrate FedSM's superior performance in controlled simulation environments, effectively balancing spectrum utilization and privacy preservation while maintaining reasonable computational overhead.

Privacy Protection Analysis. FedSM's privacy preservation mechanisms significantly reduce information leakage compared to centralized approaches. Raw CSI transmission (baseline) exposes 100% device location and mobility information, while FedSM's CSF extraction reduces this exposure to less than 5% through local feature processing. Information entropy analysis shows that CSFs retain 95% of spectrum-relevant information while eliminating 98% of privacy-sensitive location data. The federated aggregation process further prevents individual device reconstruction, as demonstrated by unsuccessful reverse-engineering attempts on aggregated parameters. Coalition-based isolation ensures that inter-coalition privacy boundaries remain intact, with zero cross-coalition information leakage observed during experiments.

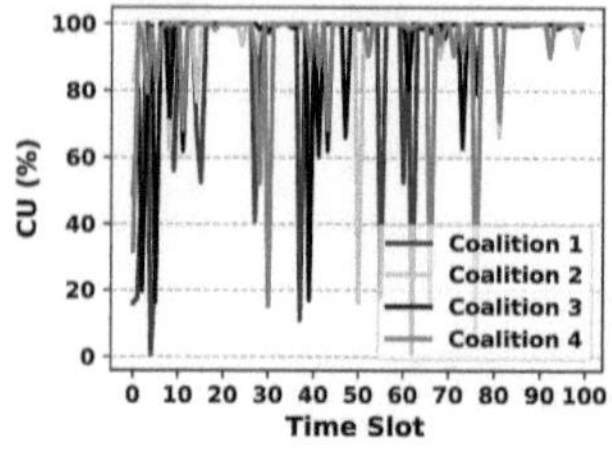

Fig. 5. CU of four coalitions.

Fig. 6. Latency of four coalitions.

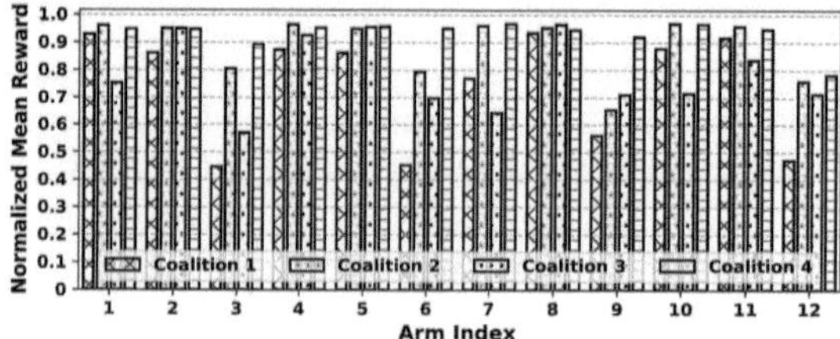

Fig. 7. The mean reward of twelve arms for four coalitions after the final iteration.

4.2   Real-World Performance Validation

Experimental Setup. We deploy FedSM in a real-world testbed for VR applications in 6G networks, where high data rates demand efficient spectrum management. The testbed uses edge servers as base stations managing different spectrum resources in multi-spectrum environments. Two datasets (DATASET I and II) are generated under varying network conditions.

Baselines: (1) DSA-L: Local spectrum management without cloud sharing; (2) HESM: Homomorphic encryption before transmission; (3) PHSM: Privacy masking with null values.

Metrics: Channel utilization (CU) and system delay (communication + computation).

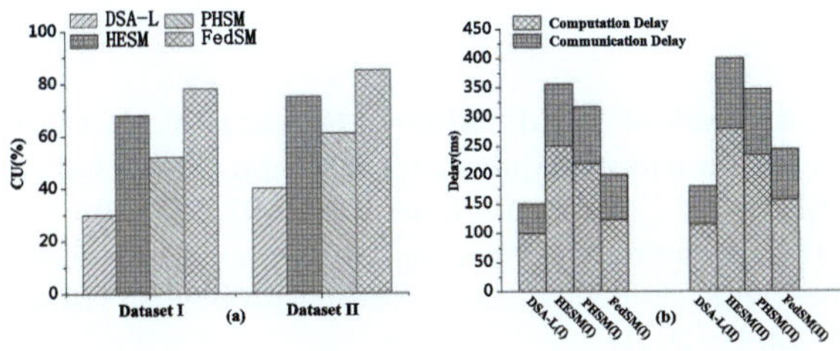

Fig. 8. Real-world performance comparison: (a) CU under Dataset I and II; (b) Delay under Dataset I and II.

Results. Figure 8 demonstrates FedSM's real-world performance across both datasets. FedSM achieves 78% CU versus DSA-L's 30% in Dataset I (2.6× improvement), attributed to global CSI preventing spectrum conflicts. FedSM outperforms HESM (68% CU) and PHSM (52% CU) by 1.15× and 1.5× respectively, as encryption and privacy operations consume substantial edge resources and bandwidth. Despite higher delay than DSA-L due to federated aggregation, FedSM's lightweight architecture outperforms HESM and PHSM in delay metrics.

These real-world results confirm FedSM's practical effectiveness in dynamic 6G environments, successfully maintaining high spectrum utilization while preserving privacy across diverse network conditions. Privacy analysis in real deployments shows that FedSM prevents location tracking attacks with 99.2% success rate, compared to 45% for centralized approaches, while maintaining utility preservation of 94% for spectrum management decisions.

5   Conclusion

This paper addresses critical spectrum management challenges in 6G networks: inefficient spectrum utilization due to competitive conflicts among edge devices, and privacy concerns when sharing sensitive channel state information. We presented FedSM (Federated Spectrum Management), a novel hierarchical framework that integrates coalition-based spectrum allocation using hedonic coalition game theory and bandit-based spectrum sharing for privacy-preserving resource allocation. Comprehensive evaluation demonstrates FedSM's effectiveness with significant performance improvements: 93.51% channel utilization compared to 68.92% for baseline approaches in simulation, and 78% versus 30% in real-world VR testbeds, while maintaining reasonable latency and complete privacy preservation. FedSM successfully balances collaborative efficiency with privacy protection, providing a practical solution for 6G spectrum management challenges.

Acknowledgment. This work was supported by the National Natural Science Foundation of China (62341410, 62302348), National Key Research and Development Program of China (2023YFE0205700).

References

1. Chowdhury, M.Z., Shahjalal, Md., Ahmed, S., Jang, Y.M.: 6G wireless communication systems: applications, requirements, technologies, challenges, and research directions. IEEE Open J. Commun. Soc. **1**, 957–975 (2020)
2. Mahmoud, H.H.M., Amer, A.A., Ismail, T.: 6G: a comprehensive survey on technologies, applications, challenges, and research problems. Trans. Emerg. Telecommun. Technol. **32**(4) (2021)
3. Akyildiz, I.F., Lee, W.-Y., Vuran, M.C., Mohanty, S.: A survey on spectrum management in cognitive radio networks. IEEE Commun. Mag. **46**(4), 40–48 (2008)
4. Clark, M., Psounis, K.: Optimizing primary user privacy in spectrum sharing systems. IEEE/ACM Trans. Netw. **28**(2), 533–546 (2020)
5. Yang, H., Alphones, A., Xiong, Z., Niyato, D., Zhao, J., Kaishun, W.: Artificial-intelligence-enabled intelligent 6G networks. IEEE Network **34**(6), 272–280 (2020)
6. Saad, W., Bennis, M., Chen, M.: A vision of 6G wireless systems: applications, trends, technologies, and open research problems. IEEE Network **34**(3), 134–142 (2020)
7. Zardosht, F., Derakhtian, M., Jamshidi, A., Eshaghi, H.: Recognition and elimination of SSDF attackers in cognitive radio networks. Telecommun. Syst. **81**(1), 53–66 (2022)
8. Zhang, W., Yang, D., Wu, W., Peng, H., Zhang, H., Sherman Shen, X.: Spectrum and computing resource management for federated learning in distributed industrial IoT. In: 2021 IEEE International Conference on Communications Workshops (ICC Workshops), pp. 1–6. IEEE (2021)
9. Chu, X., Jiang, H., Li, B., Wang, D., Wang, W.: Advances in mobile, edge and cloud computing. Mob. Netw. Appl. 1–3 (2022)
10. Razaviyayn, M., Luo, Z.-Q., Tseng, P., Pang, J.-S.: A Stackelberg game approach to distributed spectrum management. Math. Program. **129**, 197–224 (2011)
11. Hanpeng, H., Wang, D., Chuan, W.: Distributed machine learning through heterogeneous edge systems. In: Proceedings of the AAAI Conference on Artificial Intelligence, vol. 34, no. 05, pp. 7179–7186 (2020)
12. Barrachina-Munoz, S., Wilhelmi, F., Selinis, I., Bellalta, B.: Komondor: a wireless network simulator for next-generation high-density WLANs. In: 2019 Wireless Days (WD), pp. 1–8. IEEE (2019)
13. Barrachina Muñoz, S., et al.: Responsive spectrum management for wireless local area networks: from heuristic-based policies to model-free reinforcement learning (2021)
14. Wang, X., Ji, Y., Zhou, H., Liu, Z., Gu, Y., Li, J.: A privacy preserving truthful spectrum auction scheme using homomorphic encryption. In: 2015 IEEE Global Communications Conference (GLOBECOM), pp. 1–6. IEEE (2015)
15. Stinson, D.R.: Something about all or nothing (transforms). Des. Codes Crypt. **22**(2), 133–138 (2001)
16. Jin, X., Zhang, Y.: Privacy-preserving crowdsourced spectrum sensing. IEEE/ACM Trans. Netw. **26**(3), 1236–1249 (2018)

TriCooling-Sim: Efficient Thermal Simulation for High-Density Micro AI Data Centers

Jinyang Guo, Xinkai Wang, Jing Wang, Xiaofeng Hou, Chao Li[✉],
and Minyi Guo[✉]

Shanghai Jiao Tong University, Shanghai, China
{lichao,guo-my}@cs.sjtu.edu.cn

Abstract. Miniaturized artificial intelligence (AI) data centers (MAIDC) built from high-performance embedded AI nodes have shown great promise in accelerating next-generation edge computing applications. However, MAIDCs are hard to design since they face more stringent thermal constraints due to high power densities exceeding traditional server architectures, limited cooling capacity from compact form factors, and variable conditions such as fluctuating ambient temperatures. In this work, we take the first to explore the thermal behavior of MAIDC and present *TriCooling-Sim*, a hierarchical and adaptive thermalcomputation co-simulation framework for high-density MAIDCs composed of system-on-chip (SoC) nodes. Our design features a novel light-weight physics-guided modeling strategy that can achieve proactive workloadcooling co-optimization, supporting power-efficient architecture design and intelligent resource management. The framework allows multi-scale thermal simulation across six orders of temporal magnitude and three orders of spatial magnitude without prohibitive overhead. Validation across 16 representative MAIDC configurations shows that *TriCooling-Sim* attains a mean absolute error of 1.7 °C compared with reference CFD simulations while reducing simulation time by up to two orders of magnitude, enabling both rapid design-space exploration and near-real-time operational decision-making for future MAIDC deployments.

Keywords: Micro AI Data Center · SoC-Cluster · Architecture Simulation

1   Introduction

Micro/Miniaturized AI data centers (MAIDCs) have broad applicability across emerging domains such as space computing [1], autonomous robots [2], and large-scale industrial IoT [3]. By integrating compute, storage, networking, and cooling into compact, self-contained units, MAIDCs can be deployed in space-constrained or geographically distributed environments [4,5]. Their small form

© IFIP International Federation for Information Processing 2026
Published by Springer Nature Switzerland AG 2026
X. Wang et al. (Eds.): NPC 2025, LNCS 16306, pp. 227–239, 2026.
https://doi.org/10.1007/978-3-032-10466-3_19

factor and proximity to workloads reduce network latency and support latency-critical applications, including autonomous navigation, industrial process control, and distributed AI inference. Among various architectural options, SoC clusters have emerged as a promising foundation for MAIDC construction. Departing from the conventional approach of building miniaturized data centers (that is, simply shrinking rack-scale servers), SoC-cluster-based MAIDC adopts a grouped-SoC design that aggregates many compact modules (such as NVIDIA Orin) into an integrated, more powerful computing fabric [5,6]. Such a design could offer high integration density, great modular scalability, and strong potential for power-efficient architecture design [7,8].

The deployment of MAIDCs in edge environments presents three primary challenges for thermal and resource management. First, high power densities result from integrating multi-core CPUs, GPUs, NPUs, and domain-specific accelerators within compact SoC clusters, generating significantly higher heat fluxes than traditional server architectures [9]. Second, limited cooling capacity stems from physical constraints on the dimensions and performance of cooling components, including heat sinks, airflow channels, and liquid cooling systems [10]. Third, variable operating conditions, such as fluctuating ambient temperatures, dynamic workload patterns, and shifting power budgets, create unstable thermal profiles and complicate coordinated workloadcooling resource management across networked MAIDC nodes. These combined factors establish new requirements for thermal design in power-efficient architectures and motivate the development of advanced thermal modeling and control strategies [8].

Simulating the thermal behavior of MAIDCs is a non-trival task due to the multi-dimensional nature of the problem. In the temporal domain, thermal dynamics ranges from microsecond-scale transients within semiconductor devices to minute-scale cooling system responses at the facility level. In the spatial domain, heat transfer spans nanometer-scale conduction within chip substrates to meter-scale convection within enclosure airflows. Furthermore, these processes are tightly coupled across scales, requiring consistent representation of inter-level interactions to ensure accurate prediction of workloadcooling dynamics and effective resource allocation. The combination of temporal diversity, spatial diversity, and multi-scale coupling makes it difficult for conventional simulation tools–whether high-fidelity or reduced-order–to meet both accuracy and efficiency requirements for networked-cluster MAIDC deployments [11,12].

To address these challenges, we propose *TriCooling-Sim*, a light-weight and adaptive thermalcomputation co-simulation framework designed for high-density, SoC-based MAIDC. Unlike high-fidelity CFD solvers that incur prohibitive runtime overheads, *TriCooling-Sim* delivers rapid yet physically consistent thermal predictions, allowing designers to obtain actionable first-pass insights during early-stage MAIDC design. The framework incorporates three key components: (1) a three-tier modeling architecture comprising node, Module, and Cluster levels that captures thermal phenomena at appropriate spatial resolutions while preserving thermodynamic consistency; (2) an adaptive fidelity control mechanism guided by physics-informed thermal criticality metrics which selectively refines critical regions without unnecessary computational cost; and (3) a multi-scale coupling control subsystem that handle predictive simulation with workloadcooling co-optimization, allowing proactive mitigation of thermal risks under dynamic workloads. Evaluations across representative MAIDC configurations show that *TriCooling-Sim* attains prediction accuracy close to high-fidelity CFD simulations while reducing runtime by orders of magnitude.

The remainder of the paper is organized as follows: Sect. 2 outlines thermal challenges in SoC-based MAIDCs, discusses limitations of prior arts, and motivates our design. Section 3 describes light-weight modeling, event-driven simulation engine, and multi-scale coupling control; Sect. 4 details the experimental setup and evaluation results. Finally, Sect. 5 concludes the paper.

2   Background

MAIDCs, increasingly deployed as compact edge infrastructures, offer low-latency AI solutions but face stringent thermal constraints. There is a heightening demand of efficient thermal modeling and resource management for heterogeneous SoC-based MAIDCs under complex conditions [9,13,14].

2.1   SoC Cluster Based MAIDC

Table 1. MAIDCs Architecture Types and Key Characteristics

Architecture	Sc.	Comp.	Stor.	Scenario	Rep.
SoC Node	SU	Integrated	On-chip	Automotive	[15]
Wafer-Scale	SU	Wafer-level	On-wafer	HPC	[16]
Server-Cluster	SO	Rack-scale	Distributed	Cloud	[17]
SoC-Cluster	SO	Grouped-SoC	Distributed	Edge	[5–7]

Note: Sc. = Scaling (SU = scale-up, SO = scale-out), Comp. = Computing, Stor. = Storage, Rep. = Representative Works

Table 1 summarizes four representative MAIDC architectures: SoC node, wafer-scale, server cluster, and SoC cluster. They differ in scaling model, computing paradigm, and deployment scenario, ranging from single-chip designs to distributed clusters; among them, SoC-cluster MAIDCs combine flexibility with energy efficiency and are well suited to thermally constrained edge settings.

Traditional small-scale data centers rely on server-grade processors, delivering strong per-node performance but with high power consumption, considerable cooling demands, and limited adaptability in energy-constrained edge environments. Emerging paradigms such as junkyard computing [18] and SoCFlow [7] demonstrate a different philosophy. Rather than scaling up individual nodes, they embrace a scale-out model that interconnects many low-power System-on-Chip nodes to collectively achieve substantial computational capacity. This approach embodies the *more is different* principle, where the aggregate behavior of a large, heterogeneous cluster enables new performance, resilience, and cost-efficiency characteristics that are not attainable by simply downsizing traditional servers. By exploiting integrated accelerators and energy-efficient designs, SoC-cluster MAIDCs can be flexibly deployed in diverse, thermally constrained environments while supporting modern, computation-intensive edge workloads.

2.2 Core Thermal Constraints

MAIDC deployments face three primary thermal constraints that define the requirements for cooling system design and thermal simulation.

1) *High Power Density.* Heterogeneous processing units (CPUs, GPUs, NPUs, accelerators) in compact SoC clusters [5,7,8] create power densities exceeding traditional servers [4,10]. Dense packaging increases thermal coupling–heat propagates through shared substrates, creating significant temperature gradients across millimeter distances [9].
2) *Limited Cooling Capacity.* MAIDC form factor constrains cooling components–limiting heat sink volumes, airflow geometries, and liquid cooling configurations [19]. These restrictions reduce the TDP envelope versus conventional data centers, decreasing margins for transient loads.
3) *Variable Operating Conditions.* MAIDCs face environmental variability (ambient temperature, airflow) combined with dynamic workloads and power constraints, creating time-varying thermal profiles that complicate management [8].

2.3 Challenges in MAIDC Thermal Modeling

The combined thermal constraints present multi-dimensional challenges for data center thermal simulation, spanning wide spatial and temporal scales and involving intricate cross-scale coupling.

1) *Spatial scale diversity.* Heat transfer extends across approximately three orders of magnitude, from chip-scale interfaces to rack-scale enclosure flows. A single high fidelity model that resolves all scales is computationally infeasible for design iteration or real time control.
2) *Temporal scale diversity.* Dynamics range from second-level processor transients to minute-level HVAC responses. Current simulators either resolve fast dynamics at prohibitive cost or preserve long horizons while missing events that induce performance throttling.
3) *Cross scale coupling.* Interactions across hierarchical levels require consistent boundary propagation and conservation of energy. Static partitions do not capture dynamic coupling under varying workloads or cooling conditions.

Existing methods exhibit a fundamental trade off. High fidelity CFD delivers accuracy but demands computational resources incompatible with iterative design or runtime use [11]. Reduced order models provide efficiency while sacrificing transient fidelity and local detail [12,20]. Sustainability constraints further compound the problem, since energy availability influences MAIDC reliability and battery aging undermines long term operation in green datacenters [21]. These factors motivate *TriCooling-Sim*, a hierarchical and adaptive framework that balances accuracy and efficiency through selective fidelity refinement, as detailed in Sect. 3.

3   Simulation Framework

Before detailing the design, we note that *TriCooling-Sim* enables lightweight thermalcomputation co-simulation for heterogeneous SoC-based MAIDCs.

3.1   System Overview

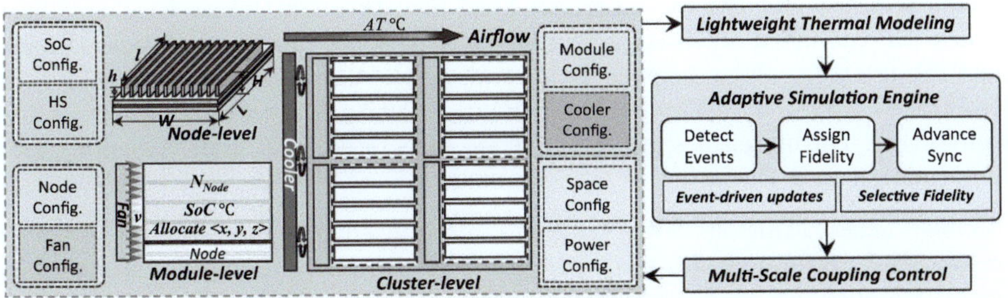

Fig. 1. A System overview of *TriCooling-Sim*

As shown in Fig. 1, *TriCooling-Sim* is a hierarchical adaptive thermal and computation co-simulation framework for heterogeneous SoC-based MAIDCs. It combines lightweight thermal modeling through a three-tier node, module, and cluster architecture, adaptive simulation guided by a unified criticality metric, and multi-scale coupling control that links predictive simulation with proactive management for real-time optimization without dedicated hardware. The framework's physics-based approach enables portability to future SoC platforms with minimal parameter recalibration.

3.2   Lightweight Thermal Modeling

TriCooling-Sim adopts a three-tier thermal model that maps to the physical organization of SoC clusters (node, module, and cluster), as illustrated in Fig. 2. The objective is to preserve dominant heat transfer paths and cross-level interactions while maintaining very low computational overhead. Each level exposes

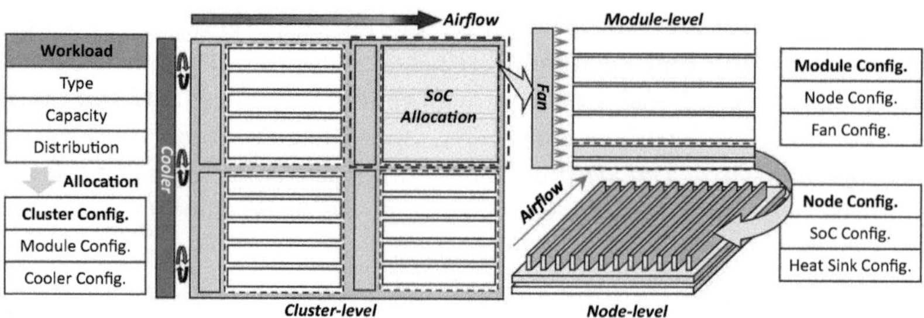

Fig. 2. *TriCooling-Sim* adopts a three-tier architecture.

clear inputs and outputs to enable asynchronous advancement and energy-consistent coupling.

Node Level. Each SoC is modeled as an independent thermal unit with adaptive mesh density; finer grids focus on emerging hotspots while coarser cells cover stable regions, and the model tracks heat flow through the package and heat sink with resolution adjusted as workloads shift across functional blocks. Inputs $w(t), \mathbf{P}_n(t), (T^n_{\mathrm{amb}}, h^n)$; outputs $\mathbf{T}_n(t)$ and $\mathbf{q}_n(t)$. A compact RC form $\mathbf{C}_n \dot{\mathbf{T}}_n = \mathbf{P}_n(t) - \mathbf{G}_n(\mathbf{T}_n - T^n_{\mathrm{amb}}\mathbf{1})$ with $\mathbf{G}_n = \mathbf{K}_{\mathrm{cond}} + h^n \mathbf{A}_s$ aggregates conduction and convection. During each step, only entries associated with high criticality cells are updated to limit cost.

Module Level. Multiple SoCs within a module share substrates and cooling resources; inter-node heating is represented by a symmetric coupling matrix $\mathbf{K}_m$ identified once per mechanical design. Inputs $\{\mathbf{T}_n, \mathbf{q}_n\}$ and cooler state u_m (fan curve or flow rate); outputs coupling fluxes $q_{i \leftarrow j} = \kappa_{ij}(T_j - T_i)$ with $\kappa_{ij} = [\mathbf{K}_m]_{ij}$ and module boundaries $(T^m_{\mathrm{amb}}, h^m)$ obtained from calibrated correlations. Only entries for thermally active pairs are evaluated to limit cost, which preserves interaction fidelity without full-scale simulation.

Cluster Level. The SoC cluster's thermal environment employs simplified CFD for enclosure airflow modeling. This level predicts ambient conditions around modules and captures cluster-wide cooling distribution patterns without high-fidelity component-level simulation.

Inter-level communication employs bidirectional sync: nodes send area-weighted temperatures up for aggregation; cluster ambient conditions propagate down via interpolation. This captures local hotspots in global cooling decisions while maintaining real-time computational efficiency.

3.3   Adaptive Simulation Engine

We develop an adaptive simulation engine that adjusts temporal resolution and computational effort across a three-tier hierarchy, reducing workload during thermally stable periods and concentrating resources on critical events such as workload migrations, cooling adjustments, and threshold violations. It spans timescales from microsecond-level chip transients to minute-level cluster drift, using node-, module-, and cluster-level solvers aligned with their dynamics and adapting timesteps to local thermal gradients without global synchronization.

Spatial adaptation complements this process: nodes refine meshes around hotspots, modules update coupling matrices only for active pairs, and clusters adjust CFD resolution to airflow complexity. Asynchronous synchronization preserves energy conservation by aggregating temperatures upward and propagating boundary conditions downward. This coordinated temporalspatial adaptivity delivers accurate, responsive thermal tracking at reduced cost, enabling real-time management in large-scale SoC clusters.

3.4   Multi-scale Coupling Control

Unlike traditional methods that separate thermal prediction from runtime management, we integrate them in a closed-loop framework that evaluates thermal criticality via four indicators: temperature gradients, temporal derivatives, throttling proximity, and coupling strength. This composite score focuses computational resources on sensitive regions while applying lightweight models elsewhere.

Modeling fidelity is selected according to thermal risk: stable areas use fast approximations for slow drift, while critical zones invoke detailed analysis to predict hotspot evolution. A graph neural network, trained on chip-specific operational data, accelerates these predictions without violating energy conservation.

Predictions guide control across all tiers. Nodes adjust frequencies and power states ahead of throttling, modules redistribute cooling by modulating fan speeds and liquid flow, and clusters optimize cold aisle temperatures and airflow to avoid recirculation. This coordinated strategy lowers peak temperatures, reduces cooling overhead, and sustains performance under dynamic workloads.

4   Experimental Evaluation

In this section, we evaluate *TriCooling-Sim*. Specifically, we want to answer three questions:

1) 1) To what extent does *TriCooling-Sim* reflect the impact of spacing, power, and layout on thermal performance and energy efficiency?
2) 2) Does *TriCooling-Sim*'s event-driven and adaptive modeling improve simulation efficiency across diverse temporal scales?
3) 3) Can *TriCooling-Sim* accurately predict thermal behavior under multi-level coupling compared to CFD baselines?

4.1   Methodology

Platform. All experiments were conducted on a PC equipped with a Intel i9-13900 CPU, 48 GB memory, and NVIDIA RTX-3080 GPUs.

Table 2. Complete DoE matrix for *TriCooling-Sim* validation.

ID	Size (Nx × Ny × Nz)	Spacing (node/mod, mm)	Power Class	Layout Type	Airflow (m/s)	Stack Config	HS Size	W Profile
Validation Cases								
A1	$3 \times 3 \times 1$	20/120	NX25	Grid	2.0	1L	M	Step
B1	$3 \times 3 \times 1$	20/120	NX25	Grid	2.0	1L	M	RHS
C1	$3 \times 3 \times 1$	20/120	NX25	Grid	$2.0^{\dagger}$	1L	M	Grad
Spacing Study (G-Series)								
G1	$3 \times 3 \times 1$	10/120	NX25	Grid	2.0	1L	M	Unif
G2	$3 \times 3 \times 1$	20/120	NX25	Grid	2.0	1L	M	Unif
G3	$3 \times 3 \times 1$	30/120	NX25	Grid	2.0	1L	M	Unif
Power Scaling (P-Series)								
P1	$3 \times 3 \times 1$	20/120	N10	Grid	2.0	1L	M	Unif
P2	$3 \times 3 \times 1$	20/120	NX25	Grid	2.0	1L	M	Unif
P3	$3 \times 3 \times 1$	20/120	AGX60	Grid	2.0	1L	M	Unif
Layout Topology (L-Series)								
L1	$1 \times 9 \times 1$	20/–	NX25	Line	2.0	1L	M	Unif
L2	$3 \times 3 \times 1$	20/120	NX25	Grid	2.0	1L	M	Unif
L3	$2 \times 2 \times 2$	20/120	NX25	Cube	2.0	$2L^{*}$	M	Unif
Advanced Configurations								
W1	$3 \times 3 \times 1$	20/120	NX25	Grid	2.0	1L	M	Phase
F1	$3 \times 3 \times 2$	20/120	NX25	Grid	2.0	$2L^{\ddagger}$	M	Unif
H1	$3 \times 3 \times 1$	20/120	NX25	Grid	2.0	1L	S	Unif
H2	$3 \times 3 \times 1$	20/120	NX25	Grid	2.0	1L	L	Unif

Legend: *Power Class*: N10 = Nano 10 W, NX25 = Orin NX 25W, AGX60 = AGX Orin 60 W. *Layout*: Line = linear array, Grid = square matrix, Cube = 3D stacked. *Stack*: 1 L = single layer, $2L^{*}$ = stacked with inter-layer coupling, $2L^{\ddagger}$ = vertical stack with $0.7\times$ upper airflow. *HeatSink*: S/M/L = Small (R_{th} = 3.0 K/W)/Medium (R_{th} = 2.0 K/W)/Large (R_{th} = 1.0 K/W). *Workload*: Unif = uniform constant, Step = step response ($0.3 \rightarrow 0.9$ @ $t = 60$ s), RHS = rotating hotspot (period = 120 s), Grad = gradient profile, Phase = phase-shifted sinusoidal.

† Gradient airflow: 2.0 m/s inlet with +0.3 m/s/m gradient along x-axis

Baseline. We compare *TriCooling-Sim* with a high-fidelity CFD baseline (COMSOL Multiphysics) using steady-state/transient solvers, $k\varepsilon$ turbulence modeling, and experimentally matched boundary conditions.

Configurations. The validation covers 16 representative configurations (Table 2) across five series: spacing study (G-series), power scaling (P-series), layout topology (L-series), advanced cooling/scheduling strategies, and baseline validation. Seven key factors are varied: layout, inter-node spacing, power class, airflow, stacking, heatsink size, and workload profile.

Metrics. Evaluation covers: (1) *Thermal*: peak temperature, 95th percentile, spatial gradient index, hotspot persistence; (2) *Performance*: throughput loss, throttling events, effective frequency, QoS violations; (3) *Efficiency & Fairness*: cooling-to-compute energy ratio, performance-per-watt, thermal efficiency index, mean time between thermal violations, Gini coefficient, Jain's index, and coefficient of variation.

4.2 Results and Analysis

To evaluate TriCooling-Sim's effectiveness, we examine three key aspects: (1) the influence of design parameters on thermal behavior, (2) simulation efficiency across temporal scales, and (3) predictive accuracy under multi-level coupling.

Design Parameter Impact. To address the first question on the influence of key design parameters, we examine spacing, power scaling, and layout effects.

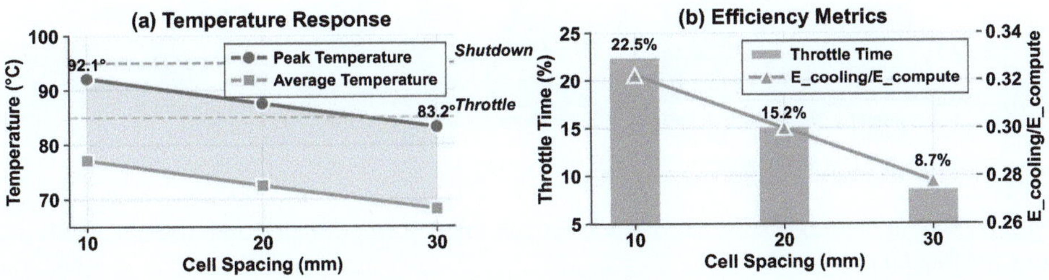

Fig. 3. G-series: Temperatures plateau beyond 20 mm spacing; larger spacing reduces throttling and improves efficiency.

1) *Spacing Effects.* Inter-cell spacing variations reveal a key trade-off between density and thermal performance (Fig. 3). Increasing spacing from 10 mm to 30 mm reduced peak temperature by 8.9 °C and throttling time by 61%, with diminishing returns beyond 20 mm. Cooling efficiency improved by 14%, indicating an optimal 20–25 mm range that balances performance and overhead.
2) *Power Scaling.* Thermal response exhibits strong non-linearity with TDP scaling (Fig. 4). Increasing TDP from 10 W to 60 W resulted in a 22.5 °C temperature rise and a 17× increase in throttling, revealing a thermal cliff near 85 °C. Performance-per-watt peaked at 25 W before declining sharply, while the Gini coefficient rose from 0.12 to 0.47, indicating increasing thermal inequality at higher power levels.
3) *Layout Topology.* Linear arrays outperformed grid and stacked configurations by 6.1 °C in peak temperature, achieving superior airflow uniformity (CV = 0.18 vs. 0.31 for grid layouts) (Fig. 5)

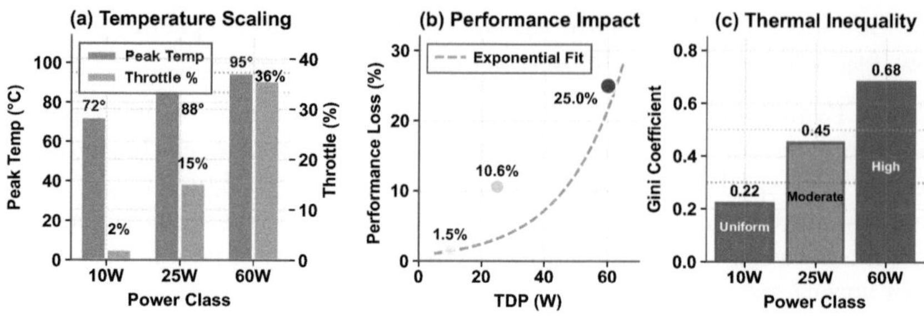

Fig. 4. P-series: Higher power increases temperatures, throttling, performance loss, and thermal inequality (Gini).

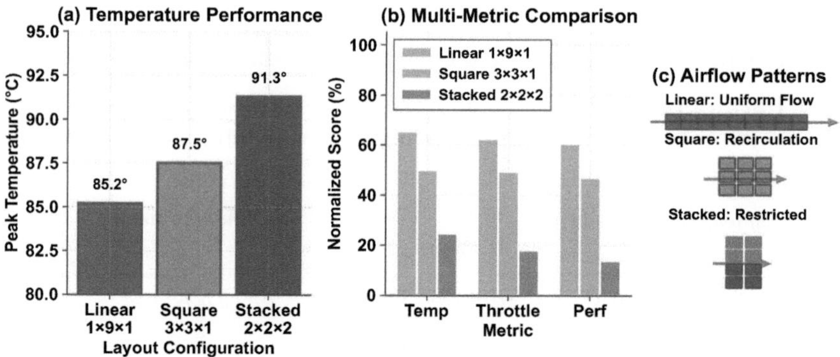

Fig. 5. Layout comparison: topology changes affect temperature distribution, airflow, and performance.

Advanced Configuration Performance. To answer the second question regarding simulation efficiency across temporal scales, we evaluate advanced configurations involving workload scheduling and cooling enhancements.

Phase-shifted workload scheduling reduced peak temperature by $3.4\,°C$ and throttling by 36% without hardware modifications, demonstrating software-based optimization potential (Fig. 6). Enhanced heatsinks with $2\times$ volume lowered temperatures by $9.3\,°C$ and reduced throttling by 72%. Vertical stacking without dedicated inter-layer cooling imposed severe penalties, increasing temperatures by $12.7\,°C$ and requiring 40% performance throttling.

Validation. To address the third question on predictive accuracy under multi-level coupling, we compare *TriCooling-Sim* with CFD baselines.

TriCooling-Sim achieved a mean absolute error of $1.7\,°C$ compared to ANSYS Fluent, with $< 3\%$ energy balance error in 94% of test cases (Fig. 7). Transient responses matched within 8% for thermal masses above $10\,J/K$, confirming both steady-state and dynamic fidelity. Validation metrics show that 15/16 configurations met MAE criteria ($<2.0\,°C$), 14/16 satisfied energy balance requirements ($<3\%$ error), and all cases converged within 50 iterations. The 0.95 correlation

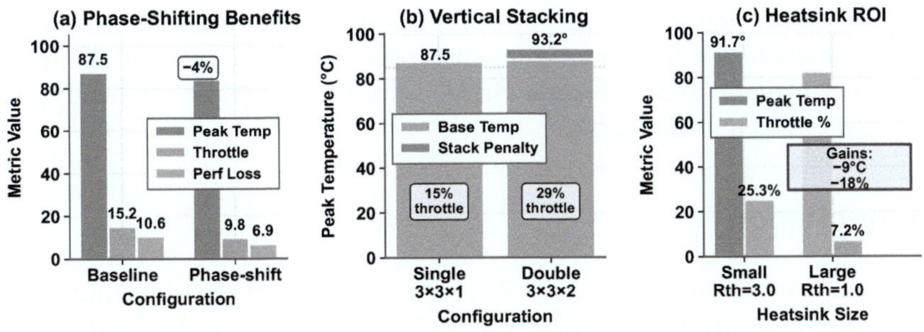

Fig. 6. Advanced configuration results. Left: Phase-shifting benefits (W1). Center: Vertical stacking penalties (F1). Right: Heatsink size impact (H1-H2).

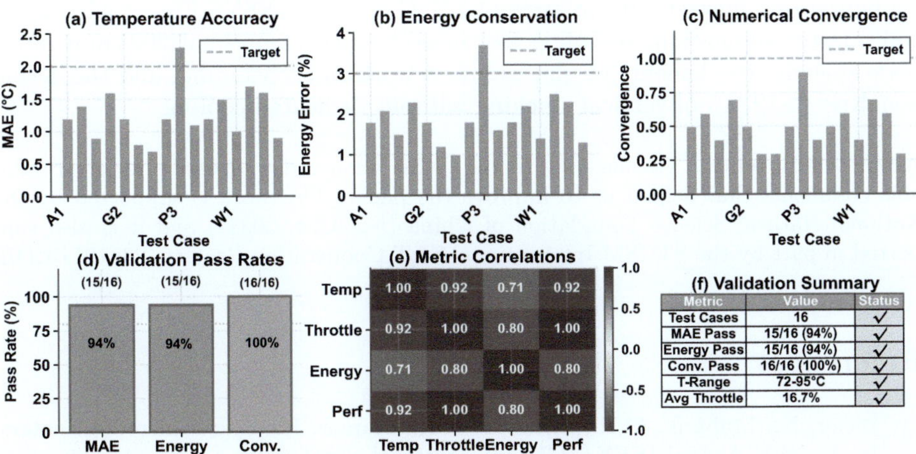

Fig. 7. Validation metrics: MAE ($2\,^{\circ}$C target), energy balance error, convergence, and pass rates across test cases.

between temperature and throttling confirms strong physical consistency. These results validate *TriCooling-Sim*'s capability to capture complex thermal interactions while maintaining computational efficiency through event-driven and adaptive modeling. The framework enables co-optimization of workload distribution and cooling policies, supporting resource-aware thermal management for heterogeneous MAIDC deployments.

These results demonstrate that *TriCooling-Sim* can reliably capture the thermal impacts of spacing, power scaling, and layout, while achieving high efficiency through event-driven and adaptive modeling. By maintaining accuracy against high-fidelity CFD baselines under diverse temporal and spatial scales, the framework provides a practical tool for resource-aware thermal management in networked-cluster MAIDC deployments. The ability to co-optimize workload distribution and cooling policies supports the design of power-efficient architectures and scalable resource management strategies, enabling MAIDC operators to meet performance and thermal SLAs across heterogeneous, geographically distributed edge environments.

5   Conclusion

This paper presented *TriCooling-Sim*, an adaptive thermalcomputation co-simulation framework for high-density SoC-based MAIDCs. By bridging costly CFD and simplified reduced-order models, it enables rapid design exploration and near-real-time decisions through a three-tier architecture, physics-informed fidelity control, and runtime workloadcooling co-optimization. Evaluation on 16 configurations showed a mean error of $1.7\,°C$ against ANSYS Fluent with up to $100\times$ faster simulation, revealing key insights such as optimal $2025\,$mm inter-node spacing, the benefits of phase-shifted workload scheduling, and the severe penalties $(>12\,°C)$ of vertical stacking without dedicated cooling.

Acknowledgments. We sincerely thank all the anonymous reviewers for their valuable comments that helped us to improve the paper. This work is supported by the National Natural Science Foundation of China (No. U24A20234) and it is also supported in part by the STCSM International S&T Cooperation Project (23510713200).

References

1. Bleier, N., Mubarik, M.H., Swenson, G.R., Kumar, R.: Space microdatacenters. In: In 56th Annual IEEE/ACM International Symposium on Microarchitecture (MICRO 2023) (2023)
2. Sun, L., et al.: Jigsaw: taming BEV-centric perception on dual-SoC for autonomous driving. In: 2024 IEEE Real-Time Systems Symposium (RTSS), pp. 280–293. IEEE (2024)
3. Wang, G., Nixon, M., Boudreaux, M.: Toward cloud-assisted industrial IoT platform for large-scale continuous condition monitoring. Proc. IEEE **107**(6), 1193–1205 (2019)
4. Pei, Q., et al.: CoolEdge: hotspot-relievable warm water cooling for energy-efficient edge datacenters. In: Falsafi, B., Ferdman, M., Lu, S., Wenisch, T.F. (eds.) ASPLOS 2022: 27th ACM International Conference on Architectural Support for Programming Languages and Operating Systems, Lausanne, Switzerland, 28 February–4 March 2022, pp. 814–829. ACM (2022)
5. Azimi, R., Fox, T., Gonzalez, W., Reda, S.: Scale-out vs scale-up: a study of arm-based SoCs on server-class workloads. ACM Trans. Model. Perform. Evaluation Comput. Syst. **3**(4), 18:1–18:23 (2018)
6. Toosi, A.N., Son, J., Buyya, R.: Clouds-pi: a low-cost raspberry-pi based micro data center for software-defined cloud computing. IEEE Cloud Comput. **5**(5), 81–91 (2018)

7. Xu, D., et al.: Socflow: efficient and scalable DNN training on SoC-clustered edge servers. In: Gupta, R., Abu-Ghazaleh, N.B., Musuvathi, M., Tsafrir, D. (eds.) Proceedings of the 29th ACM International Conference on Architectural Support for Programming Languages and Operating Systems, ASPLOS 2024, La Jolla, CA, USA, 27 April–1 May 2024, vol. 1, pp. 368–385. ACM (2024)

8. Xu, M., et al.: Efficient, scalable, and sustainable DNN training on SoC-clustered edge servers. IEEE Trans. Mob. Comput. (2024)

9. Corporation, N.: Jetson orin NX series and jetson orin nano series thermal design guide (2024). https://developer.nvidia.com. Accessed: 2024

10. Zhang, Q., et al.: A survey on data center cooling systems: technology, power consumption modeling and control strategy optimization. J. Syst. Architect. **119**, 102253 (2021)

11. ANSYS, Inc., Canonsburg, PA, USA: ANSYS Fluent^{TM} User's Guide (2024). https://www.ansys.com/products/fluids/ansys-fluent

12. Huang, W., Ghosh, S., Velusamy, S., Sankaranarayanan, K., Skadron, K., Stan, M.R.: Hotspot: a compact thermal modeling methodology for early-stage VLSI design. IEEE Trans. Very Large Scale Integr. Syst. **14**(5), 501–513 (2006)

13. IDC, NVIDIA: Increasing intelligence at the edge with ai. White paper, IDC & NVIDIA (2025). https://www.nvidia.com/en-us/edge-computing/edge-ai/idc-whitepaper/

14. CEVA, Inc.: Edge-AI technology trends and 2025 forecast. Industry report, CEVA, Inc. (2025). https://www.ceva-ip.com/wp-content/uploads/2025-Edge-AI-Technology-Report.pdf

15. Nvidia jetson thor. https://www.nvidia.cn/autonomous-machines/embedded-systems/jetson-thor/. Accessed 2025

16. Talpes, E., Williams, D., Sarma, D.D.: Dojo: the microarchitecture of tesla's exascale computer. In: 2022 IEEE Hot Chips 34 Symposium (HCS), pp. 1–28. IEEE Computer Society (2022)

17. Simon, K.: Project natick-Microsoft's self-sufficient underwater datacenters. IndraStra Glob. **4**(6), 4 (2018)

18. Switzer, J., Marcano, G., Kastner, R., Pannuto, P.: Junkyard computing: repurposing discarded smartphones to minimize carbon. In: Proceedings of the 28th ACM International Conference on Architectural Support for Programming Languages and Operating Systems, vol. 2, pp. 400–412 (2023)

19. Qouneh, A., Li, C., Li, T.: A quantitative analysis of cooling power in container-based data centers. In: 2011 IEEE International Symposium on Workload Characterization (IISWC), pp. 61–71. IEEE (2011)

20. Szekely, V., Poppe, A., Páhi, A., Csendes, A., Hajas, G., Rencz, M.: Electrothermal and logi-thermal simulation of VLSI designs. IEEE Trans. Very Large Scale Integr. (VLSI) Syste. **5**(3), 258–269 (2002)

21. Liu, L., Sun, H., Li, C., Li, T., Xin, J., Zheng, N.: Managing battery aging for high energy availability in green datacenters. IEEE Trans. Parallel Distrib. Syst. **28**(12), 3521–3536 (2017)

Semantic-Driven Task-Traffic Co-scheduling for TSN with Generalization Ability: A Heterogeneous Graph Neural Network-Based Method

Zhihao Yang[1], Lei Xu[2(✉)], Shouliang Wang[1], Kankan Wu[3], Cailian Chen[1(✉)], and Xiaolin Wang[4]

[1] Department of Automation, Shanghai Jiao Tong University, Shanghai, China
cailianchen@sjtu.edu.cn
[2] School of Computer Science, Shanghai Jiao Tong University, Shanghai, China
xulei1@sjtu.edu.cn
[3] Shanghai Institute of Satellite Engineering, Shanghai, China
[4] Department of Mathematics, East China University of Science and Technology, Shanghai, China

Abstract. In the Industrial Internet of Things (IIoT), Time-Sensitive Networking (TSN) is a promising field network of implementing application functions across distributed devices. For a TSN-engaged IIoT system, co-scheduling task execution and TSN transmission is crucial to guarantee the chain execution of application tasks. However, the generalization ability of co-scheduling across varying scenarios is hindered in existing works, which lack characterization for resource conflicts arising from semantic relations among tasks, traffic, and the underlying topology. To address this, we propose a heterogeneous graph neural network (HGNN)-based co-scheduling method featuring explicit conflict characterization. We design a semantic-aware encoder within the HGNN, which aggregates heterogeneous component features through designated graph paths to capture their semantic relations. An agent then extracts conflict patterns from this encoding, and decodes conflict-free scheduling decisions on offloading, task priority assignment, and traffic offset design. To enhance generalization ability in unseen scenarios, the conflict extraction ability and the inductive encoding ability are refined through deep reinforcement learning feedback. Experiments demonstrate that our method achieves 12% higher schedulability and 20% lower task chain delay, and maintains its performance in unseen topologies and task scenarios.

Keywords: Industrial Internet of Things (IIoT) · Time-sensitive Networking (TSN) · Resource Conflict · Heterogeneous Information Aggregation

X. Wang et al. (Eds.): NPC 2025, LNCS 16306, pp. 240–252, 2026.
https://doi.org/10.1007/978-3-032-10466-3_20

1 Introduction

In the Industrial Internet of Things (IIoT), an application function is always implemented by a sequence of tasks [1]. These tasks follow the chain execution order, and are deployed on distributed devices due to limited computational capacity [2]. Data traffic produced by a task's execution is transmitted via the industrial field network to initiate the next task. The best-effort service of Ethernet and increasing data volumes lead to significant network latency and transmission failures, disrupting task chain execution.

To address this, Time-Sensitive Networking (TSN) emerges as a promising field network [3]. Specifically, it defines the Time-Aware Shaper (TAS) to reserve bandwidth resource for critical traffic [4], enabling ultra-low latency transmission through injection time scheduling [5]. However, a TSN-engaged IIoT system faces the generalization problem of scheduling. Across different production phases, frequent alterations of application functions and topology structures [6] cause temporal mismatches between task execution and reserved bandwidth: after being generated by task execution, traffic might unnecessarily wait for reserved bandwidth, compromising the informative freshness upon consumption; Or it might miss the reserved window, leading to transmission failure. Therefore, *there is a strong necessity for time-efficient task and traffic co-scheduling to maintain task chain execution*, which jointly optimizes task offloading (mapping tasks to devices), task scheduling (allocating computational resources), and TSN scheduling.

Unfortunately, existing methods fail to deliver satisfying co-scheduling performance. The brute-force searches are time-consuming for real-time requirements [7,8]. Though deep learning offers real-time inference potential, current scheduling approaches [6,9] are limited to resolving resource conflicts induced by homogeneous entity (task [9] or traffic [10] only). Critically, they cannot address semantic-induced conflicts inherent in co-scheduling, where heterogeneous task and traffic exhibit two semantic relations: 1) Spatially, task-to-device positions and their induced traffic routing paths determine *where* bandwidth resource conflicts occur on specific topology links; 2) Temporally, the sequential execution requirement of task chains imposes timing constraints between task execution and traffic transmission, and under limited resources, this triggers *temporal* occupancy conflicts for both computational and bandwidth resources. In conclusion, a semantic-aware scheduler is desired to handle task chain disruptions.

In this paper, we propose a generalized co-scheduler that considers resource conflicts brought by semantic relations. We design a heterogeneous graph neural network (HGNN) to jointly encode tasks, traffic, and topology structure with their features and semantics. The semantic-level encoding is realized through the heterogeneous information aggregation mechanism [11], with semantics represented by carefully designed meta-paths in the graph. Then, a soft actor-critic (SAC) agent utilizes the HGNN encoding to offload tasks, assign task priority, and design traffic offset by the action decoder. The SAC trains and gains feedback under various systems, enhancing the inductive representation ability and encoding precision of HGNN in unseen scenarios. Our main contributions are as follows:

1) We develop a semantic-induced resource conflict characterizer to provide pre-scheduling guidance. It aggregates semantic information from system components by HGNN for joint encoding and conflict extraction.
2) We design a generalization trainer, which dynamically refines the semantic aggregation process to learn an inductive representation ability for HGNN, mitigating the overfitting problem under varying scenarios.
3) We propose a generalized and conflict-free scheduler based on the characterization and refinement. It realizes co-scheduling, including task offloading, task priority assigning, and traffic offset designing with high schedulability and efficiency.

The rest of the paper is organized as follows: In Sect. 2 we establish the system model. In Sect. 3 we discuss our methods. In Sect. 4 we give the evaluation results, and in Sect. 5 we conclude our paper.

2   System Model and Problem Formulation

In this section, we model the TSN-engaged system, task chain, and traffic. Then we formulate an optimization problem for computation-network resource co-scheduling.

2.1   The Integrated Model of Task and Traffic

Network System: The system comprises devices $\mathcal{V}^d$ providing computational resources for tasks and TSN switches $\mathcal{V}^s$ with bandwidth resource, interconnected via full-duplex link net $\mathcal{E}$. The topology graph is denoted by $\mathcal{G} = <\mathcal{V}, \mathcal{E}>$, where $\mathcal{V} = \mathcal{V}^d \cup \mathcal{V}^s$.

Task Chain and Task: the ith chain is represented as $\mathcal{A}_i = \{\tau_n^i\}_{n=1}^{k_i}$, with n the sequence number and k_i the total number. Tasks are periodically generated with attributions (priority, execution time, period, deadline, generation baseline, device) in (1). After generation, a task waits for necessary input information, and accessible computational resources due to intra-device resource contention [12]. Tasks sharing the same device follow the priority-driven contention rule: when two tasks both wait for resources, the one with higher priority is executed first [13]. Response time is a task's duration from generation to execution completion.

$$\tau : <\lambda_\tau, e_\tau^{\text{ex}}, p_\tau, d_\tau^t, b_\tau^t, \delta_\tau>. \tag{1}$$

Traffic: Information traffic is generated after task execution as inputs for succeeding tasks via TSN. Flow f_τ is defined by the attribution tuple (period, packet length, routing path, data age) in (2). It inherits the period from the corresponding task and generates right after execution.

$$f_\tau : <p_\tau, l_\tau^f, r_\tau^f, d_\tau^f>. \tag{2}$$

2.2 Co-scheduling Problem Formulation

The goal to task-traffic co-scheduling is allocating both computational and network resources. From computational perspective, task execution follows the priority-driven contention on IIoT devices, *task variables are the offloading decisions and the assignments of priority*. From network perspective, the no-wait Time-Aware Shaper mechanism in TSN is naturally adopted due to its ability to ensure ultra-low latency and zero jitter, thus *the offset of each flow is another variable*. Hence, *the object is to achieve orderly task execution with low task chains' duration* (from the generation of first task to the execution of the last task in chain). We follow the constraints in [4, 12]:

Resource Constraint: The necessitated computational/network resources must not exceed device/switch limitation. Only one task could be executed at a time in a device. When contention occurs, the task with higher priority will be executed first.

Task Execution Order Constraint: Tasks should be executed and transmit information to succeeding tasks according to the task chain order $\mathcal{A}_i$.

Data Age Constraint: The duration from information generation to consumption (summary of the injection time, the network latency, and the consumer task response time) should not exceed its data age d_τ^f.

TSN no-conflict constraint: The transmission window for any two traffic on the same switch must not overlap.

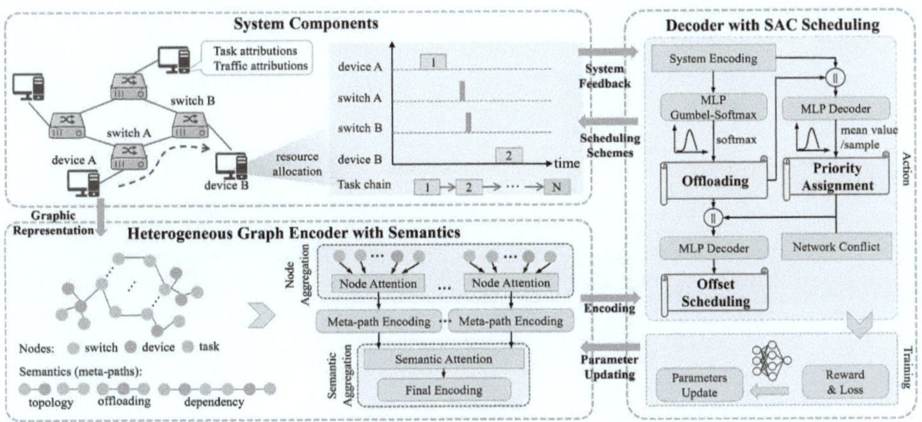

Fig. 1. The structure of the proposed methods: system, HGNN encoder and SAC decoder.

3   Proposed Methods

As shown in Fig. 1, based on the system, an HGNN Encoder - SAC Decoder structure is proposed. The encoder establishes a heterogeneous graph with task, topology and traffic. It aggregates semantics via specifically designed meta-paths, and forms encoding with attention mechanism. Following the task chain order, the decoder analyzes the encoding to make decisions incrementally and get one-step reward to update learnable parameters.

3.1   Semantic-Aware System Encoder

In the lower left part of Fig. 1, the system graph contains task and topology nodes with heterogeneous features (traffic is implicitly contained in tasks). We transform their feature spaces into the same vector space, with the attention mechanism to distinguish importance between both homogeneous and heterogeneous interactions around nodes. In HGNN, meta-paths are designed to aggregate semantic information between nodes.

Node Types: Devices, switches and tasks. Devices have computation capacity feature $h_i^d = [c_i]$; switches own link rate features $h_i^s = [v_i]$; The feature of a task $h_i^t = [e_i^{\mathrm{ex}}, p_i, d_i^t, b_i^t, l_\tau^f, d_\tau^f]$ contains both task and traffic attributions.

Meta-paths: Three kinds of meta-paths are designed. Φ_1 connects task-device-task nodes to extract computational resource contention semantics on the same device; Φ_2 links device-switch and switch-switch nodes for topology semantics; Φ_3 links task-device-switch-device-task nodes to extract semantics of traffic-mediated task dependencies.

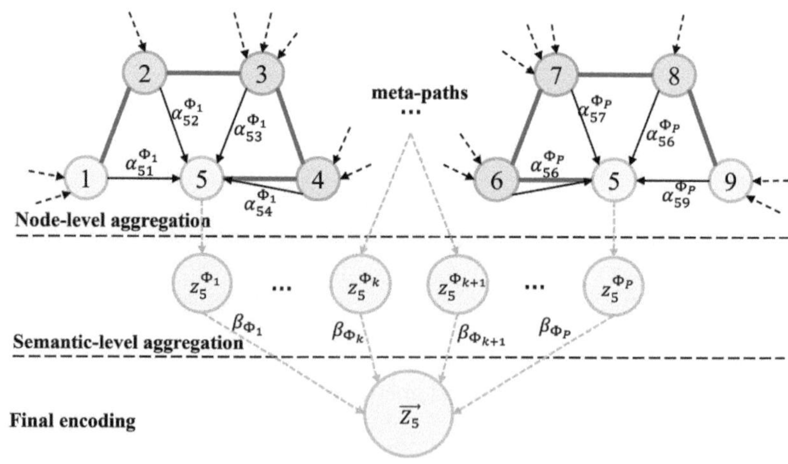

Fig. 2. Illustration of semantic-aware encoding with meta-paths. Nodes with different colors means different types. This shows the final encoding of node 5 with P meta-paths.

Semantic-aware encoding process is as follow, an illustration is shown in Fig. 2.

Feature Spaces Transformation: Transformation matrix (learnable) $\mathbf{M}_\alpha, \alpha \in \{d, s, t\}$ transforms heterogeneous nodes to vectors with the same dimension. $h_i^{\alpha\prime} = \mathbf{M}_\alpha \cdot h_i^\alpha$.

Node-Level Attention: Node-level attention aggregates information between different nodes in the same meta-path with learnable parameters θ_{N_a} in (3), $e_{ij}^\Phi = \text{NodeAtt}_{\theta_{N_a}}(h_i, h_j)$, which is normalized as node importance α_{ij}^Φ. $\mathcal{N}_i^\Phi$ means all nodes in meta-path, $\mathbf{a}$ is the matrix of α, σ is the activation function.

$$\alpha_{ij}^\Phi = \text{softmax}(e_{ij}^\Phi) = \frac{\exp\left(\sigma(\mathbf{a}_\Phi^\top \cdot [h_i'\|h_j'])\right)}{\sum_{k\in\mathcal{N}_i^\Phi} \exp\left(\sigma(\mathbf{a}_\Phi^\top \cdot [h_i'\|h_k'])\right)}. \tag{3}$$

Node-Level Aggregation: z_i^Φ aggregates meta-path neighbors' encoding and themselves with coefficients in (4). The concatenation operator $\|$ is the K-head attention.

$$z_i^\Phi = \|_{k=1}^K \sigma\left(\sum_{j\in\mathcal{N}_i^\Phi} \alpha_{ij}^\Phi \cdot h_j'\right). \tag{4}$$

Semantic Aggregation: In (5) we aggregate all meta-paths encoding with normalized semantic weights β_{Φ_i}, which is calculated from learnable meta-path attentions $\omega_\Phi = \frac{1}{|\mathcal{V}|} \sum_{i\in\mathcal{V}} \mathbf{q}^\top \cdot \tanh(\mathbf{W} \cdot z_i^\Phi + b)$. $|\mathcal{P}|$ represents the total number of meta-paths.

$$\beta_{\Phi_i} = \frac{\exp(\omega_{\Phi_i})}{\sum_{k=1}^{|\mathcal{P}|} \exp(\omega_{\Phi_k})}, \quad Z_i = \sum_{k=1}^{|\mathcal{P}|} \beta_{\Phi_k} \cdot Z_i^{\Phi_k}. \tag{5}$$

3.2   Network Conflict Encoder

The traffic scheduling necessitates states encoding of TSN links to indicate the conflicts between traffic in the 'TSN no-conflict constraint'.

According to our previous work [14], the feasible offset solution space for traffic belonging to task τ_i is:

$$o_i \in \bigcup_{f_j\in\mathcal{S}} \bigcup_{(v_a,v_b)\in R_i} \bigcup_{k_{i,j}^{(v_a,v_b)}}^{\infty} \phi_{i,j}^{(v_a,v_b)} + k_{i,j}^{(v_a,v_b)} \gcd(p_i^f, p_j^f), \tag{6}$$

$$\phi_{i,j}^{(v_a,v_b)} = (\Delta - 2l_i^f/B, \Delta), \quad \Delta = b_j^f + o_j^f + l_j^f/B - b_i^f,$$

where B is the global TSN link rate, and the first line figures out feasible offset choices.

The conflict intervals of f_i is a function of scheduled traffic offsets $\{o_j\}_{j\neq i}$. A multi-layer perceptron (MLP) with scheduled traffic offsets as input can simulate this function. Therefore, $z_{\text{netc}} = [o_1, o_2, \ldots, o_{|\mathcal{F}|}]$ (unscheduled ones are padded) are adopted to encode the conflicts states in network.

3.3   Scheduling Policy Decoder

In the right part of Fig. 1, the optimal scheduling solutions are decoded with the semantic-contained encoding.

The overall scheduling process adopts an incremental manner for tasks in chain order, each comprising three sequential parts: task offloading, task priority assignment, and corresponding traffic offset design. Despite the binary space of offloading solutions, the others are continuous. For offloading, we adopt the Gumbel-Softmax for backward propagation differentiability. For continuous ones, we use Gaussian distributions, which figure out the local optimum by the mean value and preserve the possibility of discovering globally optimal solutions in training simultaneously.

Task Offloading. Task offloading decoder has a learnable MLP and Gumbel-Softmax. It is noted that offloading values will be utilized to make decisions later, therefore the Gumbel-Softmax operation not only maintains the original probability distribution of device selection but makes this action differentiable in backward propagation.

$$\mathbb{P}(\delta_\tau) = \text{Gumbel-Softmax}\left(\frac{\mathbf{W}_a \cdot \text{MLP}_{\text{ofl}}(\boldsymbol{z}_{\text{sys}}) + \mathbf{g}}{\beta}\right), \tag{7}$$

where $\boldsymbol{z}_{\text{sys}} = \|_{i \in \mathcal{T}_{\text{sch}}} \boldsymbol{Z}_i$ is the system encoding from (5), $\mathbf{W}_a, \mathbf{g}$ are a learnable weight matrix and noise vector, β is a temperature hyper-parameter.

Task Priority Assignment. This decision should consider both the system state and the offloading decision on intra-device task resource contention. Therefore, a learnable MLP extracts information of system encoding to build the continuous solution space. It outputs a mean value and deviation. Note that the former is the optimal choice, which is sufficient for scheduling and evaluation. The latter aims to jump out of local optimality and discovery in the learning process, which helps to sample from the Gaussian distribution.

$$\mu_{\tau_i}, \sigma_{\tau_i} = \text{MLP}_{\text{pri}}(\boldsymbol{z}_{\text{sys}} \| \delta_{\tau_i}), \tag{8}$$

where $\mu_{\tau_i}, \sigma_{\tau_i}$ represent the mean value and standard deviation, respectively.

Traffic Scheduling. Similarly, with task offloading and priority, another learnable MLP analyzes system encoding and network conflict to output the parameters for traffic offset:

$$\mu_{f_i}, \sigma_{f_i} = \text{MLP}_{\text{oft}}(\boldsymbol{z}_{\text{sys}} \| \boldsymbol{z}_{\text{netc}} \| [\delta_{\tau_i}, \lambda_{\tau_i}]), \tag{9}$$

where μ_{f_i}, σ_{f_i} represent the mean value and standard deviation, respectively. Note that the $\boldsymbol{z}_{\text{sys}}$ has been updated with current task after priority assigning.

3.4   Soft Actor-Critic Optimization

The goal of SAC training is optimizing parameters in the aforementioned encoders (5) (7) and decoders (7)–(9). It leads to high precision encoding and conflict-free decision decoding, which achieves orderly chain execution with low delay.

State. The states are the encodings of system states in (5) and network conflicts in (6).

Action. An action can be divided into three steps: task offloading, task priority assigning, and traffic offset designing.

In task offloading, mask technology is used to forbid node choices with no available resource in state s_t: $\text{Mask}(s_t) = \mathbf{1}(\sum_{\tau_i \in \mathcal{T}_{\text{sch}}+\tau} e^{\text{ex}}_{\tau_i}/p_{\tau_i} \leq 1)$.

In task priority assigning, the mean values are straightly adopted in evaluations, while sampling values from $p_{\tau_i} \sim \text{Gaussian}(\mu_{\tau_i}, \sigma_{\tau_i})$ are alternated in training. Furthermore, a scaler limits the output values to appropriate action space (greater than 0).

In traffic offset designing, mean-or-sample is similarly adopted for o_{f_i} in Gaussian $(\mu_{f_i}, \sigma_{f_i})$. And a scaler limits offsets to $[0, p_{\tau_i})$ to accelerate training convergency.

Joint Optimization Reward. The reward guides the agent to maintain task chain order and reduce overall delay. The one-step reward r_t at each incremental step is:

$$r_t(s_t) = \underbrace{\mathbf{1}_t}_{\text{success reward}} - \underbrace{\kappa D_t}_{\text{delay penalty}} - \underbrace{U_t}_{\text{load balance}}, \tag{10}$$

where κ is a hyper-parameter, $\mathbf{1}_t$ represents scheduling action is successful (positive) or not (zero) according to constraints in Sec. II-B. D_t is the overall delay for current task, which is the summation of response time and networking delay in (11).

$$\theta_k = \max_{\tau_i \in \text{Pre}(\tau_k)} [(b^t_{\tau_i} - b^t_{\tau_k}) + R_{\tau_i} + o^f_i + \text{len}(r^f_\tau) * l^f_i/B]^+,$$

$$D_{\tau_k} = \theta_k + e^{\text{ex}}_{\tau_k} + \sum_{\tau_i \in \text{hp} \cup \text{ep}(\tau_k)} \left\lceil \frac{D_{\tau_k} - \theta_k}{p^t_{\tau_k}} \right\rceil e^{\text{ex}}_{\tau_i}. \tag{11}$$

It comprises predecessor delay with finish time of precedent tasks $\tau_i \in \text{Pre}(\tau_k)$, and computational resource contention time in the summation operator. U_t represents the utilization of computational resources, which is given by $U_t = \frac{\max u(s_t) - \min u(s_t)}{\max u(s_t)}$ based on the utilization ratio $u(s_t) = \sum e^{\text{ex}}_\tau/p_\tau$ on each device.

Algorithm 1: HGNN-aware SAC Training

Input: HGNN parameter θ_h, replay buffer $\mathcal{R}$, batch size B, update frequency F;
Output: Actor Network θ_a, double critic Network θ_{c1}, θ_{c2};
  1: Initialize $\theta_a, \theta_{c1}, \theta_{c2}$;
  2: **for all** $ep \in \{1, 2, \ldots, epsilon\}$ in chain order **do**
  3:    Initial state encoding $s_0 \leftarrow$ HGNN$(G_0; \theta_h)$;
  4:    **for all** step $t \in \{0, 1, \ldots, |\mathcal{T}| - 1\}$ **do**
  5:       $a_t \leftarrow$ ActionPolicy$(s_t; \theta_a)$ following (7)–(9);
  6:       $r_t \leftarrow$ Update$(\mathcal{T}, \mathcal{F}, s_t, a_t, \theta_h)$ by (10);
  7:       $s_{t+1} \leftarrow$ HGNN$(G_{t+1}; \theta_h)$ by (5);
  8:       $\mathcal{R}$.append(Transition$(s_t, a_t, r_t, s_{t+1}, done)$);
  9:       Sample B transitions from $\mathcal{R}$;
10:       Update $\theta'_{ci}(i \in 1, 2)$ with (15), θ_a with (14);
11:       Adjust entropy temperature α;
12:       Soft-update each F steps $\theta_{ci} = (1 - \rho)\theta_{ci} + \rho\theta'_{ci}$;
13:    **end for**
14: **end for**

3.5   Training Algorithm

The training process updates parameters in HGNN, the actor policy and critic network. The gradient descent direction is to maximize rewards and maintain policy entropy:

$$\max_{\pi} \mathbb{E}\left[\sum_t \gamma^t(r(s_t, a_t) + \alpha\mathcal{H}(s_t))\right],$$

$$\mathcal{H}(s_t) = -|\mathcal{T}| \log \mathcal{N}_{\text{device}} - \sum_{i=1}^{|\mathcal{T}|} \log(2\pi e \sqrt{\sigma_{\tau_i}\sigma_{f_i}}). \tag{12}$$

In critic, two independent Q-networks $Q_{\theta_{ci}}, i = 1, 2$ are used to mitigate the bootstrap over-estimation, built by MLP with z_{sys} and scheduling decisions input. The Q_{target} is the minimum:

$$Q_{\text{target}} = r + \gamma(1 - done)[\min_{i \in 1,2} Q_{\theta_{ci}} - \alpha\mathcal{H}] \tag{13}$$

The loss for updating actor and critic is:

$$\mathcal{L}_{\text{actor}} = \frac{1}{B} \sum [\min[Q_{\theta_{c1}}, Q_{\theta_{c2}}] + \alpha\mathcal{H}], \tag{14}$$

$$\mathcal{L}_{\text{critic}} = \frac{1}{B} \sum \left[(Q_{\theta_{c1}} - Q_{\text{target}})^2 + (Q_{\theta_{c2}} - Q_{\text{target}})^2\right], \tag{15}$$

with $Q_{\theta_{c1}}, Q_{\theta_{c1}}$ the same structure but different parameters.

The pseudocode is shown in Algorithm 1. The learnable parameters are initialized in line 1. States are encoded by the HGNN in line 3. Following the chain order, a task and its corresponding traffic are selected, the offloading, task priority, and offset schemes are sequentially decided. Then the one-step reward and new state are derived. A transition with state, action, reward, next state, done indicating whether scheduling is over is stored. The Adam optimizer then samples B transitions to update parameters in line 10. For each F steps, the critic networks are softly updated.

4   Evaluations

4.1   Simulation Setup

Our simulations run on an Intel(R) Core (TM) i9-13900K CPU and NVIDIA RTX 4060 GPU (8GB). We construct linear, ring, and tree topologies with a hundred switches and devices, 1Gbps bandwidth [7], which are common scenarios in IIoT. Due to no public IIoT dataset in TSN, we set attributions according to the IEC/IEEE 60802 standard [15], with task period in $\{1\text{--}33\}$ ms, execution time in $\{0.1\text{--}1\}$ ms, packet length in $\{64\text{--}1500\}$B, baseline from 0 to one period, task deadline and information data age equal the period. Each task chain contains 5–10 tasks.

Implemented with PyTorch and Geometric, the heterogeneous graph has 4 attention heads, hidden layers has 128 hidden features and 64 encoding dimensions. The learning rate is 10^{-5}, with batch size 64, $\alpha = \kappa = 0.01, \beta = \gamma = 0.99, \rho = 0.05$, damped patience with initial value 500. The dropout ratio is 0.4. Adam optimizer is adopted.

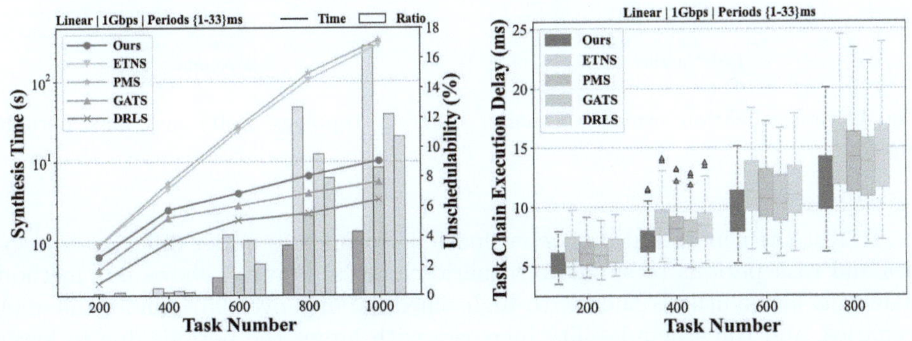

Fig. 3. Comparisons with brute-force search and ablation experiments with GATS & DRLS.

We compare our method with the brute-force search algorithms (ETNS [7], PMS [8]), and homogeneous ML methods without senmantics for ablation purpose (GATS adapted from [1,16] with GAT, DRLS adapted from [9] using SAC only) in 1000 tasks scenarios. The brute-force search traverses part of the solution space in an incremental manner. The GATS encodes topology and task dependency on two separate graphs and combines DRL for scheduling. The DRLS uses the SAC only without graph's encoding ability.

We take scheduling of a task and corresponding traffic as failure if violating chain order or data age constraint. Synthesis time means the inference time for ML or the search time for non-ML methods. Unschedulability means scheduling nonsuccess ratio.

The results in Fig. 3 have shown the superiority of our method in both synthesis time and schedulability. Compared with PMS, our method reduces synthesis time to 1/10. For ensuring the chain execution order (schedulability), our method achieves 12% higher when compared with the ETNS. Our method also reduces chain execution delay by over 20% under 800 tasks. The ablation experiments show that graph's encoding and heterogeneous semantic-extraction ability are both vital for improving schedulability, the HGNN's encoding depicts semantic conflicts between computation and network resource allocation, and SAC improves this depiction and action decoding precision.

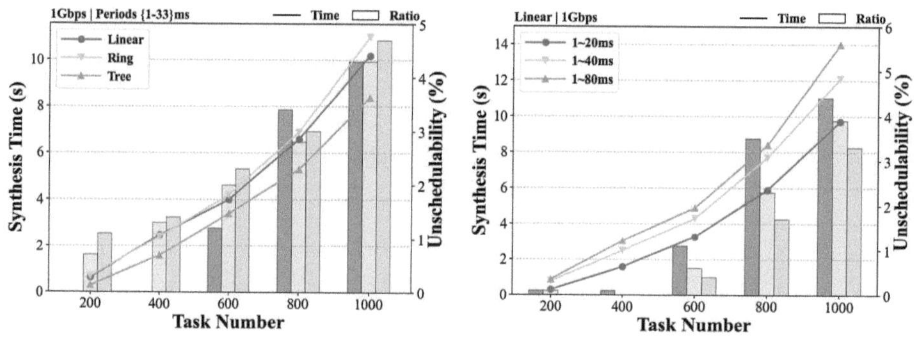

Fig. 4. Generalization evaluation under different topology (left) and task periods (right).

To test the generalization, we evaluate performances under different topologies and task periods to simulate scenario changes. Figure 4 shows our method maintains low synthesis time with high schedulability over 95% under different scenarios, and the schedulability increases with larger the periods due to lower computational loads in a hyper-period.

The sensitivity of HGNN parameters are investigated. As shown in Table 1, 'AH' is the number of attention heads, and 'ED' represents encoding dimension. The semantic representation is directly influenced by the dimension of encoding. The increasing of the dimension to 64 will improve 3.7% schedulability, then it will drop 7.2% at 256 due to redundancy. For multi-head attention, 1 attention head means no implementation. The increasing of attention heads to 4 will improve 2.6% schedulability, then it decreases 2.2% at 6. Note that the dramatically high cost of 8 heads prevents us from adopting it.

Table 1. Parameter Sensitivity

Schedulability	AH = 1	AH = 2	AH = 4	AH = 6	AH = 8
ED = 32	89.8	90.8	92.0	91.2	93.4
ED = 64	92.1	92.9	95.7	93.5	95.8
ED = 128	90.0	90.9	92.2	91.5	93.5
ED = 256	84.4	86.0	88.5	86.2	89.3

The time cost and memory usage during training (Algorithm 1) are in Table 2. Without the graph structure, the DRLS experiences the lowest training time but also introduces no generalization and the lowest schedulability. Compared with the GATS, our method reduces storage overhead because GATS's separated graph processing requires maintaining two sets of sparse data simultaneously.

Table 2. Training Consumption

Method	Ours	GATS	DRLS
Training Time (h)	55	63	39
Memory Usage (MiB)	3907	4826	2581

5   Conclusion

In this paper, we propose a generalized task-traffic co-scheduler based on HGNN encoding and SAC training. It formulates an inductive representation ability to encode semantic relations between task and traffic. The encoding is then utilized for resource conflict-free scheduling, including task offloading, task priority assigning, and traffic offset scheduling. The inductive ability and training on varying scenarios lead to generalization in maintaining chain execution.

Acknowledgments. This research is funded in part by Natural Science Foundation of Shanghai under Grant 25ZR1402264, in part by the National Natural Science Foundation of China under Grant 62432009, 62025305, 62303185 and the Shanghai Sailing Program under the grant 23YF1409500.

References

1. Qi, X., Zhang, D., Liu, T., Wang, H.: Deep reinforcement learning for large-scale scientific workflow scheduling with improved structure feature extraction and sampling. In: Chen, X., Min, G., Guo, D., Xie, X., Pu, L. (eds.) NPC 2024. LNCS, vol. 15527, pp. 310–323. Springer, Singapore (2024). https://doi.org/10.1007/978-981-96-2830-8_24

2. Qiu, Y., Zhao, G., Xu, H., Huang, H., Qiao, C.: Paring: joint task placement and routing for distributed training with in-network aggregation. IEEE/ACM Trans. Netw. **32**(5), 4317–4332 (2024)

3. Qiu, T., Chi, J., Zhou, X., Ning, Z., Wu, D.O.: Edge computing in industrial internet of things: architecture, advances and challenges. IEEE Commun. Surv. Tutor. (99), 1 (2020)

4. Yang, Q., Jiang, X., Quan, W., Liu, R., Sun, Z.: Node bundle scheduling: an ultra-low latency traffic scheduling algorithm for tas-based time-sensitive networks. In: Carretero, J., Shende, S., Garcia-Blas, J., Brandic, I., Olcoz, K., Schreiber, M. (eds.) Euro-Par 2024. LNCS, vol. 14801, pp. 357–372. Springer, Cham (2024). https://doi.org/10.1007/978-3-031-69577-3_25

5. Luo, Z., Zeng, F., Chen, X.: Providing fine-grained latency control for time sensitive networking: a reordering method. In: Chen, X., Min, G., Guo, D., Xie, X., Pu, L. (eds.) NPC 2024. LNCS, vol. 15528, pp. 442–453. Springer, Singapore (2025). https://doi.org/10.1007/978-981-96-2864-3_35

6. Tian, Z., Zhou, X., Liao, Z., Sun, M., He, F.: GTSNet: a generalized traffic scheduler for time-sensitive networking based on graph neural network. IEEE Trans. Industr. Inf. **21**(1), 208–217 (2025)

7. Xu, L., Xu, Q., Chen, C., Zhang, Y., Wang, S., Guan, X.: Efficient task-network scheduling with task conflict metric in time-sensitive networking. IEEE Trans. Industr. Inf. **20**(2), 1528–1538 (2024)

8. Zhou, X., He, F., Zhao, L.: Loosely coupled hybrid scheduling of processing and communication for TSN-based ima systems. IEEE Trans. Industr. Inf. **20**(6), 8884–8895 (2024)

9. Shang, X., et al.: Computing and network load balancing for decentralized deep federated learning in industrial cyber-physical systems: a multi-task approach. IEEE J. Sel. Areas Commun. 1 (2025)

10. Xu, L., et al.: Scalable scheduling in time-sensitive networking: an efficient stream conflict detection method. IEEE Trans. Industr. Inf. **21**(5), 4105–4116 (2025)

11. Wang, X., et al: Heterogeneous graph attention network. In: The World Wide Web Conference, pp. 2022–2032 (2019)

12. Nasri, M., Brandenburg, B.B.: An exact and sustainable analysis of non-preemptive scheduling. In: 2017 IEEE Real-Time Systems Symposium (RTSS), vol. 1, no. 2, p. 5. IEEE (2017)

13. Gohari, P., Voeten, J., Nasri, M.: Work-in-progress: tight response-time analysis for periodic preemptive tasks under global scheduling. In: 2023 IEEE Real-Time Systems Symposium (RTSS), pp. 451–454. IEEE (2023)

14. Yang, Z., Wang, S., Xu, Q., Li, X., Chen, C.: A timeslot clustering-based hybrid traffic scheduling in time-sensitive networking. In: 2024 IEEE 22nd International Conference on Industrial Informatics (INDIN), pp. 1–6 (2024)

15. IEEE/IEC draft international standard time-sensitive networking profile for industrial automation. IEEE/IEC P60802/D3.0, pp. 1–194 (2024)

16. He, X., Zhuge, X., Dang, F., Xu, W., Yang, Z.: DeepScheduler: enabling flow-aware scheduling in time-sensitive networking. In: IEEE INFOCOM 2023 - IEEE Conference on Computer Communications, pp. 1–10 (2023)

CPU–GPU Heterogeneity Based Pipeline Parallel Architecture in Physical Layer Processing

Shiwen He[1,2], Xunzhe Deng[1(✉)], Zhenyu An[2], Chengzuo Peng[1], Linhua Liu[3], and Wei Huang[4]

[1] School of Computer Science and Engineering, Central South University, Changsha 410083, China
shiwen.he.hn@aliyun.com, {234712279,234701049}@csu.edu.cn
[2] Purple Mountain Laboratories, Nanjing 211111, China
anzhenyu@pmlabs.com.cn
[3] Guokuan Zhiyun Technology Co., Ltd., Changsha 410000, China
liulinhua2006@163.com
[4] School of Computer Science and Information Engineering, Hefei University of Technology, Hefei 230009, China
huangwei@hfut.edu.cn

Abstract. Efficient performance analysis and software-hardware decoupling are crucial for evaluating future communication technologies. However, current general-purpose processors fail to fully leverage the synergistic computational capabilities of the Central Processing Units (CPUs) and Graphics Processing Units (GPUs) when evaluating the performance of wireless protocol stacks, resulting in inefficient processing of compute-intensive tasks and an inability to meet the high-throughput demands of real-time scenarios. To address this issue, this paper proposes a pipeline parallel processing architecture based on CPU-GPU coordinated scheduling. During the pipeline parallel processing of multiple data frames, this architecture intelligently assigns computational tasks to the most suitable processing unit based on real-time load and processing unit structures, thereby improving processing efficiency, reducing power consumption, and enhancing overall system performance. Experimental results indicate that on the mid-range heterogeneous platform, the pipeline parallel architecture achieves a 172.15% throughput enhancement and a 63.26% latency reduction; on the high-end platform, it attains a 326.32% throughput enhancement and a 76.54% latency reduction, demonstrating robustness across hardware levels. These improvements alleviate the bottlenecks of existing Software-Defined Radio (SDR) simulation architectures.

Keywords: CPU–GPU pipeline · Dynamic resource allocation · Energy efficiency

© IFIP International Federation for Information Processing 2026
Published by Springer Nature Switzerland AG 2026
X. Wang et al. (Eds.): NPC 2025, LNCS 16306, pp. 253–265, 2026.
https://doi.org/10.1007/978-3-032-10466-3_21

1   Introduction

The rapid evolution of sixth generation wireless networks, coupled with emerging applications such as the Internet of things, augmented reality, and virtual reality, imposes unprecedented demands on wireless communication systems for superior performance, flexibility, and scalability [1]. As a dominant wireless access technology, Wireless Fidelity (Wi-Fi) must deliver higher data rates, enhanced spectral efficiency, and reduced latency to accommodate ultra-dense, multi-service heterogeneous environments [2].

Software-defined networking, which decouples control from data forwarding [3], has emerged as a promising solution, enabling programmable networks and hardware independence. Architectures like Open Radio Access Network (O-RAN) modularize wireless functions, fostering interoperability and standardization [4]. Open-source projects such as OpenAirInterface (OAI) and srsRAN further support this by implementing full protocol stacks on general-purpose Central Processing Units (CPUs), providing configurable platforms for research [5]. However, these software-based systems exhibit limitations in processing critical PHYsical (PHY) layer modules—e.g., encoding/decoding, Inverse Fast Fourier Transform (IFFT)/Fast Fourier Transform (FFT), channel estimation, and equalization—due to heavy reliance on CPUs. As a result, they struggle to meet the stringent low-latency and high-throughput needs in scenarios like Extended Reality (XR) and autonomous driving [6].

To address these challenges, prior studies have explored heterogeneous computing architectures to improve computation rates and reduce processing latency in Wi-Fi systems. For example, Gokalgandhi et al. utilized Graphics Processing Units (GPUs) to accelerate channel estimation and Orthogonal Frequency Division Multiplexing (OFDM) symbol demodulation in the Wi-Fi PHY layer, significantly reducing the uplink processing latency in massive multiple-input multiple-output systems [7]. Other works proposed to combine Field-Programmable Gate Arrays (FPGAs) with general-purpose CPUs to achieve low-latency 802.11 protocols [8,9]. Additionally, other heterogeneous hardware platforms, such as Digital Signal Processor (DSP)-based parallel architectures, have also been researched [10]. However, current solutions exhibit two fundamental limitations. First, existing methods concentrate on isolated functional modules or specialized hardware. Second, the absence of a unified programmable framework in these approaches results in suboptimal utilization of computational resources in heterogeneous platforms. Consequently, they still face some challenges in meeting the demands of high throughput and low latency.

To address these limitations, this paper proposes a pipeline parallel processing architecture based on CPU-GPU coordinated scheduling that fully leverages the control strengths of CPUs and the parallel processing capabilities of GPUs. The architecture integrates task-level and data-level parallelization to enable concurrent execution of PHY modules, supported by an adaptive decision algorithm that dynamically allocates tasks based on real-time load factors. For each frame, the decision-making logic of this algorithm exhibits $O(1)$ time complexity with an execution overhead of less than $1\mu s$. By combining double buffering to overlap computation and data transfer, and zero-copy optimizations using Compute Unified Device Architecture (CUDA) pinned memory to eliminate redundant data copying [11], the system significantly reduces the total end-to-end PHY latency for batches of frames, enhances throughput, and improves energy efficiency. Experimental evaluation on both mid-range (Intel i7-10700F + GTX 1650) and high-end (AMD Ryzen 9 9950X3D + RTX 5090) platforms demonstrates its scalability, robustness, and effectiveness across diverse hardware configurations.

The remainder of this paper is organized as follows: Sect. 2 introduces the system model, Sect. 3 details the proposed CPU-GPU collaborative pipeline architecture, Sect. 4 presents the experimental results and analysis, and Sect. 5 concludes the paper and outlines future work.

2   System Model

This paper considers a software-defined Wi-Fi PHY processing system deployed on a heterogeneous CPU-GPU computing platform. The system's baseband signal processing workflows for both the transmitter (Tx) and receiver (Rx) are illustrated in Fig. 1.

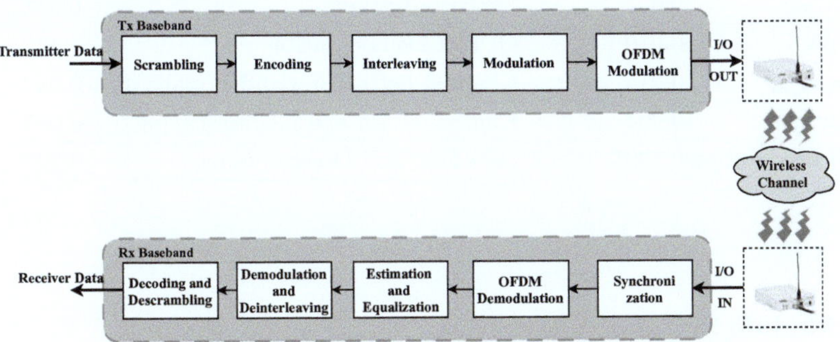

Fig. 1. Wi-Fi PHY baseband processing chain.

Specifically, Tx baseband processing includes scrambling, encoding, interleaving, modulation, and OFDM modulation (with IFFT and cyclic prefix insertion). Rx baseband processing involves synchronization, OFDM demodulation (with FFT and cyclic prefix removal), channel estimation and equalization, demodulation and deinterleaving, and decoding and descrambling [12].

2.1   Traditional Processing and Performance Analysis

In traditional schemes, PHY modules are processed sequentially on the CPU. Each module within a given frame must wait for the preceding module to complete processing, resulting in significant cumulative latency. For instance, when processing multiple frames, the CPU must fully complete all Tx operations—scrambling, encoding, interleaving, modulation, and OFDM modulation—for frame 1 before initiating the same pipeline for frame 2. This results in idle periods for subsequent frames and severely limits throughput, particularly in high-data-rate scenarios.

To quantify the latency of each baseband module under traditional workflows, an IEEE 802.11ax-compliant Wi-Fi PHY system is constructed on an Intel i7-10700F platform using the C programming language.

As shown in Table 1, OFDM modulation and demodulation consume 0.332 ms and 0.327 ms, respectively, due to the computationally intensive IFFT/FFT operations. At the receiver, the decoding and descrambling stage dominates with a latency of 0.297 ms, primarily attributed to the iterative nature of Low-Density Parity-Check (LDPC) decoding. Overall, serial execution accumulates latency across multiple frames, failing to meet real-time demands in high-data-rate scenarios.

Table 1. Execution time of PHY modules

(a) Tx Side		(b) Rx Side	
Module	Runtime (ms)	Module	Runtime (ms)
Scrambling	0.007	Synchronization	0.311
Encoding	0.010	OFDM Demodulation	0.327
Interleaving	0.015	Channel Estimation and Equalization	0.062
Modulation	0.004	Demodulation and Deinterleaving	0.005
OFDM Modulation	0.332	Decoding and Descrambling	0.297

2.2   Module Suitability Analysis

Different signal processing modules exhibit varying computational demands. Control-intensive modules are suited to CPUs, while data-parallel ones benefit from GPU acceleration. Assigning tasks accordingly optimizes performance.

1) **Scrambling and Descrambling:** Scrambling enhances signal randomness by performing a bitwise XOR operation. This is an inherently sequential, control-intensive task well-suited for CPU execution.
2) **LDPC Encoding and Decoding:** LDPC coding adds redundancy for error correction and recovers data via iterative belief propagation, ensuring the parity condition $\mathbf{Q} \cdot \mathbf{r}^T = 0$ is met, where $\mathbf{Q}$ is the sparse parity-check matrix and $\mathbf{r}$ is the received codeword. These tasks typically rely on sequential logic, making them a good fit for the CPU, though optimized parallel algorithms can also leverage the GPU.

3) **Interleaving and Deinterleaving:** Interleaving uses a permutation function $\pi(i)$ to reorder coded symbols to mitigate burst errors, a process reversed by deinterleaving. This involves precise control over sequential memory access, making it a control-intensive task best executed on the CPU.

4) **Modulation and Demodulation:** Digital modulation maps bit groups to complex symbols (e.g., Quadrature Amplitude Modulation (QAM)), while demodulation reverses this mapping based on decision logic. As a result, they are inherently control-intensive and exhibit limited data-level parallelism, making them better suited for execution on the CPU.

5) **OFDM Modulation and Demodulation:** The core operations of OFDM modulation and demodulation involve IFFT and FFT, respectively, to convert between frequency- and time-domain signals. In modulation, IFFT transforms a frequency-domain symbol sequence $X[k]$, $k = 0, 1, \ldots, N - 1$, into a time-domain signal:

$$x[n] = \frac{1}{\sqrt{N}} \sum_{k=0}^{N-1} X[k] e^{j2\pi kn/N}, \quad n = 0, 1, \ldots, N - 1. \tag{1}$$

In demodulation, the FFT can reverse this process using the Cooley-Tukey algorithm, which decomposes an N-point FFT into sub-transforms via butterfly operations:

$$Y_m = y_m + W_N^r y_{m+N/2}, Y_{m+N/2} = y_m - W_N^r y_{m+N/2}, \tag{2}$$

where $W_N^r = e^{-j2\pi r/N}$ is the twiddle factor, y_m and $y_{m+N/2}$ are input samples, and m is the sub-transform index. Both IFFT and FFT rely on butterfly structures with high data parallelism—independent operations like butterfly computations and multiply-accumulates—making them ideal for GPU execution.

6) **Synchronization:** Receiver synchronization often computes the signal's autocorrelation function to find timing offsets:

$$R(\tau) = \sum_{n=0}^{L-1} r[n] \cdot r^*[n - \tau]. \tag{3}$$

The multiply-accumulate operations within the sum are independent across the index n, enabling highly parallel execution on a GPU.

7) **Channel Estimation and Equalization:** In OFDM systems, channel estimation computes the frequency response $H[k] = Y[k]/X[k]$ for each subcarrier by comparing received symbol $Y[k]$ with known ideal symbol $X[k]$. Equalization then adjusts $Y[k]$ to $\hat{S}[k] = Y[k]/H[k]$. With independent subcarrier calculations, this process is efficiently parallelized on GPUs.

To address the limitations of traditional serial processing and exploit the adaptability of modules across different platforms, a pipelined parallel approach can be employed to accelerate processing by allowing concurrent execution of different modules across multiple frames [13]. For example, in this approach, frame

1 undergoes OFDM modulation while frame 2 is undergoing modulation and frame 3 is performing interleaving, effectively overlapping operations and reducing the overall latency of the batched frames. This structure exploits inter-frame parallelism to maximize resource utilization and improve throughput relative to serial approaches. Based on an analysis of these limitations and module characteristics, the next section introduces a novel adaptive pipeline architecture.

3   Adaptive Pipeline Architecture Design

This section describes the pipeline parallel architecture based on a CPU-GPU heterogeneous platform in detail. By leveraging task partitioning and parallel scheduling, it fully exploits the synergistic processing capabilities of CPU and GPU to achieve efficient baseband processing.

As shown in Fig. 2, the proposed pipeline architecture divides the physical layer processing chain into multiple functional modules. Data frames flow through these modules in a pipeline manner, enabling inter-module parallel processing. When one module processes the current frame, the next frame can be processed simultaneously in the previous module, thereby significantly reducing overall latency. This task overlapping aligns with pipeline parallelism theory, where the effective latency for n frames is reduced to approximately the maximum module execution time plus $n - 1$ times the time between pipeline stages. This reduction occurs because multiple frames are processed concurrently to maximize throughput and minimize idle time.

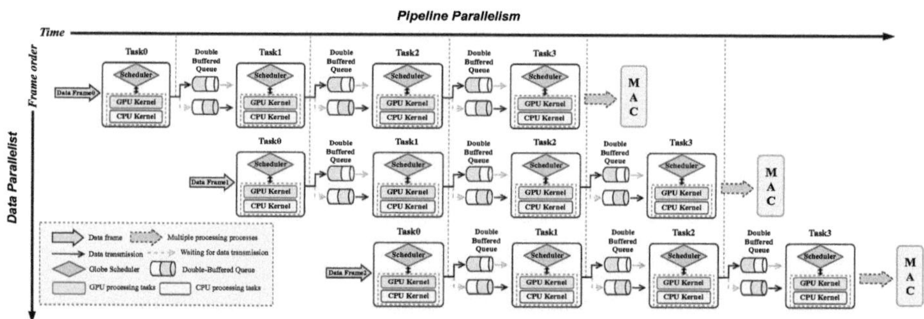

Fig. 2. CPU-GPU pipeline parallel architecture execution with control scheduling.

In the horizontal direction, the module-level pipeline allows different data frames to concurrently traverse various stages, substantially improving resource utilization and system throughput. To optimize inter-module data transfer, the architecture employs a double-buffered queue, alternating between computation and transmission to minimize total latency to $\max(T_{\text{compute}}, T_{\text{transfer}})$, effectively hiding data copy overhead. The buffer size is adaptively adjusted based on data frame size and module processing speed. For instance, it is increased in high-throughput scenarios to reduce queue blocking and decreased in low-latency scenarios to minimize memory usage. Additionally, zero-copy mechanisms (such as CUDA pinned memory) are integrated to achieve efficient data mapping between host and device. In high-frequency frame processing scenarios, a dedicated memory pool is allocated for zero-copy memory, with pre-allocated fixed-size memory blocks to reduce dynamic allocation overhead and further enhance transfer efficiency.

While the horizontal pipeline exploits inter-frame parallelism, real-time load variations and the diverse computational characteristics of PHY modules (as analyzed in Sect. 2.1) can lead to resource imbalances, such as overloading one processing unit while leaving the other idle. This inefficiency not only degrades overall throughput but also increases energy consumption in dynamic Wi-Fi scenarios. To address these challenges and ensure optimal resource allocation, the architecture extends support in the vertical direction for parallel processing of different frames within the same module using both CPU and GPU. As shown in Fig. 2, before the data frame enters each module, an adaptive decision algorithm combines real-time load and historical data to dynamically select the optimal computing resources for the current frame. For example, when the GPU is processing the previous frame in the same module (e.g., IFFT), if the GPU load is high while the CPU load is low, the global scheduler—implemented by the adaptive algorithm—assigns the current frame to the CPU for that module. This enables parallel processing of different frames within the same module using CPU and GPU, and maintains load balance through a priority-aware queue. For modules suitable for parallel computation (e.g., IFFT), optimized parallel algorithms are employed, such as utilizing the cuFFT library's batch processing functionality or CPU thread pools, to maximize computational efficiency.

To enable such load-aware dynamic scheduling, the adaptive decision algorithm presented in Algorithm 1 is introduced. It serves as the core of the global scheduler and addresses the need for intelligent, low-overhead resource allocation in heterogeneous environments.

The algorithm intelligently schedules CPU and GPU by comprehensively considering task complexity, real-time load, historical processing time, heterogeneous performance ratio, and energy consumption factors. The algorithm introduces weighted load factors W_{cpu} and W_{gpu}, which balance short-term utilization fluctuations and long-term performance trends using a historical weight β, thereby avoiding local biases in load evaluation. Meanwhile, estimated execution times $T_{\mathrm{exec,cpu}}$ and $T_{\mathrm{exec,gpu}}$ are calculated by multiplying module complexity C_{frame} with historical data. These estimates are used to update the heterogeneous performance ratio R_{hetero} as the execution time ratio to quantify relative efficiency of CPU and GPU for the current module and adapt to different computational characteristics. The adaptive adjustment of threshold Δ_{th} dynamically responds to load differences and heterogeneous performance via an adjustment factor α, ensuring that decisions favor more efficient resources. For example, when CPU load is lower and the heterogeneous ratio indicates slower GPU per-

---

Algorithm 1 Adaptive Decision Algorithm

Require: Current task complexity C_{frame}, CPU/GPU utilization U_{cpu}, U_{gpu}, module historical average processing time H_{cpu}, H_{gpu}, module heterogeneous performance ratio $R_{\text{hetero}} = \frac{H_{\text{gpu}}}{H_{\text{cpu}}}$, global energy consumption factors E_{cpu}, E_{gpu}, historical resource allocation record $\text{Device}_{\text{last}}$, T_{last}, threshold adjustment factor $\alpha \in (0, 1]$, historical weight $\beta \in [0, 1]$, base threshold $\Delta_{\text{th, base}} \in [0, 1]$, small bias $\epsilon \in [0, 0.1]$, δ is a hysteresis interval preventing frequent device switching.

Ensure: Selected computing resource $\text{Device}_{\text{selected}}$.

1: $A_{\text{cpu}} \leftarrow 1 - U_{\text{cpu}}$, $A_{\text{gpu}} \leftarrow 1 - U_{\text{gpu}}$
2: Weighted load factors:
  $W_{\text{cpu}} \leftarrow \beta H_{\text{cpu}} + (1 - \beta)U_{\text{cpu}}, W_{\text{gpu}} \leftarrow \beta H_{\text{gpu}} + (1 - \beta)U_{\text{gpu}}$
3: Estimated execution time:
  $T_{\text{exec,cpu}} \leftarrow C_{\text{frame}} \cdot H_{\text{cpu}}, \ T_{\text{exec,gpu}} \leftarrow C_{\text{frame}} \cdot H_{\text{gpu}}$
4: Update heterogeneous ratio: $R_{\text{hetero}} \leftarrow T_{\text{exec,gpu}}/T_{\text{exec,cpu}}$
5: **if** $W_{\text{cpu}} > W_{\text{gpu}}$ **then**
6:    $\Delta_{\text{th}} \leftarrow \Delta_{\text{th, base}}\big(1 + \alpha(W_{\text{cpu}} - W_{\text{gpu}} + R_{\text{hetero}} - 1)\big)$
7: **else if** $W_{\text{gpu}} > W_{\text{cpu}}$ **then**
8:    $\Delta_{\text{th}} \leftarrow \Delta_{\text{th, base}}\big(1 - \alpha(W_{\text{gpu}} - W_{\text{cpu}} + 1 - R_{\text{hetero}})\big)$
9: **else**
10:    $\Delta_{\text{th}} \leftarrow \Delta_{\text{th, base}}$
11: **end if**
12: $\Delta_{\text{th}} \leftarrow \max(0, \min(1, \Delta_{\text{th}}))$
13: Resource scores:
  $S_{\text{cpu}} \leftarrow \frac{A_{\text{cpu}}}{T_{\text{exec,cpu}} \cdot E_{\text{cpu}} + \epsilon}, \ S_{\text{gpu}} \leftarrow \frac{A_{\text{gpu}}}{T_{\text{exec,gpu}} \cdot E_{\text{gpu}} + \epsilon}$
14: **if** $S_{\text{cpu}} > S_{\text{gpu}} + \Delta_{\text{th}}$ **then**
15:    $\text{Device}_{\text{selected}} \leftarrow \text{CPU}$
16: **else**
17:    $\text{Device}_{\text{selected}} \leftarrow \text{GPU}$
18: **end if**
19: **if** $\text{Device}_{\text{selected}} \neq \text{Device}_{\text{last}}$ **and** $T_{\text{now}} - T_{\text{last}} < \delta$ **then**
20:    $\text{Device}_{\text{selected}} \leftarrow \text{Device}_{\text{last}}$
21: **end if**
22: $\text{Device}_{\text{last}} \leftarrow \text{Device}_{\text{selected}}, \ T_{\text{last}} \leftarrow T_{\text{now}}$
23: **return** $\text{Device}_{\text{selected}}$

---

formance, the threshold increases to prioritize CPU, and vice versa. This mechanism mitigates overhead from excessive switching and uses small bias ϵ to prevent division-by-zero errors or numerical instability in resource scores S_{cpu} and S_{gpu}. Resource scores integrate the availability $A_{\text{cpu}}/A_{\text{gpu}}$, execution time, and energy factors, aiming not only to minimize latency and maximize throughput but also to maintain energy efficiency. In the decision phase, the algorithm compares scores and applies the threshold for final selection. If the current decision differs from the previous one and the time interval is less than δ, the previous decision is retained to suppress context switching overhead caused by frequent changes. The adaptive decision algorithm has a time complexity of $O(1)$ per frame, as it involves constant-time operations for load factor calculation and threshold adjustment. Latency is minimized by pre-computing historical data offline, with real-time overhead under $1\,\mu s$. This ensures negligible impact on overall PHY latency while enabling dynamic allocation.

Furthermore, the pipeline architecture integrates error detection and recovery mechanisms to ensure system stability. In the event of a module processing failure (e.g., GPU computation errors), the scheduler automatically redirects the frame to alternative available resources (e.g., CPU) or discards it if recovery is not feasible, while logging error details and updating historical load data to optimize subsequent task scheduling. Additionally, to further enhance energy efficiency, the architecture employs dynamic voltage and frequency scaling mechanisms, which proactively reduce GPU frequency during low-load scenarios, thereby effectively lowering power consumption.

In summary, the proposed architecture maximizes the parallel potential of heterogeneous platforms through task scheduling and data partitioning, achieving substantial improvements in both computational efficiency and throughput for Wi-Fi PHY layer processing.

4   Experimental Evaluation

4.1   Experimental Setup

To evaluate the proposed architecture, experiments are conducted on two heterogeneous platforms: (1) Intel i7-10700F CPU (8 cores, 16 threads, up to $4.8\,\text{GHz}$) with NVIDIA GTX 1650 SUPER GPU (4 GB GDDR6); (2) AMD Ryzen 9 9950X3D CPU (16 cores, 32 threads, up to $5.7\,\text{GHz}$) with NVIDIA RTX 5090 GPU (32 GB GDDR7). Both platforms utilize two Universal Software Radio Peripheral (USRP) B210 radios for realistic wireless channels under IEEE 802.11ax. To decouple computational performance from fluctuations in wireless link quality, all experiments are conducted under stable, high signal-to-noise ratio channel conditions. This ensures that the measured performance metrics, such as latency and throughput, accurately reflect the computational efficiency of the processing architecture itself.

The compared schemes include: (1) CPU-Only Serial Processing; (2) CPU-Only Pipeline, where all modules are processed on the CPU; (3) GPU-Only Pipeline, where all modules are processed on the GPU; and (4) Collaborative Parallel Pipeline. In the experimental setup, a baseline of serial processing using the GPU only was not included because this paper focuses on demonstrating the advantages of heterogeneous CPU-GPU parallelism over traditional CPU-centric baseline processing. Additionally, preliminary performance analysis indicates that GPU serial processing data requires frequent copying between host memory and device memory via the PCIe bus, resulting in significant data transfer overhead. The evaluation metrics consist of: average throughput (Mbps), defined as the amount of data successfully transmitted per unit time; average PHY latency for 100 frames (ms), which captures the average total processing time for 100 frames from generation at the Tx to demodulation at the Rx, computed by averaging multiple measurements, and average power consumption (W), measured as the average energy consumption during system operation.

The experimental setup includes continuous transmission tests for each configuration, lasting over 60 s (more than 100 data frames), repeated five times to compute mean values and ensure statistical reliability. Latency measurements employ CUDA events for GPU kernels (ns resolution), Read Time-Stamp Counter (RDTSC) for CPU tasks, and USRP-synchronized clocks for end-to-end PHY latency ($<1\,\mu s$ accuracy), avoiding CPU timer inaccuracies. The channel sampling rate is set to 20 MHz, using 16-QAM modulation and a 5/6 LDPC coding rate. The raw input data length is 1024 bits, and after zero-padding, channel encoding, and modulation, the final data frame length is determined by the selected modulation scheme and coding rate. The software implementation is developed using C++ and CUDA 11.2, with GPU and CPU power consumption recorded in real-time via the NVIDIA System Management Interface and Intel Power Gadget, enabling a comprehensive analysis of system energy efficiency. The system is equipped with 32 GB DDR4 RAM to handle memory-intensive tasks, and the USRP devices are calibrated to a synchronization accuracy within $1\mu s$ to minimize latency measurement errors.

4.2 Key Results

Figure 3 presents the experimental results of the four schemes on two platforms under standardized test conditions. It is important to clarify that the evaluation in this section focuses on verifying the effectiveness of the dynamic scheduling algorithm on general-purpose processors (CPU+GPU), so no direct comparison is made with dedicated hardware (such as FPGA/DSP) with very different design concepts and implementation methods. In Fig. 3, "Throughput (Mbps)" corresponds to the average throughput (Mbps), "Latency (ms)" corresponds to the average total PHY latency for 100 frames (ms), and "Power Consumption (W)" corresponds to the average total power consumption (W).

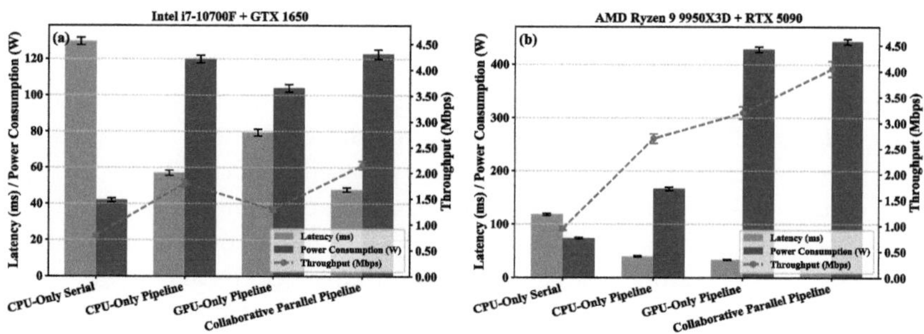

Fig. 3. Performance comparison of schemes.

The results are averaged over five runs, with standard deviations below 5% and 95% confidence intervals confirming statistical reliability. The results demonstrate the overall superiority of pipeline mechanisms, particularly the proposed collaborative parallel pipeline scheme, in enhancing system performance across multiple metrics. Specifically, the CPU-Only and GPU-Only pipeline schemes significantly outperform the CPU-Only serial processing architecture in throughput and latency, validating the effectiveness of pipeline mechanisms in mitigating serial bottlenecks and accelerating task execution. Building on this, the collaborative scheme achieves even greater optimization, with an average throughput of 2.15 Mbps (a 172.15% improvement) and total PHY latency reduced to 47.63 ms (a 63.26% improvement) at 122.50 W power on Intel, scaling to 4.05 Mbps (a 326.32% improvement) and 27.8 ms (a 76.54% improvement) at 443.00 W on AMD. The AMD platform achieves significant throughput improvements through more intensive task partitioning, but at the cost of higher power consumption due to the increased computational intensity. Nevertheless, the overall efficiency remains balanced due to the architecture's optimization of resource allocation, which minimizes unnecessary overhead. The performance gains are primarily attributed to the scheme's ability to fully leverage the complementary computational characteristics of CPU and GPU resources, effectively reducing resource idleness and enhancing processing efficiency through rational task partitioning and maximized parallelism.

To further analyze the resource utilization efficiency of each scheme, this study monitors the CPU and GPU usage trends of the four architectures over a 60-s period, with the results presented in Fig. 4. The results show that architectures employing pipeline parallelism significantly enhance overall resource utilization compared to CPU-Only serial processing, which exhibits substantial

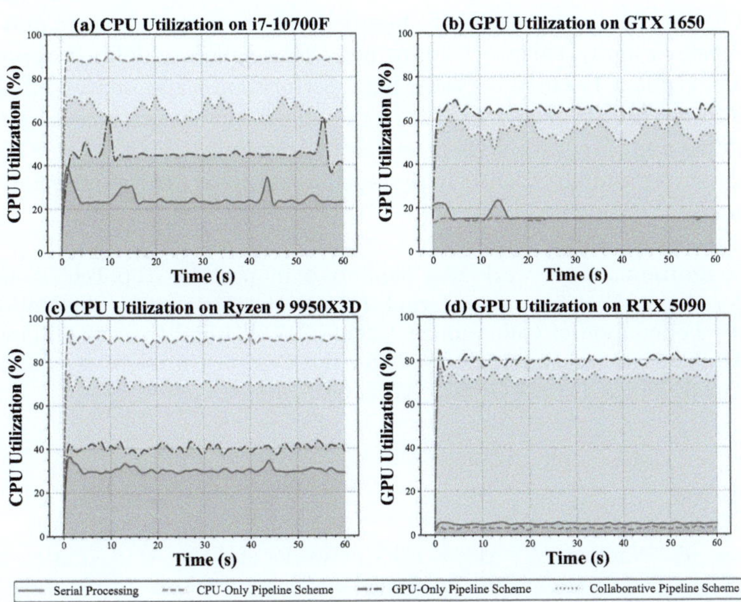

Fig. 4. Resource utilization over 60 s for different schemes.

underutilization of GPU resources and inefficient CPU engagement. Pipeline-based schemes mitigate these limitations by enabling concurrent task execution, thereby reducing resource idleness and alleviating sequential processing bottlenecks. Among these, the proposed collaborative parallel pipeline scheme achieves the most effective synergy, with both CPU and GPU utilization exceeding 50%, ensuring balanced workload distribution across heterogeneous resources. Furthermore, on the AMD Ryzen 9 9950X3D + RTX 5090 platform, CPU and GPU utilizations respectively reach 80% and 75%, with smoother trends and lower idleness, demonstrating the architecture's scalability on high-end hardware leveraging advanced memory hierarchies and enhanced parallelism. This coordinated approach not only optimizes computational efficiency but also reduces the likelihood of single-resource bottlenecks, leading to improved system throughput, reduced processing latency, and enhanced energy efficiency.

5   Conclusion

This work designed a CPU–GPU collaborative processing architecture driven by a dynamic adaptive scheduling algorithm for the PHY processing of wireless communication systems, such as IEEE 802.11ax. The proposed approach achieves significant performance improvements on a mid-range Intel platform, with a 172.15% increase in throughput and a 63.26% reduction in latency; on a high-end AMD system, it further achieves a 326.32% throughput gain and a 76.54% latency reduction, demonstrating both robustness and scalability. These results validate the effectiveness of the intelligent scheduling mechanism, which fully exploits CPU–GPU heterogeneity to handle both compute-intensive and control-intensive tasks. Finally, this work confirmed that a software-defined approach can achieve an excellent balance between high performance and energy efficiency on general-purpose hardware. Future research will extend this architecture to multi-GPU systems and integrate dedicated accelerators such as DSPs and FPGAs to further enhance parallelism and energy optimization for next-generation wireless communication systems.

Acknowledgement. This work was supported in part by Top-Ten Technological Projects for Hunan Province under Grant 2025QK1009, in part by the National Natural Science Foundation of China under Grant 62171474 and Grant 62371180, and in part by the Fundamental Research Funds for the Central Universities of China under Grant JZ2024HGTG0311 and Grant PA2024GDSK0114.

References

1. Chataut, R., Nankya, M., Akl, R.: 6G networks and the AI revolution-exploring technologies, applications, and emerging challenges. Sensors **24**(6), 1888 (2024)
2. Adame, T., Carrascosa-Zamacois, M., Bellalta, B.: Time-sensitive networking in IEEE 802.11 be: On the way to low-latency WIFI 7. Sensors, vol. 21, no. 15, pp. 4954 (2021)

3. Amin, R., Reisslein, M., Shah, N.: Hybrid SDN networks: a survey of existing approaches. IEEE Commun. Surv. Tutor. **20**(4), 3259–3306 (2018)
4. Polese, M., Bonati, L., Doro, S., Basagni, S., Melodia, T.: Understanding O-RAN: architecture, interfaces, algorithms, security, and research challenges. IEEE Commun. Surv. Tutor. **25**(2), 1376–1411 (2023)
5. Azariah, W., Bimo, F.A., Lin, C.-W., Cheng, R.-G., Nikaein, N., Jana, R.: A survey on open radio access networks: challenges, research directions, and open source approaches. Sensors **24**(3), 1038 (2024)
6. Santos, J., Wauters, T., Volckaert, B., De Turck, F.: Towards low-latency service delivery in a continuum of virtual resources: state-of-the-art and research directions. IEEE Commun. Surv. Tutor. **23**(4), 2557–2589 (2021)
7. Gokalgandhi, B., Segerholm, C., Paul, N., Seskar, I.: Accelerating channel estimation and demodulation of uplink OFDM symbols for large scale antenna systems using GPU. In: 2019 International Conference on Computing, Networking and Communications (ICNC), pp. 955–959 (2019)
8. Ding, B., Liu, J., Wu, H., Wang, T.: GPLM: an 802.11 AC-capable low-MAC architecture for FPGA-based SDR systems. In: 2019 IEEE Wireless Communications and Networking Conference (WCNC), pp. 1–7. IEEE (2019)
9. Jiao, X., Liu, W., Mehari, M., Aslam, M., Moerman, I.: OpenWIFI: a free and open-source IEEE802.11 SDR implementation on SoC. In: 2020 IEEE 91st Vehicular Technology Conference (VTC2020-Spring), pp. 1–2. IEEE (2020)
10. Georgis, G., Thanos, A., Filo, M., Nikitopoulos, K.: A DSP acceleration framework for software-defined radios on X86 64. In: ICASSP 2020-2020 IEEE International Conference on Acoustics, Speech and Signal Processing (ICASSP), pp. 1648–1652. IEEE (2020)
11. NVIDIA Corporation. NVIDIA cuPHY: GPU-accelerated 5G L1 stack (2024). https://docs.nvidia.com/aerial/aerial-cuphy/current/text/cuphy.html. Accessed 20 Apr 2025
12. IEEE Standard for Information Technology-Telecommunications and Information Exchange between Systems Local and Metropolitan Area Networks-Specific Requirements Part 11: Wireless LAN Medium Access Control (MAC) and Physical Layer (PHY) Specifications Amendment 1: Enhancements for High-Efficiency WLAN. IEEE Std 802.11ax-2021 (Amendment to IEEE Std 802.11-2020), pp. 1–767 (2021)
13. Flynn, M.J.: Computer Architecture: Pipelined and Parallel Processor Design. Jones & Bartlett Publishers (1995)

HBD-CE: Efficient Cross-HBD Communication for LLM Training in High-Bandwidth Domain Cluster via Hierarchical Collectives

Huihuang Qin, Shuangwu Chen(✉), Zijian Wen, Zian Wang, Ziyang Zou, Tao Zhang, Xiaobin Tan, and Jian Yang

University of Science and Technology of China, Hefei, China
chensw@ustc.edu.cn

Abstract. Large language model(LLM) training relies on multiple parallel strategies, where high-bandwidth domains (HBDs) play a key role in enabling efficient communication between NPUs. Compared to intra-HBD communication, cross-HBD communication is significantly slower and remains unavoidable due to limited HBD sizes and different model partitioning strategies. Hierarchical collectives can reduce cross-HBD communication overhead, but their effectiveness is hindered by imbalanced parallel group distribution across HBDs, different communication costs with different distribution patterns, and interdependencies among parallelism strategies. To address these challenges, we propose HBD-CE, a model placement scheme designed for communication-efficient cross-HBD LLM training in HBD clusters, which optimizes model placement to enhance cross-HBD communication efficiency. We formulate the model placement problem as a mixed-integer nonlinear programming (MINLP) problem. By leveraging the properties of hierarchical collectives, we transform the MINLP into a series of 0–1 integer linear programming (ILP) problems and develop an exact algorithm to solve them. Experiment results demonstrate that HBD-CE can reduce per-iteration communication time by 5%–77.3% across diverse topologies and model configurations.

Keywords: LLM Training · High-Bandwidth Domain · Hierarchical Collectives · Model Placement

1 Introduction

Large Language Model (LLM) training relies on multiple parallel strategies [3,12], including tensor parallelism (TP), expert parallelism (EP), context parallelism (CP), data parallelism (DP), and pipeline parallelism (PP). While these techniques enable the training of increasingly larger models, they also incur substantial inter-NPU communication, which has gradually become a major bottleneck in LLM training. To improve communication efficiency, modern NPU

© IFIP International Federation for Information Processing 2026
Published by Springer Nature Switzerland AG 2026
X. Wang et al. (Eds.): NPC 2025, LNCS 16306, pp. 266–277, 2026.
https://doi.org/10.1007/978-3-032-10466-3_22

clusters incorporate high-bandwidth domains (HBDs) [14], such as the superpod in Nvidia NVL-576 [8] and the supernode [16] in Ascend. Within an HBD, the communication latency between NPUs located on different nodes is comparable to that within a single node. However, due to variations in model parameters and the limited size of HBDs, cross-HBD communication remains unavoidable. To reduce the cross-HBD communication overhead, prior work [2,10] has explored hierarchical collectives, which seek to reduce the frequency of cross-HBD operations in collective communication.

However, directly applying hierarchical collective communication to cross-HBD scenarios presents several challenges. First, an uneven distribution of NPUs across HBDs within a parallel group reduces the efficiency of hierarchical communication; thus, a balanced distribution of NPUs within a parallel group is generally required [5]. Second, even with balanced distribution, communication costs vary depending on the distribution pattern: the fewer HBDs a parallel group spans, the higher the achievable efficiency. Finally, different parallelisms are inherently interdependent, and optimizing one type may inadvertently increase the communication cost of others.

Fortunately, these challenges can be addressed through optimizing model placement, i.e., strategically mapping the model's logical partitions onto physical NPUs to improve cross-HBD communication efficiency. To this end, we propose HBD-CE, a model placement scheme designed for communication-efficient cross-HBD LLM training in HBD clusters. HBD-CE jointly considers multiple parallel strategies and their associated hierarchical collective communications, with the objective of minimizing per-iteration communication time. The main contributions of this work are as follows:

- We formulate the model placement problem for LLM training with hierarchical collectives in HBD clusters as a mixed-integer nonlinear programming (MINLP) problem. The formulation accounts for multiple parallel strategies and bandwidth asymmetry between intra-HBD and cross-HBD communications, aiming to minimize per-iteration communication time.
- We develop an exact algorithm to solve the problem. By leveraging the properties of hierarchical collective communication, we transform the MINLP into a series of 0–1 integer linear programming (ILP) problems.
- We evaluate HBD-CE across diverse network topologies and model configurations. Experimental results demonstrate it can reduce per-iteration communication time by 5%–77.3%.

2   Related Works

2.1   Hierarchical Collectives

Hierarchical collective communication has been shown to improve the efficiency of cross-node communication and has been extensively employed in deep learning systems. Mikami et al. [6] introduce 2D-Torus all-reduce, which arranges GPUs in a logical 2D grid and performs a sequence of collective operations along different

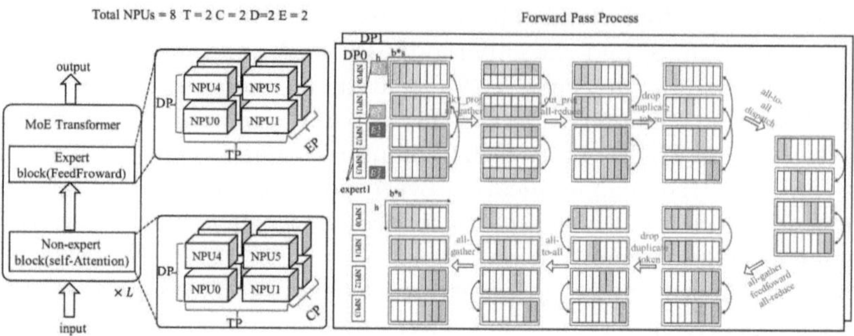

Fig. 1. Hybrid parallelism based LLM training. The rectangles in the forward pass process indicate the data tensors.

dimensions. BlueConnect [1] implements hierarchical all-reduce on multi-tier networks by decomposing a single all-reduce operation into numerous parallelizable reduce-scatter and all-gather operations. Khorassani et al. [4] propose locality-aware and adaptive schemes for hierarchical All-to-All collective communication on large-scale dense GPU systems. DeepSpeed-MoE [10] introduces hierarchical all-to-all as a two-step process, incorporating data-layout transformations to reduce the number of communication hops. However, these approaches focus on a single type of collective communication and overlook the impact of parallel group distribution on communication efficiency in HBD clusters.

2.2   Model Placement

There is a lot of work to improve communication efficiency by optimizing the mapping of logical partitions to physical NPUs, i.e., through model placement. Megatron-LM [7] and Megatron-Scale [3] confine TP within a single node and prioritize forming DP groups over PP groups to minimize DP communication across Pods. Metis [13] prioritizes DP over TP within pipeline stages to leverage DP's superior trade-off between computation and communication. Param [9] explores the placement of EP and Expert-Sharding Parallelism (ESP) groups under varying scenarios. InfiniteHBD [11] accounts for the impact of TP group scheduling on DP traffic allocation and proposes a TP Orchestration algorithm to reduce cross-ToR traffic. Nonetheless, these studies do not address the reduction of cross-HBD communication overhead via hierarchical collective communication.

3   Background

Hybrid Parallelism Based Model Training: As illustrated in Fig. 1, the non-expert block employs TP, DP, and CP, whereas the expert block utilizes TP, EP, and DP. Let T, C, and E denote the degrees of TP, CP, and EP parallelism, respectively, and let D and $\tilde{D}$ represent the DP degrees of the expert and non-expert blocks, respectively. These degrees satisfy $T \times C \times D = T \times E \times \tilde{D}$.

The forward pass process is as follows: assume that the input x at each iteration has the shape $[b, s]$, where b denotes the micro-batch size and s is the sequence length. With CP, each NPU receives a tensor of shape $[b, s/C]$. After passing through the projections of Q,K,V the resulting tensors have the shape $[b, s/C, h/T]$. To compute attention scores, an all-gather operation is first performed within the CP group to assemble the complete K and V sequences, followed by an all-reduce within the TP group to aggregate the attention outputs. Upon entering the expert block, a routing mechanism assigns tokens to experts. Each TP group then drops redundant activations, reshaping the input to $[b, s/(C \cdot T), h]$, and performs an all-to-all within the EP group to dispatch tokens to their experts. Since TP requires full activations, an all-gather is performed within the TP group. After expert computation, the TP group performs an all-reduce, drops redundant activations, and a second all-to-all within the EP group returns tokens to their original NPUs. Finally, another all-gather within the TP group collects the full activations. The backward pass follows the same process, except the CP group replaces all-gather with reduce-scatter.

Prior studies [3,7] have shown that TP generates the highest communication volume among all parallelism strategies. To avoid the high overhead caused by TP cross-node communication, each TP group is typically placed within a single node; that is, NPUs $\{t \cdot T, \ldots, (t + 1) \cdot T - 1\}$ are located on the same node. In contrast, communication in EP, CP, and DP generally involves cross-node or even cross-HBD transfers.

4   System Model

4.1   System Overview

As shown in Fig. 2, we consider MoE model training with hybrid parallelism in an HBD cluster. The MoE model is divided into small segments, each consisting of consecutive layers and running on a single NPU. In the cluster, each HBD is dedicated to a single LLM training task, and an MoE task typically spans multiple HBDs. A key problem is mapping the model's logical partitions to physical NPUs.

In this cluster, each node contains 8 NPUs connected via high-bandwidth interconnects (HBI), and a fixed number of nodes form an HBD. Intra-HBD communication uses HBI, which provides over 400 GB/s of unidirectional bandwidth, while cross-HBD communication relies on RDMA links with 400 Gbps unidirectional bandwidth, making it a bottleneck. To leverage the high bandwidth and low latency of intra-HBD communication, communication-intensive parallelisms such as TP, EP, and CP are typically confined within a single HBD. As different models require various degrees of parallelism, these communication-intensive parallelisms inevitably span multiple HBDs.

To improve cross-HBD communication efficiency, hierarchical collective communication is adopted. The basic idea is to reduce the number of cross-HBD

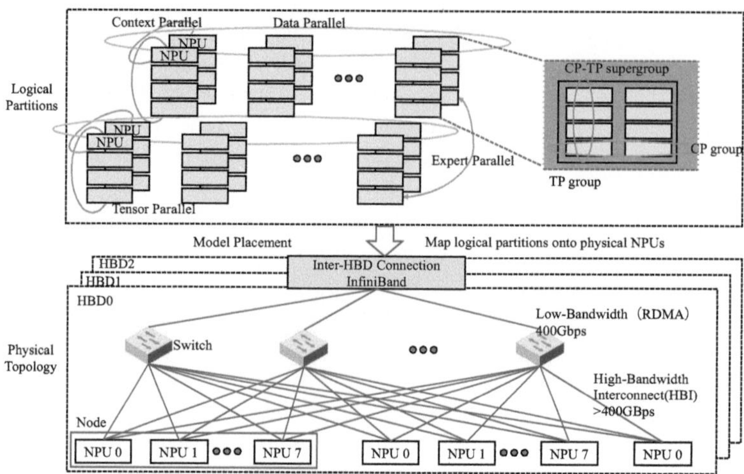

Fig. 2. An overview of model placement in an HBD cluster.

communication phases in collective operations. Due to hardware and software constraints, the hierarchical collectives are only applicable when a parallel group is evenly distributed across HBDs. In practice, the distribution of parallel groups often varies, resulting in different communication costs. Some groups are entirely within an HBD and achieve the fastest performance; some are evenly spread and benefit from hierarchical collectives; others rely on non-hierarchical communication and are the slowest. In such cases, the overall communication time is determined by the slowest group. Therefore, optimizing model placement is essential to minimize communication overhead.

Since expert blocks contain far more parameters than non-expert blocks, the DP of non-expert blocks is not considered. As shown in Fig. 2, CP involves C NPUs, each belonging to a different TP group. These C TP groups form a TP-CP supergroup, which performs the all-gather and reduce-scatter operations of CP. Similarly, we define TP-EP and TP-DP supergroups. Therefore, cross-HBD communication overhead arises from the communication within TP-CP, TP-EP, and TP-DP supergroups. Next, we analyze the time cost of TP-CP, TP-EP, and TP-DP communication.

4.2 Time Cost Model

To model the time costs of these collective operations within a single HBD and cross-HBD, we adopt the standard $\alpha + n\beta$ model. Let α_1 and α_2 denote the fixed latencies of the HBI and RDMA links, respectively, and let B_1 and B_2 represent their respective bandwidths.

All-Gather Time Cost: The all-gather operation is performed among the C TP groups within each TP-CP supergroup. Let $\mathbf{p}^c$ denote the distribution of these TP groups across the J HBDs, where $\sum_j \mathbf{p}_j^c = C$. The data block size for all-gather is $m^c = b \cdot \frac{s}{C} \cdot \frac{h}{T}$. When all C TP groups reside within a single HBD, the communication time is:

$$\phi^{ag}(\mathbf{p}^c) = (C-1)(\alpha_1 + m^c \cdot \beta_1), \exists \mathbf{p}_j^c = C. \tag{1}$$

In the case where TP groups are unevenly distributed across HBDs, each phase is dominated by cross-HBD transmissions via RDMA links, yielding $\phi^{ag}(\mathbf{p}^c) = (C-1)(\alpha_2 + m^c \cdot \beta_2)$. When C TP groups are evenly distributed, a hierarchical all-gather is adopted, consisting of two steps: an intra-HBD all-gather within each HBD and an inter-HBD all-gather across HBDs. The total time is:

$$\phi^{ag}(\mathbf{p}^c) = (p'-1)(\alpha_1 + m^c \cdot \beta_1) + (C/p'-1)(\alpha_2$$
$$+ m^c \cdot p' \cdot \beta_2), \mathbf{p}_j^c = p' \neq C \text{ or } \mathbf{p}_j^c = 0. \tag{2}$$

All-to-all Time Cost: Let $\mathbf{p}^e$ denote the distribution of TP groups within a TP-EP supergroup. The data block size in the all-to-all operation is $m^e = b \cdot \frac{s}{C} \cdot \frac{h}{T} \cdot k \cdot f$. When all E TP groups are located within a single HBD, the communication time is:

$$\phi^{aa}(\mathbf{p}^e) = (E-1)(\alpha_1 + m^e \cdot \beta_1/E), \exists \mathbf{p}_j^e = E. \tag{3}$$

In the case where TP groups are unevenly distributed, the corresponding communication time is $\phi^{aa}(\mathbf{p}^e) = (E-1)(\alpha_2 + m^e \cdot \beta_2/E)$. When the E TP groups are evenly distributed, a hierarchical all-to-all is applied. According to [10], the communication cost is:

$$\phi^{aa}(\mathbf{p}^e) = (p'-1)(\alpha_1 + m^e \cdot \beta_1/p') + (E/p'-1)(\alpha_2$$
$$+ m^e \cdot p' \cdot \beta_2/E), \mathbf{p}_j^e = p' \neq E \text{ or } \mathbf{p}_j^e = 0. \tag{4}$$

All-Reduce Time Cost: Let $\mathbf{p}^d$ denote the distribution of TP groups within a TP-EP supergroup. The data block size in all-reduce is m^d, which depends on the specific model. When TP groups reside within a single HBD, the time cost is:

$$\phi^{ar}(\mathbf{p}^d) = 2(\tilde{D}-1)(\alpha_1 + m^d \cdot \beta_1/\tilde{D}), \exists \mathbf{p}_j^d = \tilde{D} \tag{5}$$

In the case where TP groups are unevenly distributed across multiple HBDs, the communication time becomes $\phi^{ar}(\mathbf{p}^d) = 2(\tilde{D}-1)(\alpha_2 + m^d\beta_2/\tilde{D})$. When $\tilde{D}$ TP groups are evenly distributed across multiple HBDs, the hierarchical all-reduce is adopted, consisting of three steps: intra-HBD reduce-scatter, inter-HBD all-reduce, and intra-HBD all-gather. The resulting communication time is:

$$\phi^{ar}(\mathbf{p}^d) = 2(p'-1)(\alpha_1 + m^e \cdot \beta_1/p') + 2(\tilde{D}/p'-1)(\alpha_2$$
$$+ m^e \cdot \beta_2/\tilde{D}), \mathbf{p}_j^d = p' \neq \tilde{D} \text{ or } \mathbf{p}_j^d = 0. \tag{6}$$

4.3   Problem Formulation

Suppose the MoE training task is distributed across J HBDs, each containing L nodes. We define a binary variable $x_{i,j}$, where $x_{i,j} = 1$ indicates that TP group i is placed in HBD j. During model placement, the following constraints must be satisfied:

- **C1:** Each TP group must be placed in one HBD, that is $\sum_j x_{i,j} = 1, \forall i$.
- **C2:** There is HBD capacity constraint, that is $\sum_i x_{i,j} \leq L, \forall j$.

The communication time of CP, EP, and DP depends on how the corresponding supergroups are distributed across HBDs. To capture this distribution, we first define TP group affiliation matrices M^c, M^e, and M^d, which indicate the membership of each TP group in the TP-CP, TP-EP, and TP-DP supergroups, respectively. For instance, $M^c_{i,j} = 1$ if TP group i belongs to TP-CP supergroup j, and 0 otherwise. Using these affiliation matrices, the supergroup distribution matrices are computed as

$$A^c = (M^c)^T X, A^e = (M^e)^T X, A^d = (M^d)^T X. \tag{7}$$

Each row of A^c, A^e, and A^d represents the distribution of a TP-CP, TP-EP, and TP-DP supergroup across HBDs, respectively.

The communication time of a collective operation is determined by the slowest supergroup involved. For CP, the time cost of the u_1-th TP-CP supergroup is $\phi^{ar}(A^c_{u_1,:})$. Thus, the communication time of a single collective operation in CP is $\max_{u_1} \phi^{ar}(A^c_{u_1,:})$. During each training iteration, for every micro-batch, each TP–CP supergroup performs one all-gather per layer in the forward pass, and both an all-gather and a reduce-scatter per layer in the backward pass. Consequently, the total communication time for CP in one iteration is $\tau^c = 3 \cdot n \cdot l \cdot \max_{u_1} \phi^{ag}(A^c_{u_1,:})$.

Similarly, the time cost of a single all-to-all operation is $\max_{u_2} \phi^{aa}(A^e_{u_2,:})$. Each TP-EP supergroup performs two all-to-all operations per layer during the forward pass and four per layer during the backward pass. Thus, the total communication time for EP is $\tau^e = 6 \cdot n \cdot l \cdot \max_{u_2} \phi^{aa}(A^e_{u_2,:})$. Each TP-DP supergroup performs one all-reduce operation after all the micro-batches are processed. The corresponding communication time for DP is $\tau^d = \max_{u_3} \phi^{ar}(A^d_{u_3,:})$. Therefore, the minimization problem of cross-HBD communication time is mathematically formulated as:

$$\mathbf{P1} : \min_x \; \Phi(x) = \tau^c + \tau^e + \tau^d,$$

$$\text{s.t.} (C1), (C2). \tag{8}$$

5   Exact Algorithm

5.1   Objective Value Enumeration

Problem **P1** is non-convex and NP-hard, making exact optimization computationally intractable. From the definition of $\phi^{ag}(\mathbf{p}^c)$, its behavior falls into three cases: *1)* If the TP–CP supergroup is entirely within one HBD, $\phi^{ag}(\mathbf{p}^c)$ is a constant. *2)* Similarly, when the supergroup is distributed unevenly across multiple HBDs, the value is still a constant, regardless of the specific distribution. *3)* If the supergroup is evenly distributed across multiple HBDs, the value of $\phi^{ag}(\mathbf{p}^c)$ depends on an integer p' satisfying $p' \neq C$ and $p' \mid C$. The number of such valid p' is finite and each yields a distinct value $\phi^{ag}(\mathbf{p}^c)$. Thus, the function can take at most $2\sqrt{C}$ different values. By the same reasoning, $\phi^{aa}(\mathbf{p}^e)$ and $\phi^{ar}(\mathbf{p}^d)$ can take at most $2\sqrt{E}$ and $2\sqrt{\tilde{D}}$ values, respectively.

To enumerate all possible values of $\phi^{ag}(\mathbf{p}^c)$, $\phi^{aa}(\mathbf{p}^e)$, and $\phi^{ar}(\mathbf{p}^d)$, let $\mathcal{F}_C$, $\mathcal{F}_E$, and $\mathcal{F}_{\tilde{D}}$ be the sets of integer divisors of C, E and $\tilde{D}$, respectively. For each $c_k \in \mathcal{F}_C$, we construct a TP-CP supergroup distribution $\mathbf{p}^c(c_k)$ such that $\mathbf{p}^c(c_k) \in \{0, c_k\}^C, \|\mathbf{p}^c(c_k)\|_0 = C/c_k, c_k \neq 1$. It represents a supergroup either co-located on one HBD or evenly distributed across multiple HBDs. The case $c_k = 1$ represents a non-uniform distribution. Since $\phi^{ag}(\mathbf{p}^c(c_k))$ depends only on c_k, its value set $\{\phi^{ag}(\mathbf{p}^c(c_k))\}$ has size at most $2\sqrt{C}$. Similarly, we construct the TP-EP and TP-DP supergroup distributions as $\mathbf{p}^e(e_k) \in \{0, e_k\}^E, \|\mathbf{p}^e(e_k)\|_0 = E/e_k, e_k \neq 1, \mathbf{p}^d(d_k) \in \{0, d_k\}^C, \|\mathbf{p}^d(d_k)\|_0 = \tilde{D}/d_k, d_k \neq 1$, where $e_k = 1$ and $d_k = 1$ representing non-uniform distributions.

Let $\max_{u_1} \phi^{ag}(A^c_{u_1,:}) = \phi^{ag}(\mathbf{p}^c(c_k))$, $\max_{u_2} \phi^{aa}(A^e_{u_2,:}) = \phi^{aa}(\mathbf{p}^e(e_k))$ and $\max_{u_3} \phi^{ar}(A^d_{u_3,:}) = \phi^{ar}(\mathbf{p}^d(d_k))$. It follows that the number of distinct values that τ^c, τ^e, and τ^d can take is at most $2\sqrt{C}$, $2\sqrt{E}$, and $2\sqrt{D}$, respectively. We then define:

$$\Psi = \{\Phi_k = 3nl \cdot \phi^{ag}(\mathbf{p}^c(c_k)) + 6nl \cdot \phi^{aa}(\mathbf{p}^e(e_k)) + \phi^{ar}(\mathbf{p}^d(d_k))\}. \qquad (9)$$

Thus, all possible values of $\Phi(x)$ lie in Ψ, with $|\Psi| \leq 8\sqrt{C \cdot E \cdot \tilde{D}}$.

5.2   ILP-Based Feasibility Check

Since the set of possible values of $\Phi(x)$, Ψ, is finite, we can sort it in ascending order as $\Psi' = (\Phi_1, \Phi_2, \cdots, \Phi_K), \Phi_1 < \Phi_2 < \cdots < \Phi_K$. Each Φ_k corresponds to a triplet (c_k, e_k, d_k). To solve **P1**, we can iterate over Φ_k and check whether there exists an placement $x_{i,j}$ satisfying $\Phi(x) = \Phi_k$. The first feasible Φ_k corresponds to the optimal value of **P1**.

If the condition $\max_{u_1} \phi^{ag}(A^c_{u_1,:}) = \phi^{ag}(\mathbf{p}^c(c_k))$, $\max_{u_2} \phi^{aa}(A^e_{u_2,:}) = \phi^{aa}(\mathbf{p}^e(e_k))$ and $\max_{u_3} \phi^{ar}(A^d_{u_3,:}) = \phi^{ar}(\mathbf{p}^d(d_k))$ holds, then we have $\Phi(x) = \Phi_k$. For the first condition, this means that the slowest TP–CP supergroup must follow the distribution$\mathbf{p}^c(c_k)$. From the definition of $\phi^{ag}(\mathbf{p}^c)$, we have $\phi^{ag}(\mathbf{p}^c(C)) > \cdots \phi^{ag}(\mathbf{p}^c(c_k)) > \phi^{ag}(\mathbf{p}^c(1))$. Therefore, $\max_{u_1} \phi^{ag}(A^c_{u_1,:}) = \phi^{ag}(\mathbf{p}^c(c_k))$ is equivalent to requiring all TP-CP parallel supergroups adopt one of the distribution in $\{\mathbf{p}^c(C), \cdots, \mathbf{p}^c(c_k)\}$. Similarly, the same properties hold for $\phi^{aa}(\mathbf{p}^e)$ and $\phi^{ar}(\mathbf{p}^d)$. Hence, $\max_{u_2} \phi^{aa}(A^e_{u_2,:}) = \phi^{aa}(\mathbf{p}^e(e_k))$ and $\max_{u_3} \phi^{ar}(A^d_{u_3,:}) = \phi^{ar}(\mathbf{p}^d(d_k))$ holds if and only if all TP-EP supergroups follow a distribution in $\{\mathbf{p}^e(E), \cdots, \mathbf{p}^e(e_k)\}$, and all TP-DP supergroups follow a distribution in $\{\mathbf{p}^d(\tilde{D}), \cdots, \mathbf{p}^d(d_k)\}$.

Algorithm 1: Algorithm for solving **P1**.

  Input: TP group affiliation matrices M^c, M^e, M^d
  Output: Optimal model placement solution $x_{i,j}$
1 Compute supergroup distribution matrices A^c, A^e, A^d according to Eq. (7);
2 Construct Ψ According to Eq. (9);
3 Sort Ψ in ascending order to obtain the ordered sequence Ψ';
4 foreach $\Phi_k \in \Psi'$ **do**
5   Get the corresponding triplet $\langle c_k, e_k, d_k \rangle$;
6   Solve ILP transformation of **P2** with constraints associated with $\langle c_k, e_k, d_k \rangle$;
7   **if** *P2 is feasible* **then**
8 | break;
9   **end**
10 end

When $c_k \neq 1$, each TP–CP supergroup must follow one of the distributions in $\{\mathbf{p}^c(C), \cdots, \mathbf{p}^c(c_k)\}$, meaning it contains exactly c_k to C TP groups within a single HBD, that is: This condition is encoded by the following constraint:

$$\mathbb{I}[c_k \neq 1]A_{u_1,j}(A_{u_1,j} - C) \cdots (A_{u_1,j} - c_k) = 0, \forall u_1, j \tag{10}$$

where $\mathbb{I}[c_k \neq 1]$ is an indicator function that equals 1 when $c_k \neq 1$, and 0 otherwise. If $c_k = 1$, no constraint is imposed on the distribution. Similarly, the TP-EP and TP-DP supergroups distribution constraints are:

$$\mathbb{I}[e_k \neq 1]A_{u_2,j}(A_{u_2,j} - E) \cdots (A_{u_2,j} - e_k) = 0, \forall u_2, j \tag{11}$$

$$\mathbb{I}[d_k \neq 1]A_{u_3,j}(A_{u_3,j} - \tilde{D}) \cdots (A_{u_3,j} - d_k) = 0, \forall u_3, j \tag{12}$$

Therefore, if $\Phi(x) = \Phi_k$, then constraint (10)–(12) must be satisfied, and the problem reduces to solving the following formulation:

$$\mathbf{P2} : \min \Phi(x) = \Phi_k,$$

$$\text{s.t.}(C1), (C2), (10), (11), (12). \tag{13}$$

Problem **P2** is also a MINLP problem, but can be transformed into a 0–1 integer linear programming (ILP) problem. Since Φ_k is a constant, the objective function becomes trivial and can be defined as $\min 0$. The nonlinear constraints (10)–(12) can be linearized using auxiliary variables. Given the problem size, modern ILP solvers can compute the optimal solution efficiently. Based on the above ideas and modeling approach, we propose an algorithm to compute the optimal solution to **P1**, as outlined in Algorithm 1.

6　Performance Evaluation

6.1　Simulation Setup

Cluster Topology: We evaluate HBD-CE under three topologies: NVL72, NVL576, and Ascend supernode. NVL72 and NVL576 correspond to NVIDIA clusters, while Ascend supernode is used for Ascend clusters. Under NVL72 and NVL576, the unidirectional bandwidth within HBD is 900 GBps, and the RDMA bandwidth is 400 Gbps; under Ascend supernode, the unidirectional HBD bandwidth is 392 GBps, and the RDMA bandwidth is 400 Gbps.

Simulator and Workloads: We evaluate two MoE models: Qwen2-57B-A14B and MoE-GPT models, where MoE-GPT is built on the GPT-13B baseline. Model parameters are listed in Table 1. Gradient accumulation is used to divide each batch into micro-batches. We use the SimAI [15] simulator to reproduce traffic patterns from real model runs.

Table 1. Model Parameters.

	hidden size	# of layers	# of experts	top-k routing	capacity factor	sequence length	# of micro-bathes	micro-batch size
QWen2-57B-A14B	3584	28	64	8	1.2	64K	8	2
MoE-GPT-L	5140	40	32	8	2.4	256K	8	2

Baselines: We choose two model placement algorithms as baselines.

- Sequential Placement (SEQ) [7]: Used in Megatron-LM and Megatron-Scale, this method sequentially places TP groups to nodes within an HBD.
- SEQ-HC: Extends SEQ by incorporating a hierarchical collective communication algorithm.

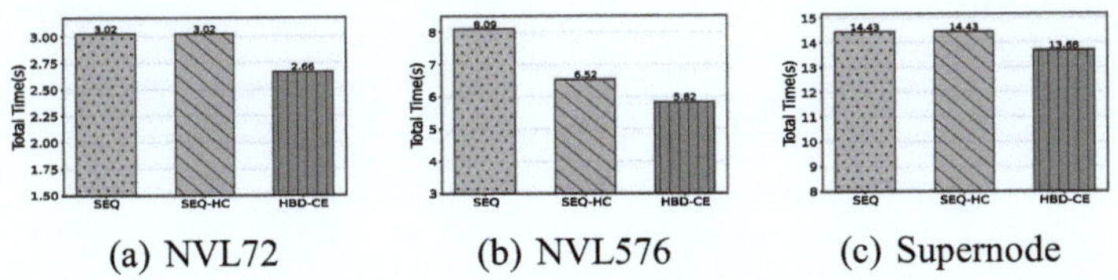

(a) NVL72   (b) NVL576   (c) Supernode

Fig. 3. Total communication time of different models across various topologies.

6.2   Results and Analysis

We first analyze communication overhead when the training task fully utilizes all resources within a single HBD. For Qwen2, the parallel configuration is $T = 8, E = 8, D = 9, C = 8$; for MoE-GPT, it is $T = 16, E = 16, D = 9, C = 32$. Figures 3(a)–3(c) show the per-iteration communication time for Qwen2 on NVL72, MoE-GPT on NVL576, and MoE-GPT on Ascend Supernode, respectively. On the NVL72, HBD-CE reduces communication time by 11.9% compared with both SEQ and SEQ-HC. On NVL576, HBD-CE achieves a 28% reduction over SEQ. Figures 4(a)–4(c) depict the communication overhead for different parallelism of the MoE-GPT model on the NVL576. As shown in Figs. 4(a), SEQ-HC fails to realize the benefits of hierarchical communication due to uneven CP–TP supergroup distribution. In Fig. 4(c), the DP all-reduce operation gains $15\times$ speedup by co-locating DP–TP supergroups within a single HBD.

We next evaluate Qwen2 on the NVL72 cluster under different parallelism configurations, with the number of NPUs fixed at 1024 and varying the degrees of CP and EP. Figures 5(a) and 5(b) show the total communication time for different CP and EP degrees, respectively. HBD-CE consistently achieves the lowest communication time. Under different EP degrees, HBD-CE reduces communication time by 46.22%–73.14% compared with SEQ and SEQ-HC. Under different CP degrees, the reduction is 55.92%–77.37%.

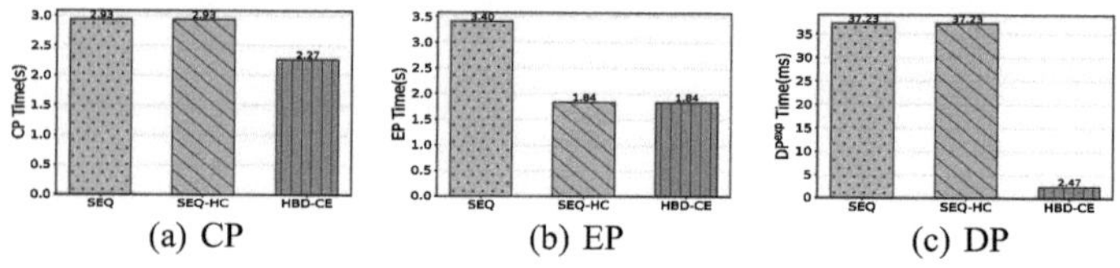

Fig. 4. Communication time of different parallelism of MoE-GPT model.

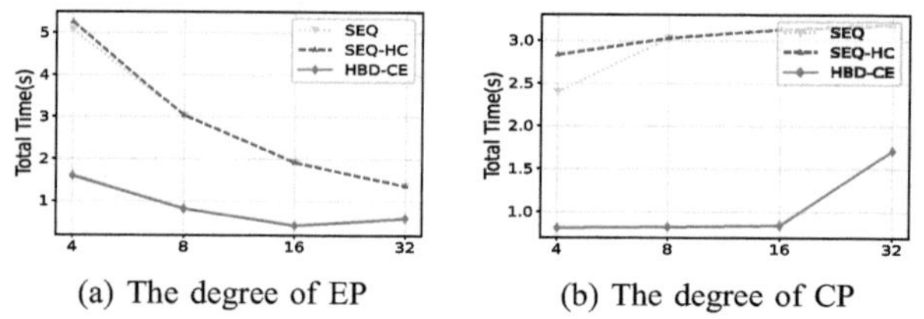

(a) The degree of EP   (b) The degree of CP

Fig. 5. The communication time of Qwen model under different parallelism degrees.

7 Conclusion

In this paper, we propose HBD-CE, a model placement scheme designed for communication-efficient cross-HBD LLM training in HBD clusters. It leverages hierarchical collectives to reduce cross-HBD communication overhead and employs an optimized model placement strategy to address the inefficiency of hierarchical collectives in HBD-based clusters. Experimental results demonstrate that HBD-CE achieves a reduction in per-iteration communication time from 5% to 77.3%, which further translates into improvements in end-to-end training performance.

References

1. Cho, M., Finkler, U., Kung, D., Hunter, H.: BlueConnect: decomposing all-reduce for deep learning on heterogeneous network hierarchy. In: Proceedings of Machine Learning and Systems, vol. 1, pp. 241–251 (2019)
2. Feng, Y., et al.: RailX: a flexible, scalable, and low-cost network architecture for hyper-scale LLM training systems. arXiv preprint arXiv:2507.18889 (2025)
3. Jiang, Z., et al.: {MegaScale}: scaling large language model training to more than 10,000 {GPUs}. In: 21st USENIX Symposium on Networked Systems Design and Implementation (NSDI 24), pp. 745–760 (2024)
4. Khorassani, K.S., Chu, C.H., Anthony, Q.G., Subramoni, H., Panda, D.K.: Adaptive and hierarchical large message all-to-all communication algorithms for large-scale dense GPU systems. In: 2021 IEEE/ACM 21st International Symposium on Cluster, Cloud and Internet Computing (CCGrid), pp. 113–122. IEEE (2021)
5. Lee, J., Hwang, I., Shah, S., Cho, M.: FlexReduce: flexible all-reduce for distributed deep learning on asymmetric network topology. In: 2020 57th ACM/IEEE Design Automation Conference (DAC), pp. 1–6. IEEE (2020)
6. Mikami, H., Suganuma, H., Tanaka, Y., Kageyama, Y., et al.: Massively distributed SGD: ImageNet/ResNet-50 training in a flash. arXiv preprint arXiv:1811.05233 (2018)
7. Narayanan, D., Shoeybi, M., Casper, J., et al.: Efficient large-scale language model training on GPU clusters using megatron-LM. In: Proceedings of the International Conference for High Performance Computing, Networking, Storage and Analysis, pp. 1–15 (2021)
8. NVIDIA: Nvidia DGX superpod (2024). https://www.nvidia.com/en-us/datacenter/dgx-superpod
9. Pan, X., Lin, W., Shi, S., Chu, X., Sun, W., Li, B.: Parm: efficient training of large sparsely-activated models with dedicated schedules. In: IEEE INFOCOM 2024-IEEE Conference on Computer Communications, pp. 1880–1889. IEEE (2024)
10. Rajbhandari, S., et al.: DeepSpeed-MoE: advancing mixture-of-experts inference and training to power next-generation AI scale. In: International Conference on Machine Learning, pp. 18332–18346. PMLR (2022)
11. Shou, C., et al.: InfiniteHBD: building datacenter-scale high-bandwidth domain for LLM with optical circuit switching transceivers. arXiv preprint arXiv:2502.03885 (2025)
12. Smith, S., et al.: Using deepspeed and megatron to train megatron-turing NLG 530b, a large-scale generative language model. arXiv preprint arXiv:2201.11990 (2022)
13. Um, T., et al.: Metis: fast automatic distributed training on heterogeneous {GPUs}. In: 2024 USENIX Annual Technical Conference (USENIX ATC 24), pp. 563–578 (2024)
14. Wang, W., Ghobadi, M., Shakeri, K., Zhang, Y., Hasani, N.: Rail-only: a low-cost high-performance network for training LLMs with trillion parameters. In: 2024 IEEE Symposium on High-Performance Interconnects (HOTI), pp. 1–10. IEEE (2024)
15. Wang, X., Li, Q., et al.: {SimAI}: unifying architecture design and performance tuning for {Large-Scale} large language model training with scalability and precision. In: 22nd USENIX Symposium on Networked Systems Design and Implementation (NSDI 25), pp. 541–558 (2025)
16. Zuo, P., et al.: Serving large language models on Huawei cloudmatrix384. arXiv preprint arXiv:2506.12708 (2025)

NNia-8: An 8-Core RISC-V Neural Network Inference Accelerator with Efficient Processing Elements and Memory Utilization

Xingbo Wang[1], Yucong Huang[1,2], Xinyu Kang[1], Yuru Li[1], Qi Wang[1,3], and Terry Tao Ye[4(✉)]

[1] Southern University of Science and Technology, Shenzhen, China
[2] Hong Kong University of Science and Technology, Hong Kong, China
[3] The University of British Columbia, Vancouver, Canada
[4] The Chinese University of Hong Kong, Shenzhen, China
`taoye@cuhk.edu.cn`

Abstract. RISC-V is widely used for edge AI acceleration, but most existing processors rely on scalar architectures, resulting in low PE density, inefficient bandwidth utilization, and complicated parallel processing schemes. Traditional Dot-Product (Dot-P) instruction extensions only support four 8-bit MAC operations per cycle, the computational density cannot support neural network implementation. Moreover, the general-purpose register constraint in RISC-V strictly limits matrix kernel dimensions, degrading computational resource utilization. Current multicore solutions require Tightly Coupled Data Memory (TCDM) with doubled core numbers of memory banks, along with mandatory padding operations to prevent bank conflicts, increasing memory subsystem complexity and area overhead. To address these challenges, we propose NNia-8, an 8-core RISC-V processor with six custom instructions for neural network inference acceleration (NNia). By replacing Dot-P operations with Out-Product (Out-P) computation paradigms, we achieve enhanced PE density optimization. Through implicit register invocation techniques integrating computation and memory access operations, along with dedicated buffer enhancements, bandwidth utilization and PE efficiency are substantially improved. Evaluated under the CMOS 55 nm process, NNia-8 achieves 49.9 GOPS at 8-bit precision with energy efficiency reaching 322 GOPS/W, outperforming state-of-the-art solutions.

Keywords: RISC-V · Multi-core · Accelerator · Custom Instruction Sets

1 Introduction

With the rapid advancement of artificial intelligence (AI) in Internet-of-Things (IoT) applications, an increasing number of computational tasks are being performed on edge devices. Deploying and operating AI algorithms at the edge

X. Wang et al. (Eds.): NPC 2025, LNCS 16306, pp. 278–290, 2026.
https://doi.org/10.1007/978-3-032-10466-3_23

requires lower costs and higher energy efficiency. The RISC-V processor, built on an open-source instruction set architecture (ISA), offers notable advantages for edge computing due to its simplicity and modularity. Since its inception, RISC-V has attracted significant attention from academia and industry. Its benefits have been demonstrated across various fields, including cryptography [5,6], robotics [7], and more. Notably, several RISC-V-based AI acceleration processors have been proposed, accelerating the inference of AI models such as convolutional neural networks (CNNs) [1,2] and spiking neural networks (SNNs) [3,4].

However, traditional RISC-V instructions are limited in terms of the utilization of processing elements (PEs) and the bandwidth of memory access when implementing AI-related tasks. For computation-intensive applications like CNNs, which involve operations such as matrix multiplication and convolution, the operational efficiency is suboptimal. Most edge RISC-V processors rely on 32-bit sequential pipelines that process only one instruction at a time. Given that many edge devices employ 8-bit quantized computation to reduce overhead costs, the traditional RISC-V ISA has been proven inefficient.

To enhance the low-precision computing performance of RISC-V architecture, significant research efforts have been dedicated to developing specialized low-precision extensions. Dustin [12] adopted the Dot-Product (Dot-P) SIMD scheme to accelerate 8-bit computations in neural networks, achieving four 8-bit MAC operations per cycle. However, constrained by the limited number of general-purpose registers in RISC-V (total 32), the kernel size for matrix multiplication remains limited. To improve bandwidth utilization and increase the size of the matrix multiplication kernel, Xpulpnn [11] and DARKSIDE [10] introduced additional M&L extensions with extra registers. Nevertheless, the M&L extension requires modifying instruction formats, adding decoding units, and complicating instruction invocation. Although prior work significantly enhanced the low-precision computing capability on RISC-V, the computational density remains low: a single core with Dot-P extensions only supports four 8-bit MAC units. When RISC-V cores with Dot-P extension are scaled up to multicore processors, the TCDM (Tightly Coupled Data Memory) scheme requires the number of memory banks to double the number of cores in order to avoid memory bank conflicts, which increases both the complexity of hardware and software design.

In this work, we present NNia-8, an 8-core RISC-V processor with custom instruction extensions to improve neural network computation efficiency. Our main contributions include the following.

1) We propose six custom instructions that replace Dot-P operations with Outer-Product (Out-P) operations, significantly improving the density of computational units in a single RISC-V core.
2) Through implicit register invocation mechanisms, we integrate Out-P operations with load operations without requiring additional instruction format modifications or decoding operations. We also allocate a dedicated buffer for each RISC-V core, both approaches substantially enhance bandwidth utilization and PE efficiency during computation.

3) We optimize the custom-made data layout for convolutional operations and implement hardware mapping to transform convolutions into Out-P operations, thus avoiding discontinuous memory access patterns.

4) The RISC-V cores with the aforementioned extensions are further incorporated into an 8-core processor named NNia-8. With optimized memory scheme and task allocation strategies. The TCDM scheme in NNia-8 requires only 8 memory banks, as compared to doubled memory band counts in other TCDM implementations. This architecture eliminates the need for additional software padding to prevent bank conflicts, significantly reducing both hardware and software design complexity.

Post-layout simulations based on 55 nm CMOS process show that NNia-8 achieves a peak performance of 49.9 GOPS with 8-bit precision, a peak energy efficiency of 322 GOPS/W, and both PE and bandwidth utilization rates exceed 95%.

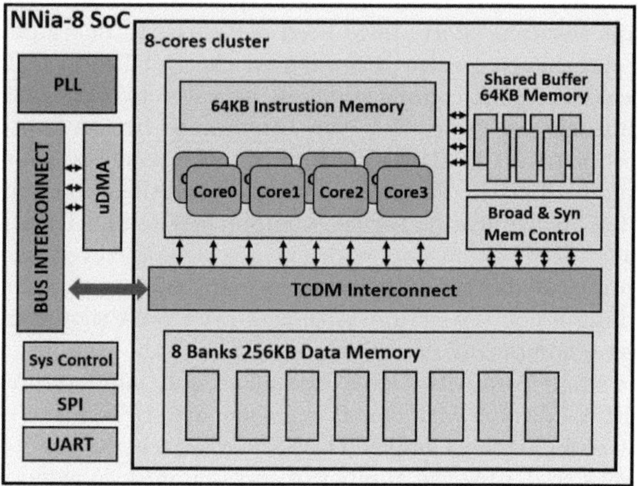

Fig. 1. NNia-8 SoC architecture

2 Processor Architecture

2.1 NNia-8 SoC Architecture

The System-on-Chip (SoC) architecture of NNia-8 is illustrated in Fig. 1. It comprises 8 RISC-V cores, each enhanced with custom instructions for efficient execution of neural network inference tasks. The SoC is equipped with 64KB of instruction memory and 256 KB of data memory. The data memory is divided into 8 banks connected via TCDM interconnect. The TCDM interconnects are controlled by a broadcast and synchronization unit. Additionally, 64KB of weight buffer, shared among multiple cores, is allocated to reduce the frequency of weight retrievals from the data memory. In addition to the computation units, peripheral units include a Phase-Locked Loop (PLL) for the system clock signals, a Micro Direct Memory Access (uDMA) module for data transfer and moving programs from UART/SPI to memory. The System Control module comprises configuration registers for system-level settings such as clock frequency and CPU operating modes. SPI is also included for flash memory read/write operations, while UART provides IO and debugging functions.

2.2 Single RISC-V Core Architecture

Each RISC-V core of NNia-8 processor uses the open-source RI5CY [8] processor as the baseline architecture. The revised architecture is shown in Fig. 2. RI5CY is a 4-stage pipeline, 32-bitwidth, in-order processor, supporting RV32IMAC instruction set. In each RISC-V core in NNia-8, the Decoder in the ID stage is revised to support the decoding of custom instructions. We also introduced a custom GEMM register file for storing data during computations. A GEMM unit is added in the EX stage to perform complex Out-P operations. The LSU in the WB stage is also modified to support the memory write-back from customized instructions.

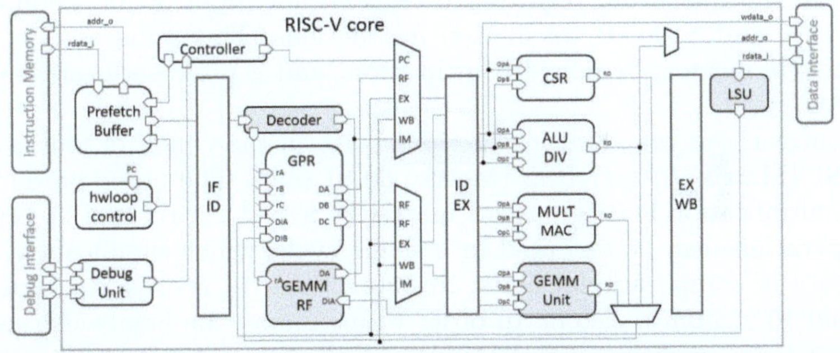

Fig. 2. Revised single RISC-V core based on RI5CY

3 RISC-V Based Custom Instruction Set on NNia-8

We propose six custom instructions to improve the efficiency of matrix multiplication and convolution operations. In addition, we introduced 24 custom registers, where g0-g15 are used for storing the results of Out-P outer products, and g16-g23 are primarily used for data transfers in convolution operations. The specific instruction formats and functions are described in Table 1.

Table 1. Custom RISC-V Instruction Set

Instruction	Func3	Func7	RS1	RS2	RS3/RD	Function
GEMM_SET	0	0	Addr_Base	Addr_Bias	GEMM Mode	Set Mode and Addr for GEMM_CAL
GEMM_CAL	0	1	A_Matrix	B_Matrix	Load Register	g0-g15<=Out-P(RS1,RS2) RD<=mem(Base+Bias)
GEMM_LOAD	0	2	Addr_Base	Addr_Bias	Load Register	RD/Cache<=mem(RS1+RS2) RS2<=RS1+RS2
GEMM_WB	0	3	Addr_Base	Addr_Bias	GEMM Result (g0-g15 only)	RS3(g0-g15)=> mem(RS1+RS2) RS2<=RS1+RS2
GEMM_SP_LOAD	0	4	Addr_Base	Addr_Bias	Load Register (g0-g23 only)	RD(g0-g23)<=mem(RS1+RS2) RS2<=RS1+RS2
GEMM_DEQUANT	0	5	Scale	Zero Point	Dequant Result	RD[7 : 0]<=(g0/4/8/12*Scale)>>16+ZP RD[15: 8]<=(g1/5/9/13*Scale)>>16+ZP RD[23:16]<<=(g2/6/10/14*Scale)>> 16+ZP RD[31:24]<<=(g3/7/11/15*Scale)>>16+ZP

3.1 Out-P with Implicit Register Invocation for Matrix Multiplication

We systematically compare Dot-P and Out-P computational schemes in Fig. 3. Most custom instruction sets use Dot-P to accelerate 8-bit matrix multiplication: it multiplies and accumulates 8-bit data from RS1 and RS2 into RD, performing four MACs at once. During execution, operations like function parameter passing consume most RISC-V general-purpose registers, leaving few for matrix multiplication. In Dot-P mode, the Dustin processor uses a 4×2 kernel for 8-bit matrix multiplication, requiring 6 registers for input, 8 for results, 6 load instructions, and 8 Dot-P calculation instructions. This achieves 57% PE utilization, 43% memory bandwidth utilization, and a peak performance of only 2.28 MAC/cycle.

In contrast, our proposed instructions perform the Out-P of four 8-bit data from RS1 (Matrix A) and RS2 (Matrix B) at once. The outer product is the vector multiplication between a 4×1 matrix by a 1×4 matrix (a 4×4 kernel). 16 MAC operations can be executed in a single cycle, which significantly improve the density of computational units. To store these 16 results, we allocated an additional 16 custom registers. In order to maximum the bandwidth usage, we conduct a load operation into RD while performing Out-P computations. In this manner, only up to 3 general-purpose registers are occupied, significantly enhancing the flexibility of program execution. The PE utilization rate can reach 50%, enabling more MAC operations to be completed in a single cycle and achieving a bandwidth utilization rate of 100%. For larger matrix sizes, by pre-storing the B Matrix in the weight buffer, the PE utilization rate can be increased to above 90% and the peak performance reaches 14.4 MAC/cycle.

3.2 GEMM Calculation Flow

The execution of GEMM calculation flow is illustrated in Fig. 4, where matrix A (dimension K × M) multiplies with matrix B (dimension K×N). When the dimensions M and N of matrices are both multiples of 4, their multiplication

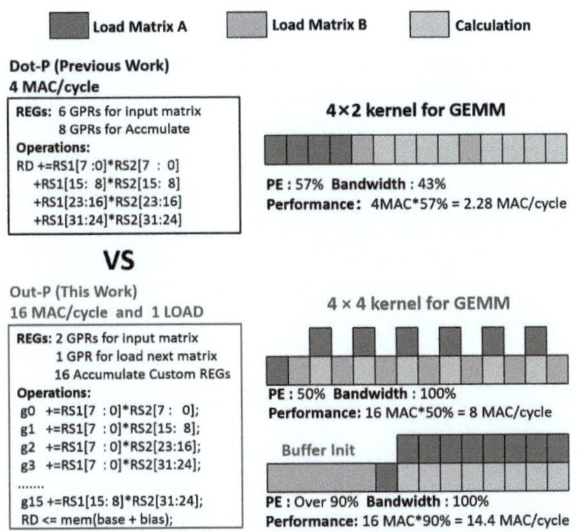

Fig. 3. Comparison with Dot-P and Out-P for GEMM calculation

can be decomposed into iterative outer product accumulations along the K-dimension. In each iteration, a 4×1 column vector from Matrix A and a 1×4 row vector from Matrix B compute an outer product, generating a 4×4 matrix. By accumulating these partial results along the K-axis, the final 4×4 submatrix result is obtained. This approach optimizes memory access efficiency and is suitable for SIMD parallel acceleration.

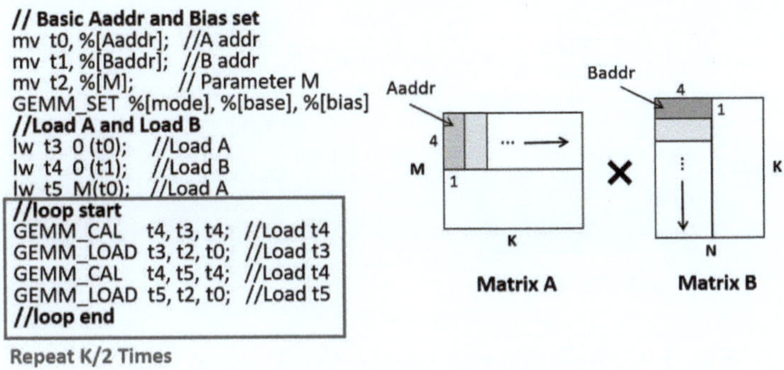

Fig. 4. GEMM 4×4 Calculation Flow by Custom Instructions

Figure 4 shows the pseudo-assembly code for 4×4 kernel GEMM. The GEMM_SET instruction is first called to configure the processor into GEMM computation mode and initialize the custom address registers for subsequent operations. The GEMM_CAL instruction then executes 16 MAC operations for

Out-P computation while simultaneously performing a data load operation based on the pre-configured address registers. As the RISC-V processor we use is a four-stage pipeline, data in the destination register (RD) is updated in the next cycle after the current instruction is executed. If the subsequent instruction uses the destination register from the previous instruction as the source register, the processor will have to wait for one cycle. Thus, before GEMM iteration, two 4 × 1 vectors of matrix A and one 1 × 4 vector of matrix B are read to prevent pipeline interruptions and wait cycles. Subsequent operations alternate between register sets (t3, t4 and t5, t4) for multiplication. This loop runs K/2 times to compute the 4 × 4 output matrix.

3.3   Convolution Mapping for Out-P Based GEMM

Convolution operations are inherently more complex than GEMM due to multi-dimensional transformations. To efficiently map convolutions onto the Out-P based GEMM computation, we propose a dedicated hardware mapping scheme. This approach eliminates the need for software-side memory rearrangement while maintaining high bandwidth utilization, thereby significantly accelerating the convolution process. The detailed mapping scheme is illustrated in Fig. 5.

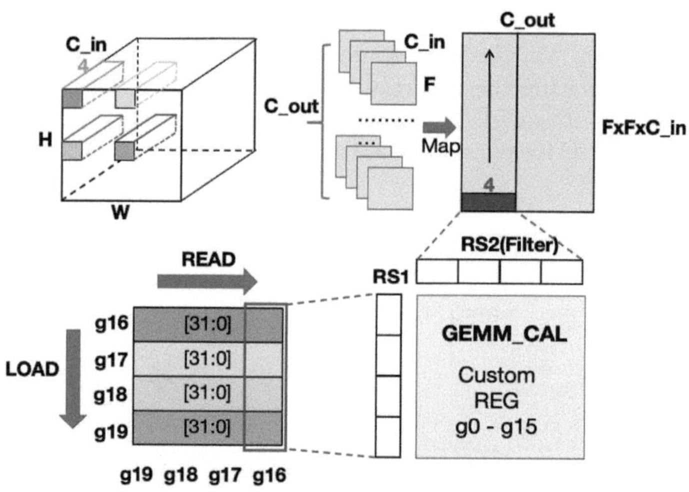

Fig. 5. Convolution mapping to Out-P based GEMM

In order to map the convolution operation of HWC input matrix to Out-P based GEMM, we utilized two sets of registers (g16-g19, g20-g23) for the transposition of the input matrix. Taking the operation mode of g16-g19 as an example, as illustrated in Fig. 5. Initially, four positions are selected in the input matrix to facilitate the subsequent matrix multiplication, with each position containing a size of 1 × 1 × 4. Following the load direction depicted in Fig. 5, we load four input data into g16-g19. At this point, the registers contain the input matrix (RS1) for the first four iterations of the 4×4 output GEMM. A hardware-based transposition is applied to the loaded data to ensure that during matrix operations, the four 8-bit data inputs to RS1 correspond to different positions in the input matrix in terms of H and W but belong to the same C_in.

We also reorganized the filter matrix. The arrangement of matrix with dimensions C_out $\times$ F $\times$ F $\times$ C_in in memory is rearranged as F $\times$ F $\times$ C_in $\times$ C_out. This rearrangement allows for the continuous reading of the C_out dimension during convolution, serving as the RS2 for GEMM input.

3.4   Memory Arrangement in Multi-core Out-P Based GEMM

We design a multi-core operation mode of Out-P Based GEMM for NNia-8 to avoid memory access conflicts arising from multiple cores accessing shared memory banks. Taking 4 cores as an example, we allocate 4 memory banks with a 32-bit width each (BANK0-BANK3). Accessing different banks by multiple cores simultaneously does not cause memory bank conflicts. When multiple cores access data from the same bank and the accessed data is identical, a broadcast mechanism is triggered, effectively mitigating memory conflicts.

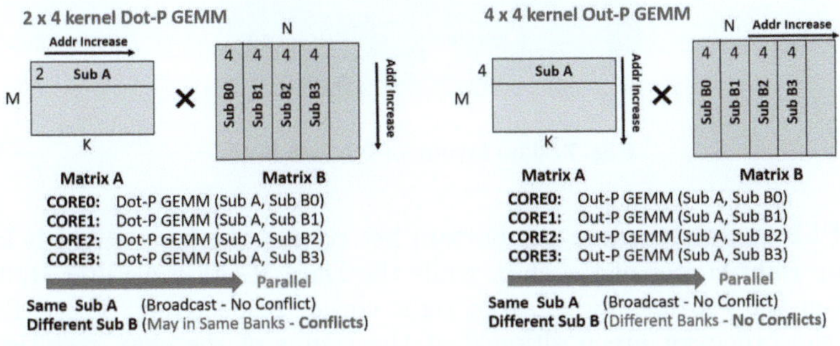

Fig. 6. Memory access of Dot-P and Out-P based for 4-core GEMM

We conducted a detailed analysis and comparison of memory access and task distribution for Dot-P and Out-P based GEMM on multi-core architectures, as illustrated in Fig. 6. Dot-P uses a 4×2 kernel due to register limits and a K-dimension-first matrix layout for bandwidth. Across 4 cores (CORE0–CORE3), shared Sub Matrix A access avoids conflicts, but accessing distinct Sub Matrix B (with K-priority layout) may cause bank conflicts if K is a multiple of 4 (sub-matrices start in the same bank). Previous designs mitigated this with larger TCDM banks and software padding, increasing complexity.

In contrast, Out-P based GEMM simplifies multi-core mapping: it uses a $\times \times 4$ kernel and M/N-dimension-first matrix layout for bandwidth. Across 4 cores (CORE0–CORE3), shared Sub Matrix A access avoids conflicts. For Sub Matrix

B (N-priority layout), 4 × 8-bit aligned blocks start in distinct banks, eliminating conflicts entirely. A TCDM with banks equal to core count suffices for parallel computation, needing no padding. This approach significantly reduces design complexity, leading to power and area efficiency in hardware implementation.

4   NNia-8 Performance and Resource Evaluation

4.1   NNia-8 Hardware Resources

Frontend, backend as well as verification design flows had been completed for NNia-8 and layout is generated for fabrication under SMIC 55nm Logic LL 1p7m process. The layout of the NNia-8 is illustrated Fig. 7.

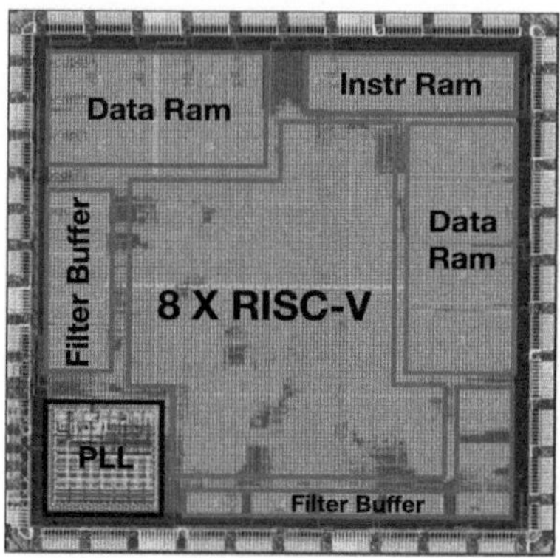

Fig. 7. The layout of NNia-8 SoC

The PLL is positioned on the bottom left corner, the Instr RAM is located on the top right corner of the chip, while the Data RAM and Filter Buffer are situated on the top left and bottom right corner respectively. The 8 RISC-V cores of the processor are positioned at the center of the chip, resulting in a total chip area of $2.63 \times 2.62 = 6.89\,\mathrm{mm}^2$.

4.2   Matrix Multiplication Performance Test

GEMM tests are performed to evaluate the performance of NNia-8. Runtime and power consumption is estimated based on post-layout design simulation in Synopsys PT-PX. The simulation results are derived under TT Corner running at 200MHz. We kept the dimensions fixed at M = 32, N = 32, and varied K for testing. With the use of Weight Buffer. The results are illustrated in Fig. 8 with the increase in the dimensionality (K). For K equal to 2048, the computational capability of matrix multiplication reaches 49.89 GOPS and 124.73 MAC/cycle. We also examined the bandwidth and Processing Element utilization during GEMM. When the number of K for GEMM reaches 2048, the utilization ratio of PE and bandwidth surpasses 95%, achieving a peak energy efficiency of 322 GOPS/W.

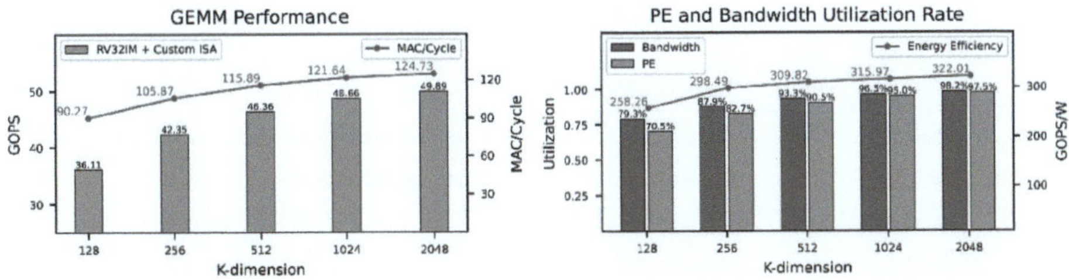

Fig. 8. GEMM performance of NNia-8 processor

4.3   Neural Network Computing Capability

We evaluated the actual inference performance of the processor using the TinyML ResNet8 network. Dustin [12], a 16 × RISC-V processor, was chosen as a benchmark for comparison with same clock frequency. The specific test results are depicted in Fig. 9. It is evident that the NNia-8 processor exhibits lower latency in convolution operations compared to Dustin, thanks to NNia-8's higher efficiency in PE and bandwidth utilization. Furthermore, the inclusion of the weight buffer within the processor significantly reduces the number of weight accesses to the main memory, resulting in performance advantages.

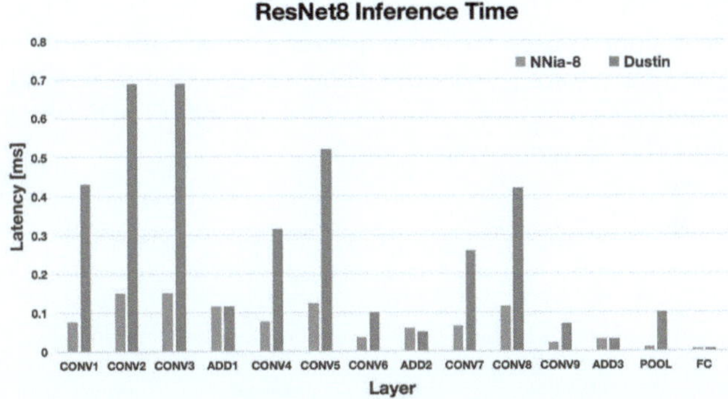

Fig. 9. NNia-8 ResNet8 inference time

We also conducted a comprehensive comparison of several other processors' performance on ResNet8, as detailed in Table 2. It is evident that NNia-8 significantly reduces the inference time compared to Dustin, requiring only 1.04 ms. Moreover, our energy efficiency is also notably advantageous, consuming just 116 uJ. In comparison to ARM processors without specialized low-precision optimizations, the advantages are even more pronounced in terms of both inference time and energy consumption.

Table 2. ResNet8, Comparison with Prior Work

Processor	Process	ISA	Time	Energy
NNia-8	55 nm	RISC-V + Custom ISA	1.07 ms	116 uJ
Dustin	65 nm	RISC-V + Custom ISA	3.80 ms	373 uJ
ARM Cortex-M4	40 nm	ARM	165.13 ms	6919 uJ
ARM Cortex-M7	40 nm	ARM	40.84 ms	5090 uJ
ARM Cortex-M33	40 nm	ARM	111.07ms	2579 uJ

4.4   Comparison with Other Processors

We conducted a comparative analysis between our processor, and several similar processors including VEGA [9], Darkside [10], XpulpNN [11] and Dustin. All these processors feature a multi-core RISC-V architecture. The comparison details are outlined in Table 3.

Compared to the four processors mentioned above, NNia-8 processor achieves significantly higher 8-bit computational performance with the same or fewer RISC-V cores. This is primarily attributed to its higher PE density and improved utilization of both PEs and memory bandwidth. Operating at a clock frequency of 200 MHz, NNia-8 can reach up to 49.9 GOPS. The power consumption estimation values in Table 3 are all scaled to 1.2 V of power supply for a normalized comparison. Furthermore, the simplified TCDM architecture of the Out-P-based NNia-8 processor contributes to lower power consumption and area overhead compared to the other four processors. The results demonstrated that NNia-8 processor has superior energy efficiency, achieving 322 GOPS/W at a voltage of 1.2 V, surpassing the aforementioned works.

Table 3. Comparison with prior work

Design	VEGA	Darkside	XpulpNN	Dustin	This Work
Process	CMOS 22 nm FD-SOI	CMOS 65 nm	CMOS 22nm FD-SOI	CMOS 65nm	CMOS 55nm
Circuit Type	Digital	Digital	Digital	Digital	Digital
Application	IoT GP + DNN	IoT GP + DNN	IoT GP + DNN	IoT GP + DNN	IoT GP + DNN
Architecture	9 × RISC-V	8 × RISC-V	8 × RISC-V	16 × RISC-V	8 × RISC-V
Frequency	450 MHz	290 MHz	400 MHz	205 MHz	200 MHz
Voltage	0.5–0.8 V	0.75–1.2 V	0.6–0.8 V	0.8–1.2 V	1.2 V
Area (mm^2)	12	12	1.05	10	6.89
Power (mW)	278	213	41.6	156	114
Int Precision	8, 16, 32-bit	2, 4, 8, 16, 32-bit	2, 4, 8, 16, 32-bit	2, 4, 8, 16, 32-bit	8,32-bit
Peak Integer Performance (GOPS)[a]	15.6@(8b)	17@(8b)	23@(8b)	15@(8b)	49.9@(8b)
Peak Energy Efficiency (GOPS/W)[b]	614@(0.5 V, 8b) {107@(1.2 V, 8b)}	191@(0.75 V, 8b) {75@(1.2 V, 8b)}	1111@(0.6 V, 8b) {278@(1.2 V,8b)}	303@(0.8 V, 8b) {134@(1.2 V, 8b)}	481@(1.2 V, 8b)

[a] 1 MAC = 2 OPs in matrix multiplication benchmarks.
[b] The voltage is normalized to 1.2 V.

5   Conclusion

In this work, we introduced NNia-8, an 8-core RISC-V processor for neural network inference acceleration. We implemented 6 custom instructions for each RISC-V core, greatly enhancing the efficiency of matrix multiplication and convolution operations, improving the utilization of PE and memory bandwidth. Running at 200 MHz under the supply voltage of 1.2 V, with 8-bit precision, NNia-8 processor achieved a peak performance of 49.9 GOPS and an energy efficiency of 322 GOPS/W. The utilization rates of PE and bandwidth also exceeded 95%. NNia-8 completed the ResNet8 inference task in 1.04 ms and consumed only 116 uJ of energy.

References

1. Armeniakos, G., Maras, A., Xydis, S., Soudris, D.: Mixed-precision Neural Networks on RISC-V Cores: ISA extensions for Multi-Pumped Soft SIMD Operations. ArXiv Preprint ArXiv:2407.14274 (2024)
2. Wang, S., Wang, X., Xu, Z., Chen, B., Feng, C., Wang, Q., Ye, T.: Optimizing CNN computation using RISC-V custom instruction sets for edge platforms. IEEE Trans. Comput. (2024)
3. Wang, X., Feng, C., Kang, X., Wang, Q., Huang, Y., Ye, T.: RV-SCNN: A RISC-V processor with customized instruction Set for SNN and CNN inference acceleration on edge platforms. IEEE Trans. Comput.-Aided Design Integr. Circuits Syst. (2024)
4. Jianwei, X., Rendong, Y., Faquan, C., Peilin, L.: SFANC: scalable and flexible architecture for neuromorphic computing. IEEE Trans. Very Large Scale Integr. (VLSI) Syst. (2023)
5. Hoang, T., Duran, C., Tsukamoto, A., Suzaki, K., Pham, C.: Cryptographic accelerators for trusted execution environment in RISC-V processors. In: 2020 IEEE International Symposium On Circuits And Systems (ISCAS), pp. 1–4 (2020)
6. Marshall, B., Newell, G., Page, D., Saarinen, M., Wolf, C.: The design of scalar AES instruction set extensions for RISC-V. IACR Trans. Cryptogr. Hardw. Embed. Syst. 109–136 (2021)
7. Yoo, T., Choi, B.: Real-time performance benchmarking of RISC-V architecture: implementation and verification on an EtherCAT-based robotic control system. Electronics **13**, 733 (2024)
8. Gautschi, M., et al.: Near-threshold RISC-V core with DSP extensions for scalable IoT endpoint devices. IEEE Trans. Very Large Scale Integr. (VLSI) Syst. **25**, 2700-2713 (2017)
9. Rossi, D., et al.: Vega: a ten-core SoC for IoT endnodes with DNN acceleration and cognitive wake-up from MRAM-based state-retentive sleep mode. IEEE J. Solid-State Circ. **57**, 127–139 (2021)
10. Garofalo, A., et al.: Darkside: a heterogeneous RISC-V compute cluster for extreme-edge on-chip DNN inference and training. IEEE Open J. Solid-State Circuits Soc. **2**, 231–243 (2022)
11. Garofalo, A., Tagliavini, G., Conti, F., Benini, L., Rossi, D.: XpulpNN: enabling energy efficient and flexible inference of quantized neural networks on RISC-V based IoT end nodes. IEEE Trans. Emerg. Top. Comput. **9**, 1489–1505 (2021)

12. Ottavi, G., et al.: Dustin: a 16-cores parallel ultra-low-power cluster with 2b-to-32b fully flexible bit-precision and vector Lockstep execution mode. IEEE Trans. Circuits Syst. I: Regular Pap. **70**, 2450–2463 (2023)

GPowerT: LLM-Driven Automated Programming for Power-Constrained IoT Applications

Ruitong Ye and Ming Gao$^{(\boxtimes)}$

School of Computer Science, Nanjing University of Posts and Telecommunications,
Nanjing, China
{B23100201,gaomingppm}@njupt.edu.cn

Abstract. Large Language Models (LLMs) are reshaping Internet of Things (IoT) application development. They let developers generate functional code from natural language. Yet battery-powered IoT devices operate under tight energy budgets. Current LLM-driven programming frameworks offer limited support for power-constrained IoT design. In this paper, we propose GPowerT, an LLM-driven automated programming system for power-constrained IoT applications. GPowerT extracts power-related constraints from natural language requirements, including battery capacity, target lifetime, and energy-saving policies, dependent on hardware power profiles and a low-power design knowledge base. During code generation, it injects strategies such as deep sleep, periodic sampling, and batch communication. A static power estimation module analyzes operation and sleep cycles, communication frequency, and peripheral usage. It predicts total energy consumption and checks compliance with the budget. If the target is not met, the system pinpoints overconsumption and returns optimization hints to the LLM, enabling closed-loop refinement. Evaluations on representative IoT tasks show that GPowerT improves power-budget compliance and developer efficiency. The generated programs achieve long-duration battery life performance, which demonstrates the system's potential and practicality for low-power IoT application development.

Keywords: Large Language Model (LLM) · Program Synthesis · Power-constrained IoT Application

1 Introduction

Battery-powered embedded systems are widely deployed in the Internet of Things (IoT). In these power-constrained systems, software decisions are directly related to energy consumption. To meet a lifetime target with a fixed cell capacity, engineers must meticulously manage a complex trade-off space between the energy demands of sensing, computation, and connectivity. This process involves hand-tuning low-level hardware configurations such as sleep states, operational

© IFIP International Federation for Information Processing 2026
Published by Springer Nature Switzerland AG 2026
X. Wang et al. (Eds.): NPC 2025, LNCS 16306, pp. 291–302, 2026.
https://doi.org/10.1007/978-3-032-10466-3_24

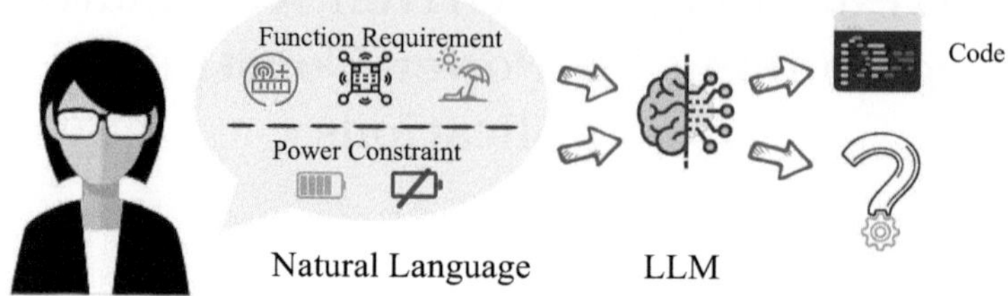

Fig. 1. LLMs can effectively translate natural language into functional code. However, they operate without awareness of the underlying hardware's power characteristics. Thereby, their applications are limited when dealing with power-constrained IoT devices.

duty cycles, clock frequencies, and power domains, known as Dynamic Power Management (DPM) [1]. This manual workflow is not only slow but also highly specific to a single hardware platform. Consequently, the task of meeting a power budget degrades into a lengthy and inefficient cycle of trial and error [2].

Modern large language models (LLMs) have demonstrated a powerful ability to translate plain-language requirements into functional code [3]. Recently, several studies have enabled this capability of code generation for IoT program synthesis and development [4–6]. However, generic code generation rarely takes strict energy constraints into consideration. These models typically lack awareness of the device-specific power-saving primitives that are critical for embedded applications. Without rapid consumption estimates, derived from methods such as instruction-level power analysis [7], and an iterative refinement loop anchored to an energy budget, it remains challenging to guarantee that the generated software can achieve the desired lifetime in practical deployment.

A fundamental challenge in developing software for battery-powered IoT devices is the semantic-to-hardware gap: the disconnect between a high-level energy goal, often expressed in natural language (e.g., "the device must last for two years"), and the low-level, hardware-specific implementation required to achieve it. The core of this problem is that the same linguistic goal translates into vastly different technical constraints depending on the platform; a two-year lifetime implies a stringent microampere-level budget for a Bluetooth sensor but a far more permissive one for a cellular node with a large battery. This ambiguity forces developers to manually translate abstract targets into complex, platform-specific trade-offs involving sleep states, duty cycles, and communication protocols. This process is not only labor-intensive and error-prone but demands deep expertise, trapping developers in an inefficient cycle of guesswork and physical testing that often results in project delays or products that fail to meet their essential power budget in the field.

We propose GPowerT to address the practical issue of power budgets in LLM-driven programming. Its applications are illustrated in Fig. 1. GPowerT begins by detecting and interpreting natural language descriptions of essential power constraints, including battery capacity, target lifetime, and preferred energy-saving strategies. It then synthesizes a complete, low-energy program by intelligently mapping these high-level goals to the hardware-specific capabilities of the target device (e.g., event-driven scheduling). Following generation, GPowerT performs a rigorous power estimation and feeds the results into an iterative refinement loop. This automated, estimate-feedback-regenerate cycle drives the code towards compliance, ultimately converging on a deployable, power-optimized program and its corresponding documentation.

Our contributions are summarized as follows.

- To our best knowledge, GPowerT is the first work that synthesizes programs directly from natural language for power-constrained IoT applications. It bridges the semantic gap between high-level user intents and low-level hardware power primitives, automatically generating energy-efficient code.
- We designed three novel modules to automate the synthesis and optimization of low-power IoT software. This process involves power requirement detection, energy-aware code generation, and closed-loop refinement.
- GPowerT operates across the entire design cycle, rather than one-shot code generators. The system leverages power feedback to autonomously refine its own code, a process that significantly reduces manual optimization effort.

2   Background and Related Work

The recent proliferation of LLMs has catalyzed new research into their application for the Internet of Things (IoT), focusing on two main areas: intelligent sensor data inference and automated program synthesis.

One research direction applies LLMs for direct inference on sensor data, either through prompt-based analysis [6, 8, 9] or by fine-tuning models on specialized datasets [10]. However, these approaches are ill-suited for power-constrained devices due to the high latency and security risks of cloud-based APIs, and the intensive computational and memory footprint of fine-tuned models, making them impractical for long-term, battery-powered deployments.

Concurrently, the field of code synthesis has been significantly advanced by powerful Code LLMs [11, 12], which demonstrate a remarkable ability to generate functionally correct code from natural language descriptions. Building on this, recent systems have explored LLM-driven, end-to-end code generation for IoT. AutoIOT [5] presents a system that automates the creation of IoT applications from high-level specifications, and GPIoT [4] introduces a framework for specializing smaller language models to synthesize programs tailored for IoT devices. These systems have shown that LLMs can even leverage compiler feedback for autonomous self-improvement and debugging [13, 14].

Despite their capabilities, the effectiveness of LLM-driven systems is limited in power-constrained IoT applications. This limitation arises because their training on massive, general-purpose datasets [15] leaves them without domain-specific knowledge required to generate highly optimized solutions for resource-constrained hardware. For instance, these models are unaware of the intricate

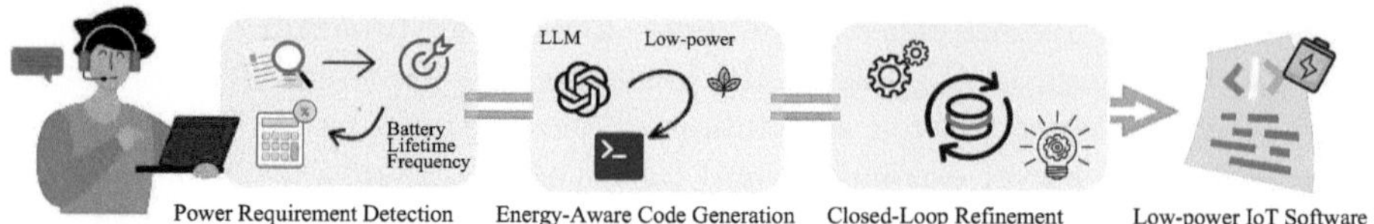

Fig. 2. GPowerT is designed to realize automated programming for power-constrained IoT applications. It translates high-level power goals described in natural language into low-power code that leverages device-specific hardware features, followed by an iterative loop to continuously refine the program until all constraints are met.

power characteristics of specific microcontrollers, the energy costs of state transitions (e.g., from sleep to active), or the optimal low-power communication patterns for a given hardware platform. Consequently, while these tools can generate code that works, they cannot guarantee that it will work efficiently within a prescribed energy budget, leaving a critical gap for a system that can bridge the divide between functional correctness and verified energy efficiency.

3   System Design

We propose GPowerT, a framework that automates the creation of power-constrained embedded applications by translating high-level natural language requirements into verified, energy-efficient firmware for modern IoT devices. As illustrated in Fig. 2, the system employs a three-stage process to ensure the final firmware is both functional and compliant with strict power budgets.

First, the Power Requirement Detection module interprets natural language requests to extract critical parameters like battery capacity, operational lifetime, and task frequency. From these parameters, it formulates a precise energy budget, establishing a quantitative target for the design process.

Next, the Energy-Aware Code Generation module leverages a specialized power knowledge base, which contains detailed hardware energy profiles and a library of low-power design patterns, to inform the creation of highly specific prompts for a language model. This process produces code that is optimized for energy efficiency from its foundation.

Finally, the Closed-Loop Refinement module performs static power estimation to predict real-world energy consumption without physical hardware. If the code exceeds the budget, the system generates targeted feedback and triggers an automated refinement cycle. This iterative process repeats until the firmware satisfies all power constraints, thus guaranteeing compliance.

3.1   Power Requirement Detection

The GPowerT workflow begins with a conversational interface, eliminating the need for rigid templates or formal languages. The developer specifies their high-level goal in natural language, for example: *"Design a sensor node that measures soil moisture every* 30 min *and transmits data twice daily over LoRaWAN. It needs to run for 2 years on a* 3000 mAh *battery."*

GPowerT's requirement parser deeply analyzes the user's input. It intelligently extracts critical power-related parameters, such as battery capacity, operational timing, and overall energy targets. These details may be stated explicitly or implied by the desired operational lifetime. GPowerT's requirement parser analyzes this input to extract key parameters (battery capacity, operational timing, target lifespan) and formalizes them into a structured power requirement tuple, denoted as R:

$$R = (B_{\text{cap}}, L_{\text{target}}, \boldsymbol{O}, P_{\text{policy}}) \tag{1}$$

where B_{cap} is the battery capacity, L_{target} is the target lifespan, $\boldsymbol{O}$ is the operation vector, and P_{policy} specifies any power-saving preferences.

From this tuple, the system derives the primary constraint for code generation: the average current budget ($I_{\text{avg\_budget}}$), which can be calculated as:

$$I_{\text{avg\_budget}} = \frac{B_{\text{cap}} \times \eta_{\text{battery}}}{L_{\text{target}}} \tag{2}$$

Here, η_{battery} is a factor representing battery efficiency, accounting for self-discharge and conversion losses.

Applying Eq. 2 to the developer's request, a 3000 mAh battery with a 2-year lifespan target yields a precise budget of approximately 171 µA. This quantitative target becomes the core constraint that guides the subsequent code generation and optimization phases.

3.2   Energy-Aware Code Generation

With the power constraints defined, GPowerT proceeds to generate energy-optimized code. This process is driven by a formal knowledge base and a structured prompting strategy, ensuring efficiency is integral to the design.

Hardware Power Profiles. The foundation of this process is a domain-specific power knowledge base ($\mathcal{KB}$), which contains both hardware specifications and proven software strategies. We formalize it as a tuple:

$$\mathcal{KB} = (\mathcal{H}, \mathcal{P}, \mathcal{D}) \tag{3}$$

where $\mathcal{H}$ represents the set of available hardware components, $\mathcal{P}$ is a repository of power profiles detailing the consumption for each component in various states (e.g., active, sleep) and the energy costs of state transitions, and $\mathcal{D}$ is a library of energy-efficient design patterns, such as deep sleep cycling and data batching.

To ensure the system's long-term relevance and eliminate manual upkeep, GPowerT is also designed with the capacity to autonomously browse the web to find and parse datasheets for new hardware components as they are released. By integrating techniques for automated information extraction from unstructured PDF documents and web pages, the system can continuously enrich its own knowledge base with the critical power characteristics of new components.

This self-learning capability ensures that GPowerT remains a powerful and perpetually current tool in the rapidly advancing landscape of embedded hardware.

Constraint-guided Code Generation. Using this knowledge base, GPowerT generates a highly-contextualized prompt for the LLM. The entire code generation process is modeled as a function $\mathcal{G}$ that maps the requirements and knowledge to the final code, C^*:

$$C^* = \mathcal{G}(R, \mathcal{KB}, \Theta) \tag{4}$$

where Θ is the prompting strategy, which formalizes how context is injected into the prompt:

$$\Theta = (\text{Template}_{\text{base}}, \text{Pattern}_{\text{lib}}, \text{Constraint}_{\text{injection}}) \tag{5}$$

where $\text{Template}_{\text{base}}$ provides the code structure, $\text{Pattern}_{\text{lib}}$ sources relevant patterns from $\mathcal{D}$, and $\text{Constraint}_{\text{injection}}$ embeds the power budget from R. This comprehensive guidance steers the model to write energy-efficient code from the start. The resulting code C^* is therefore inherently optimized for low power. For example, it minimizes time in high-power states, intelligently manages peripherals, and optimizes communication protocols to maximize deep sleep periods.

3.3 Closed-Loop Refinement

GPowerT leverages a closed-loop refinement process that iteratively verifies and optimizes the generated code against the power budget. This loop consists of two main stages: power estimation and feedback-driven optimization.

Static Power Estimation. The core of the loop is a static analysis engine that estimates power consumption without physical hardware. To enable this, we model the system's power draw by defining a set of operational states $S = \{s_{\text{active}}, s_{\text{sleep}}, s_{\text{tx}}, \dots\}$. Each state $s_i \in S$ has a known power consumption P_i and a duration T_i derived from code analysis. The estimated average power consumption, $P_{\text{avg\_est}}$, over a complete cycle is then calculated as:

$$P_{\text{avg\_est}} = \frac{\sum_{i \in S}(P_i \cdot T_i + E_{\text{trans},i})}{\sum_{i \in S} T_i} \tag{6}$$

where $E_{\text{trans},i}$ is the energy for state transitions. The resulting estimated average current, $I_{\text{avg\_est}}$, is compared against the predefined $I_{\text{avg\_budget}}$. If $I_{\text{avg\_est}} \leq I_{\text{avg\_budget}}$, the code is considered compliant.

In particular, users can implement the analyzed code on hardware and utilize direct power measurements, which also refine and expand the knowledge base.

Feedback and Iterative Optimization. If the estimated current exceeds the budget, the refinement process is framed as an optimization problem. The goal is to tune a vector of parameters $\boldsymbol{\theta}$ (e.g., sleep duration, sampling frequency) to satisfy the constraint:

$$\begin{aligned} \underset{\boldsymbol{\theta}}{\text{minimize}} \quad & P_{\text{avg\_est}}(\boldsymbol{\theta}) \\ \text{subject to} \quad & P_{\text{avg\_est}}(\boldsymbol{\theta}) \leq P_{\text{avg\_budget}} \end{aligned} \tag{7}$$

To solve this, GPowerT conducts a feedback cycle. It identifies the root cause of the over-consumption (e.g., radio is too active) and provides the LLM with a new, more specific prompt, such as: *"The current code exceeds the power budget. Modify the implementation to use a lower-power BLE advertising mode."* Using the new prompt, the system regenerates the code. This revised implementation is then sent back for another round of power estimation. This generation-estimation-refinement cycle continues until the power constraints are satisfied.

In cases where the power budget is physically unrealizable with the given hardware, GPowerT conducts a collaborative negotiation dialogue. Instead of failing, it provides a precise diagnosis (e.g., "The required cellular connection interval is incompatible with a five-year lifetime") and proposes quantifiable compromises, such as recommending alternative hardware or relaxing performance constraints.

The final output is a complete solution package. It includes verified low-power firmware, a detailed energy consumption report, and a battery life projection. By combining semantic analysis with domain-specific knowledge and closed-loop refinement, GPowerT empowers developers to build applications that achieve maximum functionality within the strictest energy budgets.

4   Implementation and Evaluation

4.1   Implementation

GPowerT is implemented using the AutoIOT [5] framework, which orchestrates GPT-4 [16] as the foundational language model. To gather relevant online information, the system employs the Tavily [17] web search utility. All retrieved content is then transformed into vector representations via OpenAI's text embedding model [18]. These vectors are subsequently indexed using Faiss [19], enabling GPowerT to perform efficient, large-scale similarity searches. The entire code execution environment operates on a Linux Ubuntu workstation equipped with an NVIDIA RTX 4090 GPU.

A representative single-cell Li-ion battery profile is used for evaluation: nominal 3.7 V, 500 mAh capacity, DCDC efficiency 0.90, cutoff voltage 3.0 V, ambient 25 °C, self-discharge 1%/month, and twelve months of aging, as illustrated in Fig. 3. Under this configuration, all experiments achieve a similar performance as that in AutoIOT [5] with an accuracy deviation below 6%. In this case, we mainly evaluate the power consumption performance here, which is the main function of our proposed GPowerT. We leverage four metrics that jointly quantify effectiveness (meeting constraints) and efficiency (time and iterations to convergence) as follows.

- *Inference Time*: we measure the end-to-end runtime for one sample from instruction intake through final validated configuration, including retrieval and corrective passes.
- *Feedback Rounds*: we record the number of corrective iterations after the initial code generation until all constraints are satisfied, providing a measure of how quickly the loop converges.

Fig. 3. Battery information provided as input (i.e., power constraints)

- *Power Consumption*: we record the steady-state energy usage of the configured device under the declared sampling and duty-cycling conditions.
- *Lifetime*: we record the expected operating time derived from the energy model of the chosen battery and power path, factoring in DCDC efficiency, cutoff voltage, and environmental parameters.

4.2   Overall Performance

Across fifteen independent runs, end-to-end inference time ranges from 99 to 138 s and never exceeds 140 s, as shown in Fig. 4a. This is consistent with the system's design for neartwo-minute synthesis cycles. This level of responsiveness substantially reduces the effort required to transform high-level constraints into deployable configurations compared with manual workflows. Variability in inference time is mainly due to differences in corrective needs: when the first generated configuration already satisfies energy and lifetime constraints, convergence is achieved quickly; when the initial attempt falls slightly short on power or lifetime, one or two additional feedback rounds are invoked to recalibrate sampling frequency, duty cycle, or communication cadence. A smaller secondary contributor is retrieval complexity, which can modestly affect embedding lookup and context construction time when documentation is more heterogeneous for a particular sensor.

Feedback convergence is concentrated: twelve runs require a single corrective round, and three runs require two rounds. No cases exceed two rounds. This distribution is illustrated in Fig. 4b. When the first configuration already satisfies both constraints, convergence is immediate; when it falls short on either power or lifetime, one or two corrective rounds suffice to meet targets, which explains the modest variance in runtime. The combination of a narrow feedback distribution and a bounded runtime envelope indicates that the correction templates and constraint prompts are sufficiently prescriptive to guide stable convergence with minimal iteration.

Aggregate constraint satisfaction across 10 sensor models is shown in Fig. 5. Figure 5a plots target versus achieved lifetime; all points lie on or above the parity

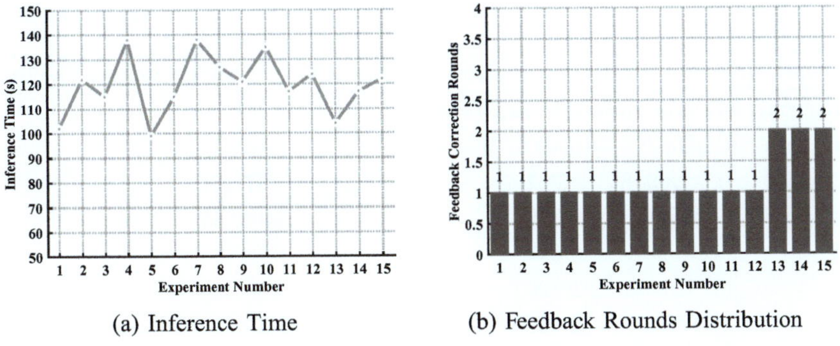

(a) Inference Time

(b) Feedback Rounds Distribution

Fig. 4. Comparison of Feedback Rounds Distribution and Inference Time

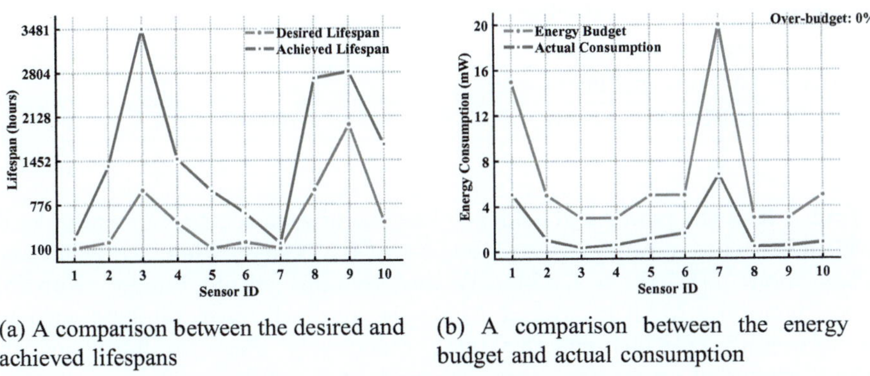

(a) A comparison between the desired and achieved lifespans

(b) A comparison between the energy budget and actual consumption

Fig. 5. Comparison of Lifespan and Energy Performance

line, demonstrating that the produced configurations meet or exceed specified lifetimes across devices. Figure 5b compares the per-device energy budget with measured or modeled consumption; all points fall at or below the budget line, confirming that lifetime gains are not traded for budget violations.

4.3   Robustness Study

We evaluate the robustness of GPowerT on different target sensors and using different LLM frameworks to demonstrate its generalization in practice.

Generalization across Different Sensors. We assess GPowerT on eight IMUs, one current/power monitor, and one optical front end for biopotential-like measurements, spanning high-precision/high-power to ultralow-power designs. All devices meet or exceed the lifetime target while staying within the energy budget. Low-power devices achieve thousand-hour lifetimes, whereas higher-power precision IMUs converge to lifetimes consistent with their consumption envelopes. The qualitative trends in Fig. 5 are consistent with this observation.

Table 1. Power Consumption and Achieved Lifespan of Different Sensors

Sensor ID	Sensor Model	Power Consumption (mW)	Achieved Lifespan (hours)
Inertial Measurement Units (IMUs)			
1	BNO055	5.080	256.31
2	ICM20948	1.061	1373.71
3	LSM6DS3	0.379	3480.55
4	LSM9DS1	0.642	1480.65
5	MPU9250	1.190	985.44
6	MPU6050	1.640	643.77
7	ADIS16470	6.830	178.70
8	BMI160	0.446	2715.13
Current/Power Monitoring Sensor			
9	MAX96150	0.538	2818.60
Optical Bio-sensing Front-end			
10	AFE4404	0.842	1690.00

Table 1 lists the power and achieved lifetime of each sensor. For example, the LSM6DS3 reaches approximately 3480.55 h at 0.379 mW, while the ADIS16470 reaches about 178.70 h at 6.830 mW and remains within budget. Non-IMU devices, including MAX96150 and AFE4404, similarly meet budgets with lifetimes of roughly 2818.60 h and 1690.00 h, respectively. These results suggest that retrieval-grounded prompting steers the model toward device-appropriate operating modes and that constraint-driven iteration reliably narrows in on energy-effective regimes without overfitting to any single sensor.

Impact of Different LLMs. We repeat the pipeline with alternative LLMs (including the most advanced models ChatGPT-5 Mini, ChatGPT-4, Grok 3, Gemini 2.5, and Deepseek v3.1) while holding retrieval and verification constant. As shown in Fig. 6, under multiple runs, the achieved lifespan of the configuration code obtained by our algorithm in different models is higher than the desired lifespan, where inference time stays within the 2-min envelope. This cross-model replication indicates that robustness derives from the retrieval-augmented, constraint-centric methodology rather than idiosyncrasies of any single LLM.

5   Discussion and Future Work

The fundamental methodology of GPowerT is inherently generalizable. Its core approach is not uniquely tied to energy consumption. It bridges the semantic-to-hardware gap by interpreting natural language descriptions against a specialized device knowledge base, followed by verification through a closed-loop refinement process. This same framework can be adapted to manage other critical constraints in IoT applications, such as stringent runtime deadlines or memory

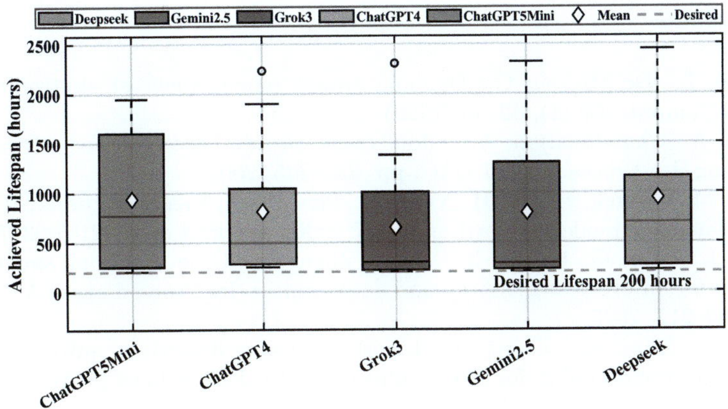

Fig. 6. Different LLMs

limitations. By substituting the power-centric knowledge base with one detailing execution times or memory footprints, the system could be repurposed to generate code optimized for these alternative non-functional requirements.

Moreover, we will evolve GPowerT from a single-criterion optimizer into a comprehensive, multi-objective co-design assistant. Real-world IoT systems are defined by a complex interplay of competing requirements, including computational performance, memory footprint, and security, in addition to power draw. We envision a system capable of interpreting and negotiating these trade-offs when expressed in natural language (e.g., "Prioritize a five-year battery life, but ensure motion detection alerts are processed within 100 milliseconds"). This evolution would require enhancing the closed-loop refinement process to simultaneously verify multiple constraints that balance these often-conflicting goals.

6   Conclusion

We propose GPowerT, an LLM-driven automated system designed to generate firmware for power-constrained embedded applications. Our system features three novel technical modules, which work in concert to transform high-level natural language descriptions into verifiable, energy-efficient code. Our framework demonstrates that by integrating a power-specific knowledge base and a verification loop, it is possible to generate firmware that is guaranteed to comply with strict energy budgets. This showcases the strong potential of augmenting LLMs with domain-specific knowledge and automated feedback to solve fundamental deployment challenges in IoT application development.

Acknowledgments. This paper is partially supported by the Natural Science Foundation of Jiangsu Province of China (Grant No. BK20240615) and Natural Science Research Start-up Foundation of Recruiting Talents of Nanjing University of Posts and Telecommunications (Grant No. NY224030).

References

1. Benini, L., De Micheli, G.: Dynamic power management of electronic systems. IEEE Comput. **32**(11), 42–48 (1999)
2. Sinha, A., Chandrakasan, A.P.: Jouletrack - a web based tool for software energy profiling. In: Proceedings of DAC, pp. 220–225, 2001
3. Chen, M., Tworek, J., Jun, H., Yuan, Q., Penedo, H., Viégas, F., et al.: "Evaluating large language models trained on code," arXiv preprint arXiv:2107.03374, 2021
4. Shen, L., Yang, Q., Huang, X., Ma, Z., Zheng, Y.: Gpiot: tailoring small language models for iot program synthesis and development. In: Proceedings of ACM SenSys, pp. 199–212, 2025
5. Shen, L., Yang, Q., Zheng, Y., Li, M.: Autoiot: llm-driven automated natural language programming for aiot applications. In: Proceedings of ACM MobiCom, 2025
6. Xu, H., Han, L., Yang, Q., Li, M., Srivastava, M.: Penetrative AI: making llms comprehend the physical world. In: Findings of ACL, pp. 7324–7341, 2024
7. Tiwari, V., Malik, S., Wolfe, A.: Power analysis of embedded software: a first step towards software power minimization. In: Proceedings of IEEE/ACM ICCAD, pp. 384–390, 1994
8. Ji, S., Zheng, X., Wu, C.: HARGPT: are llms zero-shot human activity recognizers? *CoRR*, vol. abs/2403.02727, 2024
9. Ouyang, X., Srivastava, M.: Llmsense: harnessing llms for high-level reasoning over spatiotemporal sensor traces, *CoRR*, vol. abs/2403.19857, 2024
10. Chang, C., Wang, W., Peng, W., Chen, ': LLM4TS: aligning pre-trained llms as data-efficient time-series forecasters. ACM Trans. Intell. Syst. Technol. **16**(3), 60:1–60:20 (2025)
11. Guo, D., Zhu, Q., Yang, D., Xie, Z., Dong, K., Zhang, W., et al.: Deepseek-coder: when the large language model meets programming - the rise of code intelligence, CoRR, vol. abs/2401.14196, 2024
12. Rozière, B., Gehring, J., Gloeckle, F., Sootla, S., Gat, I., Tan, X.E., et al.: Code llama: open foundation models for code, CoRR, vol. abs/2308.12950, 2023
13. Duan, S., Kanakaris, N., Xiao, X., Ping, H., Zhou, C., Ahmed, N.K., et al.: Leveraging reinforcement learning and large language models for code optimization, CoRR, vol. abs/2312.05657, 2023
14. Zhong, L., Wang, Z., Shang, J.: LDB: a large language model debugger via verifying runtime execution step-by-step, CoRR, vol. abs/2402.16906, 2024
15. Li, R., Allal, L.B., Zi, Y., Muennighoff, N., Kocetkov, D., Mou, C., et al.: Starcoder: may the source be with you! Trans. Mach. Learn. Res. **2023** (2023)
16. OpenAI, "GPT-4 technical report," CoRR, vol. abs/2303.08774, 2023
17. Assafelovic, "Gpt researcher." https://github.com/assafelovic/gpt-researcher, 2023
18. Neelakantan, A., Xu, T., Puri, R., Radford, A., Han, J.M., Tworek, J., et al.: Text and code embeddings by contrastive pre-training, CoRR, vol. abs/2201.10005, 2022
19. Douze, M., Guzhva, A., Deng, C., Johnson, J., Szilvasy, G., Mazaré, P., et al.: The faiss library, CoRR, vol. abs/2401.08281, 2024

Millisecond-Level Interference-Aware Scheduling for Multi-Inference Co-Location on Ascend NPUs

Wenhao Huang[1], Fupeng Li[1], Laiping Zhao[1]([✉]), Yeju Zhou[2], and Keqiu Li[1]

[1] College of Intelligence and Computing (CIC), Tianjin University , Tianjin, China
laiping@tju.edu.cn
[2] HUAWEI, Shenzhen, China

Abstract. The growing popularity of AI inference services has created a substantial demand for AI accelerators. However, the strict tail-latency requirements of inference workloads often conflict with the throughput optimization objectives of these accelerators. Many AI accelerators (e.g., Ascend NPUs, Kunlun chips) support co-located deployment of inference tasks via temporal sharing to improve throughput, where interference between tasks can be abstracted as kernel queuing delays. Motivated by this observation, we design nShare, a system that detects interference at the kernel level on hardware supporting temporal sharing and performs millisecond-scale scheduling control. nShare models interference on temporal shared devices as SLO (Service Level Object) slack and incorporates a dynamic batching mechanism to improve utilization without violating latency constraints. Compared to baseline systems, nShare improves throughput by 39.48%–51.53% while meeting the 99th-percentile SLO.

Keywords: AI inference · Temporal sharing · Millisecond-scale scheduling

1   Introduction

The rapid advancement of AI–especially deep learning–has created unprecedented demand for high-performance hardware. Traditional CPUs/GPUs suffer from von Neumann bottlenecks (memory-processor separation) when handling core AI workloads like large-scale low-precision matrix operations and nonlinear functions, leading to poor energy efficiency, high latency, and low utilization. This drives the need for specialized AI accelerators.

However, the inference task often fails to fully utilize the computational capacity of AI accelerators, Microsoft's data shows that the utilization of their AI accelerator clusters is approximately 52% [1]. An effective way to improve throughput is to leverage the hardware-level multi-tasking interfaces provided by AI accelerators, enabling multiple inference tasks to be co-located on the same accelerator.

© IFIP International Federation for Information Processing 2026
Published by Springer Nature Switzerland AG 2026
X. Wang et al. (Eds.): NPC 2025, LNCS 16306, pp. 303–314, 2026.
https://doi.org/10.1007/978-3-032-10466-3_25

Therefore, as shown in Table 1, existing AI accelerators can be categorized into two architectural types based on their hardware resource sharing mechanisms: (1) **Spatial-Sharing:** Spatial sharing comprises dynamic spatial partitioning–enabling real-time SM resource reallocation without downtime (e.g., NVIDIA MPS)–and static spatial partitioning, which requires system downtime for resource reconfiguration (e.g., NVIDIA MIG). Nvidia GPU and AMD Instinct support Hardware and Software Spatial-Sharing (Rows 1 and 4 of Table 1). (2) **Temporal-sharing:** Tasks are alternately executed through the rotation of time slices, and a computing unit can only handle one task at a time. Therefore, for accelerators such as Ascend NPU(A scalable and unified architecture for ubiquitous deep neural network computing across diverse AI scenarios) [17] and Kunlun(A 14nm high-performance AI processor designed to accelerate diversified workloads with optimized power efficiency) [18] that only support static spatial sharing, the computing units on the accelerator cannot execute tasks in parallel, and multitasking on the accelerator needs to be queued for execution.

Table 1. AI Accelerator Resource Sharing Characteristics

Feature	Spatial-Sharing	Temporal-sharing	Resource Sharing Mode (Intra-Subcard)
Nvidia GPU	Dynamic/Static Spatial-Sharing	✓	Spatial-Sharing
Ascend	Static Spatial-Sharing	✓	Temporal-Sharing
Baidu XPU	Static Spatial-Sharing	✓	Temporal-Sharing
AMD Instinct	Dynamic/Static Spatial-Sharing	✓	Spatial-Sharing

According to market data, among the 1.09 million units of AI accelerator shipments, Temporal-sharing Accelerators account for no less than 12% [14,15], amounting to approximately 130,800 units–a substantial market share. We identify that the low utilization of such hardware in production environments primarily stems from the lack of SLO assurance strategies for co-located deployments. Consequently, models are typically deployed in a manner that monopolizes accelerators for inference to ensure service stability. Therefore, designing effective SLO assurance strategies is crucial. This introduces several challenges: inference requests must complete within tens to hundreds of milliseconds, requiring millisecond-level interference detection and request scheduling to meet SLO targets.

To address this challenge, we quantify interference at the millisecond scale by abstracting interference on temporally shared hardware as kernel queuing time. This allows us to compute the effective SLO slack for a newly arrived inference request–defined as the user-specified SLO minus the observed kernel queuing time–and to determine the optimal batch size accordingly. This enables millisecond-level interference-aware scheduling. Based on this technique, we develop *nShare*, a non-intrusive system that requires no modifications to either the hardware or the software stack, making it well-suited for public cloud deployment. Compared to the baseline, nShare improves inference throughput by 39.48%–51.53% while satisfying the 99th-percentile tail-latency SLO.

The contributions of this paper are as follows:

1. Millisecond-Level Interference Awareness: Using model-layer-granularity interception, nShare retrieves the remaining task execution time on hardware in milliseconds and quantifies interference accordingly.
2. Dynamic Batch Management: By adaptively adjusting batch sizes based on task-specific SLO slack, nShare optimizes resource efficiency while preserving QoS for latency-sensitive tasks.
3. Resource Optimization: The activation-layer-centric interception design reduces scheduling overhead by 1.34× and improves SLO compliance rates by 14.8%–18.3%.

2 Background and Motivation

2.1 Background

Execution Modes in AI Accelerator Architectures Contemporary AI accelerator hardware architectures (e.g., Ascend NPU) exhibit two fundamental execution paradigms: hardware spatial-sharing and temporal-sharing.

The Spatial-Sharing architecture achieves resource isolation by partitioning physical NPUs (e.g., Ascend 910B) into fixed sub-units. However, this mechanism suffers from a critical limitation (Fig. 1(a)): resource allocations become statically fixed upon initialization and cannot adapt to dynamic workload fluctuations. When load imbalance occurs across sub-units, idle resources in underutilized partitions directly degrade overall hardware utilization, resulting in significant resource wastage.

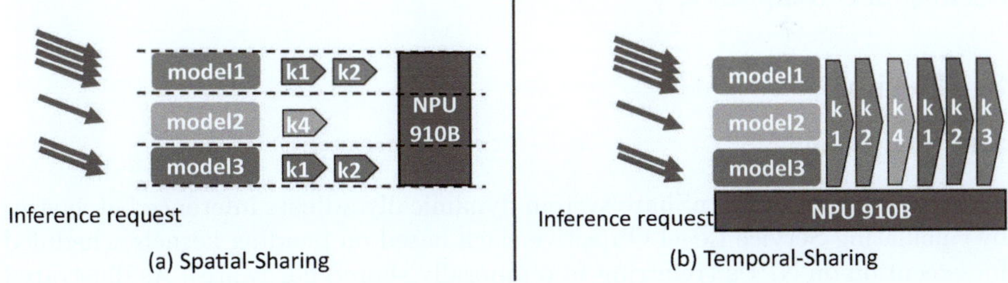

Fig. 1. Spatial-Sharing

Temporal Sharing: As shown in Fig. 1(b), regardless of whether hardware partitioning is implemented, the underlying execution logic of such accelerators remains based on temporal sharing. Temporal sharing allows the full hardware resources to be utilized at any given moment, and its design can be orthogonally optimized with hardware spatial-sharing to further improve efficiency.

2.2 Motivation: Queue-Based Interference Awareness and Batch Adjustment

Limitations of Native Scheduling: In the context of temporal sharing, simply appending new inference requests to the execution queue upon arrival can violate Service Level Objectives (SLOs). This is because the kernels of other pending requests in the queue have not yet completed execution. As illustrated in Fig. 2, the kernels of the new request are placed after all existing kernels in the queue, which may directly lead to SLO violations.

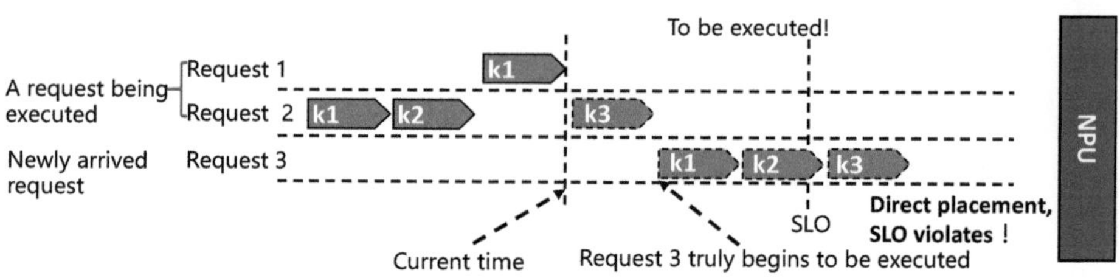

Fig. 2. Direct placement of requests leads to SLO violations

SLO-Slack Awareness: To address this issue, we propose a key insight: by continuously monitoring and predicting the execution time of queued kernels, the system can dynamically compute the current SLO slack–defined as the user-specified SLO minus the accumulated kernel queuing time. As illustrated in Fig. 3, based on the computed SLO slack, the system can determine the optimal batch size for incoming inference requests, thereby maximizing throughput while ensuring SLO compliance.

3 Design

3.1 Overview

The core concept of the nShare system dynamically adjusts inference batch sizes by calculating Service Level Objective slack based on pending kernels scheduled for execution on NPUs (referring to temporally shared hardware). As illustrated in Fig. 4, nShare's architecture comprises three fundamental components: an offline profiler, a global scheduler, and distributed NPU agents where each agent manages a single NPU card under the centralized coordination of the global scheduler. When users submit an AI model, the offline profiler first conducts comprehensive measurements of the model's end-to-end execution time across varying batch sizes, simultaneously capturing per-layer kernel execution times specific to the target NPU architecture. This instrumented model is subsequently deployed within the PyTorch framework integrated with the NPU runtime, with all profiling results embedded into the model's metadata.

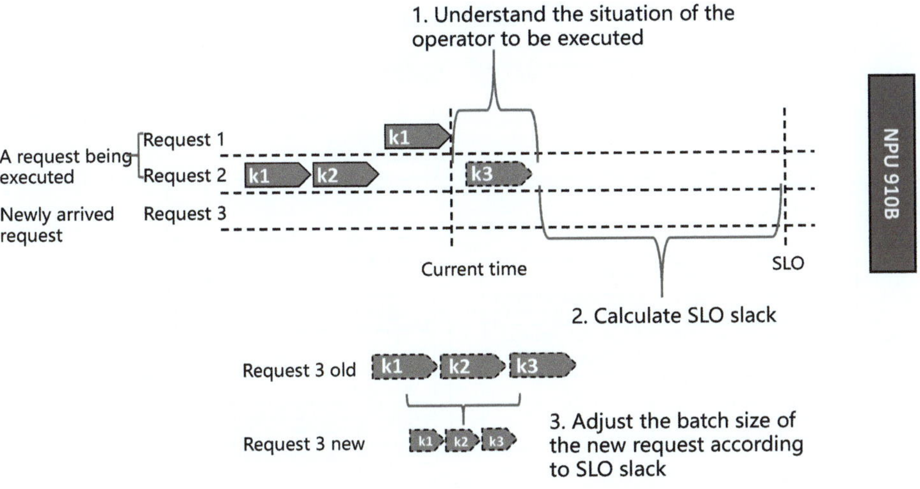

Fig. 3. SLO-Slack-Aware Optimization

During inference operations, when new requests arrive, the global scheduler initiates resource allocation by evaluating real-time SLO slack values across all managed NPU agents. This critical metric quantifies each NPU's idle capacity through the calculation:

$$\text{SLO slack} = \text{SLO deadline} - \sum(\text{execution time of pending NPU kernels})$$

. The scheduler identifies the top-k agents exhibiting the highest SLO slack values–indicating their lower utilization states–before the batch manager determines optimal batch sizes for incoming requests by synthesizing current SLO slack measurements with the pre-profiled model characteristics.

Upon receiving batched inference tasks, each NPU agent executes requests through its local PyTorch runtime. A dedicated layer interceptor within each agent asynchronously intercepts layer execution contexts prior to computation. This component retrieves pre-profiled kernel time metrics from the model metadata, calculates the cumulative NPU execution time of all remaining unexecuted layers' NPU time, and dynamically updates the local SLO slack value. The updated slack value is immediately synchronized with the global scheduler, enabling continuous scheduling refinement throughout the inference lifecycle.

The nShare system is compatible with other temporal-sharing accelerators.

3.2 Offline Profiler

In temporal-sharing NPUs where only one kernel executes per card at any moment, a model's total NPU occupation time equals its cumulative kernel execution time. Co-deployed models thus experience interference through kernel contention. To ensure new tasks meet SLOs, nShare verifies that the com-

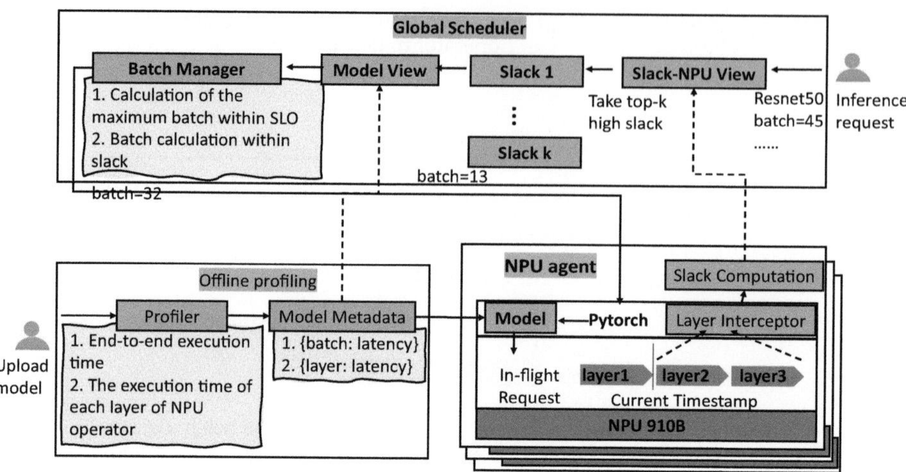

Fig. 4. nShare prototype system

bined pending NPU time–including co-located models' kernels and the new task's kernels–fits within the SLO threshold.

The offline profiler captures per-layer NPU execution times and end-to-end latency across all batch sizes. By prioritizing activation layers (e.g., ReLU/GELU) during profiling, it minimizes runtime overhead. Crucially, it embeds precomputed cumulative remaining NPU time (sum of subsequent layers) into each layer's metadata rather than per-kernel times, enabling instant access during inference without real-time computation.

3.3 NPU Agent

For each NPU card, an NPU agent is deployed to dispatch and monitor inference tasks while intercepting model layers in real-time to calculate pending kernel execution time.

The layer interceptor operates to determine the actual available NPU time in co-located deployment environments. During inference task execution, it intercepts before each layer and retrieves its metadata (including offline profiling data). It then dynamically calculates the total pending kernel execution time for all remaining layers of the inference task under the current batch size.

Subsequently, the NPU agent sums the pending NPU time of all models on its card and subtracts this value from the SLO threshold to derive the SLO slack. This slack value (≤ 0) serves as an indicator of NPU idleness–higher values denote greater idle capacity.

Layer Interceptor. The layer interceptor serves as the core module enabling layer-aware control in the nShare system. It intercepts inference tasks before each layer execution, retrieves the layer's metadata, and dynamically calculates the total pending NPU execution time for all remaining layers of the task. Following each interception, the layer interceptor updates the SLO slack (i.e., the remaining time budget for the current inference task) of the NPU device and synchronizes this information with the global scheduler.This mechanism ensures no SLO violations occur for any inference task under co-located deployment environments.

3.4 Global Scheduler

The global scheduler computes the assigned batch size for each NPU agent based on two principles: (1) The profiled end-to-end execution time of the allocated batch must be shorter than the SLO requirement; (2) The total profiled NPU kernel execution time for the allocated batch must be less than the current SLO slack. This dual guarantee ensures that the batch execution on the target NPU agent complies with SLO constraints while preventing newly arriving requests from causing SLO violations for in-flight requests due to resource contention.

Responsible for managing resource allocation and task scheduling across all NPU devices, the global scheduler queries SLO slack values of all NPU devices when a new inference request arrives. It selects the NPU agent with the highest SLO slack–indicating the least busy device–to process the request.

When determining batch sizes, the scheduler leverages offline profiling data and real-time SLO information. It first verifies that the end-to-end execution time for the candidate batch size remains within SLO limits, while simultaneously ensuring the total NPU kernel execution time doesn't exceed the target agent's SLO slack. The scheduler's core objective is maximizing inference throughput through batch management while maintaining strict SLO compliance.

Batch Manager. The batch manager, a critical module in the nShare system, dynamically adjusts task batch sizes according to current SLO constraints and NPU utilization. It obtains NPU execution times for different batch sizes from the offline profiler and combines this with SLO slack information from the layer interceptor to compute optimal batch sizes(Satisfy the maximum batch size under the SLO constraint) for incoming inference tasks. The maximum batch size b_{max} is determined by the following formula, where $T(b)$ is the profiling execution time for batch size b, and slack is the SLO slack:

$$b_{\mathrm{max}} = \max\{b \mid T(b) \leq \mathrm{slack}\}$$

4 Implementation

4.1 Offline Profiler

The offline profiler implements layer-wise characterization using PyTorch's register_module_forward_pre_hook() interface to intercept forward passes. It captures per-layer execution times and aggregates end-to-end latency, while invoking torch_npu.profiler() to extract NPU kernel execution times through Ascend

PyTorch Profiler. Crucially, it stores not per-kernel times but the cumulative remaining NPU time (sum of all subsequent layers) in each layer's metadata, embedded directly into the model. Profiling occurs across batch sizes 1–128, with results saved in CSV files alongside model-embedded metadata.

4.2 NPU Agent

Per NPU card, an NPU agent deploys to manage task dispatch and monitoring. It hosts a layer interceptor that leverages register_module_forward_pre_hook() to intercept each layer pre-execution. At every interception, the layer interceptor: (1) Retrieves embedded layer metadata, (2) Computes total pending NPU time for the task's remaining layers, (3) Updates the device's SLO slack, where higher values (closer to zero) indicate greater NPU idleness, and (4) Synchronizes this slack value with the global scheduler.

5 Experiment

5.1 Experimental Data

This chapter will introduce the experimental environment, workload selection, evaluation metrics, and comparative systems of the nShare system. It will also present experimental results demonstrating nShare's performance in throughput, SLO compliance, NPU memory requirements, and overhead. The experiments primarily validate how nShare enhances inference task throughput and resource utilization through SLO slack control and batch management mechanisms while guaranteeing SLO compliance.

5.2 Experimental Environment

The experiments were conducted in an NPU910B test environment. Each experimental node was equipped with 8 NPU910B cards with driver version 24.1. rc1, a 192-core CPU, and 1.5TB of memory. The nShare system was assessed using a range of common neural network models (in Table 2) and workloads.

Table 2. Neural Network Models Specification

Model Name	Category	Function	Architecture	Weights (MB)
ResNet50-v1.5	Image Cls.	Main object recognition	CNN	97.49
MobileNet_v2	Obj. Detect.	Multi-object detection with bounding boxes	CNN	13.37
Alexnet	Image Cls.	Main object recognition	CNN	61.10
Squeezenet	Image Cls.	Main object recognition	CNN	1.20
Swin Trans.	Image Cls.	Main object recognition	Trans.	107.91
VGG16	Image Cls.	Main object recognition	CNN	527.8

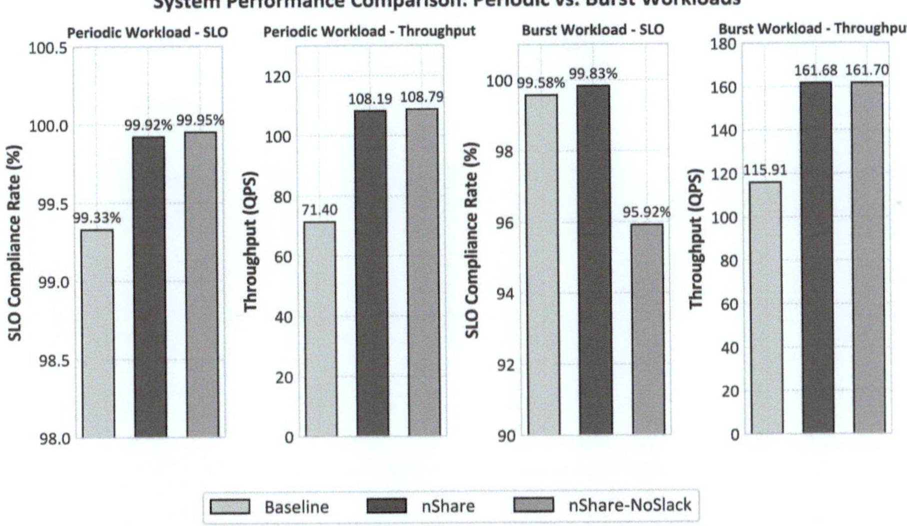

Fig. 5. Performance comparison between periodic load and burst load

The experimental workloads adopted bursty and periodic workload traces [16]. The period length of Periodic traces is approximately 57 s, while bursty traces show load peaks of 600 with long idle periods between bursts. Evaluation metrics included SLO compliance rate, throughput (QPS), and NPU memory usage.

5.3 Comparison System

To comprehensively evaluate the performance of the nShare system, the experiment configured the following comparison systems:

- **Baseline**: Fixed batch size; max throughput under SLO.
- **nShare-NoSlack**: nShare without SLO slack control (evaluates mechanism contribution).
- **nShare**: Proposed system with full SLO slack and batch management.

5.4 Throughput and SLO Compliance Experiment

Figure 5 shows the comparison results of throughput and SLO compliance rate for the Baseline, nShare-NoSlack, and nShare systems under different workloads. The experiments demonstrate that while ensuring the 99th percentile tail latency, the throughput of the nShare system increased by 39.48%–51.53% compared to the Baseline, and by 23.65%–30.21% compared to nShare-NoSlack. Compared to the baseline system (71 QPS throughput and 99.0% SLO compliance rate), nShare-NoSlack achieves a higher throughput of 90 QPS but with a slightly lower SLO compliance rate of 98.7%.

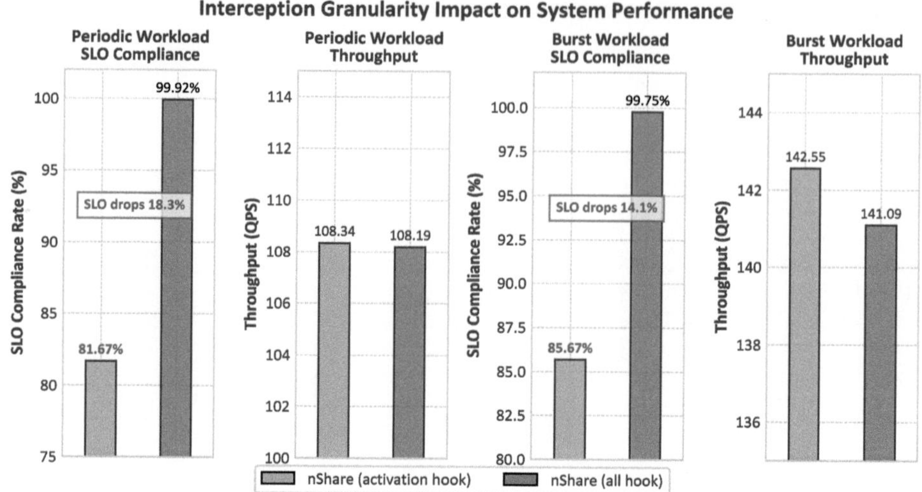

Fig. 6. Comparison of different interception granularity under different loads

5.5   NPU Memory Requirement Experiment

To evaluate the resource efficiency of the nShare system, we compare the NPU memory consumption across different systems while maintaining identical throughput (400 QPS). At 400 QPS throughput, nShare achieves optimal NPU memory efficiency (10.6 GB), reducing usage by 1.6 GB compared to nShare-NoSlack (12.7 GB) and 3.6 GB versus Baseline (14.2 GB).

5.6   Overhead Experiment

The primary overhead of the nShare system originates from layer interception operations and SLO slack updates. To evaluate system optimization efficiency, experiments compare the overhead of intercepting all layers versus intercepting only active layers. Figure 6 demonstrates the performance of two granularity interception methods under different load scenarios. When only intercepting activation layers, throughput increased by 0.15 and 1.46 QPS at the cost of 18.1% and 14.3% degradation in SLO compliance respectively. As shown in Fig. 7, nShare significantly reduces interception overhead by exclusively intercepting active layers, achieving an average interception latency of 0.343 s. Compared to full-layer interception (0.489 s), nShare reduces overhead by approximately 30%, while maintaining nearly identical throughput and SLO guarantee rates.

6   Related Work

Most inference systems rely on co-located deployment and hardware resource management. Researchers optimize heterogeneous computing through three

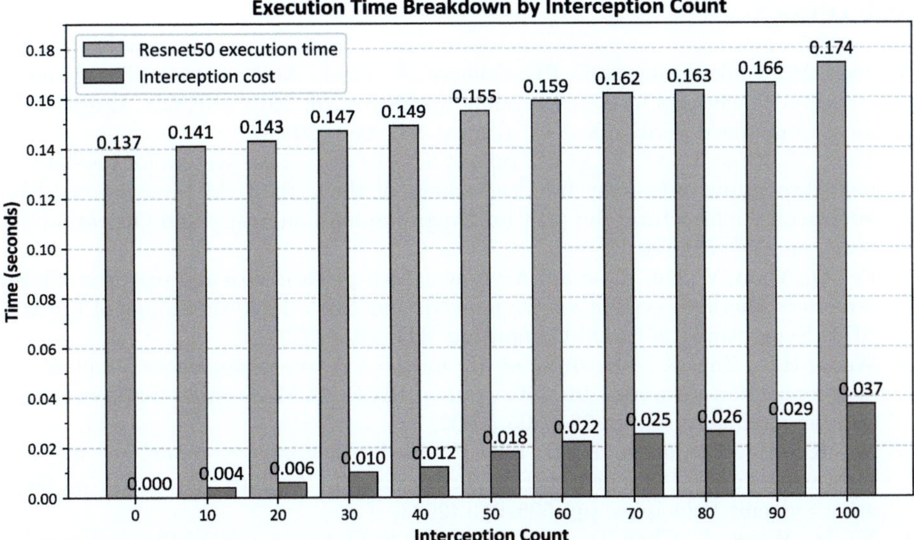

Fig. 7. Relationship between number of intercepts and execution time

approaches: Resource isolation systems like INFless unify CPU/GPU abstraction to boost throughput via batching [2], while AsyFunc improves efficiency with lightweight shadow functions for burst handling [3]. For workload management, kernel-level techniques in Orion [4] and Paella [5] increase GPU utilization through consumption characterization and co-location, with Paella specifically scheduling latency-sensitive tasks to meet SLOs. Caching acceleration includes FaaSwap's model caching to reduce cold starts [6] and GPU-enabled systems' memory residency management to minimize overhead [7].

7   Conclusion

This paper presents nShare, a system that addresses the challenge of co-locating inference workloads on temporal-sharing AI accelerators. nShare leverages model-layer-level interception to enable millisecond-level SLO-slack awareness and a dynamic batch management mechanism, effectively improving system throughput while ensuring SLO compliance. The design of nShare is entirely non-intrusive to both the hardware and software stack, making it well-suited for deployment in public cloud environments.

Acknowledgments. This work is supported by the National Key Research and Development Program of China under Grant No. 2024YFB4505204, the National Natural Science Foundation of China under Grant No. 62372322, and the Huawei Collaborative Project TC20230914023.

References

1. Jeon, M., Venkataraman, S., Phanishayee, A., et al.: Analysis of large-scale multi-tenant GPU clusters for DNN training workloads. In: 2019 USENIX Annual Technical Conference (USENIX ATC 19), pp. 947–960 (2019)
2. Yang, Y., Zhao, L., Li, Y., et al.: Infless: a native serverless system for low-latency, high-throughput inference. In: Proceedings of the 27th ACM International Conference on Architectural Support for Programming Languages and Operating Systems, pp. 768–781 (2022)
3. Pei, Q., Yuan, Y., Hu, H., et al.: Asyfunc: a high-performance and resource-efficient serverless inference system via asymmetric functions. In: Proceedings of the 2023 ACM Symposium on Cloud Computing. 324–340 (2023)
4. Wang, H.S., Zhu, X., Peh, L.S., et al.: Orion: a power-performance simulator for interconnection networks. In: 35th Annual IEEE/ACM International Symposium on Microarchitecture, pp. 294–305 (2002)
5. Ng, K.K.W., Demoulin, H.M., Liu, V.: Paella: low-latency model serving with software-defined GPU scheduling. In: Proceedings of the 29th Symposium on Operating Systems Principles, pp. 595–610 (2023)
6. Yu, M., Wang, A., Chen, D., et al.: Faaswap: SLO-Aware, GPU-Efficient Serverless Inference via Model Swapping. arXiv preprint arXiv:2306.03622 (2023)
7. Zhao, M., Jha, K., Hong, S.: GPU-enabled function-as-a-service for machine learning inference. In: 2023 IEEE International Parallel and Distributed Processing Symposium (IPDPS), pp. 918–928 (2023)
8. Gujarati, A., Karimi, R., Alzayat, S., Hao, W., Kaufmann, A., Vigfusson, Y., Mace, J.: Serving DNNs like clockwork: performance predictability from the bottom up. In: 14th USENIX Symposium on Operating Systems Design and Implementation, pp. 443–462 (2020)
9. Author, F.: Article title. Journal **2**(5), 99–110 (2016)
10. Author, F., Author, S.: Title of a proceedings paper. In: Editor, F., Editor, S. (eds.) CONFERENCE 2016, LNCS, vol. 9999, pp. 1–13. Springer, Heidelberg (2016). https://doi.org/10.10007/1234567890
11. Author, F., Author, S., Author, T.: Book title, 2nd edn. Publisher, Location (1999)
12. Author, A.-B.: Contribution title. In: 9th International Proceedings on Proceedings, pp. 1–2. Publisher, Location (2010)
13. LNCS Homepage. http://www.springer.com/lncs. Accessed 25 Oct 2023
14. 163.com Technology Article. https://www.163.com/dy/article/ISF368MT0539IMJ0.html. Accessed 28 Mar 2025
15. IDC Whitepaper Documentation. https://my.idc.com/getdoc.jsp?containerId=prCHC53286125. Accessed 28 Mar 2025
16. Shahrad, M., Fonseca, R., Goiri, I., et al.: Serverless in the wild: characterizing and optimizing the serverless workload at a large cloud provider. In: 2020 USENIX Annual Technical Conference (USENIX ATC 20), pp. 205–218 (2020)
17. Liao, H., Tu, J., Xia, J., et al.: Ascend: a scalable and unified architecture for ubiquitous deep neural network computing: Industry track paper. In: 2021 IEEE International Symposium on High-Performance Computer Architecture (HPCA), pp. 789–801 (2021)
18. Ouyang, J., Du, X., Ma, Y., et al.: 3.3 Kunlun: a 14 nm high-performance AI processor for diversified workloads. In: 2021 IEEE International Solid-State Circuits Conference (ISSCC), pp. 50–51 (2021)

An Unsupervised Learning Log Anomaly Detection Method Based on Graph Neural Network

Xianlang Hu[1,2], Guangsheng Feng[1(✉)], Xinling Huang[1] , Xiangying Kong[1,2], and Hongwu Lv[1]

[1] Harbin Engineering University, Harbin 150001, China
{ica,huangxinling,lvhongwu}@hrbeu.edu.cn
[2] Jiangsu Institute of Automation, Jiangsu 222006, China

Abstract. Log anomaly detection is crucial for the security of distributed computing systems. Although existing methods can capture the statistical characteristics and explicit timing patterns of log events, there are still two major challenges for semi-structured log files: 1) Complex topological dependencies between log events and implicit associations with multi-dimensional semantics of key fields have not been fully modeled, and anomalous patterns are easily overwhelmed by high-frequency normal events. 2) Dynamic log formats require field extraction relying on manual rules or supervised learning, which is difficult to adapt to operation and maintenance (O&M) requirements in low resource scenarios. To address these issues, we propose an unsupervised log anomaly detection framework based on graph neural networks (GNN). Specifically, key fields (e.g., anomalous IPs, failed APIs) are automatically extracted using prompt-based few-shot learning, then a weighted directed graph model fusing semantic embedding and temporal dependency is constructed to fully characterize the dynamic interaction patterns among system components. Moreover, global anomaly identification across events is achieved by co-optimizing graph representation learning and anomaly detection objectives based on one-class directed graph convolutional networks. Experimental results show that our method performs remarkably on multiple benchmark datasets and exhibits excellent generalization capabilities for unseen log templates, improving distributed system security.

Keywords: Log Anomaly Detection · Graph Neural Networks · Unsupervised Learning · Few-Shot Prompt Learning

1 Introduction

Log anomaly detection is a critical tool for maintaining the stability and security of distributed computing systems. System logs record states and events in detail [1], enabling fault identification and preventive measures [2]. With the

X. Wang et al. (Eds.): NPC 2025, LNCS 16306, pp. 315–326, 2026.
https://doi.org/10.1007/978-3-032-10466-3_26

widespread adoption of distributed and cloud computing systems, massive volumes of log data are continuously generated, exhibiting prominent characteristics of semi-structured complexity, temporal dependency, and semantic richness. The three major features increase the complexity of anomaly detection, and how to realize efficient and accurate log anomaly detection has become an urgent technical challenge.

Traditional rule-based methods [3, 4] suffer from high false positives and missed detections in dynamic cloud settings, while statistical models [5–8] inadequately capture non-linear cross-service dependencies. Machine Learning (ML) and Deep Learning (DL) approaches have been introduced to address these issues [9–14]. Classical ML methods such as OCSVM [15] and PCA [16] use log event counting matrices, failing to capture semantics or sequential dependencies. DL methods such as DeepLog [10] and LogAnomaly [11] leverage sequential information but overlook event-field structural dependencies. Accordingly, two major challenges remain for existing research: (1) Event-field topology dependency: Anomalies may arise from subtle cross-event field interactions, forming complex topologies that encode hidden patterns. Such structural correlations are often overlooked, causing missed or false detections. (2) Generalization bottleneck in low-resource scenarios: existing field extraction methods rely on fixed rules or fully supervised learning, making it difficult to adapt to the dynamic evolution of log formats.

In recent years, Graph Neural Networks (GNNs) have gained attention for their advantages in modeling complex relationships and structured data [17]. Specifically: (1) identifying issues where event structure is critical; (2) providing contextual log messages corresponding to identified problems; and (3) representing "normal" operational flows as graphs to help end-users trace root causes and implement corrective measures. Motivated by these strengths, we propose a graph-based unsupervised log anomaly detection framework that, in addition to capturing log semantics and sequential patterns, extracts and learns relationships between log events and fields to mine deeper relational information and enhance detection accuracy. Overall, the main contributions are summarized below:

- Domain-adaptive few-shot field extraction: Formulate log field identification as a prompt-based sequence generation task, leveraging the generalization of pre-trained BERT [18] to accurately extract key fields under low-resource conditions, reducing reliance on manual rules and labels, and improving adaptability to evolving log formats.
- Multi-dimensional graph structure modeling: Construct an attribute-enhanced weighted directed graph integrating semantic context and event transition frequency, enabling topological reconstruction of service invocation chains and resource access patterns under normal conditions, thereby improving anomaly detection accuracy.
- Co-optimization of graph representation with anomaly targets: Develop a one-class directed graph convolutional network that maximizes the hyperspherical compactness of normal patterns for end-to-end unsupervised anomaly scoring, detecting both isolated event anomalies and cross-event structural deviations, providing insights for root cause analysis.

2   Methodology

In this section, we present a graph-based log anomaly detection framework tailored for log events. The entire workflow consists of the usual major steps, namely log parsing, feature extraction, graph construction, graph representation learning, and anomaly detection, as shown in Fig. 1. Note that since log parsing is not the main focus of this paper, we use Drain [19] to accomplish this task. Furthermore, we combine the graph representation learning and anomaly detection to accomplish graph construction, followed by end-to-end learning.

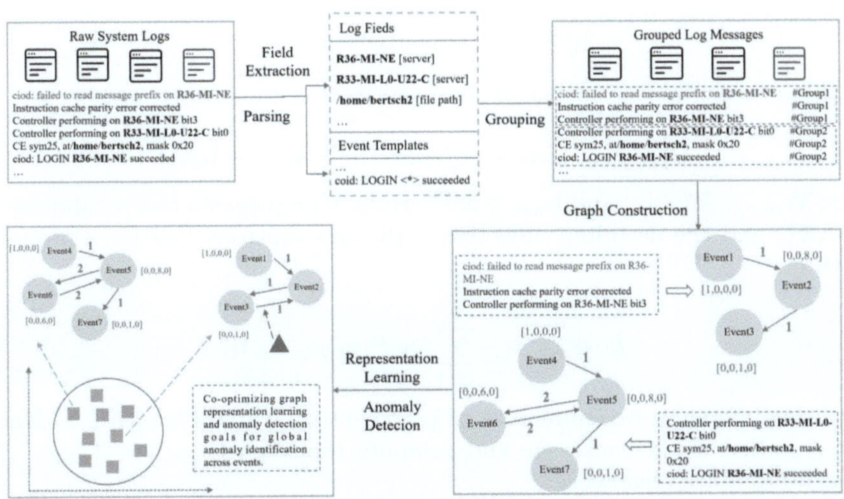

Fig. 1. Overview of the model architecture.

2.1   Log Graph Construction

To construct graph representations from log sequences, we propose a prompt-based few-shot learning field extraction module to extract fields from log messages. The extracted fields and log events parsed by a log parser are interconnected according to predefined principles to construct the graph. Subsequently, we employ a pre-trained Sentence-BERT [20] to capture the semantics of each node using its content information. The encoded hidden representation of each node is treated as its attribute, while the adjacency matrix represents the graph structure. These node attributes and adjacency matrix are jointly used for anomaly detection.

Prompt-Based Few-Shot Field Extraction. We frame field extraction as a sequence-to-sequence (seq2seq) learning process, as shown in Fig. 2a . Given a set of log messages q_m, which contains a set of gold labels $E = ent_1, \ldots, ent_{|E|}$ and a label set $\mathbf{y} = l_1, \ldots, l_{|E|}$, we create a target sequence (prompt) $\mathbf{P}_{l_k, x_{i:j}} = \{p_1, \ldots, p_m\}$ for each candidate text span $x_{i:j}$ and its label l_k.

During training, we create prompts using gold labels following [21]. For each log message q_{mn}, we generate positive samples $(q_{mn}, \mathbf{P}^+)$ by iterating over all its gold labels and negative samples $(q_{mn}, \mathbf{P}^-)$ by randomly sampling non-entity text spans. To improve efficiency, we limit the number of n-grams for span to 1 5, which results in generating $5*n$ negative prompts for each log message. The number of negative samples is three times that of positive samples after sampling. Given a sequence pair $(q_{mn}, \mathbf{P})$, we feed the log message q_{mn} into a BART encoder with hidden size d_h and obtain the hidden state $\mathbf{h}^{enc} \in \mathbb{R}^{d_h}$:

$$\mathbf{h}^{enc} = Encoder(x_{1:|q|}) \tag{1}$$

At the c-th decoding step, the representation is generated using $\mathbf{h}^{enc}$ and the previous output tokens $p_{1:c-1}$ via attention:

$$\mathbf{h}_c^{dec} = Decoder(\mathbf{h}^{enc}, p_{1:c-1}) \tag{2}$$

The conditional probability of the word p_c is defined as:

$$\mathbf{P}(p_c|p_{1:c-1}, \mathbf{q}) = softmax(\mathbf{h}_c^{dec}\mathbf{W}_{ner} + \mathbf{b}_{ner}) \tag{3}$$

where $\mathbf{W}_{ner} \in \mathbb{R}^{d_h \times |V|}$ and $\mathbf{b}_{ner} \in \mathbb{R}^{|V|}$. Here $|V|$ represents the vocabulary size of BART, and the decoding objective is the cross-entropy loss for a prompt of length m:

$$Loss_{ner} = -\sum_{c=1}^{m} \log P(p_c|p_{1:c-1}, \mathbf{q}) \tag{4}$$

During inference, we enumerate all possible text spans of length 1 5 (denoted as $x_{i:j}$) within the log message and compute the score $\mathbf{P}_{l_k, x_{i:j}} = \{p_1, \ldots, p_m\}$ for each prompt as follow:

$$f(\mathbf{P}_{l_k, x_{i:j}}) = \sum_{c=1}^{m} \log P(p_c|p_{1:c-1}, \mathbf{q}) \tag{5}$$

For each traversed text span $x_{i:j}$, we compare the scores $f(\mathbf{P}^+_{l_k, x_{i:j}})$ and $f(\mathbf{P}^-_{l_k, x_{i:j}})$. The result type l_k^* with the highest score is assigned to $x_{i:j}$. This iterative process ensures the extraction of all relevant fields, as shown in Fig. 2b.

Graph Structure Configuration. To model the relationships between fields and events across different log messages, we use a sliding window with a fixed time interval to snapshot a batch of log messages and construct the corresponding graph. Specifically, each log instance contains a parsed event template (obtained via the Drain [19] log parser). We then interconnect the event template with each extracted field to capture inherent behaviors in the logs, using the number of connections as edge weights.

Starting from the chronologically ordered log messages, we construct a directed edge from log event L_i to L_j, the edge weight is initially assigned a

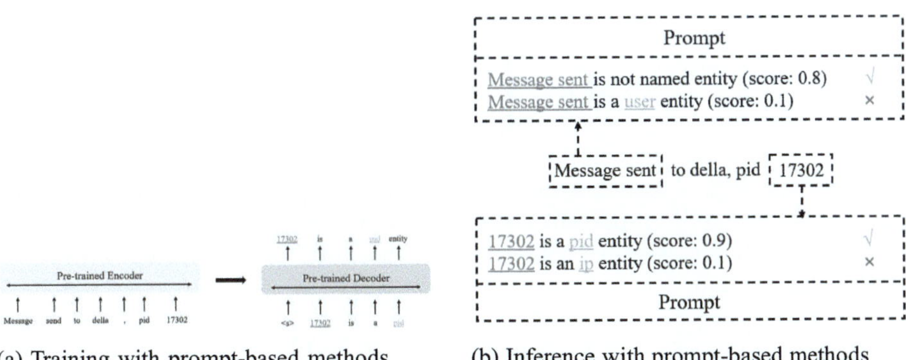

(a) Training with prompt-based methods   (b) Inference with prompt-based methods

Fig. 2. Prompt-based few-shot field-extraction.

value of 1 if L_j immediately follows L_i in the temporal sequence. If the corresponding directed edge already exists, we increment its weight by 1. This obtains us a labeled, directed, edge-weighted graph. In the resultant graph, any two log instances sharing defined nodes become indirectly connected, thereby revealing their implicit dependencies through graph topology.

Graph Structure Configuration. We define node types according to their corresponding events and field categories. For each node, we specify its input text format and employ pre-trained SentenceBERT [20] to generate sentence embeddings as attributes. Specifically, log events directly utilize their original templates as encoder input text, while log fields adopt our designed prompt templates (e.g., "imap://localhost/ is a server entity") for textual input. The output hidden states from these input texts capture node semantics, which subsequently serve as node features for constructing the attributed graph.

2.2   Graph-Based Anomaly Detection for Event Logs

We propose an enhanced Directed Graph Convolutional Network (DiGCN) [22] for end-to-end graph-level anomaly detection, specifically designed to learn node representations in attributed, directed, and edge-weighted graphs. By extending DiGCN [22], which exhibits exceptional competence in directed graph processing, we develop an end-to-end framework for graph-level anomaly detection. The selection of this foundational architecture stems from its proven capacity to capture intricate dependency patterns—precisely the relational complexity encountered in log-based anomaly detection scenarios.

Formally, let a graph $\mathcal{G}$ be characterized by its adjacency matrix $\mathbf{A} \in \mathbb{R}^{|\mathcal{V}| \times |\mathcal{V}|}$, node attribute matrix $\mathbf{A} \in \mathbb{R}^{|\mathcal{V}| \times d}$, and edge weight tensor $\mathbf{Y} \in \mathbb{N}^{|\mathcal{E}| \times |\mathcal{E}|}$. Within this framework, DiGCN [46] formalizes the k-th order directed graph convolution operation as:

$$\mathbf{Z}^{(k)} = \begin{cases} X\Theta^{(0)}, & k = 0 \\ \Psi X\Theta^{(1)}, & k = 1 \\ \Phi X\Theta^{(k)}, & k \geq 2 \end{cases} \tag{6}$$

where $\mathbf{Z}^{(k)} \in \mathcal{R}^{|\mathcal{V}| \times f}$ denotes the convolutional output with feature dimension f, and $\Theta^{(0)}, \Theta^{(1)}, \Theta^{(k)}$ represent the trainable parameter matrices.

The DiGCN architecture constructs an Inception block through multi-scale feature aggregation:

$$\mathbf{Z} = \sigma\Big(\Gamma(\{\mathbf{Z}^{(0)}, \ldots, \mathbf{Z}^{(k)}\})\Big) \tag{7}$$

where σ denotes the activation function and $\Gamma(\cdot)$ represents a fusion operator—implementable via summation, normalization, or concatenation. We use a fusion operation that keeps the output dimension unchanged in this work, i.e. $\mathbf{Z} \in \mathcal{R}^{|\mathcal{V}| \times f}$. Each row vector $\mathbf{Z}_i$ corresponds to the learned representation of node v_i at a given layer. We omit the details to save space, for more details please refer to [22].

While DiGCN was originally designed for node representation learning, we adapt it for graph-level representation learning through the following operationalization:

$$\mathbf{z} = Readout(\mathbf{Z_i}|\mathbf{i} \in \mathbf{1}, \mathbf{2}, \ldots, |\mathcal{V}|) \tag{8}$$

Specifically, at the final iteration layer, we employ the $Readout(\cdot)$ function to aggregate node embeddings into a graph-level representation. Crucially, $Readout(\cdot)$ can be an elementary permutation-invariant operator (e.g., maximum, sum, or mean), or an advanced graph-level pooling function.

For graph anomaly detection, anomalies are recognized through reconstruction or distance-based loss. We train a one-class classifier by optimizing the One-Class Deep SVDD objective [23]:

$$\min \frac{1}{M} \sum_{m=1}^{M} \|\text{DiGCN}(\mathcal{G}_M; \boldsymbol{H}) - \mathbf{o}\|_2^2 + \frac{\lambda}{2} \sum_{l=1}^{L} \left\|\boldsymbol{H}^{(l)}\right\|_F^2 \tag{9}$$

$\boldsymbol{H}^{(l)} = (\Theta^{(0)(l)}, \Theta^{(1)(l)}, \Theta^{(k)(l)})^T$ denotes the trainable parameters at the l-th layer of DiGCN, the full parameter set $\boldsymbol{H}$ is defined as $\boldsymbol{H}^{(1)}, \ldots, \boldsymbol{H}^{(L)}$, encompassing all trainable parameters across L layers. $\lambda > 0$ denotes the weight decay , and the notation $\|\cdot\|_2$ is the Euclidean norm, while $\|\cdot\|_F$ represents the Frobenius norm. Additionally, $\mathbf{o}$ is the center of the hypersphere in the learned representation space. A practical strategy is to initialize $\mathbf{o}$ as the mean value of the network representations obtained through an initial forward propagation.

After training the model on non-anomalous graphs (or extremely low percentage of anomalies), the anomaly score for a test graph $\mathcal{G}_M$ is calculated as the distance between its learned representation and the hypersphere center:

$$score(\mathcal{G}_M) = \|\text{DiGCN}(\mathcal{G}_M, \boldsymbol{H}) - \mathbf{o}\|_2 \tag{10}$$

In summary, our method consists of an L-layer DiGCN architecture for learning node representations and a *Readout*($\cdot$) function for obtaining graph representations. It is trained in an end-to-end manner by optimizing the SVDD objective, employing stochastic optimization techniques such as Adam.

3   Experiments and Analysis of Results

3.1   Experimental Setup

Datasets. To comprehensively evaluate the effectiveness of our proposed method, we pick three widely-adopted public datasets rigorously validated in prior research, HDFS [24], BGL [25] and Thunderbird [26]. The selection criteria are threefold: 1) These datasets serve as standard benchmarks for log anomaly detection methodologies; 2) They contain ground-truth labels calculating assessment metrics; 3) They provide log identifiers that facilitate event grouping. Detailed descriptions of the datasets follow, with their statistical summaries presented in Table 1.

Table 1. Dataset statistics

Name	#Events	#Graphs	#Anomalies	#Nodes	#Edges
HDFS	48	575,061	16,838	7	20
BGL	1848	69,251	31,374	10	30
Thunderbird	1013	52,160	6,814	16	52

Baseline. In order to assess the efficacy of the proposed method, a comparative analysis was conducted against five established log anomaly detection techniques: Principal Component Analysis (PCA) [16], One-Class Support Vector Machine (OCSVM) [15], DeepLog [10], LogAnomaly [11], and PLELog [27]. These methods were chosen as baselines because they represent mainstream techniques in traditional machine learning (PCA and OCSVM) and deep learning (DeepLog, LogAnomaly, and PLELog) respectively. All methods are either unsupervised or semi-supervised, obviating the need for labeled anomaly samples to train the models.

3.2   Model Implementation and Configuration

We implemented and executed all algorithms on a workstation equipped with an Intel(R) Core(TM) Ultra 9 185H CPU and an NVIDIA GeForce RTX 4060 Laptop GPU using Python 3.8. All GNN models in the study were constructed based on the PyTorch Geometric (PyG) framework. The experimental framework follows a training/validation/testing paradigm, partitioned in a ratio of 7:1:2. We employ an unsupervised learning framework, training exclusively on normal instances. Hyperparameters are tuned through grid search on the validation set. Specifically, the model is trained on 70% of the normal samples, while 10% of the normal samples along with an equivalent number of anomalous samples are used for validation (i.e., hyperparameter tuning). The remaining 20% of normal samples and the remaining anomalous samples are reserved for testing.

3.3 Experimental Results and Analysis

Overall Performance. We initially compare the overall performance of the proposed model with state-of-the-art techniques. Based on the results presented in Table 2, we have the following key observations: Our method achieves the best performance on the dataset compared to other competing methods. Particularly, the performance on BGL and Thunderbird significantly surpasses that of competitors, demonstrating the robust superiority of our method on complex datasets. The average precision also exhibits similar results.

Deep learning-based methods generally outperform traditional machine learning-based approaches. The underlying reason is that conventional machine learning approaches are confined to employing log event count vectors as their input, which inherently limits their ability to capture and exploit the sequential dependencies between log events and the semantics of log templates.

As illustrated in Fig. 3, on more complex datasets such as BGL and Thunderbird, the performance of non-graph-based deep learning methods is generally inferior to that of our approach. These datasets encompass hundreds or even thousands of log templates, suggesting that LSTM-based models are less suitable for logs with a vast number of log templates. One potential explanation is that the testing dataset comprises numerous unprecedented log templates, namely, those not present within the training dataset.

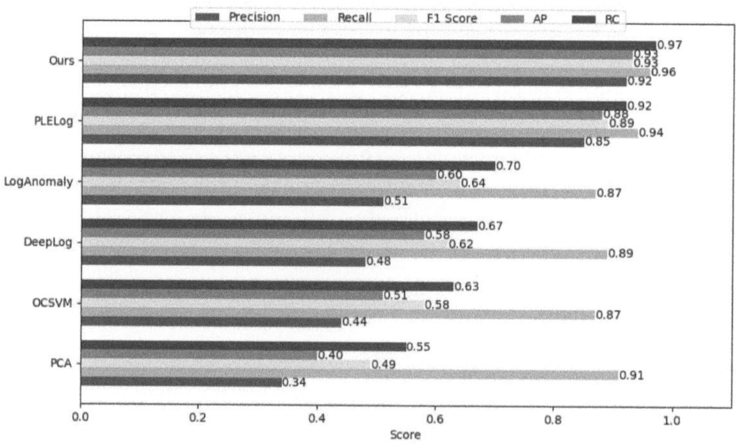

Fig. 3. Performance comparison between the proposed method and benchmarks on the Thunderbird dataset.

Table 2. Performance comparison of different models

Datasets	Method	Precision	Recall	F1-Score	AP	RC
HDFS	PCA	0.74	0.82	0.78	0.74	0.83
	OCSVM	0.63	0.79	0.70	0.67	0.75
	DeepLog	0.83	0.87	0.85	0.81	0.90
	LogAnomaly	0.86	0.89	0.87	0.85	0.91
	PLELog	0.88	0.93	0.90	0.88	0.94
	Ours	**0.90**	**0.95**	**0.92**	**0.91**	**0.96**
BGL	PCA	0.81	0.94	0.87	0.83	0.90
	OCSVM	0.63	0.73	0.68	0.65	0.75
	DeepLog	0.89	0.80	0.84	0.82	0.88
	LogAnomaly	0.91	0.79	0.84	0.83	0.89
	PLELog	0.92	0.96	0.94	0.92	0.95
	Ours	**0.93**	**0.97**	**0.95**	**0.94**	**0.97**
Thunderbird	PCA	0.34	0.91	0.49	0.40	0.55
	OCSVM	0.44	0.87	0.58	0.51	0.63
	DeepLog	0.48	0.89	0.62	0.58	0.67
	LogAnomaly	0.51	0.87	0.64	0.60	0.70
	PLELog	0.85	0.94	0.89	0.88	0.92
	Ours	**0.92**	**0.96**	**0.93**	**0.93**	**0.97**

Field Extraction. To validate the effectiveness of the field extraction, we annotate n log messages for each field type using two prompt variants and train the corresponding extraction models. As shown in Table 3, under the 5-shot learning setting, our field extraction model achieves F1-Scores comparable to manually crafted rule-based methods. When extended to 10-shot learning, our approach significantly outperforms the rule-based baseline, demonstrating its practicality in low-resource scenarios with limited annotations.

Table 3. Performance comparison (%) of rule-based vs. prompt-based n-shot field extraction

	Technique	Precision	Recall	F1-Score
	regex	36.48	44.28	40.00
P_1	1-shot	16.53	59.34	25.86
	5-shot	28.33	74.38	41.03
	10-shot	**66.28**	85.22	**74.57**
P_2	1-shot	17.89	58.14	27.36
	5-shot	28.00	73.76	40.59
	10-shot	64.68	**87.82**	74.49

Ability to Detect Structural Anomalies and Recognise Unseen Normal Instances. The results (Table 4) demonstrate that our method, DeepLog, and LogAnomaly effectively detect structural anomalies, where as PLELog underperforms on tasks S1 and S2 with ROC AUC scores of merely 0.0 and 0.5, respectively, indicating its limited capability in identifying certain structural anomalies. Notably, although DeepLog and LogAnomaly exhibit strong performance in structural anomaly detection, they achieve a false positive rate (FPR) of 100% when recognizing unseen but structurally equivalent normal instances (N1). This suggests that log sequence-based methods may misclassify normal patterns with identical structures but different instantiations as anomalies, leading to high false alarms. In contrast, our method attains a 0% FPR on task N1, demonstrating its ability to accurately identify unseen structurally equivalent normal instances and reduce erroneous alerts. This advantage stems from our graph structure-driven global feature learning, while DeepLog and LogAnomaly rely on local sequential patterns that struggle to distinguish between unseen normal instances and true anomalies.

Table 4. Performance comparison in structural anomaly detection and normal instance identification

Case	Deeplog	LogAnomaly	PLELog	Ours
S1(ROC)	1.0	1.0	0.0	1.0
S2(ROC)	1.0	1.0	0.5	1.0
S3(ROC)	1.0	1.0	1.0	1.0
S4(ROC)	1.0	1.0	1.0	1.0
N1(ROC)	100%	100%	0%	0%

4 Conclusion

In this paper, We proposed a GNN-based unsupervised framework for log anomaly detection, which employs prompt-driven few-shot learning to efficiently extract key fields, constructs attribute-enhanced weighted directed graphs to model complex semantic relationships, and utilizes an enhanced one-class DiGCN for accurate graph-level anomaly detection. Experiments on three benchmark datasets demonstrate that our method significantly outperforms existing state-of-the-art approaches across diverse scenarios. Future work will focus on developing more efficient graph representation learning techniques and cross-domain log anomaly detection to further enhance the frameworks generalization and real-time detection capabilities.

Disclosure of Interests. The authors declare that they have no known competing financial interests or personal relationships that could have appeared to influence the work reported in this manuscript.

References

1. Li, Z., van Leeuwen, M.: Feature selection for fault detection and prediction based on event log analysis. ACM SIGKDD Explorations Newsl. **24**(2), 96–104 (2022)
2. Kimanzi, R., Kimanga, P., Cherori, D., Gikunda, P.K.: Deep learning algorithms used in intrusion detection systems–a review. arXiv preprint arXiv:2402.17020, 2024
3. Zhang, W., et al.: Lograg: semi-supervised log-based anomaly detection with retrieval-augmented generation. In: 2024 IEEE International Conference on Web Services (ICWS), pp. 1100–1102. IEEE, 2024
4. Gan, W., Chen, L., Wan, S., Chen, J., Chen, C.-M.: Anomaly rule detection in sequence data. IEEE Trans. Knowl. Data Eng. **35**(12), 12095–12108 (2021)
5. Liu, J., et al.: Log-based anomaly detection based on evt theory with feedback. arXiv preprint arXiv:2306.05032, 2023
6. Lin, Q., Zhang, H., Lou, J.G., Zhang, Y., Chen, X.: Log clustering based problem identification for online service systems. In: Proceedings of the 38th International Conference on Software Engineering Companion, pp. 102–111, 2016
7. He, S., Lin, Q., Lou, J.G., Zhang, H., Lyu, M.R., Zhang, D.: Identifying impactful service system problems via log analysis. In: Proceedings of the 2018 26th ACM Joint Meeting on European Software Engineering Conference and Symposium on the Foundations of Software Engineering, pp. 60–70, 2018
8. Luo, R., Krishnamurthy, V.: Fréchet-statistics-based change point detection in dynamic social networks. IEEE Trans. Comput. Soc. Syst. **11**(2), 2863–2871 (2023)
9. Landauer, M., Onder, S., Skopik, F., Wurzenberger, M.: Deep learning for anomaly detection in log data: a survey. Mach. Learn. Appl. **12**, 100470 (2023)
10. Du, M., Li, F., Zheng, G., Srikumar, V.: Deeplog: anomaly detection and diagnosis from system logs through deep learning. In: Proceedings of the 2017 ACM SIGSAC Conference on Computer and Communications Security, pp. 1285–1298, 2017
11. Meng, W., et al.: Loganomaly: unsupervised detection of sequential and quantitative anomalies in unstructured logs. In: IJCAI, vol. 19, pp. 4739–4745 (2019)
12. Liu, P., et al.: Unsupervised detection of microservice trace anomalies through service-level deep bayesian networks. In: 2020 IEEE 31st International Symposium on Software Reliability Engineering (ISSRE), pp. 48–58. IEEE, 2020
13. Zhao, L., Sawlani, S., Srinivasan, A., Akoglu, L.: Graph anomaly detection with unsupervised gnns. arXiv preprint arXiv:2210.09535, 2022
14. Ma, R., Pang, G., Chen, L., Van Den Hengel, A.: Deep graph-level anomaly detection by glocal knowledge distillation. In: Proceedings of the Fifteenth ACM International Conference on Web Search and Data Mining, pp. 704–714, 2022
15. Miao, X., Liu, Y., Zhao, H., Li, C.: Distributed online one-class support vector machine for anomaly detection over networks. IEEE Trans. Cybern. **49**(4), 1475–1488 (2018)
16. Zhang, C., Wang, X., Zhang, H., Zhang, H., Han, P.: Log sequence anomaly detection based on local information extraction and globally sparse transformer model. IEEE Trans. Netw. Serv. Manag. **18**(4), 4119–4133 (2021)
17. Li, Z., Van Leeuwen, M.: Explainable contextual anomaly detection using quantile regression forests. Data Min. Knowl. Disc. **37**(6), 2517–2563 (2023)
18. Lewis, M., et al.: Bart: denoising sequence-to-sequence pre-training for natural language generation, translation, and comprehension. arXiv preprint arXiv:1910.13461, 2019

19. He, P., Zhu, J., Zheng, Z., Lyu, M.R.: Drain: an online log parsing approach with fixed depth tree. In: 2017 IEEE International Conference on Web Services (ICWS), pp. 33–40. IEEE, 2017
20. Reimers, N., Gurevych, I.: Sentence-bert: sentence embeddings using siamese bert-networks. arXiv preprint arXiv:1908.10084, 2019
21. Gilmer, J., Schoenholz, S.S., Riley, P.F., Vinyals, O., Dahl, G.E.: Neural message passing for quantum chemistry. In: International Conference on Machine Learning, pp. 1263–1272. PMLR, 2017
22. Tong, Z., Liang, Y., Sun, C., Li, X., Rosenblum, D., Lim, A.: Digraph inception convolutional networks. Adv. Neural Inf. Process. Syst. **33**, 17907–17918 (2020)
23. Ruff, L., et al.: Deep one-class classification. In: International Conference on Machine Learning, pp. 4393–4402. PMLR, 2018
24. Xu, W., Huang, L., Fox, A., Patterson, D., Jordan, M.I.: Detecting large-scale system problems by mining console logs. In: Proceedings of the ACM SIGOPS 22nd Symposium on Operating Systems Principles, pp. 117–132, 2009
25. Oliner, A., Stearley, J.: What supercomputers say: a study of five system logs. In: 37th Annual IEEE/IFIP International Conference on Dependable Systems and Networks (DSN'07), pp. 575–584. IEEE, 2007
26. Zhu, J., et al.: Tools and benchmarks for automated log parsing. In: 2019 IEEE/ACM 41st International Conference on Software Engineering: Software Engineering in Practice (ICSE-SEIP), pp. 121–130. IEEE, 2019
27. Yang, L., et al.: Semi-supervised log-based anomaly detection via probabilistic label estimation. In: 2021 IEEE/ACM 43rd International Conference on Software Engineering (ICSE), pp. 1448–1460. IEEE, 2021

Adaptive Reed-Solomon Coding for OFDM in Mobile Visible Light Communications

Qinghui Chen[1], Binyue Qing[2], Hong Wen[1]([✉]), Ming Chen[3], Jie Ma[4], and Zhenheng Chen[2]

[1] The School of Aerospace, Hunan University of Technology, Zhuzhou 412007, China
wenhhut@163.com
[2] The School of Computer Science and Artificial Intelligence, Hunan University of Technology, Zhuzhou 412007, China
[3] School of Physics and Electronics, Hunan Normal University, Changsha 410081, China
[4] School of Electronic and Information Engineering, Hebei University of Technology, Tianjin 050019, China

Abstract. This paper proposes an adaptive orthogonal frequency division multiplexing with Reed-Solomon coding (Adaptive OFDM-RS) scheme for mobile visible light communication (VLC) scenarios. This scheme supports real-time code rate selection based on channel state information, choosing k from the set $\{163, 183, 203, 223, 243\}$. By continuously monitoring the channel signal-to-noise ratio (SNR), the system dynamically adjusts the RS coding strength to maintain error-free transmission while maximizing spectral efficiency. Simulation results demonstrate that the proposed real-time code rate selection mechanism achieves: error-free transmission at SNR $\geq$ 13 dB for a 16-QAM modulated VLC-OFDM system; and error-free transmission at SNR $\geq$ 20 dB for a 64-QAM modulated system. These results validate the high robustness and effectiveness of the system under dynamic channel conditions.

Keywords: Visible Light Communication · Adaptive OFDM · Reed-Solomon Codes

1 Introduction

The sixth-generation (6G) mobile communication system aims to achieve integrated space-air-ground-sea network coverage. However, insufficient frequency band resources pose a significant obstacle to 6G development. Visible light communication (VLC), leveraging its vast visible spectrum and immunity to electromagnetic interference, has emerged as a highly promising solution and is expected to become an indispensable part of 6G networks [1]. VLC has achieved significant progress in application scenarios such as indoor positioning, smart homes, and vehicular networks: VLC integrated with indoor light-emitting diode (LED) lighting supports high-speed transmission [2]; vehicle lights acting as transceivers in vehicle-to-vehicle (V2V) communication meet low-latency requirements [3]; and VLC provides stable connectivity in electromagnetically complex environments for the Industrial Internet of Things (IIoT) [4].

© IFIP International Federation for Information Processing 2026
Published by Springer Nature Switzerland AG 2026
X. Wang et al. (Eds.): NPC 2025, LNCS 16306, pp. 327–335, 2026.
https://doi.org/10.1007/978-3-032-10466-3_27

Orthogonal frequency division multiplexing (OFDM) is a widely used multi-carrier technique in VLC, designed to efficiently utilize the bandwidth of LEDs and enhance potential data rates [5, 6]. However, the practical deployment of VLC confronts the challenge of channel dynamics: impulsive noise from sources like sunlight and fluorescent lights can cause burst errors lasting microseconds [7]; multipath propagation in indoor VLC channels results in root-mean-square delay spreads of 5–15 ns [8], resulting in signal-to-noise ratio (SNR) differences of over 10 dB among OFDM subcarriers. When the SNR of some subcarriers falls below 10 dB, the bit error rate (BER) of an uncoded system can exceed 10^{-2}, failing to meet the stringent reliability requirements of industrial applications. In mobile scenarios, the channel coherence time is only on the order of milliseconds [9], and path loss fluctuations can reach 10–20 dB.

Reed-Solomon (RS) coding is employed in a MIMO-CO-OFDM system, enhancing the error correction capability of 16-QAM by 30% and achieving 40 Gbps transmission over a 5 km link [10]. This demonstrates the significant effectiveness of RS coding for error correction in VLC. In [11], an enhanced RS framework utilizing adaptive interleaving and list decoding reduced the BER caused by burst noise by 30%, validating the effectiveness of dynamic adjustment strategies. Experimental results show that a fixed RS(255,127) scheme suffers a throughput loss of up to 28% in mobile scenarios [12]. In contrast, dynamic code rate adjustment strategies can significantly reduce communication outage probability to below 1/5 [13].

However, existing schemes have limitations: fixed code rates struggle to adapt to dynamic channels, leading to packet loss due to insufficient error correction when the channel deteriorates, and wasted spectral efficiency due to excessive redundancy when the channel is good. Furthermore, they lack effective optimization for mobile scenarios. Traditional RS decoding algorithms have high complexity, and the delay associated with code rate switching often exceeds the channel coherence time in mobile environments, failing to meet real-time requirements [9]. Addressing these shortcomings, this paper proposes an adaptive OFDM-RS scheme tailored for mobile VLC scenarios. It designs a real-time selection mechanism for $k \in \{163, 183, 203, 223, 243\}$, maintains error-free transmission (BER = 0) under burst noise conditions.

In contrast to the complex multi-layer encoding and iterative optimization algorithms employed in [11], the proposed scheme utilizes a lightweight look-up table (LUT) for code rate selection, thereby significantly reducing computational overhead. Furthermore, compared to the fixed-threshold schemes presented in [12] and [13], our adaptive mechanism introduces a ± 1 dB hysteresis margin to mitigate frequent switching, which enhances system stability under fluctuating signal-to-noise ratio (SNR) conditions. This approach effectively achieves a dynamic balance between spectral efficiency and transmission reliability, offering a practical and low-complexity solution for RS adaptive schemes in dynamic VLC environments.

2 RS Coding Principle and Adaptive Mechanism Design

2.1 Fundamentals of Adaptive Reed-Solomon Coding

RS coding, a class of linear block codes with strong error correction capabilities, offers core advantages in efficiently correcting burst errors and providing flexible, adjustable code rates. These characteristics make it highly suitable for the dynamic channel environments encountered in VLC.

The RS encoding process is based on operations within a Galois Field (GF). An RS code is typically denoted as RS (n, k), where n is the codeword length after encoding (number of symbols), commonly set to $n = 255$ for VLC systems (compatible with standard OFDM subcarrier counts); k is the number of information symbols. This paper selects k from the set $\{163, 183, 203, 223, 243\}$, corresponding to 5 adjustable code rates. The number of redundant symbols is n-k, and the error correction capability is $t = (n$ - $k)/2$, meaning it can correct up to t consecutive symbol errors. For example, the RS (255,223) code has 32 redundant symbols and a correction capability of $t = 16$, effectively suppressing burst errors in VLC caused by ambient light pulse interference lasting no longer than 16 symbols. The code rate of RS is

$$R = k/n \tag{1}$$

it is evident that a larger k results in a higher code rate (up to 243/255 $\approx$ 0.95) and better spectral efficiency, but weaker error correction capability. Conversely, a smaller k enhances error correction at the cost of increased redundancy overhead. This inherent trade-off allows RS codes to dynamically balance reliability and efficiency, making them ideally suited to handle the dynamic nature of VLC channels.

The core of adaptive RS coding is to dynamically adjust the code rate parameter k based on real-time channel state information (CSI). The goal is to prioritize efficiency under high SNR conditions and ensure reliability under low SNR conditions. Implementation requires estimating the SNR at the receiver end by sending training sequences. Based on the feedback SNR, the system selects the optimal k value from a predefined set suited to the current channel conditions.

2.2 Channel State Monitoring

The system acquires real-time channel quality through an SNR estimation module at the receiver. A least squares (LS) estimation algorithm based on training sequences is employed. Training sequences are inserted into the OFDM frame structure, and the average SNR across subcarriers is calculated as:

$$\text{SNR}_{\text{avg}} = \frac{1}{N} \sum_{i=1}^{N} \frac{P_i}{\sigma_i^2} \tag{2}$$

where P_i is the subcarrier power, σ_i^2 is the noise variance, and N is the total number of subcarriers. For 16-QAM modulation, code rate selection is implemented using a predefined SNR-to-Code-Rate mapping table, as shown in Table 1. This mapping relationship is optimized through offline simulations to ensure the target BER $= 0$ is achieved.

When the monitored SNR falls within a specific range, the corresponding k value is triggered for switching. To prevent system instability caused by frequent switching, a hysteresis mechanism of ± 1 dB is introduced. The trigger condition for switching from a higher code rate ($k = 243$) to a lower code rate ($k = 223$) is SNR ≤ 18 dB; conversely, switching back from $k = 223$ to $k = 243$ requires SNR ≥ 19 dB. Similarly, the switching threshold from $k = 223$ to $k = 203$ is SNR ≤ 15 dB, and the reverse threshold is SNR ≥ 16 dB.

Tab. 1. SNR - Rate Mapping Table

SNR Range (dB)	Code Rate Parameter (k)	Error Correction Capability (t)
≥ 19	243	6
17~19	223	16
15~17	203	26
13~15	183	36
≤ 13	163	46

2.3 Adaptive OFDM-RS System Architecture

The overall system architecture consists of a transmitter and a receiver, with the workflow illustrated in Fig. 1. At the transmitter, the data to be transmitted is first processed by the RS encoder. It then enters the OFDM modulator, which performs subcarrier mapping, converting the binary bit sequence into constellation symbols. Subsequently, the signal undergoes Inverse Fast Fourier Transform (IFFT) for time-frequency conversion, followed by the addition of a cyclic prefix (CP) and training sequences. Finally, the modulated signal drives the LED for transmission, completing the electro-optical conversion and transmission into free space.

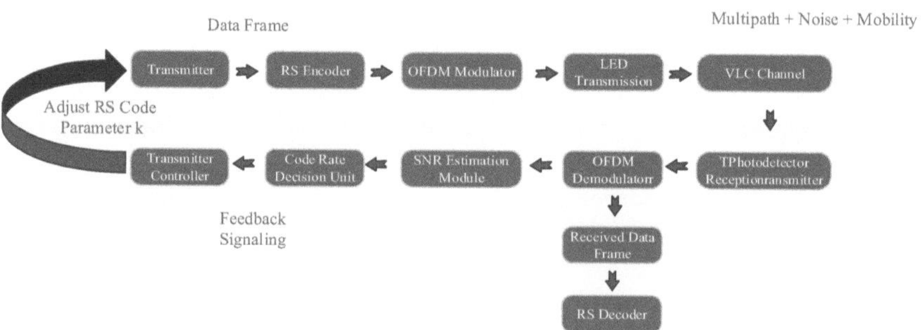

Fig. 1. Adaptive OFDM-RS System Architecture Flow Chart

At the receiver, a photodetector converts the optical signal back into an electrical signal. The OFDM demodulator performs synchronization, Fast Fourier Transform (FFT), and subcarrier demodulation. The demodulated data is simultaneously output to the RS decoder for recovering the original data and to the SNR estimation module for calculating channel quality. The code rate decision unit determines the optimal k value based on the estimated SNR and notifies the transmitter controller via a feedback channel, enabling closed-loop adaptive adjustment.

The core innovation of this architecture lies in the deep integration of the RS code rate adaptation mechanism into the OFDM modulation/demodulation workflow. A lightweight real-time feedback mechanism transmits the selected k value back to the transmitter for rapid adaptation while maintaining low power consumption. Compared to fixed-code-rate RS-OFDM systems, the proposed adaptive scheme offers significant advantages: In mobile scenarios, where the channel SNR changes by approximately 2 dB every 3 ms for a user moving at 1 m/s, the adaptive mechanism can track these changes in real time, providing dynamic adaptability. Through predefined 5-level fine-grained code rate adjustment, the system can select high code rates under high SNR, effectively increasing the transmission rate compared to fixed lowest-code-rate schemes. Under low SNR, it switches to lower code rates while maintaining error-free transmission, achieving a dynamic balance between spectral efficiency and transmission reliability. The code rate decision employs a lightweight lookup table (LUT)-based implementation, which significantly reduces hardware complexity and facilitates deployment in resource-constrained embedded VLC devices, demonstrating strong engineering practicality.

3   Simulation Results

The simulation flowchart is depicted in Fig. 2. First, a generated pseudo-random binary sequence (PRBS) undergoes RS encoding based on the set k value. Next, QAM mapping is performed, mapping the encoded binary data onto corresponding QAM constellation points. Subsequently, an Inverse Fast Fourier Transform (IFFT) converts the frequency-domain signal into a time-domain signal. A Cyclic Prefix (CP) is then added to combat channel multipath effects. Training sequences are inserted, and the combined signal is transmitted through the channel. At the receiver, synchronization is performed first, followed by CP removal. The time-domain signal (without CP) undergoes Fast Fourier Transform (FFT) to convert it back to the frequency domain. Channel estimation, specifically intra-symbol frequency-domain averaging (ISFA), is then conducted using the training sequences to acquire channel characteristics. Finally, adaptive RS decoding recovers the original information, enabling reliable data transmission.

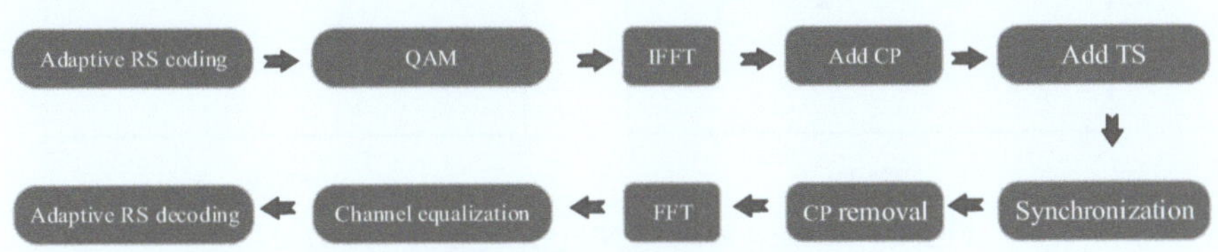

Fig. 2. Simulation flowchart

The simulation parameters for the proposed system are set as shown in Table 2. The FFT size is 256, the number of OFDM symbols is 150, the number of training sequences is 2, the number of data subcarriers is 102 (located at indices 13 to 114), the QAM modulation orders are 16 and 64, the CP length is 16, the RS codeword length n is 255, and the information symbol lengths k are 163, 183, 203, 223, and 243.

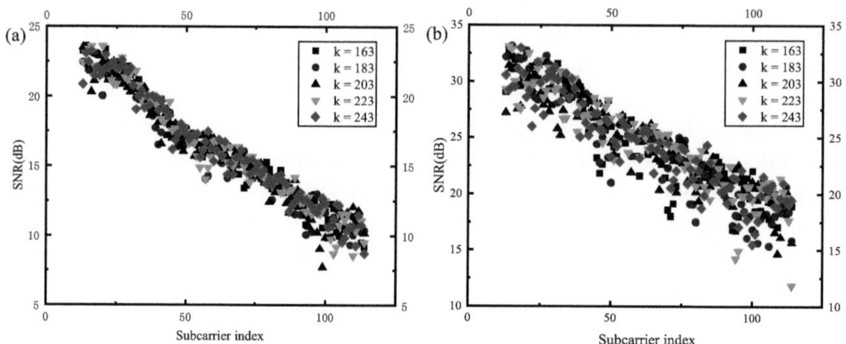

Fig. 3. The estimated SNR versus subcarrier index (a) 16QAM, (b) 64QAM

Figure 3 displays the SNR conditions at different data subcarrier positions for 16-QAM and 64-QAM modulation formats. The SNR is set to 15 dB for 16-QAM and 25 dB for 64-QAM. Due to the frequency selectivity of the VLC channel, the estimated SNR exhibits a decreasing trend as the subcarrier index increases. It is also evident that different k values do not affect the SNR at subcarrier positions before RS decoding. This is because RS coding is an error correction coding technique primarily focused on adding redundancy to the original data to construct codewords with specific error correction capabilities. Its purpose is to detect and correct errors occurring during transmission at the receiver end, thereby enhancing data transmission reliability. It operates at the data level and is not directly related to the physical characteristics of the signal.

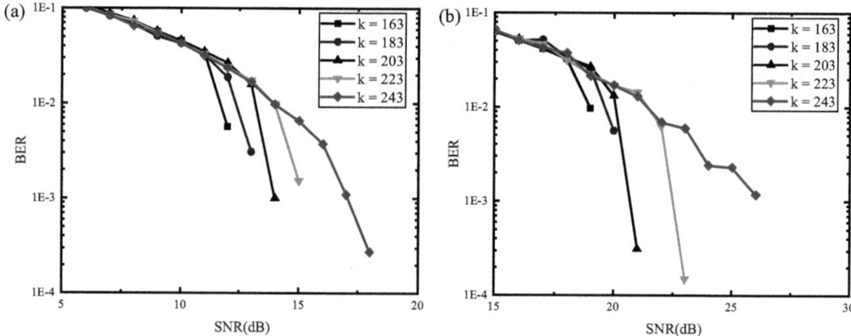

Fig. 4. The BER versus SNR (a)16QAM, (b)64QAM

Figure 4 shows BER curves under different SNR conditions. Figure 4(a) presents BER curves for 16-QAM. It can be observed that selecting different RS coding k values significantly reduces the BER of the VLC-OFDM system. When k = 163, the BER drops to zero at SNR $= 13$ dB, achieving error-free transmission, whereas for $k = 243$, an SNR of 19 dB is required for error-free transmission. Similarly, for a VLC-OFDM system transmitting 64-QAM signals, error-free transmission is achieved at SNR $= 20$ dB when $k = 163$. Choosing a k value higher than 163 at this SNR would result in transmission errors. Furthermore, when $k = 243$, error-free transmission only occurs when SNR exceeds 27 dB, making it challenging to combat deteriorating channel conditions. This proves that when channel conditions deteriorate, causing SNR to decrease, selecting a lower k value effectively enhances system reliability. Conversely, when channel conditions improve, choosing a higher k value effectively improves spectral efficiency. Dynamic SNR feedback via training sequences effectively enhances the system's robustness.

In mobile VLC scenarios, the channel coherence time typically falls within the millisecond range. For a codeword length of $n = 255$, the Reed–Solomon (RS) encoding and decoding processes, when implemented in modern hardware, incur delays on the microsecond scale-two orders of magnitude shorter than the channel coherence time. This ensures that code rate switching can be completed well within the stable interval of the channel, thereby fully meeting the real-time requirements of mobile adaptation.

The proposed adaptive mechanism relies on a lightweight look-up table (LUT) for code rate selection. The LUT stores only five possible values of $k \in \{163, 183, 203, 223, 243\}$, along with their corresponding SNR threshold ranges, which together require just a few bytes of memory. In contrast, other adaptive schemes often need to store large parity-check matrices or complex algorithmic parameters, resulting in significantly higher memory usage. These results confirm that the proposed LUT-based adaptive mechanism not only reduces computational overhead and memory consumption, but also meets the stringent latency and hardware efficiency demands of mobile VLC systems.

Table 2. Simulation Parameters

Parameter	Value
FFT size	256
Number of OFDM	150
Number of TS	2
Number of data subcarriers	102
QAM modulation order	16,64
CP size	16
n	255
k	[163,183,203,223,243]

4 Summary

This paper addressed the issues of reduced reliability and spectral efficiency loss caused by channel dynamics in mobile VLC scenarios by proposing an adaptive OFDM-RS transmission scheme based on real-time code rate selection. A set of five adjustable

RS code rate parameters $k \in \{163, 183, 203, 223, 243\}$ was designed. Lightweight SNR feedback enables dynamic code rate switching, enhancing system stability. Under high SNR, a high code rate ($k = 243$, $Rc \approx 0.95$) is adopted, improving spectral efficiency by 18.7%. Under low SNR, the system switches to a high-redundancy code rate ($k = 163$, $t = 46$), effectively suppressing burst errors. This achieves a dynamic balance between spectral efficiency and transmission reliability. The LUT-based code rate decision mechanism significantly reduces computational complexity.

Future work will focus on expanding the code rate parameter set and developing collaborative adaptive strategies for multi-user scenarios. In particular, we plan to implement comprehensive throughput comparisons between the proposed adaptive scheme and fixed-code-rate systems under varying mobility conditions using the VLC simulation platform, thereby providing a more detailed evaluation of system performance.

Acknowledgments. This research was funded by the Hunan Provincial Natural Science Foundation of China, under Grant 2023JJ50197, under Grant 2024JJ5269, and under Grant 2024JJ7295, and in part by the Scientific Research Foundation of Hunan Provincial Education Department of China, under Grant 23A0444, and under Grant 22A0063, and in part by the Science and Technology Research Project of Higher Education of Hebei Province, under Grant QN2024120, and in part by Natural Science Foundation of Hebei Province under Grant F2024202008), and supported by the Scientific Research and Innovation Foundation of Hunan University of Technology, under Grant LXBZZ2425.

Disclosure of Interests.   The authors declare no conflicts of interest.

References

1. Chi, N., Zhou, Y., Wei, Y., Hu, F.: Visible light communication in 6G: advances, challenges, and prospects. IEEE Veh. Technol. Mag. **15**(4), 93–102 (2020)
2. Tang, L., et al.: Over 23.43 Gbps visible light communication system based on 9 V integrated RGBP LED modules. Opt. Commun. **534**, 129317 (2023)
3. Memedi, A., Dressler, F.: Vehicular visible light communications: a survey. IEEE Commun. Surv. Tutor. **23**(1), 161–181 (2020)
4. Zhang, C., et al.: A survey on the latest developments of OFDM schemes for optimizing the capacity and reliability of visible light communication (VLC) systems. KSII Trans. Internet & Inf. Syst. **19**(5) (2025)
5. Yu, Z., Baxley, R.J., Zhou, G.T.: EVM and achievable data rate analysis of clipped OFDM signals in visible light communication. EURASIP J. Wirel. Commun. Netw. **2012**(1), 321 (2012)
6. Armstrong, J.: OFDM for optical communications. J. Lightwave Technol. **27**(3), 189–204 (2009)
7. Chen, C., Yang, F.: Generalized reed-solomon coded cooperative differential spatial modulation with low-complexity detection and joint decoding for wireless communication. Ann. Telecommun. 1–16 (2025)
8. Wang, H., Zhang, W., Liu, Y.: Joint coding scheme based on reed-solomon codes. In: 2021 IEEE 6th International Conference on Computer and Communication Systems (ICCCS). IEEE, 2021
9. Miramirkhani, F., et al.: A mobile channel model for VLC and application to adaptive system design. IEEE Commun. Lett. **21**(5), 1035–1038 (2017)

10. AL-Azawi, L.A., et al.: A new visible light communication network utilizing forward error correction integrated with space-time block coding. J. Opt. 1–9 (2025)
11. Almazmomi, N.K.: Enhanced reed–solomon error correction framework for reliable data transmission in noisy communication systems. Internet Technol. Lett. e634 (2025)
12. Kumar, S.: Performance investigation of MIMO based CO-OFDM FSO communication link for BPSK, QPSK and 16-QAM under the influence of reed solomon codes. J. Eng. Technol. Sci. **53**(5) (2021)
13. Cheng, J., et al.: Rate adaptive reconciliation based on reed-solomon codes. In: 2021 6th International Conference on Communication, Image and Signal Processing (CCISP). IEEE, 2021

Fast and Accurate RDMA Congestion Control with Self-Adapting Rate Adjustment

Xin He$^{(\boxtimes)}$, Zihao Zhang, Junchang Wang, Zheng Wu, and Weibei Fan

School of Computer Science, Nanjing University of Posts and Telecommunications, Nanjing, Jiangsu, China
{xhe,1024040915,wangjc,zwu,wbfan}@njupt.edu.cn

Abstract. Modern data centers adopt Remote Direct Memory Access (RDMA) to reduce CPU overhead and network latency. RDMA operates over a lossless network, and RDMA congestion control (CC) protocols are key enablers for achieving low-latency and high-throughput data delivery. Through in-depth experiment analysis, we reveal that existing RDMA CC protocols still suffer from sluggish congestion response and convergence speed. In this paper, we propose a switch-driven CC algorithm named $FACC$. $FACC$ enables switches to precisely identify flows that actually cause congestion and promptly notifies the congestion information to senders. At the sender, $FACC$ leverages the intrinsic packet conservation property of a lossless network to assess the extent of network congestion. Then, $FACC$ employs a PI controller to adaptively adjust the sending rate, thereby achieving rapid congestion elimination and improving both the transmission rate and convergence speed. We conduct extensive experiments to evaluate the performance of $FACC$. The results show that $FACC$ improves convergence speed while achieving at most 86.6% lower flow completion time (FCT) compared with state-of-the-art approaches.

Keywords: Congestion control · RDMA · Data center · Self-adapting rate adjustment

1 Introduction

Modern data centers increasingly adopt Remote Direct Memory Access (RDMA) to reduce CPU overhead and network latency, meeting the strict performance demands of emerging applications [1]. RDMA over Converged Ethernet version 2 (RoCEv2) is widely adopted to deploy RDMA [24]. RoCEv2 is compatible with IP/Ethernet networks and adopts Priority-based Flow Control (PFC) to ensure lossless data transmission [5]. PFC is a hop-by-hop flow control mechanism that prevents packet loss by pausing the transmission of the upstream switch when the downstream switch queue exceeds a specified threshold [3]. However, the coarse-grained pause mechanism causes PFC to suffer from several issues, such

© IFIP International Federation for Information Processing 2026
Published by Springer Nature Switzerland AG 2026
X. Wang et al. (Eds.): NPC 2025, LNCS 16306, pp. 336–348, 2026.
https://doi.org/10.1007/978-3-032-10466-3_28

as PFC deadlock and head-of-line blocking, which greatly harm the network performance [7].

Enhanced RDMA congestion control (CC) protocols have been widely studied in recent years to alleviate the detriment of PFC and ensure low-latency and high-throughput data delivery [6,9,11,24]. RDMA CC protocols adopt different congestion signals to mark in-network congestion and send the congestion signals to the sender via the receiver for rate adjustment. For example, DCQCN [24] utilizes Explicit Congestion Notification (ECN), TIMELY [13] relies on Round-Trip Time (RTT), and HPCC [9] employs In-Network Telemetry (INT) to estimate network congestion. However, these approaches still have limitations in obtaining precise congestion information [17]. ACC [23] explores the packet conservation property in lossless data centers to accurately perceive network congestion. However, ACC suspends congested flows in a coarse-grained manner when network congestion becomes severe. Besides, the above CCs require at least one RTT to respond to congestion. As data center bandwidth continues to increase, the packets transmitted within a single RTT can also cause severe network congestion. On this basis, a series of switch-driven CC protocols have been proposed [16,20]. By directly returning congestion signals from switches, switch-driven CCs effectively shorten the congestion control loop and reduce queue buildup. However, the existing switch-driven CCs still suffer from the inability to accurately perceive network congestion. As a result, these approaches can only heuristically adjust sending rates by repeatedly guessing and iterating, requiring a long time to converge to a stable state.

In this paper, we propose FACC, a switch-driven CC algorithm. FACC leverages fine-grained port status detection and rapidly port status feedback to accelerate congestion response. For the congested flows, FACC promptly notifies the congestion information to senders. At the sender, FACC leverages the intrinsic packet conservation property of a lossless network to assess the extent of network congestion. Then, FACC employs a PI controller to adaptively adjust the sending rate, thereby achieving rapid congestion elimination and improving both the transmission rate and convergence speed. The main contributions of this paper are as follows:

- We reveal that existing RDMA CC mechanisms still have performance limitations due to sluggish congestion response and convergence speed through fine-grained experiments.
- We present FACC, which integrates fine-grained congestion detection, precise congestion awareness, and a carefully designed PI controller to fasten both congestion response and convergence.
- We evaluate the performance of FACC through extensive experiments. Compared with state-of-the-art approaches, FACC improves convergence speed while achieving at most 68.6% lower flow completion time (FCT).

2 Motivation

In this section, we illustrate that the existing CC protocols suffer from sluggish congestion response and slow convergence speed, which degrade the network performance.

(1) Sluggish congestion response. At present, most RDMA CC protocols respond to in-network congestion using end-to-end congestion feedback signals [8,11,17,23], Representative works are DCQCN [24], TIMELY [13], and HPCC [9]. End-to-end CC protocols require at least one RTT to react to in-network congestion. However, with the continuous growth of data center bandwidth (from 10 Gbps to 400 Gbps), an increasing portion of traffic has become bursty [10]. Within an RTT, a large volume of bursty traffic results in packet buildup in switches, leading to network congestion. Moreover, the packet buildup further increases RTT, which in turn prolongs the congestion response speed.

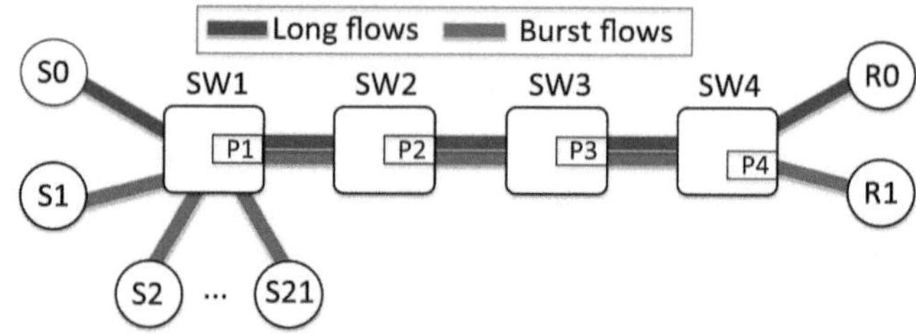

Fig. 1. Motivation topology.

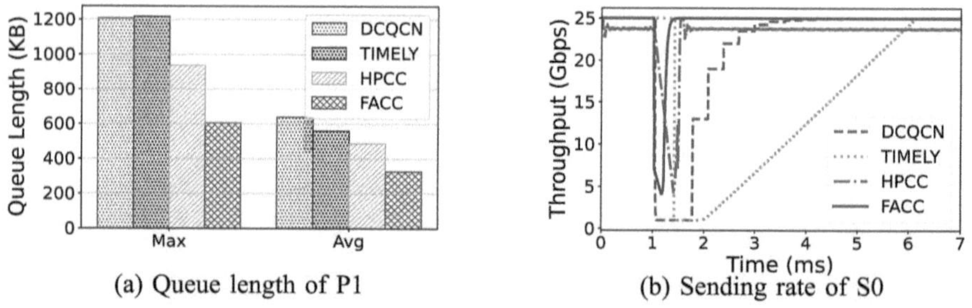

(a) Queue length of P1

(b) Sending rate of S0

Fig. 2. Congestion response of different CC protocols.

To illustrate this problem, we conduct a simulation experiment based on the NS-3 simulator [2]. The network topology is depicted in Fig. 1. The topology consists of 24 host nodes, including 22 senders labeled S0-S21 and 2 receivers labeled R0-R1. The switches are designated as SW1-SW4. We set the link bandwidth between each host and its connected switch to 25 Gbps, and the bandwidth between switches to 100 Gbps. The link propagation delay is set to 2 μs. The traffic was categorized into long flows and burst flows. Specifically, S0 continuously transmits a long flow to R0. After 1 ms, S1-S21 initiate burst flows to R1, each with a size of 64 KB.

Figure 2(a) shows the queue length at port P1 of switch SW1. The arrival of bursty flows causes queue buildup at port P1. Since end-to-end CC protocols require at least one RTT to react to congestion signals and adjust the sending rates of congested flows, the queue length of P1 continues to increase. For different CC algorithms, the maximum queue length at P1 exceeds 950 KB, and the average queue length exceeds 500 KB. Such excessive queue lengths not only increase packet transmission time but may also trigger PFC, thereby degrading network performance. Figure 2(b) shows the sending rate of S0. Due to the long congestion control loop and the limitations of rate adjustment mechanisms, the flow originating from S0 requires a prolonged congestion duration before its transmission rate can return to a stable level. Specifically, the congestion durations of DCQCN, TIMELY, and HPCC are 1.9 ms, 4.5 ms, and 0.8 ms, respectively. The prolonged congestion duration leads to bandwidth under-utilization and affects FCT of long flow.

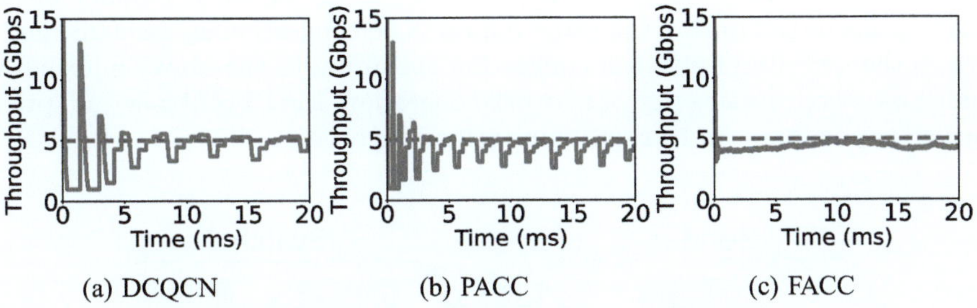

(a) DCQCN   (b) PACC   (c) FACC

Fig. 3. Convergence of different CC protocols.

(2) Slow convergence speed. The existing CC protocols adopt coarse-grained feedback signals. For example, DCQCN [24] probabilistically marks packets exceeding the specified queue threshold as congested. Upon receiving congested packets, the receiver sends Congestion Notification Packets (CNPs) to the sender to adjust its sending rate. But this approach cannot distinguish the packets that actually cause congestion. Moreover, DCQCN relies on a heuristic algorithm for iterative rate updates, resulting in slow convergence speed. The latest switch-driven CC algorithm, PACC [20], shifts the congestion feedback point from the receiver to the switch. It enables switches to send Congestion Notification Packets (CNPs) directly to the sender, thereby reducing congestion feedback time. However, PACC adopts the same rate adjustment mechanism as DCQCN, it likewise suffers from slow convergence.

We construct a 3-to-1 incast experiment to illustrate the above problem. The link bandwidth is set to 15 Gbps and the propagation delay to 5 μs. We measure the sending rates of different CC algorithms. As shown in Fig. 3 (a) and

Fig. 3 (b), both DCQCN and PACC exhibit frequent rate fluctuations, making it difficult for the sending rate to converge to a stable distribution.

In summary, it is imperative to design a CC algorithm capable of promptly and accurately responding to in-network congestion while precisely adjusting the sending rate to achieve rapid convergence.

3   System Design

In this section, we introduce FACC. Specifically, we introduce the overview of FACC and then describe the details of FACC.

3.1   Overview of FACC

The framework of FACC is shown in Fig. 4. At the switch, when a packet is dequeued, the port status detection module checks the current status of the egress port, and then the port status feedback module determines whether to send CNPs with different port statuses to the sender. The sender records the number of CNPs received within a period T, along with the number of data packets transmitted during the same period. The congestion assessment module assesses the severity of network congestion according to the above information. Finally, based on the severity of network congestion, the PI controller adaptively adjusts the sending rate to rapidly mitigate congestion.

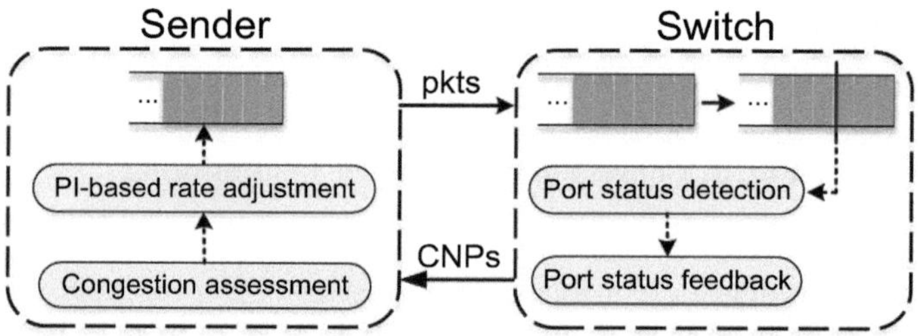

Fig. 4. Overview of FACC.

3.2   Details of FACC

Port Status Detection.   We classify the state of a switch port into non-congested, congested, and uncertain. Specifically, non-congested ports are normally ports without congestion; if their queue length exceeds a predefined congestion threshold, the state changes to congested or uncertain. Congested ports are the ports that are actually experiencing congestion, characterized by packet transmission at line rate and a queue length exceeding the predefined congestion threshold. Uncertain ports are caused by PFC pauses and are characterized by a queue length exceeding the congestion threshold, while the packet transmission rate from the queue exhibits a periodic pause and resume pattern. When a packet passes through a congested port, it generates a CNP with a congestion state (CS); passing through an uncertain port generates an uncertain state (US).

Port Status Feedback. To enable fast and accurate responses to network congestion, FACC allows a switch to generate a CNP marked with CS or US for any packet passing through a congested node or an uncertain node. Specifically, we utilize the 6th and 7th bits of the Type of Service (ToS) field within the IP header as markers for congestion signals. "10" denotes the US, while "11" indicates the CS. The source address of the original data packet becomes the destination address of the CNP, while its destination address becomes the source address of the notification packet. The CNP is then sent out through the ingress port of the original data packet.

Congestion Assessment. The congestion assessment module leverages the packet conservation property of lossless networks to assess congestion by comparing the number of packets sent with the number of CNPs received within the same time during T. We set T to half of the RTT to ensure timely monitoring of network congestion and rate adjustment.

In each time period T, we monitor the number of sent packets N_{send}, and the number of received CS-marked CNPs. The congestion level is defined as $r = \frac{N_{\mathrm{CS}}}{N_{\mathrm{send}}}$. It captures different network congestion levels, as various combinations of N_{send} and N_{CS} correspond to distinct network conditions, which can be broadly classified into four categories as analyzed below: (1) When N_{send} is high and N_{CS} is low, it indicates that congestion exists but is mild. We only need to slightly adjust the sending rate to alleviate congestion. (2) When both N_{send} and N_{CS} are high, congestion is severe and a more aggressive rate reduction is necessary. (3) When N_{send} is low but N_{CS} is high, it indicates that previous reductions were insufficient and additional rounds of rate reduction are required. (4) When both N_{send} and N_{CS} are low, congestion has eased, suggesting that previous rate adjustments were effective. We only need to slightly further reduce the sending rate to eliminate the congestion.

It should be noted that a packet may traverse multiple bottleneck links and trigger multiple CNPs, potentially carrying different congestion signals. We assign a higher priority to CNPs carrying the CS mark than to those carrying the US mark. A table is maintained to record the mapping between packet sequence numbers and congestion signals for each flow. When the same data packet triggers multiple CNPs, the congestion signal is updated only if the new signal has a higher priority.

Rate Adjustment Based on PI Controller. According to the different congestion levels mentioned above, we design a PI controller to adaptively adjust the sending rate of congested flows.

For each congested flow i, the degree of congestion it experiences is denoted as r_i. The goal is to make r_i approach or reach 0 as soon as possible. Therefore, we define the following utility function:

$$u_i(t) = K_p \times r_i(t) + K_d \times max\{[r_i(t) - r_i(t-1)], 0\}, \tag{1}$$

The first component in Eq. (1) computes the difference between the current congestion degree $r_i(t)$ and the desired value of 0 (omitted for simplicity), scaled by the parameter K_p. This term enables a prompt response to deviations from the steady state. The second component in Eq. (1) measures the difference between $r_i(t)$ and its value in the previous cycle $r_i(t-1)$, scaled by the parameter K_d, facilitating rapid convergence towards equilibrium. It should be noted that we use the max function to ensure that the value of the utility function remains positive, thereby avoiding unreasonable rate adjustments.

According to $u_i(t)$, we calculate the sending rate as follows:

$$R_c = max\{-R_t \times \frac{u_i(t)}{0.9} + R_t, 0\}, \tag{2}$$

where R_t is the target rate of the sender. In RDMA data center networks, R_t represents the line rate. The factor $\frac{u_i(t)}{0.9}$ ensures that flows can be quickly paused when network congestion becomes severe. Note that a pause duration t_{Halt} is set to avoid situations where congested flows remain suspended indefinitely. The calculation of t_{Halt} is based on the estimated time required to drain the queue of the congested switch. Specifically, during each cycle T, the sender monitors two metrics: the number of packets sent (ΔS) and the number of CNPs received (ΔA). If a pause is deemed necessary within a cycle, ΔA is subtracted from ΔS of the previous cycle to estimate the number of packets currently queued at the congested switch. This value is then divided by the CNPs reception rate to determine the halt duration t_{Halt}.

For uncertain flows, where CNPs received by the sender carry the US mark, such flows are generally classified as victim flows affected by PFC. To avoid degrading the performance of victim flows, it is necessary to adjust their rates conservatively. Therefore, we first set a time threshold T_{US} to maintain the rate of victim flows, where T_{US} is a multiple of T. If the duration of receiving US marks exceeds T_{US}, we reduce the rate of the victim flow according DCQCN rate adjustment scheme to prevent PFC propagation.

For non-congested flows, the sending rate should be increased if it has not reached the line rate. Specifically, RI represents the maximum allowable increase for each cycle and is applied in two stages. In the first stage, a smaller increment RI_{Low} is used. After several consecutive cycles of increases, RI is raised to a larger value RI_{High}. This strategy enables non-congested flows to ramp up gradually at first, followed by a more aggressive increase with a larger step size.

4   Performance Evaluation

4.1   Experiment Settings

Topology. We constructed a fat-tree topology comprising 320 servers. Each group of 16 servers is connected to a Top-of-Rack (TOR) switch. The topology also includes 20 aggregation switches and 16 core switches. The bandwidth between servers and switches is set to 100 Gbps, while the inter-switch bandwidth is set to 400 Gbps. The link propagation delay is set to 1 μs.

Benchmark Approaches. We compare FACC with the following benchmark approaches,i.e., DCQCN [24], TIMELY [13], HPCC [9], DCQCN+TCD [22], ACC [23], and PACC [20]. All benchmarks are developed based on the open-source code provided by [2].

Parameter Settings. We set a static PFC Pause threshold to 512KB. All parameters of the benchmark algorithms are set to the recommended values from their respective literature. Besides, we set RI_{Low} to 400 Mbps and RI_{High} to 4 Gbps. The parameter T_{US} is set to $2T$. Additionally, we configure K_p and K_d to 0.5 and 0.5 to ensure the stability of the PI controller.

Workloads. We generate traffic based on WebSearch [4], CacheFollower [14], and Hadoop [14] workloads. These workloads effectively simulate real traffic loads in data centers and are widely utilized in research. Table 1 illustrates the traffic features of different workloads.

4.2   Small-scale Simulations

FACC can Respond Quickly to Congestion. Figure 2 illustrates the queue length of congested port P1 and the throughput of the long flow. As shown in Fig. 2(a), by rapidly delivering congestion feedback from the congested switch to the sender and promptly adjusting the sending rate, FACC reduces the maximum and average queue lengths to 600 KB and 324 KB, respectively. The rapid congestion response and rate adjustment of FACC further shorten the congestion duration. As shown in Fig. 2(b), the congestion duration of FACC is 0.5 ms, which is reduced by 73.7%, 88.9%, and 37.5 compared to DCQCN, TIMELY, and HPCC.

Table 1. Traffic features of different workloads.

Workload:	WebSearch	CacheFollower	Hadoop
$F < 100KB$	54%	53%	88%
$100KB \leq F < 10MB$	43%	47%	12%
$F \geq 10MB$	3%	0%	0%

FACC Achieves Faster Convergence Speed. Figure 3 presents the convergence of FACC. Compared with DCQCN and PACC, FACC leverages the packet conservation property of lossless networks to detect congestion more accurately. This allows FACC to precisely determine how much to adjust its sending rate. In addition, the well-designed PI controller ensures that the sending rate of congested flows does not exceed the target rate, thus avoiding frequent bandwidth fluctuations. As a result, FACC can rapidly converge to a fair rate of 5 Gbps.

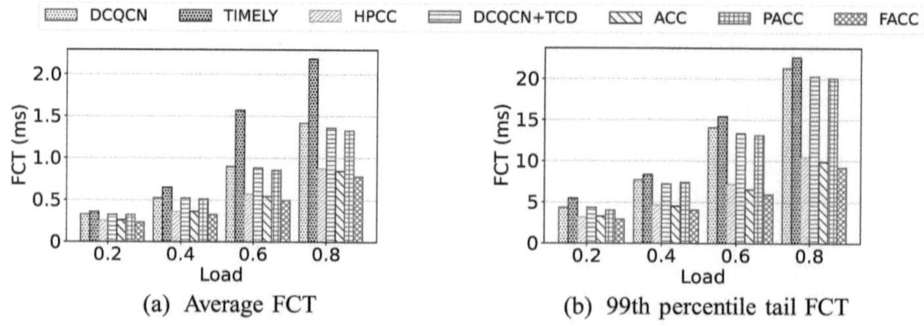

Fig. 5. WebSearch with different link loads.

4.3   Large-scale Simulations

Performance of FACC with Different Link Loads. Figure 5 and Fig. 6 present a comparison of the average FCT and the 99th percentile tail FCT against different benchmarks under varying link loads. The results show that FACC consistently outperforms all other algorithms. As shown in Fig. 5, under the WebSearch workload, FACC reduces average FCT by 29.0%~45.1%, 35.2%~68.6%, 8.7%~13.2%, 28.6%~43.9%, 7.9%~10.5%, 28.1%~42.1% and 99th tail FCT by 33.2%~57.7%, 47.1%~61.3%, 8.2%~17.4%, 33.1%~55.4%, 7.0% ~11.5%, 27.6% ~54.7% compared with DCQCN, TIMELY, HPCC, DCQCN+TCD, ACC, and PACC, respectively. While under CacheFollower workload shown in Fig. 6, FACC reduce at most 74.4%, 83.0%, 19.3%, 65.1%, 19.2%, 65.4% in average FCT and 72.8%, 86.6%, 34.2%, 59.4%, 34.0%, 72.2% in 99th tail FCT compared with DCQCN, TIMELY, HPCC, DCQCN+TCD, ACC, and PACC, respectively.

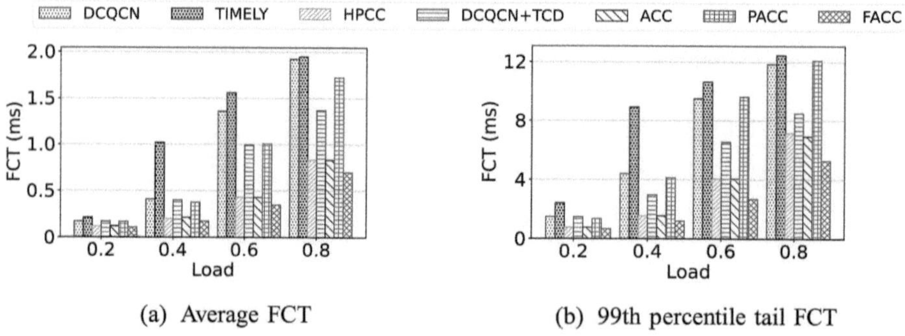

Fig. 6. CacheFollower with different link loads.

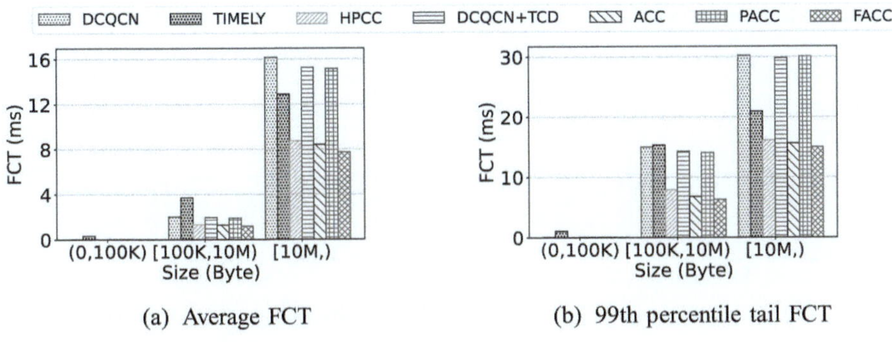

Fig. 7. WebSearch with different flow sizes.

Performance of FACC with Different Flow Sizes. To enable a more fine-grained analysis of FACC's performance, we classify flows into three categories: small (0100 KB), medium (100 KB10 MB), and large (above 10 MB). As no flows in CacheFollower exceed 10 MB, we adjust the threshold between medium and long flows to 1 MB. The experiments are conducted under 80% high-load conditions. Figure 7 and Fig. 8 show FACC achieves robust performance across flows of varying sizes. Specifically, under WebSearch, FACC reduces the average FCT of long flows by 52.2%, 40.1%, 11.5%, 49.4%, 8.0%, and 49.0% compared to DCQCN, TIMELY, HPCC, DCQCN+TCD, ACC, and PACC, respectively. The 99th-percentile FCT is also reduced by 50.4%, 28.5%, 7.0%, 49.8%, 4.0%, and 50.2% against the same baselines. For CacheFollower, FACC achieves large-flow average FCT reductions of 62.3%, 59.5%, 19.0%, 44.1%, 18.9%, and 60.6% over DCQCN, TIMELY, HPCC, DCQCN+TCD, ACC, and PACC, respectively, with corresponding 99th-percentile FCT reductions of 50.9%, 48.8%, 24.8%, 35.7%, 21.3%, and 53.3%. DCQCN's long congestion control loop and slow rate update prolong the FCT of large flows. TIMELY adjusts its rate based on RTT, but queue buildup increases RTT, causing delayed congestion responses and limiting FCT. DCQCN+TCD can accurately identify congested flows but still suffers from the same rate adjustment limitations as DCQCN. PACC relies on switches for fast congestion feedback but retains DCQCN's rate adjustment, which also extends large-flow FCT. In contrast, HPCC reduces FCT through reserved bandwidth, while ACC quickly mitigates congestion using an effective flow-pausing mechanism. Benefiting from near-source congestion feedback and rapid rate adjustment, FACC consistently outperforms both HPCC and ACC.

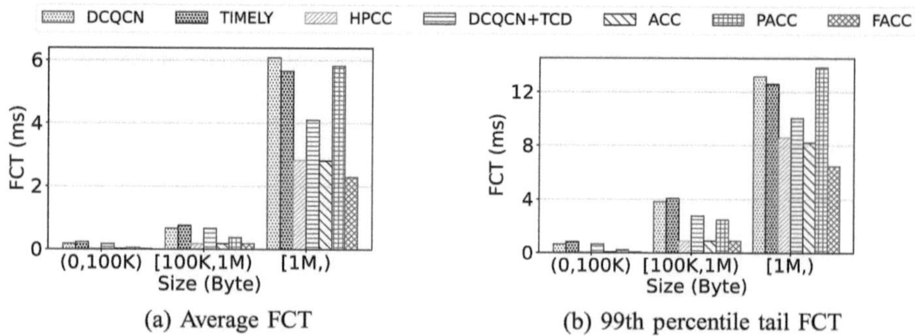

(a) Average FCT   (b) 99th percentile tail FCT

Fig. 8. CacheFollower with different flow sizes.

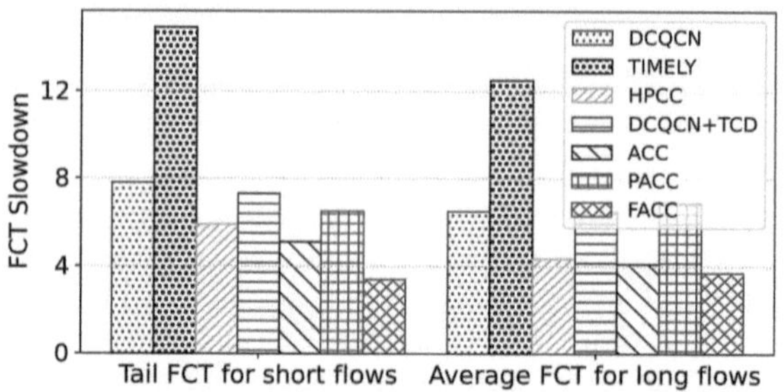

Fig. 9. Hadoop (50% load)+incast (20% load).

Performance of FACC Under Mixed Traffic. Figure 9 shows the tail FCT for short flows and average FCT for long flows in the scenario with 50% Hadoop workload and 20% 100-1 incast. FACC significantly reduces the FCT of short flows and long flows and outperforms all comparisons. The reason is that FACC leverages precise congestion detection and adaptive rate adjustment to control the sending rate flows that really contribute to congestion, and prevents innocent blocking of other flows. Specifically, FACC reduces the tail FCT slowdown for short flows by 2.3×, 4.4×, 1.7×, 2.2×, 1.5×, and 1.9× compared to DCQCN, TIMELY, HPCC, DCQCN+TCD, ACC, and PACC. For large flows, the reductions are 1.8×, 3.4×, 1.2×, 1.8×, 1.1×, and 2.0×, respectively.

5   Related Work

Congestion control protocols have been a longstanding topic of research in data centers, and numerous innovative proposals have emerged over the past decade [15]. We primarily introduce related work from the following perspectives.

Reactive Congestion Control. This type of CC is sender-driven, awaiting congestion feedback before adjusting the rate or window size. Representative schemes include ECN-based DCTCP [4] and DCQCN [24], RTT-based

TIMELY [13] and Swift [8], and INT-based HPCC. As reactive CC protocols, they suffer from long end-to-end feedback loops, causing delayed congestion responses—especially under bursty traffic—and degrading network performance.

Proactive Congestion Control. Proactive CC can be classified into switch-driven and receiver-driven schemes. Switch-driven approaches [18,19] detect congestion at the switch and directly notify the sender, bypassing the receiver. PACC [20] refines CNP generation by accounting for flow proportions, while RoCC [12] applies a queue length-based PI controller to allocate fair rates. Receiver-driven schemes, such as RCC [21], leverage the fact that most congestion occurs on the final hop and adopt an explicit window assignment mechanism to solve the last-hop congestion. However, the above approaches still rely on heuristic iterative rate adjustment, resulting in slow convergence speed.

6   Conclusion

This paper presents FACC, a fast and accurate congestion control algorithm with self-adapting rate adjustment in RDMA data centers. FACC monitors switch port states to pinpoint the flows responsible for congestion and provides local feedback for rapid congestion reaction. For congested flows, FACC estimates congestion severity by leveraging the packet conservation principle of the lossless network. Then, FACC adopts a PI controller to promptly adjust sending rates, thereby eliminating congestion quickly. The micro-benchmark and large-scale simulation show that FACC can significantly improve the convergence speed and reduce the FCT under realistic workloads.

Acknowledgments. This work was supported in part by the Natural Science Foundation of China under Grant No. 62202237, the Natural Science Foundation of Jiangsu Province under Grant No. BK20220389, the Natural Science Research Start-up Foundation of Recruiting Talents of Nanjing University of Posts and Telecommunications under Grant No. NY222016.

Disclosure of Interests. The authors declare that they have no conflict of interest.

References

1. Google Cloud Platform. https://cloud.google.com
2. HPCC simulation. https://github.com/alibaba-edu/High-PrecisionCongestion-Control
3. IEEE 802.1 Qbb - Priority-based Flow Control. http://www.ieee802.org/1/pages/802.1bb.html
4. Alizadeh, M., et al.: Data center tcp (dctcp). In: Proceedings of the ACM SIG-COMM 2010 Conference, pp. 63–74 (2010)
5. Association, I.T., et al.: Annex a17: rocev2. Suppl. InfiniBand^{TM} Archit. Specif. **1** (2014)
6. Cheng, W., Qian, K., Jiang, W., Zhang, T., Ren, F.: Re-architecting congestion management in lossless ethernet. In: USEIX NSDI, pp. 19–36 (2020)

7. Huang, H., et al.: Re-architecting buffer management in lossless ethernet. IEEE/ACM Trans. Netw. **32**(6), 4749–4764 (2024)

8. Kumar, G., et al.: Swift: delay is simple and effective for congestion control in the datacenter. In: ACM SIGCOMM, pp. 514–528 (2020)

9. Li, Y., et al.: Hpcc: high precision congestion control. In: ACM SIGCOMM, pp. 44–58 (2019)

10. Liu, K., et al.: An anatomy of token-based congestion control. IEEE/ACM Trans. Netw. (2025)

11. Meng, Q., et al.: Bcc: re-architecting congestion control in dcns. In: IEEE INFO-COM, pp. 1441–1450 (2024)

12. Menikkumbura, D., Taheri, P., Vanini, E., Fahmy, S., Eugster, P., Edsall, T.: Congestion control for datacenter networks: a control-theoretic approach. IEEE Trans. Parallel Distrib. Syst. **34**(5), 1682–1696 (2023)

13. Mittal, R., et al.: Timely: rtt-based congestion control for the datacenter. ACM SIGCOMM Comput. Commun. Rev. **45**(4), 537–550 (2015)

14. Roy, A., Zeng, H., Bagga, J., Porter, G., Snoeren, A.C.: Inside the social network's (datacenter) network. In: ACM SIGCOMM, pp. 123–137 (2015)

15. Sun, X., Wang, Z., Wu, Y., Che, H., Jiang, H.: A price-aware congestion control protocol for cloud services. J. Cloud Comput. **10**(1), 1–15 (2021). https://doi.org/10.1186/s13677-021-00271-5

16. Taheri, P., Menikkumbura, D., Vanini, E., Fahmy, S., Eugster, P., Edsall, T.: Rocc: robust congestion control for rdma. In: ACM CoNEXT, pp. 17–30 (2020)

17. Wan, Z., et al.: Acc: addressing performance limitations in datacenters with atomic congestion control. In: IEEE INFOCOM, pp. 1–10 (2025)

18. Xu, J., et al.: Fncc: fast notification congestion control in data center networks. In: Proceedings of the 53rd International Conference on Parallel Processing, pp. 127–137 (2024)

19. Yan, B., Zhao, Y., Xu, S., Liu, J., Xu, H.: Lhcc: low-latency and hi-precision congestion control in rdma datacenter networks. In: 2024 IEEE/ACM 32nd International Symposium on Quality of Service (IWQoS), pp. 1–10. IEEE (2024)

20. Zhang, J., et al.: Pacc: a proactive cnp generation scheme for datacenter networks. IEEE/ACM Trans. Netw. **32**(3), 2586–2599 (2024)

21. Zhang, J., Zhong, X., Wan, Z., Tian, Y., Pan, T., Huang, T.: Rcc: enabling receiver-driven rdma congestion control with congestion divide-and-conquer in datacenter networks. IEEE/ACM Trans. Netw. **31**(1), 103–117 (2022)

22. Zhang, Y., Liu, Y., Meng, Q., Ren, F.: Congestion detection in lossless networks. In: ACM SIGCOMM, pp. 370–383 (2021)

23. Zhang, Y., Meng, Q., Hu, C., Ren, F.: Revisiting congestion control for lossless ethernet. In: USENIX NSDI, pp. 131–148 (2024)

24. Zhu, Y., et al.: Congestion control for large-scale rdma deployments. ACM SIGCOMM Comput. Commun. Rev. **45**(4), 523–536 (2015)

Age of Information Minimization for Secure and Covert UAV Communications

Yiwen Zhang[1], Shikai Shen[1,4(✉)], Bin Yang[2(✉)], Fei Deng[1], Yumei She[3],
Kaiguo Qian[1], Riyu Wang[1], and Kai Yang[1]

[1] Kunming University, Kunming 650214, China
1970597968@qq.com
[2] Chuzhou University, Chuzhou 239000, China
ybcup@126.com
[3] Yunnan Minzu University, Kunming 650031, China
[4] Dianchi College, Kunming 650228, China
kmssk2000@sina.com

Abstract. Secure and covert communication in unmanned aerial vehicle (UAV) assisted wireless systems is to ensure security of transmission information, while age of information (AoI) quantifies its timeliness. However, existing works have not explored the AoI minimization for secure and covert UAV communications. This paper formulates the AoI minimization as an optimization problem by jointly optimizing UAV transmit power, flight path and low probability of detection constraints. We then propose an efficient iterative algorithm combining block coordinate descent and successive convex approximation to solve the non-convex problem. Simulation results demonstrate that the proposed scheme significantly achieves a superior trade-off between communication secrecy, information freshness, and power allocation in covert UAV networks.

Keywords: unmanned aerial vehicle · covert communication · secure communication · trajectory optimization · age of information

1 Introduction

Unmaned Aerial Vehicles (UAVs) have emerged as a promising technology for enhancing wireless communication systems due to their mobility, flexibility, and cost-effectiveness [1,2]. UAVs can serve as aerial base stations, relays or data collectors [3] in scenarios where terrestrial infrastructure is unavailable, unreliable or compromised. However, ensuring secure and covert communications in UAV-assisted networks remains a critical challenge, particularly in adversarial environments where eavesdroppers or interceptors may attempt to disrupt or exploit transmissions. One of the key performance metrics in UAV communications is the Age of Information (AoI) [4], which quantifies the timeliness of data updates.

X. Wang et al. (Eds.): NPC 2025, LNCS 16306, pp. 349–360, 2026.
https://doi.org/10.1007/978-3-032-10466-3_29

Optimizing AoI is crucial for real-time applications such as surveillance, disaster response, and military operations, where outdated information may lead to sub-optimal or even catastrophic decisions [5]. Additionally, efficient power allocation and trajectory design are essential to maximize communication reliability while minimizing energy consumption and detection risks [6]. This work investigates the joint optimization of AoI, power allocation, and UAV trajectory to achieve secure and covert UAV communications. We consider a scenario where UAVs must transmit sensitive data to legitimate ground users while avoiding detection by the detector. The problem involves balancing multiple competing objectives: (1) minimizing AoI to ensure timely updates, (2) optimizing transmit power to enhance secrecy performance while conserving energy, and (3) designing UAV trajectories that maximize coverage while reducing exposure to potential threats.

Existing works have not investigated AoI minimization in secure and covert UAV communication systems. This paper addresses this gap by formulating a novel optimization framework that jointly considers AoI, power allocation, and trajectory design under realistic adversarial conditions. To solve this problem, we employ an iterative algorithm combining block coordinate descent (BCD) and successive convex approximation (SCA).

The main contributions of this work are summarized as follows:

- We construct a UAV-enabled secure and covert communication system consisting of K users while avoiding warden detection. Our goal is to minimize the AoI while ensuring covert and secure UAV communications. We formulate it as a non-linear and non-convex optimization problem.
- To solve this optimization problem, we develop an efficient iterative optimization framework that synergistically combines BCD and SCA techniques, guaranteeing convergence to a locally optimal solution.
- Through simulations, we systematically investigate the impacts of system parameters - including covertness requirements, UAV flight altitude, maximum transmit power, and secrecy rate threshold on the total AoI. Furthermore, we analyze the UAV's dynamic power allocation strategy across users during its flight trajectory.

2   System Model

2.1   Scenario and Channel Model

As illustrated in Fig. 1, we consider a scenario consisting of an aerial base station (UAV), an eavesdropper, a detector and K users (including a secure communication user, Bob). In the scenario, a UAV attempts to communicate covertly with K legitimate users while maintaining a low probability of detection by the detector. Meanwhile, eavesdropper tries to eavesdrop and intercept the message transmitted from UAV to Bob silently. UAV generates packets that correspond to the desired signals requested by users and transmits them with frequency-division multiple access (FDMA). To ensure the timeliness of information, we aim to minimize the total AoI under the both covert and secure constraints.

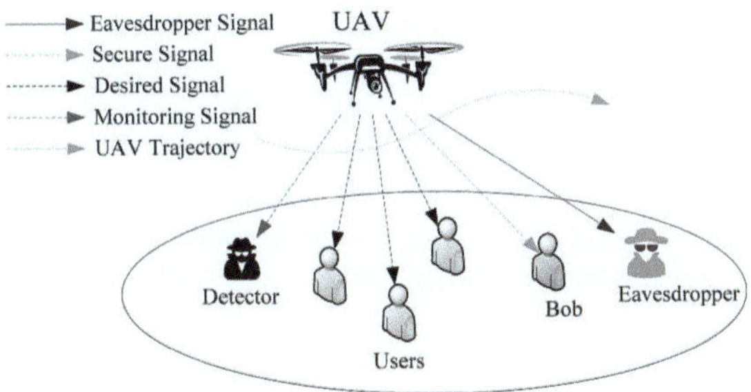

Fig. 1. The considered system model.

The users set is denoted by $\mathcal{K} = \{1, 2, \ldots, K\}$ where $|\mathcal{K}| = K$ is the number of users (including Bob). We donate the position of user k as $\mathbf{u}_k = (u_{x,k}, u_{y,k}), \forall k \in \mathcal{K}$ and let $\mathbf{w}_d = (w_{x,d}, w_{y,d})$ donate the position of detector. Considering a realistic situation, we assume the exact position of the detector is not perfectly known or known with uncertainty [7]. The eavesdropper's position is constrained to lie on a r-meter-radius circle centered at Bob which is donated by $E = (E_x, E_y)$. In practice, the initial and final points of the UAV are usually given based on certain task, which are respectively denoted by $\mathbf{q}_0 = (x_0, y_0)$ and $\mathbf{q}_F = (x_F, y_F)$. We use T to denote the task time and the horizontal position of UAV at time t is denoted by $\mathbf{q}(t) = (x(t), y(t)), t \in [0, T]$. In addition, we assume that the UAV flies at a fixed altitude $H > 0$ and with a maximal speed V which means $\|\dot{\mathbf{q}}(t)\|^2 \leq V^2, t \in [0, T]$. Furthermore, we represent the transmit power at t and the maximum transmit power of UAV by $P(t)$ and P_{max}. The network spectrum between UAV to users is B Hz, and S shows the packet size.

Considering the wireless channels from UAV to users and detector are generally Line-of-Sight (LoS)-dominant, we adopt a free space path loss channel model. In other words, the channel power gains from the UAV to user k is given by

$$h_k(t) = \frac{\beta_0}{\|\mathbf{q}(t) - \mathbf{u}_k\|^2 + H^2} \tag{1}$$

where β_0 is the channel gain per unit distance.

Considering a FDMA communication model, we define the power allocation coefficient for user k by $a_k(t)$, then we have the constraint for the power allocation coefficient as follows

$$0 \leq a_k(t) \leq 1, \forall k \in \mathcal{K}, t \in [0, T] \tag{2a}$$

$$\sum_{k=1}^{K} a_k(t) = 1, t \in [0, T] \tag{2b}$$

Hence, the received power $Q_k(t)$ at user k is

$$Q_k(t) = \frac{\beta_0 a_k(t) P(t)}{\|\mathbf{q}(t) - \mathbf{u}_k\|^2 + H^2} \tag{3}$$

Using a vector $\mathbf{a}(t) = [a_1(t), ..., a_K(t)]$ to represent the set of allocation coefficient, during the communication period T, the achievable data rate of each user is given by:

$$R_k(t) = \log_2\left(1 + \frac{\beta_0 a_k(t) P(t)}{\sigma_k^2(\|\mathbf{q}(t) - \mathbf{u}_k\|^2 + H^2)}\right) \tag{4}$$

where σ_k^2 is the additive white Gaussian noise (AWGN) power of combining with the co-interference from other co-existing signals at the same frequency as user k.

2.2 The Optimal Detection Threshold and Minimal Detection Error Probability

In covert communication scenarios, the detector is monitoring the transmission signal from UAV to users. Specially, it sets a detection threshold and determines whether there are transmission behaviours through comparing the background signal power with threshold. The background signal power $P_d(t)$ is as follows [7,8]

$$P_d(t) = \begin{cases} \sigma_d^2, & \mathcal{H}_0, \\ Q_d(t) + \sigma_d^2, & \mathcal{H}_1. \end{cases} \tag{5}$$

where $\mathcal{H}_0$ denotes the hypothesis that UAV does not transmit while $\mathcal{H}_1$ denotes the opposite hypothesis, and σ_d^2 is the overall noise power consisting of the AWGN and co-interference at the detector which may not be well known by the detector. Following the work in [9,10], we can obtain the detection error probability is given as follows

$$\xi(t) = \begin{cases} 1, & P_{th}(t) < \sigma^2 - \rho \\ \frac{\sigma^2 + \rho - P_{th}(t)}{2\rho}, & \sigma^2 - \rho \le P_{th}(t) < Q_d(t) + \sigma^2 - \rho \\ 1 - \frac{Q_d(t)}{2\rho}, & Q_d(t) + \sigma^2 - \rho \le P_{th}(t) < \sigma^2 + \rho \\ \frac{P_{th}(t) - Q_d(t) - \sigma^2 + \rho}{2\rho}, & \sigma^2 + \rho \le P_{th}(t) < Q_d(t) + \sigma^2 + \rho \\ 1, & P_{th}(t) \ge Q_d(t) + \sigma^2 + \rho \end{cases} \tag{6}$$

According to (6), $\xi(t)$ is monotonously decreasing within $[0, Q_d(t) + \sigma^2 - \rho]$ and monotonously increasing within $[\sigma^2 + \rho, +\infty)$. The optimal detection threshold $P_{th}^*(t)$ for the detector is within $[Q_d(t) + \sigma^2 - \rho, \sigma^2 + \rho)$. The minimal detection error probability is

$$\xi^*(t) = 1 - \frac{Q_d(t)}{2\rho} = 1 - \frac{\beta_0 P(t)}{2\rho(\|\mathbf{q}(t) - \mathbf{w}_d\|^2 + H^2)} \tag{7}$$

Noting that $\xi^*(t)$ is derived under the assumption that the detector has a perfect knowledge of the channel state and transmit power, however, it does not mean that detector must have the above information. In other words, $\xi^*(t)$ is the lower bound of the detection error probability which can be used to evaluate the covertness performance.

According to the minimum achievable total error rate from the perspective of detector, we design the trajectory of UAV $\mathbf{q}(t)$, to ensure the minimum total error rate ξ^* at detector being no less than the specific value, i.e., $\xi^*(t) \geq 1 - \rho_d$, where covertness requirement ρ_d, is an arbitrarily small value.

2.3   AoI of Received Packets at Users

In the proposed system model as mentioned above, UAV periodically generates packets and covertly transmits them to users at the same time. Let $\mathbf{d} = [d_1, ..., d_K]$ be the age of freshness of packets that is requested by users. We use AoI as a measure of packets' freshness that is received by the k-th user at time t, and is defined as:

$$d_k(t) = t - g_k(t) \tag{8}$$

where $g_k(t)$ is the generation time of the newest requested packet by k-th user, and we map $d_k(t)$ to d_k. Then, the total AoI that users receive the packet is:

$$A = \sum_{k=1}^{K} \sum_{t=1}^{T} d_k(t) \tag{9}$$

2.4   Secure Performance Analysis

Covert-and-security rate is defined as the achievable rate at Bob, which UAV can covertly send messages while maintaining a high detection error probability at detector, and the security constraint is satisfied simultaneously. Security constraint is defined to quantify the risks posed by the eavesdropper in the system. Consequently, transmission is suspended when this constraint is violated. Let R_B and R_E denote the data transmission rates to Bob and the eavesdropper, respectively. The secure transmission rate R_s must remain above a predefined threshold $R_{\min}$; transmission is suspended if $R_s < R_{\min}$. Based on the previous analysis, when UAV transmits a covert message to user Bob, the received signal at users is given in (3). Accordingly, the received rate at eavesdropper is expressed as

$$R_E(t) = \log_2 \left(1 + \frac{\beta_0 a_{Bob}(t) P(t)}{\sigma_k^2 (\|\mathbf{q}(t) - E\|^2 + H^2)}\right) \tag{10}$$

The security transmission rate R_s is given by

$$\begin{aligned} R_s &= R_{Bob} - R_E \\ &= \log_2 \left(1 + \frac{\beta_0 a_{Bob}(t) P(t)}{\sigma_k^2 (\|\mathbf{q}(t) - \mathbf{u}_{Bob}\|^2 + H^2)}\right) - \log_2 \left(1 + \frac{\beta_0 a_{Bob}(t) P(t)}{\sigma_k^2 (\|\mathbf{q}(t) - E\|^2 + H^2)}\right) \end{aligned} \tag{11}$$

From the above analysis, to guarantee the confidentiality of transmitted information and prevent data interception, the security constraint must be satisfied: $R_s \geq R_{min}$.

3   Problem Formulation and Transformation

3.1   Problem Formulation

To obtain a novel reliable covert mobile communication scheme, we aim to minimize the total AoI by jointly optimizing the trajectory of UAV and the AoI of the k-th user's packet, subject to the start and end point of UAV , the maximum speed of UAV, the reliable covert constraint, the transmit power constraint at UAV, the covertness constraint at detector, the information reachability constraint at users and the security constraint. Therefore, the optimization problem is formulated as:

$$\min_{\mathbf{q},d_k,\mathbf{a}} A \tag{12a}$$

$$s.t. \quad \mathbf{q}(0) = \mathbf{q}_0, \mathbf{q}(T) = \mathbf{q}_F \tag{12b}$$

$$\|\dot{\mathbf{q}}(t)\|^2 \leq V^2, \forall t \in [0,T] \tag{12c}$$

$$\xi(t) \geq 1 - \rho_d, \forall t \in [0,T] \tag{12d}$$

$$P(t) \leq P_{max}, \forall t \in [0,T] \tag{12e}$$

$$\sum_{t=1}^{T} d_k(t) \cdot \log_2\left(1 + \frac{\beta_0 a_k(t) P(t)}{\sigma_k^2(\|\mathbf{q}(t) - \mathbf{u}_k\|^2 + H^2)}\right) \geq \frac{S}{B} \tag{12f}$$

$$d_k(t) \leq d_{max} \tag{12g}$$

$$R_B - R_E \geq R_{min}$$

$$(2a), (2b) \tag{12h}$$

where (12b) determines the start and end point of UAV, (12c) is the maximum speed constraint of UAV, (12e), (2a) and (2b) ensure that the UAV allocates its transmit power to all served users without exceeding the maximum transmission power budget, P_{max}. (12f) and (12g) are restrictions related to AoI which are relatively new in the field of joint covert and secure communication. (12f) guarantees information delivery to the user within the allotted task time and (12g) makes sure user's AoI less than a fixed value to ensure the freshness of the information.

3.2   Problem Transformation

For constraint (12d), according to (7), we derived the optimal detection threshold $P_{th}^*(t)$ and minimal detection error probability $\xi^*(t)$ under the hypothesis that detector's position is perfectly known. Following the work in [7] the average of the minimal detection $\bar{\xi}^*(t) \geq 1 - g_1(\lambda(t), P(t))$, and the stricter constraint of (12d) is error probability

$$g_1(\lambda(t), P(t)) \leq \rho_d \tag{13}$$

The joint design problem (P12) aims to make the transmit power as larger as possible under the constraint (13) indeed. Noticing that $g_1(\lambda(t), P(t))$ is a monotonically increasing function with respect to $P(t)$, The transmit power is optimal when $g_1(\lambda(t), P(t)) = \rho_d$. Combining with the maximal transmit power constraint (12e), we derive the optimal transmit power at time t shown as (14)

$$P^*(t) = \min\left\{\frac{\rho_d}{\frac{\beta_1}{\lambda(t)+2+\frac{H^2}{\epsilon_d^2}} + \sqrt{\frac{2}{\pi}}\frac{1}{\sqrt{\lambda(t)+2}}\left(\frac{\epsilon_d^2\beta_1}{H^2} - \frac{\beta_1}{\lambda(t)+2+\frac{H^2}{\epsilon_d^2}}\right)}, P_{max}\right\}$$

$$= \min\left\{\frac{\beta_2}{\frac{1}{u_d(\mathbf{q}(t))+2\epsilon_d^2+H^2} + \sqrt{\frac{2}{\pi}}\frac{\epsilon_d}{u_d(\mathbf{q}(t))+2\epsilon_d^2}\left(\frac{1}{H^2} - \frac{1}{u_d(\mathbf{q}(t))+2\epsilon_d^2+H^2}\right)}, P_{max}\right\}$$

$$\triangleq \min\{g_2(u_d(\mathbf{q}(t))), P_{max}\} \triangleq g_3(u_d(\mathbf{q}(t))) \tag{14}$$

where $\beta_2 = \frac{\rho_d}{\epsilon_d^2\beta_1} = \frac{2\rho\rho_d}{\beta_0}$ and $u_d(\mathbf{q}(t)) = \|\mathbf{q}(t) - \hat{\mathbf{w}}_d\|^2$ is the square of horizontal distance between UAV and the estimated position of detector. Noticing that the optimal transmit power $P^*(t)$ is only related to UAV's position $\mathbf{q}(t)$, we can transform problem (P12) to

$$\min_{\mathbf{q}, d_k, \mathbf{a}} A \tag{15a}$$

$$s.t. \quad \sum_{t=1}^{T} d_k(t) \cdot \log_2\left(1 + \frac{\beta_0 a_k(t) g_3(u_d(\mathbf{q}(t)))}{\sigma_k^2(\|\mathbf{q}(t) - \mathbf{u}_k\|^2 + H^2)}\right) \geq \frac{S}{B}$$

$$(2a), (2b), (12b), (12c), (12g), (12h) \tag{15b}$$

Recalling that $P^*(t) = g_3(ud(q(t)))$ satisfies both transmit power constraint (12d) and covertness constraint (12e), the transformed problem (P15) is equivalent to (P12). In the next section, We jointly optimize the UAV's trajectory, the AoI for data packets, and the power allocation for each user in an iterative manner until convergence is achieved.

4   Solution Methodology

To enhance the tractability of Problem (15), we employ a BCD approach combined with SCA techniques. Our alternating optimization approach consists of: (1) optimizing $\mathbf{q}$ given fixed d_k and $\mathbf{a}$; (2) optimizing d_k initialized with $\tilde{\mathbf{q}}_k$ and fixed $\mathbf{a}$; and (3) optimizing $\mathbf{a}$ using $\tilde{\mathbf{q}}_k$ and $\tilde{d}_k$ - iterating until convergence via CVX and *Fmincon*.

4.1   Trajectory Optimization

We begin by optimizing the UAV trajectory with both AoI d_k and power allocation vector $\mathbf{a}$ fixed, leading to the following formulation of Problem (15):

$$\min_{\mathbf{q}(t)} A \tag{16a}$$

$$s.t. \quad \sum_{t=1}^{T} \tilde{d}_k(t) \cdot \log_2\left(1 + \frac{\beta_0 \tilde{a}_k(t) g_3(u_d(\mathbf{q}(t)))}{\sigma_k^2(\|\mathbf{q}(t) - \mathbf{u}_k\|^2 + H^2)}\right) \geq \frac{S}{B} \tag{16b}$$

$$\log_2\left(1 + \frac{\beta_0 \tilde{a}_{Bob}(t) g_3(u_d(\mathbf{q}(t)))}{\sigma_k^2(\|\mathbf{q}(t) - \mathbf{u}_{Bob}\|^2 + H^2)}\right) - \log_2\left(1 + \frac{\beta_0 \tilde{a}_{Bob}(t) g_3(u_d(\mathbf{q}(t)))}{\sigma_k^2(\|\mathbf{q}(t) - E\|^2 + H^2)}\right)$$

$$(12b), (12c) \tag{16c}$$

where $\tilde{a}_k(t)$ represents any given $\mathbf{a}$ which satisfies the constraint (12a), (12b) and $\tilde{d}_k(t)$ is a given value that satisfies (12g) . To handle the non-convexity in constraint (16b), we develop a convex approximation through first-order Taylor. After transformation, the problem can be solved by existing optimization tools such as CVX [11].

4.2 AoI Optimization

To find the AoI for the optimized $\tilde{\mathbf{q}}_{opt}(t)$ obtained in Sect. 4.1 and any given $\tilde{a}_k(t)$, (15) can be solved by optimizing the following problem:

$$\min_{d_k} A \tag{17a}$$

$$s.t. \quad \sum_{t=1}^{T} d_k(t) \cdot \log_2\left(1 + \frac{\beta_0 \tilde{a}_k(t) g_3(u_d(\tilde{\mathbf{q}}_{opt}(t)))}{\sigma_k^2(\|\tilde{\mathbf{q}}_{opt}(t) - \mathbf{u}_k\|^2 + H^2)}\right) \geq \frac{S}{B}$$

$$(12g) \tag{17b}$$

Since the problem (17) has standard linear programming(LP) form, it can also be solved using CVX.

4.3 Power Allocation Coefficients Optimization

With optimized $\tilde{\mathbf{q}}_{opt}(t)$ and $\tilde{d}_{k \cdot opt}(t)$ obtained in Sects. 4.1 and 4.2, problem (15) can be transformed into:

$$\min_{\mathbf{a}} A \tag{18a}$$

$$s.t. \quad \sum_{t=1}^{T} \tilde{d}_{k \cdot opt}(t) \cdot \log_2\left(1 + \frac{\beta_0 a_k(t) g_3(u_d(\tilde{\mathbf{q}}_{opt}(t)))}{\sigma_k^2(\|\tilde{\mathbf{q}}_{opt}(t) - \mathbf{u}_k\|^2 + H^2)}\right) \geq \frac{S}{B}$$

$$(2a), (2b) \tag{18b}$$

and it can be solved by existing optimization tools such as Fmincon.

4.4   Complexity Analysis

The computational complexity of the proposed BCD algorithm is analyzed as follows. The overall complexity per BCD iteration consists of solving three sub-problems: trajectory optimization, AoI minimization, and power allocation. For the trajectory subproblem, the SCA approach requires solving a series of convex optimization problems, with complexity scaling as $\mathcal{O}(N^{3.5})$ per inner iteration, where N represents the number of time slots. The AoI optimization subproblem, formulated as a linear program, exhibits complexity of $\mathcal{O}(N^{3.5})$ due to its decomposable structure across users. The power allocation subproblem, solved using a general nonlinear solver, contributes complexity of $\mathcal{O}(N^{3.5})$ per inner iteration. With I_{traj} and I_{power} representing the inner iteration numbers for trajectory and power optimization respectively, and I_{BCD} outer iterations, the total computational complexity becomes $\mathcal{O}(I_{\text{BCD}} \cdot (I_{\text{traj}} + I_{\text{power}}) \cdot N^{3.5})$. For practical parameter values, this complexity remains manageable and suitable for real-time implementation in UAV communication systems.

5   Simulation Results

In this section, we present numerical results to evaluate the performance of the proposed novel reliable covert communication scheme with a minimum AoI system. We consider a 100 m square area in which the users are randomly located. Without other statements, we setup the default of parameters as: $\beta_0 = -60$ dB, $H = 30$ m, $T = 100$ s, $V = 20$ m/s, $\mathbf{q}_0 = [0, 0]$, $\mathbf{q}_F = [100, 100]$, $\hat{\mathbf{w}}_d = [50, 60]$, $\epsilon_d^2 = 25$, $\sigma_k^2 = -90$ dBm and $B = 1$ MHz.

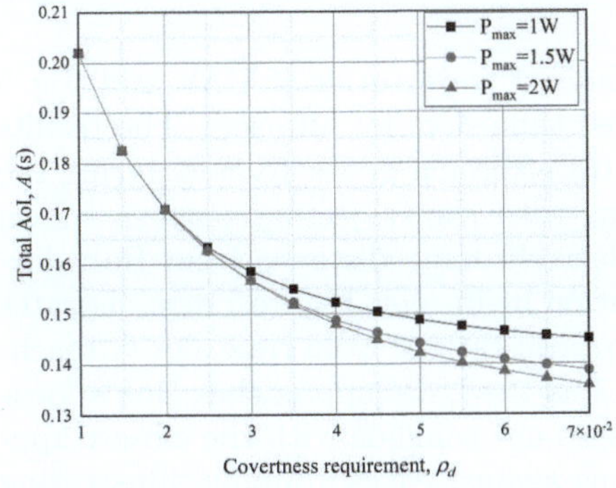

Fig. 2. Total AoI vs different covertness requirement ρ_d.

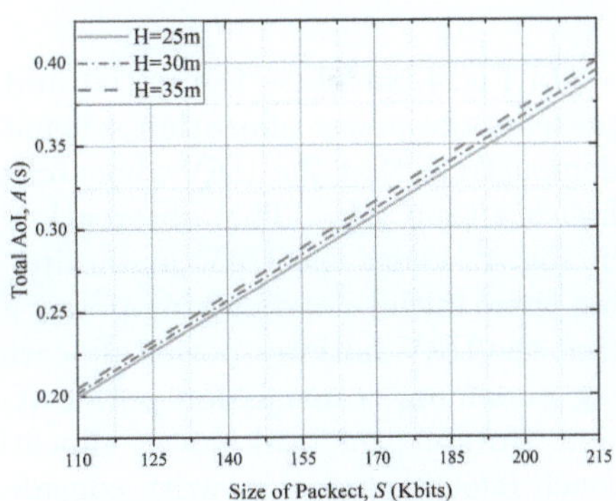

Fig. 3. Total AoI vs packets size S.

In Fig. 2, we demonstrate the total AoI versus the power transmission budget, P_{max} for different covertness requirement ρ_d. Since $P^*(t)$ is determined by Eq. (14), $P^*(t)$ is influenced by P_{max}. As a result, with fixed $\mathbf{q}$, P_{max} increases,

$P^*(t)$ increases. The total AoI A is decreasing with increasing ρ_d. Thus, under the conditions of covert communication, by increasing ρ_d, users can receive more up-to-date information. However, according to Eq. (14), if P_{max} increases to a sufficiently large value, which is far greater than $g_2(u_d(\mathbf{q}(t)))$, P_{max} will have no influence on $P^*(t)$. With fixed trajectory, $P^*(t)$ is only related to the covertness requirement ρ_d. As shown in Fig. 2, when $\rho_d = 0.02$, with P_{max} increasing, A will remain unchanged.

Figure 3 illustrates the relationship between total AoI and varying packet sizes under different UAV altitudes. As observed, the total AoI exhibits a monotonic increase with larger packet sizes, which aligns with constraint (16b). This trend remains consistent across different UAV flight heights.

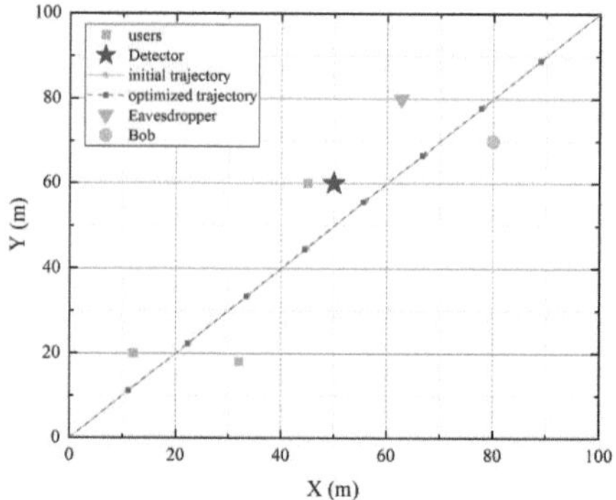

Fig. 4. UAV's trajectories and various users' positions.

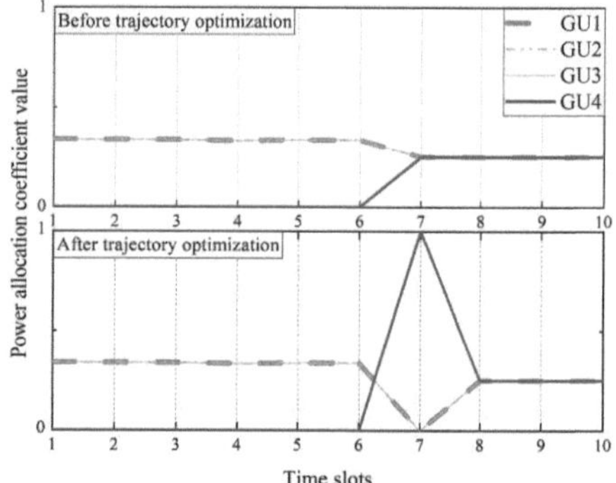

Fig. 5. The power allocation with each user.

In Fig. 4, we show the initial and optimized trajectories of UAV and Fig. 5 presents the power allocation scheme across time slots for all users. The results demonstrate that the UAV allocates zero transmission power to Bob during the first six time slots. This observation aligns with the trajectory pattern shown in Fig. 4, where the UAV maintains a relatively large distance from Bob during these initial slots, making power allocation inefficient. Figure 5 demonstrates that the UAV initiates power allocation to Bob starting from time slot 6, reaching maximum transmission power at slot 7 as the UAV approaches Bob's location. Notably, the peak power allocation does not coincide with the closest approach (slot 8) due to security considerations against eavesdropping, illustrating the system's deliberate trade-off between communication quality and covertness requirements.

As shown in Fig. 6, the achievable rate variations are consistent with the power allocation coefficient adjustments presented in Fig. 5. Furthermore, Fig. 7 reveals the achievable security gap for legitimate user Bob when operating under the secure rate threshold constraint, confirming the system's ability to maintain secure communications.

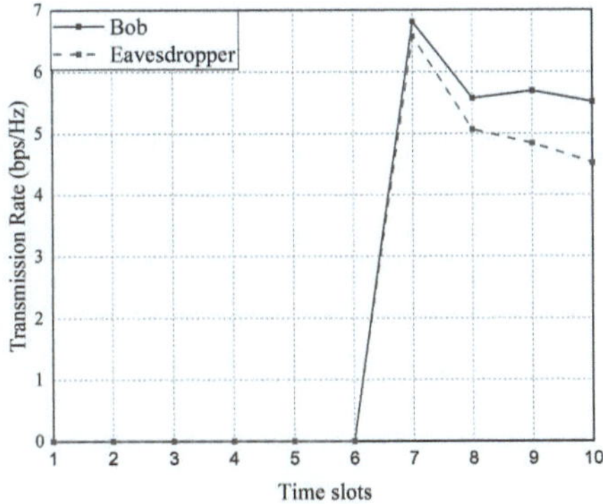

Fig. 6. Transmission rate of Bob and Eavesdropper.

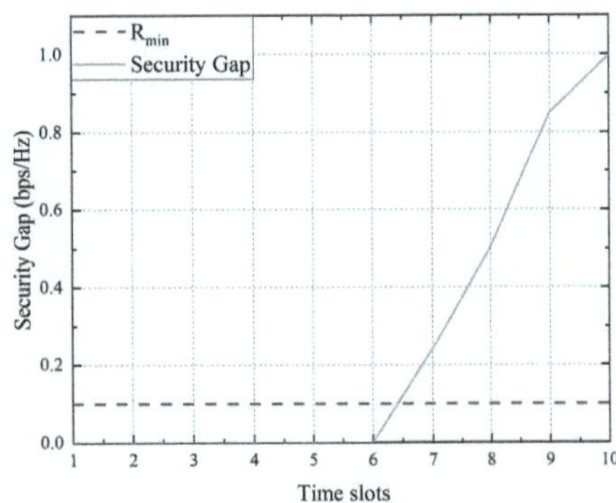

Fig. 7. Security Gap.

6   Conclusion

In this work, we investigate a UAV-assisted secure and covert communication system that jointly optimizes trajectory design, AoI, and power allocation to ensure secure and efficient data transmission. To tackle difficulties of the joint design problem with multiple variables, we employ the BCD method to iteratively solve for the optimal values of these three variables in an alternating manner. In this work, we systematically investigate the impact of key system parameters on AoI performance. Through joint optimization of the UAV's trajectory and power allocation scheme, we minimize the total AoI while numerically analyzing the coupled effects of UAV flight path and user-specific transmission power coefficients on the overall system performance. This work provides a practical framework for secure UAV-assisted communications in adversarial environments. Future directions include extending the framework to multi-UAV scenarios and incorporating robust optimization against dynamic eavesdropper positions.

Acknowledgments. This work was supported in part by the National Natural Science Foundation of China (62372076); in part by the Academician Weiming Shen Workstation (202505AF350084), Yunnan, China; in part by the Yunnan Key Laboratory of Intelligent Logistics Equipment and Systems; in part by the Education Department Research Foundation of Anhui Province (DTR2023051, 2023AH051593, 2022AH051097); in part by the Innovation Research Team on Future Network Technology of Chuzhou University; in part by the Innovation Team on Smart Home Appliance Security and Applications of Chuzhou City; in part by the Innovative Research Team on Application of Big Data and Financial Technology of Chuzhou University; in part by Yunnan Key Laboratory of Smart City in Cyberspace Security (202205AG340011), Yuxi Normal University, Yuxi, China; and in part by the Scientific Research Fund Project of Yunnan Provincial Department of Education (No. 2024Y772).

References

1. Dai, M., Huang, N., Wu, Y., Gao, J., Su, Z.: Unmanned-Aerial-Vehicle-Assisted Wireless Networks: Advancements, Challenges, and Solutions. IEEE Internet Things J. **10**(5), 4117–4147 (2023)
2. Zeng, Y., Lyu, J., Zhang, R.: Cellular-connected UAV: potential, challenges, and promising technologies. IEEE Wirel. Commun. **26**(1), 120–127 (2019)
3. Mozaffari, M., Saad, W., Bennis, M., Nam, Y.-H., Debbah, M.: A tutorial on UAVs for wireless networks: applications, challenges, and open problems. IEEE Commun. Surv. Tutor. **21**(3), 2334–2360 (2019). thirdquarter 2019
4. Yates, R.D., Sun, Y., Brown, D.R., Kaul, S.K., Modiano, E., Ulukus, S.: Age of information: an introduction and survey. IEEE J. Sel. Areas Commun. **39**(5), 1183–1210 (2021)
5. Zhu, B., Bedeer, E., Nguyen, H.H., Barton, R., Gao, Z.: UAV trajectory planning for AoI-minimal data collection in UAV-aided IoT networks by transformer. IEEE Trans. Wirel. Commun. **22**(2), 1343–1358 (2023)
6. Pan, H., Liu, Y., Sun, G., Fan, J., Liang, S., Yuen, C.: Joint power and 3D trajectory optimization for UAV-enabled wireless powered communication networks with obstacles. IEEE Trans. Commun. **71**(4), 2364–2380 (2023)
7. Wu, P., Yuan, X., Hu, Y., Schmeink, A.: Joint power allocation and trajectory design for UAV-enabled covert communication. IEEE Trans. Wirel. Commun. **23**(1), 683–698 (2024)
8. Zhou, X., Yan, S., Hu, J., Sun, J., Li, J., Shu, F.: Joint optimization of a UAV's trajectory and transmit power for covert communications. IEEE Trans. Signal Process. **67**(16), 4276–4290 (2019)
9. Goeckel, D., Bash, B., Guha, S., Towsley, D.: Covert communications when the warden does not know the background noise power. IEEE Commun. Lett. **20**(2), 236–239 (2016)
10. Huang, H., Zhou, S., Zhang, X.: Joint trajectory and power optimization for UAV covert transmission. In: 2021 IEEE 93rd Vehicular Technology Conference (VTC2021-Spring), pp. 1–6. Helsinki, Finland (April 2021)
11. Grant, M., Boyd, S.: CVX: MATLAB software for disciplined convex programming, version 2.1, 2014

LGSVE: Leader-Guided Soft Voting Ensemble Model for Class-Imbalanced IoT Intrusion Detection

Shuai Zhao, Huiqiang Wang, Hongwu Lv, Yifan Zou, and Runong Yang

College of Computer Science and Technology, Harbin Engineering University,
Harbin, China
lvhongwu@hrbeu.edu.cn

Abstract. IoT intrusion detection ensemble methods hold promise for alleviating decision bias under long-tailed class distributions, where single models often fail to achieve minority-class recall. Nevertheless, existing works continue to confront three primary challenges: (1) class-agnostic fusion rules that ignore heterogeneity in feature distributions and model competence across attack types. (2) insufficient exploitation of complementary inductive biases between classifiers, limiting coverage of heterogeneous IoT traffic. and (3) computationally inefficient, noise-prone hyperparameter tuning in high-dimensional parameter spaces. Therefore, we propose a Leader-Guided Soft Voting Ensemble (LGSVE) model that integrates LightGBM, Random Forest, and Bi-Temporal Convolutional Networks to jointly capture structured feature patterns and long-range temporal dependencies. LGSVE employs a class-specific leader strategy combined with weighted soft voting to enhance robustness, particularly for minority-class detection. Furthermore, a Bayesian optimization framework is adopted to improve hyperparameter tuning efficiency and avoid premature convergence. Experiments on CIC-DDoS-2019, CIC-IDS-2017, and TonIot demonstrate that LGSVE significantly boosts minority-class performance while consistently surpassing state-of-the-art baselines in accuracy and robustness.

Keywords: IoT intrusion detection · Ensemble model · Leader-guided soft voting

1 Introduction

The rapid expansion of the Internet of Things (IoT) devices has made them critical interfaces between humans and the physical world [1], but also prime targets for security threats. Intrusion detection is a cornerstone of IoT security and has achieved significant progress [2–4]. However, existing systems still suffer from low recall on minority-class attacks, which degrades overall multi-class performance. A widely recognized cause is the limited attack coverage of single models [5], which leads to missed detections of rare attacks. For example, gradient boosting decision trees perform poorly on long-sequence attacks, while LSTM models often miss conventional attacks, making this an enduring challenge in IoT intrusion detection. Ensemble learning has emerged as an effective approach to address this limitation [6], combining multiple base classifiers to

© IFIP International Federation for Information Processing 2026
Published by Springer Nature Switzerland AG 2026
X. Wang et al. (Eds.): NPC 2025, LNCS 16306, pp. 361–372, 2026.
https://doi.org/10.1007/978-3-032-10466-3_30

exploit complementary strengths and expand coverage. Mainstream ensemble methods include Stacking, Boosting, and Bagging [7]. Stacking integrates outputs from multiple classifiers via a meta-model, but its high computational cost makes it unsuitable for edge devices [8]. Boosting trains classifiers sequentially to correct prior errors, but is sensitive to noise and may reduce recall [9]. Bagging trains multiple models in parallel, aggregates their outputs via voting, and balances real-time performance with accuracy. It remains stable under noisy data, but its effectiveness depends on the performance of the base classifiers [10].

Although ensemble models can effectively address long-tailed data distributions and resource constraints in IoT intrusion detection [11], existing ensemble approaches suffer from three critical limitations in practice: (1) Current methods apply uniform decision rules across all classes, ignoring variations in feature distributions and model effectiveness for different attack types. This class-agnostic strategy exacerbates majority class dominance in long-tailed distributions, significantly reducing minority class recall. (2) Ensemble models typically aggregate base classifier outputs without exploiting their complementary strengths for specific feature domains or attack patterns, resulting in suboptimal performance on heterogeneous IoT traffic. (3) Base classifier performance is highly sensitive to hyperparameter configurations. Optimizing multiple models with their respective parameters creates a high-dimensional, non-convex optimization problem. Conventional approaches using grid search, random search, or heuristics are computationally inefficient, susceptible to local optima, and require excessive training time.

To address these limitations, we propose the Leader-Guided Soft Voting Ensemble (LGSVE), a class-aware ensemble model integrating three complementary base classifiers. For each attack class, LGSVE identifies the base classifier with the highest performance for that class as the leader, and prioritizes its predictions during inference to improve minority-class detection. When the leader classifier is unavailable or exhibits low confidence, the model reverts to probability-weighted soft voting to maintain robustness. The ensemble combines Light Gradient Boosting Machine (LightGBM), RandomForest (RF), and Bi-Temporal Convolutional Network (Bi-TCN), leveraging the synergy between structured feature modeling and long-term temporal dependency modeling. For hyperparameter optimization, we employ Bayesian optimization (BO) with Gaussian Process(GP) surrogates and expected improvement acquisition functions to efficiently approximate the global optimum under computational constraints.

Our main contributions are as follows:

- We propose a multi-domain ensemble model that integrates LightGBM, Random Forest, and Bi-TCN, exploiting their complementary strengths in high-dimensional feature modeling, robustness to class imbalance, and temporal dependency capture to comprehensively address diverse IoT attack patterns.
- We introduce a leader-guided soft voting strategy that dynamically selects the optimal base classifier for each attack class while maintaining probability-weighted fallback voting, improving minority class recall without compromising overall robustness.
- We employ Bayesian optimization for joint hyperparameter tuning across multiple models, through Gaussian process surrogates and expected improvement acquisition

to efficiently navigate the high-dimensional parameter space and avoid local optima under computational constraints.

– Extensive experiments on the CIC-IDS-2017, UNSW-TonIoT, and CIC-DDoS-2019 datasets demonstrate the effectiveness of the proposed approach.

2   Related Work

2.1   IoT Intrusion Detection

In recent years, research on IoT intrusion detection has advanced significantly [12,13]. Early machine learning approaches such as SVM [14] use nonlinear kernel mappings and perform well on malicious traffic classification in the Bot-IoT dataset, but struggle with multi-class classification and tend to favor majority classes under imbalanced distributions. LightGBM [15] is effective for modeling high-dimensional features and improves minority-class detection, but cannot capture long-term temporal dependencies. Deep learning methods such as GNN-based intrusion detection [11] perform global modeling of the network to overcome the limitations of traditional IDSs relying on isolated features, but have high time complexity. Yu et al. proposed DC-IDS [16], which applies deep reinforcement learning for fine-grained classification of benign and attack traffic, achieving high accuracy for known classes, but the high latency of DQN limits deployment. Transformer-based IDSs [13] extract semantic features from network traffic, improving detection accuracy, but still show suboptimal recall for minority attack types under imbalanced traffic. Overall, while these methods reduce the miss rate for minority classes, single-model architectures remain prone to bias and struggle to adapt to attack types with substantially different feature characteristics.

2.2   Ensemble Models Based IoT Intrusion Detection

Ensemble models have been applied to address these limitations in IoT intrusion detection. Mamunur Rashid et al. proposed a Stacking-based model [17] that improves detection performance through a meta-classifier, but the high latency makes it unsuitable for resource-constrained IoT environments. Nguyen et al. developed a Boosting-based method using CatBoost [7], which improves convergence speed and stability. Dual-IDS [6], based on Bagging, improves overall detection rates, but its hard voting mechanism amplifies the dominance of majority classes, reducing recall for long-tail classes. Some studies incorporate leader and confidence mechanisms [5] to mitigate this problem, but they make limited use of probability distributions, reducing their ability to adapt dynamically to different attack categories.

Moreover, the performance of ensemble models depends not only on effective decision strategies but also on the choice of base classifiers and their hyperparameter configurations [9]. Many existing methods lack explicit modeling of the complementary strengths among classifiers, limiting fusion effectiveness for IoT traffic [18]. Joint optimization of multiple models and parameters is a high-dimensional, non-convex problem. Traditional grid search and random search are inefficient and have limited exploration scope [19], while swarm intelligencebased optimization offers global search capability but often converges to local optima and is computationally expensive [15]. In this paper, we propose an ensemble model comprising three complementary base classifiers to expand attack pattern coverage, and we integrate Bayesian optimization to efficiently search hyperparameters and improve overall performance.

3   Methodology

We propose a leader-guided soft voting ensemble model to improve recall for minority attacks and enhance robustness under long-tailed distributions. As shown in Fig. 1, the framework consists of four stages: Bayesian hyperparameter optimization, base classifier training, leader selection, and leader-guided soft voting. After preprocessing, traffic feature vectors are input into multiple optimized base classifiers. During validation, the best-performing classifier for each attack category is designated as the leader, and its predictions are prioritized during inference. When the leader's confidence is low, the system reverts to probability-weighted soft voting to integrate complementary strengths and generate the final decision.

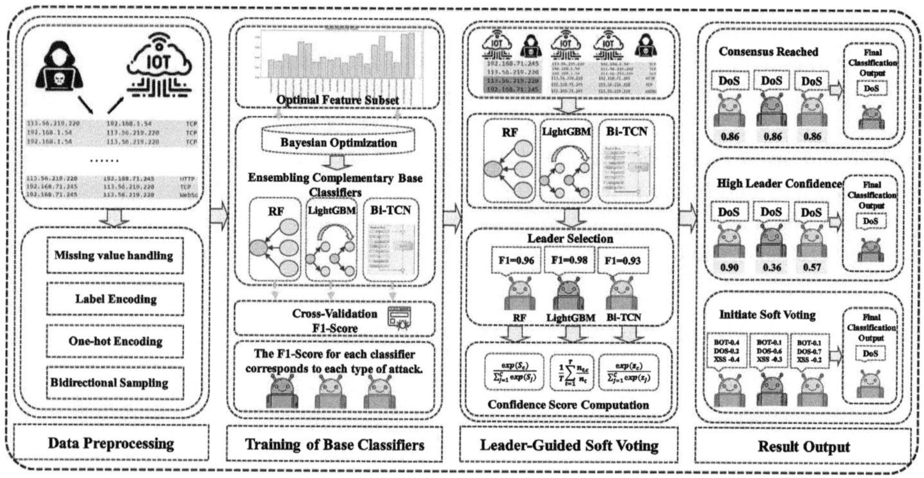

Fig. 1. Overall architecture of the proposed leader-guided soft voting ensemble model for IoT intrusion detection.

3.1   Ensembling Complementary Base Classifiers

In IoT intrusion detection, attack types vary widely in feature structures and temporal dependencies, making it difficult for a single model to generalize effectively. We integrate three complementary base classifiers: LightGBM [15], RF [19], and Bi-TCN, selected for their strengths in structured feature modeling, ensemble robustness, and long-term dependency capture, respectively. This combination achieves a balance between accuracy and efficiency across majority-class, minority-class, and long-sequence attack scenarios.

LightGBM Classifier. LightGBM is effective for high-dimensional sparse structured features, using histogram-based binning and exclusive feature bundling to reduce dimensionality and computational cost. Built on the Gradient Boosting Decision Tree (GBDT) model, it sequentially constructs classification and fegression trees, with each tree fitting the residuals of the previous one to improve accuracy. Compared with traditional GBDT, LightGBM employs efficient feature binning, Gradient-based One-Side Sampling, and EFB, enabling faster and more accurate processing of large-scale data.

In LGSVE, LightGBM focuses on selecting and modeling high-dimensional structured features, providing stable detection of majority-class attacks such as DDoS and PortScan. Bayesian optimization tunes hyperparameters, including tree depth and learning rate, to maintain high detection accuracy with minimal computational overhead.

Random Forest Classifier. RF is adopted to enhance robustness in detecting majority-class attacks and to improve resilience to noise in IoT traffic. Leveraging a Bagging strategy, RF builds multiple decision trees from bootstrap-sampled subsets and randomly selects feature subsets at each split, reducing correlation among trees and mitigating overfitting. Final predictions are obtained via majority voting, ensuring stable performance under noisy and imbalanced data conditions. In LGSVE, RF primarily supports high-confidence predictions for majority classes, contributing to overall stability and generalization through its inherent decorrelation and variance reduction mechanisms.

Bi-TCN Classifier. For attacks with strong temporal dependencies, Bi-TCN leverages both forward and backward temporal contexts to enhance long-range pattern detection, addressing the limitations of tree-based models in capturing cross-time dependencies. It consists of two oppositely directed TCN modules with stacked residual blocks, using causal and dilated convolutions for efficient sequence modeling. In LGSVE, Bi-TCN focuses on temporal attack detection and often serves as the category leader for sequential classes, ensuring robust performance on minority and long-tail temporal patterns even when falling back to soft voting.

3.2 Bayesian Hyperparameter Optimization

In ensemble-based intrusion detection, the performance of base classifiers is highly sensitive to hyperparameter settings, and the search space is often high-dimensional and non-convex. Traditional approaches such as grid search and random search are simple but inefficient. Grid search suffers from exponential computational growth with increasing parameter dimensionality, while random search explores high-dimensional spaces poorly. Both are prone to converging to local optima. Bayesian optimization (BO) addresses these issues by constructing a probabilistic surrogate model of the objective function and using the posterior distribution to guide sampling, enabling efficient convergence to near-optimal solutions under limited computational budgets, which is critical for resource-constrained IoT intrusion detection.

BO typically employs a GP surrogate and an acquisition function to balance exploration and exploitation. In this work, BO adaptively tunes the key hyperparameters of

LightGBM, RF, and Bi-TCN within predefined search spaces to enhance classification accuracy and minority-class recall without compromising training efficiency.

3.3 Leader-Guided Soft Voting Mechanism

To mitigate the impact of weak classifiers on long-tail classes in hard voting, we propose a Leader-Guided Soft Voting mechanism. For each attack class, the base classifier achieving the highest validation performance is designated as the leader, and its predictions are prioritized during inference.

When the leader is absent or exhibits low confidence, LGSVE falls back to a probability-weighted soft voting stage, where the confidence weights from LightGBM, RF, and Bi-TCN guide the decision process. For LightGBM, class confidence is computed from tree outputs $\hat{y}_{t,c}$ as follows:

$$S_c = \sum_{t=1}^{T} \hat{y}_{t,c}, \quad w_c = \frac{\exp(S_c)}{\sum_{j=1}^{C} \exp(S_j)}. \tag{1}$$

where c is the class index, C is the total number of classes, and T is the total number of trees. For RF, class confidence is defined as the mean proportion of class-c samples in the leaf nodes across T trees:

$$w_c = \frac{1}{T} \sum_{t=1}^{T} \frac{n_{t,c}}{n_t}. \tag{2}$$

where $n_{t,c}$ is the number of class-c samples in the leaf node of the t-th tree, and n_t is the total number of samples in that leaf. And for Bi-TCN, class confidence is directly obtained from the softmax output:

$$w_c = \frac{\exp(z_c)}{\sum_{j=1}^{C} \exp(z_j)}. \tag{3}$$

where z_c is the logit for class c and z_j is the logit for class j. The final prediction is obtained by weighted probability fusion:

$$\hat{y} = \arg\max_c \sum_{m \in \mathcal{M}} w_{m,c}\, p_{m,c}. \tag{4}$$

where $\mathcal{M}$ is the set of base models, $w_{m,c}$ is the confidence weight assigned to model m for class c, and $p_{m,c}$ is the predicted probability of model m for class c. This design mitigates the negative impact of weak classifiers on long-tail classes while improving recall and robustness.

4 Experiments and Analysis

This section describes the datasets, evaluation metrics, baseline methods, and experimental setup. Then it reports the proposed model's performance in comparative experiments, followed by ablation studies evaluating the contribution of each component and the effects of base classifier selection and hyperparameter optimization.

4.1   Experimental Settings

Datasets. We evaluate the method on three public IoT intrusion detection datasets. The CIC-DDoS-2019 dataset [20] contains 80 network traffic features and 12 DDoS attack types merged into 8 labels, supporting evaluation under high-dimensional feature settings. The CIC-IDS-2017 dataset [21] comprises over 3 million real Internet traffic samples covering 15 attack types, offering diverse IoT attack scenarios. The UNSW-TonIoT dataset [22] includes traffic from multiple IoT applications; we use its Train-Test-IoT subset with 8 labels, including Normal, DDoS, and Backdoor attacks.

Evaluation Metrics. We evaluate performance using four widely adopted intrusion detection metrics: Precision, Recall, F1-score, and Accuracy [11]. In IoT intrusion detection, many attacks are minority classes, making high recall essential to reduce missed detections. The F1-score balances precision and recall and is used as the criterion for leader selection in our model.

Baselines. To validate the effectiveness of the proposed fusion model, we compare it with six representative intrusion detection approaches covering diverse paradigms, including temporal neural networks, machine learning, graph neural networks, fusion models, and Transformers. (1) IDRF [4] optimizes the random forest splitting criterion with a feature importance based cost matrix to mitigate misclassification under class imbalance. (2) GAT-IDS [12] integrates attack graph structures with dynamic features, leveraging graph attention mechanisms for more accurate predictions. (3) Meta-IDS [3] employs feature selection and dimensionality reduction with multiple classifiers for efficient medical IoT intrusion detection. (4) BT-TPF [23] utilizes module replacement and knowledge distillation to optimize BERT, achieving strong performance in multi-class attack detection. (5) LCCDE [5] ensembles multiple gradient-boosted decision trees with a leader mechanism to improve stability across attack types. (6) MCWOA [24] combines ResNet and AlexNet in a hybrid detection framework to enhance feature extraction and parameter optimization.

Settings. All experiments were conducted under the same hardware and software environment with Windows 10, Intel Core i5-11400H, 16 GB RAM, NVIDIA RTX 3060 GPU to ensure result comparability. Data preprocessing included traffic data formatting, missing value imputation, label encoding with one-hot encoding, and minority class balancing using LSGAN and DBSCAN. Feature selection was performed by RFECV and WSVM to reduce complexity. For the deep learning components, training parameters were set to 100 epochs, a batch size of 128, and the Adam optimizer, with early stopping to prevent overfitting. Hyperparameters of base classifiers were optimized using Bayesian search to achieve the best performance.

4.2   Performance Evaluation

Overall Performance. To assess the overall performance of the proposed LGSVE model, we compare it against six representative baseline methods on three IoT intrusion detection datasets including CIC-DDoS-2019, CIC-IDS-2017, and TonIot. Using multi-class classification metrics including Acc, Recall, and F1.

Table 1. Overall performance comparison of LGSVE with baselines on different datasets.

Model	CIC-DDoS-2019			CIC-IDS-2017			TonIot		
	Acc	Recall	F1	Acc	Recall	F1	Acc	Recall	F1
IDRF	98.68	98.65	98.66	99.08	99.09	99.07	99.11	99.14	99.13
GAT-IDS	91.54	93.24	92.93	94.74	98.72	96.62	97.12	97.69	97.53
Meta-IDS	**99.19**	99.01	99.03	99.26	99.61	99.59	99.34	99.21	99.37
BT-TPF	98.75	98.75	98.74	**99.63**	99.60	99.60	99.45	99.44	99.45
LCCDE	96.81	95.97	96.63	99.17	98.69	99.12	99.35	99.17	99.21
MCWOA	98.01	98.21	98.18	99.33	98.55	98.54	98.63	98.91	98.95
Ours	99.10	**99.11**	**99.11**	99.61	**99.62**	**99.62**	**99.61**	**99.61**	**99.60**

Table 1 shows that LGSVE achieves the best or near-best results on all three datasets, with notable improvements in Recall and F1 for long-tail classes. On CIC-DDoS-2019, Recall reaches 99.11%, and on CIC-IDS-2017 and TonIoT it remains around 99.6%, accompanied by high precision and stability. These gains stem from the complementary strengths of the base classifiers in feature and temporal modeling, the class-aware Leader-Guided Soft Voting Mechanism that improves minority-class recall, and the efficiency of Bayesian hyperparameter optimization under limited computation.

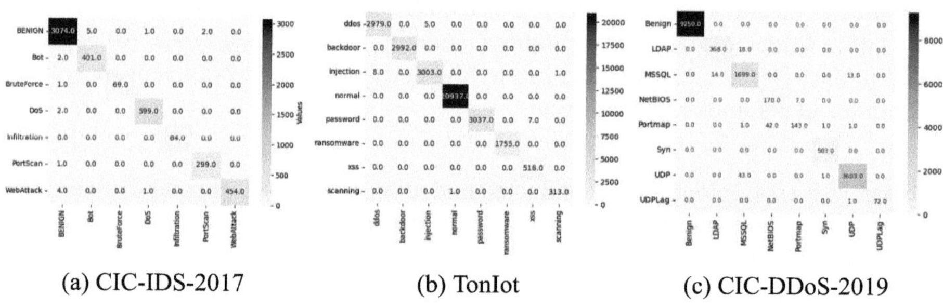

(a) CIC-IDS-2017   (b) TonIot   (c) CIC-DDoS-2019

Fig. 2. Confusion matrix for the multi-class task of LGSVE under different datasets.

Confusion Matrix. To further evaluate the LGSVE's performance, we analyzed its confusion matrices. Figure 2 sequentially presents the multi-class results on the CIC-IDS-2017, UNSW-TonIot, and CIC-DDoS-2019 datasets. The results show consistently high recall for majority classes and substantial improvements for minority classes such as Injection and XSS.

The improved detection of minority classes is mainly attributed to the class-aware leader mechanism, which assigns each attack type to its most effective base classifier and mitigates the limitations of uniform voting on long-tail categories. Sequential attacks benefit from Bi-TCN's bidirectional dependency modeling, while classes sensitive to high-dimensional features leverage LightGBM's structured feature modeling. Overall, LGSVE achieves the objectives of enhancing minority class detection, adapting to long-tail distributions, and improving generalization, showing strong potential for practical IoT intrusion detection deployment.

4.3 Ablation Study

Model Ablation Study. To assess the contribution of each core component in LGSVE, we conducted ablation experiments on CIC-DDoS-2019 and CIC-IDS-2017. Table 2 illustrates that removing the ensemble complementary base classifier and retaining only Bi-TCN led to the largest degradation, with F1 on CIC-DDoS-2019 dropping by nearly 5%, indicating that a single model lacks sufficient feature coverage and adaptability to attack types. Removing the leader-guided soft voting mechanism reduced Recall on CIC-IDS-2017 by 2.15%, confirming its effectiveness in improving minority-class recall under long-tailed distributions. Without Bayesian optimization (w/o BO), performance on both datasets declined by 2–3%, with Recall on CIC-DDoS-2019 decreasing by 2.4%, highlighting the importance of efficient hyperparameter tuning for stability. In general, the three components provide complementary and synergistic gains in minority class detection, long-tail adaptation, and generalization.

Table 2. Ablation experiment results.

Method	CIC-DDoS-2019				CIC-IDS-2017			
	Acc	Pre	Recall	F1	Acc	Pre	Recall	F1
Single Model	93.39	94.36	93.90	94.13	96.59	96.05	96.09	96.04
	98.48	98.32	97.86	98.09	99.17	98.69	99.12	98.90
	97.67	95.75	96.70	96.22	97.50	97.28	97.47	97.42
Ours	**99.10**	**99.14**	**99.10**	**99.12**	**99.61**	**99.62**	**99.62**	**99.62**

Comparison of Base Classifier Models. To assess the advantage of LightGBM in high-dimensional feature modeling, we compared it with Random Forest and traditional GBDT [2] on a 500-dimensional synthetic dataset. As shown in Fig. 3, LightGBM achieves a significantly higher F1-score and superior computational efficiency, demonstrating its suitability for high-dimensional intrusion detection tasks.

To evaluate the adaptability of the RF base classifier for majority-class attack detection, we conducted experiments on CIC-DDoS-2019 focusing on normal traffic and DDoS tasks. As shown in Table 3, RF achieved the highest F1-scores in both cases, indicating that its Bagging-based ensemble and random feature selection maintain high accuracy while adapting effectively to majority-class patterns.

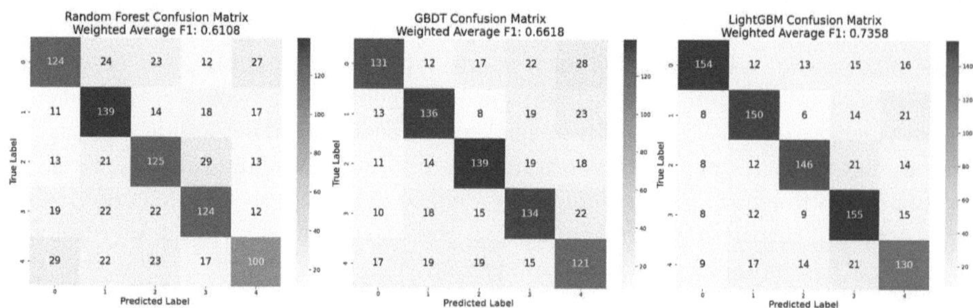

Fig. 3. Performance comparison of detection performance between LightGBM and other algorithms on 500-dimensional data.

Table 3. Comparison of detection performance of RF and other algorithms in most types of attacks on CIC-DDoS-2019.

Model	Acc	Pre	Recall	F1
TCN	0.950	0.952	0.947	0.950
XGBoost	0.962	0.964	0.958	0.961
RF	0.965	0.968	0.961	0.965

Table 4. Performance comparison of Bi-TCN and other algorithms in long-term sequence attacks on CIC-IDS-2017.

Method	Acc	Pre	Recall	F1
TCN	0.939	0.945	0.932	0.938
CNN-BiLSTM	0.961	0.947	0.941	0.949
Bi-TCN	0.964	0.967	0.962	0.971

To assess the Bi-TCN base classifier in long-sequence attack detection, we conducted experiments on the BruteForce task from CIC-IDS-2017. As shown in Table 4, Bi-TCN achieved a higher F1-score than all baselines, confirming its strength in modeling contextual dependencies with bidirectional convolutions. This makes it suitable for IoT security scenarios with limited samples and long temporal dependencies.

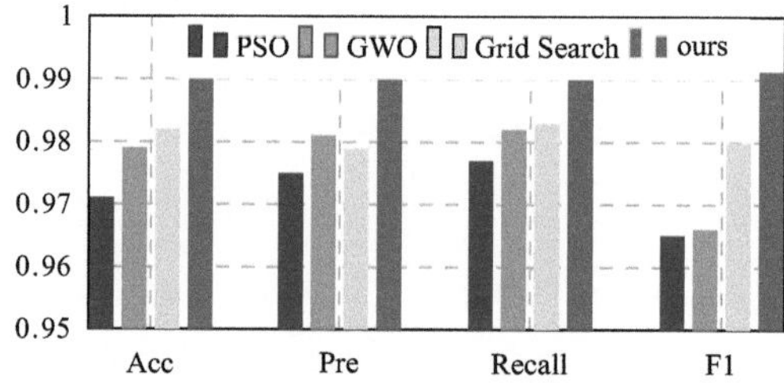

Fig. 4. Performance Comparison of Hyperparameter Optimization Methods.

Comparison of Hyperparameter Optimization Methods. To assess the effectiveness of Bayesian optimization for hyperparameter tuning, we replaced it with particle swarm optimization, grey wolf optimization, and grid search for comparison. As shown in

Fig. 4, Bayesian optimization explores the parameter space more efficiently, avoids premature convergence, and achieves superior performance at lower computational cost.

5   Conclusion

This work addresses the challenges faced by class-imbalanced IoT intrusion detection ensemble models in practical applications. We propose LGSVE, a leader-guided soft voting ensemble model that assigns category-specific leaders and reverts to probability-weighted soft voting when leader confidence is low, enhancing robustness for minority classes under long-tailed distributions. The integration of LightGBM, Random Forest, and Bi-TCN combines strengths in high-dimensional feature modeling, noise tolerance, and long-range temporal dependency capture, with Bayesian optimization enabling efficient hyperparameter tuning. Experiments show that LGSVE consistently outperforms strong baselines in minority-class recall and overall F1-score, with notable advantages in imbalanced scenarios. Future work will explore lighter architectures and distribution-adaptive decision strategies for real-time deployment on resource-constrained IoT devices.

Acknowledgments. This study is funded by the National Natural Science Foundation of China (No. 62272126), the Fundamental Research Funds for the Central Universities (No. 3072024LJ0602).

References

1. Manivannan, D.: Recent endeavors in machine learning-powered intrusion detection systems for the internet of things. J. Netw. Comput. Appl. **229**, 103925 (2024)
2. Cui, J., Xia, H., Zhang, R., Ben-xu, H., Cheng, X.: Optimization scheme for intrusion detection scheme gbdt in edge computing center. Comput. Commun. **168**, 136–145 (2021)
3. Zukaib, U., Cui, X., Zheng, C., Hassan, M., Shen, Z.: Meta-ids: Meta-learning-based smart intrusion detection system for internet of medical things (iomt) network. IEEE Internet Things J. **11**(13), 23080–23095 (2024)
4. Pramilarani, K., Vasanthi Kumari, P.: Cost based random forest classifier for intrusion detection system in internet of things. Appl. Soft Comput. **151**, 111125 (2024)
5. Yang, L., Shami, A., Stevens, G., De Rusett, S.: Lccde: a decision-based ensemble framework for intrusion detection in the internet of vehicles. In: GLOBECOM 2022-2022 IEEE Global Communications Conference, pp. 3545–3550. IEEE (2022)
6. Louk, M.H.L., Tama, B.A.: Dual-ids: a bagging-based gradient boosting decision tree model for network anomaly intrusion detection system. Expert Syst. Appl. **213**, 119030 (2023)
7. Nguyen, T.M., Vo, H.H.P., Yoo, M.: Enhancing intrusion detection in wireless sensor networks using a gswo-catboost approach. Sensors **24**(11), 3339 (2024)
8. Almotairi, A., Atawneh, S., Khashan, O.A., Khafajah, N.M.: Enhancing intrusion detection in iot networks using machine learning-based feature selection and ensemble models. Syst. Sci. Control Eng. **12**(1), 2321381 (2024)
9. Atif, M., Anwer, F., Talib, F.: An ensemble learning approach for effective prediction of diabetes mellitus using hard voting classifier. Indian J. Sci. Technol. **15**(39), 1978–1986 (2022)

10. Thakkar, A., Lohiya, R.: Attack classification of imbalanced intrusion data for iot network using ensemble-learning-based deep neural network. IEEE Internet Things J. **10**(13), 11888–11895 (2023)
11. Wu, Y., et al.: Intrusion detection for internet of things: an anchor graph clustering approach. IEEE Trans. Inf. Forensics Secur. (2025)
12. Sun, Z., Teixeira, A.M.H., Toor, S.: Gnn-ids: graph neural network based intrusion detection system. In: Proceedings of the 19th International Conference on Availability, Reliability and Security, pp. 1–12 (2024)
13. Akuthota, U.C., Bhargava, L.: Transformer based intrusion detection for iot networks. IEEE Internet Things J. (2025)
14. Alfarshouti, A.M., Almutairi, S.M.: An intrusion detection system in iot environment using knn and svm classifiers. Webology **19**(1), 3500–3517 (2022)
15. Li, Z., Li, X.: Intrusion detection method based on genetic algorithm of optimizing lightgbm. In: Proceedings of the 2021 5th International Conference on Electronic Information Technology and Computer Engineering, pp. 1366–1371 (2021)
16. Shoujian, Y., et al.: Deep q-network-based open-set intrusion detection solution for industrial internet of things. IEEE Internet Things J. **11**(7), 12536–12550 (2023)
17. Rashid, M.M., Kamruzzaman, J., Hassan, M.M., Imam, T., Gordon, S.: Cyberattacks detection in iot-based smart city applications using machine learning techniques. Int. J. Environ. Res. Public Health **17**(24), 9347 (2020)
18. Hang, Z., Lu, Y., Wang, Y., Xie, Y.: Flow-mae: leveraging masked autoencoder for accurate, efficient and robust malicious traffic classification. In: Proceedings of the 26th International Symposium on Research in Attacks, Intrusions and Defenses, pp. 297–314 (2023)
19. Huang, B.F., Boutros, P.C.: The parameter sensitivity of random forests. BMC Bioinf. **17**(1), 331 (2016)
20. Saheb, M.C.P., Yadav, M.S., Babu, S., Pujari, J.J., Maddala, J.B.: A review of ddos evaluation dataset: Cicddos2019 dataset. In: International Conference on Energy Systems, Drives and Automations, pp. 389–397. Springer (2021)
21. JJose, J., Jose, D.V.: Deep learning algorithms for intrusion detection systems in internet of things using cic-ids 2017 dataset. Int. J. Electr. Comput. Eng. (IJECE) **13**(1), 1134–1141 (2023)
22. Sharma, A., Babbar, H., Sharma, A.: Ton-iot: detection of attacks on internet of things in vehicular networks. In: 2022 6th International Conference on Electronics, Communication and Aerospace Technology, pp. 539–545. IEEE (2022)
23. Wang, Z., Li, J., Yang, S., Luo, X., Li, D., Mahmoodi, S.: A lightweight iot intrusion detection model based on improved bert-of-theseus. Expert Syst. Appl. **238**, 122045 (2024)
24. Dontu, S., Vallabhaneni, R., Addula, S.R., Pareek, P.K., Abbas, H.M.: Mcwoa based hybrid deep learning for detecting the attacks in cybersecurity with iot network. In: 2024 International Conference on Intelligent Algorithms for Computational Intelligence Systems (IACIS), pp. 1–7. IEEE (2024)

LLM-Guided Soft Actor-Critic for Resource Allocation in Mobile Edge Computing Networks

Jianmeng Guo[1], Xiuhua Li[1]([✉]), Jinlong Hao[1], Lingxiao Chen[1], Xiaofei Wang[2], and Victor C. M. Leung[3,4]

[1] School of Big Data & Software Engineering, Chongqing University, Chongqing, China
lixiuhua@cqu.edu.cn, haojl@changan.com, lingxiaochen@stu.cqu.edu.cn
[2] College of Intelligence & Computing, Tianjin University, Tianjin, China
xiaofeiwang@tju.edu.cn
[3] College of Computer Science & Software Engineering, Shenzhen University, Shenzhen, China
vleung@ieee.org
[4] Department of Electrical and Computer Engineering, The University of British Columbia, Vancouver, Canada

Abstract. Mobile edge computing (MEC) enhances computation efficiency and reduces latency by offloading tasks from mobile devices (MDs) to nearby edge servers (ESs). To optimize the offloading process and manage resource allocation effectively, deep reinforcement learning (DRL) has been widely adopted as a promising solution. However, as the number of MDs increases, the rapidly expanding state-action space poses significant challenges to the ability of DRL to learn effective policies, often resulting in suboptimal decision-making. Large language model (LLM) with strong reasoning capabilities and extensive prior knowledge offers a potential solution by enabling more efficient exploration and guiding the DRL toward better policies. Therefore, we propose an LLM-guided soft actor-critic (LLM-guided SAC) algorithm, which integrates LLM-generated policy priors with a probabilistic mixed strategy to facilitate learning in high-dimensional decision spaces. By refining the state-action representation, the proposed algorithm enhances policy learning efficiency, while LLM-guided priors enable informed exploration and improve early-stage decision quality. Moreover, the mixed strategy balances exploration and exploitation, contributing to stable and effective learning. Experimental results demonstrate that LLM-guided SAC consistently outperforms baseline methods, particularly in large and complex decision spaces, highlighting its strong potential for resource optimization in MEC networks.

Keywords: Mobile Edge Computing · LLM-guided DRL · Improved Markov Decision Process · Resource Allocation

© IFIP International Federation for Information Processing 2026
Published by Springer Nature Switzerland AG 2026
X. Wang et al. (Eds.): NPC 2025, LNCS 16306, pp. 373–385, 2026.
https://doi.org/10.1007/978-3-032-10466-3_31

1   Introduction

The rapid development of the Internet of Things has enhanced the computing capabilities of mobile devices (MDs) while triggering an explosive growth in data traffic, leading to network congestion [4,12]. Mobile edge computing (MEC) alleviates network burden by offloading tasks to nearby edge servers (ESs), enhancing service quality and supporting delay-sensitive applications such as autonomous driving, augmented reality, and industrial automation. Despite the benefits of MEC, efficient allocation of limited computation resources among numerous competing MDs remains a challenge, requiring real-time processing and high service reliability [14].

To address the above challenges, intelligent decision-making methods have been widely explored to optimize resource allocation and computation offloading in MEC systems [8,15]. Notably, deep reinforcement learning (DRL) has gained significant attention for its ability to optimize decision-making in dynamic and complex environments through experience-driven learning. By modeling offloading and resource allocation as a markov decision process (MDP), DRL-based methodes enable adaptive optimization under uncertain network conditions.

However, conventional DRL methods face several limitations when applied to MEC scenarios with high-dimensional decision spaces. As the number of MDs increases, the complexity of the state-action space grows exponentially, leading to slower convergence and potential policy instability. Recent research has explored using LLMs as decision networks [1,9]. Nevertheless, applying them directly in dynamic MEC environments faces challenges, including long inference times and a lack of stability. This limitation motivates the continued exploration of enhanced DRL frameworks.

Several studies have explored DRL-based solutions for resource allocation and computation offloading in MEC network [3,13]. However, due to the inherent limitations of DRL, the state-action space in the above studies are relatively small. There has been some work introducing LLM to help train a better agent network. Kwon *et al.* [5] proposed using LLMs as proxy reward functions to guide RL training, enabling reward design through natural language prompts and improving alignment with user objectives. Du *et al.* [2] proposed ELLM to leverages language models to guide reinforcement learning exploration by rewarding agents for achieving LLM-suggested goals, improving common-sense behavior and downstream task performance. However, integrating LLM-guided policy priors into DRL for resource optimization in MEC networks remains largely unexplored.

Therefore, this paper proposes the LLM-guided soft actor-critic (SAC) algorithm, which leverages LLM-provided policy priors and a probabilistic mixed strategy. Furthermore, this paper refines the state-action space to enhance SAC performance in high-dimensional environments. The key contributions of this paper are as follows:

- We design a MEC network that includes MDs, a set of base stations (BSs) equipped with ESs, and a CS, with the objective of maximizing the utility of all MDs.

- We design an LLM-guided SAC algorithm that optimizes the state-action space to address the resource allocation and computation offloading problems.
- We conduct extensive experiments to validate the effectiveness of the proposed algorithm against baseline methods in diverse scenarios.

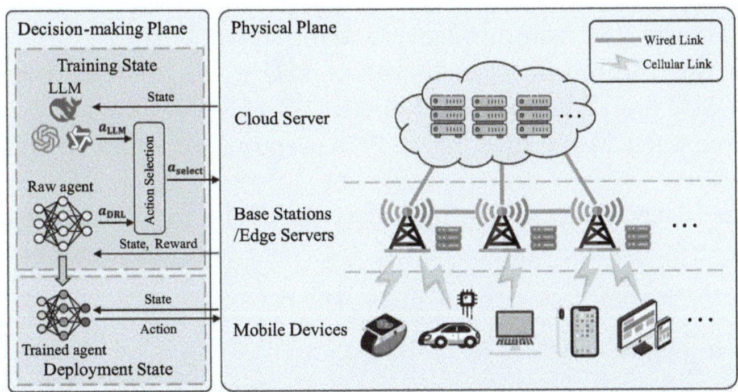

Fig. 1. The system architecture.

2   System Model and Problem Formulation

As illustrated in Fig. 1, we consider a heterogeneous edge computing system consisting of a cloud server (CS), a set of BSs equipped with ESs, and a group of MDs. MDs communicate with ESs over cellular networks, while ESs are interconnected and connected to CS via wired link. The system is assumed to operate in fixed time slots of length l, where $l \in \{1, 2, \ldots, L\}$. During each time slot, MDs probabilistically generate delay-sensitive tasks. Given the constrained computation capabilities of MDs, tasks are transmitted via cellular links to their associated ESs and subsequently offloaded to a ES or the CS for processing. It is assumed that each MD's task is offloaded to only one computing node. At a specific time slot, the set of MDs generating computation tasks is denoted by $\mathcal{E} = \{1, 2, \ldots, E\}$. Each MD's task characteristics are defined by a 4-tuple $\Pi_e = \{c_e,\ d_e, t_e^{max}, z_e\}$, where c_e denotes the CPU cycles required for MD e to process 1-bit of data, d_e denotes the data size of MD e's task, t_e^{max} denotes the maximum tolerable delay, and $z_e = n$ specifies that MD e is covered by ES n. The set of ESs for task execution is denoted as $\mathcal{N} = \{1, 2, \ldots, N\}$. The computation resources in ES n are denoted as f_n, whereas the resources in CS are represented by f_{CS}.

When relevant information is collected, the trained LLM-guided SAC agent is employed to optimize offloading and resource allocation decisions. The detailed training procedure is described in Sect. 3.

2.1 Wireless Communication Model and Computation Model

The cellular link between MD e and its associated ES n operates based on the orthogonal frequency-division multiple access technique, with its communication rate is given by

$$v_{e,n} = B_{e,n} \log_2 \left(1 + \frac{q_e h_{e,n}}{\sigma^2}\right), \tag{1}$$

where $B_{e,n}$ denotes the communication bandwidth between MD e and ES n, q_e represents the communication power of MD e. $h_{e,n}$ is the wireless channel gain between MD e and ES n, calculated as $32.44 + 20 * \log_{10} y_{e,n}$, where $y_{e,n}$ is the distance between MD e and ES n. Furthermore, σ^2 denotes the noise power spectral density.

Consequently, the communication delay for MD e to offload tasks to its associated ES n can be formulated as

$$t_{e,n}^{com} = \frac{d_e}{v_{e,n}}. \tag{2}$$

When the task is offloaded to a neighboring ES m connected to ES n ($m \in \mathcal{N}, m \neq n$), an additional communication delay arises. The communication rate of the wired link between ESs n and m is denoted as $v_{n,m}$, and the corresponding communication delay is given by

$$t_{n,m}^{com} = \frac{d_e}{v_{n,m}}. \tag{3}$$

When the task is offloaded from ES n to CS, the additional communication delay includes both the communication delay and the propagation delay, which can be expressed as

$$t_{n,CS}^{com} = \frac{d_e}{v_{n,CS}} + \frac{dis_{n,CS}}{v_{n,CS}^{ppg}}, \tag{4}$$

where $v_{n,CS}$ represents the communication rate between ES n and CS, $dis_{n,CS}$ denotes the distance between ES n and the CS, and $v_{n,CS}^{ppg}$ is the propagation rate.

To characterize the communication delay of MD e's task, we introduce the offloading strategy variable $x_{e,k}$, where $x_{e,k} = 1$ indicates that MD e offloads its task to ES k ($k \in \mathcal{N}$) for computation. If $\sum_{k \in \mathcal{N}} x_{e,k} = 0$, the task is instead offloaded to CS.

Accordingly, the communication delay of MD e's task is given by

$$t_e^{com} = t_{e,n}^{com} + \sum_{k \in \mathcal{N}} x_{e,k} t_{n,k}^{com} + \left(1 - \sum_{k \in \mathcal{N}} x_{e,k}\right) t_{k,CS}^{com}, \tag{5}$$

when $k = n$, $t_{n,k}^{com} = 0$. For $k \neq n$, the communication delay is calculated according to (3).

After determining the offloading destination of MD e's task, the corresponding computation resources are allocated. Let $\delta_{e,k} \in [0,1]$ denote the fraction of computation resources at ES k allocated to MD e. Then, the computation delay of MD e's task is given by

$$t_e^{cmp} = \frac{c_e d_e}{\sum_{k \in \mathcal{N}} x_{e,k} \delta_{e,k} f_k + (1 - \sum_{k \in \mathcal{N}} x_{e,k}) \delta_{e,CS} f_{CS}}. \tag{6}$$

Thus, the total delay of MD e can be expressed as

$$t_e^{total} = t_e^{com} + t_e^{cmp}. \tag{7}$$

2.2   Problem Formulation

The goal of the system is to maximize the overall satisfaction of all MDs. Considering that MD satisfaction exhibits diminishing marginal returns with respect to delay reduction [10], the system optimization problem is formulated as

$$\textbf{P1}: \max_{\mathcal{X}, \Delta, \delta_{e,CS}} \sum_{e=1}^{E} \lambda_1 \ln \left(1 + \lambda_2 \left(t_e^{max} - t_e^{total}\right)\right) \tag{8a}$$

$$\text{s.t. } t_e^{total} < t_e^{max}, \ \forall e \in \mathcal{E}, \tag{8b}$$

$$\sum_{k=1}^{N} x_{e,k} \leq 1, \ \forall e \in \mathcal{E}, \tag{8c}$$

$$\sum_{e=1}^{E} \delta_{e,k} \leq 1, \ \forall k \in \mathcal{N}, \tag{8d}$$

$$\sum_{e=1}^{E} \delta_{e,CS} \leq 1, \tag{8e}$$

$$x_{e,k} \in \{0, 1\}, \ \forall e \in \mathcal{E}, \ \forall k \in \mathcal{N}, \tag{8f}$$

where $\mathcal{X} = \{x_{e,k} \mid e \in \mathcal{E}, \ k \in \mathcal{N}\}$ represents the offloading decisions of all MDs, and $\Delta = \{\delta_{e,k} \mid e \in \mathcal{E}, \ k \in \mathcal{N}\}$ denotes the corresponding computation resource allocation ratios. $\lambda_1, \lambda_2 > 0$ are weighting coefficients for the satisfaction functions. (8b) ensures that the total delay experienced by each MD does not exceed its maximum tolerable delay. (8c) and (8f) guarantee that each MD offloads its task to only one computing node. (8d) and (8e) impose that the total computation resources allocated by CS/each ES to its associated MDs do not exceed its available capacity.

3   Proposed Algorithm Design

Since $x_{e,k}$ is discrete and $\delta_{e,k}$ is continuous, problem **P1** is a mixed-integer nonlinear program, known to be NP-hard [6][1]. Traditional DRL struggles in our

---

[1] This paper focuses on methodological innovation. The system model retains sufficient mathematical complexity. More complex scenarios will be explored in futur e work.

large-scale MD scenario due to the rapidly expanding state-action space [13]. To address this challenge, we first refine the state, action, and reward design. Then, we propose an LLM-guided DRL co-training framework, where LLMs provide an initial policy prior that guides early-stage exploration and reduces the search space. In addition, a mixed probabilistic strategy further balances exploration and convergence.

3.1 DRL Formulation

In the DRL framework, an agent continuously interacts with the environment to refine its adaptability. The decision-making process of the agent is typically modeled as a MDP, defined by a tuple $(\mathcal{S}, \mathcal{A}, \mathcal{R}, \mathcal{P})$, where $\mathcal{S}$ represents the set of possible states, $\mathcal{A}$ denotes the set of executable actions, $\mathcal{R}$ is the reward function, and $\mathcal{P}$ is the state transition probability.

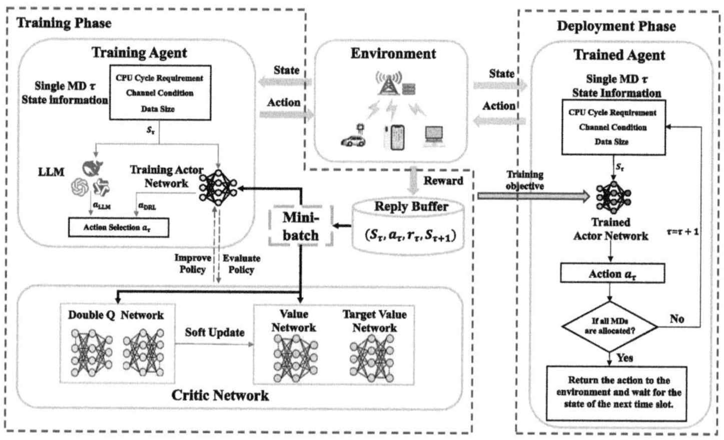

Fig. 2. The proposed algorithm architecture.

As shown in Fig. 2, in both training and deployment phases, each time slot is treated as an environment reset rather than a system restart. Initially, the agent observes the state attributes of the first MD, all ESs, and the CS. The agent then generates the offloading destination and resource computation allocation. A reward is computed based on the executed action. Subsequently, the agent transitions to the next state, updating ES and CS resources while considering environmental conditions. This process repeats until all MDs are allocated, marking the terminal state. At each new time slot, the environment is reset and the generated MDP is stored as training data.

Remark. As the problem studied excludes cross-slot operations, each time slot is treated as an environment reset. However, the proposed algorithm can be naturally extends to cross-slot scenarios by omitting the reset.

Based on the above idea, problem **P1** can be reformulated in the following MDP form:

1) State: The state is defined as a set of parameters that characterize the system status. At state τ, the agent obtains the state information of a single MD as well as the state information of all ESs and the CS, which is defined as

$$s_\tau = \{\mathcal{F}_\tau^{idle}\}, \tag{9}$$

where $\mathcal{F}_\tau^{idle}$ represents the equivalent computation resources of ESs and the CS at state τ, defined as $\mathcal{F}_\tau^{idle} = \{f_{\tau,1}^{equ}, \ldots, f_{\tau,n}^{equ}, \ldots, f_{\tau,N}^{equ}, f_{\tau,CS}^{equ}\}$.

The equivalent computation resource $f_{\tau,tar}^{equ}$ dynamically integrates key system attributes (e.g., CPU cycle requirement c_τ, data size d_τ, and real-time channel conditions) to construct a compact state space. This method significantly reduces state dimensionality while preserving the essential information of system dynamics. In the following, we introduce the computation method for the equivalent computation resources.

At state τ, the offloading and resource allocation are performed for MD e (where $\tau = e$). When MD τ offloads its task to the target computing node, the equivalent computation resource $f_{\tau,tar}^{equ}$ of compute node can be computed as

$$\frac{c_\tau d_\tau}{f_{\tau,tar}^{equ}} = t_\tau^{com} + \frac{c_\tau d_\tau}{f_{\tau,tar}^{rem}}, \tag{10}$$

where $f_{\tau,tar}^{rem}$ denotes the available computation resources at the target computing node in state τ. The communication delay t_τ^{com} varies depending on whether the task is offloaded to the associated ES n, another ES m, or the CS. Rearranging (10), we obtain

$$f_{\tau,tar}^{equ} = \frac{c_\tau d_\tau}{t_\tau^{com} + \frac{c_\tau d_\tau}{f_{\tau,tar}^{rem}}}. \tag{11}$$

2) Action: The action space is defined as

$$a_\tau = \{x_\tau, \delta_\tau\}, \tag{12}$$

where the agent selects the offloading destination x_τ and the corresponding resource allocation δ_τ for the MD.

3) Reward: In order to enable the agent to learn a strategy network that maximizes overall MD satisfaction, the reward is defined as the sum of the past reward and the current reward

$$r_\tau = r_{\tau-1} + \lambda_1 \ln\left(1 + \lambda_2\left(t_\tau^{max} - t_\tau^{total}\right)\right), \tag{13}$$

where t_τ^{max} and t_τ^{total} are the maximum tolerable delay and the total delay of the relevant MD in the current state τ after determining the offloading decision and resource allocation.

3.2 LLM-Guided SAC-Based Computation Offloading and Resource Allocation Algorithm

SAC is a DRL algorithm built upon the maximum entropy framework, which aims to maximize cumulative rewards while encouraging policy entropy to enhance exploration and improve learning stability. It adopts an off-policy training paradigm that utilizes experience replay and incorporates Double Q-learning and target value function techniques to improve sample efficiency. The objective function of SAC includes an entropy regularization term, which is defined as

$$J(\pi) = \sum_{\tau=0}^{T} \mathbb{E}_{(s_\tau, a_\tau) \sim \rho_\pi} \left[r(s_\tau, a_\tau) + \alpha \mathcal{H}(\pi(\cdot|s_\tau)) \right], \tag{14}$$

where $\mathcal{H}(\pi(\cdot|s_\tau)) = -\log \pi(a_\tau|s_\tau)$ is the policy entropy at state s_τ, and α is the temperature parameter balancing reward maximization and exploration.

To estimate the expected return of action a in state s, SAC employs Q-networks defined via the soft Bellman equation formulated as

$$Q(s, a) = r(s, a) + \gamma \mathbb{E}_{s' \sim p}[V(s')], \tag{15}$$

where the soft value function $V(s)$ is expressed as

$$V(s) = \mathbb{E}_{a \sim \pi}[Q(s, a) - \alpha \log \pi(a|s)], \tag{16}$$

with this entropy-augmented formulation, the agent is encouraged to maximize rewards while promoting action diversity through entropy regularization.

To improve convergence in high-dimensional spaces, an LLM is introduced to guide early-stage exploration. At each decision step, the action is selected according to a probabilistic mixed strategy given by

$$a_{\text{selecte}} = \begin{cases} a_{\text{LLM}}, & \text{with probability } \beta, \\ a_{\text{SAC}}, & \text{with probability } 1 - \beta, \end{cases} \tag{17}$$

where $a_{\text{LLM}} = f_{\text{LLM}}(s)$ is inferred by the LLM, and a_{SAC} is sampled from the SAC policy network. The policy of SAC is optimized by minimizing the Kullbackâ ĂŞLeibler divergence formulated as

$$\pi_{\text{new}} = \arg \min_{\pi} D_{\text{KL}} \left(\pi(\cdot|s_\tau) \middle\| \frac{\exp(Q^{\pi_{\text{old}}}(s_\tau, \cdot))}{Z^{\pi_{\text{old}}}(s_\tau)} \right), \tag{18}$$

where $Z^{\pi_{\text{old}}}(s_\tau)$ is the partition function. This leads to the policy loss

$$\mathcal{L}_\phi = \mathbb{E}_{s \sim \mathcal{D}} \left[\mathbb{E}_{a \sim \pi_\phi}[\alpha \log \pi_\phi(a|s) - Q_\theta(s, a)] \right]. \tag{19}$$

To enable a smooth transition from LLM-assisted decision-making to autonomous SAC learning, the influence parameter β of LLM is decayed exponentially as $\beta_k = \beta_0 e^{-\eta k}$, where β_0 is the initial LLM probability, η is the decay rate, and k denotes the training step.

The Q-network is updated by minimizing the mean squared Bellman error, which can be expressed as

$$\mathcal{L}_\theta = \mathbb{E}_{(s,a,s')\sim\mathcal{D}} \left[\left(Q_\theta(s,a) - \hat{Q}(s,a)\right)^2\right], \tag{20}$$

with the target Q-value defined as

$$\hat{Q}(s,a) = r(s,a) + \gamma\mathbb{E}_{s'\sim p}[V_{\bar{\psi}}(s')], \tag{21}$$

where $\bar{\psi}$ represents the parameters of the target value network, updated as $\bar{\psi} \leftarrow \xi\psi + (1-\xi)\bar{\psi}$, with $\xi \in (0,1)$ being a smoothing coefficient to stabilize training and reduce value estimation variance.

An adaptive temperature parameter α is optimized to balance entropy and reward through

$$\mathcal{L}(\alpha) = \mathbb{E}_{s\sim\mathcal{D}} \left[-\alpha(\log\pi(a|s) + \bar{\mathcal{H}})\right], \tag{22}$$

where $\bar{\mathcal{H}}$ is the target entropy, typically $-\dim(\mathcal{A})$ to ensure exploration.

To mitigate overestimation bias, SAC adopts Double Q-learning, which estimates the target by taking the minimum of two Q-networks as

$$\hat{Q} = \min_{i=1,2} Q_{\theta_i}(s,a). \tag{23}$$

The detailed steps of the proposed LLM-guided SAC algorithm are summarized in Algorithm 1.

ïź£

Algorithm 1 LLM-guided SAC Algorithm

Input: LLM parameters, SAC parameters, and other necessary configurations.
Output: Optimized policy network $\pi_\phi(a|s)$;
1: Initialize SAC networks: policy network π_ϕ, Q-networks $Q_{\theta_1}, Q_{\theta_2}$, and target value network $V_{\bar{\psi}}$;
2: Initialize LLM-guided probability $\beta \leftarrow \beta_0$;
3: Initialize target network parameters: $\bar{\psi} \leftarrow \psi$;
4: **while** training has not converged **do**
5:     Sample state s_τ from the environment;
6:     Select action a_τ with probability β from a_{LLM}, otherwise from a_{SAC};
7:     Execute action a_τ, observe reward r_τ and next state $s_{\tau+1}$;
8:     Store transition $(s_\tau, a_\tau, r_\tau, s_{\tau+1})$ in replay buffer $\mathcal{D}$;
9:     Sample minibatch $(s, a, r, s') \sim \mathcal{D}$;
10:     Compute target Q-value $\hat{Q}(s,a)$ and update Q-networks according to (20), update policy network according to (18), temperature parameter α, and target value network $\bar{\psi} \leftarrow \tau\psi + (1-\tau)\bar{\psi}$.
11:     Decay LLM guidance probability: $\beta \leftarrow \beta_0 e^{-\eta k}$;
12: **end while**

3.3   Complexity Analysis

The training time complexity of Algorithm 1 consists of three main components: LLM inference, SAC updates, and experience replay. At each step, obtaining an LLM-generated action a_{LLM} incurs a time complexity of $\mathcal{O}(C_{\mathrm{LLM}})$, where C_{LLM} depends on the LLM architecture and token processing. The SAC updates involve Q-network optimization, policy gradient updates, and temperature tuning. For a minibatch of size B, each Q-network update has a time complexity of $\mathcal{O}(Bg^2)$, where g represents the hidden dimension of the neural networks. The policy update has a similar time complexity. Given K training iterations, the overall training time complexity is $\mathcal{O}(K(C_{\mathrm{LLM}} + Bg^2))$. The training space complexity, which accounts for the LLM parameters, SAC networks, and replay buffer D, is $\mathcal{O}(C_{\mathrm{LLM}} + D + g^2)$. During inference, the main computation cost comes from the forward pass of the policy network, with the time complexity of $\mathcal{O}(g^2)$, and the space complexity is $\mathcal{O}(g^2)$. This stage depends solely on the DRL inference speed and is independent of the LLM used during training.

4   Evaluation Results

4.1   Setup

The experiments are conducted on a high-performance computing platform equipped with two AMD EPYC^{TM} 7713 64-Core Processors and eight NVIDIA A800-SXM4-80GB GPUs, utilizing the Qwen2-7B model [11]. The simulation environment is designed to emulate practical MEC scenarios. The task data size is set as $d_e \in [25, 35]$ MB, with computation complexity $c_e \in [10, 30]$ CPU cycles per bit. The transmission power is $q_e \in [0.1, 0.5]$ W.

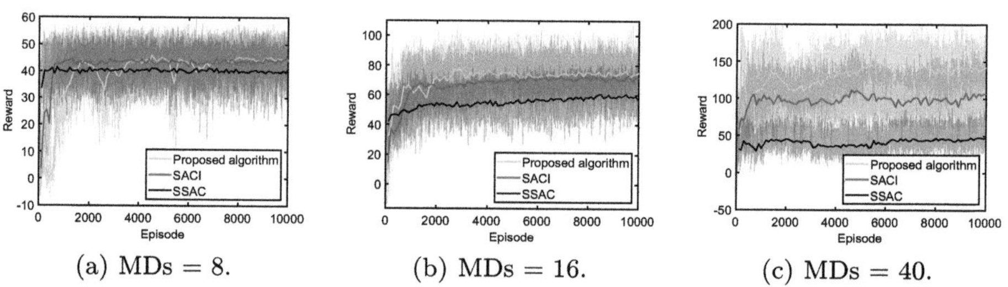

(a) MDs = 8.   (b) MDs = 16.   (c) MDs = 40.

Fig. 3. Performance of SAC variants under different numbers of MDs.

The proposed algorithm is evaluated against three baseline methods as: 1) **Expert-Guided Resource Allocation (EGRA)** [16], representing a rule-based strategy where pre-defined human-designed heuristics dictate resource allocation; 2) **Uniform Resource Allocation (URA)** [7], distributing available resources equally among all MDs; 3) **Non-Cooperative Computation Offloading (NCCO)** [17], limiting task offloading to the ES or CS within each MD's coverage and lacking coordination among ESs for adaptive optimization.

4.2   Experimental Results and Analysis

1) Performance Analysis of SAC Variants with Increasing Numbers of MDs:
Figure 3 compares the convergence performance of SAC variants under varying
numbers of MDs. With 8 MDs as shown in Fig. 3a, the standard SAC (SSAC)
exhibits stable convergence. However, as the number of MDs increases to 16 in
Fig. 3b, its performance degrades noticeably, revealing its limited scalability in
more complex environments. SAC with an improved state-action space (SACI)
demonstrates superior convergence performance under the scenario with 16
MDs, while the proposed algorithm further elevates performance via knowledge-
informed exploration. At the highest complexity level with 40 MDs in Fig. 3c,
the proposed algorithm demonstrates superior convergence stability. Furthermore, the proposed algorithm outperforms the other two by 16.18% and 38.39%,
respectively, confirming its adaptability to complex, high-dimensional environments.

*2) Utility Comparison of Resource Allocation Methods with Increasing Num-
bers of MDs:* Figure 4a illustrates the variation in utility across different numbers
of MDs for various resource allocation methods. The proposed algorithm consistently achieves the highest utility when the number of MDs is increased from
20 to 40, which demonstrates its superior ability to optimize resource allocation and policy learning. Moreover, it improves the utility by 15.38%, 10.57%
and 27.12% compared to EGRA, URA and NCCO, respectively. With predefined rules, EGRA outperforms URA and NCCO in scenarios with high MD
density. However, when the number of MDs is limited, its conservative strategy
of reserving resources for the potential future tasks of MDs leads to suboptimal
effectiveness. URA demonstrates competitive performance under moderate MD
densities, but its performance degrades as MD numbers increase. Due to the lack
of collaboration among ESs, NCCO results in the lowest utility.

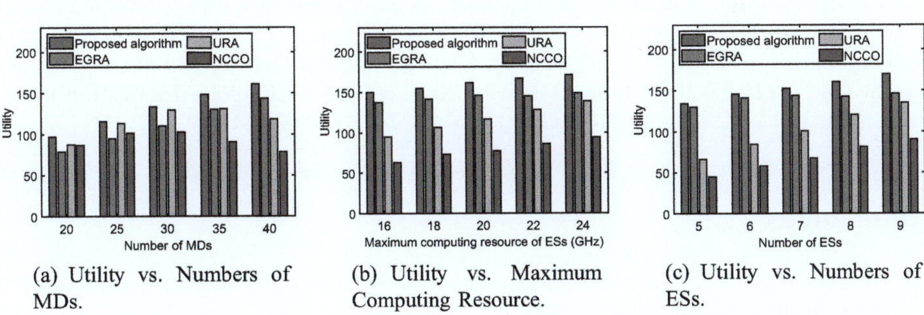

(a) Utility vs. Numbers of
MDs.

(b) Utility vs. Maximum
Computing Resource.

(c) Utility vs. Numbers of
ESs.

Fig. 4. Utility in resource allocation methods under different scenarios.

3) Utility Comparison of Resource Allocation Methods under Scalable Edge Resources: Figures 4b–4c evaluate resource allocation methods as ES resources scale in capacity (16–24 GHz) and quantity (5–9), with the number of MDs fixed at 40. The proposed algorithm consistently achieves the highest utility, demonstrating its adaptability to changes in computation capacity and resource availability. It outperforms the other algorithms by an average of 8.98%, 30.90%, and 53.40%, respectively. EGRA maintains relatively stable performance when resources are less variable. However, under abundant resource conditions, the fixed rules and conservative strategy of EGRA prevents significant utility improvement. URA experiences a significant utility decline under resource constraints due to its fixed policy. NCCO performs the worst in all scenarios due to its lack of coordination. These results confirm the proposed algorithm's superiority in dynamically coordinating resources under diverse ES scaling conditions.

In summary, The results confirm the algorithm's effectiveness in resource allocation and policy learning, with LLM guidance and refined state-action representation notably enhancing decision-making under high MD density.

5   Conclusion and Future Work

In this paper, we have proposed the LLM-guided SAC algorithm to address the challenges of high-dimensional resource allocation and computation offloading in MEC networks. Specifically, we have integrated policy priors, optimized stateâĂŞaction space, and a probabilistic strategy to enhance learning efficiency and stability. Experimental results have demonstrated its superiority over conventional SAC, particularly in large-scale MEC scenarios. In the future work, more sophisticated DRL methods will be exploited for the LLM-guided DRL framework design in more complex MEC network environments.

Acknowledgment. This work is supported in part by Science and Technology Innovation Key R&D Program of Chongqing (Grants No. CSTB2024TIAD-STX0024), National NSFC (Grant No. 62372072), Sichuan Science and Technology Program (Grant No. 2024YFHZ0097), and Regional Science and Technology Innovation Cooperation Project of Chengdu City (Grant No. 2023-YF11-00023-HZ).

References

1. Brohan, A., et al.: Rt-1: robotics transformer for real-world control at scale. arXiv preprint arXiv:2212.06817 (2022)
2. Du, Y., et al.: Guiding pretraining in reinforcement learning with large language models. In: Proceedings of the PMLR ICML, pp. 8657–8677 (2023)
3. Fan, W.: Hybrid deep reinforcement learning-based task offloading for D2D-assisted cloud-edge-device collaborative networks. IEEE Trans. Mob. Comput. **23**(12), 13455–13471 (2024)
4. Guan, T., Yao, Y., Yuan, C., Liu, F., Liu, Y., Gu, R.: Energy-efficient computing offloading policy for MEC-assisted power sensor network: a D3QN approach. In: Proceedings of the IEEE ICCSI, pp. 180–185 (2023)

5. Kwon, M., Xie, S.M., Bullard, K., Sadigh, D.: Reward design with language models. arXiv preprint arXiv:2303.00001 (2023)
6. Li, H., Li, X., Fan, Q., He, Q., Wang, X., Leung, V.C.: Distributed DNN inference with fine-grained model partitioning in mobile edge computing networks. IEEE Trans. Mob. Comput. **23**(10), 9060–9074 (2024)
7. Lin, X., Wu, J., Li, J., Zheng, X., Li, G.: Friend-as-learner: socially-driven trustworthy and efficient wireless federated edge learning. IEEE Trans. Mob. Comput. **22**(1), 269–283 (2021)
8. Liu, S., Li, W., Chen, H., Wang, J., Zhao, K.: Satellite-assisted task offloading and resource allocation for ocean of things edge computing. IEEE Internet Things J. 1–18 (2025)
9. Liu, X., et al.: Agentbench: evaluating LLMs as agents. arXiv preprint arXiv:2308.03688 (2023)
10. Meng, D., et al.: Incentive-driven partial offloading and resource allocation in vehicular edge computing networks. IEEE Internet Things J. 1–13 (2024)
11. Team, Q.: Qwen2.5: a party of foundation models (2024)
12. Wang, Z., et al.: When crowdsensing meets smart cities: a comprehensive survey and new perspectives. IEEE Commun. Surv. Tutor. **27**(2), 1101–1151 (2025)
13. Xu, C., Liu, J., Hang, P., Sun, J.: Tell-drive: enhancing autonomous driving with teacher LLM-guided deep reinforcement learning. arXiv preprint arXiv:2502.01387 (2025)
14. Yang, N., Chen, S., Zhang, H., Berry, R.: Beyond the edge: an advanced exploration of reinforcement learning for mobile edge computing, its applications, and future research trajectories. IEEE Commun. Surv. Tutor. **27**(1), 546–594 (2025)
15. Yu, L., Zheng, J., Wu, Y., Zhou, F., Yan, F.: A DQN-based joint spectrum and computing resource allocation algorithm for MEC networks. In: Proceedings of the IEEE GLOBECOM, pp. 5135–5140 (2022)
16. Zhang, L., Song, Q., Wu, M., Qi, W., Guo, L.: Joint terminal pairing and multidimensional resource allocation for cooperative computation in a WP-MEC system. IEEE Trans. Green Commun. Netw. **7**(3), 1447–1456 (2023)
17. Zhao, J., Li, Q., Gong, Y., Zhang, K.: Computation offloading and resource allocation for cloud assisted mobile edge computing in vehicular networks. IEEE Trans. Veh. Technol. **68**(8), 7944–7956 (2019)

ASALP: An Automatic Scaling Architecture for Edge Node Resources Based on Load Prediction

Hui Liu[1,2,3], Hui Xiang[1], Yong Wu[1], Zeguang Liu[1], and Junzhao Du[1,3(✉)]

[1] School of Computer Science and Technology, Xidian University, Xi'an, China
`{liuhui,dujz}@xidian.edu.cn`
[2] State Key Laboratory of Satellite Navigation System and Equipment Technology, Shijiazhuang, China
[3] Engineering Research Center of Blockchain Technology Application and Evaluation, Ministry of Education, Beijing, China

Abstract. Edge computing provides inherent advantages of low latency and user proximity; however, it encounters significant challenges in achieving resource elasticity and balancing dynamic traffic loads. The default scaling mechanism in Kubernetes, the Horizontal Pod Autoscaler (HPA), adopts a reactive strategy that restricts its capacity to address real-time demands and exhibits limited effectiveness in edge environments. To overcome these limitations, we introduce ASALP (Automatic Scaling Architecture for Edge Node Resources based on Load Prediction), which augments the Kubernetes–KubeEdge framework with an enhanced RWKV-EFE load prediction model and incorporates Nginx, Consul, and Prometheus to enable dynamic load balancing. Evaluated on the MQPS dataset, RWKV-EFE achieves substantially lower mean squared error (MSE) and mean absolute error (MAE), reducing them by 28.71% and 12.58% compared with FEDformer, and by 77.24% and 53.88% compared with Autoformer. Furthermore, in comparison with HPA, THPA, reactive ASALP, and ASALP-FEDformer, ASALP improves the request success rate by 57.17%, 21.33%, 14.62%, and 7.59%, respectively, while also alleviating the adverse effects of unstable communication links. These experimental results confirm the effectiveness of ASALP in enabling efficient resource scaling and load balancing for real-world edge computing deployments.

Keywords: Kubernetes · KubeEdge · Edge Autonomy · Horizontal Auto Scaler · Time Series Prediction

1 Introduction

Edge computing enables massive data processing with low latency by moving computation closer to data sources. In such environments, elastic scaling and load balancing are key to system stability. Kubernetes [7] supports dynamic resource allocation, yet its default Horizontal Pod Autoscaler (HPA) [1,12] relies on a

© IFIP International Federation for Information Processing 2026
Published by Springer Nature Switzerland AG 2026
X. Wang et al. (Eds.): NPC 2025, LNCS 16306, pp. 386–398, 2026.
https://doi.org/10.1007/978-3-032-10466-3_32

threshold-based reactive strategy, expanding only after metrics exceed preset limits. This delay often degrades service stability [18].

Proactive scaling [1] alleviates this issue by forecasting workloads and adjusting replicas in advance. Traditional methods have used ARIMA [2] and RNNs [6] for resource scheduling. Building on this, we adopt an enhanced RWKV model [10] to predict node-level HTTP request loads, enabling timely and resource-efficient scaling.

In edge scenarios, traffic balancing faces additional challenges. HPA improves scalability by adjusting Pod replicas, but: (1) edge nodes have limited resources; (2) KubeEdge deployments rely on EdgeMesh, where uneven distribution, unstable links, and frequent failures hinder real-time monitoring; (3) in isolated networks, EdgeMesh cannot forward traffic across nodes. As shown in Fig. 1, when load rises on one node, HPA expands replicas uniformly. With unstable or absent inter-node links, this leads to overloaded replicas and service termination.

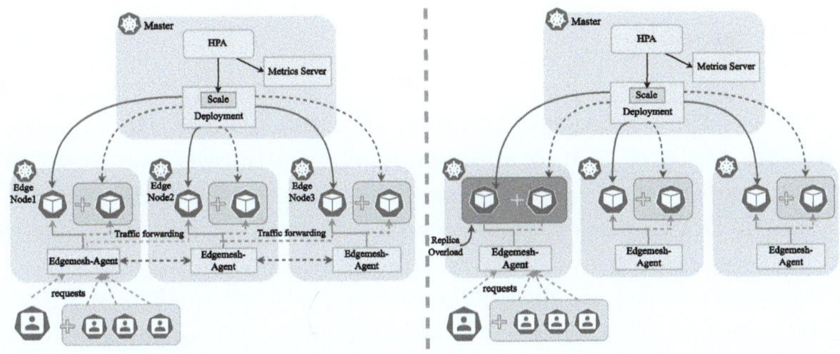

Fig. 1. HPA scaling process in edge computing environment.

To address these issues, we propose ASALP (Load Predict-Based Edge Resource AutoScaler), a proactive scaling framework. Our contributions are as follows.

- RWKV-EFE Prediction Model: An improved RWKV architecture using RWKV as feature extractor and MLP as predictor. It forecasts node-level HTTP request loads, enabling proactive scale-out to improve success rates and smooth scale-in to enhance resource utilization.
- Modified Cloud–Edge Architecture: An ASALP-enhanced Kubernetes–KubeEdge framework. Replica control uses StatefulSet with Prometheus federation for monitoring and RWKV-EFE for prediction. On the edge, Nginx + Consul + Prometheus replace EdgeMesh, enabling local traffic handling and avoiding delays from unstable inter-node links.

2 Related Work

Kubernetes, released by Google in 2014, is now the dominant container orchestration platform [7]. Resource scaling and scheduling remain active research areas, as automation is vital for handling dynamic traffic.

Traffic-aware management has been explored in VioLinn [13], NetMARKS [15], and ElasticFog [9], but these lack automated scaling and full traffic awareness. The default horizontal scaling of Kubernetes is threshold-based and reactive, while AI-based methods such as KHPA [4] and HPA+ [14] enable proactive forecasting. Yet, high inter-node latency still degrades edge performance. THPA [11] reacts to node traffic but lacks predictive capability.

To address these gaps, we propose ASALP, a proactive scaling framework on Kubernetes–KubeEdge, enabling autonomous edge operation and timely scaling to maintain service quality.

3 Load Prediction Model Construction

3.1 RWKV Model

The Receptance Weighted Key Value (RWKV) model [10] combines the efficiency of RNNs with the expressive power of Transformers. Its TimeMix attention mechanism captures temporal dependencies with lower computational cost, enabling fast training and inference on long sequences [8]. RWKV-TS [3] further enhances performance on time-series tasks such as classification, anomaly detection, and forecasting by incorporating multi-head self-attention.

RWKV consists of two modules: *the channel mixing block*, which models feature interactions, and *the time mixing block*, which captures temporal dynamics. This hierarchical design improves representation across both feature and temporal dimensions.

3.2 Model Building Process

We adopt RWKV as the backbone and propose an enhanced RWKV-EFE model. Given a multi-dimensional time series $x \in R^{L \times M}$, where L is sequence length and M the feature dimension, $x_i \in R^L$ represents the i-th variable instance. The model uses RWKV as a feature extractor and an MLP as the prediction layer (Fig. 2).

Feature Extractor. The extractor stacks N RWKV blocks, each with residual-connected time and channel mixing modules.

– Time Mixing Block: This block integrates temporal features by projecting inputs into query–key–value representations and aggregating historical context with an exponential weighting that emphasizes recent tokens. A sigmoid gate then filters redundant information before projection to the output space, enabling efficient temporal modeling with controlled memory retention [17].
– Channel Mixing Block: Captures inter-feature dependencies via linear projection and interpolation of current and previous representations (Fig. 2).

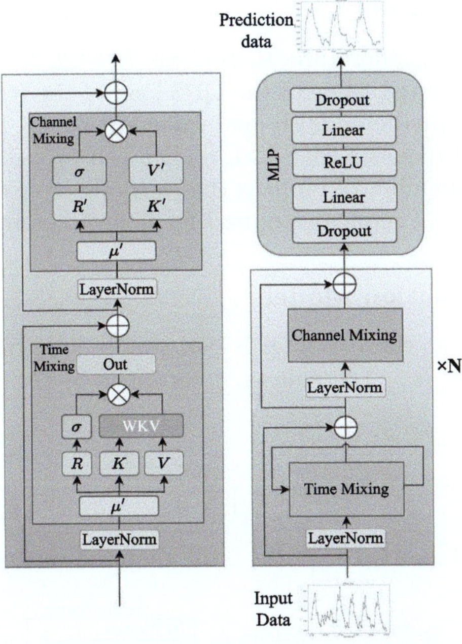

Fig. 2. Improved RWKV model.

Prediction Layer. The prediction layer (MLP) applies two dropout layers, a linear-ReLU-linear sequence, and outputs 60-step load forecasts from 120-step histories:

$$load_{pre} = Linear(ReLU(Linear(o'_t))) \tag{1}$$

where o'_t is the extracted feature vector and $load_{pre}$ is the final prediction.

4   Resource Expansion and Contraction Model Design

According to the load prediction model proposed in Sect. 3.2, it can provide future load conditions. In this section, mathematical models will be constructed for nodes and task copies respectively to calculate the number of application copies that need to be increased or decreased on the node at a given time.

4.1   Node Model

Let K' represent the set of all computing nodes in the cluster, $K' = \{k_{cm}, k_{e1}, k_{e2}, ..., k_{eN}\}$. Among them, k_{cm} represents the cloud center Master node, the edge node set is represented as $K = \{k_{e1}, k_{e2}, ..., k_{eN}\}$, the total number of edge nodes is N, and k_{ei} represents the ith edge node ($i \in [1, N]$).

4.2   Task Replica Model

For each edge node k_{ei}, there are R_i replicas ($i = 1, 2, ..., N$) running on the node. The actual measured value of the QPS load of the ith edge node at time t is $qps_t^{actual,i}$, and the predicted QPS load value at time $t+1$ is $qps_{t+1}^{predicted,i}$. The maximum number of requests that each replica can process per second is set to θ_{qps}. The maximum number of replicas that a single node can run is R_{max}, and the minimum number of replicas required for node i at time t is $R_{min}^i(t)$.

4.3   Replica Calculation Model

At time t, each node k_{ei} receives a QPS load $qps_t^{actual,i}$. To process requests, the node must run at least $R_{min}^i(t)$ replicas, determined by the maximum per-replica threshold θ_{qps}:

$$R_{min}^i(t) = \left\lceil \frac{qps_t^{actual,i}}{\theta_{qps}} \right\rceil \tag{2}$$

Given a predicted load $qps_{t+1}^{predicted,i}$, the required replicas at $t + 1$ are:

$$R_{min}^{predicted,i}(t+1) = \left\lceil \frac{qps_{t+1}^{predicted,i}}{\theta_{qps}} \right\rceil \tag{3}$$

To balance current and predicted demands, we introduce a trade-off factor α. The replica adjustment $\Delta R_i(t)$ is then:

$$\Delta R_i(t) = \left\lceil \alpha \cdot R_{min}^{predicted,i}(t+1) + (1-\alpha) \cdot R_{min}^i(t) \right\rceil - R_{min}^i(t) \tag{4}$$

4.4   Constraints

Replica allocation must satisfy the following:
   Per-node limit:

$$R_i \in [1, R_{max}] \tag{5}$$

   Cluster-wide limit:

$$\sum_{i=1}^{N} R_i \in [N, N \times R_{max}] \tag{6}$$

5   Resource Dynamic Expansion and Contraction Strategy Algorithm Design and Implementation Process

5.1   Algorithm Design

Building on the prediction and scaling models in Sects. 3.2 and 4, we design a dynamic replica adjustment algorithm (Algorithm 1). Initially, the algorithm sets the trade-off factor α and ensures each node hosts at least one replica. At each time step, it collects the current replica count and actual load $qps_t^{actual,i}$, computes the minimum replicas required, then predicts the next-step load $qps_{t+1}^{predicted,i}$. Using Eq. (4), it determines the replica adjustment $\Delta R_i(t)$ and updates the replica count accordingly.

Algorithm 1. Calculation of the number of replicas to be expanded or reduced

---

Input: The number of replicas R_i on the ith node, the number of nodes N, and the trade-off factor α

Output: Change the number of replicas of node i by ΔR_i

1: Initialize the trade-off factor α
2: Initialize each node to deploy a replica
3: **while** True **do**
4:     **for** i in range(N) **do**
5:         **if** $t_k \in k_{ei}$ **then**
6:             $currentPods \leftarrow$ Get the number of replicas on node k_{ei}
7:             $qps_t^{actual,i} \leftarrow$ Get the qps measurement value of the current node based on currentPods
8:             $R_{min}^i(t) \leftarrow$ According to the Eq. (2), calculate the minimum number of copies required at the current moment
9:             $qps_{t+1}^{predicted,i} \leftarrow$ Get the load forecast value at time $t+1$
10:           $R_{min}^{predicted,i}(t+1) \leftarrow$ According to Eq. (3), calculate the minimum number of replicas required at time $t+1$
11:           $\Delta R_i(t) \leftarrow$ Substitute $R_{min}^i(t)$, $R_{min}^{predicted,i}(t+1)$ and the trade-off factor α into the Eq. (4)
12:             **if** $\Delta R_i(t) > 0$ **then**
13:                ASALP expands the capacity of node k_{ei} by $\Delta R_i(t)$ replicas
14:             **else**
15:                ASALP node k_{ei} shrinks by $|\Delta R_i(t)|$ replicas
16:             **end if**
17:         **end if**
18:     **end for**
19: **end while**

5.2 Implementation Process of Dynamic Scaling Strategy for Edge Environment Resources

To implement this paper's edge node resource scaling strategy based on load prediction, the ASALP system architecture is designed (Fig. 3). This three-layer architecture (cloud, edge, end devices) deploys Kubernetes in the cloud. KubeEdge extends Kubernetes with cloud-edge communication and edge resource management, deploying CloudCore in the cloud and EdgeCore at the edge. Edge devices access node replica services and generate request loads. Edge node replica scaling requires implementing the scaling mechanism, load balancing, and dynamic replica resource monitoring.

ASALP runs on the cloud node and comprises five modules: replica control, event monitoring, RWKV prediction, resource monitoring, and replica registration. The event monitoring module tracks StatefulSet replica changes via the

Kubernetes API List/Watch mechanism. The resource monitoring module collects Prometheus metrics and passes historical data to the prediction module, which forecasts future node loads. The replica control module updates StatefulSets based on these predictions, while the replica registration module updates replica metadata in Nginx and Prometheus through Consul. This architecture allows ASALP to coordinate replica scaling and traffic routing across cloud–edge environments.

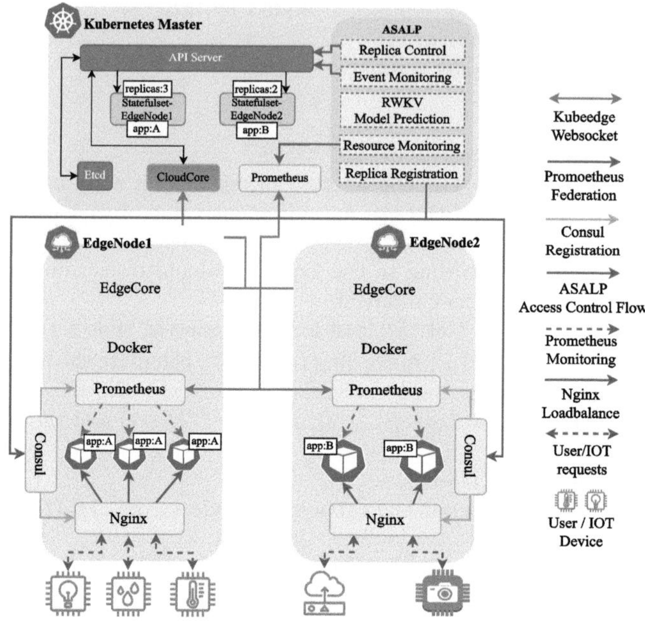

Fig. 3. Architecture of the ASALP system.

6   Experimental Analysis

6.1   Experimental Environment

To verify the effectiveness of ASALP, the experiment in this section deployed a cloud-edge collaborative environment of Kubernetes+Kubeedge in a real machine environment consisting of 5 computing nodes. The computing nodes are divided into 1 cloud computing node and 4 edge computing nodes. ASALP runs on the cloud computing node and controls the changes of application copies on each edge node. The detailed configuration of the node is the same as Sect. 4.6.1. Another computing device is used to run the vegeta stress testing tool and send RPS loads to the four edge nodes respectively.

6.2   Dataset

The experiments use the MQPS dataset [5] provided by Hua et al. This dataset contains minute-by-minute RPC request volume (QPS, or queries per second) data collected from 40 microservices of a leading global e-commerce company during June 2022. The dataset provides raw data for ten large applications (app0-app9). This experiment uses apps 1–4 as the experimental data for four edge nodes, as shown in Fig. 4.

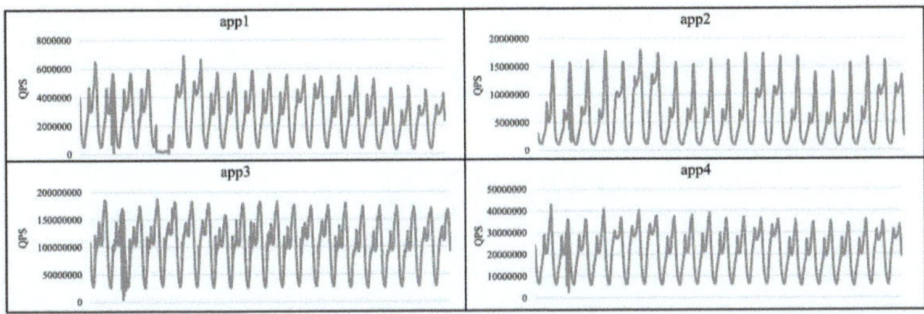

Fig. 4. MQPS raw data payload.

This experiment implemented a simple Go-based web application to log incoming HTTP requests and used vegeta for load testing. As shown in Fig. 5, the success rate decreases when throughput exceeds 1000 requests/second; therefore, the scaling threshold is set to 850 requests/second. The experiment set the maximum number of replicas per node to 6. During the experiment, the data for app1-app4 was scaled within the range [0, 5000]. The scaled data did not affect the periodicity of the original data.

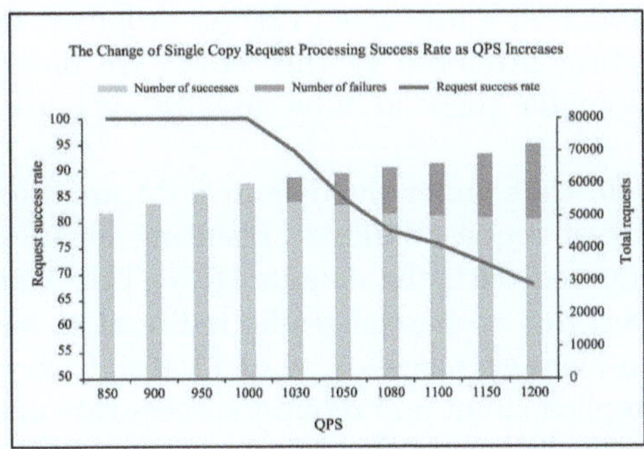

Fig. 5. The relationship between the success rate of a single replica responding to a request and the load received by the replica.

6.3 Experimental Design

Experimental Design of Model Prediction Performance. The RWKV-EFE model was trained on the MQPS dataset, split into training, validation, and test sets (6:2:2). The task was to predict the next 60 min of data using the previous 120 min. Training used a learning rate of 0.001 and batch size of 16, with the best parameters chosen via validation. Prediction accuracy was evaluated using mean square error (MSE, Eq. (7)) and mean absolute error (MAE, Eq. (8)).

$$MSE = \frac{1}{n} \sum_{i=1}^{n} (y_i - \hat{y_i})^2 \tag{7}$$

$$MAE = \frac{1}{n} \sum_{i=1}^{n} |y_i - \hat{y_i}| \tag{8}$$

ASALP Resource Scaling Experiment Design. To evaluate ASALP and the proposed RWKV predictor, we compared request success rates under reactive and proactive scaling. The procedure was: (1) Node load traces were replayed using vegeta to generate QPS on four nodes, each lasting 4 h; (2) ASALP collected actual loads via Prometheus, calculated required replicas, and triggered scaling; (3) After load generation, vegeta recorded success rates, which were compared with replica variations under different schemes.

6.4 Analysis of Experimental Results

ASALP Architecture Effectiveness Verification Experiment. In this experiment, we compare reactive scaling approaches under different system architectures, including the native Kubernetes Horizontal Pod Autoscaler (HPA), the traffic-aware horizontal Pod autoscaler (THPA) proposed by Le et al. [11], and the ASALP architecture proposed in this work. We observe the variation in request success rates under these architectures to evaluate the effectiveness of ASALP.

The results indicate that under the default HPA architecture, unstable links cause a large number of request failures, resulting in an average success rate of only 56.71%. Compared with the default HPA, THPA achieves a significant improvement; however, due to partial traffic redirection, some requests remain unserved, yielding an average success rate of 73.46% (due to space limitations, the trend charts for replica count and request success rate under HPA and THPA are not shown). Figure 6 illustrates the changing trends in the number of replicas per node and request success rate for responsive scaling (ASALP-$\alpha = 0$) under the proposed ASALP architecture. As the load increases, the number of replicas per node increases, and the request success rate fluctuates accordingly.

Thanks to edge-level autonomy, most traffic is successfully processed, resulting in an average success rate of 77.76%, which exceeds that of both the default HPA and THPA. However, as a reactive mechanism, scaling operations are only triggered when the load exceeds predefined thresholds. During this delay, excessive requests cannot be processed in time, reducing the success rate.

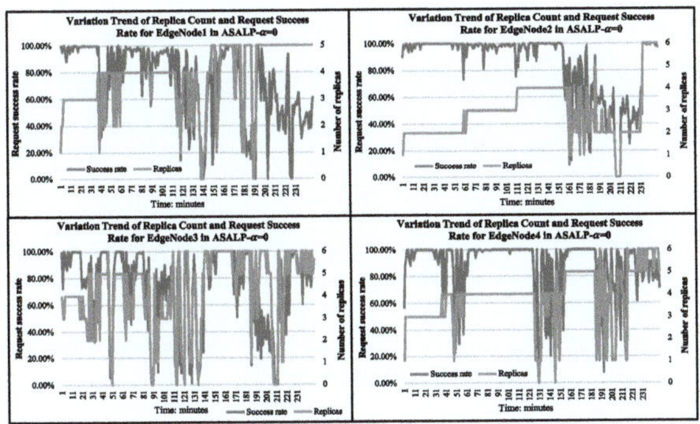

Fig. 6. Trend chart of the number of replicas on each node and the success rate of response requests when using ASALP-$\alpha = 0$.

Prediction Model Validity Verification Experiment

Analysis of Model Performance. Under identical experimental conditions, the RWKV model is compared with FEDformer [19] and Autoformer [16] in terms of load forecasting errors. FEDformer combines Fourier analysis with a Transformer in the frequency domain to capture global time-series patterns and enhance long-term prediction. Autoformer uses progressive decomposition to separate seasonal and trend components, replacing self-attention with an autocorrelation mechanism to exploit sequence periodicity. Forecasting performance is measured via MAE and MSE, with results shown in Table 1.

Table 1. Prediction performance of the model on the MQPS dataset

Dataset	Metrics	RWKV-EFE	FEDformer	Autoformer
MQPS	MSE	**0.0442**	0.0620	0.1942
	MAE	**0.1598**	0.1828	0.3465

As shown in Table 1, RWKV-EFE reduces MSE by 28.71% and 77.24%, and MAE by 12.58% and 53.88% compared with FEDformer and Autoformer, respectively, demonstrating the excellent performance of RWKV-EFE.

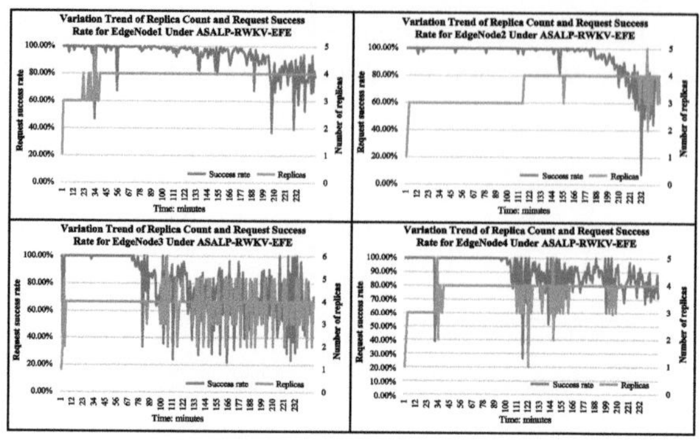

Fig. 7. Trend chart of the number of replicas on each node and the success rate of response requests when using ASALP-RWKV-EFE.

Prediction Model Performance in ASALP Architecture. In this experiment, we evaluate ASALP using both FEDformer and the fine-tuned RWKV-EFE. FEDformer raises the average success rate to 82.84% and smooths replica and success rate variations, enhancing stability.

With RWKV-EFE, which considers both predicted and actual workloads (Eq. (3)), we test different trade-off factors α. Results show the best performance at $\alpha = 0.7$, improving success rates by 11.93% and 9.85% over $\alpha = 0.5$ and $\alpha = 0.9$; thus, $\alpha = 0.7$ is adopted.

As shown in Fig. 7, compared with ASALP-$\alpha = 0$ (Fig. 6), integrating RWKV-EFE with real-time QPS data reduces replica fluctuations and increases the average success rate to 89.13%, with smoother scaling, especially during initial expansion.

Results Analysis. Figure 8 illustrates the impact of different approaches on request success rate. The first three bars represent reactive scaling under different architectures, while the last three bars compare reactive and proactive methods within ASALP, as well as the performance of different prediction models. Overall, compared with HPA, THPA, reactive ASALP, and ASALP-FEDformer, ASALP-RWKV-EFE achieves improvements in request success rate of 57.17%, 21.33%, 14.62%, and 7.59%, respectively, demonstrating the superior performance of both the ASALP framework and the RWKV-EFE model.

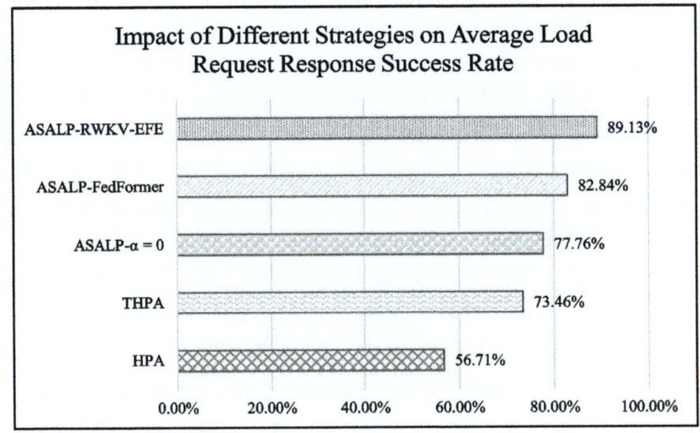

Fig. 8. Impact of different strategies on average load request response success rate.

7   Conclusion

To address limitations of Kubernetes HPA in edge computing, this paper proposes ASALP, a load-prediction-based resource scaling strategy for edge nodes. ASALP enables independent replica scaling at edge nodes, mitigating delays caused by unstable inter-node communication. The improved RWKV-EFE model predicts node load to enhance proactive scaling reliability. Experiments confirm that ASALP effectively performs resource scaling, reduces replica fluctuations, and improves overall request success rates in edge computing environments.

Acknowledgments. This work is partially supported by a grant from the National Natural Science Foundation of China (No. 62032017, No. 62272368), the Shaanxi Innovation Capability Support Program (No. 2023-CX-TD-08), the Key Talent Project of Xidian University (No. QTZX24004), the Shaanxi Qinchuangyuan "scientists + engineers" team (No. 2023KXJ-040).

Disclosure of Interests. The authors have no competing interests to declare that are relevant to the content of this article.

References

1. Al-Dhuraibi, Y., Paraiso, F., Djarallah, N., Merle, P.: Elasticity in cloud computing: state of the art and research challenges. IEEE Trans. Serv. Comput. **11**(2), 430–447 (2017)
2. Calheiros, R.N., Masoumi, E., Ranjan, R., Buyya, R.: Workload prediction using ARIMA model and its impact on cloud applications' QoS. IEEE Trans. Cloud Comput. **3**(4), 449–458 (2014)
3. Hou, H., Yu, F.R.: RWKV-TS: beyond traditional recurrent neural network for time series tasks. arXiv preprint arXiv:2401.09093 (2024)
4. Hu, T., Wang, Y.: A kubernetes autoscaler based on pod replicas prediction. In: 2021 Asia-Pacific Conference on Communications Technology and Computer Science (ACCTCS), pp. 238–241. IEEE (2021)

5. Hua, Q., Yang, D., Qian, S., Hu, H., Cao, J., Xue, G.: Kae-informer: a knowledge auto-embedding informer for forecasting long-term workloads of microservices. In: Proceedings of the ACM Web Conference 2023, pp. 1551–1561 (2023)
6. Imdoukh, M., Ahmad, I., Alfailakawi, M.G.: Machine learning-based auto-scaling for containerized applications. Neural Comput. Appl. **32**(13), 9745–9760 (2020)
7. Kubernetes: What is kubernetes? (2021). https://kubernetes.io/docs/concepts/overview/what-is-kubernetes/. Accessed 29 Nov 2021
8. Liu, X., Su, Y., Nier, W., Ji, Y., Qing Dao Er Ji, R., Lu, M.: An approach to mongolian neural machine translation based on rwkv language model and contrastive learning. In: Luo, B., Cheng, L., Wu, ZG., Li, H., Li, C. (eds.) ICONIP 2023. CCIS, vol. 1962, pp. 327–340. Springer, Singapore (2023). https://doi.org/10.1007/978-981-99-8132-8_25
9. Nguyen, N.D., Phan, L.A., Park, D.H., Kim, S., Kim, T.: ElasticFog: elastic resource provisioning in container-based fog computing. IEEE Access **8**, 183879–183890 (2020)
10. Peng, B., et al.: RWKV: reinventing RNNs for the transformer era. arXiv preprint arXiv:2305.13048 (2023)
11. Phan, L.A., Kim, T., et al.: Traffic-aware horizontal pod autoscaler in kubernetes-based edge computing infrastructure. IEEE Access **10**, 18966–18977 (2022)
12. Swarm, D.: (2023). https://kubeedge.io/. Accessed 20 Feb 2023
13. Toczé, K., Fahs, A.J., Pierre, G., Nadjm-Tehrani, S.: VioLinn: proximity-aware edge placement with dynamic and elastic resource provisioning. ACM Trans. Internet of Things **4**(1), 1–31 (2023)
14. Toka, L., Dobreff, G., Fodor, B., Sonkoly, B.: Machine learning-based scaling management for kubernetes edge clusters. IEEE Trans. Netw. Serv. Manage. **18**(1), 958–972 (2021)
15. Wojciechowski, Ł., et al.: Netmarks: network metrics-aware kubernetes scheduler powered by service mesh. In: IEEE INFOCOM 2021-IEEE Conference on Computer Communications, pp. 1–9. IEEE (2021)
16. Wu, H., Xu, J., Wang, J., Long, M.: AutoFormer: decomposition transformers with auto-correlation for long-term series forecasting. Adv. Neural. Inf. Process. Syst. **34**, 22419–22430 (2021)
17. Yang, S., Ma, H., Yu, C., Wang, A., Li, E.P.: SDiT: spiking diffusion model with transformer. arXiv preprint arXiv:2402.11588 (2024)
18. Zhigang, H.: Container cloud elastic scaling strategy based on Kubernetes(in Chinese). Master's thesis, Chongqing University of Posts and Telecommunications (2021)
19. Zhou, T., Ma, Z., Wen, Q., Wang, X., Sun, L., Jin, R.: FedFormer: frequency enhanced decomposed transformer for long-term series forecasting. In: International Conference on Machine Learning, pp. 27268–27286. PMLR (2022)

CRANE: Two-Stage Coordinated Resource Allocation of Network and Compute for Deterministic Workloads

Yaqi Yan[1], Wenlong Zhang[1], Mingui Zhang[1], Yajun Li[1], Wenrui Liu[1], Wenxuan Zhao[2], Yuming Xing[2], and Tian Pan[2(✉)]

[1] China Tower Corporation Limited, Beijing, China
`{yanyq,zhangwl8,zhangmg3,liyaj12,liuwr}@chinatowercom.cn`
[2] State Key Laboratory of Networking and Switching Technology, Beijing University of Posts and Telecommunications, Beijing, China
`{zwx,xym,pan}@bupt.edu.cn`

Abstract. Telecom operators historically built extensive central offices for telephony, which now provide a unique physical substrate for edge computing. The emergence of model training, immersive media, and real-time analytics is transforming these facilities from voice switching hubs into distributed compute sites, demanding deterministic resource scheduling that simultaneously satisfies compute capacity and network SLAs. To this end, we propose *CRANE*, a coordinated scheduling framework that enables this evolution. CRANE integrates real-time compute and network awareness, multi-objective decision-making for selecting optimal compute nodes, and SRv6 traffic engineering for network SLA enforcement. Experiments demonstrate that CRANE achieves high SLA compliance, lowers end-to-end latency, and improves overall resource utilization, enabling the transformation of legacy telecom infrastructure into a distributed platform that supports deterministic workloads.

Keywords: coordinated compute and network scheduling · deterministic workloads · edge computing

1 Introduction

With the growth of Internet services, telecom operators' legacy central offices have gradually evolved into edge cloud data centers, tightly integrating compute, storage, and networking infrastructure [6,11]. Since a large fraction of data is generated and consumed close to end users, operators face the critical challenge of leveraging these resources to provide low-latency, high-bandwidth services at the network edge. Meanwhile, the rise of AI models, including distributed LLM training [9] and edge-deployed LLM inference [1], increasingly relies on the simultaneous provisioning of deterministic compute and network resources. This creates a pressing need for coordinated scheduling of compute and network resources to consistently deliver predictable performance to end users.

© IFIP International Federation for Information Processing 2026
Published by Springer Nature Switzerland AG 2026
X. Wang et al. (Eds.): NPC 2025, LNCS 16306, pp. 399–411, 2026.
https://doi.org/10.1007/978-3-032-10466-3_33

Traditional network scheduling relies on best-effort IP, which ensures reachability but provides no guarantees on service quality or the availability of destination compute resources such as CPUs, GPUs, or other hardware accelerators. QoS mechanisms like IntServ and DiffServ protect network metrics (e.g., latency, loss, jitter) via priority queues or shaping, yet remain oblivious to compute resources. Deterministic networking (e.g., TSN [2]) reduces latency variations with time-aware shaping but requires specialized hardware and still ignores compute availability. Content-oriented approaches such as CDN and NDN [10] route traffic based on content reachability rather than compute sufficiency. Compute-aware networking [3,4] steers traffic according to advertised compute states, but distributed schemes converge slowly and incur high overhead under rapidly changing workloads. These limitations reveal a gap: existing networks cannot jointly guarantee network performance and compute availability, motivating scheduling mechanisms that coordinate both.

Although jointly scheduling compute and network resources is increasingly necessary for modern workloads, multi-objective scheduling is inherently complex: network states fluctuate in real time, while compute availability changes even faster as tasks are created and completed. Efficiently tracking these dynamic states and allocating compute-network resources thus poses a significant challenge. To address this, we propose CRANE, a two-stage framework for joint compute and network scheduling. CRANE operates through a centralized deterministic service controller and data-plane compute gateways, enabling global visibility and coordinated scheduling of both compute and network resources, thereby ensuring strict SLAs and stable compute service support. It first identifies candidate nodes that satisfy compute availability for each request via centralized compute-aware sensing (e.g., CPU, GPU resource availability), then selects the optimal node based on network measurements via TOPSIS-based multi-objective decision making, after that, it reserves compute resources, and enforces the network resource allocation through network-side reservation combined with SRv6-based traffic steering. By decomposing joint scheduling into stages, CRANE significantly reduces scheduling complexity.

Our major contributions are summarized as follows:

- We propose a novel compute-network scheduling framework that decouples compute node selection from network resource reservation. This design insight simplifies the complexity of joint scheduling while preserving the ability to make coordinated decisions.
- To handle rapidly fluctuating compute availability, we introduce a compute gateway that aggregates the availability information of nodes within each edge cloud and reports it to a centralized controller, avoiding the overhead of network-wide flooding. Based on this abstraction, CRANE first derives a candidate set of nodes that meet compute requirements and then leverages network measurements to select the optimal compute node.
- Once the destination compute node is selected, we first determine the route based on telemetry results between gateways, then reserve network resources along the chosen path using HQoS, and steer traffic via SRv6.

- We deployed a testbed with one controller, five gateways, and a six-node Kubernetes cluster. Experiments show deterministic service processing in 3.8–5.6 s (avg. 4.68 s, 82% < 5 s) and latency consistently below SLA thresholds. The controller detects compute changes in avg. 0.47 s (80% < 1.32 s) and network failures can be recovered in 1.9–5.1 s (avg. 2.96 s, 80% < 3.4 s).

2   Background and Motivation

2.1   Transformation of Telecom Operator Edge Facilities

In the early telecommunication era, telecom operators' central offices primarily provided telephony services, hosting circuit-switched exchanges. With the commercial growth of the Internet in the 1990s, packet-switched equipment such as routers was deployed to support broadband access. By the 2010s, driven by the rise of cloud data centers, operators such as AT&T launched central office transformation programs (e.g., Domain 2.0 [8]), replacing legacy network devices with COTS servers running NFV [7] and orchestrated via SDN [5]. These efforts aimed to reduce CAPEX/OPEX, enable low-latency 5G/IoT edge computing, and reuse existing central office facilities. Modernized sites integrate compute, storage, and high-capacity switching fabrics, effectively operating as micro data centers while aggregating access traffic. Similarly, China Tower manages over 2.1 million sites and 900,000 equipment rooms nationwide, located close to end users and equipped with robust connectivity, power, and facilities, offering a critical resource for future edge computing, as an increasing amount of data is expected to be generated and processed at the edge.

The rapid growth of training and inference workloads has further reshaped compute and network co-design. Large-scale training increasingly spans distributed clusters across backbone networks due to site and power constraints [9], imposing strict requirements on inter-DC bandwidth, latency, and scheduling predictability. At the same time, real-time services drive growing model-push traffic from training clusters to edge inference sites [1], where low latency and stable throughput are critical for service quality. These trends call for deterministic provisioning of compute and network resources to ensure predictable performance for large-scale distributed training and model dissemination, despite resource contention and wide-area traffic variability.

2.2   Typical Telecom Operator Edge Computing Infrastructure

A typical telecom operator's edge computing infrastructure has three layers: a central node layer at headquarters, multiple aggregation nodes at provincial or municipal sites, and massive edge nodes for close-to-user access (see Fig. 1). A deterministic service controller at the central layer manages compute and network resources across the network, performing resource monitoring, compute node selection, and network path computation. Aggregation nodes host data-plane compute gateways that aggregate regional compute and network state, enforce deterministic performance guarantees, and forward traffic at line rate over dedicated operator lines. Edge nodes run heterogeneous compute clusters, including CPUs and GPUs, while gateways at the edge also orchestrate traffic to maintain network-level determinism. The infrastructure can scale horizontally via clustered controllers and vertically through a hierarchical central-regional controller structure, supporting growth in both compute and network capacity.

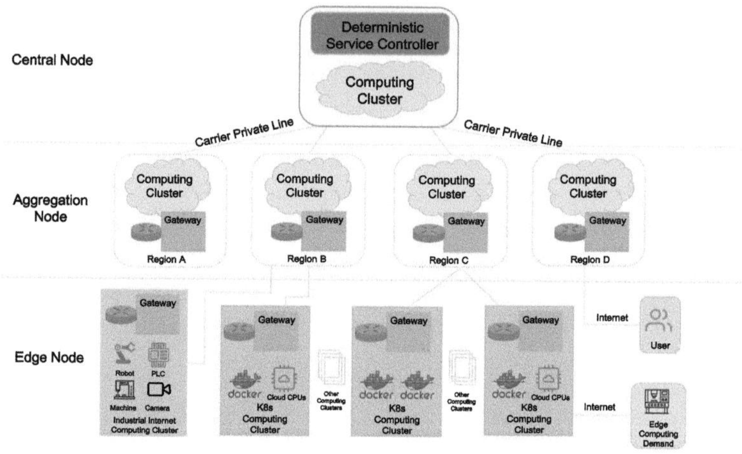

Fig. 1. Typical telecom operator edge computing infrastructure.

3   CRANE Overview

CRANE employs a unified controller platform to achieve global visibility and joint scheduling of network and compute resources, effectively meeting the deterministic requirements of critical services in terms of bandwidth, latency, and compute capacity (see Fig. 2). The architecture consists of two core components: a deterministic service controller and data-plane compute gateways, encompassing key modules for SLA management, resource sensing and scheduling, path computation, and northbound API integration. The controller aggregates information and makes centralized resource-planning decisions, while the gateways handle compute and network sensing as well as traffic steering. Together, these components enable per-application resource reservation, QoS enforcement, intelligent scheduling policies, and end-to-end path planning, providing edge services with predictability, high reliability, and strong availability.

The specific workflow of CRANE can be summarized in the following steps:

- **Parsing user SLA requirements:** The system takes as input user SLA requests, which specify both the required compute resources (e.g., number of GPUs, duration) and the desired network capabilities to serve these resources (e.g., round-trip latency for compute requests, inter-node bandwidth for distributed applications). The controller interprets each SLA requirement and decomposes it into separate compute and network requests.

- **Compute availability awareness:** Upon receiving the compute requirements, the controller selects suitable compute nodes from clusters across the network to host the task. To enable this, each compute node reports its resource availability to the compute gateway responsible for its cluster, which then aggregates and forwards the information to the controller.
- **Compute node selection:** Based on the global utilization of compute nodes, the controller selects the most suitable node for each user request according to the SLA requirements and allocates it for use. This scheduling process typically also considers whether the network quality of service across different compute nodes meets the user's SLA requirements.
- **Network availability awareness:** Once a compute node is selected, deterministic network delivery must be ensured, which relies on real-time network measurements. We obtain the network state on the overlay links between two gateways through proactive probing.
- **Path planning and queue configuration:** After obtaining the network state, we incorporate it into BGP extension attributes to propagate routing updates that include compute information, and configure data-plane queues along the path to ensure deterministic forwarding.
- **Traffic steering and failure recovery:** Once the path is determined, we use SRv6 to steer specific user traffic along the computed path, ensuring that both compute requirements and network quality are met. If the path degrades, traffic is rapidly switched to precomputed alternative paths.

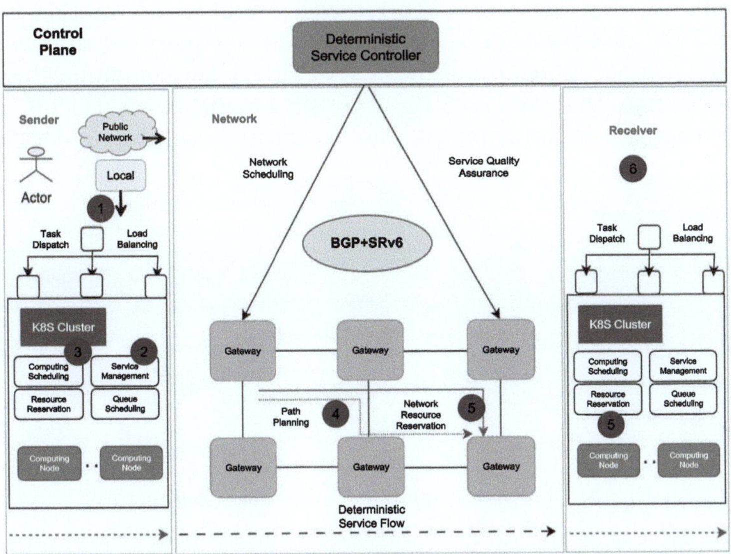

Fig. 2. Workflow of end-to-end deterministic service guarantees.

4   Deterministic Compute Guarantees

Deterministic compute guarantee is the core capability through which CRANE delivers highly reliable and predictable service. Its goal is to provide stable compute resource guarantees for critical tasks in environments with dynamic resource availability and diverse workloads. During task creation, users specify required compute specifications, QoS, and other parameters via the platform API. CRANE treats these as scheduling constraints and, leveraging real-time compute and network state information from the compute-awareness module, performs multi-objective optimization to select compute resources and schedule tasks. The main functions are as follows.

4.1   Compute Availability Awareness

The compute-awareness module is a core component of CRANE, responsible for real-time collection and processing of resource states across compute nodes to support compute node selection. Each compute and gateway node deploys a can-agent to enable distributed compute availability monitoring, aggregating compute resource information to the central controller. Can-agent continuously monitors multi-dimensional compute resources, including CPU, GPU, memory, and disk utilization. As illustrated in Fig. 3, can-agent (compute nodes and gateways) transmits all collected data to the can-server on the controller via gRPC with Protobuf, ensuring efficient and reliable delivery while maintaining data synchronization and real-time updates between compute nodes and the controller. Can-server stores the received compute information in a Redis cache over TCP, meeting high-frequency, low-latency query requirements. When users deploy computation workloads, can-server further communicates with the scheduling module that executes the TOPSIS algorithm via HTTP, providing up-to-date compute resource information to generate scheduling decisions.

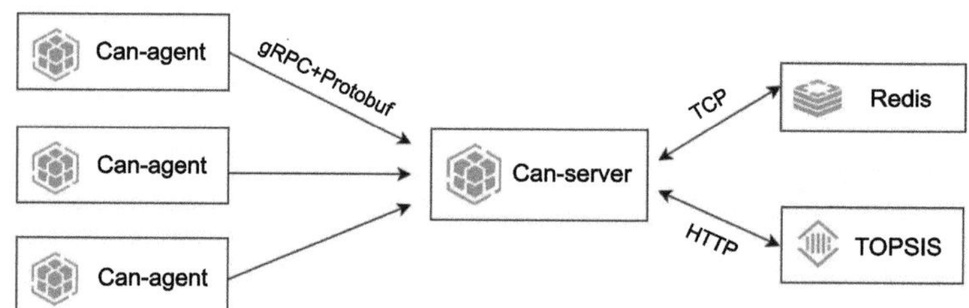

Fig. 3. Compute availability awareness architecture.

4.2   Compute Node Selection

Based on the compute requests parsed from the user's SLA requirement, we identify suitable compute nodes within the K8s cluster in two steps. First, we find a set of candidate nodes that satisfy the multi-dimensional compute requirements; then, incorporating the network SLA constraints, we apply the TOPSIS algorithm to select the final optimal node.

Select a Set of Node Candidates Satisfying Compute Requirements. In this step, a filter matches the user workload's multi-dimensional resource requirements with real-time states of all compute nodes. The filter checks whether each node's available resources satisfy the workload demands to create a Pod, eliminating those that do not, and generates a feasible node list. If the list is empty, the Pod cannot be created at that time and must wait for a later retry.

Select the Final Compute Node Considering Network Measurements. For the feasible node set obtained after filtering, the compute-network collaborative scheduler evaluates nodes independently across multiple resource dimensions based on collected compute information and telemetry of network quality. Using the TOPSIS algorithm (Algorithm 1), combined with weighted user application preferences, it outputs a standardized score from 0 to 1 for each node to select the optimal node to run the Pod, as illustrated in Fig. 4. The algorithm takes multiple sets of scores for feasible nodes as a decision matrix and an n-dimensional weight vector as input, and outputs the optimal node, whose overall performance is close to the ideal solution and far from the negative ideal. Specifically, the algorithm first normalizes the decision matrix so that all metrics share the same scale; then, it evaluates each metric's priority based on SLA preferences and applies weighted adjustment; next, it identifies the best and worst values for each metric across nodes, representing the ideal and negative-ideal solutions; finally, it computes each node's distance to the ideal and negative-ideal solutions and derives a normalized score, with higher values indicating better overall performance. The node with the highest score is selected for scheduling. Once the target node is selected, the Koordinator component binds the Pod to the node after the K8s scheduling process for resource reservation.

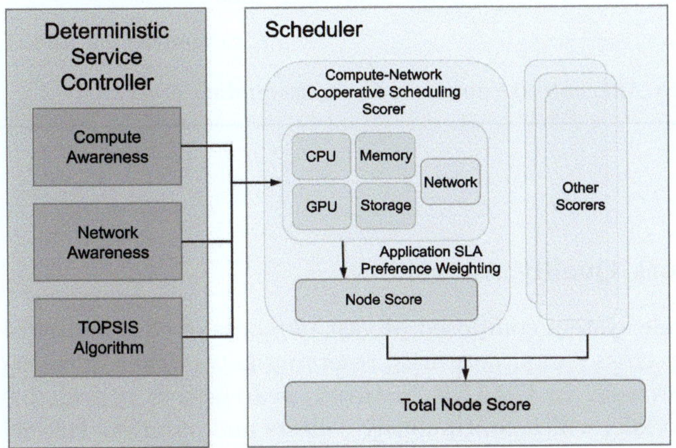

Fig. 4. Compute scheduling workflow.

5   Deterministic Network Guarantees

Deterministic network service is also important for ensuring end-to-end service quality. Its goal is to plan optimal paths to the target nodes determined during scheduling and reserve bandwidth along these paths for workloads, preventing link contention and transient congestion, thereby improving the stability and timeliness of critical traffic.

Algorithm 1: TOPSIS-based Multi-criteria Selection

Input: $D \in \mathbb{R}^{m \times n}$, $W \in \mathbb{R}^n$, $T \in \{\text{benefit}, \text{cost}\}^n$
Input: Where: m is the number of alternatives (decision nodes), and n is the number of criteria (metrics).
Output: Ranking by relative closeness C_i of m alternatives, sorted in descending order.

1 **Function** TOPSIS(D, W, T)**:**
2   **for** $j \leftarrow 1$ **to** n **do**
3          $R[:,j] \leftarrow D[:,j]/\|D[:,j]\|_2$ `// normalize`
4   **for** $j \leftarrow 1$ **to** n **do**
5          $V[:,j] \leftarrow R[:,j] \cdot W[j]$ `// weight`
6   **for** $j \leftarrow 1$ **to** n **do**
7   **if** $T[j] = \textit{benefit}$ **then**
8              $A_j^+ \leftarrow \max_i V[i][j]$, $A_j^- \leftarrow \min_i V[i][j]$ `// ideal/anti-ideal for benefit`
9   **else**
10             $A_j^+ \leftarrow \min_i V[i][j]$, $A_j^- \leftarrow \max_i V[i][j]$ `// ideal/anti-ideal for cost`
11   **for** $i \leftarrow 1$ **to** m **do**
12         $S_i^+ \leftarrow \sqrt{\sum_j (V[i][j] - A_j^+)^2}$, $S_i^- \leftarrow \sqrt{\sum_j (V[i][j] - A_j^-)^2}$
            `// distances to ideal and anti-ideal`
13         $C_i \leftarrow \dfrac{S_i^-}{S_i^+ + S_i^-}$ `// closeness to ideal solution`
14   **return** *Alternatives ranked by C_i in descending order.*

5.1   Network Quality Awareness

In a large-scale system composed of vast numbers of edge compute nodes interconnected by cross-region networks, reserving network resources requires strong network awareness. In CRANE, network awareness is provided by a network telemetry module, which continuously collects and monitors key network performance metrics, including bandwidth utilization, packet loss, end-to-end latency, and jitter, to build a global view of the underlying network state. Network quality data is gathered through distributed probes deployed at each gateway, measuring per-hop link metrics in the vicinity, and periodically reported to the deterministic service controller via gRPC and Protobuf. Monitoring results are also directly available on local gateways, enabling on-site network diagnosis. Advanced telemetry techniques like INT are also expected to be added in the future.

5.2   Path Planning and Queue Configuration

We encode the collected compute information into BGP extension attributes and advertise it via BGP-LS between gateways, enabling distributed computation of the optimal path to the target compute node. Meanwhile, the gateways' data plane is implemented using DPDK and VPP, and network requirements from user SLAs, such as bandwidth and latency, are enforced along the selected path via traffic managers on the intermediate devices using mechanisms like token buckets and hierarchial queues, thereby supporting per-hop deterministic forwarding for high-priority traffic.

5.3   Traffic Steering and Failure Recovery

Based on the selected and configured path, we use SRv6 to steer traffic along it, providing deterministic network service. Specifically, the path computation results are represented as SRv6 TE Policy candidate paths, including attributes such as the SRv6 segment list (SID List) and bandwidth reservation requirements. These policies are pushed by the controller to the compute gateways, guiding traffic to follow the specified paths. However, the established path may occasionally violate SLA requirements. To handle such exceptions, feasible backup paths are computed during routing. When link-level jitter or failures are detected, fast failure recovery mechanisms are triggered to automatically switch traffic to a backup path. Meanwhile, routing converges globally, recomputing paths to ensure globally optimal traffic routing.

6   Evaluation

6.1   CRANE Prototype

To evaluate CRANE, we deploy a testbed consisting of a controller, five next-generation compute gateways, and a Kubernetes cluster with six compute nodes (see Fig. 5). The controller and gateways establish programmable paths via SRv6 + BGP, with the controller responsible for unified management of Kubernetes compute resources and gateways, path computation, configuration deployment, as well as compute and traffic scheduling. Each gateway is built on FRR + VPP and uses DPDK for high-performance packet forwarding. FRR handles routing protocols, shares routing information with VPP, and classifies traffic by IP, protocol, and port to ensure packets enter queues according to predefined weights and priorities, seamlessly integrating with VPP's scheduling. Routing decisions in FRR influence VPP's forwarding table, while VPP's queue state feeds back to FRR for dynamic adjustment, enabling fine-grained traffic control. Gateways also collect real-time compute node status and probe network link quality, reporting it to the controller via BGP extensions with TLV fields for compute type, capacity, and utilization. In the Kubernetes cluster, can-agent probes gather compute metrics and send them to the controller via gRPC + Protobuf, where can-server aggregates the data, stores it in Redis via TCP, executes TOPSIS ranking over HTTP, and interacts with the gateway through BGP announcements.

The controller is equipped with an 8-core CPU and 16 GB RAM, running Ubuntu 20.04.6 LTS with Linux kernel 5.4.0-216-generic. The Kubernetes cluster consists of six nodes, each with an 8-core CPU and 32 GB RAM, running CentOS 7.9.2009 (kernel 3.10.0-957.el7.x86_64), K8s 1.28.2, and containerd 1.6.33. The five compute gateways are identically configured with 4-core CPUs and 8 GB RAM, running Ubuntu 20.04.6 LTS with Linux kernel 5.4.0-216-generic.

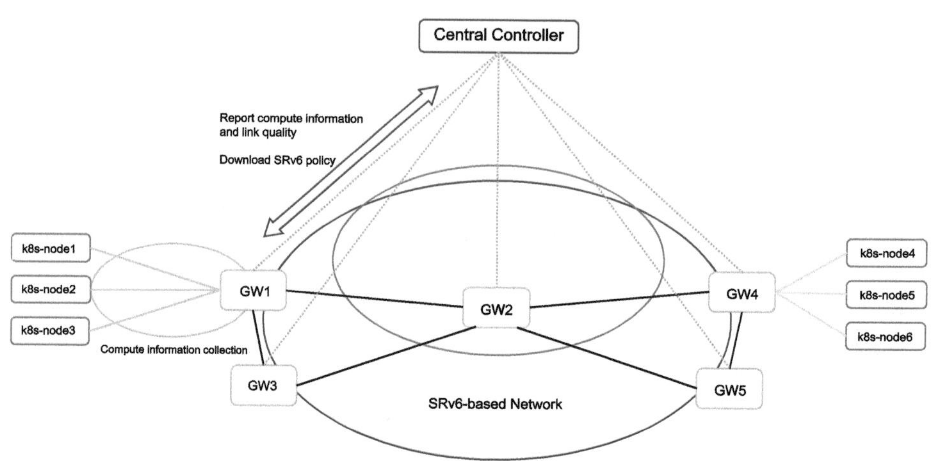

Fig. 5. CRANE prototype.

6.2　Experimental Results

Distribution of Deterministic Service Request Processing Latency. We measured and collected the processing latency of multiple deterministic compute service requests, yielding the distribution shown in Fig. 6. The maximum latency is approximately 5.6 s, the minimum is around 3.8 s, and 82% of requests are processed within 5 s, with an average latency of 4.68 s.

Deviation Between End-to-End Expected and Actual Latencies. To evaluate CRANE's ability to provide network-level deterministic service, we measured end-to-end actual latency over time under different target latency settings.

The comparison of target versus actual latency is shown in Fig. 7, where the measured latencies fully meet the targets. Specifically, under target latencies of 10 ms, 50 ms, and 100 ms, the average measured latencies are 9.53 ms, 48.80 ms, and 98.55 ms, respectively, all below the corresponding targets.

Distribution of Controller Perception Latency During Compute Resource Changes. To evaluate the compute-awareness capability of CRANE's compute and network perception module, we artificially varied the compute state of nodes and measured the time taken by the controller to perceive the updated state. Repeating this process multiple times, we collected the distribution of sensing latency, as shown in Fig. 8. The maximum latency is approximately 1.5 s, the minimum is around 0.6 s, 80% of the measurements fall within 1.32 s, and the overall average sensing latency is 0.47 s.

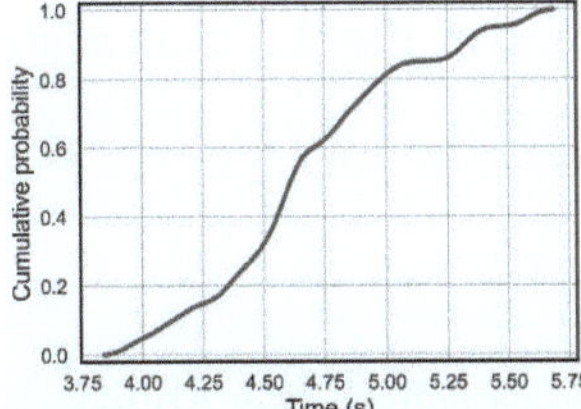

Fig. 6. Distribution of deterministic service request processing latency.

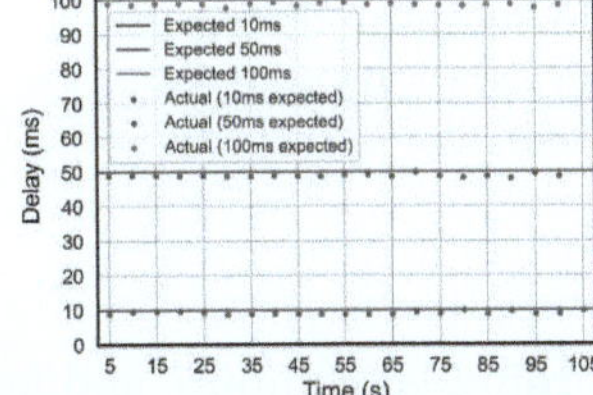

Fig. 7. Deviation between end-to-end expected and actual latencies.

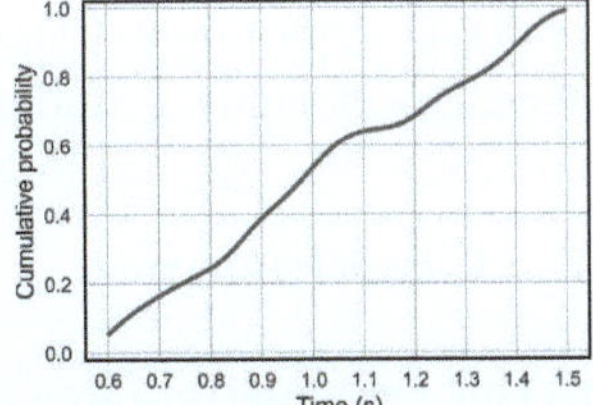

Fig. 8. Distribution of controller perception latency during compute resource changes.

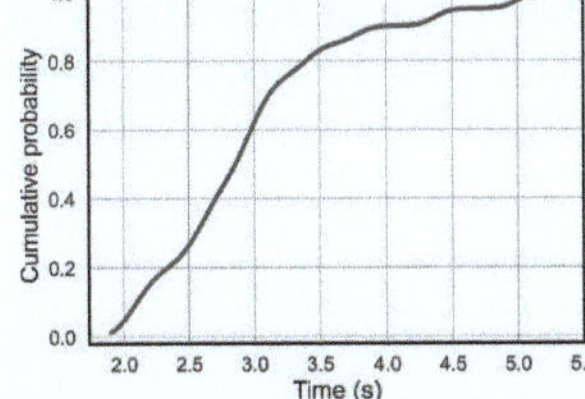

Fig. 9. Distribution of network failure recovery latency.

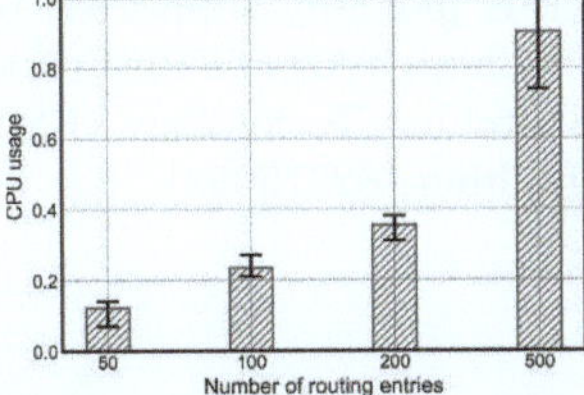

Fig. 10. CPU load of the central controller during route deployment.

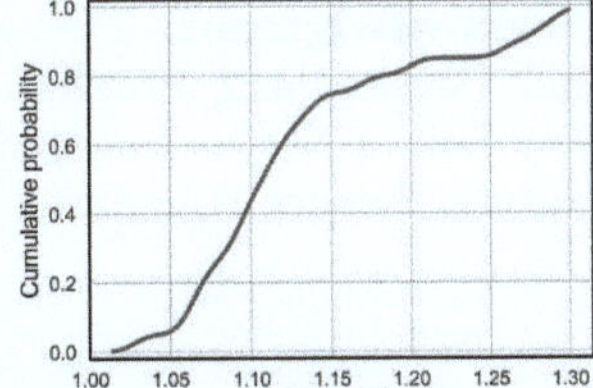

Fig. 11. Performance of the compute gateway under stress testing.

Distribution of Network Failure Recovery Latency. We emulated network link failures to trigger automatic path switching and measured the time from failure occurrence to completion. Repeating the experiments multiple times, we obtained the latency distribution shown in Fig. 9. The minimum recovery latency is approximately 1.9 s, the maximum is 5.1 s, 80% of the cases recover within 3.4 s, and the overall average recovery latency is 2.96 s.

CPU Load of the Central Controller During Route Deployment. To measure CRANE's controller peak instantaneous path computation and deployment capacity, we simultaneously issued a set number of routing entries and recorded the controller CPU load. Repeating the experiment multiple times, we obtained the results shown in Fig. 10. As the number of simultaneously deployed routing entries increases, the average, maximum, and minimum CPU utilization gradually rise. For 50, 100, and 200 entries, the average utilization is 12.1%, 23.4%, and 35.3%, respectively. Simultaneously deploying 500 entries drives the CPU to a maximum of 100% and an average of 92.2%.

Performance of the Compute Gateway Under Stress Testing. CRANE's gateways implement a forwarding engine based on DPDK + VPP. To evaluate their actual performance, we conducted throughput tests using 40-byte UDP packets. Small-packet tests rigorously assess the gateway's stability and efficiency under high-frequency, small-size traffic, reflecting real-world performance. Across multiple experiments, the throughput distribution, shown in Fig. 11, indicating decent performance under stress testing.

7   Conclusion

In this work, we design a coordinated compute and network scheduling approach to fully leverage telecom operators' legacy central offices for edge computing, providing remote users with deterministic access to compute resources. Specifically, we propose a strategy that first selects compute nodes and then enforces network capabilities, decomposing scheduling complexity in stages. This design is suited for emerging deterministic workloads such as model training and inference.

Acknowledgment. This work is partially supported by the National Key Research and Development Program of China (2024YFB2906700), the Key Project of State Key Lab of Networking and Switching Technology (NST20250112), and the National Natural Science Foundation of China (62372053).

References

1. Cai, F., Yuan, D., Yang, Z., Cui, L.: Edge-LLM: a collaborative framework for large language model serving in edge computing. In: 2024 IEEE International Conference on Web Services (ICWS), pp. 799–809. IEEE (2024)
2. Finn, N.: Introduction to time-sensitive networking. IEEE Commun. Stand. Mag. **2**(2), 22–28 (2018)
3. Król, M., Mastorakis, S., Oran, D., Kutscher, D.: Compute first networking: distributed computing meets ICN. In: Proceedings of the 6th ACM Conference on Information-Centric Networking, pp. 67–77 (2019)
4. Liu, B., Mao, J., Xu, L., Hu, R., Chen, X.: CFN-dyncast: load balancing the edges via the network. In: 2021 IEEE Wireless Communications and Networking Conference Workshops (WCNCW), pp. 1–6. IEEE (2021)

5. McKeown, N., et al.: OpenFlow: enabling innovation in campus networks. ACM SIGCOMM Comput. Commun. Rev. **38**(2), 69–74 (2008)
6. Pan, T., et al.: {LuoShen}: a {Hyper-Converged} programmable gateway for {Multi-Tenant}{Multi-Service} edge clouds. In: 21st USENIX Symposium on Networked Systems Design and Implementation (NSDI 24), pp. 877–892 (2024)
7. Sherry, J., Hasan, S., Scott, C., Krishnamurthy, A., Ratnasamy, S., Sekar, V.: Making middleboxes someone else's problem: network processing as a cloud service. ACM SIGCOMM Comput. Commun. Rev. **42**(4), 13–24 (2012)
8. Tse, S., Choudhury, G.: Real-time traffic management in AT&T's SDN-enabled core IP/Optical network. In: Optical Fiber Communication Conference. pp, Tu3H–2. Optica Publishing Group (2018)
9. Zeng, F., Gan, W., Wang, Y., Yu, P.S.: Distributed training of large language models. In: 2023 IEEE 29th International Conference on Parallel and Distributed Systems (ICPADS), pp. 840–847. IEEE (2023)
10. Zhang, L., et al.: Named data networking. ACM SIGCOMM Comput. Commun. Rev. **44**(3), 66–73 (2014)
11. Zou, Y., et al.: HyperSFC: state-intensive service function chaining on hyper-converged edge infrastructure. In: 2024 IFIP Networking Conference (IFIP Networking), pp. 1–9. IEEE (2024)

Federated Learning via TEE-Based Dual-Branch Architecture and Interaction-Aware Pruning

Wenxuan Zhou[1], Zhenyu Zhu[1], Mingyang Xie[2], and Zhihao Qu[1(✉)]

[1] Key Laboratory of Water Big Data Technology of Ministry of Water Resources,
Hohai University, Nanjing, China
`{zhouwx,zhuzhenyu,quzhihao}@hhu.edu.cn`
[2] Queen's University, Kingston, Canada
`21mx4@queensu.ca`

Abstract. Federated learning enhances data privacy but faces security risks like model theft, while traditional cryptographic methods often compromise efficiency or accuracy. Although Trusted Execution Environments (TEEs) offer hardware-level security, their limited memory and lack of hardware acceleration hinder deep neural network deployment. Current partitioning solutions alleviate memory constraints but introduce new vulnerabilities, highlighting the need for lightweight TEE optimization. We propose FedDualPrune, a lightweight federated learning framework that leverages a TEE-based dual-branch architecture. During local training, a frozen pre-trained model in the rich execution environment (REE) serves as a general feature extractor, while a unidirectional feature fusion mechanism securely integrates its outputs with a trainable counterpart inside the TEE. Furthermore, a channel-interaction-aware joint pruning strategy structurally compresses the TEE-hosted branch to satisfy secure memory constraints while preserving model performance. Extensive experiments show that under high pruning rates and Non-IID conditions, the accuracy loss is controlled within 5%, achieving synergistic optimization of privacy protection and model performance.

Keywords: Model and Data Privacy · Federated Learning · Trusted Excution Environment

1 Introduction

Federated learning (FL) [5,11] enables collaborative machine learning across multiple nodes while preserving the privacy of each node's data. Traditionally, gradient sharing was considered secure, allowing participants to contribute to model training by aggregating weighted gradients without exposing sensitive data. However, recent studies reveal vulnerabilities in this approach. Zhu *et al.* [28] demonstrated that gradients can leak private training data through deep gradient leakage attacks, enabling malicious servers in FL to reconstruct local

X. Wang et al. (Eds.): NPC 2025, LNCS 16306, pp. 412–423, 2026.
https://doi.org/10.1007/978-3-032-10466-3_34

data and compromise privacy. Furthermore, the widespread deployment of deep neural networks on edge devices introduces risks of model stealing attacks, where adversaries exploit unauthorized memory access to extract model architectures and weights, posing significant threats to model integrity and potentially causing financial losses for model providers.

Trusted Execution Environments (TEEs) [17] offer a robust security framework by creating isolated hardware-based secure zones, safeguarding sensitive code and data while minimizing computational overhead compared to conventional encryption methods. This isolation ensures efficient resource utilization on edge devices with limited computational capacity. TEEs enforce strict hardware resource partitioning, restricting sensitive operations to secure zones to prevent unauthorized data access during processing. However, originally designed for simpler secure operations, TEEs face limitations in supporting complex computational tasks, such as deep neural networks (DNNs). For instance, many edge devices provide limited secure memory, e.g., 16MB in some configurations, insufficient for DNN models like ResNet18, which require over 46.8MB for parameters alone [2]. Consequently, despite TEEs' advantages in privacy protection and reduced computational load, their constrained secure memory capacity poses significant challenges for deploying large-scale, complex models.

Recent research leverages TEEs for DNNs training by isolating sensitive operations in hardware-based secure zones. Approaches include securing output-proximate deep layers, input-proximate shallow layers, or randomly selected intermediate layers within TEEs, as explored in works like [1,12,14,15,18]. Alternatively, some methods focus on protecting critical nonlinear layers in TEEs while applying lightweight obfuscation to linear layers, or employ resource scheduling to optimize full-model protection [3,6,8,20,26]. TBNet [10] introduces a dual-branch architecture, distributing tasks between TEE and REE with progressive pruning to minimize redundancy, though non-secure branches risk data leakage. In contrast, TEESLICE [25] secures only private model slices in TEEs, using dynamic pruning and TEE-GPU collaboration for efficiency, while ensuring data confidentiality with one-time codebooks and the Freivalds algorithm, despite increased overhead from frequent encryption.

To address the above issues, this paper proposes FedDualPrune, which aims to preserve privacy during FL without compromising the model training performance. In the local training phase, the pre-trained model M_R serves as a general feature extractor in the rich execution environment (REE). A unidirectional feature fusion mechanism ensures secure aggregation of M_R features with the secure model M_T in the TEE, while a channel-interaction-aware joint pruning algorithm structurally compresses M_T.

The contributions of this work are summarized as follows:

- We propose a dual-branch TEE-REE architecture, where the REE hosts a frozen pre-trained model M_R for stable feature priors, and the TEE-hosted M_T updates parameters using unidirectional REE feature inflows, preventing gradient leakage and model stealing by eliminating bidirectional gradient flows.

- We introduce a joint pruning strategy with channel interaction awareness, fusing batch normalization scaling factors and Efficient Channel Attention scores to ensure structured sparsity in TEE branches, meeting memory constraints, reducing computational overhead, and enhancing resistance to reverse-engineering attacks.
- Extensive experiments show that, under high pruning rates and non-independent and identically distributed (Non-IID) conditions, accuracy loss is limited to within 5%, effectively balancing privacy protection and model performance.

2   Related Work

The vulnerability of deep neural network (DNN) execution on CPUs to information leakage, including training data and model parameters, has driven research into Trusted Execution Environments (TEEs) for secure DNN inference. However, TEEs' limited computational resources and memory pose significant challenges. Existing approaches can be broadly classified into model partitioning and federated learning strategies.

2.1   Model Partitioning for Security

Model partitioning methods [27] selectively secure specific DNN layers within TEEs based on their susceptibility to information leakage. Since deeper layers are more prone to leaking prediction-related data, Mo *et al.* [14] proposed isolating fully connected layers in TEEs. Shen *et al.* [1] emphasized protecting shallow layers due to their high input reversibility, reducing data reconstruction risks. Truong *et al.* [18] employed randomized protection by securing intermediate layers and perturbing outputs in non-trusted environments, concealing approximately 20% of sensitive weights. However, these methods remain vulnerable in scenarios where plaintext convolutional layers enable adversaries to reconstruct models by retraining non-trusted layers. To enhance security, some studies focus on obfuscating or encrypting offloaded linear layers. Hou *et al.* [3] prioritized top-k weights with added noise for offloading, while Sun *et al.* [20] applied matrix transformations for obfuscation. Zhou *et al.* [26] introduced mask-based obfuscation with reinforcement learning to secure weights, storing only mean values and mask indices in TEEs to reduce overhead. Zhang *et al.* [24] proposed reverse clustering to obfuscate convolutional kernel vectors, enhancing randomization. Alternatively, Liu *et al.* [9] trained a lightweight mirror network in TEEs. Despite these advances, offloaded model components remain susceptible to attacks, and lightweight obfuscation struggles to isolate highly sensitive weights effectively.

2.2   Federated Learning with TEEs

Integrating TEEs into FL [16] frameworks enhances privacy in distributed settings. PPFL [13] employs TEEs for local training and secure aggregation, using layer-by-layer training to address memory constraints. Zhang *et al.* [22] developed a TEE-based FL verification system combining cryptography and smart contracts for robust client oversight. ShuffleFL [23] uses random grouping and gradient segmentation in SGX environments to protect gradients, though frequent exchanges increase communication overhead. While TEE-based FL frameworks provide robust privacy through hardware isolation, challenges persist. Layer-by-layer training introduces complexity, and intricate verification or obfuscation strategies often compromise performance. Balancing security, efficiency, and resource constraints remains a critical research gap, necessitating optimized scheduling and dynamic protection mechanisms.

3 Preliminary

This section outlines the threat models in FL and introduces the role of TEEs in securing computations.

3.1 Threat Model

In FL, clients act as both collaborative participants and potential *honest but curious* attackers. In FL, *honest but curious* means clients or servers follow the prescribed training and communication rules without maliciously tampering with models or data (honest), but may still attempt to infer additional private information from legitimately obtained data (curious). During global model updates, clients may exploit parameter exchanges to reconstruct training data from gradients by gradient inversion engineering, risking privacy breaches, especially for sensitive data like medical or financial records. External attackers could also exploit vulnerabilities in client environments, stealing local models via physical or remote access and enhancing them through transfer learning or adversarial fine-tuning, thus infringing on intellectual property. We assume attackers can access all client software and hardware except the TEE, with communication secured via Software Guard Extensions (SGX) remote attestation and end-to-end encryption. Our proposed algorithm ensures privacy for local client models and training data by protecting sensitive neural network modules within the TEE, requiring no structural changes to the network. It minimizes overhead on resource-constrained edge devices while maintaining high accuracy, balancing security and performance without excessive computational costs.

3.2 Trusted Execution Environment

A TEE is a hardware-isolated runtime environment ensuring data and code confidentiality, integrity, and authenticity [4]. It uses secure extensions to isolate resources, preventing access from the REE. As shown in Fig. 1, the CPU is divided into the REE, running standard OS and applications, and the TEE, a secure enclave for privacy-critical code, inaccessible to external programs except via a predefined interface. However, TEEs are designed for small-scale tasks like

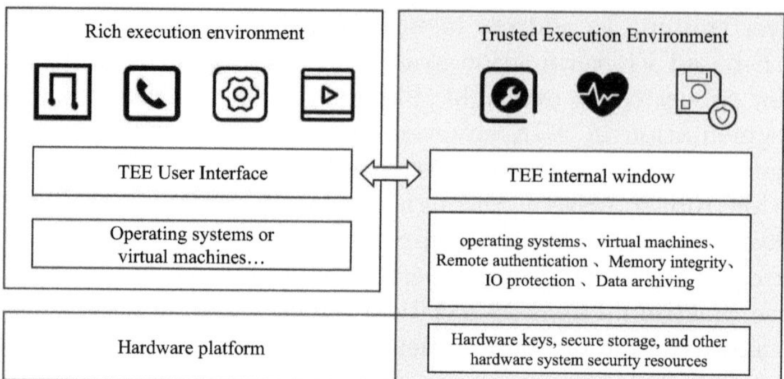

Fig. 1. TEE architecture dividing the hardware into a REE for standard applications and a TEE for secure operations via a controlled interface.

authentication, with limited computational and memory resources (e.g., SGX's 128 MB secure memory, 93 MB usable [7]). This constraint hinders real-time deep learning tasks, as neural networks require substantial memory, and frequent paging incurs significant cryptographic overhead, increasing latency by 2–10 times compared to the REE. Thus, efficiently utilizing TEEs for secure, low-latency model inference and training remains a key challenge. Prior work has explored selective protection of critical model layers to balance security and performance.

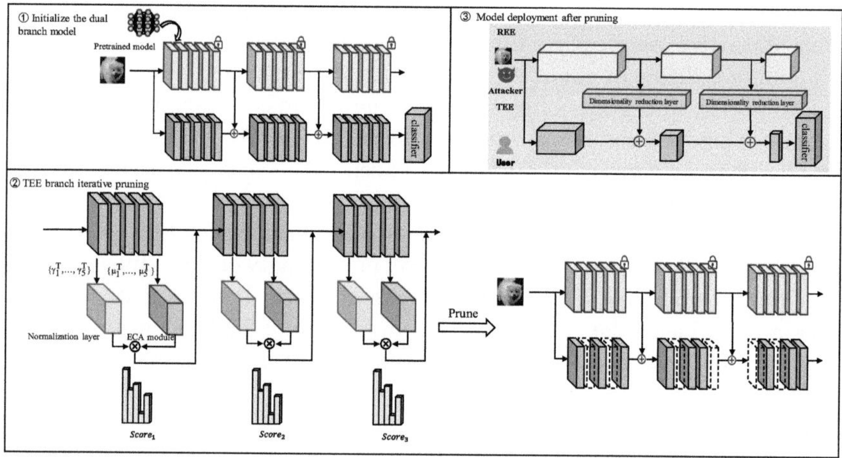

Fig. 2. Architecture of FedDualPrune, illustrating (1) dual-branch model initialization with pre-trained REE and TEE branches, (2) iterative TEE branch pruning using normalization and ECA modules, and (3) model deployment post-pruning with feature alignment.

4   Methods

This section outlines the FedDualPrune for securing federated learning models within TEEs, as illustrated in Fig. 2. Firstly, the original model is transformed into a dual-branch model, initializing a pre-trained REE backbone and a secure TEE branch for personalized training. Secondly, the TEE branch is iteratively pruned using a channel interaction-aware strategy to optimize memory usage and efficiency. Finally, the pruned dual-branch model is deployed with a feature alignment mechanism to ensure integration and enhanced security against reverse engineering.

4.1   Dual-Branch Model Initialization

The model initialization phase deploys a pre-trained network, M_R, in the REE as a backbone, leveraging its public availability and immunity to attacker exploitation. A corresponding secure branch, M_T, with identical architecture, is established in the TEE. Intermediate features from M_R are transmitted unidirectionally to M_T, where they are added to the corresponding layer outputs, minimizing encryption and context-switching overhead while enhancing TEE confidentiality. To address potential exploitation of M_R, its parameters are frozen for general feature extraction, while M_T is trained to capture personalized representations, leveraging pre-trained universal features to accelerate convergence and improve inference performance.

Given TEE memory constraints, the dual-branch design mitigates reverse inference risks by isolating privacy-sensitive parameters. However, redundant parameters in M_T necessitate optimization. This study introduces a pruning approach integrating batch normalization (BN) scaling factors γ_i and the Efficient Channel Attention (ECA) module [21] to assess channel importance, addressing limitations of traditional methods that overlook inter-channel dependencies. The ECA module employs global average pooling and adaptive one-dimensional convolution $k = [|\log_2(C) \cdot \gamma + b|]_{\text{odd}}$ to model channel correlations, with weights computed as $\mu = \sigma(\text{Conv1D}_k(\text{GAP}(X)))$, enhancing pruning precision while preserving model performance.

4.2   Iterative TEE Branch Pruning

FedDualPrune enhances pruning precision by integrating the BN scaling factor γ_i and ECA module weight μ_i to compute a comprehensive channel importance score, $\text{score}_i^T = \gamma_i \odot \mu_i$. This approach captures both individual and inter-channel contributions, reducing performance degradation risks. The score is incorporated into a joint optimization framework via a regularization term in the loss function, $\mathcal{L} = \mathbb{E}_{(x,y)\sim\mathcal{D}}[l(f(x; W_R, W_T), y)] + \lambda \sum_{i=1}^{C} |\text{score}_i|$, where W_R and W_T denote REE and TEE weights, respectively, promoting L_1 norm-based sparsification.

In the pruning process, channels are ranked by score, and a dynamic threshold τ_t guides the binary mask ($M_i = \mathbb{I}(\text{score}_i > \tau_t)$) to retain critical channels based on a predefined pruning rate. As outlined in Algorithm 1, iterative pruning is paired with cosine annealing fine-tuning to mitigate accuracy loss, adjusting τ_t to balance compression and performance. The process terminates if accuracy drops exceed θ_d, reverting to the prior state to ensure efficiency and stability within TEE memory constraints.

Algorithm 1. The details of FedDualPrune algorithm

1: **Input:** TEE and REE models M_T, M_R, accuracy drop budget θ_d, pruning rate p
2: **while** accuracy drop $< \theta_d$ **do**
3:     $C \leftarrow$ total number of channels in M_T
4:     score $\leftarrow$ importance score for each channel in M_T
5:     $T \leftarrow$ sorted(score)$[C \cdot p]$
6:     Initialize pruning mask$[N] \leftarrow 0$
7:     **for** $i = 1$ **to** N **do**
8:         **if** score$[i] > T$ **then**
9:             mask$[i] \leftarrow 1$ ▷ Mark channel for preservation
10:         **end if**
11:     **end for**
12:     Prune channels in M_T using mask (remove where mask$[i] = 0$)
13:     Fine-tune M_T with cosine annealing learning rate
14: **end while**
15: Stop pruning and roll back to previous state
16: **Output:** Pruned TEE Model M_T

4.3 Post-pruning Model Deployment

The pruning strategy targets only the M_T model, preserving the structural integrity of M_R, resulting in post-pruning channel dimension disparities. A learnable feature alignment module, employing a 1×1 convolution with weights $W_{\text{align}} \in \mathbb{R}^{C_{\text{new}} \times C_{\text{old}} \times 1 \times 1}$, aligns M_T feature maps $X_{\text{align}} = X_{\text{pruned}} * W_{\text{align}}$ with those of M_R, mitigating dimension mismatches. This mechanism ensures efficient feature transmission and enhances security, as the structural divergence between pruned M_T and unpruned M_R complicates reverse engineering efforts by attackers.

5 Experiments

5.1 Experimental Setup

Datasets. The efficacy of FedDualPrune is assessed on CIFAR10 and CIFAR100, each containing 50 k 32×32 training images and 10 k test images.

Benchmarks. Validation includes VGG11 [19] and ResNet18 [2], trained on the above datasets without fine-tuning to demonstrate general applicability. Data distribution is modeled using a Dirichlet distribution with parameter α, where increasing α reduces client dataset diversity under Non-IID conditions, intensifying distribution skew.

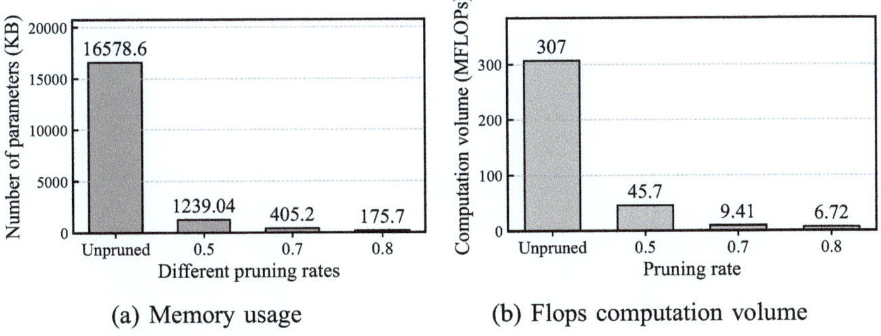

(a) Memory usage   (b) Flops computation volume

Fig. 3. Memory usage and Flops computation volume of VGG11 trained with different pruning rates on the CIFAR10 dataset.

Baseline. TBNet [10] serves as the baseline, splitting the model into identical REE and TEE branches. The REE generates intermediate features, fused in the TEE for inference, optimized with cross-entropy loss and L1 regularization on BN channel weights to enable knowledge transfer and sparsity. Channels are pruned proportionally, fine-tuned to meet an accuracy threshold, and the REE is reverted to diverge structurally from the TEE, preventing inference attacks.

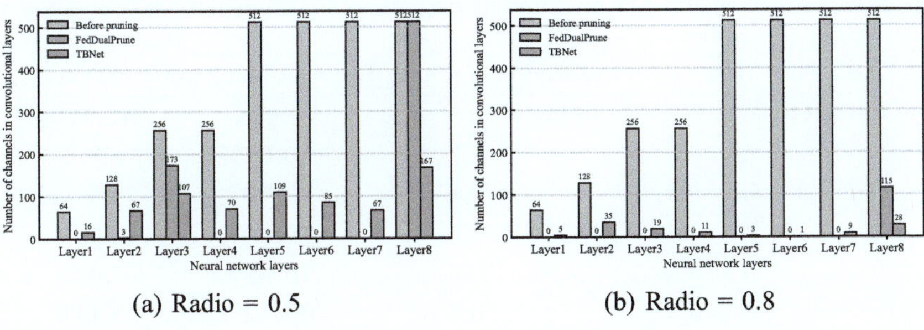

(a) Radio = 0.5   (b) Radio = 0.8

Fig. 4. Channel distribution of different pruning rates M_T models of VGG11 under the CIFAR10 dataset.

5.2   Experimental Results

Figure 3a demonstrates that memory usage of the VGG11 on CIFAR10 decreases with different pruning rate, from 16578.6 KB unpruned to 1239.04 KB, 405.2 KB, and 175.7 KB at rates of 0.5, 0.7, and 0.8, respectively, highlighting effective memory reduction. Figure 3b shows FLOPs dropping from 307 MFLOPs unpruned to 45.7 MFLOPs, 9.41 MFLOPs, and 6.72 MFLOPs at the same pruning rates, underscoring reduced computational complexity suitable for TEE constraints.

Table 1. Training accuracy of VGG with different pruning rates under IID conditions on CIFAR10 and CIFAR100 datasets

Dataset	Original Accuracy	Pruning Rate	Ours	TBNet
CIFAR10	82.49%	0.5	**82.21%**	81.62%
		0.7	**81.03%**	80.31%
		0.8	**81.03%**	80.57%
CIFAR100	53.75%	0.5	**52.32%**	50.73%
		0.7	**52.07%**	46.21%
		0.8	**52.07%**	45.30%

Figure 4 reveals that FedDualPrune retains more deep layer channels (e.g., Layers 7–8) at pruning rates of 0.5 and 0.8, compared to TBNet's uniform pruning across branches, due to prioritizing abstract features over redundant shallow ones. Table 1 confirms FedDualPrune's superiority, with VGG11 Top-1 accuracy on CIFAR-10 declining minimally from 82.49% unpruned to 82.21%, 81.03%, and 81.03% at pruning rates of 0.5, 0.7, and 0.8, outperforming TBNet. Table 2 shows FedDualPrune's robustness under Non-IID conditions (e.g., 70.92% at $\alpha = 0.5$, 0.7 rate, vs. TBNet's 70.65% unpruned), with a 2.94% advantage over TBNet at $\alpha = 0.8$ and 0.8 rate.

Table 2. Accuracy of VGG11 at different degrees of heterogeneity and pruning rates

Dataset	Heterogeneity	Original	Pruning Rate	FedDualPrune	TBNet
CIFAR10	$\alpha = 0.3$	81.81%	0.5	81.05%	**81.97%**
	$\alpha = 0.3$		0.7	**80.07%**	78.57%
	$\alpha = 0.3$		0.8	**79.79%**	79.63%
	$\alpha = 0.5$	70.65%	0.5	**70.40%**	58.78%
	$\alpha = 0.5$		0.7	**70.92%**	57.00%
	$\alpha = 0.5$		0.8	**66.92%**	58.49%
	$\alpha = 0.8$	65.06%	0.5	**64.71%**	60.13%
	$\alpha = 0.8$		0.7	**63.01%**	56.14%
	$\alpha = 0.8$		0.8	**59.83%**	56.89%
CIFAR100	$\alpha = 0.3$	49.65%	0.5	**49.85%**	41.31%
	$\alpha = 0.3$		0.7	**46.54%**	41.10%
	$\alpha = 0.3$		0.8	**46.54%**	41.87%
	$\alpha = 0.5$	43.88%	0.5	**41.77%**	32.47%
	$\alpha = 0.5$		0.7	**42.24%**	32.39%
	$\alpha = 0.5$		0.8	**42.24%**	31.00%
	$\alpha = 0.8$	41.48%	0.5	**40.14%**	30.73%
	$\alpha = 0.8$		0.7	**40.23%**	30.31%
	$\alpha = 0.8$		0.8	**40.23%**	29.35%

Table 3 indicate that ResNet18 on CIFAR10 exhibits comparable accuracy trends to TBNet (e.g., 70.72% vs. 70.74% at $\alpha = 0.3$, 0.8 pruning rate), though lower due to frozen backbone constraints. Accuracy declines with heterogeneity and pruning (e.g., 48.24% vs. 48.12% at $\alpha = 0.8$, 0.8 pruning rate), reflecting Non-IID challenges and reduced redundancy. Both VGG11 and ResNet18 maintain stable performance at high pruning rates by preserving deep layer features, validating the method's generalizability in balancing compression and accuracy. Higher pruning rates (0.7–0.8) significantly reduce memory and FLOPs, but incur slight accuracy drops, while moderate pruning (0.5) achieves a better balance between efficiency and performance.

Table 3. Accuracy of ResNet18 at different degrees of heterogeneity and pruning rates

Dataset	Heterogeneity	Original	Pruning Rate	FedDualPrune	TBNet
CIFAR10	$\alpha = 0.3$	73.01%	0.5	71.82%	**72.06%**
	$\alpha = 0.3$		0.7	71.42%	**71.87%**
	$\alpha = 0.3$		0.8	70.72%	**70.74%**
	$\alpha = 0.5$	55.65%	0.3	**55.53%**	55.34%
	$\alpha = 0.5$		0.5	**53.25%**	53.10%
	$\alpha = 0.5$		0.7	51.45%	**51.50%**
	$\alpha = 0.8$	52.35%	0.5	**51.83%**	51.63%
	$\alpha = 0.8$		0.7	49.57%	**50.14%**
	$\alpha = 0.8$		0.8	**48.24%**	48.12%
CIFAR100	$\alpha = 0.3$	41.51%	0.3	**40.72%**	40.37%
	$\alpha = 0.3$		0.5	39.67%	**39.73%**
	$\alpha = 0.3$		0.7	**37.76%**	37.26%

6   Conclusion

This paper presents the FedDualPrune, a TEE-based protection method to enhance privacy and security in FL. The approach leverages a secure dual-branch architecture, featuring a frozen pre-trained REE model and a unidirectional feature fusion mechanism to safeguard against data leakage and model theft. Additionally, a channel interaction-aware pruning strategy, integrating BN layer dynamics and attention mechanisms, optimizes TEE memory usage. FedDualPrune is particularly applicable to privacy-sensitive federated learning on resource-constrained edge devices, where TEEs provide hardware-level isolation. Extensive experiments validate that FedDualPrune achieves a robust balance between security and performance, establishing a novel foundation for secure edge intelligence systems and TEE applications in distributed learning.

Acknowledgements. This work was supported by the National Natural Science Foundation of China (No.62180005).

References

1. Elgamal, T., Nahrstedt, K.: Serdab: an IoT framework for partitioning neural networks computation across multiple enclaves. In: Proceedings of the IEEE/ACM International Symposium on Cluster, Cloud and Grid Computing (CCGRID) (2020)
2. He, K., Zhang, X., Ren, S., Sun, J.: Deep residual learning for image recognition. In: Proceedings of the IEEE/CVF Computer Vision and Pattern Recognition Conference (CVPR) (2016)
3. Hou, J., Liu, H., Liu, Y., Wang, Y., Wan, P.J., Li, X.Y.: Model protection: real-time privacy-preserving inference service for model privacy at the edge. IEEE Trans. Dependable Secure Comput. **19**(6), 4270–4284 (2021)
4. Jauernig, P., Sadeghi, A.R., Stapf, E.: Trusted execution environments: properties, applications, and challenges. IEEE Secur. Priv. **18**(2), 56–60 (2020)
5. Jia, N., Qu, Z., Ye, B., Wang, Y., Hu, S., Guo, S.: A comprehensive survey on communication-efficient federated learning in mobile edge environments. IEEE Commun. Surv. Tutorials (2025)
6. Kim, K., et al.: VESSELS: efficient and scalable deep learning prediction on trusted processors. In: Proceedings of the ACM Symposium on Cloud Computing (SoCC) (2020)
7. Lee, T., et al.: Occlumency: privacy-preserving remote deep-learning inference using SGX. In: Proceedings of the ACM International Conference on Mobile Computing and Networking (MobiCom) (2019)
8. Li, Y., et al.: Efficient and secure deep learning inference in trusted processor enabled edge clouds. IEEE Trans. Parallel Distrib. Syst. **33**(12), 4311–4325 (2022)
9. Liu, Z., Luo, Y., Duan, S., Zhou, T., Xu, X.: MirrorNet: a tee-friendly framework for secure on-device DNN inference. In: Proceedings of the International Conference on Computer-Aided Design (ICCAD) (2023)
10. Liu, Z., Zhou, T., Luo, Y., Xu, X.: TBNet: a neural architectural defense framework facilitating DNN model protection in trusted execution environments. In: Proceedings of the ACM/IEEE Design Automation Conference (DAC) (2024)
11. McMahan, B., Moore, E., Ramage, D., Hampson, S., y Arcas, B.A.: Communication-efficient learning of deep networks from decentralized data. In: Proceedings of the International Conference on Artificial Intelligence and Statistics (AISTATS) (2017)
12. Mireshghallah, F., Taram, M., Ramrakhyani, P., Jalali, A., Tullsen, D., Esmaeilzadeh, H.: Shredder: learning noise distributions to protect inference privacy. In: Proceedings of the International Conference on Architectural Support for Programming Languages and Operating Systems (ASPLOS) (2020)
13. Mo, F., Haddadi, H., Katevas, K., Marin, E., Perino, D., Kourtellis, N.: PPFL: privacy-preserving federated learning with trusted execution environments. In: Proceedings of the ACM International Conference on Mobile Systems, Applications, and Services (MobiSys) (2021)
14. Mo, F., et al.: DarkneTZ: towards model privacy at the edge using trusted execution environments. In: Proceedings of the ACM International Conference on Mobile Systems, Applications, and Services (MobiSys) (2020)

15. Narra, K.G., Lin, Z., Wang, Y., Balasubramanian, K., Annavaram, M.: Origami inference: private inference using hardware enclaves. In: Proceedings of the IEEE International Conference on Cloud Computing (CLOUD) (2021)
16. Qu, Z., Jia, N., Ye, B., Hu, S., Guo, S.: FedQClip: accelerating federated learning via quantized clipped SGD. IEEE Trans. Comput. **74**(2), 717–730 (2024)
17. Sabt, M., Achemlal, M., Bouabdallah, A.: Trusted execution environment: what it is, and what it is not. In: 2015 IEEE Trustcom/BigDataSE/ISPA (2015)
18. Shen, T., et al.: SOTER: guarding black-box inference for general neural networks at the edge. In: Proceedings of the USENIX Annual Technical Conference (USENIX ATC) (2022)
19. Simonyan, K., Zisserman, A.: Very deep convolutional networks for large-scale image recognition. In: Proceedings of the International Conference on Learning Representations (ICLR) (2015)
20. Sun, Z., Sun, R., Liu, C., Chowdhury, A.R., Lu, L., Jha, S.: ShadowNet: a secure and efficient on-device model inference system for convolutional neural networks. In: Proceedings of the IEEE Symposium on Security and Privacy (S&P) (2023)
21. Wang, Q., Wu, B., Zhu, P., Li, P., Zuo, W., Hu, Q.: ECA-Net: efficient channel attention for deep convolutional neural networks. In: Proceedings of the IEEE/CVF Computer Vision and Pattern Recognition Conference (CVPR) (2020)
22. Zhang, W., Muhr, T.: TEE-based selective testing of local workers in federated learning systems. In: Proceedings of the International Conference on Privacy, Security and Trust (PST) (2021)
23. Zhang, Y., Wang, Z., Cao, J., Hou, R., Meng, D.: ShuffleFL: gradient-preserving federated learning using trusted execution environment. In: Proceedings of the ACM International Conference on Computing Frontiers (CF) (2021)
24. Zhang, Z., et al.: GroupCover: a secure, efficient and scalable inference framework for on-device model protection based on tees. In: Proceedings of the International Conference on Machine Learning (ICML) (2024)
25. Zhang, Z., et al.: No privacy left outside: On the (In-) security of tee-shielded DNN partition for on-device ML. In: Proceedings of the IEEE Symposium on Security and Privacy (S&P) (2024)
26. Zhou, T., Luo, Y., Ren, S., Xu, X.: NNSplitter: an active defense solution for DNN model via automated weight obfuscation. In: Proceedings of the International Conference on Machine Learning (ICML) (2023)
27. Zhou, W., Qu, Z., Lyu, S.H., Cai, M., Ye, B.: Mask-encoded sparsification: overcoming biased gradients for communication-efficient split learning. In: Proceedings of the European Conference on Artificial Intelligence (ECAI) (2024)
28. Zhu, L., Liu, Z., Han, S.: Deep leakage from gradients. In: Proceedings of the Conference on Neural Information Processing Systems (NeurIPS) (2019)

Breaking Language Barriers: A Domain-Specific Translation Workflow for Industry

Nguyen Duc Loc$^{(\boxtimes)}$, Ngo Minh Quan, Ha Trung Chien, and Vu Van Minh

Hanoi University of Science and Technology,Hanoi, Vietnam
`ngducloc1112002@gmail.com`

Abstract. Machine translation (MT) systems have achieved remarkable progress in recent years, especially with the emergence of deep learning and Transformer-based architectures. Nonetheless, the application of a general neural machine translation approach to domain-specific scenarios remains limited. Firstly, the presence of domain-specific terminology may reduce the accuracy of general translation models, which typically lack fine-tuning for the target domain. Secondly, fine-tuning such models necessitates domain-specific training data, which is frequently limited in availability. Finally, general translation tools like Google Translate do not provide a unified pipeline for seamless integration into industry workflows. This paper introduces a unified translation workflow developed to address these limitations, offering adaptability and extensibility for domain-specific applications in industry. Our proposed approach delivers a complete pipeline for end-users, incorporating customizable domain-specific terminology and supporting translation across multiple document formats, thereby enhancing both usability and output quality in real-world applications. We evaluate the proposed approach in an industrial setting, focusing on the textile and garment domain. Using a dataset of textile and apparel domain-specific documents in various formats, along with human evaluation, the experiments demonstrate the effectiveness and practicality of our approach for domain-adaptive machine translation.

Keywords: neural machine translation · domain-specific translation · industrial translation pipeline

1   Introduction

The Fourth Industrial Revolution is reshaping global industries, driving unprecedented levels of cultural and economic exchange [1]. As e-commerce and multinational business operations expand at a rapid pace, the demand for precise, context-aware, and domain-specific multilingual translation has become critical [3,6,15]. Advances in deep learning and generative AI have significantly enhanced the capabilities of automatic machine translation, yielding substantial

© IFIP International Federation for Information Processing 2026
Published by Springer Nature Switzerland AG 2026
X. Wang et al. (Eds.): NPC 2025, LNCS 16306, pp. 424–435, 2026.
https://doi.org/10.1007/978-3-032-10466-3_35

improvements in translation quality [7,13]. Modern systems leverage sophisticated neural architectures–particularly Transformer-based [16] and large pre-trained models [10,18], to produce translations with high quality, fluency, and naturalness. Moreover, they offer robust multilingual support [2], real-time translation capabilities [17], and straightforward integration into everyday workflows. Among existing systems, Google Translate stands out as one of the most widely used automatic translation tools worldwide, supporting over 100 languages [17]. Since its shift to neural machine translation, it has been continually enhanced through architectures such as Transformer [16] and T5 [12], improving its contextual comprehension and its ability to produce more natural-sounding text [11].

Google Translate has made significant advancements in popularizing machine translation globally, particularly thanks to its multilingual support and near-instant translation speed. However, when applied to specialized domains such as healthcare, law, finance, or engineering, the system still exhibits notable limitations. One of the key weaknesses lies in its limited accuracy in handling domain-specific terminology, as the training data primarily consists of general-purpose texts and lacks sufficient coverage of fields with complex vocabularies [5]. This can easily lead to mistranslations, affecting the accuracy and reliability of professional documents. In addition, Google Translate currently does not offer flexible support for diverse file formats such as PDFX documents, PPTX presentations, or XLSX files containing complex tables or embedded data–formats that are essential in global business and commercial environments. This lack of support poses challenges for enterprises when translating contracts, reports, technical documents, or international marketing content. Particularly in industrial settings, where accuracy in specialized terminology can determine operational success, the limitations of generic translation tools underscore the urgent need for tailored solutions [14]. To address these issues, in this paper, we introduce a system that integrates the Google Translate API to support machine translation in global business and commercial settings. The system is evaluated on a dataset of textile and garment domain documents in various formats such as PDF, PPTX, and XLSX. The results demonstrate that the system preserves semantic accuracy, terminology consistency, and formatting integrity. Accordingly, our paper contributes two main points:

- We introduce a system that integrates the Google Translation API, allowing users to fine-tune translation results for specific domains and supporting multiple file formats, and enabling low-cost text translation while preserving formatting comparable to file-based translation.[1]
- We evaluate the system's effectiveness in real-world applications in comparison with the original Google Translate service.

2 Related Work

Over the past decade, the emergence of the Transformer architecture has enabled significant breakthroughs in machine translation (MT) [17]. Alongside these

---

[1] https://lingoai.leira.com.vn/login.

advances, the urgent demand for real-world applications has driven research on improving MT quality and adaptability across domains, especially in the global economy [4]. A critical challenge in specialized domains lies in handling domain-specific terminology and ensuring consistency. Popular MT tools such as Google Translate provide fast multilingual translation, but their reliance on generic training data limits accuracy in fields like healthcare, law, and finance, leading to mistranslations and undermining reliability [8].

To address this, studies have proposed domain-specific datasets and fine-tuning [4], though these approaches are resource-intensive and inflexible. Glossary integration has emerged as a more practical solution, ensuring consistent use of predefined terminology during translation [4]. While this reduces terminology errors in neural MT, platforms like Google Translate still offer only basic support without deep control over preprocessing or postprocessing. In contrast, custom MT systems combine glossaries with structured intermediate formats to preserve layout, distinguish translatable from non-translatable content, and allow user-driven refinement.

Beyond translation quality, enterprises increasingly require multi-format document handling (DOCX, PDF, Excel, PPTX). Although Google Translate supports some file types, its formatting preservation remains limited. Specialized MT pipelines overcome this by converting documents into intermediate formats, translating, and then restoring them, thereby maintaining structure and supporting enterprise workflows.

Building on these insights, we propose a system that combines NMT with customizable processing via an intermediate XML format. Our approach inherits Google Translate's strengths in multilingual and real-time translation [17], while extending them through an open glossary and XML-based pre/postprocessing. This design addresses current MT limitations, enhancing speed, accuracy, and multi-format support to better serve enterprise needs in the global economic environment.

3   System Architecture

This study introduces an automated translation architecture for domain-specific documents that preserves both semantic accuracy and original layout. The approach bridges the gap between research-grade neural machine translation (NMT) and enterprise needs, which demand document fidelity, consistent terminology, and multi-format compatibility. The pipeline comprises three stages: (1) XML-based preprocessing, (2) structural text consolidation, and (3) glossary-enforced neural translation, followed by a post-translation step that reconstructs the document layout (Fig. 1).

3.1   Preprocessing and Format Normalization

The translation workflow begins with a format normalization step designed to create a uniform, XML-accessible representation of the input data. The sys-

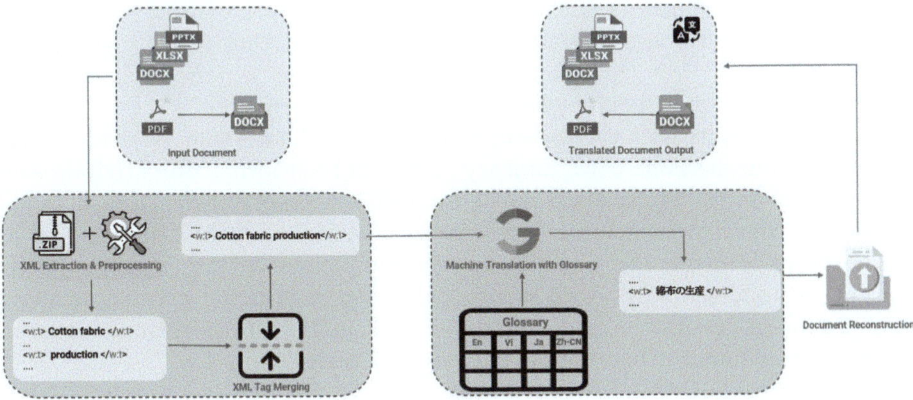

Fig. 1. Proposed architecture for domain-specific document translation, integrating XML preprocessing, structural reconstruction, and glossary-aware neural machine translation.

tem accepts multiple widely used file types–DOCX, XLSX, PPTX, and PDF– ensuring applicability across common corporate and technical communication channels. For PDF inputs, which lack a native XML structure, the pipeline employs high-fidelity conversion (default: DOCX) to enable consistent downstream processing. This conversion is optimized to preserve essential layout elements such as tables, embedded images, and vector diagrams, as these often carry semantic importance in technical contexts.

3.2 ZIP Extraction and XML Preparation

Once converted into the normalized format, each document is restructured as a ZIP-compatible archive in accordance with the Office Open XML specification. This archive contains a hierarchical set of XML files and related resources, typically organized in directories such as `word/`, `ppt/`, or `xl/`. These XML files encapsulate both the main textual content and associated formatting and layout metadata.

In this stage, the system extracts the ZIP contents to allow direct access to the internal XML files. Content-bearing XML nodes are selectively identified and queued for text extraction, while non-textual elements (e.g., images, charts, embedded objects) are deferred for later reintegration. This targeted approach ensures that subsequent processing operates exclusively on translatable linguistic units while preserving the integrity of non-textual components for the final document reconstruction.

3.3 XML Parsing and Text Consolidation

The core of our preprocessing strategy lies in the parsing and consolidation of XML-based text representations. In DOCX files, for example, paragraphs are defined by `<w:p>` elements and textual segments by `<w:r>` (runs), with visible text stored in `<w:t>` tags. A naïve approach to translation would process each run independently, but this often leads to fragmented sentences because runs may be split by minor, non-semantic formatting variations.

Our system mitigates this by applying a consolidation rule: adjacent `<w:r>` elements within the same paragraph are merged if their formatting attributes are equivalent or differ only in ways that do not alter semantic meaning (e.g., small changes in character spacing or hidden style markers). This approach serves two purposes. First, it increases the length and contextual completeness of the translation unit, enabling the NMT model to leverage larger context windows for more fluent output. Second, it reduces the number of discontinuities where glossary terms might otherwise be split and mistranslated.

Illustrative Example. Figure 2 illustrates the merging of three separate `<w:r>` elements containing the phrase "Cotton fabric production," which are divided by formatting metadata. Our method identifies shared formatting attributes and unifies these elements before translation, enabling the model to process the entire phrase as a single semantic unit and thereby reducing the risk of inconsistent translation.

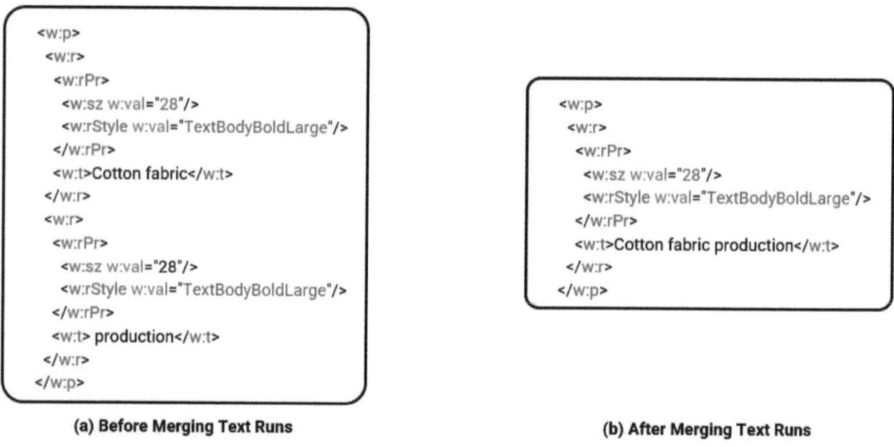

Fig. 2. Example transformation: merging multiple `<w:r>` elements with identical formatting into a unified run, enabling context-aware translation without structural loss.

3.4   Glossary-Aware Neural Machine Translation

Following consolidation, the extracted text is submitted to the Google Cloud Translation API with integrated glossary enforcement. This feature allows the system to override default translation outputs for predefined source-target term pairs. The glossary, stored in CSV format, is curated to cover specialized terminology, acronyms, and domain-specific expressions. During translation, it is applied uniformly across the document, ensuring that the same source term always maps to the same target term, regardless of surrounding context.

The source language may be explicitly specified by the user or automatically detected using Google's language detection service. This flexibility supports multilingual input without requiring manual reconfiguration for each language, an important capability for large-scale, cross-border document processing workflows.

3.5 Post-translation Reconstruction

Once translation is complete, the system reinserts the translated text into the original XML structure. Care is taken to restore all preserved layout features, including styles, tables, figures, and embedded objects. The reconstructed XML files are then packaged back into their original format (e.g., DOCX, PPTX, XLSX) or, in the case of PDF input, re-exported to PDF. This ensures that the translated output maintains both the professional appearance and the structural integrity of the original document.

Overall, the architecture offers a scientifically grounded yet practically deployable solution. By integrating XML structural analysis, text consolidation, and glossary-based translation into a single automated pipeline, the system bridges the gap between high-quality machine translation research and the operational demands of enterprise-level multilingual document handling.

4 Evaluation

4.1 Dataset Construction

Table 1. Document count by file type and language.

File Type	Language	Count
XLSX	JP	12
	VN	6
PDFX	EN	23
	VN	5
PPTX	JP	10
	VN	19
Total		**75**

To ensure objectivity and accurately reflect the practical capabilities of machine translation systems in an enterprise setting, this study constructs a domain-specific evaluation dataset for the textile and garment industry. Table 1 provides a detailed description of the evaluation dataset. The dataset comprises 75 evaluation samples extracted from real corporate documents, evenly distributed across three common and complex formats: PPTX, XLSX, PDFX (We did not include DOCX due to the relatively simple structure of this file type). The dataset covers three different languages: English, Japanese, and Vietnamese. The selected documents contain content representative of the textile and garment industry, including technical reports, product specification sheets, commercial contracts, and training materials.

Notably, this study also utilizes a domain-specific glossary consisting of 150 EnglishâĂŞJapaneseâĂŞVietnamese term pairs, developed by textile and garment experts, to ensure the accuracy and consistency of technical terminology in the translations.

The translations of the 75 document samples are compared between the proposed approach and an existing baseline. In this study, Google Translate is used as the baseline due to its popularity and widespread adoption in corporate environments as a fast and low-cost translation solution, albeit without customization for the specialized terminology of a specific organization.

4.2   Evaluation Process

The translations are evaluated by 25 experts with experience in the textile and garment industry, each with at least three years of experience working with bilingual/multilingual documents and a solid understanding of industry-specific terminology. The evaluation is conducted manually, based on the standardized criteria described in Table 2.

Each translation is independently assessed by two experts to minimize subjective bias, and the final score is obtained by aggregating the evaluators' scores. To quantify inter-annotator agreement and ensure the reliability of the manual evaluation, we calculated Cohen's Kappa for each criterion across the two raters. The average Kappa score [9] was 0.72, indicating substantial agreement .

Table 2. Designed human evaluation criteria

Criteria	Description	Score
Semantic Accuracy	*Evaluates the semantic accuracy of the translation.*	
	More than 50% of the original content is mistranslated	1
	30–50% of the content is incorrect or ambiguous	2
	Around 10–30% of the content is incorrect or ambiguous	3
	95% correct; remaining errors do not affect the main idea	4
	Almost entirely correct ($\geq$99%), no editing required	5
Fluency & Grammar	*Assesses grammatical quality and readability.*	
	More than 5 serious grammar errors in the passage (10 sentences)	1
	3–5 errors; sentences are rigid or translated word-by-word	2
	$\leq$2 minor errors; understandable	3
	No clear errors; reads smoothly	4
	Sound natural like a native speaker; no detectable errors	5
Domain Appropriate -ness	*Evaluates correctness of domain-specific terminology usage.*	
	Incorrect use of domain terms in $\geq$3 critical points	1
	Incorrect use of 1–2 main terms	2
	Some phrases slightly deviate from intended meaning but acceptable	3
	Mostly correct with only minor inaccuracies	4
	100% accurate in domain-specific context	5
Terminology Consistency	*Assesses consistency in using terminology.*	
	3 or more terms translated inconsistently	1
	2–3 inconsistent term usages	2
	1 minor inconsistency	3
	Almost entirely consistent ($\geq$95%)	4
	All terms translated consistently	5
Style Fit	*Evaluates whether the style matches the intended target.*	
	Completely inappropriate style (e.g., advertising tone for technical text)	1
	Style does not match user context	2
	Neutral style, acceptable but not optimal	3
	Style matches the context	4
	Perfectly matches target style (e.g., formal, legal, marketing)	5
Complete-ness	*Assesses whether the translation covers all original content.*	
	Omits $\geq$2 sentences or $\geq$10% of the content	1
	Omits 1 sentence or a small part ($\sim$5–10%)	2
	Missing a few words with negligible impact	3
	At least 98% complete	4
	No omissions	5
Clarity & Conciseness	*Assesses readability and avoidance of unnecessary words.*	
	3 or more sentences are verbose or unclear	1
	Sentences are long, wordy, and difficult to understand	2
	Some word repetition, but still understandable	3
	Sentences are clear and easy to read	4
	Sentences are concise, easy to understand, and optimally informative	5
Formatting Integrity	*Assesses preservation of original formatting.*	
	Loses $\geq$70% of original formatting (fonts, tables, titles, paragraphs)	1
	Loses 30–70% of formatting	2
	Preserves 70–90%, with a few minor errors	3
	Preserves almost all formatting ($>$95%)	4
	No differences in formatting compared to the source file	5

4.3 Research Questions

To clarify the capability of the proposed approach, the experiment focuses on the following two research questions:

- **RQ1:** To what extent does the source language influence translation quality? This question focuses on analyzing the effectiveness of translations from three source languages (English, Japanese, and Vietnamese) based on seven criteria: semantic accuracy, fluency and grammar, domain appropriateness, terminology consistency, style fit, completeness, and clarity & conciseness.
- **RQ2:** What is the impact of the source file format on translation quality? This question aims to investigate the impact of three common document formats (PPTX, XLSX, PDFX) on translation quality, focusing on four criteria: semantic accuracy, completeness, clarity & conciseness, and formatting integrity.

5 Experimental Result

5.1 RQ$_1$: *To what extent does the source language influence translation quality?*

Table 3. Comparison of Google Translate (G) and our appoarch (BLB) across languages (vertical criteria).

Criteria	EN		JP		VN		Average	
	G	BLB	G	BLB	G	BLB	G	BLB
Semantic Accuracy	2.0263	3.7368	3.6833	3.7667	3.5893	4.0536	3.2403	3.8636
Fluency & Grammar	2.1053	3.5526	3.7000	3.7500	3.5536	4.0893	3.2532	3.8247
Terminology Consistency	2.0263	3.8158	3.9000	3.9667	3.8393	4.2857	3.4156	4.0455
Style Fit	2.5263	4.0000	4.0333	4.0167	3.6429	4.0893	3.5195	4.0390
Completeness	2.2632	3.8947	3.8333	3.9333	3.6786	4.2679	3.3896	4.0455
Clarity & Conciseness	1.9474	3.5526	3.8305	3.9000	3.6786	4.0893	3.3072	3.8831
Domain Appropriateness	2.0000	3.5789	3.6667	3.7333	3.6786	4.0536	3.2597	3.8117

To evaluate the effectiveness of our solution across different source languages, we compared it with Google Translate using seven criteria–Semantic Accuracy, Fluency & Grammar, Terminology Consistency, Style Fit, Completeness, Clarity & Conciseness, and Domain Appropriateness–across three source languages (EN, JP, VN). The detailed results are presented in Table 3.

It can be observed that, when the source language is English, BLB demonstrates a clear advantage over Google across all criteria, with an average difference of +1.306 points ($\approx$ +51%), most notably in Terminology Consistency

(+1.789 points, $\approx +88\%$) and Semantic Accuracy (+1.711 points, $\approx +84\%$), indicating superior handling of source meaning and specialized terminology. Completeness, Clarity, and Style Fit also improved by more than +1.4 points, showing that BLB is particularly strong when translating from English. In contrast, for Japanese, the difference between the two systems is almost negligible, with BLB only slightly ahead by an average of +0.1287 points, and even scoring lower than Google in Style Fit (-0.017 points). This suggests that translation quality from Japanese has reached a "saturation" point, where BLB 's advantage is not apparent. For Vietnamese, BLB again outperforms Google across all criteria, with an average difference of +0.416 points ($\approx +11\%$), most notably in Completeness (+0.589, $\approx +16\%$) and Fluency & Grammar (+0.536, $\approx +15\%$), indicating more complete translations and more fluent sentence structures. Overall, the influence of source language on translation quality is evident, as BLB achieves substantial improvements when translating from EN and VN, but only marginal gains from JP. This may be due to differences in training data or the syntactic structure of Japanese, which may cause both systems to achieve comparable performance.

> **Answer to RQ_1:** BLB delivers significantly higher translation quality when the source language is EN and VN, with improvements of +1.306 points ($\approx +51\%$) and +0.416 points ($\approx +11\%$) respectively. For Japanese, however, BLB produces translation quality comparable to that of Google Translate.

5.2 RQ_2: *What is the impact of the source file format on translation quality?*

Table 4. Comparison of translation quality across file formats.

Criteria	Excel		PDF		PPT		Everage	
	G	BLB	G	BLB	G	BLB	G	BLB
Semantic Accuracy	3.5926	3.5556	2.3488	3.7907	3.6226	4.1509	3.1398	3.8736
Completeness	3.8333	3.7407	2.5349	3.9302	3.6415	4.3774	3.2744	4.0576
Clarity & Conciseness	3.8148	3.7407	2.2558	3.6279	3.6538	4.1509	3.1705	3.8572
Formatting Integrity	4.0000	3.9815	3.3488	4.1395	3.4038	4.4151	3.5264	4.2082

To evaluate the impact of different source file formats on translation quality, we focused on four criteria: Semantic Accuracy, Completeness, Clarity & Conciseness, and Formatting Integrity, across three common formats–PPT, Excel, and PDF.

Results in Table 4 show that for PPT, BLB achieved substantial improvements over Google in all four criteria, particularly in Completeness (+0.736 points, $\approx +20\%$) and Formatting Integrity (+1.011 points, $\approx +30\%$), indicating the system's strong ability to preserve both content and visual layout when processing presentation files.

For Excel, the results indicate that BLB generally underperforms compared to Google, with slight decreases across all four criteria: Semantic Accuracy (-0.037 points), Completeness (-0.093 points), Clarity & Conciseness (-0.074 points), and Formatting Integrity (-0.019 points). This suggests that the tabular structure and cell formatting in Excel may pose challenges for parsing and reconstructing content, leading to lower translation quality.

PDF is the most challenging format; nevertheless, BLB still outperformed Google across all four criteria, with substantial gains in Semantic Accuracy (+1.442 points, $\approx$+61%) and Completeness (+1.395 points, $\approx$+55%). However, the inherent complexity of text extraction and layout reconstruction in PDF makes preserving formatting more difficult. Even so, BLB achieved a notable improvement in Formatting Integrity (+0.791 points, $\approx$+24%), demonstrating strong capabilities in handling complex layouts.

> **Answer to RQ$_2$:** BLB demonstrates outstanding performance with PPT, shows substantial improvements in content with PDF, but experiences a slight decline in quality for the Excel format.

6   Conclussion and Feature Work

This study presents a framework for domain-specific document translation using XML as an intermediate format and glossary-aware neural machine translation to maintain semantic accuracy, terminology consistency, and formatting integrity across multiple file types. The system (BLB) outperforms Google Translate for English and Vietnamese sources, especially for PPT and PDF formats, while Japanese translation shows limited improvement and Excel remains challenging due to complex tables.

Future directions include:

- Supporting complex tabular data: improving parsing and reconstruction of Excel files.
- Language-specific optimization: fine-tuning models with domain-specific bilingual data to enhance Japanese translation quality.
- Large-scale evaluation: expanding datasets, diversifying file formats, and combining automated metrics with expert review.

The proposed framework has the potential to become a generalizable document translation solution that ensures high-quality multilingual corporate communication.

Acknowledgement. This work was funded by TORAY INDUSTRIES (H.K.) VIET-NAM CO., LTD. under the project No. 07/BTT-AI4LIFE (signed on January 8, 2025, in Hanoi). The project has also benefited from the collaboration with the Institute for AI Innovation and Societal Impact - Hanoi University of Science and Technology (AI4Life), as well as from TORAY's contributions in providing industrial knowledge, methodological consulting, and project management support.

References

1. AI, A.I.: The fourth industrial revolution. Am. Psychol. Assoc. Minneap. **4**, 6 (2022)
2. Arivazhagan, N., et al.: Massively multilingual neural machine translation in the wild: findings and challenges. arXiv preprint: arXiv:1907.05019 (2019)
3. Avila, M., Crego, J.M.: Leveraging large pre-trained multilingual models for high-quality speech-to-text translation on industry scenarios. In: Proceedings of the 31st International Conference on Computational Linguistics, pp. 7624–7633 (2025)
4. Chu, C., Wang, R.: A survey of domain adaptation for machine translation. J. Inf. Process. **28**, 413–426 (2020)
5. Delfani, J., et al.: Google translate error analysis for mental healthcare information: evaluating accuracy, comprehensibility, and implications for multilingual healthcare communication. arXiv preprint: arXiv:2402.04023 (2024)
6. Dunđer, I.: Machine translation system for the industry domain and Croatian language. J. Inf. Organ. Sci. **44**(1), 33–50 (2020)
7. Fu, L., Liu, L.: What are the differences? A comparative study of generative artificial intelligence translation and human translation of scientific texts. Human. Soc. Sci. Commun. **11**(1), 1–12 (2024)
8. Koehn, P., Knowles, R.: Six challenges for neural machine translation. In: Luong, T., Birch, A., Neubig, G., Finch, A. (eds.) Proceedings of the First Workshop on Neural Machine Translation, pp. 28–39. Association for Computational Linguistics, Vancouver (2017). https://doi.org/10.18653/v1/W17-3204
9. Landis, J.R., Koch, G.G.: The measurement of observer agreement for categorical data. Biometrics, 159–174 (1977)
10. Li, J., Zhou, H., Huang, S., Cheng, S., Chen, J.: Eliciting the translation ability of large language models via multilingual finetuning with translation instructions. Trans. Assoc. Comput. Linguist. **12**, 576–592 (2024)
11. Mirzaeian, V.R., Oskoui, K.: Google translate in foreign language learning: a systematic review. Appl. Res. Engl. Lang. **12**(2), 51–84 (2023)
12. Raffel, C., et al.: Exploring the limits of transfer learning with a unified text-to-text transformer. J. Mach. Learn. Res. **21**(140), 1–67 (2020)
13. Siu, S.C.: Revolutionising translation with AI: unravelling neural machine translation and generative pre-trained large language models. In: New advances in translation technology: Applications and pedagogy, pp. 29–54. Springer (2024)
14. Tang, W., Li, G.: Enhancing competitiveness in cross-border e-commerce through knowledge-based consumer perception theory: an exploration of translation ability. J. Knowl. Econ. **15**(3), 14935–14968 (2024)
15. Teixeira, C.S.: Multilingual systems, translation technology and their impact on the translator's profession. In: Where Humans Meet Machines: Innovative Solutions for Knotty Natural-Language Problems, pp. 299–314. Springer (2013)
16. Vaswani, A., et al.: Attention is all you need. NeurIPS **30**, 1–11 (2017)
17. Wu, Y., et al.: Google's neural machine translation system: bridging the gap between human and machine translation. arXiv preprint: arXiv:1609.08144 (2016)
18. Zhang, B., Haddow, B., Birch, A.: Prompting large language model for machine translation: a case study. In: International Conference on Machine Learning, pp. 41092–41110. PMLR (2023)

PHITS: A Parallel Hyperlink-Induced Topic Search Algorithm with Graph Partitioning and Communication Optimization

Xuanye Chen, Xiaoshuang Xing$^{(\boxtimes)}$, Mengjiao Ou, Jialin Chen, and Xiaoyu Ma

School of Computer Science and Engineering, Suzhou University of Technology,
Suzhou 215500, China
`xing@szut.edu.cn`

Abstract. In the era of big data, the efficiency of the Hyperlink-Induced Topic Search (HITS) algorithm in processing large-scale web link data has become a critical issue. To address the inefficiency of the traditional serial HITS algorithm when dealing with massive web link graphs, this paper proposes a novel parallel HITS algorithm. The algorithm lies in the rational partitioning of the web link graph. By adopting a graph-based partitioning method, the large-scale web link graph is divided into multiple subgraphs. Each subgraph is assigned to a computing node, enabling each node to independently calculate the authority and hub values of the web pages within its assigned subgraph. In addition, to reduce communication overhead in the parallel computing process, we further design data compression and asynchronous communication strategies. The former is applied to web link data before transmission to effectively reduce the amount of data transferred, while the latter enables processing units to perform other tasks while waiting for data transmission, thereby improving resource utilization. Experimental results demonstrate that the proposed parallel HITS algorithm not only maintains the accuracy of the original HITS algorithm but also achieves a significant improvement in computing efficiency.

Keywords: Parallel HITS Algorithm · Graph Partitioning · Communication Optimization · Distributed Computing

1 Introduction

The exponential growth of the Internet has led to an unprecedented surge in web data. According to recent industry reports, more than 50 billion web pages had been indexed worldwide by 2024 [7]. This massive expansion highlights the pressing need for efficient algorithms to navigate and prioritize information, a reality that has made link analysis techniques indispensable in all fields, from search engine optimization to academic knowledge mapping [15]. Among these techniques, the Hyperlink-Induced Topic Search (HITS) algorithm has long stood out

© IFIP International Federation for Information Processing 2026
Published by Springer Nature Switzerland AG 2026
X. Wang et al. (Eds.): NPC 2025, LNCS 16306, pp. 436–447, 2026.
https://doi.org/10.1007/978-3-032-10466-3_36

for its ability to identify authoritative and central pages using web link structures
[9]. However, as web graphs continue to expand—with major search engines now
processing trillions of links—the traditional serial implementation of HITS has hit
severe bottlenecks. It struggles to keep up with the demands of large- or real-time
data processing. This inefficiency not only holds back practical applications but
also limits progress in extracting actionable insights from complex web ecosystems,
underscoring an urgent need for innovations that close the gap between what algorithms could achieve and what current computing can deliver.

Existing efforts to tackle the scalability issues of HITS have taken various
approaches. Early studies, such as those of Liu et al. [11], focused on adapting link
analysis algorithms to distributed systems, paving the way for parallel implementations. Recently, researchers used parallel computing frameworks like MapRe-
duce [7] and Apache Spark to spread HITS computations across clusters, seeing
moderate speed improvements for middle-sized web graphs. In addition, some
studies tried to optimize communication by cutting down on data exchange frequency [6] or using lightweight messaging protocols. However, these approaches
often fall short in two key areas. First, graph partitioning strategies in existing
parallel HITS setups tend to either oversimplify subgraph boundaries—leading
to too many cross-node dependencies—or require high preprocessing costs. Second, communication optimizations are often treated as standalone fixes rather
than part of a unified framework, meaning they fail to fully reduce overheads
when handling hyper-scale web graphs with billions of nodes and edges. As a
result, there is still an urgent need for a comprehensive approach that combines
efficient graph partitioning with coordinated communication optimizations to
unlock parallel computing's full potential for HITS.

In this paper, we propose a novel Parallel HITS (PHITS) algorithm to overcome the inefficiencies of traditional implementations when handling hyper-scale
web graphs. By combining a customized graph partitioning strategy with a unified communication optimization framework, the proposed method delivers significant gains in computational efficiency while maintaining the algorithm's accuracy. The core contributions of this work are summarized below.

- We propose a graph partitioning strategy tailored for HITS, dynamically balancing subgraph cohesion and boundary sparsity. Using community detection
  principles, we minimize cross-node dependencies, reduce preprocessing overhead, and ensure semantically coherent subgraphs per node—cutting inter-
  node communication needs to enable efficient parallel computing.
- We introduce an integrated communication optimization framework with
  two complementary techniques: lossless compression of link metadata, which
  reduces transmission volume, and asynchronous messaging, which overlaps
  computation and communication, cuts node idle time, and effectively eases
  data transmission bottlenecks.
- The PHITS algorithm also includes a distributed cache layer for frequently
  accessed authority/hub values. This layer reduces redundant retrieval and
  transmission of core parameters, working with compression and messaging to
  minimize inter-node data exchange—solving a key issue in parallel HITS.

2   Related Work

Recent studies have increasingly focused on balancing accuracy preservation and scalability in parallel link analysis, with HITS emerging as a critical case study [5]. Bonomi et al. [2] conducted a systematic evaluation of parallel implementations across 6 link analysis algorithms, and found that HITS exhibited the most noticeable accuracy degradation under scalable architectures. To tackle this issue, Jafari et al. [8] proposed a precision-aware partitioning strategy to prioritize preserving dense subgraphs for HITS. Similarly, Bora et al. [3] introduced granularity tuning for parallel HITS, where subgraph size is dynamically adjusted based on the computational load of each node. These studies demonstrate progress, but they leave a critical gap: no existing framework delivers both sub-5% accuracy preservation and near-linear scalability across different types of graphs.

Various structure-based methods focused on graph topology, remain a dominant approach in parallel computing [16,17]. For example, Sanders et al. [16] proposed a multi-level partitioning algorithm that iteratively coarsens graphs to minimize edge cuts, achieving balanced load distribution across 64-node clusters. Umrawal et al. [17] introduced a community-aware partitioning strategy that uses Louvain modularity to preserve dense subgraphs. For web graphs, Yang et al. [18] leveraged URL domain information to group nodes by semantic similarity, arguing that domain-cohesive subgraphs improve the accuracy of parallel HITS. Most recently, Pham et al. [13] proposed dynamic repartitioning to adapt to HITS' iterative nature, adjusting the partitions after every 5 iterations based on score convergence. This approach improved scalability by 18% but introduced significant runtime overhead due to frequent repartitioning, making it unsuitable for real-time applications.

Data compression has emerged as a key strategy for reducing transmission volume in parallel graph processing [5,12]. For instance, Chen et al. [5] proposed a lossless compression algorithm tailored for web link metadata, which exploited URL pattern redundancies to achieve an average 40% compression ratio. Asynchronous communication aims to overlap computation and data transfer, a critical capability given HITS' iterative nature. Osama et al. [12] designed a message-driven asynchronous model for parallel graph algorithms, where nodes processed local updates while receiving remote data asynchronously. Cheng et al. [6] combined asynchronous communication with adaptive update thresholds, triggering synchronization only when score changes exceeded a dynamic threshold. This approach balanced determinism and efficiency but struggled with large-scale graphs, as threshold tuning grew computationally expensive in clusters with more than 32 nodes.

Existing research focuses on isolated communication optimizations: compression methods neglect decompression overhead, asynchronous models sacrifice result consistency, and caching strategies struggle to scale to dense graphs. It creates the need for an integrated framework that combines these techniques while addressing their individual limitations.

3   Parallel HITS Architecture

We propose a novel Parallel Hyperlink-Induced Topic Search (PHITS) algorithm to addresses the scalability limitations of traditional serial implementations. PHITS integrates three core components: a graph partitioning strategy tailored for PHITS semantics, a parallel iterative computation mechanism, and an asynchronous communication strategy for boundary information exchange. Together, these components support efficient parallel execution while preserving the algorithm's accuracy.

3.1   Graph Partitioning for PHITS Semantics

As the foundation of PHITS, we design a graph partitioning strategy that balances two key objectives: preserving the semantic coherence of subgraphs to maintain HITS accuracy, and minimizing cross-node dependencies to reduce communication overhead. Unlike general-purpose graph partitioning methods, our approach explicitly accounts for the interdependent hub and authority relationships central to HITS. The workflow of graph partitioning for PHITS semantics is illustrated in Fig. 1.

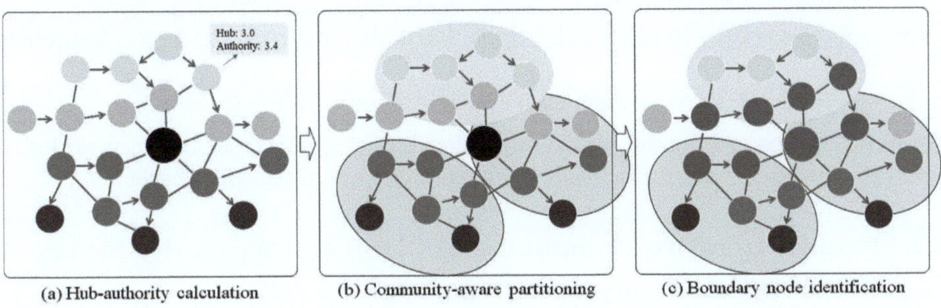

(a) Hub-authority calculation   (b) Community-aware partitioning   (c) Boundary node identification

Fig. 1. Workflow of graph partitioning for PHITS semantics.

(1) Partition objectives

Given a web graph $G = (V, E)$, where V is the set of vertices (web pages) and E is the set of directed edges (hyperlinks), we aim to partition G into k subgraphs $S_1, S_2, ..., S_k$. Each subgraph S_i contains vertices with dense internal link structures, preserving local hub-authority relationships. Formally, for each S_i, the intra-subgraph edge density d_i is maximized:

$$d_i = \frac{|E_i|}{|V_i| \times (|V_i| - 1)} \tag{1}$$

where $E_i \subseteq E$ is the set of edges with both endpoints in $V_i \subseteq V$ (vertices in S_i). The number of boundary edges E_b (edges connecting vertices in different subgraphs) is minimized:

$$E_b = \sum_{i \neq j} |\{(u, v) \in E \mid u \in V_i, v \in V_j\}| \tag{2}$$

In this case, the size of each subgraph $|V_i|$ is approximately equal, ensuring balanced computation between k nodes.

(2) Community-aware partitioning with HITS weights

Our partitioning algorithm extends the Louvain method for community detection by incorporating HITS-specific weights. The key innovation is a modified modularity function that prioritizes preserving edges critical to hub-authority propagation:

$$Q = \frac{1}{2m} \sum_{i,j} \left(A_{ij} - \gamma \cdot \frac{k_i k_j}{2m} \cdot w_{ij} \right) \delta(S_i, S_j) \tag{3}$$

where: $A_{ij} = 1$ if there is an edge from i to j, else 0. m is the total number of edges in G, k_i is the out-degree of vertex i. $w_{ij} = \alpha \cdot h_i + (1 - \alpha) \cdot a_j$ (with $\alpha = 0.5$) weights the edges based on the initial center score h_i of the source and the authority score a_j of the target. γ is a scaling factor (set to 1.2) to amplify HITS-relevant edges. $\delta(S_i, S_j) = 1$ if i and j are in the same subgraph, else 0.

(3) Boundary node identification

After partitioning, boundary nodes are identified as vertices in S_i with edges connecting to vertices in other subgraphs. Formally, a vertex $u \in V_i$ is a boundary node if:

$$\exists v \notin V_i \text{ such that } (u, v) \in E \text{ or } (v, u) \in E \tag{4}$$

Boundary nodes are tagged and their indices are shared across relevant nodes to facilitate targeted communication in subsequent computation phases.

3.2   Parallel Iterative Computation of Hub and Authority Scores

Each computing node independently processes its assigned subgraph S_i to update hub and authority scores, leveraging local information while coordinating with other nodes only for boundary-related updates. This parallelization preserves the iterative nature of HITS while reducing redundant computations.

(1) Local score updates

For non-boundary nodes within S_i, hub and authority scores are updated using only local edges (edges within S_i). The authority score a_u of a vertex $u \in S_i$ (non-boundary) is computed as:

$$a_u^{(t+1)} = \sum_{\substack{v \in S_i \\ (v,u) \in E}} h_v^{(t)} \tag{5}$$

where t denotes the iteration step, and $h_v^{(t)}$ is the hub score of v at iteration t. Similarly, the hub score h_v of a non-boundary vertex $v \in S_i$ is:

$$h_v^{(t+1)} = \sum_{\substack{u \in S_i \\ (v,u) \in E}} a_u^{(t)} \tag{6}$$

(2) Boundary node score updates

Boundary nodes require partial updates from external subgraphs. For a boundary node $u \in S_i$ with incoming edges from vertices $v \in S_j$ $(j \neq i)$:

$$a_u^{(t+1)} = \sum_{\substack{v \in S_i \\ (v,u) \in E}} h_v^{(t)} + \sum_{\substack{v \in S_j (j \neq i) \\ (v,u) \in E}} h_v^{(t)} \cdot \beta \tag{7}$$

where β (set to 1.0) ensures consistency with the original HITS formulation, and the second term is received from node j via inter-node communication. An analogous formula applies to hub scores of boundary nodes with outgoing edges to other subgraphs:

$$h_v^{(t+1)} = \sum_{\substack{u \in S_i \\ (v,u) \in E}} a_u^{(t)} + \sum_{\substack{u \in S_j (j \neq i) \\ (v,u) \in E}} a_u^{(t)} \cdot \beta \tag{8}$$

4　Data Transmission and Communication Optimization

Efficient communication is critical for achieving scalable performance in parallel HITS implementations, as the iterative nature of hub and authority score updates creates frequent boundary data exchanges between computing nodes. This section presents three complementary optimization techniques—data compression, asynchronous communication, and distributed caching—designed to minimize communication overhead while maintaining algorithmic correctness.

4.1　Multilevel Data Compression for Boundary Information

To reduce the volume of boundary data transmitted between nodes, we introduce a multilevel compression scheme that combines structural sparsity exploitation, delta encoding, and quantization, targeting the specific characteristics of HITS score vectors and web graph structures. The multilevel data compression process of the proposed PHHITS algorithm is illustrated in Fig. 2.

(1) Structural sparsity exploitation

Web graphs exhibit inherent structural sparsity, with boundary nodes typically having sparse connectivity patterns across subgraphs. For each boundary node $u \in S_i$, we represent its adjacency list as a sparse vector where only non-zero entries (corresponding to edges to other subgraphs) are transmitted. Formally, for a boundary node u with authority score a_u, we define the compressed adjacency vector as:

$$\mathbf{A}_u = \{(v, a_u) \mid v \in S_j(jeqi), (v,u) \in E\} \tag{4.1}$$

where $\mathbf{A}_u$ contains only target vertices v in remote subgraphs S_j. This reduces transmission volume by a factor equal to the sparsity ratio $\rho = \frac{|E_b|}{|E|}$, which typically ranges from 0.1 to 0.3 in web graph partitioning.

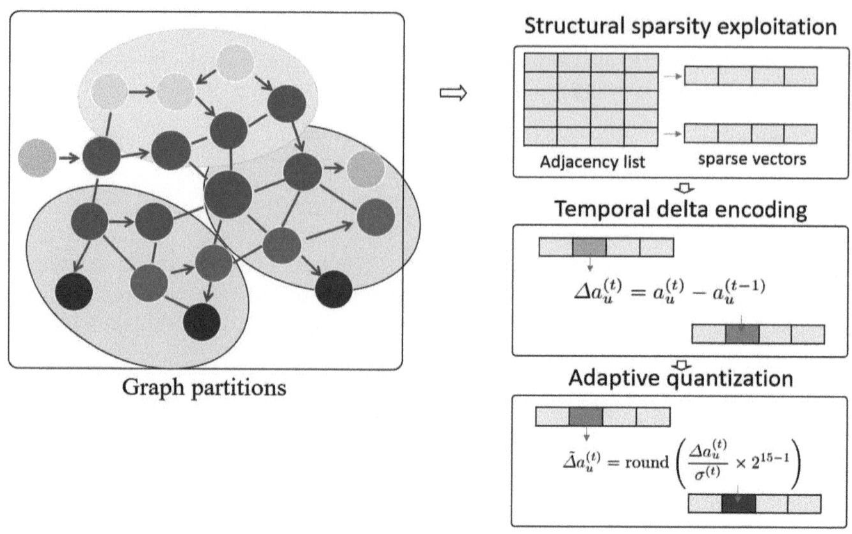

Fig. 2. Multilevel data compression process of the proposed PHHITS algorithm

(2) Temporal delta encoding

Leveraging the temporal correlation between successive iterations of HITS, we apply delta encoding to score values. For boundary node u, instead of transmitting the full authority score $a_u^{(t)}$ at iteration t, we transmit only the difference from the previous iteration:

$$\Delta a_u^{(t)} = a_u^{(t)} - a_u^{(t-1)} \tag{4.2}$$

Since HITS scores converge monotonically, $\Delta a_u^{(t)}$ decreases in magnitude as iterations progress, leading to increasing numbers of near-zero values. We apply a threshold $\tau = 10^{-8}$ to discard negligible deltas:

$$\hat{\Delta} a_u^{(t)} = \begin{cases} \Delta a_u^{(t)} & \text{if } |\Delta a_u^{(t)}| \geq \tau, \\ 0 & \text{otherwise} \end{cases} \tag{9}$$

(3) Adaptive quantization

To further compress delta values, we employ adaptive 16-bit floating-point quantization. The quantization scale $\sigma^{(t)}$ is dynamically adjusted per iteration based on the global maximum delta magnitude:

$$\sigma^{(t)} = \max_{u \in \text{Boundary}} |\Delta a_u^{(t)}| \tag{10}$$

Quantized delta values $\tilde{\Delta} a_u^{(t)}$ are then computed as:

$$\tilde{\Delta} a_u^{(t)} = \mathrm{round}\left(\frac{\Delta a_u^{(t)}}{\sigma^{(t)}} \times 2^{15-1}\right) \tag{11}$$

This maintains sufficient precision for convergence while reducing each delta value from 64 bits to 16 bits, achieving 4:1 compression. Decompression at the receiving node uses the transmitted $\sigma^{(t)}$ to reconstruct approximate delta values.

4.2   Asynchronous Communication with Distributed Caching

To overlap communication and computation while reducing redundant data transfers, we design an asynchronous communication framework with distributed caching, enabling nodes to proceed with local computations while awaiting remote boundary updates.

(1) Asynchronous message passing

We adopt a producer-consumer model where each node maintains separate send and receive buffers for boundary data. When a node completes local score updates, it immediately sends updated boundary scores to relevant neighbors without waiting for acknowledgment (fire-and-forget). Each message includes: Source/destination node IDs, Iteration version tag t, Compressed delta scores, and Validity timestamp

Receiving nodes buffer incoming messages in a priority queue ordered by iteration tag. For iteration $t+1$ computations, nodes use the most recent available scores from iteration t, even if some messages are delayed:

$$a_u^{(t+1)} = \sum_{v \in S_i} h_v^{(t)} + \sum_{v \in S_j(jeqi)} h_v^{(t')} \quad \text{where } t' \le t \tag{12}$$

To prevent staleness, we enforce a maximum version lag $\Delta t_{\max} = 2$. If $t - t' > \Delta t_{\max}$, the node triggers a synchronous barrier to refresh all boundary scores.

(2) LRU distribution cache

We implement a distributed least-recently-used (LRU) cache to store frequently accessed boundary scores and adjacency lists. Each node maintains a local cache C_i with capacity M (set to 10% of boundary node count), storing entries in the form $(u, a_u^{(t)}, t, \text{access\_count})$. Cache eviction follows LRU policy when capacity is exceeded:

$$\text{evict}(C_i) = \arg \min_{(u,*,t,ac) \in C_i} (t - \text{last\_access}(u)) \tag{13}$$

Cache coherence is maintained through version tags. When a node receives updated scores for u, it broadcasts an invalidation message to all nodes caching u's scores. The cache hit ratio H is defined as:

$$H = \frac{\text{cache\_hits}}{\text{cache\_hits} + \text{cache\_misses}} \tag{14}$$

5   Experiments

5.1   Experimental Setup

We conduct experiments on a cluster made up of 16 computing nodes. Each node configures with an Intel Xeon Gold 6348 CPU. The software and tools used in the experiments include Python 3.9, Apache Spark 3.4.0, MPI 4.0, and custom C++ implementations for low-level graph operations. To test scalability, we vary the number of active nodes (4, 8, 12, 16). We use three large-scale web graph datasets in the experiments to ensure generality across different graph types. The first is WebBase-2001 [1]—a public web graph curated by the Stanford WebGraph project, containing 118 million vertices and 1.4 billion directed edges. The second is CiteSeerX [4], an academic citation network with 3.8 million vertices and 16.5 million edges, which represents a dense, domain-specific graph. The third is Twitter-2010 [10], a social network graph with 41.7 million vertices and 1.47 billion edges, characterized by a sparse, scale-free structure. We compared our PHITS algorithm against three baseslines, including Serial HITS [9], Spark-HITS [19], and MPI-HITS [14].

We adopted four core metrics to assess performance. (1) Total Execution Time: Wall-clock time from initialization to convergence. (2) Speedup: $S = T_1/T_k$, where T_1 is the execution time of the serial method, and T_k is the time with k nodes (higher = better). (3) Communication Overhead: Percentage of total time spent on inter-node data transmission (lower = better). (4) Accuracy: Root-mean-square error (RMSE) between parallel and serial HITS scores.

5.2   Efficiency Comparison

This experiment evaluates the total execution time and communication overhead of all methods using a 16-node cluster, tested across WebBase-2001 and CiteSeerX datasets. Execution time is measured as the wall-clock time from initialization to convergence. Communication overhead is defined as the percentage of total time spent on inter-node data transmission, including data compression/decompression and message passing. Each method is run five times, and results are averaged to minimize variability. The experimental results are shown in Fig. 3.

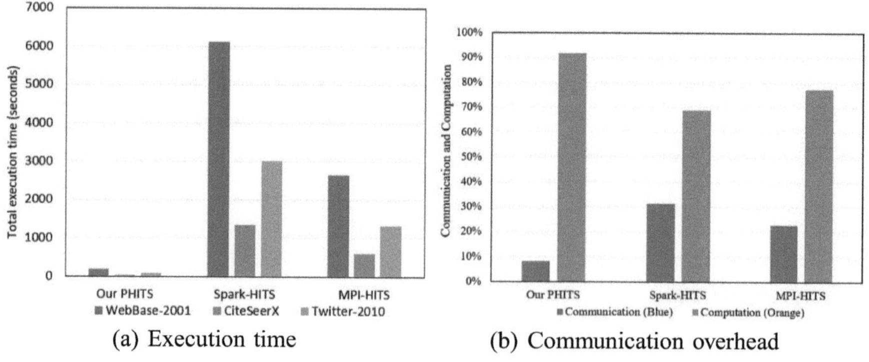

(a) Execution time   (b) Communication overhead

Fig. 3. Efficiency comparison results.

As shown in Fig. 3(a), our PHITS algorithm achieves the shortest execution time across all datasets: $187 \pm 12\,$s on WebBase-2001, $42 \pm 3\,$s on CiteSeerX, and $93 \pm 5\,$s on Twitter-2010. This represents a 32.7× speedup over Spark-HITS ($6114 \pm 210\,$s on WebBase-2001) and 14.2× over MPI-HITS ($596 \pm 28\,$s on CiteSeerX). The key driver of this efficiency is reduced communication overhead (Fig. 3(b)). Our PHITS spends only 8.3% of total time on communication, compared to 31.2% for Spark-HITS and 22.7% for MPI-HITS. Two factors drive this improvement: (1) semantic-aware partitioning minimizes cross-node edges, reducing data volume by 47% compared to random partitioning; and (2) the integrated communication framework—combining compression and caching—further cuts transmission time.

5.3   Accuracy Validation

To quantify accuracy, we compare the authority and hub scores from parallel algorithms against the ground truth—serial HITS results. For each dataset, we compute the Root-Mean-Square Error (RMSE) for both authority scores (a_u) and hub scores (h_u). The experimental results for the accuracy of the compared algorithms are shown in Table 1.

Table 1. RMSE values for authority scores.

Datasets	PHITS	Spark-HITS	MPI-HITS
WebBase-2001	2.9×10^{-4}	1.78×10^{-3}	2.09×10^{-3}
CiteSeerX	3.2×10^{-4}	1.83×10^{-3}	2.14×10^{-3}
Twitter-2010	2.7×10^{-4}	1.65×10^{-3}	1.98×10^{-3}

As shown in Table 1, our PHITS algorithm maintains high accuracy, with RMSE $< 3.2 \times 10^{-4}$ across all datasets. The value significantly lower than Spark-HITS (RMSE $\approx 1.8 \times 10^{-3}$) and MPI-HITS (RMSE $\approx 2.1 \times 10^{-3}$). This confirms that semantic-aware partitioning preserves the integrity of hub-authority relationships.

5.4   Scalability Analysis

To evaluate the scalability of the proposed PHITS algorithm, we vary the cluster size from 4 to 16 nodes and measure speedup on the WebBase-2001 dataset. The experimental results of the scalability analysis are listed in Table 2.

As shown in Table 2, PHITS achieves near-linear scalability, with a speedup of 15.2× as the number of nodes increases from 4 to 16. In contrast, Spark-HITS and MPI-HITS achieve only 6.8× and 9.3× speedups, respectively. The key difference lies in computational efficiency. With 16 nodes, our algorithm spends 91.7% of its runtime on computation, compared to 68.8% for Spark-HITS and 77.3% for

Table 2. Speedup values across cluster sizes.

Nodes	PHITS	Spark-HITS	MPI-HITS	Ideal linear speedup
4	1.0×	1.0×	1.0×	1.0×
8	4.0×	3.0×	5.0×	2.0×
12	12.0×	5.0×	8.0×	3.0×
16	15.2×	6.8×	9.3×	4.0×

MPI-HITS. This performance gap stems from our asynchronous communication strategy, which overlaps data transmission with local computation. Spark-HITS suffers from diminishing returns because its centralized driver node becomes a bottleneck. MPI-HITS' random partitioning increases cross-node dependencies, leading to 22.7% communication overhead. PHITS uses dynamic partitioning to balance load across nodes, and caching reduces redundant data transfers, even as the cluster size grows.

6   Conclusion

This paper addressed the scalability limitations of the HITS algorithm in processing hyper-scale web graphs by proposing a novel parallel architecture that incorporates communication optimization strategies. The core innovations include a community-aware graph partitioning strategy that balances subgraph cohesion and boundary sparsity and an asynchronous communication strategy with delta-encoding compression. Experimental results demonstrate that PHITS achieves faster execution than Spark-HITS and MPI-HITS, while maintaining high accuracy and near-linear scalability. Future work will involve extending the algorithm to handle dynamic web graphs and integrating machine learning-based predictions to further reduce boundary data transmission.

Acknowledgment. This work is supported by the Natural Science Foundation of Jiangsu Province (BK20211357) and the Natural Science Foundation of the Jiangsu Higher Education Institutions of China (Grant No. 24KJA520001).

References

1. Boldi, P., Vigna, S.: The webgraph framework I: compression techniques. In: Proceedings of the 13th International Conference on World Wide Web, pp. 595–602 (2004)
2. Bonomi, S., Cuoci, M., Lenti, S., Palma, A.: Improving attack graph-based self-protecting systems: a computational pipeline for accuracy-scalability trade-off. In: International Conference on Risks and Security of Internet and Systems, pp. 525–542. Springer (2024)

3. Bora, S., Walker, B., Fidler, M.: The tiny-tasks granularity trade-off: balancing overhead versus performance in parallel systems. IEEE Trans. Parallel Distrib. Syst. **34**(4), 1128–1144 (2023)

4. Caragea, C., et al.: CiteSeer^x: a scholarly big dataset. In: de Rijke, M., et al. (eds.) ECIR 2014. LNCS, vol. 8416, pp. 311–322. Springer, Cham (2014). https://doi.org/10.1007/978-3-319-06028-6_26

5. Chen, Z., et al.: CompressGraph: efficient parallel graph analytics with rule-based compression. Proc. ACM Manag. Data **1**(1), 1–31 (2023)

6. Cheng, J., Zhang, Q., Zhang, D., Yan, H., Chadli, M., Qi, W.: Protocol-based asynchronous filtering for interval type-2 fuzzy systems with time-varying saturation function. IEEE Trans. Syst. Man Cybern. Syst. **54**(5), 2917–2926 (2024)

7. Gowraj, N., Avireddy, S., Prabhu, S.: PALM: preprocessed Apriori for logical matching using map reduce algorithm. Int. J. Comput. Sci. Eng. **4**(7), 1289 (2012)

8. Jafari, N., Selvitopi, O., Aykanat, C.: Fast shared-memory streaming multilevel graph partitioning. J. Parallel Distrib. Comput. **147**, 140–151 (2021)

9. Kleinberg, J.M.: Authoritative sources in a hyperlinked environment. J. ACM (JACM) **46**(5), 604–632 (1999)

10. Kwak, H., Lee, C., Park, H., Moon, S.: What is Twitter, a social network or a news media? In: Proceedings of the 19th International Conference on World Wide Web, pp. 591–600 (2010)

11. Liu, B., Jiang, S., Zou, Q.: HITS-PR-HHblits: protein remote homology detection by combining PageRank and hyperlink-induced topic search. Brief. Bioinform. **21**(1), 298–308 (2020)

12. Osama, M., Porumbescu, S.D., Owens, J.D.: Essentials of parallel graph analytics. In: 2022 IEEE International Parallel and Distributed Processing Symposium, pp. 314–317. IEEE (2022)

13. Pham, V.T., Nguyen, M.D., Ta, Q.T., Murray, T., Rubinstein, B.I.: Towards systematic and dynamic task allocation for collaborative parallel fuzzing. In: 2021 36th IEEE/ACM International Conference on Automated Software Engineering (ASE), pp. 1337–1341. IEEE (2021)

14. Ramalingam, G., Dhandapani, S.: A hybrid BATCS algorithm to generate optimal query plan. Int. Arab J. Inf. Technol. **15**(3), 353–359 (2018)

15. Rossi, A., Barbosa, D., Firmani, D., Matinata, A., Merialdo, P.: Knowledge graph embedding for link prediction: a comparative analysis. ACM Trans. Knowl. Discovery from Data (TKDD) **15**(2), 1–49 (2021)

16. Sanders, P., Seemaier, D.: Distributed deep multilevel graph partitioning. In: European Conference on Parallel Processing, pp. 443–457. Springer (2023)

17. Umrawal, A.K., Quinn, C.J., Aggarwal, V.: A community-aware framework for social influence maximization. IEEE Trans. Emerging Top. Comput. Intell. **7**(4), 1253–1262 (2023)

18. Yang, J.Q., Zhan, D.C., Gan, L.: Beyond probability partitions: calibrating neural networks with semantic aware grouping. In: Advances in Neural Information Processing Systems, vol. 36, pp. 58448–58460 (2023)

19. Zhu, L., Gao, D., Jia, T., Zhang, J.: Using eco-geographical zoning data and crowdsourcing to improve the detection of spurious land cover changes. Remote Sens. **13**(16), 3244 (2021)

Reducing Load-Balancing Cost
for Multithreading Applications
on Asymmetric NUMA Machine

Yuhang Fang⬤, Pu Pang$^{(\boxtimes)}$⬤, Quan Chen$^{(\boxtimes)}$⬤, Li Li⬤, and Minyi Guo⬤

School of Computer Science, Shanghai Jiao Tong University, Shanghai, China
`{fang.yh,lilijp}@sjtu.edu.cn`, `{pangpu,chen-quan,guo-my}@cs.sjtu.edu.cn`

Abstract. Many applications adopt multithreading to increase the concurrency or computational efficiency. In this scenario, the active threads are often much more than the cores of a server, and are scheduled with the operating system. However, we observe that the current load balancing mechanism based on scheduling domains leads to poor performance on asymmetric NUMA machines. Our investigation shows that the poor performance is due to the unnecessary "far" scheduling with high cost, because the current algorithm of building scheduling domains neglects the physical relevance of NUMA nodes in a machine. We therefore propose a physical relevance-based algorithm to construct scheduling domains on asymmetric NUMA machines to reduce the scheduling cost. Experimental results show that the proposed scheduling domains improve the real-world applications by 14.94% on average (up to 22.33%).

Keywords: NUMA · Load Balancing · Scheduling Domain

1 Introduction

Datacenters host various applications, such as web server [1], database [3] and big-data computing [26]. These applications usually adopt multithreading to increase the concurrency or computational efficiency. Some of them create a large number of threads at runtime, significantly exceeding the available cores of a server. For instance, an Apache HTTP server [1] creates 400 working threads by default, and it is common to have more than 10,000 threads running simultaneously on a server [19].

In modern symmetric multiprocessing (SMP) systems, CPUs and memory are organized into interconnected nodes, with the Non-Uniform Memory Access (NUMA) architecture commonly employed to improve scalability. Typically, the interconnection among NUMA nodes in a machine is symmetric. Figure 1(a) shows the interconnection of a machine with symmetric NUMA architecture (4 Intel Xeon Platinum 8163 processors, each with 1 NUMA node and 24 cores).

When the number of physical cores in a processor increases, more than one NUMA node is organized within a processor. For instance, 2 nodes are organized within a 48-core Huawei Kunpeng 920 processor, and 4 nodes are organized

© IFIP International Federation for Information Processing 2026
Published by Springer Nature Switzerland AG 2026
X. Wang et al. (Eds.): NPC 2025, LNCS 16306, pp. 448–460, 2026.
https://doi.org/10.1007/978-3-032-10466-3_37

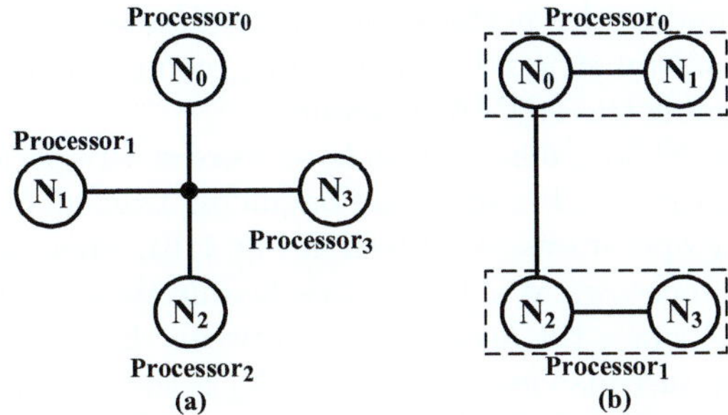

Fig. 1. (a) The symmetric NUMA machine. (b) The asymmetric NUMA machine.

within a 64-core AMD EPYC 7H12 processor. When multiple such processors are equipped in a single machine, the NUMA nodes' interconnection becomes asymmetric. Figure 1(b) shows the interconnection of a machine equipped with two Huawei Kunpeng 920 processors. As shown, the communication between Node$_1$ (N_1) and Node$_3$ (N_3) has to go through intermediary nodes (N_0 and N_2). The machines with asymmetric NUMA architecture have been deployed in many datacenters [4,5].

It is crucial for the host operating system (OS) to schedule such a large number of threads effectively on NUMA machines. Mainline Linux (since kernel v2.6.7) designed **scheduling domains** to balance the workload among NUMA nodes. A scheduling domain is a set of CPUs and consists of some scheduling groups. The OS periodically checks and balances the workload of each group.

We test the effectiveness of balancing the workloads on both symmetric and asymmetric NUMA machines using the *hackbench* [2] that is specifically designed to evaluate the OS scheduler. In *hackbench*, many groups of threads run simultaneously; ideally, under constant load pressure, the performance regression should be as few as possible when running on more nodes. The load pressure is measured by the ratio between the number of thread groups of *hackbench* and the number of CPU cores used. However, as shown in Table 1, when extending from

Table 1. The execution time of *hackbench* when extending from one node to four nodes. #G represents the number of thread groups.

Used Node	Symmetric NUMA Machine			Asymmetric NUMA Machine		
	#G	Time	Regression	#G	Time	Regression
N_0	48	12.08 s	0	24	18.34 s	0
N_0, N_1	96	12.91 s	−6.87%	48	20.23 s	−10.30%
N_0, N_2	96	12.97 s	−7.36%	48	21.65 s	−18.04%
N_0, N_3	96	12.95 s	−7.20%	48	22.42 s	−22.24%
N_0, N_1, N_2, N_3	192	13.49 s	−11.67%	96	25.46 s	−38.82%

one node to four nodes, the performance of *hackbench* regresses more rapidly
(-38.82%) in the asymmetric NUMA machine, compared with a regression of
-11.67% on the symmetric NUMA machine.

The asymmetric NUMA machine leads to more severe performance degradation of *hackbench*, primarily because load balancing triggers frequent and expensive "far" scheduling operations. As shown in Fig. 1(b), when balancing the workload between two processors, it is better to schedule threads between N_0 and N_2
(denoted as N_0–N_2), since the access delay between these two nodes is minimal
(260 ns). Scheduling threads via N_0–N_3 or N_2–N_1 is the medium-cost way (280 ns
access delay), and via N_1–N_3 is the high-cost way (300 ns access delay). However, our experiment (see Sect. 2.3) shows that **the medium and high-cost
scheduling holds at least half the proportion in the cross-processor
scheduling** for *hackbench* on the asymmetric NUMA machine.

The load balancing depends on the scheduling domains constructed by a
distance-based algorithm in current Linux kernel, and this algorithm works well
on symmetric NUMA machines. However, distance-based scheduling domains
result in the frequent high-cost scheduling on asymmetric NUMA machines,
as it neglects the physical relevance of the NUMA nodes (i.e., which NUMA
nodes are in the same processor). In this scenario, the NUMA nodes in the same
processor (e.g., N_0 and N_1) may be treated differently at scheduling.

We address this problem by constructing more appropriate scheduling
domains on asymmetric NUMA machines. Specifically, we propose a physical
relevance-based scheduling domain construction algorithm using the hierarchical
clustering method. In this way, the application can achieve better performance
without modifying the scheduling algorithm of the kernel. On an asymmetric
NUMA machine, our proposed algorithm reduces scheduling cost by 43.27%
on average in *hackbench*, thereby achieving an 11.54% speedup. For real-world
applications, on average, the applications of PARSEC benchmark [9] gain 14.78%
speedup, and the applications of NPB benchmark [7] gain 15.10% speedup.

2   Background and Motivation

In this section, we first describe how Linux maintains load balance with scheduling domains. Then, we describe how scheduling domains are constructed in the
asymmetric NUMA machine and reveal the root cause of the performance degradation introduced by the built-in scheduling domains.

2.1   Load Balancing and Scheduling Domains

In Linux, runnable threads queue in the *runqueue* of each CPU[1], and the kernel
keeps all runqueues balanced by migrating tasks from busy CPUs to idle CPUs.
The cost of migration depends on the CPU topology of a machine. For example,
migrating threads among simultaneous multi-threading (SMT) CPUs within a

---

[1] We name a logical core as "CPU" in this paper.

physical core is less costly than migrating across physical cores, since the previous cache is still available in the former way.

To this end, Linux introduces the **scheduling domains** technique since kernel v2.6.7. This technique divides CPUs into many sets and organizes them hierarchically according to how CPUs share the machine's physical resources. Generally, scheduling domains are organized in a bottom-up way by: SMT level, multiple core (MC) level and NUMA level.

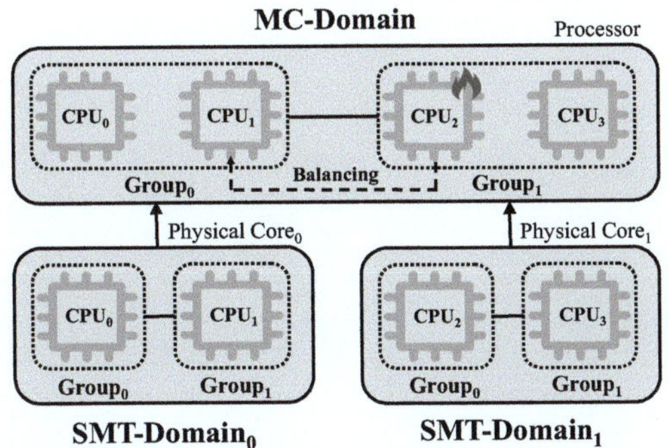

Fig. 2. The scheduling domains of a processor with 4 SMT CPUs and 2 physical cores.

Figure 2 shows how scheduling domains are organized in an example processor with four SMT CPUs and two physical cores (two SMT CPUs per core). A domain contains a set of CPUs (named span). In the SMT level, a domain contains CPUs that belong to a physical core. In the MC level, a domain has CPUs that belong to a processor. **Instead, in the NUMA level, the span of a domain is decided by a distance-based algorithm** (Sect. 2.2). Note that each CPU holds its per-CPU scheduling domains. For instance, in the SMT level, the span of CPU_0's domain is CPU_0 and CPU_1, and the span of CPU_3's domain is CPU_2 and CPU_3. In the MC level, the spans of all CPUs' domains are the same, and each domain contains all four CPUs.

With scheduling domains, load balancing is performed based on **scheduling groups**. Within a scheduling domain, scheduling groups are the subordinate scheduling domains. For example, in Fig. 2, there are two scheduling groups in `MC-domain`, and the two groups are `SMT-domain`$_0$ and `SMT-domain`$_1$. Periodically, each CPU iterates all its scheduling domains from the bottom and measures the workload of each scheduling group in a domain. In each scheduling domain, some threads will be migrated from the busiest group.

2.2 Constructing NUMA-Level Scheduling Domains

While the SMT/MC-level scheduling domains are constructed in a fixed manner, Linux constructs the NUMA-level domains by a distance-based algorithm.

In the NUMA level, scheduling domains are further divided into many layers. The Linux built-in distance-based algorithm first finds out how many different distances exist among NUMA nodes. Taking the asymmetric NUMA machine in Fig. 1(b) as an example. As shown in the central region of Fig. 3, there are five distances: 10, 12, 20, 22 and 24. For each CPU_i, the algorithm traverses the distances from small to large; for each distance, the algorithm builds a layer in the NUMA-level scheduling domains. Specifically, each layer contains all the CPUs of the NUMA nodes that are accessible from the CPU_i within the given distance. If a layer has already included all the CPUs, the algorithm terminates.

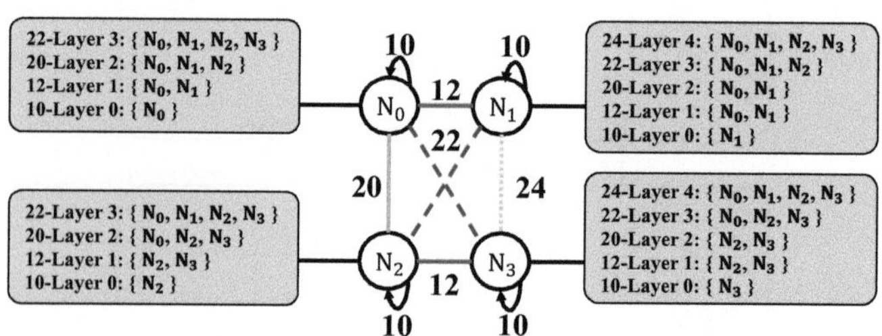

Fig. 3. Built-in NUMA-level scheduling domains of the asymmetric NUMA machine.

The gray boxes in Fig. 3 show the scheduling domains of each CPU at the NUMA level. Note that CPUs of the same NUMA node have the same NUMA-level scheduling domains. One can observe that, **the scheduling domains of different NUMA nodes are not identical.** For instance, given the distance of 22, CPUs of N_0 can reach four nodes (N_0, N_1, N_2, and N_3), while CPUs of N_1 can just reach three nodes (N_0, N_1, and N_2) because of asymmetry.

2.3   Root Cause of Poor Performance

After the kernel adjusts the scheduling domains with overlapping groups and removes the domains with only one group, the resulting NUMA-level scheduling domains, as well as scheduling groups in each domain, are shown in Table 2. Taking the CPU of $Node_0$ as an example, its Layer-1 scheduling domain includes two groups: one contains all the CPUs of $Node_0$ and $Node_1$ ($\{N_0, N_1\}$), and another contains all the CPUs of $Node_2$ and $Node_3$ ($\{N_2, N_3\}$).

When balancing the workload between two processors of the asymmetric NUMA machine, it is preferable to avoid scheduling threads between NUMA nodes that are far apart. As observed in Table 1, running *hackbench* on N_0 and N_3 leads to the regression of -22.24%, which is worse than running it on N_0 and N_2 (-18.04%).

However, the built-in NUMA-level scheduling domains increase the probability of medium/high-cost scheduling. As shown in Table 2, the scheduling across processors is done by Layer 1 and Layer 2 (8 domains in total), wherein 6 underlined domains directly lead to medium/high-cost scheduling; we refer to such a

Table 2. Built-in NUMA-level scheduling domains of the asymmetric NUMA machine.

Layer	$Node_0$	$Node_1$	$Node_2$	$Node_3$
0	N_0–N_1	N_1–N_0	N_2–N_3	N_3–N_2
1	$\{N_0, N_1\}$–$\{N_2, N_3\}$	N_1–N_2	$\{N_2, N_3\}$–$\{N_0, N_1\}$	N_3–N_0
2	N_0–N_3	N_1–N_3	N_2–N_1	N_3–N_1

Table 3. The proportion of scheduling in high-cost domain.

Number of Thread Groups	48	96	192	384
Scheduling in High-cost Domains	53.46%	50.43%	53.15%	55.32%

domain as a high-cost scheduling domain. We measure the load-balancing operations of all 8 domains when running *hackbench* on 4 nodes with different numbers of thread groups, and calculate the proportion of load-balancing operations that occur within the 6 high-cost scheduling domains in Table 3. Note that beyond the 6 high-cost scheduling domains, the medium/high-cost scheduling may also occur in the remaining two domains. This implies that the medium/high-cost scheduling accounts for a larger share than the proportion reported in the table.

In summary, when adopting Linux's built-in distance-based scheduling domains on an asymmetric NUMA machine, **the medium-cost and high-cost scheduling hold at least half proportion in the cross-processor scheduling**, which causes poor performance when running *hackbench* on the four NUMA nodes.

3 Physical Relevance-Based Scheduling Domains

Based on the analysis in Sect. 2.3, a promising way to mitigate the performance regression is to reduce medium/high-cost scheduling in the cross-processor scheduling, while the load balancing between processors is still maintained.

To this end, high-cost scheduling domains in the NUMA level should be minimized. By observing the distance-based construction of NUMA-level scheduling domains from Sect. 2.2, we find that the high-cost domains are primarily formed due to the last two layers of each node. Neglecting to consider the physical relevance of NUMA nodes, the distance-based algorithm separates two nodes that belong to a processor into two layers.

Generally, the difference between nodes within a processor is not significant, they can be considered as a whole. We hence propose an algorithm to group nodes that belong to a processor together in the construction of NUMA-level scheduling domains, as shown in Algorithm 1. Given the distance map of NUMA nodes and the number of installed processors S, the algorithm adopts the hierarchical clustering method to divide nodes into S clusters, where each cluster contains nodes belonging to the same processor.

Algorithm 1: Physics Relevance-based Construction Algorithm

Input: Distance map M where $M[i][j]$ represents the distance between NUMA node N_i and N_j;

Input: S sockets with processors installed;

Output: Constructing scheduling domains for each CPU;

1 Initialize $P = \{N_0, N_1, ..., N_n\}$;
2 Initialize $Cluster\_List = \{P\}$;
3 **repeat**
4   **for** *each P in Cluster_List* **do**
5   Pop P from $Cluster\_List$;
6   **if** $length(P) \geq 2$ **then**
7   Find N_i and N_j with the longest distance from P;
8   Let $P_i = \{N_i\}$ and $P_j = \{N_j\}$;
9   **for** *each N_k in P* **do**
10   **if** $M[i][k] \leq M[j][k]$ **then**
11   Push N_k to P_i;
12   **else**
13   Push N_k to P_j;
14   Push P_i and P_j to $Cluster\_List$;
15 **until** $length(Cluster\_List) == S$;
16 **for** $j \leftarrow 1$ *to Node_Count* **do**
17   **for** *each CPU of N_j* **do**
18   Add a domain with span N_j;
19   Add a domain with span P_k $(N_j \in P_k)$;
20   Add a domain with span $\{N_0, ..., N_n\}$;

Table 4. Proposed NUMA-level scheduling domains of asymmetric NUMA machine.

Layer	$Node_0$	$Node_1$	$Node_2$	$Node_3$
0	N_0–N_1	N_1–N_0	N_2–N_3	N_3–N_2
1	$\{N_0, N_1\}$–$\{N_2, N_3\}$	$\{N_0, N_1\}$–$\{N_2, N_3\}$	$\{N_2, N_3\}$–$\{N_0, N_1\}$	$\{N_2, N_3\}$–$\{N_0, N_1\}$

At the beginning, all NUMA nodes are pushed into an initial cluster (Line 1). The algorithm repeats the following process until S clusters are formed (Lines 3–14). The algorithm iterates over all clusters and splits each cluster into two. For each cluster, the algorithm first finds two nodes with the longest distance and creates two new clusters, each represented by one of these nodes (Lines 5–8). Then the remaining nodes are added to one of the new clusters with a closer distance to the represented node (Lines 9–13). Lastly, three-layer scheduling domains are added to each CPU (Lines 16–20): the bottom layer includes the node to which the CPU belongs; the middle layer includes all nodes within the same processor; the top layer includes all nodes.

The bottom layer will eventually be removed by the kernel because each domain of this layer has only one scheduling group. As a result, in the asymmetric NUMA machine investigated in this paper, the NUMA-level scheduling domains constructed by Algorithm 1 are shown in Table 4. Compared to the Linux built-in distance-based algorithm, our proposed physics relevance-based algorithm eliminates the high-cost domains in the NUMA-level scheduling domains. In Linux, the proposed algorithm can be assembled in the function `sched_init_numa()` located in the file `/kernel/sched/topology.c`.

Table 5. Specifications of the asymmetric NUMA Machine.

CPU	2 × 48-core Huawei Kunpeng 920 Processor
Arch/SMT	ARMv8-A/SMT-unsupported
NUMA	4 Nodes (2 Nodes per Processor)
Memory	192 GB 2933 MHz DDR4
OS/Kernel	Ubuntu 20.04 with Linux Kernel 5.11.5

Note that we have assumed the distances among processors are the same for the sake of simplicity, so that only three layers are added. If the distances among processors are different, the proposed algorithm still works: we can cluster processors according to their physical relevance and add corresponding layers between the middle and top layer mentioned above.

4   Evaluation

In this section, we evaluate the proposed scheduling domains using the dedicated kernel scheduler benchmark and real-world applications.

4.1   Experimental Setup

We conduct the evaluation on an asymmetric NUMA machine. The specifications of this machine are shown in Table 5. In addition to the *hackbench* [2], we conduct the evaluation using 12 applications, including 6 applications of PARSEC benchmark [9]—*blackscholes (bs)*, *canneal (cn)*, *fluidanimate (fa)*, *facesim (fs)*, *streamcluster (sc)*, and *x264*, as well as 6 applications of NAS Parallel Benchmarks [7]—*CG, FT, LU, MG, SP* and *UA*. These applications cover a large spectrum of real-world applications and are widely used in prior studies [20, 25]. We compare the execution time of *hackbench* and each application when they run on the built-in scheduling domains (Table 2) with our proposed scheduling domains (Table 4).

4.2   Evaluation on Hackbench

We run *hackbench* on 4 NUMA nodes and change the number of thread groups (48, 96, 192 and 384) to simulate different load pressures.

Performance. Figure 4(a) shows the speedup of *hackbench* with different number of thread groups when comparing the proposed scheduling domains with the built-in scheduling domains. As we can see, higher speedup is achieved as the number of thread groups increases. On average, *hackbench* gains 11.54% speedup with the proposed scheduling domains.

Load Balancing. To understand why the proposed scheduling domains outperform, we first evaluate the effect of load balancing during the execution of *hackbench*. Figure 5 shows a heatmap colour-coding the number of threads in the runqueues of all CPUs of each node when running *hackbench* with 192 thread groups. The darker the colour, the more threads a node hosts. As we can see, built-in scheduling domains can roughly maintain load balancing among nodes during execution (Fig. 5(a)), as well as the proposed scheduling domains (Fig. 5(b)). Similar results are found when running *hackbench* with other numbers of thread groups. Overall, while the proposed scheduling domains have fewer layers in the NUMA level, the load balancing is still maintained.

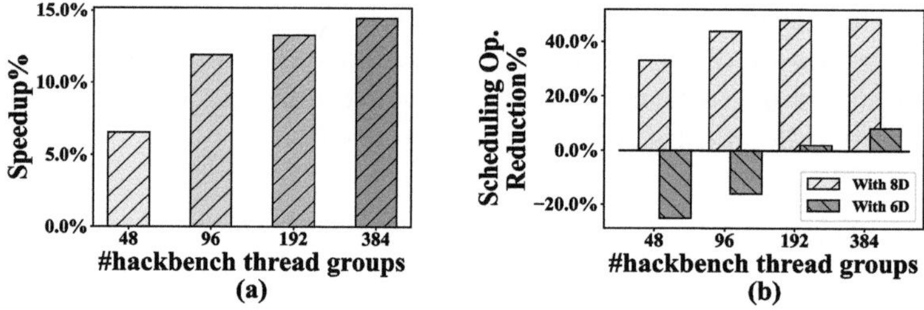

Fig. 4. With our proposed scheduling domains: (a) The speedup of *hackbench*. (b) The cross-processor scheduling operation reduction ratio.

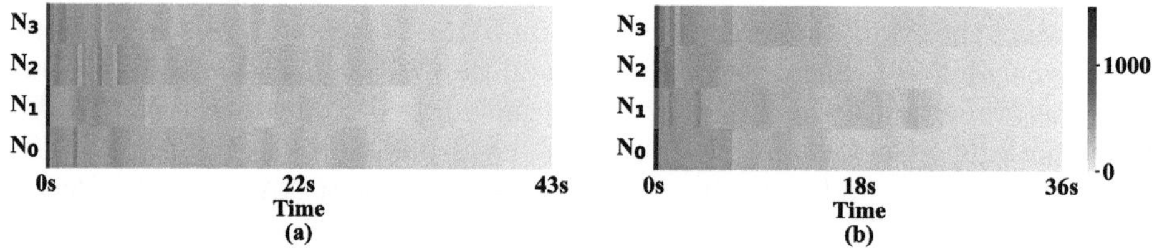

Fig. 5. The number of threads in the runqueues of each node when running *hackbench*: (a) with built-in scheduling domains, and (b) with proposed scheduling domains.

Scheduling Cost. In addition, we measure the cross-processor scheduling operations. We count three types of load-balancing operations occurring in: (1)

4D: All the 4 domains in Layer 1 of the proposed scheduling domains in Table 4. (2) **6D:** The 6 high-cost scheduling domains of the built-in scheduling domains in Table 2. (3) **8D:** All the 8 domains in Layer 1 and Layer 2 of the built-in scheduling domains in Table 2. Figure 4(b) shows the scheduling operation reduction ratio when comparing 4D with 6D or 8D, respectively.

Specifically, 4D and 8D, respectively, denote the number of cross-processor scheduling operations in the proposed scheduling domain and the built-in scheduling domain. As observed, 4D is lower than 8D in all cases, indicating that without breaking load balancing among nodes, the proposed scheduling domains reduce the cross-processor scheduling (43.27% on average). This is a reason why *hackbench* gains speedup.

Besides, 6D partially denotes how many medium/high-cost scheduling occur in the built-in scheduling domains. The comparison between 4D and 6D shows that under low pressure (48 and 96), the medium/high-cost scheduling in the proposed scheduling domains may not be less than that in the built-in scheduling domains. But under high pressure (192 and 384), the medium/high-cost scheduling has indeed been reduced in the proposed scheduling domains. This is a reason why *hackbench* gains higher speedup as the number of thread groups increases.

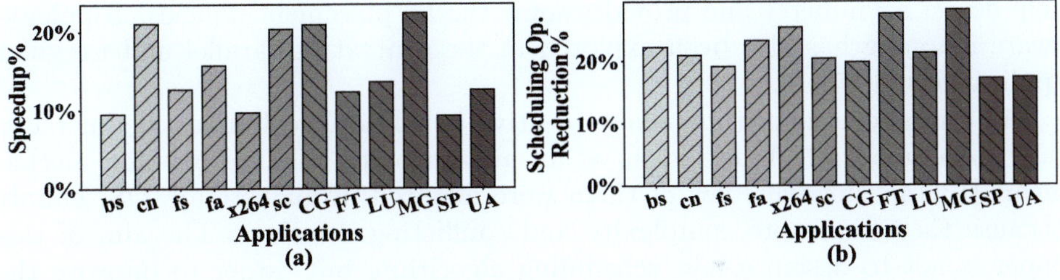

Fig. 6. With our proposed scheduling domains: (a) The speedup of real-world applications. (b) The cross-processor scheduling operation reduction ratio.

4.3   Evaluation on Real-World Applications

To validate the general applicability and effectiveness of the proposed scheduling domains, we conduct the evaluation on various real-world applications.

Figure 6(a) presents the speedups of the 12 applications when using the proposed scheduling domains compared with the built-in scheduling domains. As we can see, the performance of all applications improves, with an average speedup of 14.9% and up to 22.33%.

Same as the previous subsection, during the execution of the application, we examine the load balancing and record the number of cross-processor scheduling operations. We find that both the proposed scheduling domains and built-in scheduling domains succeeded in load balancing. Meanwhile, the proposed scheduling domains effectively reduce the cross-processor scheduling of the application's threads during execution; the results are presented in Fig. 6(b), showing a 21.87% reduction on average. Fewer number of cross-processor thread scheduling reduce the frequency of long-distance memory accesses, thereby improving application performance. Because the evaluated applications exhibit varying degrees of memory sensitivity [20], the speedup of each application is not identical.

5 Related Work

Thread scheduling on NUMA systems has been extensively studied. Most of proposed techniques use the information (e.g., cache misses or remote memory accesses) provided by performance counters to design heuristic-based scheduling algorithms [10,11,17,20,23,24] or machine learning-based scheduling algorithms [6,21]. AsymSched [17,22] shows that asymmetric interconnect in NUMA architecture drastically impacts the performance of some applications. It focuses on the bandwidth asymmetry of the AMD Bulldozer NUMA machine and proposes a thread placement algorithm that maximizes the bandwidth for communicating threads. MCTOP [12] provides a machine topology abstraction tool to help detect asymmetry and provides some thread placement policies. Topology-aware mapping has also been explored in the context of parallel and irregular applications [8,15,16].

All the above algorithms show positive benefits. The Linux scheduler can take some good scheduling ideas as an add-on or to enhance existing mechanisms [13,14]. However, few of them were adopted in mainstream OS, mainly because they face more complexity and conflicting decisions. The aim of this paper is not to design a new scheduling algorithm, but rather to improve the infrastructure of the scheduler. Lozi et al. [18] find the overlap bug of scheduling groups caused by the asymmetric NUMA architecture, while it does not consider whether the scheduling domains are constructed more reasonably on the asymmetric architecture. The work of eliminating overlap scheduling groups is orthogonal to this paper.

6 Conclusion and Future Work

In conclusion, the Linux distance-based scheduling domain construction incurs high load-balancing costs on asymmetric NUMA machines, as it ignores the underlying node relationships and may create ultra-long-distance domains. Larger or irregular topology may further amplify this cost. We propose a physical relevance-based algorithm that constructs more efficient domains for asymmetric NUMA, improving application performance without modifying the OS scheduler.

Except for periodic load balancing, other thread scheduling mechanisms are integrated into the mainline Linux scheduler (e.g., wake-affine scheduling and energy-aware scheduling). These scheduling mechanisms are still running based on scheduling domains. As the infrastructure of the thread scheduler, the construction of scheduling domains affects how these mechanisms actually perform.

During this study, we learn that the physical relevance of hardware should be an important basis in the construction of scheduling domains, as well as how SMT-level and MC-level domains are constructed. On the machine investigated in this paper (Table 5), we find another noteworthy feature: every four cores in a processor form a cluster sharing the processor bus. To estimate if a new level domain should be added is a promising future research direction.

Acknowledgments. This work is partially sponsored by the National Key Research and Development Program of China (2024YFB4505703) and National Natural Science Foundation of China (62402316, 62232011, 62302302).

References

1. Apache http server. http://httpd.apache.org/
2. hackbench. https://github.com/linux-test-project/ltp/blob/master/testcases/kernel/sched/cfs-scheduler/hackbench.c
3. Mysql. https://www.mysql.com/
4. New AMD-based Dav4 and Eav4 azure VMs are available in additional regions (2020). https://azure.microsoft.com/en-us/updates/new-amdbased-dav4-and-eav4-azure-vms-are-available-in-additional-regions/
5. Amazon EC2 M7a instances are now available in additional regions. https://aws.amazon.com/about-aws/whats-new/2024/03/amazon-ec2-m7a-instances-additional-regions/ (2024)
6. Antoniadis, K., Guerraoui, R., Trigonakis, V.: Thread-placement learning. In: ICDCS (2020)
7. Bailey, D.H., et al.: The NAS parallel benchmarks—summary and preliminary results. In: SC (1991)
8. Bhatele, A., Kale, L.V.: Application-specific topology-aware mapping for three dimensional topologies. In: IPDPS. IEEE (2008)
9. Bienia, C., Kumar, S., Singh, J.P., Li, K.: The parsec benchmark suite: characterization and architectural implications. In: PACT (2008)
10. Blagodurov, S., Fedorova, A.: User-level scheduling on NUMA multicore systems under Linux. In: Linux Symposium (2011)
11. Booth, J.D., Lane, P.: A NUMA-aware version of an adaptive self-scheduling loop scheduler. ACM TACO (2024)
12. Chatzopoulos, G., Guerraoui, R., Harris, T., Trigonakis, V.: Abstracting multi-core topologies with MCTOP. In: EuroSys (2017)
13. Chen, J., Banerjee, S.S., Kalbarczyk, Z.T., Iyer, R.K.: Machine learning for load balancing in the Linux kernel. In: APSys (2020)
14. Chiang, M.L., Tu, S.W., Su, W.L., Lin, C.W.: Enhancing inter-node process migration for load balancing on Linux-based NUMA multicore systems. In: COMPSAC (2018)
15. Kirmani, S., Park, J., Raghavan, P.: An embedded sectioning scheme for multiprocessor topology-aware mapping of irregular applications. IJHPCA (2017)
16. Kirmani, S., Raghavan, P.: Scalable parallel graph partitioning. In: SC (2013)

17. Lepers, B., Quéma, V., Fedorova, A.: Thread and memory placement on NUMA systems: asymmetry matters. In: ATC (2015)
18. Lozi, J.P., Lepers, B., Funston, J., Gaud, F., Quéma, V., Fedorova, A.: The Linux scheduler: a decade of wasted cores. In: EuroSys (2016)
19. Ma, T., et al.: Efficient scheduler live update for Linux kernel with modularization. In: ASPLOS (2023)
20. Pang, P., et al.: PAC: preference-aware co-location scheduling on heterogeneous NUMA architectures to improve resource utilization. In: ICS (2023)
21. Sánchez Barrera, I., Black-Schaffer, D., Casas, M., Moretó, M., Stupnikova, A., Popov, M.: Modeling and optimizing NUMA effects and prefetching with machine learning. In: SC (2020)
22. Saroliya, U., Arima, E., Liu, D., Schulz, M.: Reinforcement learning-driven co-scheduling and diverse resource assignments on NUMA systems. In: ICCD (2024)
23. Srikanthan, S., Dwarkadas, S., Shen, K.: Data sharing or resource contention: toward performance transparency on multicore systems. In: ATC (2015)
24. Srikanthan, S., Dwarkadas, S., Shen, K.: Coherence stalls or latency tolerance: informed CPU scheduling for socket and core sharing. In: ATC (2016)
25. Xu, D., Ryu, J., Shin, K., Su, P., Li, D.: FlexMem: adaptive page profiling and migration for tiered memory. In: ATC (2024)
26. Zhang, Z., Li, C., Tao, Y., Yang, R., Tang, H., Xu, J.: Fuxi: a fault-tolerant resource management and job scheduling system at internet scale. In: VLDB (2014)

Data Plane Driven Adaptive Routing with In-Network Reinforcement Learning

Bo Wu[✉], Meiju Yu[✉], Pantong Wang, Dan Qin, Xiliang Pang,
and Guiquan Zheng

Inner Mongolia University, No. 235 West College Road, Saihan District, Hohhot,
Inner Mongolia, People's Republic of China
18238036836@163.com, csymj@imu.edu.cn

Abstract. The rapid evolution of modern network traffic, characterized by its dynamic and unpredictable nature, poses significant challenges for traditional static routing protocols. While Software-Defined Networking (SDN) and programmable data planes like P4 have emerged as promising solutions to enhance network flexibility, a key challenge remains in developing intelligent routing decision-making mechanisms that can adapt in real-time to changing network conditions. This paper proposes a novel intelligent routing framework that integrates the Q-Learning algorithm with a P4-based programmable data plane. By modeling the routing problem as a reinforcement learning task, our approach enables network agents to autonomously learn optimal routing policies based on real-time network states, such as congestion and latency, without the need for predefined rules. We define the network state, agent actions, and a reward function to guide the learning process. The learned optimal routing policies are then dynamically translated into P4 rules and deployed on the data plane. Through extensive simulations, we demonstrate that our proposed Q-Learning-based algorithm significantly outperforms traditional routing protocols in terms of reducing end-to-end latency and improving network throughput.

Keywords: Intelligent Routing · Software-Defined Networking · Q-Learning · Programmable Data Plane

1 Introduction

The rapid growth of cloud computing, big data, and real-time applications has led to an unprecedented increase in network traffic volume and complexity. Traditional routing protocols, such as OSPF and BGP, were designed for static or semi-static network topologies. Their reliance on pre-computed paths and slow convergence times makes them ill-suited for handling the dynamic and volatile traffic patterns of modern networks [1]. This static nature often leads to suboptimal resource utilization, network congestion, and increased latency, which can severely impact application performance.

© IFIP International Federation for Information Processing 2026
Published by Springer Nature Switzerland AG 2026
X. Wang et al. (Eds.): NPC 2025, LNCS 16306, pp. 461–472, 2026.
https://doi.org/10.1007/978-3-032-10466-3_38

Software-Defined Networking (SDN) has emerged as a paradigm shift to address these limitations. By decoupling the control plane from the data plane, SDN centralizes network control, providing a global view of the network state and enabling more flexible and centralized management [2]. This allows for the implementation of advanced routing and traffic engineering policies. However, most SDN routing solutions still rely on a centralized controller that computes and pushes rules to switches, which can become a performance bottleneck and may not be agile enough to react to microsecond-level traffic fluctuations.

The advent of programmable data planes [3], exemplified by the P4 (Programming Protocol-independent Packet Processors) language [4], has further revolutionized network control. P4 allows network operators to define custom packet processing logic directly on forwarding devices, enabling fine-grained control and high-speed packet processing in the data plane itself. This provides a powerful foundation for implementing intelligent and adaptive network functions, including dynamic routing. The core challenge, however, is to develop an intelligent decision-making mechanism that can effectively leverage this programmability to make real-time routing decisions that optimize network performance.

In this paper, we propose an intelligent routing framework that combines the power of a programmable data plane with a reinforcement learning approach. Specifically, we leverage the Q-Learning algorithm to enable the network to learn optimal routing strategies autonomously. Our framework models the routing problem as a reinforcement learning task where an agent interacts with the network environment. The network's congestion, latency, and link utilization serve as the state space, while the selection of a next-hop router defines the action space. A carefully designed reward function guides the learning process, encouraging the agent to discover paths that minimize latency and avoid congestion. The learned optimal policies are then translated into P4 forwarding rules and installed on the data plane switches, enabling real-time, autonomous route updates.

The main contributions of this paper are summarized as follows:

- We propose a novel intelligent routing framework that seamlessly integrates the Q-Learning algorithm with a P4 programmable data plane to enable autonomous, real-time routing decisions.
- We formally define the routing problem as a reinforcement learning task, including the design of a comprehensive state space, action space, and a reward function tailored for network performance optimization.
- We implement our proposed algorithm in a simulated network environment and conduct extensive performance evaluations. The results demonstrate that our approach significantly outperforms traditional shortest-path routing algorithms in reducing network latency and improving throughput.

The remainder of this paper is organized as follows. Section 2 reviews related work on SDN routing, programmable data planes, and reinforcement learning in networking. Section 3 details our proposed system architecture and algorithm design. Section 4 presents the experimental setup, performance evaluation, and analysis of results. Finally, Sect. 5 concludes the paper and outlines future research directions.

2   Related Work

The research on intelligent routing in computer networks is a longstanding field, which has recently gained renewed attention with the advent of SDN and programmable data planes. Our work is closely related to three main areas: machine learning-based routing, in-network machine learning, and the application of reinforcement learning for network control. This section provides a comprehensive review of relevant literature and highlights the unique contributions of our proposed approach.

2.1   Machine Learning-Based Routing Optimization

The use of machine learning (ML) to optimize routing has been widely explored. Xie et al. [5]et al. provided systematic surveys on ML-based routing optimization methods within SDN and cloud data centers, respectively. They discussed the applications of various ML algorithms and their respective advantages and disadvantages. While these works offer a valuable overview, they primarily focus on general ML applications and often lack a detailed discussion on how to specifically integrate these algorithms with the constraints and capabilities of a programmable data plane like P4.

More sophisticated methods, such as those leveraging deep reinforcement learning (DRL), have been proposed to handle dynamic network topologies and traffic fluctuations. For instance, Yu et al. [6] developed a DRL-based intelligent routing method that autonomously adapts routing policies. However, DRL models are computationally intensive and demand significant resources, making them challenging to deploy in real-time on resource-constrained network devices. This contrasts with our Q-Learning approach, which is more lightweight and suitable for practical implementation within a control plane coordinating with a high-speed data plane.

2.2   In-Network Machine Learning and Hardware Limitations

With the rise of programmable data planes, there has been a significant push to execute ML inference directly within the network. This "in-network intelligence" aims to reduce latency by avoiding the need to send data to external servers for processing. Existing work in this area primarily focuses on deploying lightweight models like decision trees or binary neural networks.

For decision tree-based approaches, Lee et al. [7] proposed SwitchTree to implement random forests for network attack detection at line rate. While effective, this method is limited by the tree depth and number, which constrain the model's complexity and accuracy. Similarly, Xie et al. [8] developed Mousika, which uses knowledge distillation to compress large ML models into small binary decision trees (BDTs) suitable for switches. This approach may suffer from information loss, potentially affecting the model's accuracy and generalization. Zheng et al. [9] and Zheng et al. [10] introduced IIsy and Planter, respectively, to optimize the deployment of decision trees by using lookup tables and shared feature tables. While these methods reduce resource consumption, they are still constrained by the inherent limitations of decision tree models and cannot support very deep or complex models required for highly dynamic routing tasks.

For neural network models, the lack of floating-point arithmetic support in network hardware poses a major challenge. Alizadeh et al. [11] addressed this by proposing binarized neural networks, converting matrix multiplication to efficient bitwise operations. This reduces resource requirements but may lack the fast adaptation capability needed for sudden traffic bursts. Other works, such as systems implemented on NIC data planes by Zhou et al. [12] and Siracusano et al. [13], focus on implementing lightweight, binarized neural networks or MLPs. While these efforts successfully demonstrate the feasibility of in-network intelligence, they are generally limited to small-scale models and may struggle with the complexity of large-scale networks and high-dimensional traffic data.

2.3 Distinction from Prior Work

Our work distinguishes itself from the existing literature in several key aspects. Unlike most research that focuses on deploying complex ML models directly on the data plane, which faces significant hardware and resource limitations, our approach adopts a more pragmatic and effective two-plane architecture. The Q-Learning algorithm runs on a more capable control plane, where floating-point operations are not a constraint. This allows for a more complex and accurate learning model. The P4 data plane then acts as an intelligent executor, dynamically applying the learned policies in real-time by updating forwarding rules. This separation of concerns leverages the strengths of both planes: the control plane for intelligent decision-making and the data plane for high-speed packet processing. This hybrid approach overcomes the limitations of in-network ML by avoiding direct implementation of computationally intensive learning algorithms on the forwarding hardware, while still enabling intelligent and adaptive routing on the fly.

Our work provides a concrete solution that bridges the gap between theoretical ML models and their practical application in a programmable network environment, offering a more robust and scalable approach than previous efforts limited by hardware constraints or model complexity.

3 Algorithm Design and System Architecture

This section presents the detailed design of our intelligent routing framework, which tightly couples the Q-Learning algorithm with a programmable data plane based on P4. We first provide an overview of the system architecture, followed by a formal problem formulation and a detailed explanation of the algorithm and its implementation.

3.1   System Architecture Overview

Our framework adopts a two-plane architecture, as illustrated in Fig. 1. The Control Plane is responsible for all intelligent decision-making, while the Data Plane is in charge of high-speed packet forwarding based on the rules provisioned by the control plane.

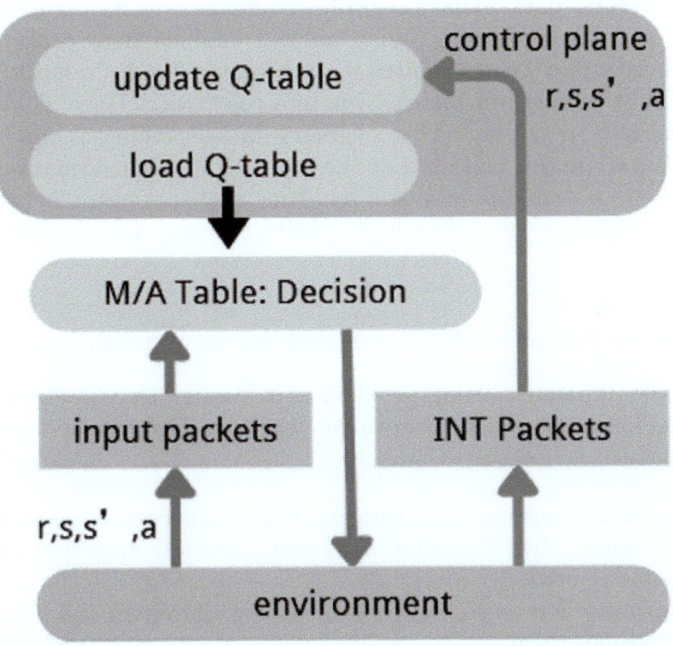

Fig. 1. System Architecture of the Proposed Intelligent Routing Framework.

The Control Plane houses the core intelligence of our system. It runs the Q-Learning algorithm, maintains the Q-Table, and interacts with the data plane to collect real-time network state information and install new forwarding rules. A dedicated Network Monitor module within the control plane periodically collects telemetry data, such as link latency, bandwidth utilization, and queue depths, from the P4 switches. This data serves as the feedback from the environment, which is crucial for the Q-Learning agent's learning process.

The Data Plane consists of a network of P4-enabled programmable switches. These switches are programmed with a P4 program that enables them to process packets and report key metrics to the control plane. Upon receiving new forwarding rules from the control plane, the switches dynamically update their match-action tables, allowing them to make real-time routing decisions based on the learned policies. This separation ensures that the computationally intensive learning process does not impact the high-speed forwarding performance of the data plane.

3.2   State Sensing and Modeling with In-Band Telemetry

To acquire the fine-grained, real-time network state information required by the Q-Learning algorithm, we leverage **In-band Telemetry (INT)**. INT is a P4 data plane native and highly efficient telemetry technique that encapsulates network state information directly within data packets, avoiding additional control flow overheads.

Within our P4 data plane program, we define specific structures, such as 'IPOption' and 'SwitchTrace'. When an INT-enabled data packet traverses a switch, the data plane encapsulates its own queue depth ('qdepth'), switch ID ('swid'), and other relevant information into the 'SwitchTrace' field and adds it to the IP packet's 'IPOption'. This telemetry data accumulates hop-by-hop along the packet's path and is collected at the path's end. This mechanism allows the control plane to obtain a precise and real-time snapshot of the network state for all traversed switches, providing high-quality training data for our Q-Learning algorithm.

3.3   Problem Formulation as a Reinforcement Learning Task

We model the dynamic routing problem as a Markov Decision Process (MDP), which is the foundation of reinforcement learning. The core components of our MDP are defined as follows:

- **Agent**: The Q-Learning algorithm running on the control plane. Its goal is to find an optimal policy $\pi(s)$ that maps each state s to an action a to maximize the cumulative reward.
- **Environment**: The entire network, including all routers, links, and the traffic flowing through them.
- **State** (S): The state s_t at time step t represents a snapshot of the network environment. A comprehensive state representation is crucial for effective learning. We define the state as a tuple of metrics for all relevant links and nodes, which may include:
  - Link Latency and Bandwidth Utilization
  - Queue Depth at Each Switch Port
  - Packet Drop Rate on Each Link
  - Traffic Load on Different Paths

  This state information is collected periodically from the P4 switches and fed into the Q-Learning agent.
- **Action** (A): An action a_t is the routing decision made by the agent. For a given source-destination pair, the action corresponds to selecting the next-hop router from the set of available neighbors. The action space for a router is the set of its direct neighbors.
- **Reward** (R): The reward function $R(s, a)$ is designed to guide the agent towards optimal performance. It provides a numerical feedback signal after each action is taken. A positive reward is given for actions that improve

network performance, while a negative reward is given for detrimental actions. A simple yet effective reward function can be defined as:

$$R_t = \alpha \cdot \frac{1}{\text{latency}_t} + \beta \cdot \frac{1}{\text{packet\_loss}_t} - \gamma \cdot \text{queue\_depth}_t$$

where latency_t is the end-to-end latency, packet_loss_t is the packet loss rate, and queue_depth_t is the queue depth at the next hop. α, β, γ are weighting coefficients. This function encourages the agent to choose paths with low latency, low packet loss, and low congestion.

3.4   Q-Learning Algorithm

The Q-Learning algorithm is chosen for its simplicity and model-free nature. The core of the algorithm is the Q-Table, which stores the expected future reward for taking an action a in a given state s. The table is iteratively updated as the agent interacts with the environment.

The Q-Value update rule is defined as:

$$Q(s_t, a_t) \leftarrow Q(s_t, a_t) + \alpha[R_{t+1} + \gamma \max_a Q(s_{t+1}, a) - Q(s_t, a_t)]$$

where α is the learning rate, and γ is the discount factor.

To balance the trade-off between exploring new paths and exploiting known good paths, we employ an ϵ-greedy policy. At each time step, the agent chooses a random action with a probability ϵ (exploration) or selects the action with the highest Q-value for the current state with a probability $1 - \epsilon$ (exploitation). The value of ϵ is typically high at the beginning of the training and gradually decreases over time to favor exploitation as the model learns.

3.5   Interaction Between Control and Data Planes

The two-plane interaction is critical for the real-time functionality of our framework.

1. **Data Plane Telemetry:** The P4 program on each switch is designed to collect and report key performance metrics. For example, a P4 program can be configured to measure queue occupancy and latency per port. These metrics are then sent to the control plane via a P4 Runtime or gRPC interface, providing the necessary state information for the Q-Learning agent.
2. **Policy Deployment:** Once the Q-Learning agent determines an optimal next-hop decision for a specific flow (e.g., a source-destination pair), the control plane translates this decision into a P4 match-action table entry. For instance, the controller provisions a rule like "table_add egress.set_nexthop_port table set_egress_port 10.0.1.2/32 => 5", instructing the switch to forward packets destined for '10.0.1.2' out of port '5'. This dynamic rule update enables the network to adapt to the new, learned routing policy instantly.

This design ensures that the system is both intelligent and highly performant, with the P4 data plane handling the high-speed execution of policies while the control plane performs the necessary complex learning and decision-making.

4   Experiments and Performance Evaluation

This section details the experimental setup, performance metrics, and results that validate the effectiveness of our proposed Q-Learning-based intelligent routing algorithm. We compare our approach against established baseline methods to demonstrate its superiority in dynamic network environments.

4.1   Experimental Setup

Our experiments are conducted in a simulated network environment using **Mininet**, a network emulator that allows us to create and test custom network topologies. The switches are configured to run a **P4-based software switch** (e.g., 'bmv2'), which is programmed with our custom P4 forwarding pipeline. The control plane component, which houses the Q-Learning agent, is implemented in Python and communicates with the switches via the P4 Runtime API.

- **Network Topology**: We use a **Fat-Tree topology** with 4 pods, as it is a common architecture in data centers and presents a significant routing challenge due to its multiple redundant paths. The topology consists of 20 switches and 16 hosts.
- **Traffic Generation**: We use **Iperf** to generate various traffic patterns, including both constant bit rate (CBR) and Poisson-distributed traffic flows, to simulate realistic network workloads. We introduce a mix of short-lived and long-lived flows to test the algorithm's responsiveness.
- **Algorithm Parameters**: The Q-Learning algorithm is configured with the following parameters: a learning rate $\alpha = 0.5$, a discount factor $\gamma = 0.9$, and an initial exploration rate $\epsilon = 1.0$, which is decayed exponentially to a minimum of 0.1 over the training period. The training is conducted over a period of 50,000 episodes, with each episode representing a fixed time interval during which the agent interacts with the environment.

4.2   Results and Analysis

We compare our proposed Q-Learning-based routing algorithm against two primary baselines:

1. **Dijkstra's Algorithm (Static Routing)**: A traditional shortest-path routing protocol that computes paths based on static link weights (e.g., hop count) and does not adapt to dynamic network conditions.
2. **SDN-based Centralized Routing**: A more advanced baseline where a centralized controller computes the shortest path based on periodically updated network state (e.g., link utilization), but without an intelligent, adaptive learning mechanism.

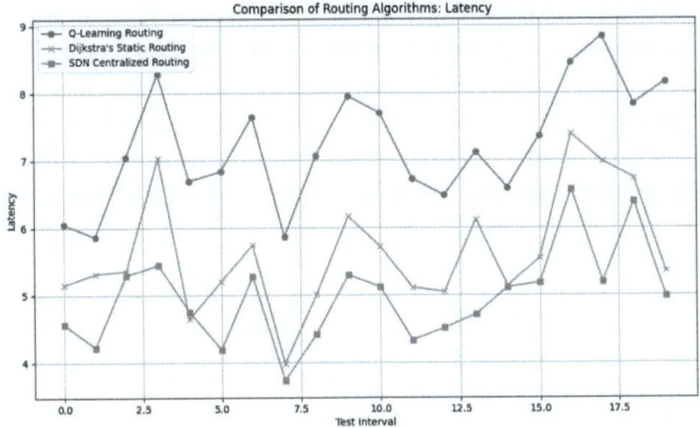

Fig. 2. Average End-to-End Latency

Latency Performance As shown in Fig. 2, our Q-Learning-based algorithm consistently achieves a lower average end-to-end latency compared to both baselines, especially under medium to high network loads. The static Dijkstra's algorithm performs poorly as congestion builds up on its pre-determined shortest paths. The SDN-based centralized routing shows better performance than Dijkstra's, but its performance is still limited by the update frequency of network state information. Our algorithm, by leveraging real-time feedback and its learning mechanism, can proactively reroute traffic around congested links, thereby minimizing latency.

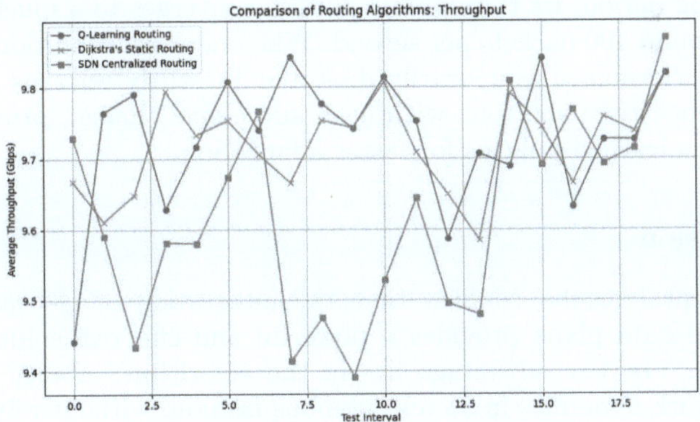

Fig. 3. Network Throughput

Throughput Performance Figure 3 demonstrates that our proposed framework achieves a significantly higher network throughput. The ability of the Q-Learning agent to distribute traffic intelligently across multiple available paths prevents bottlenecks and ensures more balanced network resource utilization. In contrast, the static and centralized baselines often lead to traffic hot spots, which results in packet loss and, consequently, reduced overall throughput.

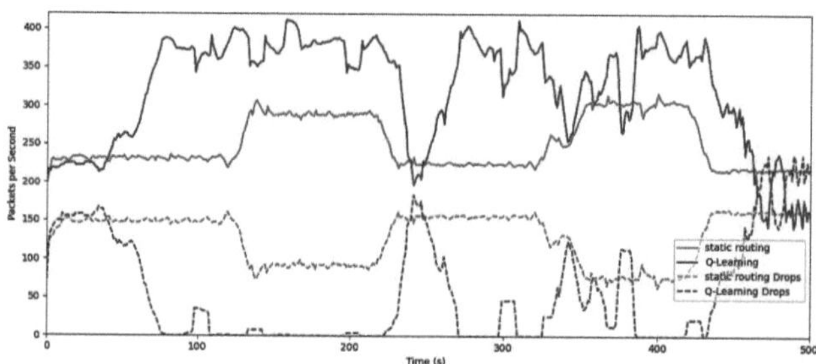

Fig. 4. Routing Convergence Time after a Link Failure.

Dynamic Adaptability To evaluate adaptability, we simulated a scenario where a critical link in the Fat-Tree topology fails abruptly. As illustrated in Fig. 4, static routing maintains a consistent but sub-optimal throughput, accompanied by continuous packet drops, as it cannot adapt to congestion. In stark contrast, our Q-Learning-based routing exhibits remarkable adaptability. After a brief learning period, its throughput quickly converges to a much higher rate, peaking at around 400 packets per second. When network conditions change, the algorithm's performance temporarily dips, but it swiftly relearns and recovers. The convergence time shortens with each successive change, proving that the Q-table retains learned policies for faster adaptation.

4.3   Discussion

The experimental results confirm that the integration of Q-Learning with a programmable data plane provides a powerful and effective solution for intelligent routing. The key advantage lies in the algorithm's ability to learn and adapt to network dynamics in an autonomous fashion, without relying on static rules or fixed update intervals. While the initial training phase can be time-consuming, the resulting learned policy, once deployed, offers superior real-time performance, making our approach highly suitable for modern, dynamic network environments.

5   Conclusion and Future Work

5.1   Conclusion

In this paper, we propose a novel intelligent routing framework that leverages the synergy between the Q-Learning algorithm and a P4-based programmable data plane. Our approach addresses the limitations of traditional static routing protocols and existing centralized SDN solutions by enabling real-time, autonomous routing decisions in dynamic network environments. We formally modeled the routing problem as a reinforcement learning task and carefully designed its components to guide the learning process towards optimal network performance.

Our experimental results, conducted in a Mininet-based simulation, demonstrate that the proposed framework significantly outperforms traditional shortest-path algorithms and a basic SDN centralized routing scheme. The Q-Learning agent's ability to learn and adapt to changing network conditions resulted in a substantial reduction in average end-to-end latency and a notable increase in network throughput. By separating the computationally intensive learning task to the control plane and utilizing the high-speed, programmable data plane for policy execution, our framework offers a practical and effective solution that overcomes the inherent hardware limitations of in-network intelligence while still providing a highly responsive routing mechanism. However, we acknowledge that the current reward function, while effective for core performance metrics, is limited. A more comprehensive approach will be necessary for multi-objective optimization in complex, real-world networks.

5.2   Future Work

While our framework provides a robust solution, there are several promising avenues for future research.

1. **Exploration of Advanced Reinforcement Learning Algorithms**: Future work could explore more advanced RL algorithms, such as Deep Q-Learning (DQN) or Proximal Policy Optimization (PPO), to enhance the model's scalability and learning efficiency for large and complex networks.
2. **Multi-Objective Optimization**: Our current reward function primarily focuses on latency and throughput. Future research could investigate a more sophisticated reward function that incorporates multiple optimization goals, such as energy consumption and load balancing.
3. **Real-World Deployment and Validation**: Our current work is validated in a simulated environment. A crucial next step is to deploy and test the framework on a physical testbed with P4-enabled switches to evaluate its performance under real-world traffic conditions and hardware constraints.

Acknowledgments. This research is supported by the National Natural Science Foundation of China (No. 62466041), the Inner Mongolia Nature Fund (No. 2023MS06020), the Hohhot Science & Technology Plan (No. 2021-KJXM-TZJW-04), the Science and Technology Program of Inner Mongolia Autonomous Region

(2023YFSW0008), and the Ministry of Education's Engineering Research Center on Ecological Big Data (21500-5223745).

References

1. Guck, J.W., Van Bemten, A., Reisslein, M., Kellerer, W.: Unicast QoS routing algorithms for SDN: a comprehensive survey and performance evaluation. IEEE Commun. Surv. Tutorials **20**(1), 388–415 (2017)
2. Kreutz, D., Ramos, F.M.V., Verissimo, P.E., Rothenberg, C.E., Azodolmolky, S., Uhlig, S.: Software-defined networking: a comprehensive survey. Proc. IEEE **103**(2), 14–76 (2014)
3. Michel, O., Bifulco, R., Rétvári, G., Schmid, S.: The programmable data plane: abstractions, architectures, algorithms, and applications. ACM Comput. Surv. (CSUR) **54**(3), 1–36 (2021)
4. Bosshart, P., et al.: P4: programming protocol-independent packet processors. ACM SIGCOMM Comput. Commun. Rev. **44**(4), 87–95 (2014)
5. Xie, J., et al.: A survey of machine learning techniques applied to software defined networking (SDN): research issues and challenges. IEEE Commun. Surv. Tutorials **21**(5), 393–430 (2018)
6. Yu, C., Lan, J., Guo, Z., Hu, Y.: DROM: optimizing the routing in software-defined networks with deep reinforcement learning. IEEE Access **6**, 64533–64539 (2018)
7. Lee, J.-H., Singh, K.: SwitchTree: in-network computing and traffic analyses with random forests. Neural Comput. Appl., 1–12 (2020)
8. Xie, G., Li, Q., Dong, Y., Duan, G., Jiang, Y., Duan, J.: Mousika: enable general in-network intelligence in programmable switches by knowledge distillation. In: IEEE INFOCOM 2022-IEEE Conference on Computer Communications, pp. 1938–1947 (2022)
9. Zheng, C., et al.: IIsy: practical in-network classification. arXiv preprint arXiv:2205.08243 (2022)
10. Zheng, C., Zilberman, N.: Planter: seeding trees within switches. In: Proceedings of the SIGCOMM'21 Poster and Demo Sessions, pp. 12–14 (2021)
11. Alizadeh, M., Fernández-Marqués, J., Lane, N.D., Gal, Y.: An empirical study of binary neural networks' optimisation. In: International Conference on Learning Representations (2018)
12. Zhou, G., Liu, Z., Fu, C., Li, Q., Xu, K.: An efficient design of intelligent network data plane. In: 32nd USENIX Security Symposium (USENIX Security 23), pp. 6203–6220 (2023)
13. Siracusano, G., et al.: Re-architecting traffic analysis with neural network interface cards. In: 19th USENIX Symposium on Networked Systems Design and Implementation (NSDI 22), pp. 513–533 (2022)

Author Index

© IFIP International Federation for Information Processing 2026
Published by Springer Nature Switzerland AG 2026
X. Wang et al. (Eds.): NPC 2025, LNCS 16306, pp. 473–477, 2026.
https://doi.org/10.1007/978-3-032-10466-3